Ethiopia, Eritrea & Djibouti

Frances Linzee Gordon

LONELY PLANET PUBLICATIONS
Melbourne • Oakland • London • Paris

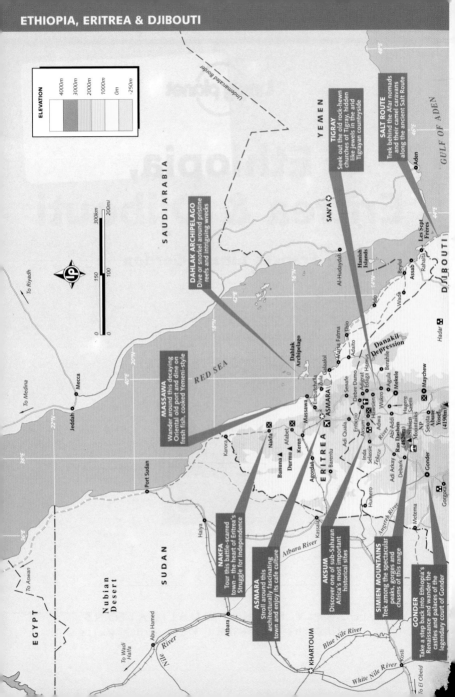

ELEVATION

4000m
3000m
2000m
1000m
0m
-250m

DAHLAK ARCHIPELAGO
Dive or snorkel around pristine reefs and intriguing wrecks

TIGRAY
Seek out the old rock-hewn churches of Tigray, hidden like jewels in the arid Tigrayan countryside

SALT ROUTE
Trek behind the Afar nomads and their camel caravans along the ancient Salt Route

MASSAWA
Wander around this decaying Oriental old port and dine on fresh fish, cooked Yemeni-style

NAKFA
Tour this battle-scared town – the heart of Eritrea's Struggle for independence

ASMARA
Stroll around this architecturally fascinating town and enjoy its cafe culture

AKSUM
Discover one of sub-Saharan Africa's most important historical sites

SIMIEN MOUNTAINS
Trek among the spectacular peaks, gorges and chasms of this range

GONDER
Take a step back into Ethiopia's Renaissance and wander the castles and palaces of the legendary court of Gonder

300mi
200km
150
100
0

To Riyadh
To Medina
Mecca
Jeddah
To Aswan
To Wadi Halfa
Abu Hamed
EGYPT
Nubian Desert
SUDAN
Atbara
Haiya
Kassala
KHARTOUM
Blue Nile River
White Nile River
To El Obeid
Nile River
Atbara River

SAUDI ARABIA
RED SEA
Port Sudan
Karora
Nakfa
Banuna
Durmu
Afabet
Keren
Agordat
Barentu
Adi Quala
ERITREA
Adi Arkey
Tekeze
Inda Selasie
Debark
Metema
Gorgora
Gonder
Humero
Ansereb River

YEMEN
SAN'A
Al-Hudaydah
Hanish Islands
GULF OF ADEN
Aden
Les Sept Frères
Rahaïta
Assab
Beylul
DJIBOUTI
Hadar
Dahlak Archipelago
Massawa
Embatcalla
Ghatelai
ASMARA
Zula
Maq'ia Fatma
Adaito
Thio
Ido
Wade
Danakil Depression
Senafe
Debre Damo
Edaga Hamus
Adigrat
Adwa
Aksum
Hawsien
Wukro
Agula
Mekele
Berahile
Maychew
Hagere Salem
Sankta Maria
Ras Dashen (4620m)
Simien Mountains NP
Abune Yosef (4190m)
Adi Abbi
Ras Dashen

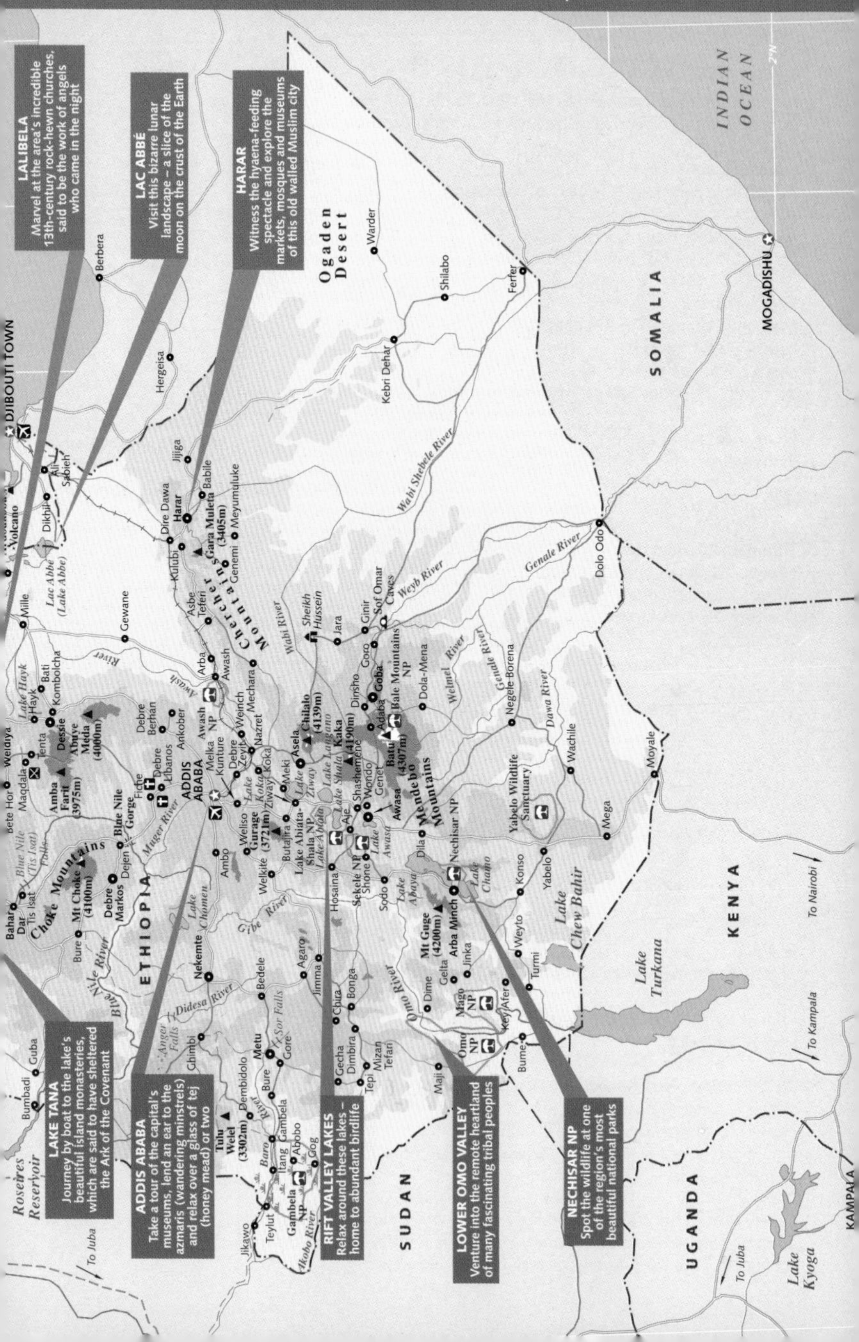

LALIBELA
Marvel at the area's incredible 13th-century rock-hewn churches, said to be the work of angels who came in the night
LAC ABBÉ
Visit this bizarre lunar landscape – a slice of the moon on the crust of the Earth
HARAR
Witness the hyaena-feeding spectacle and explore the markets, mosques and museums of this old walled Muslim city
LAKE TANA
Journey by boat to the lake's beautiful island monasteries, which are said to have sheltered the Ark of the Covenant
ADDIS ABABA
Take a tour of the capital's museums, lend an ear to the azmaris (wandering minstrels) and relax over a glass of tej (honey mead) or two
RIFT VALLEY LAKES
Relax around these lakes – home to abundant birdlife
LOWER OMO VALLEY
Venture into the remote heartland of many fascinating tribal peoples
NECHISAR NP
Spot the wildlife at one of the region's most beautiful national parks
ETHIOPIA
SUDAN
KENYA
UGANDA
SOMALIA
INDIAN OCEAN
Ogaden Desert
DJIBOUTI TOWN
ADDIS ABABA
MOGADISHU
KAMPALA
Berbera
Hergeisa
Jijiga
Dire Dawa
Harar
Babile
Gara Muleta (3405m)
Chercher Mountains
Awash
Awash NP
Debre Zeyit
Nazret
Asela
Chilalo (4139m)
Kaka (4190m)
Batu (4307m)
Bale Mountains NP
Goba
Dinsho
Sof Omar Caves
Sheikh Hussein
Mendebo Mountains
Shashemene
Awasa
Dila
Nechisar NP
Arba Minch
Mt Guge (4200m)
Lake Abaya
Lake Chamo
Lake Chew Bahir
Lake Turkana
Lake Kyoga
Yabelo Wildlife Sanctuary
Yabelo
Konso
Moyale
Mega
Negele-Borena
Dolo Odo
Genale River
Weyb River
Wabi Shebele River
Kebri Dehar
Shilabo
Ferfer
Warder
Gewane
Mille
Lac Abbe (Lake Abbe)
Dikhil
Ali Sabieh
Kombolcha
Dessie
Lake Hayk
Weldiya
Magdala
Abuye Meda (4000m)
Amba Farit (3975m)
Debre Berhan
Debre Libanos
Fiche
Blue Nile Gorge
Blue Nile (Tis Isat) Falls
Bahar Dar
Tis Isat
Choke Mountains
Mt Choke (4100m)
Debre Markos
Dejen
Bure
Nekemte
Lake Chomen
Gibe River
Didesa River
Bedele
Jimma
Agaro
Bonga
Chira
Metu
Gore
Sor Falls
Anger Falls
Chimbi
Dembidolo
Tulu Welel (3302m)
Gambela
Gambela NP
Baro River
Itang
Abobo
Gog
Teylut
Jikawo
Akobo River
Gecha
Dimbira
Tepi
Mizan Tefari
Maji
Omo NP
Mago NP
Omo River
Jinka
Dime
Key Afer
Turmi
Weyto
Bume
Hosaina
Sodo
Butajira
Gurage (3721m)
Weliso
Welkite
Ambo
Lake Ziway
Lake Langano
Lake Abiata-Shala NP
Lake Shala
Wondo Genet
Sekele NP
Lake Awasa
Muger River
Awash River
Blue Nile River
Roseires Reservoir
Bumbadi
Guba
To Juba
To Kampala
To Nairobi

Ethiopia, Eritrea & Djibouti
1st edition – November 2000

Published by
Lonely Planet Publications Pty Ltd ABN 36 005 607 983
90 Maribyrnong Street, Footscray, Victoria 3011, Australia

Lonely Planet offices
Australia Locked Bag 1, Footscray, Victoria 3011
USA 150 Linden St, Oakland, CA 94607
UK 10a Spring Place, London NW5 3BH
France 1 rue du Dahomey, 75011 Paris

Photographs
Many of the images in this guide are available for licensing from
Lonely Planet Images.
email: lpi@lonelyplanet.com.au
Web site: www.lonelyplanetimages.com

Front cover photograph
In Ethiopia, coffee is served with great ceremony – Dahlak Kebir,
Dahlak Archipelago
(Frances Linzee Gordon)

Title page photographs
Ethiopia: (Frances Linzee Gordon)
Eritrea: (Frances Linzee Gordon)
Djibouti: (Frances Linzee Gordon)

ISBN 0 86442 292 X

text & maps © Lonely Planet Publications Pty Ltd 2000
photos © photographers as indicated 2000

Printed by The Bookmaker International Ltd
Printed in China

Contents – Text

NORTH OF ADDIS ABABA

SOUTH OF ADDIS ABABA

WEST OF ADDIS ABABA

EAST OF ADDIS ABABA

ORAL LITERATURE IN THE HORN

ERITREA
313

FACTS ABOUT ERITREA
315

FACTS FOR THE VISITOR
335

GETTING THERE & AWAY
350

GETTING AROUND
353

ASMARA
355

NORTH OF ASMARA
377

EAST OF ASMARA
382

WEST OF ASMARA
396

Contents – Maps

The Author

Frances Linzee Gordon

Frances grew up in the highlands of Scotland, but later went to London University where she read Latin. Deciding modern languages might be a bit more useful, she lived and worked in continental Europe for a couple of years, doing various things such as researching bark beetle behaviour for the European Union. After returning to London, she worked for a travel trade publisher and read French and European law, politics and economics with the University of Lille at the French Institute. She is a Fellow of the Royal Geographical Society, holds a licentiateship at the Royal Photographic Society and has qualifications in nine languages.

Frances' first 'travel article' was written under duress following a school scholarship to Venice at the age of 17. Still travelling and still under duress, she now writes guidebooks and travel articles for her sins; she has co-authored Lonely Planet's *Morocco* and contributed to *Africa on a shoestring*, *Western Europe* and *Mediterranean Europe*. She is currently studying part-time for an MA in African and Middle Eastern history and Arabic at the School of African and Oriental Studies in London – and more usefully for upcoming wine-tasting exams. She has a passion for all forms of dangerous sport, electric blankets and above all, pickled onions.

FROM THE AUTHOR

My thanks to Yash Senturk and Frank Ohrtman for Internet research; Robin and Patricia Linzee Gordon for botanical expertise; Dr Philip Linzee Gordon for medical expertise; Richard Bendy and James Gray for – some! – research on the Simiens; and to Mike Street and Marianne Scott for information on architecture in Eritrea.

At Lonely Planet, thanks in particular to Virginia Maxwell, Vince Patton and especially Geoff'll-Fix-It-Stringer, who should take full credit for this publication.

In Ethiopia

Many letters were received, and thanks in particular must go to Vince Gainey of FARM-Africa.

Thanks also to Dr Adem Ibrahim, Minister of Health; Tesfaye Hundessa, Director of EWCO; Leykun Abunie; Engineer Solomon Kassaye, General Manager, NUPI; Tesfaye Maru, Ethiopian Mapping Authority; Worku Abate, Ministry of Information and Culture; Teyib Abba Foggi, Head of Culture, Jimma; Bisrat Negatu, MD, Ethiopian Airlines; Joseph Yohannes; Kagnew Fesseha;

8 The Author

Peter Talkington; John Summers; Demeke Berhane, Head of Manuscript and Archival Materials; Jara Haile Mariam, Head of CRCCH; Dr Jonas; Dr Bertrand Hirsch; and Matewos Fufa, Bureau Head of Oromia Trade, Industry and Tourism.

Thanks to Karen Laurenson and Dr Claudio Sillero for Ethiopian wolf information; Enkalatay Sani, Chief of Konso; Negusie Tesfa, Braile Farm; the writer Asfaw Damte; Florence Napthen, British Vice Consul; Lulseged Retta; Brigadier General Fresenbet Amde; Tamrat Bekele, Addis Tribune; Alemayehu Makonnen, Shell Ethiopia; Atakilti Hagege, Director of Tourism, Tigray.

To Ato Makonnen, Bahir Dar Travel Agency; Wondwossen Lakew; Ato Moges; Moges Kassa. Many thanks to Dr David Phillipson, Director of the digs, Aksum; Noël Siver, Conservator; Wondimu Yohannes, Mayor of Aksum; Fisseha Zibelo; Tesfaye Behonegen, Lalibela Municipality; Gudissa Lefe, Acting Warden of Senkele National Park; Hailu Beyene Dogoma, Culture Head, Dila; Tilahun Tute; Kirubel Zekkariyes, Head of Administration in Awasa; Gessesse Dessie, Head of Wondo Genet College of Forestry.

In Harar, Abdunasir Idris; Abdulhafiz Mawi; Yimaj Idris; Abdunasir Edris. Thanks to Tony Hickey; Denis Gérard for excellent reproductions of old photographs; Chadden Hunter for gelada baboon information; Habteselassie Asemare; and Dawit Abebe for his beautiful drawings.

Thanks to Lt Alo Afkihea, Deputy Police Commissioner, Asaita; Zewdu Shaul; Mohammed Said Meki; Alo Aydihas; Mohammed Yayo; Amsalu Temesger; Akililu Tilahun, Head of Culture, Nekemte; Berhaneselassie Lemma, Gambela Tourism Office; Kumneger Tsige, Gambela National Park; Meuze Tilaye and Teferi Gedlu, Tepi Coffee Plantation; Sisay Asrat, Manager, Bebeka Coffee Plantation; and Habtewold Habtemikael, Trade, Industry & Tourism Department, Bonga.

For help and hospitality, thanks to Hanna and Peter Williams; Omar Bagarsh; Menbere Girma; Tesfaye Gesessa; Olivier Vetter; Professor Richard and Rita Pankhurst; Ahmed Zekaria, Curator, National Museum; the Honorable Maître Artiste Laureat Afewerk Tekle; Ayalneh Mulatu; Dr Hailu Araya and his wife.

Above all thanks to Yusuf Abdullahi Sukkar, Commissioner of Tourism, who facilitated everything for me and who put his hardworking staff at my disposal: Menbere Girma; Almas; Ato Mattias; Mekonen Shiferaw; Dr Theodros Atlabachew; Habtamu Bekele; Tefera Kifetew; and in particular Zeyede Haile, Makonnen Shiferaw, and Hailu Mulatu.

To all the people of Ethiopia:

መኖን ፡ ከልከሰው ፡ ይንተፍእ ፡ ሁ ፡ ንከብ ፡ ለሞይኖሜ ፡ ኢ ኩ ፡ ከወሬ ፡ ኩ ።

In Eritrea

Thanks to Ahmed Haji Ali, Minister of Tourism; Bissirat Dessalegn; Yishak Yared, Ministry of Information; Rusom Semeri, Head of the Demining Unit; Berhanu Abraha, Ministry of Health; Kifle Wold-eselassie, DG, Ministry of Fisheries; Million Ghirmay and Semere Haile, Assab; Solomon Tsehaye, Cultural Affairs Bureau. Thanks to Mebrahtu Neguse, Eritrean Shipping Lines; Zereit Teweldebrhan, Director, Southern Regional Administration; Hamid Mohamed Jebber, Administrator, Dahlak Kebir; Yakob Gebregziabher, Mohammed Abdullah Abhada, Ali Issa Ahmed and Solomon Nigusei, Municipality of Assab.

Thanks to Dr Hagos Yohannes, Wildlife Conservation, and Dr JC Hillman, Ministry of Marine Resources, for access to their own work. To Tedros Kebbede, Director, ETS; Dahlak Kebir; Ahmed Issa Gabobeh, Ambassador to Djibouti, Eritrea; Carlo Prevosto and crew aboard the Fidel; Musie Misghina, Governor of Nakfa; Osman Abdela Buluh, Mayor of Assab; Yasin Gaim, Chief of Immigration, Assab; and Tewolde Andu, Mayor of Massawa. To Gabriel Tzeggay and Shumondi Bereket, for maps; Tekleab Tezare; the Sultan of Rahaita for his hospitality and class in Afar; the VSOs Katy Weiner, Fiona Maine, Sam Grimsditch, Ken Gurr, and Paul Satterthwaite; and particularly Segid Mehari.

Above all, thanks to Dr Yoseph Libsekal, Head of the National Museum, for access to his own notes and for wonderful tours.

To all the proud, independent and admirable people of Eritea: thank you.

In Djibouti

Thanks to Mohammed Ahmed Sultan, Ministry of Culture; Djaffar Guedi Hersi, Ministry of Transport; Abdo Farah Badar, Director of Tourism; Saïd Ahmed Warsama and Guedda Mohamed Ahmed, l'ISERST; Abdi Ismael Jackson, Djibouti Port; Dr Kassim Issak, PNLS; Baragoïta Saïd, Caravane du Sel Travel Agency; Philippe Lambrect, British Honorary Consul; Fouad Daoud Youssouf, artist, for his drawings; Zyad Doualeh; Omar Maalin Nour, the brave, blind poet; Aden Farah Samatar; Solomon, Ethiopian Airlines; Ali Aboubaker, IRIS; Ali Barkat Siradj, La Nation; Chehem Watta, PNUD; the Association SITTI; Madame Françoise Trikoff, Centre Culturel Français; Jean de Chatelperon, Air France; Marc Raynal, Centre Hôpitalier des Armées. Thanks particularly to Mohammed Abdillahi, Assistant Director, Tourism; Lt Colonel Abdillahi Abdi Farah, Head of Immigration; Nagib Abdou, Banque Indosuez; and Assowe Rirache and Alexandre Horak for great assistance and generosity researching Djibouti's diving.

For hospitality as well as assistance with research, thanks to the Prime Minister, Barkat Gourad Hamadou; Moussa Chehem,

Minister of Foreign Affairs; Mohamed Abdo Ahmed, Assistant Commissioner of Obock; Nimaan Abdillahi, Chamber of Commerce; Ismaël Guedi Hared; Dr Tony Caminiti; Abdourahman Boreh and Carawan Cassim; Marie-Jeanne Pillon and Patricia, French embassy; Jean-Dominique Pénel; Lt Guedid Abdon; and finally Youssef the nomad, who allowed me to stay with him and his family in the bush.

Above all, to Mr Ismaël Houssein Tani, Directeur de Cabinet, for facilitating with a phonecall anything I required and for his friendship.

To all the people of Djibouti: thank you. Your welcome, your warmth and your hospitality will never be forgotten.

This book is dedicated to my twin brother, Andrew, for years my companion, confidant and accomplice in all things.

This Book

From the Publisher

This first edition of Ethiopia, Eritrea & Djibouti was edited by Susan Holtham with able assistance from Kerryn Burgess, Isabelle Young, Hilary Rogers, Julia Taylor, Michelle Glynn and Virginia Maxwell. Mapping and design was coordinated by Katie Butterworth with cartographic assistance from Vince Patton (design), Hunor Csutoros (mapping and climate charts), Rodney Zandbergs (technical assistance) and Anna Judd (legend).

The illustrations were drawn by African artists Dawit Abebe, Fouad Daoud Youssouf and Kahssai Tzegumenghistu. Katie Butterworth created the chapter ends. The cover was designed by Vicki Beale with assistance from Margie Jung and cartographic assistance from Jim Miller. Quentin Frayne produced the language chapter and based it on Tilahun Gabriel's and Catherine Snow's *Ethiopian Amharic* phrasebook.

Foreword

ABOUT LONELY PLANET GUIDEBOOKS

The story begins with a classic travel adventure: Tony and Maureen Wheeler's 1972 journey across Europe and Asia to Australia. Useful information about the overland trail did not exist at that time, so Tony and Maureen published the first Lonely Planet guidebook to meet a growing need.

From a kitchen table, then from a tiny office in Melbourne (Australia), Lonely Planet has become the largest independent travel publisher in the world, an international company with offices in Melbourne, Oakland (USA), London (UK) and Paris (France).

Today Lonely Planet guidebooks cover the globe. There is an ever-growing list of books and there's information in a variety of forms and media. Some things haven't changed. The main aim is still to help make it possible for adventurous travellers to get out there – to explore and better understand the world.

At Lonely Planet we believe travellers can make a positive contribution to the countries they visit – if they respect their host communities and spend their money wisely. Since 1986 a percentage of the income from each book has been donated to aid projects and human rights campaigns.

Updates Lonely Planet thoroughly updates each guidebook as often as possible. This usually means there are around two years between editions, although for more unusual or more stable destinations the gap can be longer. Check the imprint page (following the colour map at the beginning of the book) for publication dates.

Between editions up-to-date information is available in two free newsletters – the paper *Planet Talk* and email *Comet* (to subscribe, contact any Lonely Planet office) – and on our Web site at www.lonelyplanet.com. The *Upgrades* section of the Web site covers a number of important and volatile destinations and is regularly updated by Lonely Planet authors. *Scoop* covers news and current affairs relevant to travellers. And, lastly, the *Thorn Tree* bulletin board and *Postcards* section of the site carry unverified, but fascinating, reports from travellers.

Correspondence The process of creating new editions begins with the letters, postcards and emails received from travellers. This correspondence often includes suggestions, criticisms and comments about the current editions. Interesting excerpts are immediately passed on via newsletters and the Web site, and everything goes to our authors to be verified when they're researching on the road. We're keen to get more feedback from organisations or individuals who represent communities visited by travellers.

Lonely Planet gathers information for everyone who's curious about the planet – and especially for those who explore it first-hand. Through guidebooks, phrasebooks, activity guides, maps, literature, newsletters, image library, TV series and Web site we act as an information exchange for a worldwide community of travellers.

Research Authors aim to gather sufficient practical information to enable travellers to make informed choices and to make the mechanics of a journey run smoothly. They also research historical and cultural background to help enrich the travel experience and allow travellers to understand and respond appropriately to cultural and environmental issues.

Authors don't stay in every hotel because that would mean spending a couple of months in each medium-sized city and, no, they don't eat at every restaurant because that would mean stretching belts beyond capacity. They do visit hotels and restaurants to check standards and prices, but feedback based on readers' direct experiences can be very helpful.

Many of our authors work undercover, others aren't so secretive. None of them accept freebies in exchange for positive write-ups. And none of our guidebooks contain any advertising.

Production Authors submit their raw manuscripts and maps to offices in Australia, USA, UK or France. Editors and cartographers – all experienced travellers themselves – then begin the process of assembling the pieces. When the book finally hits the shops, some things are already out of date, we start getting feedback from readers and the process begins again ...

WARNING & REQUEST

Things change – prices go up, schedules change, good places go bad and bad places go bankrupt – nothing stays the same. So, if you find things better or worse, recently opened or long since closed, please tell us and help make the next edition even more accurate and useful. We genuinely value all the feedback we receive. A well travelled team reads and acknowledges every letter, postcard and email and ensures that every morsel of information finds its way to the appropriate authors, editors and cartographers for verification.

Everyone who writes to us will find their name listed in the next edition of the appropriate guidebook. They will also receive the latest issue of *Planet Talk*, our quarterly printed newsletter, or *Comet*, our monthly email newsletter. Subscriptions to both newsletters are free. The very best contributions will be rewarded with a free guidebook.

We may edit, reproduce and incorporate your comments in all Lonely Planet products, such as guidebooks, Web sites and digital products, so let us know if you don't want your comments reproduced or your name acknowledged.

Send all correspondence to the Lonely Planet office closest to you:

Australia: Locked Bag 1, Footscray, Victoria 3122
USA: 150 Linden St, Oakland, CA 94607
UK: 10a Spring Place, London NW5 3BH
France: 1 rue du Dahomey, 75011 Paris

Or email us at: talk2us@lonelyplanet.com.au

For news, views and updates see our Web site: www.lonelyplanet.com

HOW TO USE A LONELY PLANET GUIDEBOOK

The best way to use a Lonely Planet guidebook is any way you choose. At Lonely Planet we believe the most memorable travel experiences are often those that are unexpected, and the finest discoveries are those you make yourself. Guidebooks are not intended to be used as if they provide a detailed set of infallible instructions!

Contents All Lonely Planet guidebooks follow roughly the same format. The Facts about the Destination chapters or sections give background information ranging from history to weather. Facts for the Visitor gives practical information on issues like visas and health. Getting There & Away gives a brief starting point for researching travel to and from the destination. Getting Around gives an overview of the transport options when you arrive.

The peculiar demands of each destination determine how subsequent chapters are broken up, but some things remain constant. We always start with background, then proceed to sights, places to stay, places to eat, entertainment, getting there and away, and getting around information – in that order.

Heading Hierarchy Lonely Planet headings are used in a strict hierarchical structure that can be visualised as a set of Russian dolls. Each heading (and its following text) is encompassed by any preceding heading that is higher on the hierarchical ladder.

Entry Points We do not assume guidebooks will be read from beginning to end, but that people will dip into them. The traditional entry points are the list of contents and the index. In addition, however, some books have a complete list of maps and an index map illustrating map coverage.

There may also be a colour map that shows highlights. These highlights are dealt with in greater detail in the Facts for the Visitor chapter, along with planning questions and suggested itineraries. Each chapter covering a geographical region usually begins with a locator map and another list of highlights. Once you find something of interest in a list of highlights, turn to the index.

Maps Maps play a crucial role in Lonely Planet guidebooks and include a huge amount of information. A legend is printed on the back page. We seek to have complete consistency between maps and text, and to have every important place in the text captured on a map. Map key numbers usually start in the top left corner.

Although inclusion in a guidebook usually implies a recommendation we cannot list every good place. Exclusion does not necessarily imply criticism. In fact there are a number of reasons why we might exclude a place – sometimes it is simply inappropriate to encourage an influx of travellers.

Introduction

Located at the eastern tip of the African continent, Ethiopia, Eritrea and Djibouti, along with neighbouring Somalia, jut tusk-like into the Indian Ocean, giving rise to the area's rather exotic and alluring title, the Horn of Africa.

The Horn has long attracted travellers – seaborne merchants have for centuries jostled and fought for trade on the region's shores – but it is only quite recently that the tourist has set foot here. And though visited much less often than other East African countries, Ethiopia, Eritrea and Djibouti hold remarkable – and incredibly little known – attractions.

Though neighbouring and – at different times in history – joined, the three countries today are as diverse in topography, culture and tradition as can be imagined. Unfortunately, the recent prolonged armed conflicts

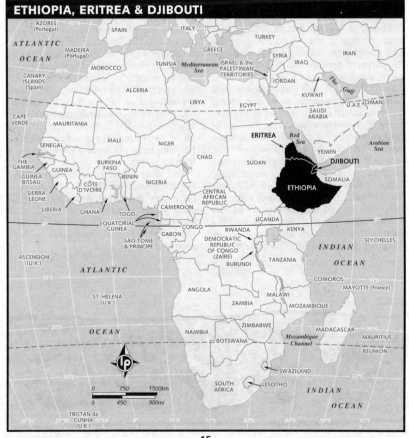

ETHIOPIA, ERITREA & DJIBOUTI

in the region have highlighted these differences.

The tiny enclave of Djibouti once formed part of French Somaliland and still retains a very French influence. Though the climate is torrid and the cost of living high, the country can still claim some special attractions. Lying at the convergence of three tectonic plates, Djibouti boasts exceptional geology. The landscape, though incredibly bleak in parts, can be extraordinarily beautiful. No less exceptional is the country's diving. Situated at the crossroads of the Red Sea and Indian Ocean, Djibouti's nomadic people have an intriguing culture, and, born perhaps from an inhospitable climate, a strong sense of hospitality.

Though it formed part of Ethiopia for years, Eritrea is very different from her larger neighbour. Colonised by the Italians, the European heritage is still evident in the pasta, cappuccino and Cinquecento cars. Beautiful Asmara, safe and clean and with outstanding architecture, must rank among the most attractive capital cities on the continent. Eritrea is also home to some significant archaeological remains: from ancient Aksumite ruins right up to the poignant war remnants of its 30-year Struggle for Independence with Ethiopia. Though arid, Eritrea's landscape can be beautiful, and like Djibouti, its Red Sea coral reefs are rich, pristine and undiscovered. The Eritrean people, proud, independent and industrious, welcome the visitor warmly to this country they fought so hard to free.

Ethiopia, almost the only African country to have escaped European colonialism, has retained much of its cultural identity. With its ancient history, its long connection with Christianity and its complex culture, Ethiopia is a fascinating country to visit. It's known above all for its exceptional historical attractions, including centuries-old rock-hewn churches and grand castles. Home to some famous archaeological finds, Ethiopia is known as the Cradle of Humanity; archaeologically speaking, Ethiopia is to sub-Saharan Africa what Egypt is to North Africa.

In contrast with its international image as a land of desert and famine, the word 'diverse' is the only way to describe Ethiopia. Diverse in geography, peoples and wildlife, the country offers correspondingly diverse attractions. The Simien and Bale Mountains offer very scenic trekking, the rivers of the south offer white-water rafting and fishing, and the country's parks have good wildlife and exceptional bird-watching. The southwestern regions offer memorable encounters with tribes considered among the most fascinating on the continent. With its 'little bit of everything' but also much of each, Ethiopia turns out to be a country rich in tourism potential.

Providing a great combination of differing attractions, the Horn of Africa makes for a very rewarding destination. Mythicized by the ancients for its exotic allure and rich resources, the Horn of Africa is today yet barely on the tourism map – but it soon will be.

Ethiopia

Pelicans enjoying a dip at dusk

White-backed vulture

Yellow-billed stork

Abyssinian ground hornbill

Beep! Beep! Vultureine guineafowls on the move

Bearded vultures are seen in the highlands.

Ethiopia

This is the land of the eighth harmony
in the rainbow: Black.
It is the dark side of the moon
brought to light.

Ethiopian poet Tsegaye Gebre-Medhin, *Africa,*
Traveller's Literary Companion,
In Print Publishing, UK, 1994

There are no two ways about it: Ethiopia
has an image problem. Mention Ethiopia,
and most people think of desert, famine and
war. Incredibly, Ethiopian Airlines – one of
Africa's most successful commercial airlines – still fields roundabout inquiries as to
whether passengers will get anything to eat
on its planes!

Though poor materially, Ethiopia boasts
extraordinary cultural, historical and natural wealth. In historical terms, it has the
longest archaeological record of any country on Earth; in religious terms, it was the
first country in the West after Armenia to
adopt Christianity; in natural terms, it
boasts an exceptional number of endemic
species and more birds than any other
African country except South Africa.

Among its attractions are 2000-year-old
Aksum, described as one of the last of the
great civilisations of antiquity to be revealed to modern knowledge; the beautiful
13th-century rock-hewn churches of Lalibela; and the 17th-century castles of
Gonder.

Right up until the latter half of the 19th
century, the country remained almost unknown to outsiders and it wasn't until the
latter half of the 20th century that visitors
began to set foot here. Even today, the attractions of Ethiopia remain little known.
A land still visited by the very few, a trip
here will afford the traveller a real sense of
discovery.

Ethiopia's isolation – along with its
unique political independence (it was almost the only country on the continent to
avoid colonisation) – has ensured that its
culture has remained remarkably intact, un-
polluted and undiluted by outside influence. The country retains its own particular language and script, its own food and
drink, its own church and saints, even its
own calendar and clock. Endlessly fascinating, it defies any categorisation or gen-
eralisation; Ethiopia is like no other
country in Africa.

Here, life simply goes on as it has for millennia, heedless of the modern world. The
centuries-old churches are still filled with
priests thumbing the old parchment, ancient
ceremonies continue to be re-enacted and old
ancestral traditions are rigidly adhered to.
You can encounter men who claim to receive visions directly from God, priests with
a gift for prophecy and wandering minstrels
reciting verses. In Ethiopia, one truly has the
impression of stepping back a thousand
years.

Isolated from within as well as from without, Ethiopia's rugged terrain has also seen
the development of great cultural diversity;
some of the ethnic groups that inhabit the
south-west, such as the Mursi lip stretchers
and Karo body painters, are among the most
fascinating on the African continent.

Despite the international indifference and
neglect, facilities for travellers are not lacking. The country boasts an excellent national
airline; plenty of enterprising tour operators;
and hotels to suit all tastes, including one
ranked as the most luxurious on the continent. For the budget traveller, hotels and
food are cheap, buses are reasonably comfortable and safe, bus routes are extensive
and the dollar goes on forever.

With a history as rich as anything found
in North Africa, with birds and animals as
interesting as anything in East Africa, with
tribal groups as fascinating as any in West
Africa and with climate and scenery as
pleasant as that in Southern Africa, Ethiopia
turns out to be a country far richer than
many imagine.

Ethiopia is Africa's best-kept secret. It is
the continent's 'dark side of the moon'; get
there before it's brought to light.

ETHIOPIA

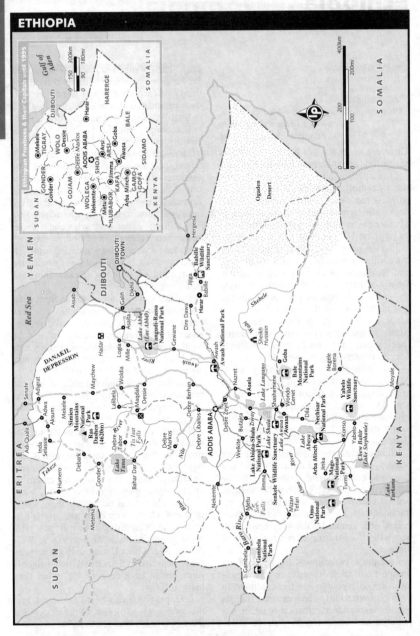

Facts about Ethiopia

HISTORY

Ethiopia has a long, rich and colourful history and a little knowledge about its past greatly enhances a trip around the country.

More than any other nation on the continent, Ethiopia refutes the amazingly persistent Western chauvinistic idea that 'sub-Saharan African has no culture'. Ethiopia is one of the oldest Christian civilisations in the world, and with the longest archaeological record of any country on Earth, it is also credited with being the original home of humanity.

Cradle of Humanity

During the last 40 years, some extraordinary prehistoric finds have been unearthed in the region (the most of famous of which is Lucy, see the boxed text 'Lucy in the Sky') earning Ethiopia the prestigious title of the 'Cradle of Humanity'.

Other Finds In December 1992, another find rocked the world of paleoanthropology. A joint American-Japanese team unearthed at Aramis, close to Hadar, over 50 fragments of skull, teeth, jaw and arm bone. These remains belonged not only to several different creatures (in fact a whole group numbering between 17 to 20 individuals) but also to a totally new species. Dating to some 4.4 million years ago, Lucy looked positively modern by comparison. Christened *Australopithecus ramidus*, the creature's ape-like features combined with the typical hominid characteristics such as smaller teeth, has led to the suggestion that the ape was Darwin's famous 'missing link' – a crucial transitional point from ape to human.

Yet more excitement came with the American-Ethiopian excavations of 1992–94 in the Gona Valley, south-west of Hadar. Several thousand stone tools were discovered, thought to date back between 2.5 to 2.6 million years. They were the oldest yet found in the world.

ETHIOPIA AT A GLANCE

Capital City: Addis Ababa

Population: 58 million

Time: 3 hours ahead of GMT

Land Area: 1,098,000 sq km

International Telephone Code: ☎ 251

GDP/Capita: US$102

Currency: Birr (Birr8 = US$1 approx)

Languages: Amharic (national language)

Greeting: *Tadiyass*

Highlights

- Explore Aksum's tombs, ruined palaces and beautiful obelisks

- See the awesome complex of rock-hewn churches at Lalibela

- Witness the feeding of the hyaenas in the Muslim walled city of Harar

- Get lost in sub-Saharan Africa's busiest outdoor market, the Merkato, in Addis Ababa's west

- Brave the notorious roped ascent up to the holy site of the Damo monastery in Tigray

- Catch a dhow out to the centuries-old Lake Tana island monasteries

Lucy in the Sky

On 30 November 1974, there was an international sensation: in a dried-up lake near Hadar in the far north-east of Ethiopia, the fossilised remains of a very remote human ancestor were found. Named Lucy or, more evocatively, *Denkenesh* or *Birkinesh* (You are wonderful) in Ethiopian Amharic, she was then the oldest-known hominid in the world, dated at least 3.2 million years old. Today, her remains are conserved in the National Museum in Addis Ababa.

Darwin was right, and Lucy seemed to prove it: man's 'nearest ally' was the ape, and its original home was in Africa. Belonging to the group *Australopithecus afarensis*, Lucy was a hominid: a kind of half-human – half-ape, distinguished above all by its erect walk. Hominids represent a major step on the evolutionary ladder towards modern man.

But Lucy was special, not just for her incredible age, but for her anatomy, too. Her skeleton seemed to suggest that our ancestors – contrary to previous theories – began to walk *before* they developed bigger brains. Standing just over a metre high, and weighing no more than 30kg, the little creature had a tiny brain, yet her other features were unmistakably human: the pelvis, legs and above all her V-shaped jaw. Similar to our own, it differed totally from the box-like, parallel-tooth formation of her ape ancestors.

Named after the Beatles' song *Lucy in the Sky*, which happened to be playing in the archaeologists' camp at the moment of discovery, Lucy continues to intrigue. According to her discoverer, Donald Johanson, many aspects about her still provide 'ongoing riddles'.

Meanwhile, similar finds of a comparable age are being unearthed in another very rich paleoanthropological site, the Omo Valley in southern Ethiopia. In 1998, a US team began investigating the region. The area is thought to be brimming with animal and human fossils.

Paleoanthropology is still in its infancy in Ethiopia and it's very likely that more finds – perhaps just as sensational as Lucy – await discovery. Although finds in southern Africa have recently challenged Ethiopia's claims to being the cradle of humanity, the Ethiopian Rift Valley remains an extremely important source of information on this still very obscure period in our early history.

Prehistory

Important prehistoric remains include recently discovered Late Stone Age paintings and engravings, as well as evidence of very early cereal cultivation. Some cereals, such as *tef*, a grass, are thought to be indigenous; others such as wheat and barley may have come down the Nile from Egypt several millennia back.

Land of Punt

Ethiopia is believed to have formed part of the ancient Land of Punt, an area on the southern Red Sea coast which had attracted the trading ships of the Egyptian Pharaohs for millennia.

Although Eritrea, on the coast, is the most likely site of the land (see the boxed text 'Land of Punt' under History in the Facts about Eritrea section later in this book), it is very likely that some export items such as gold, myrrh, ivory and slaves issued from the Ethiopian interior.

Very little is known about Ethiopia at this time (c.3500 BC), but it is thought that the northern region saw much migration from surrounding areas. By around 2000 BC, strong contacts had been established between the people of northern Ethiopia and Eritrea and the inhabitants of southern Arabia across the Red Sea.

Pre-Aksumite Civilisation

The cultural significance of the meeting of the southern Arabians and the Ethiopians was enormous. A number of Afro-Asiatic languages emerged, including an early Ge'ez (a kind of Latin and a forerunner of Amharic), which is spoken by Christian priests in Ethiopia and Eritrea to this day.

Most significant was the rise, in the first millennium BC, of a remarkable civilisation in the Horn. The influence of southern

Arabia was clear in the Semitic language, the Sabaean script and in the worship of the same gods. The new civilisation in Ethiopia, which appeared to mushroom overnight, was confined to very small settlements and benefited from specialist crafts, skills and technologies previously unknown in Ethiopia – all apparently indicative of settlers bringing with them imported knowledge.

Noting the similarity, and disinclined to believe that such a civilisation could be African, scholars for years concluded that the culture was Arabian, transplanted from across the Red Sea by Sabaean settlers migrating between 1000 to 400 BC. But in just the last few years, scholars have begun to argue with greater conviction that this civilisation was indeed African. And that although undoubtedly influenced by Sabaean ideas, it developed from local effort and initiative. If proved correct, histories of the Horn will have to be completely rewritten.

Whatever the origin, the civilisation was a very important one. The most famous relic of the times is the extraordinary stone 'temple' of Yeha, lying to the north of Aksum. Thought to date to between 800 and 500 BC, it was probably Ethiopia's first capital.

The remains of many other buildings also exist, including the large and remarkable sites of Metera, Tocanda and Keskese in southern Eritrea.

Kingdom of Aksum

At the beginning of the first millennium AD, there arose in the highlands of Ethiopia and Eritrea a unique African civilisation. During seven centuries, it grew to number among the most powerful kingdoms of the ancient world.

Aksum is thought to have owed its importance to its position, lying at the pivot of an important commercial crossroads. To the north-west lay Egypt, and to the west, near the present-day Sudanese border, were the rich, gold-producing lowlands. To the north-east, in present-day Eritrea, was the Aksumite port of Adulis, positioned at the crux of an extensive trading route that stretched from Egypt and

---

Divine Travellers

Ethiopia, meaning 'Land of the Burnt Faces', got its name from the Greeks. The Greeks saw the country as a remote, far-off realm, populated with incredible people and extraordinary animals. According to the Greek historian Diodorus Siculus, Ptolemy II used to return from hunting expeditions in Ethiopia in the 3rd century BC with wild exotic animals, which were 'objects of amazement' to the Greeks.

The Greek poet Homer (writing in 800 BC) spoke of the people as the 'blameless Ethiopians'. The Greek gods themselves were said by Diodorus in the 1st century BC to have been impressed by their piety. Homer, in the *Iliad*, writes that some of them even deigned to visit the remote land. Celestial travellers purportedly included Zeus himself, the king of the gods; the goddess Iris, who fancied taking part in some sacrificial rites there; and Poseidon the sea god, who 'lingered delighted' at the sumptuous Ethiopian feasts.

---

the Mediterranean, all the way to India and Ceylon. Trade flourished and the kingdom boomed.

Aksum also enjoyed a good geographical location. Spreading out around the town were fertile and well-watered agricultural lands, further exploited by the use of well-designed dams, wells and reservoirs.

The kingdom's greatest assets and those that made up the bulk of its exports, were its natural resources: frankincense, grain, animal skins, rhino horn, apes and particularly ivory. Wildlife at this time was abundant and ten of thousands of elephants were reported to roam the region. Ivory was one of the most highly prized nonprecious products in the Egyptian world.

The *Periplus of the Erythraean Sea*, written by a Greek-speaking Egyptian sailor or merchant around the 1st century AD, describes Aksum's imports. Most came from Egypt, Arabia and India, and ranged from dyed cloaks and cheap unlined coats to glassware, and iron for making spears, swords and axes. Syrian and Italian wine and olive oil (then considered a luxury)

Rock Art

Rock art is notoriously difficult to date; nevertheless, some Ethiopian rock paintings are thought to date back at least 10,000 years. Still very little studied, the paintings provide an invaluable glimpse into the social, economic, religious and artistic life of Stone Age man.

Rock art is found particularly in the (old) provinces of Tigray (north), Harerge (east) and Gamo-Gofa (south-west), and varies from simple engravings to beautifully executed carvings and delicate colour paintings. Depictions include domestic and wild animals (such as zebu cattle, lions and elephants) and human subjects with bows and arrows, spears and shields. Additionally, various enigmatic and abstract signs and symbols have been found. The latter, difficult to interpret, may well reveal much information about the period.

were also imported, as was much gold and silver plate for the king.

During its heyday between the 3rd and 6th centuries, the kingdom of Aksum stretched east across the Red Sea into large parts of southern Arabia, and west into the Sudanese Nile Valley. Aksumite society was rich, well organised and technically and artistically advanced. During this era, an unparalleled coinage in bronze, silver and gold was produced, extraordinary monuments were built and, exerting the greatest influence of all on future Ethiopia, Christianity was introduced.

The Coming of Christianity

Although the Ethiopian church claims that Christianity first reached Aksum at the time of the Apostles, it did not become the state religion until the beginning of the 4th century. King Ezana's stone inscription makes reference to Christ, and his famous coins bear the Christian Cross – the first in the world to do so.

The end of the 5th century AD saw the arrival of the famous Nine Saints, a group of Greek-speaking missionaries who established well-known monasteries in the north of the country, including Debre Damo. At

this time, the Bible was first translated from Greek into Ge'ez, the early language of Ethiopia.

The arrival of Christianity was a major turning point in Ethiopian history. The religion was to have an enormous influence on the country, shaping not just its spiritual and intellectual life, but also its cultural and social life, including its art and literature. Today around half the population of Ethiopia is Orthodox Christian.

Soon to account for the other half, and hot on the heels of Christianity, came a new religion to Ethiopian shores: the religion of Islam.

The Coming of Islam

According to tradition, the Prophet was nursed by an Ethiopian woman. Later, the Muslim Hadith (collection of traditions about Mohammed's life) recounts that Mohammed sent some of his followers to Ethiopia in AD 615, to avoid persecution in Arabia. Among the group was the Prophet's own daughter and son-in-law and future successor, Uthman.

At Aksum, the refugees were shown hospitality and, it is said, King Armah liked them so much that he didn't wish to let them go. However, at the end of the persecution the refugees returned safely to Arabia.

Good relations between the two religions continued until at least the death of King Armah. Thereafter, as Islam's fortunes waxed, those of Christian Aksum began to wane; a conflict of interests was inevitable.

The Demise of Aksum

Islam's expansion in the area was concomitant with the rise in the fortunes of the Arabs, fast becoming the new masters of the Red Sea. Little by little, Aksum became increasingly isolated: trade and the economy slumped, coins ceased to be minted, and hard times set in. Aksum's commercial domination of the region was over. However, to this day, Aksum occupies a very special position in Ethiopian history and consciousness. From its decline in the early 12th century, right up to the present day, Aksum has remained a kind of religious and

Christianity Arrives by Accident

No one knows for certain how Christianity first came to Ethiopia. According to an apparently contemporary account by the Byzantine ecclesiastical historian, Rufinus, it arrived on Ethiopian shores by accident rather than by design.

The story begins with the Christian merchant, Meropius, who was returning one day from a voyage to India accompanied by his two young students. On their way back home to Tyre in Syria, the boat put in for water on the coast of Africa, but was attacked by unfriendly natives.

Meropius was killed in the struggle, but the boys, Frumentius and Aedesius, were taken to the court of the Aksumite king. There Frumentius became the king's secretary and treasurer and Aedesius became cup-bearer.

Soon Frumentius began to establish many churches in the kingdom, and eventually travelled to Alexandria in Egypt, the most important centre of eastern Christianity at the time. There he urged the great patriarch Athanasius to appoint a bishop to Ethiopia. The old patriarch agreed, and appointed the virtuous Frumentius himself. Frumentius became Ethiopia's first bishop and for the next 1500 years, the country obtained its patriarchs from Alexandria.

spiritual capital in the eyes of many of Ethiopia's Christian population.

The Zagwe Dynasty

After the decline of Aksum, political power began to shift southwards. In the early 12th century, a new capital was established under a new power: the Zagwe dynasty. Based in the mountains of Lasta not far from Lalibela, its capital was initially known as Adafa.

The dynasty reigned from around AD 1137 to 1270 – over 130 years – yet the period is one of the most obscure in Ethiopian history. Seemingly, no coins were minted, no stones inscribed and no chronicles written.

Unlike the kingdom of Aksum, no accounts of the dynasty by foreign travellers survive and, positioned further from the coast, far fewer imported items have been found – objects that might have provided clues to this enigmatic period. In addition, the dynasty is traditionally treated as a kind of embarrassment in Ethiopian history. The Zagwes were seen as usurpers in the long Solomonic dynastic line.

Nevertheless, the period is an extremely important one in the cultural history of Ethiopia. During the reign of three of its kings: Yemrehanna Kristos, Lalibela and Na'akuto La'ab, the astonishing rock-hewn churches of Lalibela were constructed, which are today one of Ethiopia's top attractions (see the North of Addis Ababa section).

It is not certain what brought the Zagwe dynasty to an end; probably a combination of infighting within the ruling dynasty, as well as local opposition from the clergy. In AD 1270, the dynasty was overthrown. Political power shifted once again, this time to the province of Shoa. There, Yekuno Amlak set himself on the throne and established a new dynasty that would reign for the next 500 years.

The Solomonic line had been 'restored', and the Middle Ages were about to dawn in Ethiopia.

The Middle Ages

Compared to the previous period, medieval Ethiopia is quite well documented, thanks to the royal chroniclers of the court, and to various reports made by foreign travellers.

The Middle Ages were both a continuation of the past with its all-powerful monarchy and influential clergy, and a break with it. Trade was now conducted by barter with pieces of iron, cloth or salt (see the boxed text 'Salt for Gold' under Danakil Desert in the North of Addis Ababa section) rather than with a minted currency, and the kingdom's capitals had become 'itinerant'. Capitals were little more than vast moving military camps.

Culturally, the period was important for the significant output of Ge'ez literature,

The Lost City

Aksum's relatively rapid decline and disappearance is still a mystery, though many explanations have been offered.

The environmental argument suggests that Aksum's ever-increasing population led to over-cropping of the land, deforestation and eventually soil erosion. The climatic explanation claims that a kind of 'global warming' took place, which finished Aksum's agriculture and led eventually to drought and famine. The military argument claims that Aksum was undermined by continual incursions from neighbouring tribes, such as the Beja from the north-west of the country.

According to the traditional explanation, Aksumite power was usurped around the 9th century by the dreaded warrior queen, Gudit (or Judit), a Pagan or Jew, who killed the ruling king, burnt down the city and sabotaged the stelae. Intriguingly, this legend seems to be born out by at least two documents written at about this time.

᚛᚛᚛᚛᚛᚛᚛᚛᚛᚛᚛᚛᚛᚛᚛᚛᚛᚛᚛᚛᚛᚛᚛᚛᚛᚛

including the nation's epic, the Kebra Negast (see under Arts later in this section).

It was also at this time that contacts with European Christendom began to increase. With the rising threat of well-equipped Muslim armies in the East, Europe was seen as a kind of Christian superpower.

Europe, for its part, dreamed of winning back Jerusalem from the 'Saracens', and welcomed the important strategic position offered by Ethiopia – at the time, almost the only Christian kingdom outside Europe. Ethiopia even became a candidate for the location of the legendary Kingdom of Prester John. According to the legend, an immensely wealthy and powerful Christian monarch reigned in a far-off land in the East, who would join the kings of Europe in a mighty crusade against the infidel.

In the early 15th century, the first European embassy arrived in Ethiopia, sent by the famous French aristocrat Duc de Berry. Ethiopians in their turn began to travel to Europe, particularly to Rome, where many joined churches established there.

The Muslim – Christian Wars

The first few decades of the 16th century were plagued by some of the most costly, bloody and wasteful fighting in Ethiopian history, in which the empire, its institutions and its culture came quite close to being wiped out.

From the 13th century, relations with the Muslim emirates of Ifat and Adal (which lay between the Ethiopian highlands and the Red Sea) began to show signs of strain. Competition was growing over control of the valuable trade routes, and tension was increasing.

Mahfuz In the 1490s, animosities came to a head. A skilled and charismatic Muslim warrior named Mahfuz established himself at the port of Zeila, in present-day Somalia. There he declared a *jihad* (holy war) against Christian Ethiopia and made no less than 25 annual raids into the highlands of Shoa. Mahfuz was finally defeated by Emperor Lebna Dengel, but not before he had carried off huge numbers of Ethiopian slaves and cattle.

Mohammed Gragn the Left-Handed

The famous Ahmed Ibn Ibrahim al Ghazi, nicknamed Mohammed Gragn the Left-Handed, was an even more legendary figure. After overthrowing Sultan Abu Bakr of Harar, Mohammed then declared his intention of continuing the jihad of Mahfuz. Carrying out several raids into Ethiopian territory, he managed to defeat Emperor Lebna Dengel himself in March 1529. Mohammed then embarked on the conquest of all of Christian Ethiopia. Well supplied with firearms from Ottoman Zeila and southern Arabia, which he pragmatically exchanged for captured Christian slaves, the Muslim leader had, by 1532, overrun almost all of eastern and southern Ethiopia.

In 1535, Emperor Lebna Dengel appealed in desperation to Portugal – already active in the region. In 1541, an army of 400 well-armed musketeers arrived in Massawa (present-day Eritrea), led by Dom Christovão da Gama, son of the famous mariner Vasco da Gama.

Mohammed met the Portuguese army near Lake Tana, defeated it and captured and beheaded the overly confident commander, Dom Christovão.

By 1543, the new Ethiopian emperor, Galawdewos, had assembled a new army. Joining ranks with the surviving Portuguese force, he met Mohammed at Wayna Daga in the west. This time, the huge numbers proved too much for Mohammed – he was killed and his followers fled. Keen to follow up his victory, Galawdewos turned on the rich trading Muslim city of Harar. But advancing too hastily and without the back-up of his main army, the emperor also lost his life.

Aftermath The Muslim-Christian Wars had been incredibly costly. Thousands of people lost their lives, the Christian monarchy was nearly wiped out, and the once mighty Muslim state of Adal lay in ruins. Many of the most beautiful churches and monasteries in Ethiopia – along with their precious manuscripts, church relics and regalia – lay in ashes.

Oromo Migrations
Following the imam's death, and filling the power vacuum left behind, a new threat to the Ethiopian empire arose. A Cushitic people, the Oromos (then known as the Gallas), originating from the south and present-day Kenya, began a great migration northwards. For the next 200 years, armed conflict between the empire and the Oromos sporadically broke out. For the empire, the expansion meant not just the loss of territory, but more seriously, the loss of vital tax revenue.

The Jesuits
At the beginning of the 17th century, the Oromo threat led several emperors to seek help from the Jesuits, who were backed in their cause by the well-armed Portuguese. Two emperors, Za-Dengel and Susenyos, even went as far as conversion to the Jesuits' Catholicism. But in attempting to impose the faith on the state, the emperors provoked widespread rebellion; Za-Dengel was overthrown and, in 1629, Susenyos' draconian measures to convert his people incited civil war. Much bloodshed followed

Itinerant Courts

During the Ethiopian Middle Ages, the business of most monarchs consisted of waging wars, collecting taxes and inspecting the royal domains.

Obliged to travel continuously throughout their far-flung empire, the kings lived a kind of perpetual nomadic existence.

And with the rulers went their army, courtiers and servants. In addition there were the judges, prison officers, priests, merchants, prostitutes and a whole entourage of artisans: butchers and bakers, chefs, tailors and blacksmiths. Camps could spread over 20km; for transportation, 50 to 100,000 mules were required.

The retinue was so vast that it rapidly exhausted the resources of the locality; four months was usually the maximum permissible stay and ten years had to pass before the spot could be revisited.

The put-upon peasantry were said to dread the royal visits as they dreaded the swarms of locusts. In both cases, everything that lay in the path of the intruders was devoured.

– 32,000 peasants are thought to have lost their lives at the hands of the emperor's army. Susenyos was forced to back down, and the Orthodox faith was re-established.

On Susenyos' death, his son Fasiladas kicked out the meddling Jesuits, and forbade all foreigners from setting foot in his empire. For nearly 130 years, only one European, a French doctor Charles Poncet (see the boxed text 'Emperor Iyasu'), was allowed to enter Ethiopia.

Though the Jesuits' interference had caused great suffering and bloodshed in Ethiopia, they did leave behind one useful legacy: books. Pero Pais wrote the first serious history of the country. Other writings included detailed accounts of Ethiopia's cultural, economic and social life.

With the Ottoman hold in the east, and the Oromo entrenchment in the south, the political authority of Shoa had become increasingly circumscribed. It was time to relocate – once again – the centre of power.

Emperor Iyasu

...A great emerald glitter'd on his forehead and added majesty to him...[the emperor was] clad with a vest of blue velvet, flower'd with gold, which trail'd upon the ground. His head was cover'd with a muslin, strip'd gold, which fram'd a sort of crown after the manner of the ancients, and which left the middle of his head bare. His shoes were wrought, after the Indian fashion, with flowers beset with pearls...The throne, of which the feet were of massy silver, was plac'd at the bottom of a hall, in an alcove cover'd with a dome all shining with gold and azure.

French traveller Charles Poncet, from *A Voyage to AEthiopia* (trans), 1709, republished by the Hakluyt Society, 1949

The Rise of Gonder

In 1636, following the tradition of his fore-fathers, Emperor Fasiladas, decided to found a new capital. Gonder – the chosen site near Lake Tana – proved to be different from its predecessors. The town became a permanent capital, the first in Ethiopian history, and was to flourish for the next 200 years.

By the end of the 17th century, the city of Gonder boasted magnificent palaces, beautiful gardens and extensive plantations. The court was the site of sumptuous feasts and extravagant court pageantry and attracted visitors from around the world. The town was also the site of a thriving market, which drew rich Muslim merchants from across the country.

Under the ample patronage of church and state, the arts and crafts flourished. Beautiful churches were built, among them the famous Debre Berhan Selassie, which can be seen to this day. Outside Gonder, building projects included the remarkable island churches of Lake Tana.

But Gonder's court soon proved to be rotten to the core and, in 1706, Emperor Iyasu was assassinated. In the struggle for succession over the next 24 years, no less than four monarchs held power. The royal bodyguard, the clergy, the nobles, even the ordinary citizens, all conspired. Assassination, plotting and intrigue became the order of the day, and the ensuing chaos was like something out of Shakespeare's *Macbeth*, or the worst excesses of the late Roman Empire. Emperor Bakaffa's reign (1721–30) restored brief stability, during which time new palaces and churches were built, and literature and the arts once again thrived.

But on Iyasu II's death in 1755, the Gonder kingdom was back in turmoil. The provinces started to rebel, and ethnic rivalries surfaced at court, coming to a head in a power struggle between the Oromo, who had become increasingly absorbed into the court, and the Tigrayan ruler, Ras Mikael Sehul. Assassination and murder again followed, central government fell apart, and the emperors became little more than puppets in the hands of the rival feudal lords and their powerful provincial armies. The country disintegrated and civil war became the order of the day. From a kind of renaissance, Ethiopia had stepped right back into the dark ages.

Ethiopian historians later referred to the period after Iyasu II's death as the era of the *masafent* or judges, after the references in the Book of Judges 21:25, to a time when 'there was no king in Israel: every man did that which was right in his own eyes'.

Emperor Tewodros

Right up until the middle of the 19th century, Ethiopia continued to exist as separate fiefdoms. In the mid-19th century, however, there arose from among the feuding lords one who dreamed of unity. Kassa Haylu had a curious background. The son of a western chief, he was brought up in a monastery, later became a *shifta* (bandit), and then a kind of Robin Hood figure: looting the rich to give to the poor.

He quickly attracted followers and began to defeat the rival princes, one after another, until in 1855 he had himself crowned Emperor Tewodros. The new monarch soon began to show himself not just as a capable leader and strong ruler but as a unifier, innovator and reformer as well.

Choosing as his base the natural fortress of Maqdala, around 112km east of Debre Tabor, Tewodros began to formulate mighty plans. Among the emperor's many projects were the establishment of a national army, an arms factory and a great road network. His policies included a major program of land reform, the abolition of the slave trade and the promotion of Amharic (the vernacular) in place of the classical written language, Ge'ez. Tewodros even tried to strengthen the institution of marriage.

But these reforms met with deep resentment and opposition from the land-holding clergy, the rival lords and even the common faithful. Tewodros' response was ruthless and sometimes brutal. Like a Shakespearean tragic hero, Tewodros suffered from fatal flaws: an intense pride, a fanaticism for his cause and an inflated sense of destiny, which eventually would bring him into conflict with other forces, too.

Frustrated by failed attempts to enlist European and particularly British support for his modernising programs, Tewodros impetuously imprisoned some British functionaries present at his court. Initially successful in extracting concessions, Tewodros overplayed his hand, and his plan badly miscarried. In 1869, Sir Robert Napier set out from Britain at the head of 32,000 men. His mission was to free the hostages held at Maqdala. Far better equipped, far superior in numbers and backed-up by rival Ethiopian lords, the British army inflicted appalling casualties on Tewodros' men, many of them armed with little more than shields and spears.

Refusing to surrender and with his offer of peace rebuffed, Tewodros – playing the tragic hero to the last – penned a final dramatic and bitter treatise, put a pistol in his mouth and shot himself. The British, with their mission accomplished, put Maqdala to the flames, looted its royal treasures (including crowns and over 500 precious manuscripts now in museums and private collections in Britain), and rode away.

Tewodros' defeat gravely weakened Ethiopia, which was watched carefully by other colonial powers, hungry for expansion.

Emperor Yohannes

In the wake of the British there arose another battle for succession. With superior weaponry (won from the British in exchange for support of the expedition to Maqdala) Kassa Mercha of Tigray managed to defeat his opponent, the newly crowned Emperor Tekla Giorgis, at the battle of Assam in 1871.

Proclaiming himself Emperor Yohannes the following year, Kassa's reign lasted 17 years. In contrast to Tewodros, Yohannes staunchly supported the church and, being much more of a realist, believed that unity of his country could only be achieved through a kind of federalism.

In exchange for keeping their kingdoms, the local lords were obliged to recognise the emperor's overall power, and to pay taxes to his state. In this way, Yohannes secured the religious, political and financial backing of his subjects.

Yohannes proved himself a skilful soldier, too. In 1875, after the Egyptians had advanced into Ethiopia from Eritrea, Yohannes drew them into battle and beat them resoundingly, once at Gundat in 1875 and again at Gura in 1876. His victories not only ended any Egyptian designs on the territory, but brought him much captured weaponry – turning his army into the first well-equipped force in Ethiopian history.

But soon another power threatened: the Italians. The opening of the Suez Canal in 1869 hugely increased the strategic value of the Red Sea, which became again a passageway to the East and beyond.

In 1885, the Italians arrived in Massawa, Eritrea, and soon blockaded arms to Yohannes. Furious at their failure to impede the arrival of the Italians, Yohannes accused the British of contravening the Hewett Treaty, signed in 1884. Privately, the British welcomed the arrival, both to counter French influence in Djibouti, and to deter Turkish designs on the coast.

In the meantime, the Mahadists (or Dervishes) were raising their heads to the West. Filling the power gap left by Egypt, they overran Sudan. In 1888, a large Dervish army arrived in Ethiopia. Defeating the army sent against them, they sacked Gonder, and torched many of its churches.

Yohannes rushed to meet the Dervishes at Qallabat in 1889 but, at the close of another Ethiopian victory, he fell, mortally wounded with a sniper's bullet.

Emperor Menelik

Menelik, Prince of Shoa since 1865, had long aspired to the throne. Confined by Tewodros for ten years at Maqdala, he was yet reportedly much influenced by his captor, dreaming like Tewodros of the unification and modernisation of his country.

After his escape from Maqdala and ascendancy in Shoa, Menelik concentrated on consolidating his own power, and embarked on an aggressive, ruthless and sometimes brutal campaign of expansion, occupying territories to the south, south-west and south-east, forcing many new ethnic groups under the yoke of his empire.

Relations with the Italians were at first good; Menelik had been seen as a potential ally against Yohannes. On Yohannes' death, the Italians recognised Menelik's claim to the throne and, in 1889, the Treaty of Wechale was signed. In exchange for granting Italy the region that was later to become Eritrea, the Italians recognised Menelik's sovereignty and gave him the right to import arms freely through Ethiopian ports. However, a dispute over a discrepancy in the purportedly identical Amharic and Italian texts (the famous Article 17) led to disagreement. According to the Italian version, Ethiopia was obliged to approach other foreign powers through Italy – in effect reducing Ethiopia to the status of an Italian protectorate. Relations began to sour.

In the meantime, the Italians continued their expansion in their newly created colony of Eritrea, and soon were spilling into Ethiopian territory, also – well beyond the confines agreed to in both treaties.

Despite Italian attempts to subvert the local chiefs of Tigray, the chiefs chose instead to side with Menelik. However, the Italians managed to defeat Ras Mangasha and his Tigrayan forces and were soon in occupation of the Ethiopian town of Mekele in 1895.

Provoked at last into marching north, Menelik assembled his forces and met the Italians in Adwa in 1896. To international shock and amazement, the Italian armies were resoundingly defeated (see the boxed text 'The Battle of Adwa' under Adwa in the North of Addis Ababa section).

In the following months, diplomatic missions were sent to Ethiopia from across the world and international boundaries were formally drawn up. Ethiopia as an independent country was born.

The Battle of Adwa was one of the biggest and most significant in African history – numbering among the very few occasions when a colonial power was defeated by a native force. To the rest of Africa, Ethiopia became a beacon of independence in a continent almost entirely enslaved by colonialism.

Menelik was responsible for another great achievement, too: the modernisation of his country. During his reign, the old Shoan capital of Ankober had been abandoned and the new site of Addis Ababa founded. Electricity and telephones were introduced, bridges, roads, schools and hospitals built, banks and industrial enterprises established.

The greatest technological achievement of the time was undoubtedly the construction of Ethiopia's first railway, which reached Addis Ababa in 1915. Linking Addis Ababa to Djibouti, it contributed greatly to the growth of Addis Ababa and the expansion of Ethiopian trade (see the boxed text 'The Railway' under Dire Dawa in the East of Addis Ababa section).

Iyasu

Menelik managed to die a natural death in 1913. Iyasu, his raffish young grandson and nominated heir, proved to be very much a product of the 20th century. Continuing with Menelik's reforms, he also showed a 'modern' secularist, nonsectarian attitude.

The young prince took several Muslim as well as Christian wives, built mosques as well as churches, and took steps to support the empire's periphery populations that had for years suffered at the oppressive hands of the Amhara settlers and governors.

Despite ever-deepening opposition from the church and nobility, Iyasu and his councillors managed to push through a few reforms, including the improvement of the system of land tenure and taxation.

After also upsetting the allied powers with his dealings with Germany and Austria, some of the nobles found a pretext to act against him. Accused nominally of 'abjuring the Christian faith', the prince was deposed, Zewditu, Menelik's daughter, was proclaimed empress, and Ras Tafari the prince regent.

Ras Tafari

On coming to power, Ras Tafari boasted more experience and greater maturity than Iyasu, particularly in the field of foreign affairs. In an attempt to improve the country's international image, the Ethiopian slave trade was at last abolished.

In 1923 Tafari pulled off a major diplomatic coup: Ethiopia was granted entry into the League of Nations. Membership not only firmly placed Ethiopia on the international political map, but also gave it some recourse against its grasping, colonial neighbours.

Continuing the tradition begun by Menelik, Tafari showed himself to be an advocate of reform. A modern printing press was established as well as several secondary schools and an airforce. In the meantime, Tafari was steadily outmanoeuvring his rivals. In 1930, the last rebellious noble was defeated and killed in battle. A few days later the sick empress also died, and Tafari assumed the throne.

Emperor Haile Selassie

On 2 November 1930, Tafari was crowned Emperor Haile Selassie. The extravagant spectacle that was staged – attended by representatives from around the world – proved to be a terrific public relations exercise, and even led to the establishment of a new faith (see the boxed text 'Rastafarians' under Shashemene in the South of Addis Ababa section).

Memories of His Majesty

It was a small dog, a Japanese breed. His name was Lulu. He was allowed to sleep in the Emperor's great bed. During various ceremonies, he would run away from the Emperor's lap and pee on dignitaries' shoes. The august gentlemen were not allowed to flinch or make the slightest gesture when they felt their feet getting wet. I had to walk among the dignitaries and wipe the urine from their shoes with a satin cloth. This was my job for ten years.

From *The Emperor* by Ryszard Kapucinski, Vintage International, 1989

The following year, the country's first written constitution was introduced. In it, the emperor was granted virtually absolute power, and his body was declared sacred. Although a two-house parliament was established, consisting of a senate (nominated by the emperor from among his nobles) and a chamber of deputies (elected from those with property), it was little more than a chamber for self-interested debate.

Since his regency, the emperor had been steadily bringing the country under centralised rule. For the first time, the Ethiopian state was unambiguously unified.

Italian Occupation

By the early 20th century, Ethiopia was the only state in Africa to have survived the European Scramble (see the boxed text 'Scramble for Africa' under History in the Facts about Eritrea section). However, Ethiopia's position – poised uneasily between the two Italian colonies of Eritrea and Somalia – made her a very enticing morsel. Any attempt by the Italians to link or develop its colonies would make expansion into Ethiopia inevitable. When Mussolini seized power in 1922, Italian colonial ambitions burgeoned, and the inevitable happened.

From 1933, in an effort to undermine the Ethiopian state, Italian agents, well oiled with funds, were dispatched to subvert the local chiefs, as well as to stir up ethnic tensions. Britain and France, nervous of pushing Mussolini further into Hitler's camp,

Italy's Dirty War

During the Italian campaign in Ethiopia, hundreds of tons of bombs were dropped on civilian as well as military targets including international Red Cross hospitals and ambulances. The countryside was set on fire with incendiary devices, and vast quantities of the internationally banned mustard gas was used. The campaign had cost Italy 4350 men. An estimated 275,000 Ethiopians lost their lives. It wasn't until 1996 that the Italian Ministry of Defence finally admitted this.

refrained from protests and looked on in silence.

When Italy claimed a pretext for its invasion (the Wal Wal incident of 1934, in which there was a minor skirmish between an Italian and Ethiopian force) Britain, France and the US all declared themselves neutral. An arms embargo was declared on both Italy and Ethiopia; in Italy's case, it was almost meaningless.

Invasion On 2 October 1935, an Italian force, overwhelmingly superior in both ground and air forces, invaded Ethiopia from Eritrea. First the northern town of Aksum fell, then Mekele.

Following the complete contravention of its covenants, the League of Nations was obliged to issue sanctions against Italy. However, these proved to be little more than a slap on the wrist. Although their effect was eventually felt on Italy's domestic economy, the measures were wholly ineffectual in either deterring or slowing down Italy's aggression abroad.

Even more risibly pro-Italy was the Hoare-Laval proposal of 1936, which suggested that Ethiopia should cede to Italy all territory then occupied by the Italians as well as economic rights over many other areas – all in return for a 'passageway to the sea'.

If, as should have happened, the Suez Canal had been closed to the Italians, or an oil embargo put in place, the Italian advance – as Mussolini was later to admit – would

have been halted within weeks. The lives of thousands of men, women and children would have been spared.

Campaigning Mussolini was in a hurry. Terrified that the international community would eventually come to its senses and impose more serious embargoes, and keen to keep Italian morale high, Il Duce pressed for a swift campaign.

Impatient with progress made, he soon replaced his first general, De Bono, with Pietro Badoglio, and authorised him 'to use all means of war – I say all, both from the air and from the ground'. Implicit in the instructions was the use of mustard gas – then strictly banned by the 1926 Geneva Convention.

Ethiopian resistance was stiff, and despite overwhelming odds, succeeded in launching a major counter offensive (known as the Christmas Offensive) at the Italian position at Mekele at the end of 1935.

However, following the first Battle of Tembien, the Italians were soon on the offensive again. Backed by hundreds of planes, cannons and weapons of every type, the Italian armies swept across the country. In May 1936, Mussolini triumphantly declared 'Ethiopia is Italian'.

Emperor Haile Selassie meanwhile had fled Ethiopia (some Ethiopians never forgave him for it) to escape the invader, as well as to lay the cause of Ethiopia before the world. On 30 June 1936, he made his famous speech to the League of Nations in Geneva. Despite his appeal, the league responded by lifting sanctions – against Italy – in the same year. Despite widespread popular opposition to Italy's conquest, the conquest was recognised by most of the world, barring only the USSR, the US, Haiti, Mexico and New Zealand.

Occupation Ethiopia was promptly merged with Eritrea and Somalia to become the new colonial territory of Africa Orientale Italiana (or Italian East Africa). During this time, the Aksum stele was famously removed to Rome – its return is currently under discussion.

Hoping to turn Abyssinia (Ethiopia) into an important economic base, the Italians were prepared to invest heavily in the colony. From 1936, as many as 60,000 Italian workers poured into the colony and were put to work on the country's infrastructure.

Resistance Spirited Ethiopian resistance to Italian rule continued throughout its brief duration. Italy's response to this patriotic movement was famously brutal. Mussolini personally ordered all rebels to be shot, and insurgencies were put down using large-scale bombing, poison gas and machine-gunning from the air.

Vigorous resistance continued, however, culminating in an attempt on the life of the much-hated Italian viceroy Graziani in February 1937. In reprisal, the Fascists carried out a three-day massacre in Addis Ababa, in which several thousand Ethiopians were shot, beheaded or disembowelled.

The patriotic movement was mainly based in Shoa, Gojam and Gonder, but drew support from all parts of the country; many resistance fighters were women. Small underground movements worked in Addis Ababa and other towns; its members were known as *wust arbagna* (insider patriots).

Graziani's response was simple 'Eliminate them, eliminate them, eliminate them' (a statement that chillingly echoes Kurtz's 'Exterminate all the brutes' in Conrad's *Heart of Darkness*). But resistance grew, and the Italians, though in control of the major towns, never succeeded in conquering the whole country.

The outbreak of WWII in 1939, for which the Ethiopian patriots had long-awaited, changed the course of events. Italy's declaration of war against Britain in 1940, caused Britain at last to reverse its policy of tacit support of Italian expansion in Ethiopia. The Italians in East Africa now threatened not only British and British-run neighbouring colonies such as Sudan, but also the important sea route to India.

Britain initially offered assistance to the Ethiopia patriots on the Sudan-Ethiopia border. Later, at the beginning of 1941, the British launched three major attacks on Italian East Africa, including one led by Emperor Haile Selassie, who had flown back from England for the liberation of his country.

Though not then widely recognised, the Ethiopian patriots played a major role in the campaign for liberation both before, during and after the liberation of Addis Ababa. On 5 May 1941, the emperor and his men entered Addis Ababa. The Italian occupation was over.

Post-War Ethiopia

The British, who had entered the country as liberators, seemed at first to have replaced the Italians as occupiers. In 1944, however, an Anglo-Ethiopian agreement returned to Ethiopia its independence at last.

The 1940s and 1950s saw much postwar reconstruction, including – with US assistance – the establishment of a new government bank, a national currency, and the country's first national airline, Ethiopian Airlines, in 1946.

New schools were also developed and, in 1950, the country's first institution of higher education was established: the University College of Addis Ababa (later the Haile Selassie I University and now Addis Ababa University).

In 1955, the Revised Ethiopian Constitution was introduced. Although for the first time, the legislature included a fully elected chamber of deputies, the government remained autocratic and real power continued to lie with the emperor.

The End of Music

Since the revolution, every song, old or new, has been censored. Some are played with verses deleted, some have been shelved permanently...Love songs have been banned from radio and TV for good. Now during listener-choice programs, one hears people dedicating martial music to their loved ones.

Alem Mezgebe, *Ethiopia: The Deadly Game,* **writing on the Derg in Aug 1978**

Cause of Death Unknown

No one knows for certain how the emperor met his end. The most accepted theory is that he was smothered with a pillow as he slept in his bed. The perpetrator of this crime against 'the Chosen One of God', was none other than the man who had engineered his downfall: Lieutenant-Colonel Mengistu Haile Mariam.

Evidence for the crime? A certain ring spotted on Mengistu's middle finger; the ring of Solomon – as it was rumoured to be – was said to have been plucked from the murdered emperor's hand.

In the capital that day, the news ran as follows:

Addis Ababa, August 28, 1975. Yesterday Haile Selassie I, the former Emperor of Ethiopia, died. The cause of death was circulatory failure.

The Ethiopian Herald, 29 August 1975

Ethiopia's almost untarnished history of independence also gave it a particular diplomatic authority vis-a-vis other African states. In 1962 Addis Ababa became the headquarters of the Organisation of African Unity (OAU) and, in 1958, of the United Nations Economic Commission for Africa (ECA).

Discontent Despite the modernisation process, dissatisfaction began to grow during the 1950s both with the country's slow pace of development, and with the autocratic rule of the emperor. Taking advantage of a state visit to Brazil in December 1960, the emperor's imperial bodyguard staged a coup d'etat. Though put down by the army and airforce, it signalled the beginning of the end of imperial rule in Ethiopia.

After 1965, discontent simmered among the students, who protested against land tenure, corruption and the appalling famine of 1972–74 in Tigray and Wolo, in which an estimated 200,000 peasants died.

The emperor, now an old man in his eighties, seemed more preoccupied with foreign affairs than with internal ones. His government was slow and half-hearted in its attempts to reform. Measures often miscarried because of opposition from the landlord-dominated assembly.

Meanwhile, international relations were also deteriorating. The newly established state of Somalia claimed the ethnic Somali-inhabited region of the Ogaden in Ethiopia. In 1964, war finally broke out.

In 1962, Ethiopia abrogated the UN-sponsored federation with Eritrea and unilaterally annexed the Eritrean state, provoking separatist Eritreans to launch a bitter guerrilla war.

The Fall of the Emperor During 1974, an unprecedented wave of teacher, student and taxi strikes broke out in Addis Ababa, and even mutinies in the armed forces began to be reported. At crisis point, the prime minister and his cabinet resigned and a new one was appointed with the mandate to carry out far-reaching constitutional reforms. But it was too late: by this time an increasingly powerful and radical military group had emerged, which soon replaced the new prime minister with their own.

Gaining in power, this group (known as the Derg or Committee, see following) began to arrest the old ministers, leading aristocrats and close confidants of the emperor. Finally, using the media with consummate skill, they began to undermine the authority of the emperor himself.

On 26 August 1975, footage from BBC journalist Jonathan Dimbleby's well-known TV report on the Wolo famine was famously flashed in between clips of sumptuous palace banquets. The following day the emperor was deposed, unceremoniously bundled into the back of a Volkswagen beetle, and driven away. The absolute power and divine right of rule of Ethiopia's millennium-old dynasty was finished forever.

The 1974 Revolution The radicals soon dissolved parliament and established a provisional military government; the Provisional Military Administrative Council (PMAC), became known as the Derg (Committee).

However, bitter power struggles and clashes of ideology soon splintered the Derg, culminating in the famous Death of the Sixty in which, in a single night on 23 November 1974, 57 high-ranking civilian and military officials were executed.

Emerging from the chaos was a certain Colonel Mengistu Haile Mariam, who conveniently piggy-backed on both the wave of popular opposition to the old regime, and the Marxist-Leninist ideology of left-wing students. But the political debate soon degenerated into violence. In 1977, the famous 'Red Terror' was launched to suppress all political opponents. At a conservative estimate, 100,000 people were killed and several thousand more fled abroad.

The Socialist Experiment On 20 December 1974, a socialist state was declared. In 1975, the Derg carried out a series of revolutionary reforms. Under the adage Ityopya Tikdem or 'Ethiopia First', banks, businesses and factories were nationalised as was rural and urban land. Over 30,000 peasant associations were also set up. Raising the status of the Ethiopian peasants, the campaign was initially much praised internationally, particularly by Unesco.

In the meantime, the external threats posed by Somalia and secessionist Eritrea were increasing. In July 1977, Somalia invaded Ethiopia. Thanks to the intervention of the Soviet Union, which flooded socialist Ethiopia with Soviet state-of-the-art weaponry, Somalia was beaten back. In Eritrea, however, the secessionists continued to thwart Ethiopian offensives.

The Fall of Mengistu Opposition to the Derg had existed since the Death of the Sixty in 1974, culminating in an unsuccessful coup d'etat in May 1989. Opposition parties during this time included the Marxist EPRP, and later various ethnically based regional liberation movements, including those of the Afar, Oromo, Somali and particularly Tigrayan peoples.

Another appalling famine followed a drought in 1984–5, in which hundreds of thousands more people died. Failed

---

Star Pupils

After 17 years of fighting for freedom, Ethiopia's leaders emerged well schooled in the art of warfare, but less well versed in the skills of modern government. After deciding that you can teach old dogs new tricks, twenty senior government officials enrolled for an MBA at the well-known British distance-learning institution, the Open University.

When the final exams came around, a certain Meles Zenawi was gripped by a bout of nerves. On spying the 'no smoking' sign in the examination room, he exclaimed, 'I have spent the last 17 years fighting a civil war but I have never been so frightened as I am now. There's no way I'll sit the exam without a fag!'.

Declaiming the newly learnt philosophy of participative decision making, the prime minister insisted on a vote and smoking was permitted during the exam.

Fourteen of the 20 government officials graduated with an MBA, and Meles – demonstrating true leadership by example – took third place in one of the exams out of 1400 candidates worldwide.

---

government resettlement campaigns, communal farms and 'villageisation' programs aggravated the disaster.

The different opposition groups eventually united to form the Ethiopian People's Revolutionary Democratic Front (EPRDF), which in 1989, began its historic march towards Addis Ababa.

Mengistu's time was up. Doubly confronted by the EPRDF in Ethiopia and the EPLF in Eritrea, with the fall of his allies in Eastern Europe, and with his state in financial tatters and his own military authority in doubt, Mengistu opted to flee the country. On 21 May 1991, he boarded a plane to Zimbabwe, where he remains to this day. Seven days later, the EPRDF entered Addis Ababa.

The Road to Democracy

After the war of liberation from the Derg, the leaders of both Ethiopia and Eritrea continued to show determination and zeal as they rebuilt their countries.

Stop Press:
The Ethiopian-Eritrean War

Though receiving much international news coverage, the Ethiopian-Eritrean conflict affects only a tiny area of each country at the border. For the traveller, the only major implication is that passage between the two countries is no longer possible. Permits to some places in Eritrea may be required. The dispute, though tragic, represents no apparent danger to the traveller.

In June 2000 Ethiopia launched a major offensive and had not only won back 'occupied' territory but had also penetrated Eritrean land. A preliminary cease-fire was signed between the two sides on 18 June. The plan called for the creation of a 25km buffer zone along the border, to be patrolled by a UN peace-keeping force, along with the main areas of contention including Badme, Zala Ambassa and Bure. Though the document signed was not a final cease-fire, it is the most encouraging step towards the end of two years of fierce fighting.

In July 1991, a transitional charter was endorsed, which gave the EPRDF-dominated legislature a four-year, interim rule under the executive of the TPLF leader, Meles Zenawi. Mengistu's failed socialist policies were first and foremost abandoned, and de facto independence granted to Eritrea.

In 1992, extensive economic reforms began, including the relaxing of all direct economic controls and the introduction of a radical form of federal devolution to the new regional states: Tigray, Afar, Amhara and Banshangul (north of Addis Ababa) and Gambella, Kaffa, Oromo and Somali (south of Addis Ababa). In contrast to the former provinces (which were clockwise around the border: Tigray, Wollo, Harerge, Bale, Sidamo, Gamo-Gofa, Kafa, Ilubador, Welaga, Gojam and Gonder, plus Shoa and Arsi in the middle) these were to be demarked along mainly linguistic-ethnic lines. See the map 'Ethiopian Provinces & their Capitals until 1995' attached to the country map.

In August 1995, the Federal Democratic Republic of Ethiopia was proclaimed, a series of elections followed, and the constitution of the second republic was inaugurated. Meles Zenawi formed a new government. Soon the leaderships of both Ethiopia and Eritrea were hailed, in US President Clinton's own words, as belonging to a 'new generation of African leaders'.

Neighbourly Disputes

However, all of the progress made by Ethiopia and Eritrea in the decade since independence was seriously undermined at the end of 1997. In November, Eritrea introduced its own currency to replace the old Ethiopian birr. The new currency, the nakfa, represented not just an historic break with Ethiopia, but an economic one, too – annulling the de facto currency union that had existed until then.

Disagreement over Eritrea's exchange-rate regime followed, and in early 1998, arguments started over bilateral trade relations, too. Resulting tensions between the countries escalated into a major military conflict that erupted in May–June 1998 over a 390-sq-km area called the Yirga Triangle (or Badme after the major town in the area).

Although the Eritreans were initially blamed for the initial 'occupation' and subsequent intransigence over attempts to resolve the dispute peacefully, the EPRDF lost considerable international sympathy with its policy of deporting, in the first 15 months of the conflict, an estimated 50,000 people of Eritrean origin (though most were Ethiopian citizens) to Asmara in Eritrea.

The small nature of the disputed terrain as well as the ferocity of the fighting, intensity of national sentiment, and the vitriol exchanged between the two leaders, demonstrated that the war turns not on territorial or material ambitions, but rather on national pride and prestige. The dispute has been likened to two bald men fighting over a comb. Both leaders seem reluctant to lose face by appearing to back down; despite international efforts to resolve the conflict, the situation remains at an impasse.

In the meantime, the economies of both Ethiopia and Eritrea are suffering enormously, international credibility has been lost and many aid organisations have broken off assistance for as long as the conflict lasts. Tens of thousands of troops have lost their lives on both sides. The remarkable progress made both by Ethiopia and Eritrea during the 1990s has been halted, and possibly even reversed.

Relations with Somalia, which has long harboured anti-government insurgency groups, worsened as the country became implicated in the Eritrea-Ethiopia dispute.

GEOGRAPHY

With a land area of 1,098,000 sq km Ethiopia measures five times the size of Britain or about twice the size of Texas. Ethiopia's topography is incredibly diverse, boasting 20 mountains above 4000m, as well as one of the lowest points on the Earth's surface: the Danakil Depression.

Two principal geographical zones can be found in the country: the cool highlands and the hot lowlands that surround them.

Ethiopia's main topographical feature is the vast central plateau (the Ethiopian highlands), which has an average elevation of between 1800–2400m. It is here that the country's major peaks are found including Ras Dashen (4620m), Ethiopia's highest mountain and the fourth highest in Africa.

The mountains are also the source of four large river systems, the most famous of which is the Blue Nile. Rising in Lake Tana, and joined later by the White Nile in Sudan, it supplies a massive 90% of the Nile's water, which nurtures the fertile Nile Valley of Egypt to the north. (Since 1991, disagreement with Egypt has arisen over Ethiopia's harnessing of the waters of the Blue Nile for irrigation and hydroelectric schemes.) The other principal rivers are the Awash, the Omo and the Wabe Shebele.

The Rift Valley, which runs all the way down to Mozambique, bisects southern Ethiopia diagonally. Averaging around 50km wide, several lakes can be found on the valley floor, including the well-known chain lying to the south of Addis Ababa.

The northern end of the East African Rift Valley opens into the infamous Danakil Depression, one of the hottest places on Earth. This semidesert is also home to several salt lakes.

CLIMATE

Ethiopia's climate reflects its topography.

The highlands are classed as temperate with an average daytime temperature of 16°C. Most rain occurs between mid-June to mid-September when around 1000mm fall. Rainstorms can be violent. In the notoriously drought-susceptible areas in the north-east, however, rainfall is much more erratic. Rainfall in the lowlands is around half that of the highlands, but some areas also experience 'small rains' falling between March and April.

The southern Rift Valley, with an average elevation of around 1500m, is classed as moderate to hot, and shares a similar rainfall pattern to the highlands. In the Bale Mountains in the south, snow sometimes falls. At the other end of the scale, temperatures in the Danakil Depression can touch 50°C, and rainfall in the region is practically zero.

The far south and the eastern lowlands are hot and dry. The western lowlands are hot and humid and are the most 'tropical' area of

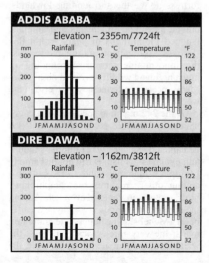

Funny Frogs

A huge 32% of frog species are endemic to Ethiopia. During a recent expedition to the Harenna Forest in the Bale Mountains, four entirely new species were discovered in the space of just three weeks. Many of the frogs have made peculiar adaptations to their environment. One species swallows snails whole, another has forgotten how to hop and a third has lost its ears!

Ethiopia. In the south-west, the main rains occur from March to June, and the small rains in November.

ECOLOGY & ENVIRONMENT

The farmer who eats his chickens as well as all their eggs will have a bleak future
Tigrayan proverb

Biodiversity & Endemism

Reflecting its geography, Ethiopia has a very wide range of ecosystems – from high peaks and semitropical forest to salt lakes and desert. For details of the range of Ethiopia's habitats see Flora & Fauna following.

The highlands provide a very particular habitat. Rising like a kind of vast natural fortress above the surrounding lowlands, the Ethiopian central plateau is home to a unique assemblage of plants and animals. Isolated for millions of years within this 'fortress environment' and unable to cross the inhospitable terrain surrounding it, much highland wildlife evolved on its own. Many species are found nowhere else in the world.

Of the 242 mammal species in the country, no less than 28 are endemic. In 1919, the last large mammal species on Earth to be named by science was Ethiopia's mountain nyala. Endemism is rife not just among Ethiopia's mammals and flora, but also among other creatures too: amphibians, birds, reptiles, insects and even fish. Among the endemic mammals are Swayne's hartebeest, Menelik's bushbuck, the mountain nyala, the very rare African wild ass, the walia ibex, the famous Ethiopian wolf, the gelada baboon, and six species of rodent including the molerat.

Ethiopia's highland flora is no less exceptional for the same reason. The country is classed as one of the 12 'Vavilov centres' in the world for crop plant diversity, and is thought to possess extremely valuable pools of crop plant genes.

Environmental Problems

Like many sub-Saharan African countries, three factors above all have taken their toll on Ethiopia's environment: war, famine and demographic pressure. Additionally, Ethiopia has not benefited from the investment and development of wildlife conservation that occurred in colonised countries of Africa.

Although limited conservation has long been practised – the Aksumite state set aside designated areas for hunting, and King Zara Yaqob in the 15th century is known to have replanted the Menagesha Forest – national legitimised conservation programs are still in their infancy, long delayed by war.

War During the civil war in Ethiopia, whole forests were torched to smoke out rebel forces. Large armies, hungry and with inadequate provisions, turned their sights on the land's natural resources; much wildlife was wiped out.

The armed conflict that continues between warring tribes in the Omo and Mago National Parks also impedes wildlife conservation efforts.

Demographic Pressures Ethiopia's population has quadrupled in the last 65 years, and is growing at a rate of 3%. As living space, firewood, building materials, agricultural land and food is increasingly sought, more pressure is put on the land and its resources, and larger and larger areas of wildlife habitat are lost.

In Gambela in western Ethiopia, the presence of the tsetse fly has made cattle rearing impossible. (In the parts of the Omo Valley where the tsetse fly is prevalent, and humans are scarce, wildlife flourishes. The fly, the carrier of sleeping sickness, has even been called the 'protector of wildlife'.) The Anuak people who live in the west are obliged, like many Ethiopian tribes, to supplement their diet with meat from the bush. With their traditional spears, the wildlife population was sustainable, but with the introduction of rifles and machine guns in the 20th century, animal populations have been decimated.

Ethiopia has long suffered from a cycle of recurrent drought – an average of one drought every ten years. During these periods, food becomes scarce and wildlife has to compete, usually unsuccessfully, with domestic animals. Sometimes wildlife becomes a source of food in itself (see the boxed text 'Famine' under Economy later in this section).

Harmful Agricultural Practices More cattle are reared in Ethiopia than in any other country in Africa, with an estimated 25 million head reported – nearly one for every two Ethiopians. Livestock is kept in Ethiopia both for social prestige and as security in times of hardship. However, such huge numbers exert enormous demands on the land.

About 95% of Ethiopia's original forest is believed to have been lost to agriculture and human settlement. The highlands are the worst affected area. Here, for seven millennia, farming has been practised and land cleared. Today, 85% of Ethiopia's population gain their livelihood from agriculture.

A direct result of deforestation, soil erosion represents an extremely serious threat in Ethiopia. As land becomes less and less productive, the ever-present threat of famine looms larger and larger. Almost no steps to combat soil erosion have yet been taken.

Harmful Commercial Practices The demand for firewood has led to much destruction of habitat. The thick acacia woodland surrounding Lake Abiata was devastated after the war by disbanded soldiers turning it into charcoal.

On a larger scale, commercial farms set up in 1976 near the waters of Lake Chamo and, more recently, Lake Abiata, have been responsible for eutrophication, the process in which algae, affected by chemical waste seeping into the water, in turn release toxins. At Lake Chamo, many Burchell's

zebras died; at Lake Abiata, the lesser flamingos were the main victims.

Lake Abiata also provides the main source of food for the colonies of great white pelicans on the nearby Lake Shala islands. The latter are one of seven nesting sites of the bird in the whole of Africa.

In 1990, a soda ash mining factory was established to the north of Lake Abiata. Contamination of the lake led to a decrease in the fish population, and a dramatic fall in the population of pelicans.

Hunting & Poaching Hunting and poaching over the centuries has decimated the country's once large populations of elephant and rhino. Since Aksumite times, huge numbers of animals were hunted for the export trade, including giraffes, monkeys and apes. Rhinos were hunted for their horns, hippos for their hides and, above all, elephants for their tusks. Today, hunting is officially controlled by the government; it may even provide the most realistic and pragmatic means of ensuring the future survival of Ethiopia's large mammals.

Poaching, however, continues to pose a serious threat to animals. Ivory and rhino horn continue to fetch astronomical prices in Asia. The black rhino is now on the verge of extinction in Ethiopia.

Protective Measures
Ethiopia's parks were set up during the time of Emperor Haile Selassie. In order to create Western-style conservation projects, land was forcefully taken from the peasants – a measure much resented by the local people. When the Derg government fell in 1991, there was a brief period of anarchy, when park property was looted and wildlife killed. Wildlife authorities are now actively trying to encourage the participation of the local people in the conservation of wildlife: educational programs are on the agenda.

After the end of the civil war in 1991, the old parks (established in the 1960s and 1970s) were redefined, and hunting and grazing within them again banned. The Simien Mountains National Park has been declared a Unesco World Heritage Site.

Spot the Endemic Flora

Ethiopia has more unique species of flora than any other country in Africa. In September and October, look out particularly for the famous yellow daisy known as the Meskel flower, which carpets the highlands; it belongs to the Bidens family, of which six are endemic. In towns and villages, look out for the endemic yellow-flowered *Solanecio gigas*, which is commonly employed as a hedge. Around Addis Ababa, the tall endemic *Erythrina brucei* tree can be seen. Look out for the indigenous Abyssinian rose in the highlands such as in the lower hills of the Bale Mountains. Also in the Bale Mountains, look out for the endemic species of globe thistle (*Echinops longisetus*).

Future efforts to preserve wildlife will include the captive breeding and relocation of certain species, such as the Ethiopian wolf, and the establishment of private wildlife ranches. It is hoped that the latter will provide not only wildlife protection, but local employment and revenue for the government, which can then be reinvested.

Commercial hunting is now subject to strict hunting controls and is permitted only in certain areas. Permits are expensive: a licence to bag an elephant costs $12,000, whether or not an elephant is even seen! Revenue earned from commercial hunting is theoretically reinvested into the local communities.

Ethiopia is now a party to the Cites convention (Convention on International Trade in Endangered Species of Wild Fauna and Flora). More than 135 countries have signed the treaty, which has banned trade in certain species such as elephant and rhino, and controls the trade in others.

Ongoing Obstacles

Despite the attempts at reform, major shortcomings remain. Though a new and comprehensive wildlife policy (the National Conservation Action Plan) has been drawn up, it still awaits enactment. A clear government environmental agenda is also lacking, and funds for conservation are far from forthcoming; currently all development aid comes from nongovernmental organisations (NGOs). As in many developing countries, wildlife and the national parks are not a major source of revenue, so are not accorded much importance. In Ethiopia, the development of agriculture and food sufficiency is the prime objective of the government. A shortage of personnel with adequate experience or qualifications in conservation is another serious obstacle to progress.

Although grazing in the park is officially banned, the practice remains rampant, since law enforcement is often insufficient or nonexistent. Additionally, many local administrators are afraid of disaffecting the people who have elected them to power, plus they often know little about the animals under their charge. Senkele, Abiata Shala and the Simien Mountains National Park are all overrun by human populations.

When attempts *are* made to enforce the law, conflicts occasionally break out. In 1997, a park warden was shot and wounded at Awash National Park by the local herdsmen he was attempting to apprehend.

For more information on wildlife conservation, contact the Ethiopian Wildlife Conservation Organisation (☎ 44-44-17) PO Box 386, Addis Ababa.

FLORA & FAUNA

Although Ethiopia lacks the large and spectacular animal herds found in Kenya, its wildlife is no less interesting. In some ways it's more interesting, since many animals and birds are unique – they are found nowhere else in the world. See Biodiversity & Endemism under Ecology & Environment previously for more information on endemic flora and fauna. See also the special section 'Birds in Ethiopia'.

Major Habitats

Eight major habitats can be found in Ethiopia. Each has its own distinct flora and fauna, as well as its own particular environmental problems.

Desert & Semi-Desert Scrubland The Dankalia region, Omo delta and Ogaden

Desert all fall into this category. Vegetation is typically characterised by highly drought-resistant plants such as small trees, shrubs and grasses, including acacia. Succulent species include euphorbia and aloe.

Irrigation schemes have destroyed much vegetation in the Awash and the Gode valleys in the Afar and Somali regions in the south-east, and many of the large state-run farms practise environmentally 'unfriendly' agriculture.

Larger mammals include the (extremely rare) African wild ass, Grevy's zebra, Soemmering's gazelle and Beisa oryx. Birds include the ostrich, secretary bird, Arabian, Kori and Heuglin's bustard, Abyssinian roller, red-cheeked cordon bleu and crested francolin.

Small-Leaved Deciduous Forest These woodlands can be found all over the country apart from the western regions, at an altitude of between 900m and 1900m. Vegetation consists of drought-tolerant shrubs and trees with either leathery persistent leaves or small deciduous ones. Trees include various type of acacia. Herbs include *Acalypha* and *Aerva*.

The demand for firewood to supply cites has destroyed much woodland, and wind erosion is now posing a further threat.

Large mammals include Grevy's zebras, hartebeests, greater and lesser kudus and Beisa oryx. Birds include the white-bellied go-away bird, superb starling, red-billed quelea, helmeted guinea fowl, secretary bird and Ruppell's long-tailed starling.

Broad-Leaved Deciduous Forest These forests occur mainly in western and north-western parts of the country. Bamboo is also found in the western valleys.

Agricultural expansion and the demand for firewood threatens these forests.

Wildlife includes hartebeests, greater and lesser kudus, gazelles, buffaloes, common elands, elephants and De Brazza's monkeys. Bird species include the gambaga flycatcher, red-cheeked cordon bleu, bush petronia and black-faced firefinch.

Moist Evergreen Forest These forests can be found in the south-western and western parts of the country. Vegetation consists of tall and medium-sized trees and under-storey shrubs.

Uncontrolled commercial logging (supplying the timber industry) as well as large-scale clearance for coffee plantations is the most serious threat to the forests and vast areas have been lost.

Wildlife includes Menelik's bushbucks, bushpigs, forest hogs and De Brazza's monkeys. The very colourful birdlife includes the Abyssinian black-headed oriole, Abyssinian hill babbler, white-cheeked turaco, scaly throated honeyguide, scaly francolin, emerald cuckoo and the yellow-billed coucal.

Lowland Semi-Evergreen Forest These forests can be found in western Ethiopia around Gambela. Vegetation consists of semi-evergreen tree and shrub species as well as grasses.

With human settlement in the region and the expansion of Gambela town, the forest is fast disappearing. Additionally, the Abobo dam has flooded much of the forest.

Wildlife includes elephants, cheetahs, giraffes, lions and the white-eared kob. Birds include Adim's storkss, openbill stork, pelicans and egrets. The famous shoebill has not been seen since 1973.

Dry Evergreen Montane Forest & Grassland This habitat is found in much of the highlands, and in the north, north-west, central and southern parts of the country. The habitat is particularly important as the home of a large number of endemic plants. Tree species include various types of acacia, olive and Euphorbia. Africa's only rose the *Rosa abyssinica* is also found here, with its sweet smell and creamy-coloured petals.

Agriculture, practised for millennia, has destroyed much of the natural vegetation and still poses the biggest threat.

Wildlife includes leopards, gazelles, jackals and hyaenas. Birds include the Abyssinian longclaw, black-headed siskin, yellow-fronted parrot, black-winged lovebird,

Gelada Baboon

The gelada baboon *(Theropithecus gelada)* is one of Ethiopia's most fascinating endemic mammals. Not in fact a baboon at all, it makes up its own genus of monkey.

Of all the nonhuman primates, it is by far the most dexterous. It also lives in the largest social groups (up to 800 have been recorded), and is the only primate that feeds on grass and has its 'sexual skin' on its chest and not on its bottom – presumably because it spends so much time sitting on its bottom!

It also has the most complex system of communication of any nonhuman primate and the most sophisticated social system: the females decide who's boss, the young males form bachelor groups, and the older males perform a kind of grandfather role looking after the young.

Although the males sport magnificent leonine manes, their most striking physical feature is the bare patch of skin on their chest. This has given rise to their other popular name: the 'bleeding heart baboon'. The colour of the patch indicates the sexual condition not just of the male (his virility), but also his female harem (their fertility), like a kind of communal sexual barometer.

Unfortunately, the gelada is gravely threatened, and because of climatic changes its habitat (precipitous mountain pockets of up to 4200m) is fast disappearing. It will almost certainly become extinct – one of the first victims of global warming.

blue-winged goose, half-collared kingfisher and wattled ibis.

Afro-Alpine Vegetation This unique habitat is found in the national parks of the Bale and Simien Mountains. In the Bale Mountains the endemic giant lobelia *(Lobelia rhynchopetalum)* is particularly well known, which in flower can stand up to 6m high. Also endemic is a species of globe thistle and the so-called 'soft thistle'. A very common sight is the red hot poker. In the Bale Mountains, Heather is known for its huge size and can grow into trees of up to

10m. On the high plateaus at around 4000m, many varieties of gentian can be found; the little grey bush found everywhere is the *Helichrysum splendidum* named for its bright yellow flowers. Ragwort also flourishes.

Expanding barley cultivation is proving the biggest threat to the habitat as well as grazing and the demand for firewood. Few trees remain beyond the introduced eucalyptus. Soil erosion is a major problem.

For wildlife and bird species, see National Parks following.

Wetlands These are found along the Baro River and around Gambela in the west as well as in the highlands and the north-west. Along rivers or *wadis* (dry riverbeds) look out for the fig and tamarind trees.

Crocodiles and hippos infest many rivers. Birdlife is particularly abundant in these areas and includes Rouget's rails and white-winged flufftails in the swamps, and the Senegal thick-knee and red-throated bee-eater in riverbank habitats.

Endangered Species

According to the accounts of early travellers to Ethiopia, the country was once home to huge numbers of animals. In AD 525, Cosmos Indicopleustes of Byzantium reported tame giraffes and elephants at the kingdom of Aksum, kept apparently for the amusement of the court and to pull the royal chariots.

The Byzantine writer and traveller, Nonosus, claimed to have seen 5000 elephants in a single herd near Adwa in the north of the country. Even as late as the turn of the 19th and 20th centuries, the game hunter Harrison reported a herd of 100 elephants in the Middle Awash area.

Flora and fauna today is much reduced. Currently 151 flowering species, 21 mammal species and 17 species of birds are classed by the International Union for the Conservation of Nature and Natural Resources (IUCN) as endangered. Numbering among them are: the Ethiopian wolf, the black rhino, the walia ibex, the dibatag (a type of antelope), the African wild ass, the Swayne's hartebeest, the Tora hartebeest and the Grevy's zebra. Endangered birds include Prince Ruspoli's turacos, Sidamo long-clawed larks and Ankober serins (see also the special section 'Birds of Ethiopia').

NATIONAL PARKS

There are nine national parks and three wildlife sanctuaries in Ethiopia. The latter await the awarding of full national park status. Most parks were designed to create at least one stronghold for Ethiopia's endemic mammals. The Simien and Bale Mountains National Parks are more famous as trekking destinations, though wildlife at the latter is easily seen without much hiking. Bale Mountains National Park is also a must for birders. See the individual listings throughout the chapter for details of entrance fees.

Awash NP (827 sq km) Accommodation is in a very basic caravan site. Habitats include arid and semi-arid woodland and some riverine forest. Wildlife includes greater and lesser kudus, Soemmering's gazelles, Beisa oryx, Swayne's hartebeests, lions (rare) and kori bustards. Large mammals recorded (63), birds recorded (392). Established for range of larger mammals (easily seen). Quite easily accessible (210km east of Addis Ababa). See the East of Addis Ababa section.

Babille Elephant Sanctuary (6982 sq km) Accommodation is in the village of Babille. Habitats include semi-arid open woodland. Established to protect indigenous elephant subspecies *Loxodonta africana oreleansi*. This elephant sanctuary is disrupted badly by incursions of Somali refugees and livestock. Elephants very rare; definitely not worth a special visit. Difficult to reach (570km east of Addis Ababa). See under Awash to Dire Dawa in the East of Addis Ababa section.

Bale Mountains NP (2471 sq km) Accommodation is in a self-catering lodge, basic hotels at Dinsho and camping. Habitats include Afroalpine, high mountain and montane vegetation. Wildlife includes Ethiopian wolves, Menelik's bushbucks, mountain nyalas and giant molerats. Large mammals recorded (64), birds recorded (270). Established to protect endemics: mountain nyala and Ethiopian wolf (both commonly seen); other mammals also easily seen. Beautiful scenery; great trekking. Must for birders, many endemics easily seen.

Quite easy to get to (400km south-east of Addis Ababa). See the South of Addis Ababa section.

Gambela NP (5060 sq km). Accommodation is in Gambela town or in Gog. Habitats include semi-arid woodland and deciduous woodland. Wildlife includes savanna Nile lechwe, white-eared kobs, elephants, roan antelopes, tiangs, shoebills and whale-headed storks. Large mammals recorded (41); birds recorded (154). Established for larger mammal species typical of neighbouring Sudan. Park suffers from Sudanese poaching and influx of refugees and has yet to be developed. Difficult to get to (850km west of Addis Ababa). Definitely not worth special trip. See under Around Gambela in the West of Addis Ababa section.

Kuni-Muktar WS Accommodation is in the town of Asbe Teferi. Habitats include two small hills with forested peaks. Wildlife includes mountain nyalas and Menelik's bushbucks. Large mammals recorded (20); birds recorded (24). Established to protect the mountain nyala. Not worth a special visit. Difficult to get to (350km east of Addis Ababa). See the East of Addis Ababa section.

Lake Abiata-Shala NP (887 sq km) Hotels and camping on the lake as well as on nearby Lake Langano; hotels at Arsi Negele. Habitats include savanna and acacia woodland. Wildlife includes the great white pelican, lesser flamingo, white-necked cormorant and Grant's gazelle. Large mammals recorded (31); birds recorded (299). Established for huge numbers of aquatic birds. Attractive scenery. Good accessibility by public transport (208km south of Addis Ababa). See the South of Addis Ababa section.

Mago NP (2162 sq km) Camping is possible. Habitats include semi-arid open woodland and savanna. Wildlife includes the elephant, cheetah, giraffe, lelwel, hartebeest, buffalo, tiang and black rhino. Large mammals recorded (56); birds recorded (153). There are also local tribes here. Established to protect large mammals of the plains (elephants, buffaloes, giraffes etc). Very difficult to get to but worthwhile (785km south-west of Addis Ababa). See under Lower Omo Valley in the South of Addis Ababa section.

Nechisar NP (514 sq km). Accommodation is in hotels in nearby Arba Minch as well as camping. Savanna habitat. Wildlife includes the Swayne's hartebeest, Burchell's zebra, greater kudu, crocodile, Nechisar nightjar and kori bustard. Large mammals recorded (37); birds recorded (188). Established for abundant wildlife on plains, especially Burchell's zebras and Swayne's hartebeests. Many crocodiles and hippos in lakes. Beautiful scenery.

Easily accessible from Arba Minch; (500km south-west of Addis Ababa). See the South of Addis Ababa section.

Omo NP (4068 sq km) Camping is possible. Habitats include savanna and deciduous woodland. Wildlife includes common elands, elephants, black rhinos, cheetahs, giraffes and buffaloes. Large mammals recorded (57); birds recorded (306). Local tribes are very colourful. Established to protect wilderness and prolific plains wildlife. Poaching by Surma people a problem. Very inaccessible but worthwhile (886km south-west of Addis Ababa). See under Lower Omo Valley in the South of Addis Ababa section.

Senkele NP (54 sq km) Accommodation is in the village of Aje. Savanna habitat. Wildlife includes Swayne's haartebeests. Large mammals recorded (13); birds recorded (91). Established to protect the Swayne's hartebeest. Quite hard to get to (320km south of Addis Ababa). See under Around Shashemene in the South of Addis Ababa section.

Simien Mountains NP (179 sq km) Camping is possible and there are hotels in nearby Debark. Habitats include the Afro-alpine, high mountain. Wildlife includes the walia ibex (common), Ethiopian wolf, gelada baboon and lammergeyer (easily seen). Large mammals recorded (21); birds recorded (63). Established for spectacular mountain scenery; best place for trekking. Quite easily accessible (875km north of Addis Ababa). See the North of Addis Ababa section.

Yabelo WS (2496 sq km) Accommodation is in hotels in nearby Yabelo. Savanna habitat. Wildlife includes the Streseman's bushcrow, white-tailed swallow and Swayne's hartebeest. Large mammals recorded (20); birds recorded (194). Established to protect the Swayne's hartebeest (now greatly reduced) but more important for endemic birds. Quite difficult to get to (500km south of Addis Ababa). See the South of Addis Ababa section.

Yangudi-Rassa NP (4731 sq km) Accommodation is in the village of Gewane. Semidesert habitat. Wildlife includes the African wild ass, oryx, gerenuk, Soemmering's gazelle, cheetah and ostrich. Large mammals recorded (36); birds recorded (136). Established to protect the African wild ass, but park is in contentious area and is not developed/maintained. Not worth a special trip. Difficult to get to (500km north-east of Addis Ababa). See under Awash to Asaita in the East of Addis Ababa section.

GOVERNMENT & POLITICS

The second republic, formally known as the Federal Democratic Republic of Ethiopia, came into being in August 1995. It consists of a federation of nine states governed by a bicameral legislature. The 548-member Council of People's Representatives (CPR) is the executive arm, and the smaller Federal Council (FC) serves as the senate, with a merely supervisory role.

The EPRDF (see History earlier in this section), which evolved from the coalition of armed groups that overthrew the Derg in May 1991, holds 90% of the CPR's seats and its members control all the major regional state councils.

The Oromo Liberation Front (OLF) is the one conspicuous absentee from the coalition. Withdrawing in protest from the transitional government in July 1992, it was later banned and remains in opposition.

The president has a mainly ceremonial role. The prime minister is the head of state and appoints the 16-member cabinet. Reflecting the new republic's principle of ethnic federalism, cabinet members are drawn from different ethnic groups. This has led both to accusations of 'political appointeeism' on the one hand, and empty political appeasement on the other.

The real power, especially in foreign and economic affairs, is said to lie with EPRDF staff outside the cabinet – in particular from the ex-Tigrayan People's Liberation Front (TPLF). Nevertheless, the effort to acknowledge its multicultural and multiethnic society makes Ethiopia stand almost alone in Africa.

Opposition groups to the government, though vociferous, have proved largely ineffectual, unable to mobilise much support and lacking in clear political agendas. Among them are the Addis Ababa–based Coalition of Alternative Forces for Peace and Democracy in Ethiopia (CAFPDE), and the various regional factions including Afar, Oromo, Ogaden Somali and Amhara groups. Armed conflict continues between the government and the OLF, the Ogaden National Liberation Front (ONLF) and the Ethiopian Unity Front. In July 1998, major intercommunal disturbances blew up between the Gedeo and Oromo-Guji peoples, with an estimated 3000 people killed.

Despite the new regional boundaries, the bulk of the population continues to use the old historic geographical names such as Shoa and Gonder. For information on the old and new provinces see The Road to Democracy under History earlier in this section.

Since 1991, the government has come a long way from the repressive regime of the Derg: the oppressive security apparatus is being dismantled and there is greater freedom of speech, expression and political organisation.

In the May 2000 elections, Meles Zenawi, the incumbent prime minister, and his EPRDF party convincingly won another term in office.

ECONOMY

The Ethiopian economy suffers from two major and persistent weaknesses: food insecurity and a near total dependency on coffee for foreign exchange earnings.

Agriculture provides the livelihood of 85% of the population, but drought, pests and severe soil erosion have all kept agricultural yields notoriously erratic and low. Per capita income is estimated at around US$115 – making Ethiopia one of three poorest countries in the world. Agriculture accounts for a huge 50% of Ethiopia's GDP. During the 1980s and 1990s, however, food imports to feed Ethiopia's population sometimes exceeded 1 million tonnes per year. Recent measures to combat the problem include the increased use of fertilisers, pesticides, irrigation systems.

Though not officially promoted by the government, one plant that has proved lucrative is the notorious chat plant (see the boxed text 'Chat Among the Pigeons' in the East of Addis Ababa section), which regularly earns Ethiopia around US$30 million per annum. Incredibly, it is the third largest export earner. Most of it is exported to Djibouti and Somalia, where it meets the steady and high demand from the locals.

Placing the Ethiopian economy in a particularly vulnerable position is the notoriously volatile international price of coffee. Over two-thirds of the country's foreign earnings come from coffee. Diversification

Human Rights

Compared with many African countries, Ethiopia's human rights record isn't bad, and the government seems keen to improve it further. In May 1998, an international council was called to consider the establishment of a National Human Rights Commission, and in June 1998, Ethiopia acceded to the African charter on Human and People's Rights.

But there's still room for improvement: more than 10,000 political detainees are thought to be held, most without charge or trial. 'Disappearances' of government opponents are still reported; prison conditions are grim, with medical treatment either delayed or denied; and the freedom of the press is notoriously restricted, with at least 20 journalists languishing in jail for criticism of the government.

into horticulture, such as the production of fresh flowers or spices, is among the initiatives currently encouraged. Other hopes lie in the country's rich, and as yet unexploited, mineral deposits including gold, iron ore and potassium.

Attempts have also been made to bolster manufacturing, accounting presently for just 4.4% of GDP, particularly in the area of food processing. In 1997, French and South African companies announced plans to build new breweries in the country.

Though inheriting a Marxist economy in 1991 that was additionally badly worn by years of war, and with very little experience in economic management, the government hasn't done badly in attempts at reform (see the boxed text 'Star Pupils' earlier in this section). The transition though very cautious and slow, has been reasonably successful and steady.

Wholesale privatisation is apace: of hotels, state farms, restaurants, shops and factories. Foreign investment in recent years is being vigorously encouraged; by far the biggest foreign investor to date is the Midroc group, controlled by the half-Ethiopian Sheikh Alamoudi of Saudi Arabia. Alamoudi's many ventures include the new ultra-luxurious Sheraton Hotel in Addis

Famine

From time immemorial, Ethiopia has been prone to cyclical drought. Since the early 1970s, the country's name has become synonymous in the West with drought, disaster and famine. In May 2000, horrifying pictures of famine again shocked the world.

In the past, the causes have had less to do with environmental factors – Ethiopia remains a remarkably fertile country – and more to do with the inequitable and oppressive social, political and economic relations that have long existed between the people and its rulers.

It is hoped that, in the future, a combination of improved agriculture, measures to combat soil erosion and the development of irrigation systems will help make Ethiopia self-sufficient at last. The prime minister, himself from the notoriously famine-prone region of Tigray, has made the fight against famine something of a personal crusade.

In the meantime, the image of Ethiopia as a desertified land wracked by drought and famine has widespread economic repercussions. It is the single greatest obstacle to the development of its tourism industry – the one sector that could earn it millions of dollars.

Ababa and gold prospecting at Leba Dembi. His name is so often attached to property development and new projects, that he is referred to sometimes as 'the emperor'!

Tourism is thought to have the greatest growth potential of any economic activity in Ethiopia. Civil war, famine, state socialism and the recent conflict with Eritrea, have dealt a severe blow to the growth of the industry which, in the 1970s, counted 75,000 visitors a year. Although the government allocates a minuscule 0.04% of its budget on the industry, the private sector has proved much more proactive and visionary, as borne out by the rash of hotels mushrooming up in Addis Ababa and some of the provincial capitals.

POPULATION & PEOPLE

In the past, war, slavery, epidemic diseases and famine have all taken their toll on Ethiopia's population. The 20th century saw the abolition of slavery (in 1917), and the introduction of modern medicine and foreign food aid. These factors increased the population from 15 million in 1935 to an estimated 58 million in 1998. Today, Ethiopia is the most populous nation in sub-Saharan Africa after Nigeria. Growing by a hefty rate of 3% per year, the population is predicted to reach a huge 111 million by 2020. However, AIDS, which at the beginning of 1998 affected an estimated 9.3% of the population, will inevitably slow future growth.

Over 90% of the people inhabit the countryside. Life expectancy is currently 49 years.

EDUCATION

Providing education for Ethiopia's youth is a major challenge (over half the population is under 16), and along with the improvement of the nation's health, is a top government priority – at least it was before the war broke out. Only 25% of the population is literate (a third that of neighbouring Kenya).

Currently, school attendance is also far below other African countries: just 28% of children attend primary school; only 15% of children make it to secondary school.

Other schools include missionary, 'community' (such as the British, American, Indian and Italian schools in Addis Ababa), and church schools. There is one university in the country: the Addis Ababa University, built by Emperor Haile Selassie in 1961.

Many better-off Ethiopians go abroad for secondary education, particularly to Europe, Canada and the US, traditionally returning to join the state's civil service.

ARTS

Encompassed on all sides by the enemies of their religion, the Aethiopians slept near a thousand years, forgetful of the world, by whom they were forgotten.

Edward Gibbon, *The History of the Decline and Fall of the Roman Empire*, 1776–1788

More than any other country in sub-Saharan Africa, Ethiopia is known for its culture.

With its long and prestigious history and early connections with the Christian church, its culture is ancient and rich. Additionally, it was the only country on the continent to escape colonialism; its culture has survived largely intact.

The development of Ethiopia's culture has been profoundly influenced by three things: the dominance of the Amhara people, the country's historical, geographical and political isolation and by its nature as an enclave of Christianity within a wholly Islamic area.

Dominating the country's history, politics and society, the Amhara have imposed their own language and their own culture on the country. All but one of the Ethiopian emperors were Amhara, and it was under their aegis that the country's most famous monuments were built.

The church – traditionally enjoying almost as much authority as the state – is responsible for both inspiring Ethiopia's art, and stifling it with its great conservatism and rigorous adherence to convention.

Firmly moulded by the church, some Ethiopian art has been accused of 'sterility', and lack of innovation. However, there is much in Ethiopian art that is both original and innovative. Long neglected and ignored, the cultural contributions of Ethiopia's other ethnic groups are only now receiving due credit and attention. The contribution to dance, for example, or to the country's vast and rich oral literary tradition is very significant. See the National Museum and the Ethnological Museum in the Addis Ababa section as well as the special section 'Oral Literature in the Horn'.

Dance

Dance forms an extremely important part of the lives of most Ethiopians, and almost every ethnic group has its own distinct variety. Although the *iskista* movement is the best known (see the boxed text), there are myriad others. Dance traditionally serves a variety of very important social purposes: from celebrating religious festivities (such as the *shibsheba* or priestly dance), to celebrating social occasions such as weddings

Dancing the Iskista

When dancing the *iskista*, the shoulders are juddered up and down, backwards and forwards, in a careful rhythm, while the hips and legs are kept motionless. Sometimes the motion is accompanied by a sharp intake of breath, making a sound like the word 'iskista', or alternatively by a *zefen*, a loud, high-pitched and strident folk song.

and funerals and, in the past, to stoking up warriors before departing for battle.

Still found in rural areas are dances in praise of nature, such as after a good harvest or when new sources of water are discovered, and dances that allow the young 'warriors' to show off their agility and athleticism. Look out for the *fukara* or 'boasting' dance, which is often performed at public festivals. A leftover of less peaceful times, it involves a man holding a spear, stick or rifle horizontally above his shoulders while moving his head from side to side and shouting defiantly at the 'enemy'. Among the tribes of the Omo Valley in the south, much dance incorporates jumping and leaping up and down, a little like the dances of the Massai of Kenya. All dancing is in essence a social, communal activity, and you'll often be expected to join in. If you do give it a go, you'll win a lot of friends.

Music

Amharic traditional music consists largely of a continual repetition of a series of limited musical themes. However, the music was designed to suit the subject matter – usually solemn religious occasions and, though simple, can be very beautiful.

Church Music Yared the Deacon is traditionally credited with inventing church music, with the introduction in the 6th century of a system of musical notation.

Church music known as *aquaquam* uses just the drum, in particular the *kabaro*, as well as the *tsinatseil* or sistrum, a kind of sophisticated rattle, thought to be directly descended from an ancient Egyptian

Peoples of Ethiopia

The Italian historian, Conti Rossini, once described Abyssinia as a 'museo di popoli' (a museum of peoples). The 83 languages and 200 dialects spoken in Ethiopia give an indication of the country's incredible ethnic diversity. See also the boxed texts 'Peoples of the Lower Omo River' and 'The People of Konso' in the South of Addis Ababa section. The major tribal groups include the following:

Oromo People

Thought to originate from the south and from present-day Kenya, the Cushitic Oromo were once nomadic pastoralists and skilful warrior horsemen (see Oromo Migrations under History earlier in this section). Today, most are sedentary farmers or cattle breeders. The Oromo are Muslim, Christian and animist in religion, and are known for their egalitarian society, which is based on the famous *gada* or age-group system. A man's life is divided into age-sets of eight years. In the fourth set (between the ages of 24 and 32), men assume the right to govern their people. The Oromo are estimated to form the largest ethnic group (around 54%). For more on the Oromo see the East of Addis Ababa section.

Amhara & Tigrayan Peoples

In the centre and north of the country live the Semitic Amharas and Tigrayans, traditionally tillers of the soil. Their staple cereal is the famous *tef*, a local indigenous type of millet, which is responsible for the Ethiopian *injera* or pancake (see Food in the Facts for the Visitor section).

In the past, the Amharas and to a lesser extent the Tigrayans, proved themselves as great warriors, skilful governors and astute administrators. This century-old domination was always much resented by other tribal groups, who saw it as little more than a kind of colonialism.

Fiercely independent, devoutly Christian and fanatically attached to their land, the Amhara and Tigrayans disdain all manual labour with the single exception of agriculture – DIY is a notion completely lost on the average highlander. The Amhara form the second largest ethnic group (24%), and the Tigrayans the third largest (5%).

The Gurage People

The Gurage, Semitic-Cushitic in origin, are said to be the descendants of military colonists to the north. Most practise herding or farming, and the *enset* plant (see the boxed text 'Enduring Enset' in the South of Addis Ababa section) is their favoured crop. Known as great workers, clever improvisers – even counterfeiters – and skilled craftspeople, the Gurage will apply themselves to any task. Many work as seasonal labourers for the highlanders. Their faith is Christian, Muslim or animist, depending on the area in the south from which they originate.

---

instrument used for the worship of Isis. Only percussion instruments are used since their function is to mark the beat for chanting and dancing. The *maquamia* (prayer stick) also plays an essential role in church ceremony, and with hand-clapping is used to mark time. Very occasionally a *meleket* or trumpet is used, such as to lead processions.

You'll get plenty of opportunities to hear church music in Ethiopia. In the often beautiful surroundings of the old churches, with the colour of the priestly robes, and the heady perfume of incense, it can be quite mesmerising.

Secular Music Secular music, strongly influenced by church music, usually combines song and dance, emphasises rhythm, and blends both African and Asian elements. The music of the Amharas and Tigrayans in the highlands, as well as that of the peoples living near the Sudanese border, is heavily influenced by Arab music, and is very strident and emotive. Many visitors find it all a bit overwhelming.

Wind as well as percussion instruments are used for secular music. The *begenna* is a type of harp similar to that played by the ancient Greeks and Romans. The most

Peoples of Ethiopia

Harari People

Also Semitic in origin are the Harari people (also known as Adare), who have long inhabited the walled Muslim city of Harar in the east of the country. The people are particularly known for their distinct two-storey houses known as *gegar* (see the boxed text 'Traditional Adare Houses' under Harar in the East of Addis Ababa section) and for their very colourful traditional costumes, still worn by many Harari women today. In the past, the Harari were known as great craftspeople – they were weavers, basket-makers and bookbinders – as well as renowned Islamic scholars.

Somali People

The arid lowlands of the south-east dictate a nomadic or semi-nomadic existence for the Cushitic Somali people. Somali society is Muslim, strongly hierarchical, tightly knit and based on the clan system, which requires intense loyalty from its members. In the harsh environment in which they live, fierce competition for the scant resources leads to frequent and sometimes violent disputes over grazing grounds and sources of water.

Afar People

The Cushitic Afar people inhabit the famous Dankalia region, which stretches across the region (in Eritrea's south-east and into Ethiopia's east) and is considered one of the most inhospitable environments in the world. The people are famously belligerent and proud, and in the past won social prestige for themselves and their clan through the murder and castration of a member of an opposing tribe (see the boxed text 'The Dreaded Danakils' in the East of Addis Ababa section). For more information on the Afars and Somalis, see the special section 'A Museum of Peoples' and the boxed text 'Murder Most Foul' under Population & People in the Facts about Eritrea and Facts about Djibouti sections respectively.

Sidama People

The heterogeneous Cushitic Sidama people originate from the south-west, and can be divided into five different groups: the Sidama proper, the Derasa, Hadiya, Kambata and Alaba. Most Sidama are farmers who cultivate cereals, tobacco, enset and coffee. The majority are animists and many ancient beliefs persist, including a belief in the reverence of spirits. Pythons are believed to be reincarnations of ancestors and are sometime kept in houses as pets. The Sidama social organisation, like the gada system of the Oromo, is based on an age-group system. See the boxed text 'Sidamo Style' under Awasa in the South of Addis Ababa section.

---

popular instrument in the country is the *krar*, a kind of five or six-stringed lyre, which is often heard at weddings, or to attract customers to traditional pubs or bars. The *masenko* is a single-stringed fiddle and is the instrument of the *azmaris* or wandering minstrels (see the boxed text 'Mincing Minstrels' under Entertainment in the Addis Ababa section).

In the highlands, particularly the Simien and Bale Mountains, shepherd boys can be found with reed flutes. The *washint*, about 50cm long, with four holes, makes a bubbling sound said to imitate running water. It is supposed to keep the herds close by and to have a calming effect on the animals.

Song Songs are traditionally passed down from generation to generation, and every ethnic group has their own repertoire, from *musho* (household songs) and *lekso* (laments for the dead) to war songs, hunting songs and lullabies for the cradle and caravan.

Ethiopian male singing in the highlands is often in falsetto. The most characteristic element of female singing is the high-pitched trilling – a kind of tremulous and vibrating

Kebra Negast

Written during the 14th century by unknown author(s), the Kebra Negast or Glory of Kings, is considered Ethiopia's great national epic. It is more than a literary work – like the Quran to Muslims or the Old Testament to the Jews, it is a repository of Ethiopian national, religious and cultural sentiment.

Though a collection of many legends, the story of Solomon and Sheba is the most important. Though based on a Biblical passage in Kings, the Ethiopian version goes much further, claiming not only that Sheba (known as Makeda) was Ethiopian, but that she had a son by Solomon. Menelik, their offspring, is then said to have later stolen the Ark of the Covenant from Jerusalem and taken it to Ethiopia, where it apparently resides to this day in Aksum (see the boxed text 'The Tabot' later in this section).

The epic is notoriously shrouded in mystery – perhaps deliberately so. It may even represent a kind of massive propaganda stunt to legitimise the rule of the so-called 'Solomonic kings', who came to power in the 13th century and who, the book claims, were direct descendants of the kings of Israel.

ululation, which can be heard on all solemn, religious occasions.

Modern Music Ethiopian modern music is diverse and subject to outside influences, ranging from classical Amharic to jazz and blues. Modern classical singers and musicians include the late Assefa Abate, Kassa Tessema and the female vocalist, Asnakech Worku, both of the latter known for their singing and krar playing. Girma Achanmyeleh, who studied in England, is known for his piano playing. The composer Mulatu Astatike, is well known for his jazz.

Amharic popular music has a great following with the young. Unlike many other African countries, it is generally much preferred to the Western variety, and can be heard in all the bars, and discos of the larger towns. For visitors, it takes some getting used to.

The most famous Ethiopian pop singers have huge followings. Among them are Mohammud Ahmed, an easy-on-the-ear Sinatra type; the female vocalist Aster Awoke, who now lives in America; and the particularly popular (with the ladies) Tilahun Gessesse, a kind of Ethiopian Julio Iglesias. In 1997 he almost died following an attempted murder – many suspect a female hand.

Literature
Ge'ez Inscriptions in Ge'ez (the ancestor of modern Amharic) date from Aksumite times. During the Aksumite period, the Bible was translated from Greek into Ge'ez.

The year 1270 is considered to mark the 'golden age' of Ge'ez literature, in which many religious works were translated from Arabic, as well as original writing produced. In the early 14th century the Kebra Negast (see the boxed text) was written.

During the Muslim-Christian wars in the 16th century a huge amount of literature was destroyed and production ground to a halt. By the 17th century Ge'ez was in decline as a literary language and had long ceased to serve as the vernacular.

Amharic Amharic, today the official language of Ethiopia, was the national language of the Amharas. It was Emperor Tewodros who first gave encouragement to the local language in an attempt to promote national unity. The chronicles of his reign were written in Amharic. During the emperor's day – and in continuation of the trend begun in the 14th century – many songs and poetic laudatory songs were written to praise the ruler's qualities and 'munificence'.

Under the Derg, both writing and writers were suppressed. Be'alu Girma is a well-known example of one of the many artists who 'disappeared' at the hands of the Derg.

Poetry Poetry, along with dance and music, is used on many religious and social occasions, such as weddings or funerals. Rhymed verse is almost always chanted or sung in consonance with the rhythm of music.

Poetry places great stress on meaning, understanding of metaphor and allusion.

Keeping warm while studying the holy scriptures

Afar camel vendor

The delicious tilapia fish can be found on Lake Ziway, part of the northern group of Rift Valley lakes.

A raincoat, Ethiopian-style

Dressed as a traditional Abyssinian warrior for the Timkat festival

FRANCES LINZEE GORDON

Hamar woman, Omo Valley

Beautifully adorned Karo woman and child in the Omo Valley

Karo woman in her finery

A Karo warrior

Selling pineapples on the roadside near Dila

FRANCES LINZEE GORDON

In Ge'ez poetry, the religious allusions demand an incredibly thorough knowledge of Ethiopian religious legends and the Bible.

Folk Literature Perhaps the source of the greatest originality and creativity is the vast folk literature of Ethiopia – most of it in oral form. It encompasses everything from proverbs, tales and riddles, to magic spells and prophetic statements. See the special section 'Oral Literature in the Horn'.

Theatre

Ethiopia boasts one of the most ancient prolific and flourishing theatrical traditions in Africa. Addis Ababa is home to no less than five state theatre companies and state-supported *kinet* (performance arts) groups litter the regions. The University of Addis Ababa also has a special drama department.

Ethiopian theatre has also played an important part in the country's history. Because Ethiopian theatre is written in Amharic, however, it is practically unknown outside the country. Having largely resisted European influence, it has also preserved its own very local flavour and outlook.

Ethiopian theatrical conventions include minimal drama, sparse characterisation (with actors often serving as symbols) and plenty of long speeches. Verse form is often still used and rhetoric remains a very important element of Ethiopian plays.

Serious drama is seen as upper-class entertainment; the general public tend to prefer the variety shows. Many theatre companies have separate sections for both 'genres'.

Architecture

Ethiopia boasts some extraordinary architecture. Though some monuments – such as the castles of Gonder – show foreign influence, earlier building styles, such as those developed during the Aksumite period, are believed to be wholly indigenous, and are of a high technical standard.

Ethiopia's monumental architecture is almost wholly religious. Since the Ethiopian monarchs had no permanent capital (except during the Gonder period), few royal palaces were built.

The 'Aksumite style' of stone masonry is Ethiopia's most famous building style. Walls were constructed with field stones set in mortar and sometimes finely dressed corner stones. In between lay alternating layers of stone and timber, recessed then projected, and with protruding ends of round timber beams, known as 'monkey heads'. The latter are even symbolically carved into the great obelisks. The Aksumites were undoubtedly master masons. The style is seen in some of the early medieval churches such as Debre Damo and the motifs continue to serve in modern design today.

Monuments The monolithic granite stelae of the pre-Aksum and Aksumite period are without doubt Ethiopia's most extraordinary architectural achievement. For detailed information, see the boxed text 'A Quick Guide to Aksum's Stelae' under Aksum in the North of Addis Ababa section.

Traditional Churches Ethiopia has been called a country of churches. Churches are spread all over the landscape and are most often perched upon hills, dominating community life physically and psychologically. (The word *Debre* means 'mountain' in Ge'ez and often prefixes the names of monasteries.)

Churches vary in size from little and round to large rectangular and octagonal buildings. Famous rectangular churches include the very beautiful church at Debre Damo (see the Debre Damo section of this chapter) and the old church of St Mary of Zion at Aksum (see the Aksum section).

Ethiopian churches have several entrances. The eastern entrance leads to the *maqdas*, the Holy of Holies, and is reserved exclusively for the priests. It is here that the sacred *tabot* (the Ark of the Covenant) rests. The southern entrance is for women, the northern one for men. The western entrance can be used by both sexes, but inside, the men go to the left (north) and the women to the right (south).

Rock-Hewn Churches The churches of Lalibela are Ethiopia's most famous rock-hewn churches. Dating from the Zagwe

The Tabot

According to Ethiopian tradition, the *tabot*, the Ark of the Covenant, was abducted from Jerusalem and brought to Ethiopia in the first millennium BC, where it has remained ever since.

Today, every Ethiopian church has a replica of the Ark (or more precisely the Tablets of Law that are housed in the Ark) known as the tabot, which is kept in the inner sanctuary. It is the single most important element of the church, giving the church its sanctity.

During important religious festivals, the tabot is carried in solemn processions, accompanied by singing, dancing, the beating of staffs or prayer sticks, the rattling of the *sistra* (rattle) and the beating of drums – a scene wholly reminiscent of those described in the Old Testament.

They carried the ark of God on a new cart...David and all the house of Israel were dancing before the Lord with all their might, with songs and lyres and harps and tambourines and castanets and cymbals.
2 Sam. vi. 3–5

period, they are considered among the finest early Christian architecture in the world.

The churches are unique in that many stand completely free from the rock – unlike the Coptic churches of Egypt. The buildings show extraordinary technical skill in the use of line, proportion and decoration, and in the remarkable variety of styles. Some of the churches are in the shape of a cross, others are rectangular.

Lalibela's churches are the apex of a rock-hewing tradition that probably predates Christianity and has resulted in nearly 400 churches across the country.

The rock-hewn churches of the Tigray region, though less famous and spectacular, are no less remarkable; many almost certainly predate Lalibela, and date perhaps as far back as the 5th century. They represent the beginning of the rock-hewing tradition.

For detailed information on Ethiopia's rock-hewn churches, see the North of Addis Ababa section.

Castles of Gonder The town of Gonder and its imperial enclosure represent another peak in Ethiopian architectural achievement.

Although Portuguese, Moorish and Indian influences are all evident, the castles are nevertheless a very Ethiopian synthesis. Some have windows decorated with red volcanic tuff, and barrel- or egg-shaped domes.

For detailed information, see Gonder in the North of Addis Ababa section.

Painting
Religious Painting Most painting is limited to religious subjects – particularly the life of Christ and the saints. Every church in Ethiopia is decorated with abundant and colourful murals, frescos or paintings (see the boxed texts 'Know Your Ethiopian Saints' in the North of Addis Ababa section).

Ethiopian painting is characterised by a kind of naive realism. Everything is expressed with vigour and directness using bold colour, strong line and stylised proportions and perspective. Like the stained glass windows in European Gothic churches, the paintings served a very important purpose: to instruct, inspire and instil awe in the illiterate and uneducated.

Modern Painting Borrowing freely from the past, but no longer constrained by it, modern Ethiopian painting shows greater originality of expression, and like theatre, is a flourishing medium. Until recently, the artist was considered a mere craftsmen but as Western influence has spread the artist has attained a more professional standing.

The vast stained-glass window in Africa Hall in Addis Ababa is the work of one of Africa's best-known painters, Afewerk Tekle. Many of his most famous paintings can be seen in the form of posters stuck up in hotels, restaurants and cafes around the country (see the boxed text 'Afewerk Tekle' in the Addis Ababa section).

SOCIETY & CONDUCT
Traditional Culture
See also Women Travellers in the Facts for the Visitor section.

Marriage Most Ethiopians live with their families until marriage. Young men in the towns traditionally lead a fairly free lifestyle. Sexual adventures – at least until marriage – are considered fairly normal for men. A woman's virginity before marriage is only preferred in the towns, but is a pre-requisite in the rural areas.

In rural areas, the traditional form of marriage is called *kal kidan*. Arranged by the parents of the couple, a civil and binding marriage contract is drawn up. A long engagement follows, until the bride is declared fit for marriage by her parents – sometimes when she has reached puberty.

Marriages are usually celebrated with several days of feasting, which can place a huge financial burden on the two families. After marriage, the couple usually join the household of the husband's parents. After a couple of years, they will request a plot of land from the village on which to build their own house. January is a very popular month for weddings, when the harvest is over, the weather is dry, and there are no fasting periods to restrict the wedding feasts.

Increasingly, and particularly in the urban centres, marriage follows the Western pattern both in an individual's choice of partner and in the wedding ceremony – complete with white wedding gown and iced cake. Nevertheless, Ethiopian families still play a big role in brokering marriages. Instead of exchanging goats, cows etc, the families exchange a predetermined number of gifts, including TVs and videos. The dowry can range anywhere between Birr3000 to 50,000. Polygamy is forbidden by the Ethiopian penal code.

Divorce is still relatively easy in Ethiopia and marriage can be dissolved at the request of either party – usually adultery is given as justification. In theory, each partner retains the property he or she brought into the marriage, though sometimes allowances are made for the 'wronged' partner. Legally, women in Ethiopia enjoy a relatively equitable position compared to some African countries.

Dos & Don'ts

Names Customs vary greatly according to the ethnic group, but many Ethiopians –

Illuminated Manuscripts

Illuminated manuscripts represent without doubt one of Ethiopia's greatest artistic achievements. The best manuscripts were prepared by monks and priests for the kings, the court and the largest and wealthiest churches and monasteries in the 14th and 15th centuries. These were characterised by beautifully shaped letters, attention to minute detail, and elaborate ornamentation. Pictures were included in the text to bring it to life and make it more comprehensible.

The binding consisted of thick wooden boards often covered with tooled leather. The volume was then placed into a case with straps made of rough hides so that it could be slung over a shoulder. Made of goatskin, some required the hides of 150 animals.

On the blank pages at the beginning or at the end of the volume, look out for the formulae *fatina bere* 'trial of the pen' or *bere' sanay* 'a fine pen', as the scribes tried out their reeds. Some are also dated and contain a short blessing for the owner as well as the scribe.

Unfortunately, huge numbers have been pillaged from Ethiopia by soldiers, travellers and explorers. Few manuscripts date prior to the 14th century because they didn't survive the mass destruction of the churches by the Muslims and Dervishes in the 10th and 16th centuries respectively. Don't miss the chance to see these illuminated manuscripts – the priests of the churches are usually happy to show off their 'treasures'.

particularly the Amharas and Tigrayans, take their father's first name as their second name.

If you ask an Ethiopian their name, they will give you their first name only. When introducing yourself, do the same. Surnames are hardly used in Ethiopia. A woman's name does not change on marriage.

Ethiopians are always addressed, formally and informally, by their first names. To formalise an address, you just add *Ato* (Mr) for a man and *Weizero* (Mrs) for a woman. See also the boxed text 'What's in a name?'.

What's in a Name?

Ethiopian Christian names usually combine a religious name with a secular name.

Common male secular names include *Hagos* 'Joy', *Mebratu* 'Light', and *Desta* (also for women) 'Pleasure'. For women, names include *Ababa* 'Flower', *Belainesh* 'You're the Best', *Zawditu* 'Crown', and *Terunesh* 'You're Wonderful'.

Some Ethiopian names have particular meanings. *Mitiku* or *Mitke* means 'Substitute' and *Kassa* 'Compensation', given to children after the death of a brother or sister. *Masresha*, roughly meaning 'Distraction', is given after a family misfortune. *Bayable* means 'If he Hadn't Denied It', applied to a bastard-child whose father refuses to acknowledge it. *Tesfaye* means 'My Hope', often given to a child by a poor or single mother who looks forward to her child's future success in life. Other names can mean 'That's the Last!' or 'No More!' after a long string of children.

Many Christian names are compounds made up of two names. *Wolde* means 'Son of', *Gebre* 'Servant of', *Haile* 'Power of', *Tekle* 'Plant of', *Habte* 'Gift of'; so that *Gebre-Yesus* means 'Son of Jesus', *Habte-Mikael* 'Gift of Michael' etc.

The *Yedabo sim* (literally 'Name of the Bread') is the tradition of giving a bride a new second name on her wedding day.

Names are very important in Ethiopia, and the exchange of names – rather like the exchange of addresses in the West – is the first important stage in forming a friendship. If someone has performed a service for you, ask his/her name. Many children will ask 'What is your name?', which however irritating after the 1000th time is an overture to friendship, not just the practising of English.

Dress Ethiopians are conservative in their dress and it is much appreciated if visitors follow suit. Sleeveless shirts and shorts are looked down upon, particularly in rural areas, and are a big no-no in the churches or mosques. Nor are they advised in the Muslim city of Harar (see Dos & Don'ts in the Facts about Djibouti section later in this book for Islamic etiquette). Ethiopian women traditionally never expose their shoulders, knees, cleavage or waist in public.

If visiting government offices or on business, a tie and decent shirt for a man is a minimum, a jacket helps and a suit is preferred. Dress in Ethiopia is important and an effort to look smart is seen as showing respect to those you are meeting. See also the boxed text 'Church Etiquette' under Responsible Tourism in the Facts for the Visitor section.

Greetings The Ethiopian highlanders attach great importance to etiquette. Greetings are characterised by an incredibly lengthy exchange of inquiries; the longer the exchange, the greater the friendship. Questions turn on the health of the family, the crops, weather, animals etc. It is also common to 'send regards' to relatives even if you've never met them. Once you've made an Ethiopian acquaintance, you'll be expected to follow this ritual, too. Neglecting to do so is considered very impolite. It's also customary to do this before getting down to any business matter.

Greetings are often accompanied by a nod or quick head bow – which shows respect. This is also a way of showing thanks or appreciation for something. Low bowing is still normal before distinguished people. In the past, children would prostrate themselves completely before their fathers and grandfathers and kiss their feet.

Handshaking is generally reserved for equals. Sometimes hands remain joined for the duration of the conversation. As a *faranji* or foreigner, you will be expected to shake hands with everyone even if you enter a room full of people. If hands are dirty or wet, you will be offered a wrist, with the hand hanging down rather limply. Children – foreign and local – are expected to extend a hand, too. It is polite also to kiss babies or young children, even if you've just met them.

Kissing on the cheek is very common among friends and relatives of either sex, but in Ethiopia, three kisses are given (right, left, right), and they are interspersed with the greeting formulae (see previous). The cheek is touched rather than kissed, though kissing noises are made. 'Long-lost' friends may kiss up to five times.

Other Etiquette When receiving a gift, both hands must be extended. Only one is seen as showing reluctance or ingratitude.

Friends of the same sex can often be seen holding hands in the street, or with arms wrapped around one another. But opposite-sex couples – even married ones – never display affection in public.

When attracting someone's attention, such as a waiter or porter, it is polite to call *yikerta* (excuse me). In restaurants, waiters aren't ignoring you – simply clap your hands to call them when you need them. Whistling or snapping your fingers is considered rude. Don't be offended by waiters snatching away your plates the moment you've finished; it's considered impolite to leave dirty dishes in front of customers. See also the boxed text 'Eating Etiquette' under Food in the Facts for the Visitor section.

If you're sitting in a cafe and someone joins your table, it's customary to pay for his/her coffee or drink when you come to pay for yours. The same will be done for you and isn't, as some guidebooks have thought, a kind of special 'welcome-to-Ethiopia-treatment for foreigners'. It's also customary to invite those rendering services to you, such as guides or drivers, to coffee or meals.

Punctuality is important as tardiness is seen as a sign of disrespect. Conversely, you may be kept waiting, which is sometimes a demonstration of the other person's prestige or status. Deference to authority is also important – to policeman, officials etc. You'll find your trip is smoother if you bear this in mind. Smiling works wonders, too. Many Africans see Westerners as arrogant, proud and imperial, but a smile is instantly returned.

See also Dangers & Annoyances and Photography & Video – both in the Facts for the Visitor section.

RELIGION
Faith is an extremely important part of an Ethiopian's life. Christian Ethiopians bring

Rude Noises

Making rude noises of any sort is considered the height of bad manners by most Ethiopians. Considered the worst foreign offenders of the worst offence (rude, smelly noises) are the Italians, whose lack of attention or ensuing hilarity is considered deeply shocking, and the French, whose 'subterfuge' is considered somewhat deceitful. If you do breach this strict rule of social conduct, a quick *yikerta* (excuse me) is probably the best way out!

God into everyday conversation just as much as their Muslim counterparts who will say 'thanks be to God', 'God willing' 'God forbid' etc. Some Ethiopians even thank God in speeches or include Him in the list of acknowledgments in books.

Pre-Christianity
Earliest Aksum is thought to have practised the worship of serpents. Later, such beliefs were replaced by the southern Arabian–derived deification of the sun, moon and stars. The pantheon also included Astar, a kind of Arabian equivalent to Zeus, the Greek king of the gods. Mahrem, like Ares, was the God of war, and Baher, like Poseidon, the god of the sea. Quite contrary to the Graeco-Roman mythology, the sun was regarded as female, the moon as male.

The pre-Christian symbols of the sun and crescent moon can be seen on the famous stelae of Aksum to this day. The moon remains an important element in Ethiopian folk culture. When Christianity became the Aksumite state's official religion in the early 4th century BC, the gods were forgotten.

Christianity
Although the population is split fairly evenly between Muslims (35%) and Christians (45%), it is Orthodox Christianity that has traditionally dominated the country's past. The official religion of the imperial court right up until Emperor Haile Selassie was deposed in 1974, it has heavily influenced the political, social and cultural life

Passports to the Promised Land

Moses and Solomon may be biblical names to most but, to over 20,000 Ethiopian Jews, the names of these biblical characters became their passports to the Promised Land in two dramatic rescue operations that captured the imagination of the Western world.

In 1985, some 7000 Ethiopian Jews were plucked from the brink of famine and airlifted to Israel in Operation Moses. Trekking through the desert to Khartoum, they then flew via Europe en route to Israel in a mission cloaked in a veil of secrecy to avoid any undue publicity that would hamper the rest of the rescue. Inevitably, many thousands who embarked on the overland journey from Ethiopia died along the trail to Sudan.

Then in 1991, as the country plunged deeper into civil war and opposition rebels were on the verge of overthrowing the Marxist regime and capturing Addis Ababa, Israel staged another dramatic rescue: Operation Solomon. In the short space of 36 hours, a staggering 14,000 Jews were airlifted to Israel. To add to the drama, seven babies were born during the 36-hour transit.

Since their arrival in Israel, however, the Ethiopians have been at the centre of a dispute regarding their religious authenticity, including a request by the chief rabbinate that they go through a symbolic conversion process. Nevertheless, they claim their lineage is linked to King Solomon (hence the name of the 1991 airlift), though some scholars believe they are descendants of the Tribe of Dan: one of the 12 lost tribes of Israel dispersed after the Babylonian exile in 586 BC.

Dan Goldberg

of the highlands. Today, the church continues to carry great clout among the Ethiopian people and sees itself as the great guardian of ancient Ethiopian traditions, directly inherited from Aksum.

Ethiopia's connection with Christianity is an ancient and distinguished one. With the sole exception of Armenia, it can claim to have been the first country in the world to have adopted Christianity as its state religion. Christianity in the past has also served as Ethiopia's only true unifying factor; though, by the same measure, it has also legitimised the oppression of the people by its rulers.

Ethiopian Orthodox Christianity is thought to have its roots in Judaism – parts of the country were Judaic before conversion to Christianity. This would explain many of the Judaic elements in the church, such as the food restrictions, including the way animals are slaughtered. Even the layout of the traditional round church is considered Hebrew in origin. Ancient Semitic and pagan elements also persist.

The church plays an important part in daily life, regulating many social and even dietary traditions – such as the customary Wednesday and Friday fasts and the Lent, Advent and *Kweskwam* (40 days preceding the feast of the flight to Egypt) fasts. There are also a huge number of feasts; of which 33 days honour the Virgin Mary alone.

Circumcision is generally practised on boys, marriage is celebrated in the presence of a priest, and confession is usually only made during a grave illness. The sacrament of confirmation has fallen into disuse. Church services normally take place on Sunday morning at 6 am and last at least two hours. There are no pews or stools in a church, as it is customary to stand or lean hour after hour on a prayer stick.

Islam

Ethiopia's connection with Islam is as distinguished as its connection with Christianity. Ethiopia's oldest and holiest mosque is that at Negash, north of Wukro in Tigray, believed to date originally from the 8th century. The shrine of Sheikh Hussein in the Bale region is also greatly venerated and attracts national and international pilgrims (see Sheikh Hussein in the South of Addis Ababa section).

The most famous Muslim city is the walled city of Harar, an important Islamic centre in its own right. Long renowned as a centre of learning, it is also home to an incredible number of important shrines and mosques.

Most Muslims inhabit the eastern, southern and western lowlands, but there are also significant populations in the country's major 'Christian' towns including Addis Ababa. For general information on Islam see Religion in the Facts about Djibouti section later in this book.

The Falashas

Falashas (Ethiopian Jews) have inhabited Ethiopia since the 14th century. Actively engaged in various wars to defend their independence and freedom, they are now thought to number no more than a few thousand: war, persecution and emigration have greatly reduced their numbers. Tiny populations remain north of Lake Tana in the northwest; their beliefs combine a fascinating mixture of Judaism, paganism and Christianity (see the boxed text 'Passports to the Promised Land').

Paganism

Paganism is still commonly found among the country's Cushitic peoples, in particular in the lowland areas of the west and south (see also the boxed text 'Peoples of Ethiopia' earlier in this section), and accounts for an estimated 11% of the population.

Paganism ranges from animism (associated with trees, springs, mountains and stones etc) to totemism found among the Konso, in which animals are ritually slaughtered and then consumed by the people. Elements of ancestor worship, are still found among the Afar. The Oromo traditionally believe in a supreme celestial deity known as Wak, whose eye is the sun.

LANGUAGE

Since Ethiopia was never really colonised, European languages never took a grip as they did in other African colonised countries. Amharic, an indigenous language, is

> ## Ethiopian Eloquence
>
> The Amharas, like the ancient Romans, place great value on eloquence. Considered the mark of a cultured and refined man, eloquence cannot, unlike other status symbols, be bought. A good speaker employs clear and slow expression, and makes ample use of metaphor, allusion and double meaning – a kind of literary gymnastics.
>
> Ambiguity, thought to originate from centuries of political instability and courtly intrigue, has become an art in itself and is valued above all. The skilled speaker is said to be able to answer any question put to them in the most eloquent and beautiful, but entirely vague, manner possible. It is also said that a litigant can win a point or even a legal case with an apt poetic reference or witty innuendo.
>
> The Ethiopian love of wordplay can be seen today in the innumerable marketing slogans and quips of travel agencies, banks, even hotels – some frankly verge on the bizarre.

Semitic (like Arabic) in origin, and is the national language. Twelve million or so Amhara people speak it and it is the second language of around one-third of the population. It is also the official language of the media and the government. In the absence of any European languages, it is by far the most useful language. English is generally only spoken by the urban educated population (and often not all that well). Outside the towns, you're on your own. Ethiopia's many ethnic groups have their own languages and resent speaking Amharic (the language of the 'colonisers'). If you can stretch to a few phrases in the other languages – even hello – you'll cause delight and the world will be yours!

See Books in the Facts for the Visitor section and also the Language chapter.

BIRDS IN ETHIOPIA

The birds of Ethiopia are so numerous, so diverse and so colourful that even the die-hard nonbirder will find it difficult, given time, not to become hooked. More than 830 species have been recorded, compared to 250 in the UK, and although other African countries claim more species, Ethiopia boasts the special distinction of possessing a high number of endemics (birds found only in that country). Of these, 16 are found only in Ethiopia and 14 are semi-endemic, shared only with Eritrea.

Additional advantages of birding in Ethiopia are the relative ease of spotting many of the species (including at least 20 of the semi-endemics or endemics), the possibility of birding on foot (due to the scarcity of dangerous animals), and the small number of tourists found at the sites.

The best time to visit Ethiopia for birding is between November and February; July and August are when the heaviest rain falls. While it is possible to spot birds all day, the best time is from dawn to 11 am and from 5 pm to dusk.

The following section is designed for both the novice and the hard-core twitcher.

Habitats

One of the reasons for the high degree of endemism in Ethiopia is the country's topography. A large part of the country is little more than a giant highland plateau surrounded on all sides by arid land. Its isolation has permitted the evolution of unique forms and species.

The plateau supports a surprising range of habitats. The Great Rift Valley, with its large freshwater and saline lakes, runs through the central highlands of Ethiopia from north to south. The highlands, which rise to 4620m, support montane forest, juniper woodland, crags and escarpments, and grassland.

Elsewhere, crater lakes and acacia savanna are found, and to the east of the highlands are large areas of semidesert.

Endemics of Ethiopia

Abyssinian catbird (Parophasma galinieri)
Abyssinian longclaw (Macronyx flavicollis)
Ankober seedeater or serin
    (Serinus ankoberensis)
Black-headed siskin (Serinus nigriceps)
Degodi lark (Mirafra degodiensis)
Golden-backed or Abyssinian woodpecker
    (Dendropicos abyssinicus)
Harwood's francolin (Francolinus hardwoodi)
Nechisar nightjar
    (Caprimulgus nechisarensis)
Prince Ruspoli's Turaco (Tauraco ruspolii)

Salvadori's seedeater or serin
    (Serinus xantholaema)
Sidamo long-clawed lark
    (Heteromirafra sidamoensis)
Spot-breasted plover (Vanellus
    melanocephalus)
Stresemann's or Abyssinian bush crow
    (Zavattariornis stresemanni)
White-tailed swallow (Hirundo megaensis)
Yellow-fronted parrot (Poicephalus flavifrons)
Yellow-throated seedeater or serin
    (Serinus flavigula)

Tip

Always ask permission before birding on private property. Be particularly careful around airports, bridges, military camps and royal palaces. Photography is strictly forbidden in these areas.

Cities & Towns

Contrary to popular belief, the urban landscape is surprisingly full of birdlife. A common sight in towns all over the world are the **swifts, swallows** and **martins** nesting under the eaves of buildings. **Sparrows, starlings** and **pigeons** are also familiar denizens of human settlements.

Birds to look out for particularly in urban Ethiopia include the **dusky turtle dove** and **Swainson's sparrow**. At airports, keep an eye out for the large flights of the semi-endemic **white-collared pigeon**.

One bird you can't fail to notice in towns and villages throughout the country is the **black kite**. It visits Ethiopia from North Africa and the Middle East and is much maligned as a scavenger. In fact it provides an invaluable waste-disposal service, cleaning up the city's waste. Its piercing and beautiful cry is unmistakable.

Forests

Forests and woodland now cover only a small proportion of Ethiopia's total land area, and in many parts the natural, indigenous forest has been replaced either by pastoral and agricultural land or by plantations of the imported eucalyptus tree.

Nevertheless, forests are home to a large variety of birds, among them **woodpeckers, warblers, birds of prey** and the beautiful **hoopoe**. Though numerous, woodland birds are often hard to spot; it is their song that most often gives them away.

The endemic **Abyssinian catbird** is one of the star ornithological attractions of Ethiopia. Other forest species include the semi-endemic **black-headed forest oriole** and the endemic **golden-backed woodpecker**.

Deserts

Arid and semidesert regions are found in the far south and east of Ethiopia. The number and variety of species are reduced in this harsh environment, but the habitat still supports some interesting birds that have learnt to adapt to it.

Species of **lark, ostrich, sandgrouse** and smaller and larger **bustards** are all found here. **Finches** can also be seen feeding around the droppings of camels. If you're wondering about the dainty little birds scattering in front of your vehicle, they are **Namaqua doves**, a common sight throughout the drylands of southern Ethiopia.

Waterways

Lakes, swamps, marshes and rivers can support an astonishing variety of birds. However, during hot months, watering holes, streams and even large rivers can dry up, so many water birds have had to adapt by becoming migratory or nomadic.

Different groups of birds use waterways in different ways. Some rout along the shore in search of prey, others probe the mud with long beaks, or stride into deep water on tall legs. Some, like the kingfisher, have learnt to use patience and immobility as artifice, perching on overhanging vegetation before diving into the water after prey.

Ethiopia's lakes are famous for their birdlife and more than 50% of all the country's species have been recorded in the vicinity of the lakes. Among the attractions are the **great white pelican**, **greater and lesser flamingos** and the large numbers of **waders**, **ducks** and **kingfishers**.

Grasslands

In recent years, large areas of grassland have been lost to grazing and agriculture. Nevertheless some species, such as the **finch**, have adapted well to this modern-day habitat. Grassland species include the **lark**, **pipit**, various **birds of prey** and 'game' birds such as the **bustard**.

The highland grassland plateaus of Ethiopia are particularly rich in endemic or semi-endemic species. The Bale Mountains harbour no fewer than 16 of them. Some birds, such as the endemic **black-headed siskin**, prefer higher altitudes. In season, several species of **harriers** can be seen diving for rodents in the high-altitude grasslands.

Other birds found in mountainous regions include various species of **starling**, which feed on the high-altitude giant lobelia plant; thrush; and various species of **sunbird**. Visiting **storks** and **cranes** can often be found feeding in boggy mountain patches.

Lowland grassland provides a habitat in particular for seedeaters and insectivores. The **weaverbird** has adapted well to this environment, and the pendulous nest it builds from the acacia trees is unmistakable. The starling is also common, as is the **red-billed oxpecker**, which can be seen perched on the back of domestic animals, ridding them of ticks and other parasites.

Where to See Birds

The following is a summary of Ethiopia's principal bird sites. It can be used either to plan a kind of ornithological itinerary, or, for those with other interests as well as birds, as a kind of pointer for things to look for while travelling around the country. Visitors keen only to see birds should allow a minimum of 10 days to cover all the areas listed.

For more details on the sites and the bird species in each area, refer to the relevant section of this book.

In & Around Addis Ababa

Birds in Ethiopia are so abundant that travellers will notice them almost everywhere. Even in and around the capital, Addis Ababa, visitors can expect to see at least eight endemics or semi-endemics. The **black-winged lovebird** is one example; it makes its way through the sky like a miniature helicopter.

North of Addis Ababa

The seasonally wet highland grasslands of the Sululta Plains, 31km north of Addis Ababa, support a good number of waders including the **black-winged lapwing**. Around 30km further north, the Blue Nile gorges around Debre Libanos are home to at least seven endemics or semi-endemics, among them the **banded barbet**, **Rueppell's chat** and **white-billed starling**.

Tip

Don't always assume that birds are best approached on foot. Some birds tolerate vehicles remarkably well, and good roadside views and photos can be had from a car window.

Further north, the town of Bahar Dar is situated on the shores of the huge freshwater Lake Tana. There is good birdlife along the lakeshore.

One site not to be missed is the Blue Nile Falls, 32km south-east of Bahar Dar. The 45m-high falls create a kind of subtropical microclimate that attracts several colourful species including the endemic **yellow-fronted parrot**.

Between Bahar Dar and Aksum are the spectacular Simien Mountains. Although the area's birdlife is not as rich as that found in the Bale Mountains, the scenic crags and escarpments provide an unparalleled opportunity to see the soaring **lammergeyer**. Sightings of this immense bird and its incidental companion, the semi-endemic **thick-billed raven**, are almost guaranteed.

East of Addis Ababa

Around 20km south-east of Addis Ababa, on the Nazret road, are the Akaki wetlands. With its open river, marshes, waterfall and seasonal lakes, this is a great spot for birds. The wetlands boast a decent variety of **waders**, **ducks** and sometimes **flamingos**. The semi-endemic **wattled ibis** and **red-chested wheatear** are both commonly spotted there.

Around 30km further along the same road is Debre Zeyit, the site of a collection of crater lakes which are home to a wide variety of waders and ducks as well as the endemic **white-winged chat**.

The rocky escarpment near the little village of Ankober, north-east of Addis Ababa, has become a more recent fixture on the birder's itinerary, on account of the discovery in 1976 of the endemic and very localised Ankober serin.

Around 200km due east of Addis Ababa lies the Awash National Park, one of the best places for birding in Ethiopia.

The Dire Dawa–Harar area provides the bird-watcher with a variety of habitats including semi-arid bush, highland grassland and waterways. A bonus to this area is that much of the region's avifauna overlaps with species from the Ogaden region of south-east Ethiopia, an area currently unsafe for travellers.

South of Addis Ababa

South of Debre Zeyit, the string of Ethiopian Rift Valley lakes are home to a huge selection of water birds including, during the northern winter, a large number of Palearctic **waders** and **waterfowl** and a few semi-endemics such as the **brown sawwing**.

Lake Ziway, with its large expanses of aquatic vegetation, attracts some interesting water birds including herons and storks. The acacia savannas and the cliff-lined shores of Lake Langano provide a habitat for the hornbill, fan-tailed raven and helmet shrike.

The saline waters of Lake Abiata and Lake Shala are known as the feeding and nesting grounds of large numbers of **greater and lesser flamingos** and the **great white pelican**. In the northern winter, the shores attract a good number of **waders** and **ducks**.

On Lake Awasa, the **African pygmy-goose** can sometimes be spotted, along with various species of **stork**, **ibis**, **crake**, **heron** and **coot**.

At the southern end of the Ethiopian Rift Valley, the varied habitats around Arba Minch, such as the freshwater lakes Chamo and Abaya, the

Tip

Consider the services of local guides: their knowledge of species and habitats is sometimes unsurpassed, and their employment brings very useful revenue to the local community.

The Strange Case of the Vanishing Turaco

In a remote patch in the deep south of Ethiopia lives one of the country's rarest, most beautiful and most enigmatic birds. The Prince Ruspoli's turaco was first introduced to the world in the early 1890s. It was 'collected' by an Italian prince who gave his name to the bird as he explored the dense juniper forests of southern Ethiopia.

Unfortunately, the intrepid prince failed to make a record of his find, and when he was killed shortly afterwards near Lake Abaya following an encounter with an elephant, all hope of locating the species seemed to die with him.

In subsequent years, other explorers searched in vain for the bird. None were successful until the turaco finally reappeared in the 1940s. Just three specimens were obtained; then the turaco disappeared again. It was not until the early 1970s that the bird was again spotted.

To this day, the turaco is considered Ethiopia's most elusive endemic bird. Almost nothing is known about the species, and its nest and eggs have never been seen. The turaco is registered in the *Red Book* of 'very endangered species of the world'.

However, recent sightings in the juniper forest of the Yabelo Wildlife Sanctuary, and in fig and acacia undergrowth in the west, suggest that the bird may not, after all, be as elusive as it would have us believe.

lowland riverine forest and the acacia woodland, attract a wide variety of birds, including **weavers**, **sunbirds** and **waxbills**.

The thickly forested hills of Wondo Genet, south of Shashemene, are home to an excellent variety of birds including many semi-endemics such as the **thick-billed raven** and the **Abyssinian slaty flycatcher**.

The Bale Mountains National Park is a favourite among birders and is famous as the home of a large number of Ethiopian endemics and semi-endemics (16 in total). The park protects a wide range of habitats, from juniper and Hagenia woodland and montane forest, to high-altitude alpine and heather moorland. Endemics include the **Abyssinian longclaw**, **Abyssinian catbird**, and **spot-breasted lapwing**, which is so common that a sighting is almost guaranteed.

South of the Bale Mountains are various spots which, though rather inaccessible, are home to some of Ethiopia's most rare endemics, such as **Prince Ruspoli's turaco**, the **Sidamo lark**, **Degodi lark** and **Stresemann's bush crow**. The areas around Negele, Yabelo and Mega are particularly good, but Bogol Manyo is currently unsafe.

West of Addis Ababa

The Jimma-Bonga area in western Ethiopia has some extensive montane forests, and the birds associated with them include **woodpeckers**, **warblers**, **birds of prey** and **hoopoes**.

The Gefersa Reservoir, 18km outside Addis Ababa, is a good place to spot water birds, including two semi-endemics, the **blue-winged goose** and the **wattled ibis**.

Tip

Keep an eye out for fruiting trees. Many Ethiopian birds including Turacos, hornbills and barbets are attracted to them.

Bird Species

Of the 10 bird families endemic to the African mainland, eight are represented in Ethiopia; only rockfowl and sugarbird are absent. Families that are particularly well represented are the **falcon**, **francolin**, **bustard** and **lark**.

Ethiopia boasts the largest number of endemic and semi-endemic species in mainland Africa after South Africa, including the **Abyssinian catbird**, **Rouget's rail**, the **white-cheeked turaco** and **Heuglin's bustard**. The nonendemics, which include the ubiquitous **Abyssinian roller** and the **blue-breasted bee-eater**, are also diverse and colourful. During the northern winter, some 200 species of Palearctic migrants cross into Ethiopia from Europe and Asia, via the Sahara Desert, Arabian Peninsula and Red Sea. These migrants add significantly to the already abundant African resident and intra-African migrant populations.

Of the 836 species recorded in Ethiopia, 19 are considered threatened, and five are classified as near-threatened.

Organised Tours

In Ethiopia, various travel agencies offer bird tours (see Organised Tours in the Getting Around section of this chapter). In the UK, a number of travel agencies specialise in bird tours, including the following:

Birdquest   (☎ 01254-826317, fax 826780, ✉ birders@birdquest.co.uk)
Cygnus Wildlife   (☎/fax 01736-711280)
Ornitholidays   (☎ 01243-821230, fax 829574)
Sunbird   (☎ 01767-682969, fax 692481).

Publications

To date, there is no comprehensive field guide to the birds of Ethiopia. For most people, however, the Collins illustrated checklist *Birds of Eastern Africa* by Ber van Perlo will suffice.

The Ethiopian Wildlife and Natural History Society, PO Box 60074, Addis Ababa, publishes the annual journal *Walia*. The society has also recently published *Important Bird Areas of Ethiopia*, an excellent 300-page inventory covering the entire country.

Ethiopia's Endemic Birds, published by the Ethiopian Tourism Commission in Addis Ababa, is a small, but useful, illustrated booklet on the country's endemics and semi-endemics. *Birds of Africa* (Fry et al), volumes I to IV, is a good source of reference for the more serious birder, though it's hardly for use in the field.

The comprehensive *Checklist of the Birds of Ethiopia* by EK Urban and LH Brown is available from Addis Ababa's university bookshop. It lists all of Ethiopia's birds, as well as their range, status, abundance and time of breeding.

Bird-watching reports on Ethiopia are available in English from Steve Whitehouse (☎ 01905-454541), who runs an information service on bird-watching abroad. His address is 6 Skipton Crescent, Berkeley Pendesham, Worcester WR4 OLG, UK.

For tape recordings of Ethiopian birds (UK£7.50), contact Steve Smith at 42 Lower Buckland Rd, Lymington, Hampshire SO41 9DL, UK.

Facts for the Visitor

SUGGESTED ITINERARIES

In terms of tourism and travel, Ethiopia can simply be divided into four main parts: north, south, west and east, with Addis Ababa acting like a pivot in the centre and providing a convenient base. In a nutshell, the north is home to the major historic sites; the south is where much of the best birding and wildlife is, as well as where some of the most interesting tribal groups can be found; the west makes for good off-the-beaten-track exploration; and the east boasts the old Muslim town of Harar. Ethiopia's attractions are very diverse – from serious history to challenging trekking and heavy birding!

Given Ethiopia's size and the state of most roads, travelling by bus is very slow and time-consuming. The only way of speeding up road travel is by renting your own vehicle (outside Addis Ababa, a 4WD is essential). Taking a couple of flights can cut out whole days on the road.

Addis Ababa is situated roughly at the centre of the country, and at the centre too of the air, rail and road transportation network. Well supplied with hotels and restaurants of all categories, it makes a good springboard for travel to the regions surrounding it, which are otherwise as good as separated from one another. Addis Ababa itself is worth a couple of days, with several good museums and its famous outdoor market.

Historic Sites

Ethiopia's best-known and most well-trodden travellers trail is the so-called historical route, which takes you on a tour of northern Ethiopia. The circuit includes all the most famous historic and religious sites, including 'the big four': Bahar Dar, Aksum, Gonder and Lalibela. A loop from Addis Ababa covers over 2000km. By road, you're looking at around 10 days' travel and a very sore bottom before you've even got off the bus.

Ethiopian Airlines has flights that connect all four towns. You could see them all, with time to visit the sites, in a week – at a push.

If you have a little longer, the outlying churches of Lalibela are well worth exploring and make terrific treks by mule or on foot.

A good compromise on cost and time is to use both bus and plane, taking in the scenery but not wasting too many days on the road. Not a bad itinerary is to bus from Addis Ababa as far as Gonder or Aksum, then miss out the less picturesque southern loop by flying back to Addis Ababa via Lalibela.

With another week, you could also visit the rock-hewn churches of Tigray. You'll need your own vehicle or else plenty of time to reach many of these churches.

To the east of Addis Ababa lies the Muslim town of Harar, which can be visited in around four days from Addis Ababa, by bus or by the somewhat slower train (as far as Dire Dawa).

Wildlife & Natural Sites

The west and south are great places for exploration off the beaten track, but in almost every corner of Ethiopia there is scenic country to be explored. Ethiopia has huge potential for trekking (an epic route might include a trek from Aksum to Lalibela crossing the Simien Mountains on the way).

The Bale Mountains National Park is the best place for wildlife, particularly endemic mammals and birds (unlike in the Simien Mountains National Park, you don't need to trek to see the animals). One day will give you a glimpse of the animals and birds, two will increase your chances of seeing an Ethiopian wolf, and three to four will allow a decent trek. The journey to or from Addis Ababa takes between one and 1½ days, depending on whether you are driving or on a bus. Ethiopian Airlines flies to Goba.

To trek in the Simien Mountains, you'll need a minimum of three days. The journey from Addis Ababa to Debark takes 1½ days by bus; Ethiopian Airlines flies to Gonder. Six to eight days are better, particularly if you're planning to climb Ras Dashen.

The Awash and Nechisar National Parks are also good for wildlife and are around two or three days' journey from Addis Ababa.

If you're keen on birds, the Rift Valley lakes as well as Wondo Genet in the south are easily accessible from Addis Ababa and can be easily appreciated in two days. Both are good for birds (see the special section 'Birds in Ethiopia').

The Blue Nile Falls are easily accessible from Bahar Dar in the north and can be seen while on the historical route.

The west is rich in natural beauty (but not wildlife) and is great for off-the-beaten-track exploration. To go west as far as Gambela National Park, you'll need around 10 days by bus including the loop back to Addis Ababa.

See also Flora & Fauna, and National Parks, in the Facts about Ethiopia section earlier.

Cultural Experiences

The tribal groups of the remote Omo Valley in the south are most often visited through tours from Addis Ababa, and require a minimum of eight days, or more if you don't take a tour. Public transport runs to some places, but you'll need at least three weeks for travelling in this way. See the boxed text 'Peoples of the Lower Omo Valley' in the South of Addis Ababa section.

PLANNING
When to Go

There's some truth to the old Ethiopian Tourism Commission (ETC) slogan '13 Months of Sunshine'. Although there's a rainy season from mid-June to the end of September, sunshine is practically guaranteed. The country is incredibly green at this time, particularly towards the end of the season. The wildflowers in September and early October are stunning. Additionally, you may well have the tourist sites to yourself. However, if you're trekking, camping or planning to explore the west or south by car, the dry season (October to May) is definitely a better time to travel.

If you're planning a trip to the Omo Valley, note that the main rains occur from March to June (and the light rains in

Too Few Hours in the Day

Because of the Horn's proximity to the equator, the length of the days varies little. Dawn breaks practically on the dot of 6.30 am, dusk falls at 6.30 pm – something to bear in mind if you're trekking.

November). The region becomes almost impassable with the rains.

Weather-wise, the ideal time is from November to January, though airfares tend to go up during this period, and some hotels can be filled with tour groups.

Finally, it's well worth trying to coincide with one of Ethiopia's major festivals (see Public Holidays & Special Events later in this section), particularly Timkat or Meskel.

Maps

In Ethiopia, the map produced by the ETC (1987; 1:2,000,000) isn't at all bad, though it's a little out of date. It's available from some of the larger hotels and souvenir shops in Addis Ababa and costs Birr53. The map of the capital on the back is quite useful.

The Ethiopian Mapping Authority (☎ 51-64-51, fax 51-51-89), PO Box 597, Addis Ababa, sells more detailed maps of some parts of the country (such as 1:50,000 maps), but you'll need special permission from the government to buy them. You could start by contacting the ETC in Addis Ababa (see Maps in the Addis Ababa section).

Of the maps currently available outside the country, the best is that produced by International Travel Maps (1998; 1:2,000,000). Though the scale is the same as that of the ETC map, it's much more up to date. The Cartographia map of Ethiopia, Eritrea and Djibouti (1996; 1:2,500,000) comes second, and isn't a bad choice for the region, though the coverage of Djibouti is too small to be useful.

If you're planning on trekking in the Simien Mountains, the well-respected Institute of Geography, University of Berne, Switzerland, produces a useful trekking map (1980; 1:100,000), complete with suggested routes, proposed camp sites, trekking

World Heritage Sites

The following places have been declared World Heritage Sites by Unesco:

Aksum (stelae)
Lalibela (churches)
Gonder (architecture)
Tiya (prehistory)
Hadar (prehistory and discovery place of Lucy)
Omo Valley (prehistory)
Simien Mountains (natural beauty)

In the future, Harar (ancient town) and Konso (anthropological interest) should be declared Unesco sites also.

distances and hours, and locations of wildlife and viewpoints.

Most major map suppliers stock maps produced outside Ethiopia, including Stanfords in London (☎ 020-7836 1321, fax 7836 0189, ✉ sales@stanfords.co.uk), 12–14 Long Acre, London WC2E 9LP, UK.

RESPONSIBLE TOURISM

Ecotourism is a concept still little known in Ethiopia. However, a tiny effort on the part of the traveller is a good start in the right direction. Here are a few pointers:

- Water is an extremely precious and scarce resource in some parts of Ethiopia such as Tigray and Wolo (where Aksum and Lalibela respectively are found). Try not to waste it in hotels by letting taps and showers run unnecessarily.
- Support local businesses, initiative and skills by shopping at local markets, buying authentic crafts and giving to local charities (as opposed to international ones).
- Resist the temptation to buy any genuinely old artefacts, such as manuscripts, scrolls and bibles, sold in shops and by hawkers around the country. Ethiopia has already lost a vast amount of its heritage. Any such items found in your bag at the airport will be confiscated anyway.
- Be sensitive to wildlife. Litter, campfires, off-road driving and loud music can harm or disturb animals and nesting birds.

See also Photographing People and Tipping later in this section.

The following two excellent organisations in the UK can provide more information for concerned travellers:

Tourism Concern (☎ 020-7753 3330, fax 7753 3331) 177–181 Holloway Rd, London N7
Centre for the Advancement of Responsive Travel or CART (☎ 0732-352757) 70 Dry Hill Park Rd, Tonbridge, Kent TN10 3BX

Church Etiquette

Churches in Ethiopia are considered very hallowed places. The following are a few pointers when visiting these:

- Always remove shoes before entering a church.
- Try and wear clothing that covers all parts of the body.
- Never try to enter the inner Holy of Holies, which is reserved strictly for the priests.
- Avoid smoking, eating or drinking in a church, or talking or laughing loudly.
- Be sensitive when taking photos.
- Resist the temptation to photograph old manuscripts in sunlight, even if the priests offer to move the manuscripts into the sun for you, as sunlight can cause great damage.
- During prayer time, try not to stray into the areas reserved for the opposite sex.
- A contribution to the church is greatly appreciated after a visit.

TOURIST OFFICES
Local Tourist Offices

All matters of tourism come under the aegis of the government-run ETC in Addis Ababa. The enterprising but very underfunded ETC has in the past produced a series of interesting booklets on Ethiopia's culture and attractions. Where the ETC can help greatly is with facilitating travel in the country. If you're planning to travel in very remote regions or are preparing an expedition, the ETC can write official letters, and help you obtain visas etc.

Independent regional tourist offices can be found in the provincial capitals. Staff in these offices usually do their best to help, but have little experience in accommodating or dealing with tourists directly; in the past, most tourism to Ethiopia has been in the form of package tours. Frankly, a visit is rarely worth the effort, and you can expect to leave with little more than brochures.

Considerations for Responsible Trekking

Trekking can greatly disturb the natural environment. Please consider the following tips when trekking and help preserve the ecology and beauty of the Ethiopian mountains.

Rubbish
- *Always* carry out your rubbish, even cigarette stubs, orange peel and particularly those tiny pieces of silver foil. Be kind and considerate; carry out rubbish left by others.
- To minimise the waste you must carry out, use reusable containers or stuff sacks.
- Never bury your rubbish: digging disturbs soil and ground-cover and encourages erosion. Buried rubbish will more than likely be dug up by animals, who may be injured or poisoned by it. It may also take years to decompose, especially at high altitudes.

Human Waste Disposal
- Contamination of watercourses by human faeces can lead to the transmission of hepatitis, typhoid and intestinal parasites such as giardia, amoebas and roundworms. It can cause severe health risks not only to members of your party, but also to local residents and wildlife.
- Where there is no toilet, bury your waste. Dig a small hole at least 15cm deep and a minimum of 100m from any watercourse. Cover the waste with soil and a rock.

Washing
- Don't use detergents or toothpaste in or near watercourses, even if they are biodegradable.
- For personal washing, use biodegradable soap and a water container at least 50m away from the watercourse. Disperse the waste water widely to allow the soil to filter it fully before it finally makes it back to the watercourse.
- Wash cooking utensils 50m from watercourses using a scourer or sand instead of detergent.

Low Impact Cooking
- Don't depend on open fires for cooking. The cutting of wood for fires in popular trekking areas can cause rapid deforestation.
- Cook on a lightweight kerosene, alcohol or shellite (white gas) stove and avoid those powered by disposable butane gas canisters.
- If you are trekking with a guide and porters, share the stoves with the whole team.

Fires
- Fires may be acceptable below the tree line in more remote areas.
- If you light a fire, use an existing fireplace rather than creating a new one.
- Don't surround fires with rocks as this creates a visual scar.
- Use only dead, fallen wood.
- Remember the adage 'the bigger the fool, the bigger the fire'.
- Use minimal wood, just what you need for cooking.
- In alpine areas, ensure that all members have enough clothing so that fires are not a necessity for warmth.
- Ensure that you fully extinguish a fire after use. Spread the embers and douse them with water. A fire is only truly safe to leave when you can comfortably place your hand in it.

The best sources of practical information are the many enterprising travel agencies in the capital. The government-run National Tourist Organisation (NTO), not far from the ETC, is very good for practical advice.

Tourist Offices Abroad
No national tourist office exists abroad. The Ethiopian embassies and consulates try to fill the gap, but generally just hand out the usual tourist brochures.

An excellent organisation in the UK is the Anglo-Ethiopian Society, 154 Connell Cres, London W5 3BP, founded in 1948 'to foster knowledge of Ethiopian culture'. It holds lectures, has quite a well-stocked library on Ethiopia and Eritrea, and publishes a tri-annual news file. Annual membership – open to all – costs UK£8.

VISAS & DOCUMENTS
Visas

All visitors except Kenyan and Djiboutian nationals need visas to visit Ethiopia. These should be obtained from the Ethiopian embassy in your home country before arrival in Ethiopia (see under Embassies & Consulates following). If there is no diplomatic representation in your country, you can obtain a tourist, business or transit visa on arrival. Transit visas issued on arrival are for a maximum of 72 hours.

Some Ethiopian embassies abroad may require the following: an onward air ticket, a visa for the next country you're planning to visit, a yellow-fever vaccination certificate, and proof of sufficient funds. To obtain a business visa, you'll need a covering letter from your company.

If you're coming to Ethiopia with a one-way ticket, it's a very good idea to carry proof of your intention to travel to other countries. A valid visa for the next country you plan to visit is usually sufficient, or evidence of ample funds (such as travellers cheques or credit cards).

Presently, Ethiopian law allows for multiple-entry visas to be issued only to those with bona fide business visas, and those working for NGOs or the government. The exception to the rule is US citizens, who benefit from a reciprocity agreement. There are plans in the future to alter the law in favour of tourism.

Tourist Visas In general, tourist visas are issued for single entry, cost around US$65, and are valid for one month only, starting from the date of arrival in Ethiopia. If you're spending more than a month in Ethiopia, you'll need to plan your itinerary so that you're back in Addis Ababa in time to renew your visa (see Visa Extensions following). If this is difficult, you may be able to come to a special agreement with immigration – just explain your situation clearly, and be very polite and patient.

Transit Visas Transit visas should be obtained in the same way as tourist visas (at the Ethiopian embassy in your home country) and in most countries cost just US$1.50 less than a full tourist visa; they are valid for seven days. They are also available to select nationalities upon arrival, but for 72 hours only.

Business Visas Business visas cost around US$150 and are valid for one month, for a single entry. Journalists must obtain a special permit from the Ministry of Information (☎ 11-11-24), PO Box 1020, Addis Ababa. This can take months to be processed, and there's usually a hefty fee thrown in as well.

Visa Extensions The immigration office (☎ 55-38-99), PO Box 5741, Addis Ababa, extends visas for a period of one to 90 days for Birr105 (for all nationalities). The office

---

Cautious Copies

It's a very good idea to photocopy important documents or note down various details before you set off on your travels. Leave one copy of the following with someone at home and keep another with you, separate from the originals:

- passport data page and visa page
- travel insurance policy
- air tickets
- credit cards and 24-hour telephone numbers of issuers (in case of loss)
- driving licence and international driving licence

It's also a good idea to store details of your vital travel documents in Lonely Planet's free online Travel Vault in case you lose the photocopies or can't be bothered with them. Your password-protected Travel Vault is accessible online anywhere in the world – create it at www.ekno.lonelyplanet.com

is just north-west of the centre. Visas normally take 24 hours to be processed, though if it's urgent you can obtain an extension the same day, or even within one hour (but you'll need to show proof of 'urgency' with air tickets etc). The office is open from 8.30 am to 12.30 pm and 1.30 to 5.30 pm weekdays.

Visas can be extended again and again (for 90 days at a time) up to a maximum period of nine months. Note that immigration will not extend your visa until the old one is four days (or less) away from expiring. If you're stuck somewhere, you can, in theory, send your application through your embassy, who should extend it on your behalf (if you have good enough reasons to persuade them). A maximum of four days after your visa expiry is considered the 'grace period', but don't risk it. There's a penalty charge of a further Birr105 for latecomers.

If you're extending your business visa, you'll need to bring a letter from your company explaining your business and your need for an extension.

Travel Insurance

A travel insurance policy to cover theft, loss and above all medical problems is a very good idea for travel in the Horn. A variety of policies are available. Check that the policy includes all the activities you want to do. Some specifically exclude 'dangerous activities' such as motorcycling, whitewater rafting, and – if you're going to Eritrea or Djibouti – diving. Sometimes even trekking is excluded. Above all, check that the policy covers an emergency flight home – a good idea in most Third World countries, where blood transfusions are not always safe. You may prefer a policy that pays doctors or hospitals directly rather than you having to fork out on the spot and claim later. However, doctors and hospitals in Ethiopia normally expect immediate cash payment. If you have to claim later, it's essential to keep all documentation.

Other Documents

An international driving licence is required in Ethiopia. If you're bringing your own car, you'll need all the appropriate documentation (see Land in the Getting There & Away section).

Travellers to Ethiopia require evidence of a yellow-fever vaccination. Officially, a vaccination against cholera is also required for anyone who has visited or transited a cholera-infected area within six days prior to arrival in Ethiopia.

EMBASSIES & CONSULATES
Ethiopian Embassies & Consulates

For the Ethiopian embassies in Eritrea and Djibouti see Embassies & Consulates in the

---

Your Own Embassy/Consulate

It's important to realise what your embassy can or cannot do if you get into trouble when abroad. Generally speaking, it won't help much if you've got in a tangle through your own fault. Remember that you're bound by the laws of the country you are in. Your embassy will not be sympathetic if you end up in jail after committing a crime locally, even if such actions are legal in your own country.

In genuine emergencies, you might get some assistance, but only if other channels have been exhausted. For example, if you need to get home urgently, a free ticket home is exceedingly unlikely – the embassy would expect you to have insurance. If you have all your money and documents stolen, it might assist with getting a new passport, but a loan for onward travel is out of the question.

Most embassies in the Horn strongly advise registering with them if you're spending some time in the country (more than a couple of weeks), or are planning to visit remote places or anywhere security is less than 100%. If you do have an accident, assistance will be much easier and faster to organise if you're registered.

Embassies are also a good (if somewhat overcautious) source of information on current security in the country, and areas that are presently off-limits. With the sunny optimism of the tourism industry combined with the dark alarmism of the embassies, you should get a reasonably balanced picture of goings-on in the country.

other chapters. Ethiopia has diplomatic representation in the following countries:

Canada (☎ 613-235 6637) Suite 208, 112 Kent St, Tower 8, Ottawa
Egypt (☎ 202-347 7805, fax 347 9002) PO Box 12, Midan Bahlawi, Dokki, Cairo
France (☎ 1-47-83-83-95, fax 43-06-52-14) 35 Ave Charles Floquet, 75007, Paris (also represents Spain)
Germany (☎ 228-233 041, fax 233 045) Brentanostrasse 1, D-5300, Bonn 1
Kenya (☎ 2-723035, fax 723401) PO Box 45198, Nairobi
Saudi Arabia (☎ 2-5250 383, fax 5250 428) PO Box 459, Jeddah 21411
Spain (see France)
UK (☎ 020-7589 7212, fax 7221 3780) 17 Princes Gate, London, SW7 1PZ
USA (☎ 202-2342 281, fax 3287 950) 2134 Kalorama Rd Northwest, Washington DC 20008

Embassies & Consulates in Ethiopia

Countries with diplomatic representation include the following (see the Addis Ababa maps for locations):

Australia (see Canada)
Austria (☎ 71-21-44)
Belgium (☎ 61-18-13)
Canada (☎ 71-30-22) (also represents Australia)
Djibouti (☎ 61-30-06)
Egypt (☎ 55-30-77)
Eritrea (☎ 51-29-40) (currently closed because of the conflict)
France (☎ 55-00-66)
Germany (☎ 55-04-33)
Ghana (☎ 71-14-02)
Ireland (☎ 61-33-66)
Israel (☎ 61-09-99)
Italy (☎ 55-15-65)
Japan (☎ 51-10-88)
Kenya (☎ 61-00-33)
Netherlands (☎ 71-11-00)
Saudi Arabia (☎ 44-80-10)
Somalia (☎ 71-22-11)
Spain (☎ 55-02-22)
Sudan (☎ 51-64-77)
Sweden (☎ 51-66-99)
Switzerland (☎ 71-05-77)

UK (☎ 61-23-54)
USA (☎ 55-10-02)
Uganda (☎ 51-30-88)
Yemen (☎ 71-09-90)

CUSTOMS

Many import-export restrictions were introduced during the Mengistu regime–including a rigorous censorship of books and cassettes leaving and entering the country. However, these controls are now being gradually relaxed.

Antiquities

As far as the traveller is concerned, the most important (and necessary) restriction may concern the protection of antiquities. If you buy any souvenir that either is or looks remotely antique, you'll need a clearance permit from the Department of Inventory and Inspection at the Centre for Research and Conservation of Cultural Heritage (CRCCH) of the National Museum in Addis Ababa (☎ 11-36-84). It's found to the left of the National Museum (see National Museum in the Addis Ababa section). The office is open Monday, Wednesday and Friday from 8.30 am to 12.30 pm (Friday until 11.30 am) and from 1.30 to 5.30 pm (call to arrange an appointment for other times). To avoid queues, come before 10.30 am or after lunch before 3.30 pm.

Souvenirs are also limited to the value of US$500 per person (see also the boxed text 'List of Banned Souvenirs' following). If you don't get a permit and your bags are searched at the airport or – as always happens – are x-rayed, you risk having your souvenirs confiscated. If you're sending objects by post, cargo or freight you'll still need a permit. If you're at all in doubt about your souvenirs, check with the office, and don't rely on the assurances, 'permits' or slips of paper from the souvenir-shop keepers. If you buy anything that you think might cause you a problem, make sure you get a receipt and an assurance from the shopkeeper that you can change it if denied an export permit. If export permission is denied (this doesn't happen very often), you'll be advised to take your souvenir back to the shop where you bought it. If something is of outstanding interest, it will be bought from you by the museum. Items are never confiscated by the department, only at the airport.

A permit costs Birr1 per three items; you'll need to list among other things where and when you bought your souvenir, and give a telephone number – use your hotel's. Once the object has been inspected, you can wrap it up. Then the package is carefully sealed and stamped. Bring your own wrapping paper, masking tape or cardboard boxes. Hang on to the permits; you'll need to show them at the airport.

Endangered Species

Ethiopia is a party to the Convention on International Trade in Endangered Species of Wild Fauna and Flora or Cites (see Ecology & Environment in the Facts about Ethiopia section). It's therefore illegal to export any endangered species or their products, such as ivory, tortoiseshell or leopard skins – all sadly found in Ethiopian shops.

Other Items

Other items requiring permits include sporting firearms; apply for a permit from the Ethiopian Wildlife Conservation Organisation (☎ 44-44-17), PO Box 386, Addis Ababa. Professional film, recording or video equipment requires a permit from the Ministry of Information (see Business Visas earlier). If you're sending food – even Ethiopian spices – you'll need a certificate from the Ministry of Agriculture (☎ 51-80-40, fax 51-29-84), PO Box 62347, Addis Ababa.

If you're bringing a video camera or laptop computer with you, you may be required to register it on your passport as you enter Ethiopia.

Two litres of spirits and 200 cigarettes or 100 cigars may be imported duty free.

Currency Declaration Forms

Upon arrival in Ethiopia, all visitors must complete a currency declaration form. There is no limit to the amount of currency that can be brought in, but no more than Birr10 can be exported and imported.

In Search of Souvenirs

During the last several hundred years, thousands of manuscripts and other national treasures, including gold and silver crosses and even a giant stele (!), have left Ethiopia as 'souvenirs'. In March 1997, the famous 7kg gold cross was stolen from the church of Medhane Alem in Lalibela. It'll probably never be recovered.

Today, tourists, antique dealers and even diplomats are responsible for the disappearance of most works of art. In 1996, a German tourist removed several items from the National Museum at Aksum.

Controls are now imposed. Though they can seem irksome for the traveller, without them, and at the current rate of 'souvenir' removal, it is thought that Ethiopia would have lost most of her treasures by 2020.

The form records the amount of foreign currency you are bringing into Ethiopia– travellers cheques as well as cash. All foreign currency transactions you make in Ethiopia should then be recorded on the form. When you leave the country, the amount of foreign currency in your possession should tally with the amount declared on your form, minus the transactions made. Officially, you should have spent US$30 per day during your stay in Ethiopia.

Note that if you have more than the equivalent of US$150 in birr left over at the end of your trip and need to convert it back into dollars, you'll need to show your currency declaration form, air ticket, passport and valid visa, and sometimes exchange receipts and hotel bill settlements too!

Although you'll be asked to surrender the form as you leave, the forms are in practice rarely checked. But you should still abide by the procedure, just in case.

MONEY
Currency

Ethiopia's currency is the birr. It is divided into 100 cents in 1, 5, 10, 25 and 50 cent coins, and 1, 5, 10, 50 and 100 birr notes. The exchange rate is determined by a weekly auction.

List of Banned Souvenirs

The following list is adapted from the official catalogue of objects that are now denied export permits. Be warned that currently *all* parchment is being denied permission.

- Animal and plant fossils and any prehistoric items such as stone tools, bones or pottery
- Anything of outstanding anthropological or ethnographical interest
- Anything with an ancient inscription on it
- Old processional or hand crosses that bear the names of kings or religious leaders, or any currently in use at churches or monasteries
- Any items (including manuscripts, books, documents or religious objects such as chalices, crosses and incense burners) currently serving in churches
- Any old wooden items
- Ivory
- Coins and paper money not currently in circulation
- Wildlife products
- Any items of exceptional artistic interest whether old or modern
- Art with outstanding historical value, such as engravings with historical figures
- Any items formerly belonging to the emperor, his family or Ethiopian nobles

Exchange Rate

In the past couple of years the average exchange rate has fluctuated between Birr7 and Birr8 to the US dollar.

Australia	A$1	=	Birr4.78
Canada	C$1	=	Birr5.47
Euro	€1	=	Birr7.67
France	10FF	=	Birr11.70
Germany	DM1	=	Birr3.92
Japan	¥100	=	Birr7.51
New Zealand	NZ$1	=	Birr3.73
UK	UK£1	=	Birr12.26
USA	US$1	=	Birr8.09

Exchanging Money

US dollars are the best currency to carry both in cash and in travellers cheques; you are required to pay for certain things in US dollars, such as internal air tickets and airport departure tax. For these it's a very good idea to bring, say, US$100 in US$10 notes. Changing birr back into dollars is a hassle (see Currency Declaration Forms under Customs earlier in this section), and banks are not always open when you need them.

Cash Outside the capital, you have to rely entirely on cash. Furnish yourself with a good wad of small notes – Birr1 in particular – as you'll inevitably need these for tips at restaurants, for children showing you the way, for photographs etc. See also Tipping later in this section.

Banks The state-owned Commercial Bank of Ethiopia offers foreign exchange facilities, and has branches in the major towns throughout the country. The one notable exception is in the town of Lalibela, though there are plans to open one there soon too.

Opening hours in the capital are from 8 am to 4 pm (usually with a lunch break between noon and 2 pm) weekdays, and on Saturday from 9 am to noon (although the Hilton Hotel branch of the Commercial Bank in the capital keeps longer hours – see Money in the Addis Ababa section). Outside the capital, hours vary from region to region, but banks are always open at least in the morning, and usually for a couple of hours in the afternoon.

More and more private banks are opening in the capital; these normally keep longer hours than the Commercial Bank, and are much quicker with money exchanges. Travellers cheques and all major currencies are accepted.

All major currencies can be exchanged in the capital; sometimes only US dollars can be exchanged outside of Addis Ababa. Banks charge a commission of 1.3–1.5%. Remember to take your passport, as sometimes it's needed even for exchanging cash, and don't forget your currency declaration form; you'll need to get each transaction recorded and officially stamped (see

Currency Declaration Forms under Customs earlier in this section).

There are currently no ATMs in Ethiopia.

Travellers Cheques Most major banks across the country exchange travellers cheques. In the capital, a few major hotels and travel agencies also accept them. Like cash, travellers cheques are best carried in US dollars.

The Commercial Bank of Ethiopia charges a 0.5% service charge, a 'postage' charge of Birr2–4 for each five cheques cashed, and a 'revenue stamp' of 20¢ per cheque. Private banks charge around the same.

Credit Cards Some of the larger hotels of the capital, some airlines (including Ethiopian Airlines) and a few travel agents now accept credit cards; American Express (AmEx) is the one most commonly accepted, though Visa is increasingly accepted too. A commission of up to 5% is sometimes charged; you should inquire in advance of transactions.

Outside the capital, credit cards are useless.

International Transfers In theory, transfers by telex should take no more than four days, though in practice it's often much longer, depending on the competence of both sender and receiver banks. Some travellers have reported delays of between four and six weeks; the installation of computers in the near future should speed up the process.

Transfers can be made in all the major currencies and there's no limit to the amount. The Commercial Bank charges a service fee of 25¢ per Birr100 transferred. You'll need to give an address in Addis Ababa (your hotel) and passport number. A payment order can be received currently by telex order only.

If you need a transfer urgently, Western Union (see Money in the Addis Ababa section) is the best bet, though it's not cheap and takes a bit of organising. The whole process should take no more than a day.

Black Market Unofficial moneychangers hang around the Merkato and Piazza areas in Addis Ababa. The black market is in decline as the official and free rates for the Ethiopian birr converge; it's rare to find a rate much above 10% more than that offered by the banks. Remember that the black market is still illegal, and penalties range from hefty fines to imprisonment. If you do indulge, stick to the shops, and be very wary of other places – particularly Merkato and the Piazza, where's there's a good chance of being swindled or even robbed.

Security

If you're travelling at all off the beaten track, you'll need to carry a fair amount of cash with you. Fortunately, the risk of theft and pickpocketing is low and diminishes further outside the capital (though you'll still need to be vigilant). Ethiopian hotels have a reputation for being fairly safe too.

In the capital, the risk of pickpocketing or robbery is very low compared to many African capitals. However, you should be cautious in the Piazza and above all Merkato areas; the latter is notorious for pickpockets (see Dangers & Annoyances later in this section and also in the Addis Ababa section).

Any pockets – particularly the back ones – are easy targets. A money belt, ideally concealed under clothing, is still the best way of carrying around cash and documents. Money pouches, on the other hand, are often conspicuous and are easily cut. Some travellers also like to keep an emergency stash of, say, US$100 hidden in some place removed from the rest of their funds. This can prove a life-saver after a theft.

Most travellers experience no problems in Ethiopia; those who do were usually easy targets (they left belongings unattended, for example). With a little preparation and vigilance, trips should be unmarred by such incidents.

Costs

For most day-to-day costs, Ethiopia is a very inexpensive country in which to travel, even by African standards. Budget travellers can get by very adequately with US$10 per day (particularly outside the capital), and even US$7 is possible. The cheapest hotels cost around US$2. For other

Guidelines for Guides

Few official guides exist in Ethiopia, and none are subject to regulation. Unfortunately, the profession – as in many developing countries – can attract rather mercenary characters in for an easy buck.

Some guides, particularly in the more touristy areas, have become 'spoilt'. When their expectations are not met, they feign either hysterics or a monumental sulk. For some travellers, a trip to a site can be ruined by such an incident.

To avoid 'misunderstandings', the following are a few tips for dealing with guides:

- Choose a guide you're happy with – test their knowledge of English and of the sites in advance, perhaps over a coffee.
- Make sure your itinerary and expectations are very clearly understood before starting – such as exactly what you want to see and in exactly how much time.
- Negotiate a fee in advance with the guide, and make it clear that it is paid on the condition that you are happy with their services.
- If the service has been good, you can tip a bit extra, but don't be pressured into tipping. It's unwise to overtip as it can unfairly raise the expectations of the guide.

everyday costs, you can expect to pay the following: a main course costs from Birr5 in the cheaper restaurants to Birr50 in the more expensive ones; a bottle of local beer likewise ranges from Birr3 to Birr11; local wine costs Birr10 to Birr50. Bus travel works out at around US$1 per 100km.

However, don't forget to allow for extra costs such as guides or national park or historic site entrance fees. Admission fees to historic sites vary from Birr10, to Birr100 for Lalibela. You should budget in another US$200 to cover these for duration of your trip.

If your time is restricted, you may want to consider some internal flights. For the historical route, you're looking to pay US$75 to US$100 per leg.

If you're staying in mid-range hotels in the capital, and want a wider choice of food and entertainment, you should budget for around US$50 per day (see Accommodation and Food later in this section).

The one area in which Ethiopia is expensive is in car hire and organised tours. The toll exacted by poor roads on vehicles, and the very high customs duty, make car hire particularly pricey. As tourism is still relatively undeveloped, most tours are custom-made and so are expensive

If you're keen to visit a remote area that is only really accessible in a private vehicle, such as the Omo Valley, there are two ways of keeping prices down. Either you can try and organise your own group before you approach a travel agency, or you can try contacting one of the larger agencies well in advance of your trip to see if you can tag onto an organised group (see Organised Tours in the Getting Around section).

Tipping

Tipping is considered a part of everyday life in Ethiopia, and helps supplement often very low wages. If someone acts as an informal guide or porter, it is usual to offer them 'tea money' – a nominal amount to show appreciation for their services.

It's worth bearing in mind too that tipping is a vital source of revenue for the nation's poor in those countries where there is no social welfare system. The maxim 'little but often' is a good one, and even very small tips are greatly appreciated.

By the same measure, it is a great mistake to overtip. Though this is tempting, and often provoked by feelings of guilt, you're not doing anyone any favours. Grossly distorted tips raise unfairly the expectations of the locals, undermine the social traditions of the country, and are very likely to spoil the trips of future tourists, who will then be seen as little more than walking banks or Santa Clauses. In addition, local 'guides' can start to select only those travellers who look lucrative, and can react very aggressively if their expectations are not met. The fairest system for all concerned is to stick to a percentage and not exceed it by more than, say, 20–50% maximum.

If a so-called professional person helps you (or someone drawing a regular wage), it's probably better to show your appreciation in other ways: shaking hands, exchanging names, the offer of a cigarette, or an invitation to a coffee and pastry are all local ways of expressing gratitude (see also Society & Conduct in the Facts about Ethiopia section).

Bargaining

Overcharging tourists is fairly rare, particularly in the rural areas, and prices are usually fixed. Despite the fact that around half the population are Muslim, with the inevitable Arab influence, haggling over prices can offend Ethiopians. However, all the usual discounts apply for long stays in hotels, for extended car hire etc, and you should ask for them.

The one exception, where haggling is almost expected, is in the local markets and with the local taxi and *gari* (horse-drawn cart) drivers. Haggling is meant to be an enjoyable experience, and if you're light-hearted and polite about it, you'll end up with a better price.

POST & COMMUNICATIONS
Post

Ethiopia has quite an efficient and reliable postal service. Stamps for postcards cost 60¢ to Europe, and 75¢ to the USA or Australia; a letter up to 10g costs 85¢ to Europe, and Birr1.10 to the USA or Australia. Letters should take between five and eight days to arrive in Europe; eight to 15 days for the USA or Australia. All mail to Ethiopia is delivered to PO boxes only.

There's a free poste restante service in Addis Ababa (send to 'Poste Restante, Addis Ababa, Ethiopia') and in many of the larger towns. When you collect it, make sure you check under your first name as well as your surname, as Ethiopians tend to go by their first name.

If you want to save money on phone calls you can send an 'I'm still alive' international telegram back home, which costs

Tips for Tipping

Tipping can be a constant source of worry, hassle or grief for travellers. The following guide has been compiled with the help of an Ethiopian.

- In the smaller restaurants in the towns, service is included, and Ethiopians don't tip unless the service has been exceptional (Birr2–5).
- In bars and cafes, sometimes loose coins are left. However, in the larger restaurants accustomed to tourists, around 10% will be expected.
- In the larger hotels, staff will expect a bare minimum of Birr5–10 per service.
- Outside the large hotels, luggage handlers will expect a tip of around Birr2 per bag, and guides between Birr5 and Birr10, though you should tip a bit more if the service has been exceptional.
- At the historic sites, Birr10 is reasonable for one or two hours' service with a guide, then around Birr5 for every hour after that (see also the boxed text 'Guidelines for Guides' earlier).
- For the assistance of a child, Birr1 is plenty.
- Taxi drivers in Addis Ababa could expect around Birr1–2 added to the fare, and car 'guards' (often self-appointed) the same.
- At traditional music and dance shows in the bars, restaurants and hotels, an audience shows its appreciation by giving generously (around Birr10), by placing money on the dancers' foreheads or in their belts.

just Birr1.20/1.60/2.20 per word for the USA/Europe/Australia, plus 10% of the total. It should take just two days to arrive.

The post office opening hours across the country are from 8 am to noon and from 1 to 4 pm weekdays, and on Saturday morning. In Addis Ababa the post office hours are longer.

Parcel Post & Courier Services Surface mail from the main post office in Addis

Ababa takes between five and seven months for Europe, the USA and Australia, and costs an average of Birr105 per parcel plus an average of Birr21 per kilogram, depending on the country.

Airmail parcel post (maximum weight 31kg) takes eight to 10 days for Europe and 10 to 12 days for Asia, Australia and the USA. It costs an average of Birr77 per parcel, plus Birr16 per kilogram, plus Birr25 per 0.5kg air credit. Parcels are accepted from 8 to 11.30 am and 1 to 3.30 pm weekdays, and Saturday mornings.

Even faster is the Express Mail Service or EMS (☎ 15-20-72), which delivers mail weighing 0.5–20kg. The service takes between three and five days to deliver worldwide. The first 0.5kg costs an average of Birr125, depending on the country, plus Birr42.5 for each additional 0.5kg. The EMS service is open from 8 am to noon and 1 to 5.30 pm Monday to Saturday, and from 10 am to noon Sundays and holidays.

All parcels are subject to a customs inspection, so leave them open. Don't forget the souvenir clearance permit (see Customs earlier in this section).

Various courier services have offices in Addis Ababa including DHL. Parcels cost Birr300/320/330 for the first 0.5kg to Europe/USA/Australia (plus Birr65/70/75 for each additional 0.5kg). Sending documents only costs Birr100 less. Delivery takes three to four days worldwide.

Telephone & Fax

Ethiopia's telephone system is pretty efficient, especially when compared with some parts of Africa. It's also fairly reasonably priced.

When calling Ethiopia from abroad, use the country code (☎ 251). When calling abroad from Ethiopia, use (☎ 00) followed by the country code.

International calls and faxes are best made from the telecommunications offices found in all the main towns and the capital. To telephone, you'll be asked if the call is for up to three minutes or 'open'. A deposit of Birr100/200 must then be paid for a three-minute/open call, then you must wait

to be assigned a cabin. Unfortunately, only one call at a time can be made, then you have to queue up again. The early evening tends to be the busiest time, when you can expect to wait up to an hour.

International rates are the same all day, and costs are calculated per minute: Birr20 for the USA, Birr14–20 for Europe, and Birr24 for Australia, New Zealand or Japan, plus 70¢ for the cabin. Collect calls can be made to the UK/USA/Canada only, but you still have to pay a 'report charge' of Birr4.50/5.85/7.20, plus a Birr10 (refundable) deposit.

Domestic calls cost Birr1.50–3, and you must leave a Birr10 deposit. Sometimes it's difficult to get through (lines sound engaged or seem to be unanswered), and a bit of patience is required.

Telephone cards are available in denominations of Birr25, 50 and 100.

After hours, it's possible to make calls and send or receive faxes from the larger hotels, but rates are expensive (up to 20% more). Faxes cost from Birr37/46/55 per page to Europe/USA/Australia. When calling, contact the following services:

Directory assistance	☎ 97
International operator	☎ 98
Domestic operator	☎ 99

Major town codes include:

Addis Ababa, Debre Zeyit, Akaki, Debre Berhen, Ambo	☎ 01
Nazret	☎ 02
Dessie, Asaita, Lalibela	☎ 03
Mekele, Adwa, Aksum, Adigrat	☎ 04
Dire Dawa, Harar, Jijiga	☎ 05
Awasa, Shashemene, Arba Minch	☎ 06
Jimma, Nekemte, Gambela	☎ 07
Gonder, Bahar Dar	☎ 08

eKno Communications Card

There's a wide range of local and international phonecards. Lonely Planet's eKno Communication Card is aimed specifically at independent travellers and provides budget international calls, a range of messaging services, free email and travel information – for local calls, you're usually better off with a local card. At the time this book went to print, eKno telephone services did not yet cover the countries in this book, though new countries are being added all the time. You can join online at www.ekno.lonely planet.com. Check the eKno Web site for access numbers in other countries and updates on super budget local-access numbers and new features.

Email & Internet Access

Addis Ababa is the only place in Ethiopia where the Internet can be accessed by travellers, and just a handful of places provide the service currently (see Email & Internet Access in the Addis Ababa section).

Travelling with a portable computer is a great way to stay in touch with life back home, but unless you know what you're doing it's fraught with potential problems. If you plan to carry your notebook or palmtop computer with you, remember that the power supply voltage in the countries you visit may vary from that at home, risking damage to your equipment. The best investment is a universal AC adaptor for your appliance, which will enable you to plug it in anywhere without frying the innards. You'll also need a plug adaptor for each country you visit – often it's easiest to buy these before you leave home (see Electricity later in this section).

Your PC-card modem may or may not work once you leave your home country – and you won't know for sure until you try. The safest option is to buy a reputable 'global' modem before you leave home, or buy a local PC-card modem if you're spending an extended time in any one country. Keep in mind that the telephone socket in each country you visit will probably be different from the one at home, so ensure that you have at least a US RJ-11 telephone adaptor that works with your modem. You can almost always find an adaptor that will convert from RJ-11 to the local variety. For more information on travelling with a portable computer, see www.teleadapt.com or www.warrior.com.

Major Internet service providers such as AOL (www.aol.com), CompuServe (www.compuserve.com) and IBM Net (now www.attbusiness.net) may have the relevant dial-in nodes for travel throughout the Horn; it's best to download a list of the dial-in numbers before you leave home. If you access your Internet email account at home through a smaller ISP or through your office or school network, your best option is either to open an account with a global ISP, like those mentioned above, or to rely on cybercafes and other public access points to collect your email.

If you do intend to rely on cybercafes, you'll need to carry three pieces of information with you to enable you to access your Internet email account: your incoming (POP or IMAP) mail server name, your account name and your password. Your ISP or network supervisor will be able to give you these. Armed with this information, you should be able to access your Internet email account from any Web-connected machine in the world, provided it runs some kind of email software (remember that Netscape and Internet Explorer both have mail modules). It pays to become familiar with the process for doing this before you leave home. A final option for collecting email through cybercafes is to open a free eKno Web-based email account online at www.ekno.lonelyplanet.com. You can then access your email from anywhere in the world from any Web-connected machine running a standard Web browser.

INTERNET RESOURCES

The World Wide Web is a rich resource for travellers. You can research your trip, hunt down bargain air fares, book hotels, check on weather conditions or chat with locals and other travellers about the best places to visit – or avoid.

The Lonely Planet Web site (www.lonely planet.com) is a great place to start your Web explorations. Here you'll find succinct summaries on travelling, postcards from other travellers and the Thorn Tree bulletin board, where you can ask questions before you go, or dispense advice when you get back.

You can also find travel news and updates to many of our most popular guidebooks. The subWWWay section links you to the most useful travel resources elsewhere on the Web.

More and more sites on Ethiopia are mushrooming up on the Web. The following are among the most useful:

Addis Tribune is good for the latest news on current affairs, culture, the economy, sport and other goings-on.
www.addistribune.ethiopiaonline.net

CyberEthiopia is like a kind of Ethiopian *Yahoo!*, with quite useful information catgorised into different sections.
www.cyberethiopia.com

Ethiopian Airlines includes the latest news on domestic and international flights, reservation options and schedules.
www.ethiopian-airline.com

Ethiopian News is a fairly comprehensive Web guide to Ethiopia that gives updated daily news as well as business links and cultural information. There's also a chat service and a very useful calendar of upcoming events and public holidays.
www.ethio.com

Ethiopian Tourism Net is probably the best place to start for a concise overview of the country's main attractions. The capital and different regions are covered in fair detail. It also offers quite a lot of practical tips.
www.tour.ethiopiaonline.net

International Lesbian & Gay Association is a good site with some relevant stuff for travellers to the Horn.
www.ilga.org

Travel Health Online is an excellent way to quickly evaluate your 'disease risk summary' in the region.
www.tripprep.com

BOOKS

Books tend to be published in different editions by different publishers in different countries. As a result, a book might be a hardcover rarity in one country, while it's readily available as a paperback in another. Fortunately, bookshops and libraries search by title or author, so your local bookshop or library is best placed to advise you on the availability of the following recommendations.

In the UK, the Africa Bookshop (☎ 020-7240 6649, fax 7497-0309, ✉ info @africabookcentre.com), 38 King St, London W2, is a great place to browse for books on Ethiopia, and can order any not held in stock. Ask for the very helpful Daniel Lofters. L'Harmattan (☎ 01-46-34-13-71), 16, rue des Ecoles, 75005, Paris, is a kind of French equivalent.

For older books, there are various second-hand book stalls you can try in Addis Ababa (see under Information in the Addis Ababa section).

There are innumerable books on Ethiopia; what follows is just a very small but reasonably eclectic selection which are among the more widely available. More 'academic' books have been avoided, but are plentiful for those with a deeper interest.

For a selection of health guides, see Health later in this section.

Lonely Planet

The *Ethiopian Amharic phrasebook* is highly recommended for any independent traveller spending more than a week in Ethiopia, and is currently the only Amharic phrasebook available outside Ethiopia. *Read this First: Africa* is an indispensible guide both for predeparture planning and for those new to travelling. The pocket-sized *Healthy Travel Africa* has a lot in it to keep you healthy, and *Trekking in East Africa* has a small section on trekking in Ethiopia to get you started.

Guidebooks

The government-sponsored *Spectrum Guide to Ethiopia*, though a bit out of date, is still informative and is lavishly illustrated with first-class photos. If you're still hesitating about visiting Ethiopia, this will help you decide for sure.

If you read Italian, *Etiopia* by Andrea Semplici is a very comprehensive, if rather idiosyncratic, guide to Ethiopia. Though practical details and maps are a bit lacking, the depth of research and sheer enthusiasm for the country compensate.

Much the best German guide is the *Äthiopien Reise Know-How* by Katrin Hildemann and Martin Fitzenreiter. In French, the *Introduction á l' Ethiopie* by Marc Aubert is probably the best bet.

Travel

Dervla Murphy's *In Ethiopia with a Mule* is an entertaining read if you like the how-to-make-the-journey-as-gruelling-and-un-comfortable-as-possible genre.

Wilfred Thesiger's *Life of My Choice* includes reminiscences of the author's childhood and early adult years in Ethiopia, including the lavish coronation of the Emperor Haile Selassie (see Books in the Facts for the Visitor section in the Djibouti chapter for his *Danakil Diary*).

Philip Marsden-Smedley's *A Far Country* is another travelogue, but is better researched than most and gives some interesting insights into Ethiopia at the end of the 1980s.

Evelyn Waugh's *Remote People* includes some wry impressions of both Ethiopia and Djibouti on the way to and from Ethiopia in the 1930s. *Black Mischief*, one of Waugh's funniest books, describes an English-educated emperor trying to modernise his country, and is drawn partly from the Abyssinia of the 1930s. *Waugh in Abyssinia* is the author's account of Ethiopia in 1935, when he was sent as a correspondent to cover the Italian-Ethiopian conflict.

The delightful *A Cure for Serpents* by the Duke of Pirajno recounts the duke's time as a doctor in the Horn. Beautifully and engagingly written, the book describes encounters with famous courtesans, noble chieftains, Berber princes and giant elephants – even Nefasti the Ethiopian lioness, who fell in love with the author.

Two new travel accounts published in 1999 include *Eccentric Graces* by Julia Stewart and *One Hop Too Far* by Jane Graham, both aid workers in Ethiopia and Eritrea.

History & Politics

Two of the most recent and thoroughly readable histories of Ethiopia are Harold G Marcus' *Ethiopia*, and Richard Pankhurst's *The Ethiopians*.

If you're intrigued by the fascinating ancient civilisation of Aksum, the newly published *Ancient Ethiopia* by David W Phillipson is a must and is an easy read. The author directed archaeological research at Aksum during most of the 1990s. Though older, and now a little out of date, Stuart Munro-Hay's *Aksum: An African Civilisation of Late Antiquity* is well respected.

If you're really into the history of the country, considered among the modern 'classics' are Edward Ullendorff's *The Ethiopians*, and Richard Greenfield's *Ethiopia: A New Political History*.

For a view from 'the other side', J Spencer Trimingham's *Islam in Ethiopia* is unsurpassed. Outstanding for its insight into Amharic culture (with the possible exception of a rather wayward chapter six!) is Donald N Levine's imaginative *Wax & Gold*. *Greater Ethiopia* by the same author is one of a number of other anthropological-orientated works on the country.

The Emperor by Ryszard Kapuscinski consists of a series of interviews by a Polish journalist with the servants and closest associates of the deposed Emperor Haile Selassie. At times grotesque, bizarre and even sad, the accounts give a great insight into the imperial court of the day.

If you read French, the newly published *Histoire de l'Ethiopie* by Berhanou Abebe is an excellent history.

A modern classic of historical travel writing is Alan Moorehead's *The Blue Nile*, which is the story of the river, its people and its 'discovery' by Europeans. It's a engrossing book, as much an adventure story as a history.

Language

For those keen to take their Amharic beyond the pale, *Colloquial Amharic* by David Appleyard is a comprehensive teach-yourself course, complete with cassettes.

Cheap and widely available in the capital is *Amharic for Foreigners* by Semere Woldegabir, which though rather dismally presented isn't a bad introduction to basic grammar and vocabulary.

See also Lonely Planet earlier in this section.

General

African Zion: The Sacred Art of Ethiopia was originally published as a catalogue to

Bad Bad Press

In the summer of 1973, a young British journalist scooped a sensational story in East Africa. Jonathan Dimbleby's BBC film *Ethiopia: The Unknown Famine* shook the world and caused an international sensation. Within just one year, the emperor – formerly lauded by the BBC – had been overthrown and murdered, the ancient tradition of kingship was brought to an end, and a new regime installed whose rule proved to be far more brutal, calamitous and costly in human life than the one it had replaced.

Though it's unfair to blame the film – as some have done – for the appalling events that it heralded, it undoubtedly contributed as a catalyst, and was used both as a pretext and as a kind of international sanction for the overthrow of the old regime. The power of international media and the dangers of 'irresponsible journalism' have never been made more apparent.

Although Ethiopia benefited – albeit rather tardily – in the short term from international aid, the harrowing images, along with those projected by the global musical fundraiser Live Aid in 1985, were to deal Ethiopia a great blow in public relations, from which, nearly 30 years later, has still not recovered. It will probably take at least another 50 years to do so. In the meantime, Ethiopia continues to be seen by the world as a land of desert and famine. Although famine does still seriously threaten some parts in the north, Ethiopia's bad image is still the single greatest obstacle to the development of its tourist industry, which, ironically, would contribute millions of dollars to its economy.

In the meantime, Ethiopian Airlines continues to field inquiries from its passengers about whether they will get anything to eat on international flights.

accompany the exhibition of the same name during the early 1990s. It contains a series of interesting essays and notes on various aspects and periods of Christian art from the Ethiopian Orthodox church, as well as some stunning photographs of old manuscripts, coins and crosses.

Art That Heals by Jacques Mercier is an interesting and well-illustrated hardcover exploration of the ancient Ethiopian traditional belief that art and healing are inextricably connected. The French *Æthiopia* is an excellent and well-illustrated tome on all things cultural, with a series of essays by many of the leading authorities on the subjects.

The *Collins Guide to Wildflowers of East Africa* is a useful and well-illustrated guide. For bird books, see the special section 'Birds in Ethiopia'.

If you enjoy poring over coffee-table books check out *African Ark* by Carol Beckworth and Angela Fisher. It has stunning photographs of the peoples of the Horn with accompanying text. *The Mountains of Rasselas* by Thomas Pakenham, the author of the excellent *Scramble for Africa*, is an account of Pakenham's two journeys through Ethiopia, and is well written and illustrated. The well-illustrated *Journey Through Ethiopia*, by Mohamed Amin et al, makes a good souvenir of a trip to Ethiopia.

One of the best-known books on Ethiopia is Graham Hancock's *The Sign and the Seal*, which has been likened to a great detective story. The author spent ten years trying to solve one of the greatest mysteries of all time: the bizarre 'disappearance' of the Ark of the Covenant. Though the book has raised an eyebrow or two among contemporary historians, it is an absolute must for any visitor to Ethiopia, and however tenuous the facts, gives a great insight into the country's history and culture.

If you're trying to get your children interested in Ethiopia, try *Ethiopia: The Roof of Africa* by Jane Kurtz. Elizabeth Laird has spent time collecting some of the delightful traditional oral literature of Ethiopia in *When the World Began*.

If you fancy preparing a deft *doro wat* for your friends when you get back home, *Exotic Ethiopian Cooking* by DJ Mesfin is a great easy-to-follow cookbook, with recipes ranging from Ethiopian bread and false-banana dishes to *tella* (homebrewed beer), *tej* (honey wine) and *katikala* (Ethiopian vodka).

If you're inspired to know more about the poet Rimbaud, *Arthur Rimbaud: Collected*

Poems published by Penguin gives the original French with an English translation. *Somebody Else* by Charles Nicholl is a new account of the poet's travels in Africa, including Ethiopia.

For information on the fascinating tribes of the Omo Valley, David Turton has written various papers and publications such as *Movements, Ethnicity & Warfare in the Omo Valley*.

The Ethiopian Orthodox Church, published by the Ethiopian Church Mission in Addis Ababa, is excellent for those keen to find out more about this ancient institution. Steven Kaplan's *The Holy Men and Christianisation of Early Solomonic Ethiopia* is also interesting.

Ben Parker's *Ethiopia: Breaking New Ground* (an Oxfam publication) makes mention of some of the fascinating Ethiopian traditional agricultural practices.

FILMS

It wasn't until the mid-1950s that sub-Saharan Africa began to make its own films, and not until the 1960s that a credible cinema industry began to emerge – notably in French-speaking African countries such as Senegal. Initial efforts were hampered by a lack of financial resources and technical know-how.

Ethiopia, which was never colonised, missed out on the 'benefit' of colonial support enjoyed by other countries. However, some films were still produced. Solomon Bekele was one of the pioneers of Ethiopian cinema and is best known for his Amharic feature film *Aster*. Ethiopia's most famous English-speaking film-maker is Haile Gerima, whose latest film *Adwa* (released in early 2000) deals with a recurring theme: the battle of Adwa (see the boxed text 'The Battle of Adwa' under Aksum in the North of Addis Ababa section later in this chapter).

Various documentaries have been made on Ethiopia, the most famous of which was Jonathan Dimbleby's *Ethiopia: The Unknown Famine*. Though it helped establish the young journalist's career, its long-term effect on Ethiopia is contentious (see the boxed text 'Bad Bad Press').

Press Law

The private papers are considered fairly neutral in their political stance – neither particularly for nor against the government. Censorship laws have relaxed considerably since the Derg – but still not entirely. At least 20 journalists have been arrested since the 1992 Press Law came into effect, and held without trial for publishing articles critical of the government. These included, in 1998, four journalists from the newspaper *Tobia*, and Abay Haile, the editor of *Agere*, who died untried in prison in February 1998.

Other documentaries have been made on the battle of Adwa, the poet Rimbaud, and the struggle for freedom against the Derg. In 1998, a Hollywood-produced biography of the famous athlete Haile Gebreselassie was released, entitled *Endurance*, and was well received internationally (see the boxed text 'An Interview with Africa's Giant – Haile Gebreselassie' later in this section).

NEWSPAPERS & MAGAZINES

The best-known English language newspapers are the daily (except Sunday), government-owned *Ethiopian Herald*, the thrice-weekly, privately owned *Monitor*, and the weekly, privately owned *Addis Tribune*. Other weekly private newspapers include the *Reporter* and the *Sun*. The *Berissa* is a weekly Oromo paper, the *Yezareyity* is Amharic, and *Al Ahem* is Arabic.

All are published in Addis Ababa and, apart from the *Ethiopian Herald*, are only available in the capital. The *Ethiopian Herald* can usually be found in the Mega Enterprise bookshops in the towns, though sometimes it's a few days old.

The well-respected *Addis Tribune* is a good source of information on forthcoming entertainment and cultural events in Addis Ababa. Of all the papers, it is probably the one most of interest to travellers. The weekly *Press Digest* and *7 Days Update* (both Birr15) give useful summaries of the most important stories from the week's Amharic and English press. International newspapers

ETHIOPIA

Photo Paranoia

A relic perhaps of the oppressive Derg regime is a universal distrust of the camera. Stories abound in Ethiopia of unsuspecting tourists having cameras or film snatched from them by heavy-handed policemen. And for no apparent reason other than possession of a camera.

At entrances to banks or other official buildings, bags are routinely searched. It's not 'Gun? Gun?' or 'Grenade? Grenade?', that the friskers demand, it is 'Camera? Camera?' No one seems sure why.

Some areas in Ethiopia, such as military and police installations, airports, bridges, government buildings, residences and royal palaces are classed as 'sensitive'. Anyone caught photographing from, at or around these places is likely to unleash a terrible fury – not just from the civil and military police, but from ordinary Ethiopian civilians too. Penalties for contravening this law range from confiscation of film and camera, to between three months' and one year's imprisonment. Camera-clutchers travelling in Ethiopia are best advised to keep a low profile.

A different kind of war has been waged on the video camera. At many of the major tourist sites in Ethiopia, a separate fee for video cameras is now charged (usually US$15 to US$30). The pretext is that your souvenirs may be used for 'commercial purposes'. Binoculars are treated with equal suspicion – birders beware.

such as the *International Herald Tribune* are available in the larger hotels in the capital. There are newspaper reading rooms in the international cultural centres in Addis Ababa (see under Information in that section).

RADIO & TV

Radio Ethiopia broadcasts in six local languages, plus English and French for around 1½ hours each per day. English-language radio can be heard from 1.30 to 2 pm and 7 to 8 pm weekdays. The BBC World Service can be received on radios with shortwave reception, though frequencies vary according to the time of day (try 9630, 11940 and 17640).

Ethiopia's single television channel broadcasts every weekday evening from around 6 pm to midnight (from noon on the weekends). From 10.30 pm to midnight there is a broadcast in English. Some of the larger hotels have satellite dishes that receive CNN.

PHOTOGRAPHY & VIDEO

Ethiopia uses the PAL system. This differs from France (which uses the SECAM system), and the USA, Canada and Japan (which use NTSC). The three systems are not compatible.

Film & Equipment

Decent print film is quite widely available in the capital and costs around Birr27 for a 36-exposure Kodak film. Some slide film is also available. Outside Addis Ababa, it's difficult to find film except in the larger towns, and products may not always be fresh.

Photographic equipment is pretty limited in Addis Ababa; the best place to head is the Piazza, where there are a few shops stocking such things as tripods and camera bags. In the larger hotels, such as the Hilton, a limited selection of compact cameras are on sale, but prices are high.

Photo development in the capital is of a good quality, can be done in around 45 minutes, and represents good value: from Birr50 for 36 exposures (see Other Services under Information in the Addis Ababa section).

Photographing People

It's vitally important to be sensitive to people when photographing. Many Ethiopians – particularly outside the capital or in the bush – are unused to tourists pointing cameras at them. Many may feel seriously threatened or compromised, particularly the women. Always smile at your subject and ask permission first – even with basic sign language. Best of all, use a local as a kind of interpreter or go-between. Never take a photo if permission is denied.

The people in some areas, such as those in the Omo Valley, are more accustomed to photographers, and understandably want to benefit from it too – they may ask for money. For some groups, tips from photog-

Tips for Photographers in the Horn

In hot regions the single most important consideration when trying to take photos or video footage is the heat. Never ever leave equipment or film in a car or in the sun, and try and get film processed as soon after exposure as possible. Extreme heat can wreck equipment and play havoc with film colour.

As in all tropical or semitropical countries, the morning and late afternoon are the best time to take photos and videos – before 8 am and after 4 pm, ideally, when light is gentler and there's less contrast between light and shade. Spot-metering – if you have it – is great for photographing faces, particularly dark ones, in difficult lighting conditions.

One advantage of the hours of sunlight is that lower speeds of film are possible. In sunny conditions, ISO50 slide film or ISO100 print film can yield clear, fine-grained and colour-saturated pictures. But don't forget that in areas with dense tropical vegetation, where there's less light, you'll need film up to the speed ISO200 or even ISO400.

A flash is useful for indoor scenes such as dance spectacles. A small zoom lens of some sort is a great addition, not only for wildlife in the Horn but for getting great 'portrait' shots of the very colourful people (but don't forget to show sensitivity and tact).

Make sure you bring plenty of batteries with you. Outside the capitals, batteries are often old, or of very poor quality. If you're planning to recharge your video camera, make sure you have an adaptor that protects it from power surges (see also Electricity following).

Try and keep your equipment tucked away and clean when not in use or travelling. Dust can wreak havoc with the electronics, and spray from the sea can quickly corrode both camera body and lenses. A UV filter on each lens is a must as a protector as well as a filter. A dust blower (either compressed air or manual) is essential, as is a decent lens cloth.

---

raphers is their only source of income. However, the fee should always be agreed in advance (see Tipping earlier in this section).

Be sensitive in areas such as *tej beats* (local pubs) or even restaurants; eating and particularly drinking is rather a private thing in Ethiopia. Drinking alcohol is still considered slightly shameful, and people understandably will not appreciate cameras poked in their faces.

TIME

Ethiopia is three hours ahead of GMT/UTC. When it's noon in Ethiopia, it's 1 am the previous day in Los Angeles, 4 am in New York, 9 am in London, and 11 pm the same day in Sydney.

For many travellers to Ethiopia, one of the most curious idiosyncrasies of the country is the way time is expressed. Time is measured – in fact perfectly logically – with the 12-hour day. This means that the Ethiopian clock begins just after daybreak, at 1 o'clock (7 am our time), and ends when dusk starts to fall, at 12 o'clock (6 pm our time). Instead

of using 'am' or 'pm', Ethiopians use 'in the morning', 'in the evening' and 'at night' to indicate the time of day.

The system is used widely, though the 24-hour clock is used occasionally among some private businesses. Be careful to ask if a time quoted is according to the Ethiopian or 'European' clock, particularly where important schedules such as bus departure times are concerned, with: *be habesha/faranji akotater no?* – is that Ethiopian/ foreigner's time?

Until you get used to the system, the easiest way to translate local time into Western time is by adding six hours to it. Alternatively, you may want to 'go Ethiopian' and set your clock by the local one, and start getting up at 'midnight'!

CALENDAR

The other great Ethiopian idiosyncrasy you'll need to get used to is the calendar. Based on the Julian system, it is roughly 7½ years 'behind' the Western Gregorian calendar. The year 2000–01 is thus '1993' in the Ethiopian calendar, while '1994' begins in September 2001. Just to confuse you thoroughly, the Ethiopian fiscal year begins on 8 July, and the Ethiopian New Year is rung in on 11 September.

The Julian calendar is named after Julius Caesar, and developed as a result of a dispute over the exact date of Christ's birth. It is made up of 12 months of 30 days each and a 13th month of five or six days. Hence the ETC's challenge to 'Visit Ethiopia and be seven years younger'!

ELECTRICITY

Ethiopia's electricity supply is 220v, 50 cycles AC. Power cuts are common during the rainy season, when storms can bring down the lines; a torch and plenty of batteries are essential.

If you're planning to take a laptop with you, make sure you have something to protect it against the variations in current, as power surges occur frequently (see Email & Internet Access earlier in this section).

A variety of sockets are found around the country. A relic from the Italian period, a good many take the continental, two-pin, earth prong (two round prongs), rated at 600 watts.

It's a good idea to bring an adaptor. Visitors from the USA and Canada (with120v at 60Hz) should be careful to choose one appropriate for their equipment; appliance performance may be affected or even damaged otherwise. Newer appliances are made to run at both 50 and 60 Hz.

LAUNDRY

A good, usually 24-hour, laundry service is offered by all hotels, from the very cheapest to the most expensive. Prices correspond with the room rates: budget hotels will charge little, smart hotels will charge a great deal. In the smaller hotels, clothes are hand-washed.

In Addis Ababa and some of the larger towns, both laundry and dry-cleaning services are offered. Sleeping bags can be cleaned if yours has got wet while trekking, or just a bit too pongy.

TOILETS

Both the sit-down and squat types of toilet are found in Ethiopia, reflecting European and Arab influences respectively.

In the highlands, the sit-down type tends to prevail. In the Muslim lowlands, the squat style is more commonly found (but only in the cheaper hotels). Toilet paper is very rare in either; you're best advised to carry your own.

In the country, Ethiopian toilets can be a bit traumatic for the uninitiated. The most common arrangement is a rickety and smelly old shack, with two planks, a hole in the ground, and all the flies you can fit in between. You may suddenly discover that you can survive the next 1000km without a toilet stop after all.

In the smaller villages, the inhabitants simply mark an area outside the village, point you in that direction, and off you trot.

If you're caught short in the towns, the hotels are the best places to head, and unlike in the west, wouldn't dream of turning you away in your moment of need.

See also the boxed text 'Considerations for Responsible Trekking' under Responsible Tourism earlier in this section for toilet training on the mountains.

HEALTH

One who hides his illness has no medicine; one who hides his problem has no remedy.
Ethiopian proverb

Travel health depends on three things: your predeparture preparations, your daily healthcare while travelling, and how you handle any medical problem that may arise.

While the Horn boasts a fabulous selection of tropical diseases, and the potential dangers can seem quite horrifying, in reality few travellers experience anything more than an few undignified trots to the toilet. Don't let the following information put you off.

Predeparture Planning

Adequate health insurance is essential (see Travel Insurance under Visas & Documents earlier in this section). Medical facilities in Ethiopia are limited. Although most doctors are well trained, supplies and modern equipment are lacking even in Addis Ababa. Emergency assistance is also limited outside the capital. While there's no undue cause for alarm, travellers are best advised to travel well-prepared: adequately immunised, with their own supplies of prescription drugs and with a reasonable medical kit (see the boxed text 'Medical Kit Check List').

Immunisations Plan ahead for immunisation – ideally six weeks before travel. Some vaccinations require more than one injection. Most vaccinations are required a minimum of ten days before departure. If you are pregnant or suffer from allergies, you should inform your doctor.

In the UK you can contact the travel clinic at the well-respected Hospital for Tropical Diseases (☎ 020-7637 9899) in London.

Carry proof of your vaccinations, particularly the yellow-fever vaccination, which is required for entrance to Ethiopia, Eritrea and Djibouti.

Malaria Medication Malaria is a serious health risk for travellers to the Horn. Of the 2000 annual cases of malaria reported in the UK, over half are the potentially more dangerous falciparum malaria. This is mainly acquired in Africa, where chloroquine resistance is widespread.

Antimalarial medication is essential for the Horn. Your doctor will recommend what type, which depends on your medical history, possible side effects, and whether medication is for a child, adult, or pregnant woman.

A treatment dose of medication is a good idea if you're travelling to risk areas.

See also Malaria under Insect-Borne Medical Problems later in this section'.

Travel Health Guides If you're planning to be away for a long period or visiting remote areas, a health guide is sometimes a good idea.

CDC's Complete Guide to Healthy Travel, Open Road Publishing, 1997. The US Centers for Disease Control & Prevention recommendations for international travel.

Medical Kit Check List

The following is a list of items you should consider including in your medical kit – consult your pharmacist for brands available in your country. Those marked with an asterisk are essential for travel in the Horn.

☐ **Antibiotics*–** consider including these if you're travelling well off the beaten track; see your doctor as they must be prescribed, and carry the prescription with you

☐ **Antihistamine –** for allergies such as hay fever; to ease the itch from insect bites or stings; and to prevent motion sickness

☐ **Antiseptic*** (such as the excellent povidone-iodine) – for cuts, including those from coral

☐ **Aspirin or paracetamol** (acetaminophen in the US) – for pain or fever

☐ **Bandages, Band-Aids** (plasters) and other wound dressings – useful for blisters when trekking

☐ **Calamine lotion, sting relief spray or aloe vera –** to ease irritation from sunburn and insect bites or stings; handy after a night in one of the fleapit budget hotels

☐ **Cold and flu tablets, throat lozenges and nasal decongestant**

☐ **Insect repellent*, sunscreen*, lip balm and eye drops**

☐ **Loperamide* or diphenoxylate –** gut-paralysing drugs that 'block' diarrhoea; only to be used in emergencies, eg, when you must travel

☐ **Multivitamins –** consider for long trips, when dietary vitamin intake may be inadequate

☐ **Rehydration mixture* –** to prevent dehydration, eg, due to severe diarrhoea; particularly important when travelling with children

☐ **Scissors, tweezers and a thermometer** (note that mercury thermometers are prohibited by airlines)

☐ **Sterile kit*–** in case you need injections in a country with medical hygiene problems; discuss with your doctor

☐ **Water purification tablets or iodine**

Vaccinations for the Horn

Cholera – the current injectable vaccine against cholera is poorly protective and has side effects, so it is not always recommended. However, if you're spending long periods in risky areas, you might as well err on the side of caution.

Diphtheria & Tetanus – a booster every 10 years maintains immunity. Tetanus vaccination is particularly important in the Horn.

Hepatitis A – this is a real risk in the Horn, and a vaccination is strongly recommended. Hepatitis A vaccine (eg Avaxim, Havrix 1440 or VAQTA) is administered with an initial injection, followed by a booster six to 12 months later. Though the vaccination can be expensive, it provides long-term immunity – around 10 years. Alternatively, an injection of gamma globulin can provide short-term protection against hepatitis A: from two to six months, depending on the dosage. It is reasonably effective and, unlike the vaccine, is protective immediately. Hepatitis A vaccine is also available in a combined form: Twinrix, with a hepatitis B vaccine. Three injections over a six-month period are required, the first two providing substantial protection against hepatitis A.

Hepatitis B – vaccination against hepatitis B is strongly recommended, and involves three injections, with a booster at 12 months. More rapid courses are available if necessary.

Meningococcal meningitis – a single injection gives good protection against the major epidemic forms of the disease for three years and vaccination is advisable for travel to the Horn. Protection may be less effective in children under two years.

Polio – a booster is only necessary every 10 years; make sure you're up to date.

Rabies – vaccination is a good idea for those spending a month or longer in the Horn, especially if cycling, handling animals, caving or travelling to remote areas, and for children (who may not report a bite). A pre-travel rabies vaccination involves three injections administered over 21 to 28 days. If bitten or scratched by an animal, two booster injections of vaccine are required. Those without an initial vaccination require more.

Tuberculosis – the risk of contracting TB in the Horn is usually very low, unless you're living or working closely with local people in high-risk areas. If you're a VSO worker, check out the situation in advance. Vaccination against TB is recommended for children and young adults living in these areas for three months or more.

Typhoid – vaccinations are strongly recommended if you are travelling for more than a couple of weeks in the Horn. It's available either as an injection or as capsules.

Yellow Fever – a yellow-fever vaccination certificate is now a legal requirement for entry into Ethiopia, Eritrea and Djibouti.

Healthy Travel Africa, Isabelle Young, Lonely Planet Publications, 2000. A very useful pocket-sized compendium of all the diseases, symptoms and remedies you can possibly think of, plus some sound practical advice on how to stay healthy.

Travel with Children, Maureen Wheeler, Lonely Planet Publications, 1995. Includes advice on travel health for younger children.

Where There Is No Doctor, David Werner, Macmillan, 1994. A very detailed guide intended for someone such as a Peace Corps worker going to work in a developing country.

You could also check out some of the excellent travel health sites on the Web: follow the links from the Lonely Planet Web site, and see also Internet Resources earlier in this section.

Other Preparations If you're going on a long trip, a check-up with your dentist is a very good idea; good dentists are very hard to come by in the Horn. If you wear glasses take a spare pair as well as your prescription.

If you require a particular medication take an adequate supply in case it's not available locally. A note of the generic name (rather than the brand) will make getting replacements easier. A letter from your doctor stating that you require the medication should circumscribe any other problems.

Basic Rules

Food There is an old colonial adage that says: 'If you can cook it, boil it or peel it you can eat it...otherwise forget it'. Vegetables and fruit can also be washed with purified water.

Beware of ice cream that is sold in the street or anywhere it might have been melted and refrozen; if there's any doubt (eg, if there's a power cut in the last day or two, which is a problem in Djibouti and Ethiopia), steer clear. Shellfish such as mussels, oysters and clams are dubious. Undercooked meat is also a risk, particularly in the form of mince (see Intestinal Worms and the boxed text 'Would You Like Worms with That?' later in this section).

Busy local places are often better than empty 'smart' places. If the place is crowded, clean and well run, it's normally OK. Contrary to what you might expect, sizzling street food is often safer than the elaborate buffets put on by the expensive hotels, where food is allowed to sit around for long periods.

Nutrition If your diet is poor or limited in variety, if you're travelling hard and fast and missing meals, or if you're simply not eating enough, you can soon start to lose weight and place your health at risk. The following will contribute to a well-balanced diet – essential to good health when travelling:

- Cooked eggs, beans, lentils (*mësër* in Amharic) and nuts are safe ways to get protein.
- Fruit you can peel is a safe way to get vitamins.
- Grains including rice and bread are good for fibre.
- Vitamins and iron pills are good for supplements (if eating a well-balanced diet is difficult).
- Drinking lots of water is essential in hot climates. Don't rely on feeling thirsty to indicate when you should drink (not needing to urinate or small amounts of very dark yellow urine are

danger signals). Always carry a water bottle with you.

- Adding a little salt to food can help to avoid muscle cramp caused by the excessive loss of salt through sweating.

Water The number-one rule is be careful of the water and especially ice. If you don't know for certain that the water is safe, assume the worst. Reputable brands of bottled water or soft drinks should be fine and are widely available in the Horn. A water bottle is a good idea.

Take care with fruit juice, particularly as tap water may have been added. Milk is sometimes dodgy if it's unpasteurised, though boiled milk is fine if it is kept hygienically. Tea or coffee should also be OK, since the water is normally boiled.

The simplest way of purifying water is to boil it thoroughly. At high altitude, water boils at a lower temperature, so in order to kill germs, it needs to be boiled for longer.

A water filter is a good idea if you're planning on trekking or spending long periods in remote areas. There are two main kinds of filter. The most sophisticated filters take out all parasites, bacteria and viruses and make water safe to drink. Though expensive, they can save on buying bottled water. Simple filters (which can even be a nylon mesh bag) take out dirt and larger foreign bodies from the water and are used in combination with chemical solutions.

Of the chemical solutions, chlorine tablets will kill many pathogens, but not some parasites like giardia and amoebic cysts. Iodine is more effective and is available in tablet form. Follow the directions carefully and remember that too much iodine can be harmful.

Medical Problems & Treatment

Self-diagnosis and treatment can be risky, so you should always seek medical help. In the Horn, most people consult pharmacists for initial symptoms of diseases. They are usually quite well qualified, are very helpful, usually speak good English (or French in Djibouti) and are very familiar with the symptoms of the most common diseases such as giardia.

Although drug dosages are given in this section, they are for emergency use only. Correct diagnosis is vital. In this section generic names for medications have been included – check with a pharmacist for brands available locally.

Note that antibiotics should ideally be administered under medical supervision. Take only the recommended dose at the prescribed intervals and use the whole course, even if the illness seems to be cured. Stop immediately if there are any serious reactions. Some people are allergic to commonly prescribed antibiotics such as penicillin; carry this information (eg, on a medical bracelet) when travelling.

For information on dangerous animals including snakes, see Dangers & Annoyances later in this section. See also Hazardous Marine Life in the special section 'Marine Life in the Red Sea'.

Cuts & Scratches Any cut should be washed well and treated with an antiseptic such as povidone-iodine. Where possible avoid bandages and Band-Aids, which can keep wounds wet. Coral cuts are notoriously slow to heal and if they are not adequately cleaned, small pieces of coral can become embedded in the wound. In the heat, infection happens very quickly; look after cuts and try and avoid scratching mosquito bites.

Diarrhoea Simple things like a change of water, food or climate can all cause a mild bout of diarrhoea, and a few bolts for the toilet with no other symptoms is not indicative of a major problem. Diarrhoea affects over half of all travellers to the tropics.

The best solution is to rest for 24 hours, and drink lots of clear fluids (3–4L). Alcohol should be avoided. If you're hungry, opt for bland food such as boiled rice, potatoes or biscuits.

Dehydration is the main danger with diarrhoea, particularly in children or the elderly, as dehydration can occur quite quickly. Fluid replacement (at least equal to the volume being lost) is the most important thing to remember. Weak black tea with a little sugar, or soda water, or soft drinks allowed to go flat and diluted 50% with clean water are all good.

With severe diarrhoea a rehydrating solution is preferable to replace lost minerals and salts. Commercially available oral rehydration salts (ORS) are very useful; add them to boiled or bottled water. In an emergency you can make up your own solution: six teaspoons of sugar and a half teaspoon of salt added to a litre of boiled or bottled water. Urine is the best guide to the replacement required – if you have small amounts of concentrated urine, you need to drink more. Drink small amounts of water often, and stick to a bland diet as you recover.

Gut-paralysing drugs such as loperamide or diphenoxylate can be used to bring relief from the symptoms, although they do not actually cure the problem. Only use these drugs if you do not have access to toilets, such as if you *must* travel. These drugs are not recommended for children under 12 years.

Diarrhoea with blood or mucus (dysentery), any diarrhoea with fever, profuse watery diarrhoea, persistent diarrhoea not improving after 48 hours and severe diarrhoea suggest more serious illnesses such as cholera (see Less Common Diseases later in this section). Gut-paralysing drugs should be avoided.

A simple stool test can diagnose the bug causing your diarrhoea. Where this is not possible, the recommended drugs for bacterial diarrhoea (the most likely cause of severe diarrhoea in travellers) are norfloxacin 400mg twice daily for three days or ciprofloxacin 500mg twice daily for five days. These are not recommended for children (who should be given co-trimoxazole) or pregnant women (ampicillin or amoxycillin is usually recommended).

Giardiasis & Amoebic Dysentary Two other causes of persistent diarrhoea in travellers are amoebic and giardiasis dysentery.

Giardiasis, quite common among travellers in both Ethiopia and Eritrea, is caused by a common parasite, *Giardia lamblia*. Symptoms include stomach cramps; a bloated stomach; very watery, foul-smelling diarrhoea; sulphurous burping; and sometimes nausea.

Amoebic dysentery, caused by the protozoan *Entamoeba histolytica*, is characterised by a gradual onset of low-grade diarrhoea, often with blood and mucus. Cramping abdominal pain, vomiting and fever are less likely than in other types of diarrhoea. Symptoms of both diseases may disappear for a few days and then return, and will persist until treated; they can also cause other health problems. If you think you have giardiasis or amoebic dysentery, you should seek medical advice. Tinidazole or metronidazole are the recommended drugs. Treatment is a 2g single dose of tinidazole or 250mg of metronidazole three times daily for five to 10 days. It's important to avoid all alcohol at this time.

Fungal Infections Fungal infections occur more commonly in hot weather and are usually found on the scalp, between the toes (athlete's foot) or fingers, in the groin and on the body (ringworm). Moisture encourages infection. Ringworm (a fungal infection, not a worm) is transmitted by infected animals or people. If you do get an infection, wash the infected area at least daily with a disinfectant or medicated soap and water, and rinse and dry well. Apply an antifungal cream or powder like tolnaftate. Wash all towels and underwear in hot water, change them often and let them dry in the sun.

Hepatitis Hepatitis is a general term for inflammation of the liver. It is a common disease in the Horn, caused by different viruses, and can lead to serious long-term problems such as chronic liver damage and liver cancer.

Symptoms include fever, chills, headache, fatigue, feelings of weakness and aches and pains, followed by loss of appetite, nausea, vomiting, abdominal pain, dark urine, light-coloured faeces, jaundiced (yellow) skin and yellowing of the whites of the eyes.

Hepatitis A and E are transmitted by contaminated food and drinking water. If infected, rest, drink lots of fluids, eat lightly and avoid fatty foods. Hepatitis B, C and D

AIDS in Africa

Sub-Saharan Africa is home to two-thirds of the world's 33.4 million people infected with AIDS; some 5000 die daily on the continent. It is estimated that by 2005, the figure will have increased to 13,000 daily – a number that will bring the AIDS death toll in the region to above that of the two world wars combined.

In 1997, the percentage of HIV-infected people in Ethiopia was calculated at 7.4% – around 2½ million. By 2009, it is estimated that the mortality rate for the age group 15–49 years old will have increased by a staggering 57%. AIDS is now the single greatest threat to economic development in Africa.

are spread through contact with infected blood or body fluids. The disease is usually transmitted through sexual contact, contact with blood via small breaks in the skin, and dirty needles. Note that vaccinations, acupuncture, tattooing and body piercing in developing countries can be potentially as dangerous as intravenous drug use.

If you do need an injection, ask to see the syringe unwrapped in front of you, or take a needle and syringe pack with you. However, fear of infection should never preclude treatment of serious medical conditions.

The disease can also be spread through infected blood transfusions. Although blood is now in theory screened for transfusions in the Horn, it probably can't be guaranteed.

There are vaccines against hepatitis A and B, but there are currently no vaccines against the other types of hepatitis (see the boxed text 'Vaccinations for the Horn' earlier in this section). Following the basic rules about food and water (hepatitis A and E) and avoiding risky situations (hepatitis B, C and D) are important preventative measures.

HIV/AIDS Infection with the Human Immunodeficiency Virus (HIV) may lead to Acquired Immune Deficiency Syndrome (AIDS), which is a fatal disease. HIV/AIDS is spread in exactly the same way as are hepatitis B, C and D.

Ethiopia and Djibouti have a large number of prostitutes; unprotected sexual contact with these sex workers is unwise to put it mildly. Good quality condoms in Ethiopia are now subsidised and cost just 25¢ (less than half a US dime).

Meningococcal Meningitis

This serious disease can be fatal, and recurring epidemics are reported in sub-Saharan Africa. A fever, severe headache, sensitivity to light and neck stiffness that prevents forward bending of the head are the first symptoms. There may also be purple patches on the skin. Death can occur within a few hours, so urgent medical treatment is required.

Sexually Transmitted Infections (STIs)

HIV/AIDS and hepatitis B can be transmitted through sexual contact – see the relevant headings earlier for more details.

Other STIs include gonorrhoea, herpes and syphilis; sores, blisters or rashes around the genitals and discharges or pain when urinating are common symptoms. In some STIs, such as wart virus or chlamydia, symptoms may be less marked or not observed at all, especially in women. Chlamydia infection can cause infertility in men and women, before any symptoms have been noticed. Syphilis symptoms eventually disappear completely but the disease continues and can cause severe problems in later years.

While abstinence from sexual contact is the only 100% effective prevention, using condoms is also effective. STIs are treated with specific antibiotics, though there is no known cure for herpes or HIV.

Typhoid

Typhoid fever is a serious gut infection caused by contaminated water and food, and requires immediate medical attention. Early symptoms include headaches, body aches, a slow pulse and a fever that gradually increases until it reaches around 40°C (104°F). Vomiting, abdominal pain, diarrhoea or constipation may also occur. In the second week, pink spots may appear on the body; trembling, delirium, weakness, weight loss and dehydration may occur. Unless treated, serious complications may follow.

Insect-Borne Medical Problems

See also Less Common Diseases later in the Health section.

Intestinal Worms

These little parasites are quite common in the Horn. Worms may be ingested through food such as undercooked meat. The Ethiopian tradition of eating raw meat as well as the delicacy *kitfo* (raw mince) is the cause of widespread tapeworm infestation, particularly outside the capital. An infusion prepared from the bark of the kosso tree *(Hagenia abyssinica)* is the traditional treatment. See also the boxed text 'Would You Like Worms with That?' under Food later in this section.

Worms such as hookworms can also enter through your skin. You should always wear shoes when walking outside. Infestations may not show up for several months. Although they are not generally serious, they can cause health problems later if not treated. A stool test when you return home isn't a bad idea to check for parasites.

Bilharzia (Schistosomiasis)

This disease is transmitted by minute worms that infest certain varieties of freshwater snails. There is a high risk of bilharzia in all of Ethiopia's rivers, streams and lakes and any dammed water, apart from Lake Langano, which is believed to be free of the disease.

The worm enters through the skin and attaches itself to the intestines or bladder. The infection often causes no symptoms until the disease is well established. Symptoms (which may appear several weeks or even years later) include a high fever, abdominal pain and blood in the urine. Damage to internal organs is irreversible. A blood test is the best diagnosis, but should not be taken until a number of weeks after exposure. Avoid swimming or bathing in fresh water. If you do get wet, dry off quickly and dry your clothes as well.

Malaria

This potentially fatal disease is prevalent in areas below 1800m and is spread by the *Anopheles* mosquito, most commonly found near permanent or temporary pools of still water, where it breeds.

Prophylactics are essential in Djibouti, Eritrea and some parts of Ethiopia, such as the Omo Valley and the western lowlands around Gambela.

The disease is a major public health problem in Ethiopia, with between one and two million clinical cases reported each year. Unfortunately, one of the most dangerous strains of malaria, and that most resistant to chloroquine, *Plasmodium falciparum*, is responsible for 60–70% of malaria cases in Ethiopia and Eritrea.

Though malaria is generally absent in Ethiopia at altitudes above 1800m, epidemics have occurred in areas above 2000m. The central plateau, Addis Ababa, the Bale and Simien Mountains, and most of the northern historical route areas are traditionally considered 'safe' areas, but not wholly risk free.

For short-term visitors, it's probably wise to err on the side of caution. If you're thinking of travelling outside these areas, you should definitely take prophylactics. Most transmission takes place after the rainy season, from August or September to November, and after the light rains from March to April or May.

Symptoms of malaria range from fever, chills and sweating, headache, diarrhoea and abdominal pains to a vague feeling of ill-health. Seek medical help immediately if malaria is suspected. Without treatment, malaria can quickly become more serious and can be fatal.

If medical care is not available, malaria tablets can be used for treatment. Note that you need to take a malaria tablet that is different from the one you were taking when you contracted the disease.

For mefloquine, the standard dose is two 250mg tablets and a further two six hours later. For Fansidar, it's a single dose of three tablets. If you were previously taking mefloquine and cannot obtain Fansidar, then other alternatives include malarone (atovaquone-proguanil; four tablets once daily for three days), quinine sulphate (600mg every six hours) or halofantrine (three doses of two 250mg tablets every six hours). Note that halofantrine is no longer recommended by the WHO as emergency standby treatment because of side effects, and should only be used if no other drugs are available.

Note also that malaria usually takes between one week and three months to develop, though it can take a year. Be vigilant for possible symptoms when you return home, and don't forget to finish your course of tablets.

The best way of avoiding malaria is by avoiding mosquito bites; the following tips will also reduce your risk of infection:

- Wear light-coloured clothing, long trousers and long-sleeved shirts.
- Use mosquito repellents containing the compound DEET on exposed areas.
- Avoid perfumes or aftershave.
- Use a mosquito net impregnated with mosquito repellent (permethrin).
- Mobil Insecticide Spray is widely available in Ethiopia, and is great for pre-turning-in raids in your hotel room; the mosquitoes sound like WW1 fighter planes coming down!

Dengue Fever This viral disease is also transmitted by mosquitoes and is fast becoming one of the major public health problems in the tropics. Unlike the malaria mosquito, the *Aedes aegypti* mosquito is most active during the day, and is found mainly in urban areas, in and around human dwellings.

Symptoms of dengue fever include a sudden onset of high fever, headache, joint and muscle pains (hence its old name, 'breakbone fever') and nausea and vomiting. A rash of small red spots sometimes appears three to four days after the onset of fever.

Of the four strains, the haemorrhagic fever (DHF) is the most dangerous and can be fatal. It usually affects residents of the country rather than travellers, and is characterised by heavy bleeding.

Recovery from all strains may be prolonged, with tiredness lasting for several weeks. If you suspect infection, you should seek immediate medical attention. Aspirin should be avoided, as it increases the risk of haemorrhaging. There is no specific treatment and no vaccine for dengue fever. Like malaria, the best way of avoiding dengue fever is avoiding mosquito bites.

Bedbugs

One seasoned expat in Ethiopia made his own particular suggestions for combatting bedbugs in cheap hotels:

- Switch the light on in the night and play hunt-the-bug with a damp bar of soap
- Wear a dog flea collar in bed or have a quick dust-down with anti-flea dog talc
- Sleep in the car

Bedbugs & Lice Bedbugs are quite common in some of the cheaper hotels in the rural areas of Ethiopia and Eritrea. Dirty mattresses and bedding – evidenced by spots of blood on bedclothes or on the wall – are favourite haunts. An enclosed sleeping net is the only protection against them. Bedbugs leave itchy bites in neat rows. Calamine lotion or a sting relief spray may help.

Lice can cause itching, and can infest your hair (head lice), your clothing (scabies) or your pubic hair (crabs). Lice are caught through direct contact with infected people or by sharing combs, clothing and the like. Powder or shampoo treatment will kill the lice. Infected clothing should be washed in very hot, soapy water and left in the sun to dry.

Bites & Stings Unless you receive multiple stings, bee, wasp and hornet stings are usually only painful rather than dangerous. Travellers who are allergic to stings should bring with them antihistamine treatments. Scorpions are found in the Danakil region of Ethiopia, Eritrea and Djibouti, and often shelter in shoes and clothing. The sting is notoriously painful, but is rarely life threatening. For information on biting or stinging marine creatures, see the special section 'Marine Life of the Red Sea'.

Ticks Ticks are found in certain dry rural areas of the Horn. They can cause skin infections and other more serious diseases such as typhus. If a tick is found attached, press down around the tick's head with tweezers, grab the head and gently pull upwards. Avoid pulling the rear of the body as

this may squeeze the tick's body contents through the attached mouth parts into the skin, increasing the risk of infection and disease.

Less Common Diseases The following diseases pose a small risk to travellers, and so are only mentioned in passing. If you suspect you have any of these diseases seek medical advice immediately. There are vaccinations for cholera, rabies (partially), tetanus, typhoid, tuberculosis and yellow fever (see the boxed text 'Vaccinations for the Horn' earlier in this section).

Cholera – outbreaks of cholera are generally widely reported, so you can usually avoid such areas. Cholera is the worst of the watery diarrhoeas. If there is a delay in getting to hospital, then start taking tetracycline. The adult dose is 250mg four times daily. It is not recommended for children under nine years or for pregnant women. Tetracycline may help shorten the illness, but fluid rehydration is essential to prevent death.

Filariasis is a mosquito-transmitted parasitic infection found in many parts of Africa. Possible symptoms include fever, pain and swelling of the lymph glands, swelling of a limb or the scrotum, skin rashes and blindness.

Leishmaniasis is a group of parasitic diseases transmitted by sandflies, which are found in some parts of the Horn. Cutaneous leishmaniasis affects the skin tissue, causing ulceration and disfigurement; visceral leishmaniasis affects the internal organs.

Rabies – many species of animals can be infected by this fatal virus, including dogs, cats, bats, monkeys and other wild animals. The disease is transmitted through the animal's saliva; any bite, scratch or even lick should be immediately scrubbed with soap and running water. Alcohol or iodine solution should then be applied; even whisky or gin will do in the absence of anything else. A course of injections needs to be administered at once to prevent the onset of symptoms and death.

Sleeping Sickness or Trypanosomiasis is found in many parts of tropical Africa, including Ethiopia – particularly in the Omo Valley. The disease is borne by the tsetse fly, though only a small percentage of the insects actually carry it. The fly, about twice the size of a housefly, is recognisable by the scissorlike way it folds its wings when at rest. The flies are attracted to large moving objects such as safari buses, to perfume and aftershave and to dark colours. Swelling at the site of the bite, five or more days later, is the first sign of infection; two to three weeks later, fever follows. The disease can be fatal unless treated.

Tetanus – the germ that causes tetanus is found in the soil and in animal faeces. It enters the body via breaks in the skin. The first symptom may be discomfort in swallowing, or stiffening of the jaw and neck; this is followed by painful convulsions of the jaw and eventually the whole body.

Tuberculosis (TB) is a bacterial infection usually transmitted from person to person by coughing. Occasionally, it is transmitted through consumption of unpasteurised milk (boiled milk, yoghurt and cheese are safe). Transmission is usually only through close household contact with infected people.

Typhus is spread by ticks, mites or lice. Symptoms initially include fever, chills, headache and muscle pains. Often a large painful sore appears at the site of the bite. Nearby lymph nodes are also swollen and painful. A few days later a body rash appears. Though serious, typhus can be treated under medical supervision.

Yellow Fever is a viral disease endemic in many African countries and is transmitted by mosquitoes. The initial symptoms are fever, headache, abdominal pain and vomiting. Seek medical care urgently and drink lots of fluids.

Environmental Hazards

Altitude Sickness Travellers trekking in the Bale or Simien Mountains (with some areas over 4000m) are most likely to suffer from altitude sickness, though new arrivals even in Addis Ababa (at 2400m) sometimes experience mild symptoms for the first 48 hours or so.

Lack of oxygen at high altitudes (over 2500m) affects most people to some extent, and occurs because less oxygen reaches the muscles and the brain, requiring the heart and lungs to compensate by working harder.

Symptoms of Acute Mountain Sickness (AMS) usually develop during the first 24 hours at altitude but may be delayed up to three weeks. Mild symptoms include headache, lethargy, dizziness, difficulty sleeping and loss of appetite. In Asmara, Eritrea, you may notice these symptoms if you have just flown in from a low altitude.

Severe symptoms – which can develop without warning – include breathlessness, a dry irritated cough, severe headache, lack of coordination and balance, confusion, irrational behaviour, vomiting, drowsiness and unconsciousness.

There is no hard-and-fast rule as to what is too high: AMS has been fatal at 3000m, although 3500 to 4500m is the usual range.

Treat mild symptoms by resting at the same altitude until recovery, usually a day or two. Paracetamol or aspirin can be taken for headaches. If symptoms persist or become worse, however, *immediate descent* is necessary; descending just 500m can help. Drug treatments should not be used to avoid descent or to enable further ascent.

The following pointers will help you avoid AMS:

- Ascend slowly – have frequent rest days, spending two to three nights at each rise of 1000m.
- Sleep if possible at a lower altitude than the greatest height reached during the day. Once above 3000m, avoid increasing the sleeping altitude by more than 300m per day.
- Drink extra fluids. Moisture is lost as you breathe in the dry mountain air, and as you sweat (even imperceptibly).
- Eat light, high-carbohydrate meals for more energy.
- Avoid alcohol (which increases dehydration), sedatives and sleeping pills.

Heat Exhaustion & Heatstroke Dehydration and salt deficiency can cause heat exhaustion. Drink sufficient liquids and avoid activities that are too physically demanding. Salt deficiency is characterised by fatigue, lethargy, headaches, giddiness and muscle cramps; salt tablets may help, but adding extra salt to your food is better.

Heatstroke is a serious, occasionally fatal condition that can occur if the body's heat-regulating mechanism breaks down and the body temperature rises to dangerous levels. Long, continuous periods of exposure to high temperatures and insufficient fluids can leave you vulnerable to heatstroke. The symptoms are feeling unwell, not sweating very much (or not at all) and a high body

Everyday Health

Normal body temperature is up to 37°C (98.6°F). More than 2°C (4°F) higher indicates a high fever.

The normal adult pulse rate is 60 to 100 per minute (children 80 to 100; babies 100 to 140). As a general rule the pulse increases about 20 beats per minute for each 1°C (2°F) rise in fever.

⋘⋘⋘⋘⋘⋘⋘⋘⋘⋘⋘⋘⋘⋘⋘⋘⋘⋘⋘⋘

temperature (39° to 41°C or 102° to 106°F). Where sweating has ceased, the skin becomes flushed and red. Severe, throbbing headaches and lack of coordination will also occur, and the sufferer may be confused or aggressive. Eventually victims will become delirious or convulse. Hospitalisation is essential, but in the interim, get victims out of the sun, remove their clothing, cover them with a wet sheet or towel and fan them continually. Give fluids if they are conscious.

Hypothermia Though it can get cold in the mountains of Ethiopia, particularly if you're trekking in the higher peaks, hypothermia shouldn't be a problem unless you're inadequately equipped.However, it's surprisingly easy to progress from very cold to dangerously cold because of a combination of wind, wet clothing, fatigue and hunger, even if the air temperature is above freezing.

Symptoms of hypothermia are exhaustion, numb skin (particularly toes and fingers), shivering, slurred speech, irrational or violent behaviour, lethargy, stumbling, dizzy spells, muscle cramps and violent bursts of energy.

To treat mild hypothermia, first get the person out of the wind and/or rain, remove their clothing if it's wet and replace it with dry, warm clothing. Give them hot liquids – not alcohol – and some high-kilojoule, easily digestible food. Do not rub victims: instead, allow them to slowly warm themselves.

The early recognition and treatment of mild hypothermia is the only way to prevent severe hypothermia, which is a critical condition.

Motion Sickness Some roads in Ethiopia and Eritrea are very winding and rolling; motion sickness is common among the locals.

If you suffer from motion sickness, take pills with you. You should eat lightly before and during a trip, sit near the centre in buses and cars (or near the wing on an aircraft, or close to midships on boats) and avoid reading and cigarette smoke.

If you find yourself without pills, peppermint and ginger are natural preventatives.

Prickly Heat Prickly heat is an itchy rash caused by excessive perspiration trapped under the skin. It usually strikes people who have just arrived in a hot climate. Keeping cool, bathing often, drying the skin and using a mild talcum or prickly heat powder or resorting to air-conditioning may help.

Sunburn In the tropics, in the desert and at high altitude you can burn surprisingly quickly, even through cloud. Use sunscreen, a hat, and a barrier cream for your nose and lips. Protect your eyes with good quality sunglasses, particularly if you're near water or sand.

Women's Health

Gynaecological Problems Antibiotic use, synthetic underwear and contraceptive pills can lead to fungal vaginal infections, especially when travelling in hot climates. Fungal infections are characterised by a rash, itch and discharge and can be treated with a vinegar or lemon-juice douche, or with yoghurt. Nystatin, miconazole or clotrimazole pessaries are the usual treatment. Maintaining good personal hygiene and wearing loose-fitting clothes and cotton underwear may help prevent these infections.

If you're in need of medical attention, there are various excellent women's clinics in Addis Ababa.

Pregnancy Pregnancy is not an ideal period for travelling. However, if you must travel, these are a few things to bear in mind: check that your insurance covers prenatal complications, premature labour, delivery abroad or speedy evacuation home.

Discuss your travel plans with your doctor, particularly vaccinations and anti-malarial medication.

Check that medical aid is readily available and that facilities are adequate. Ensure that the area where you will be going screens blood transfusions for HIV and hepatitis. Air travel is usually not possible after the 35th week of pregnancy (though the policies of individual airlines differ – check in advance).

WOMEN TRAVELLERS

Compared with many African countries, Ethiopia is pretty easy-going for women travellers, so long as you're aware of a few unspoken codes of etiquette (see Society & Conduct in the Facts about Ethiopia section). If you respect the local ways, you'll find Ethiopians a very polite, respectful and charming people, and you should experience few problems.

Attitudes Towards Local Women

Establishing the status of the local women in a society – and how they behave and are expected to behave – is very important for woman travellers in any country, and the Horn is no exception.

In Ethiopia as well as Eritrea and Djibouti, drinking alcohol, smoking, and wearing excessive make-up and 'inappropriate' clothes are all indications to the male population of 'availability' – since this is also the way the local prostitutes behave. Chewing qat (a stimulating herb) among men is also typical behaviour among prostitutes. No 'proper' Ethiopian women would be seen in a bar either. In restaurants, at markets, about town and even at discos, women are always accompanied, if not by male relatives, then by a good rabble of female friends. Women in bars are almost always 'bar girls' (see the boxed text 'Prostitution in Ethiopia' later in this section). Addis Ababa is the one exception, where women have greater freedom.

The social stigma attached to prostitution in the West is lacking in Ethiopia (and to a

---

Bring Me a Blanket

To watch the pebbles dance in rhythm to the thick lashes of rain,
To see petals falling, to hear the rooftop sing,
Snugly wrapped in a blanket,
No uneasiness to discomfort the mind;
This is happiness.
But wait. I am not that woman whose life a beast of burden has made;
That woman whose wet rags outline her cold, emaciated body;
And whose every step is a picture of weariness.

From Serifu's Metaferia's poem 'The Rainy Season in Bullukko', 1968

---

lesser degree in Eritrea). A huge number of prostitutes exist in the country; many girls are students, trying to make ends meet. Others are widows, divorcees or refugees – all with little or no hope of finding other forms of employment. With no social security system either, it is often their only means of survival. Though not exactly a respected profession, prostitution is considered a perfectly viable means of making a living for such women. Some very beautiful or accomplished prostitutes can even become well-known figures in society.

Visiting a prostitute is considered a fairly normal part of a young boy's adolescence and bachelor life. Once married, it is considered 'shameful', however, and married men who can afford it often keep permanent mistresses or 'girlfriends' instead. Virginity in girls before marriage is still widely expected and prized, at least in the small towns and rural areas.

Many women in Ethiopia (and to a far greater extent in the rest of the Horn) have undergone the most extreme form of female genital mutilation, known as infibulation (see the boxed text 'Female Circumcision – A Scream So Strong, It Would Shake the Earth' in the West of Addis Ababa section later in this chapter).

Since the downfall of the Derg, there has been an effort to improve the status of women in Ethiopia. At a national level, positive discrimination has been introduced in

Female Phobia

In some of the monasteries and holy sites of Ethiopia and Eritrea, an ancient prohibition forbids women from setting foot in the holy confines. But the holy fathers believe in going by the book: the prohibition extends not just to women but to all female creatures, even she donkeys, hens and nanny goats!

favour of women, both in university entrance requirements (lower for girls than for boys) and in the workforce. However, in most rural areas, a woman's life remains incredibly hard: her day is one of perpetual toil.

If you want to get in touch with Ethiopian women, contact the Ethiopian Women's Promotion Centre (☎ 62-05-52, fax 61-59-02, ✉ EWPC@telecom.net.et), PO Box 0111/970 Addis Ababa.

Attitudes Towards Foreign Women

Because of Hollywood cinematic 'glamour', foreign women in many developing countries are often seen as 'easier' than local women. Additionally, with Ethiopia's relatively permissive society, foreign women are sometimes seen as an exotic alternative to local fun.

'Respectable' Ethiopian women – even if they're game – are expected to put up at least a show of coyness and modesty. For long, and still in rural areas, this was a part of the wedding night ritual for Amhara brides: a fierce struggle with the groom was expected of them. Consequently, many Ethiopian men may mistake your 'nos' for 'yes pleases' (this concept is known in Amharic as *maqderder*). Be very careful not to get yourself in a compromising situation. Ethiopian men are expected to behave roughly and forcefully to overcome what is seen as superficial reluctance. If you mean no, don't spare anyone's feelings, make it absolutely clear from the start. And if you slap an Ethiopian, do it twice: the number one is very unlucky in Ethiopia! However, as in any difficult situation, it's best to diffuse it with humour.

Accepting an invitation to an unmarried man's house, under any pretext, is considered a latent acceptance of things to come. Dinner invitations often amount to 'foreplay' before you are expected to head off to some seedy hotel. Even a seemingly innocent invitation to the cinema can turn out to be little more than a invitation to a good snog in the back row!

Adultery is quite common among many of Ethiopia's urban population, particularly among the men, but also among women. So long as it is not blatant, it is tolerated remarkably well. For this reason, a wedding ring on a woman traveller – bogus or not – has absolutely no deterrent value in the Horn. In fact, quite the reverse! Married women seem to be considered easier prey.

Women travellers in the company of a male traveller are sometimes 'ignored' in conversation, or when ordering at a restaurant, or asking directions etc. This is considered a sign of respect for the woman, not a slight; conversation is seen to be properly directed through the men.

Safety Precautions

The best advice always is: 'When in Rome ...' If you want to go out at night, particularly outside Addis Ababa, try and find a male companion, or at least a couple of female companions. Be wary of certain invitations and the signals your dress and behaviour may be giving off (see Attitudes Towards Local Women). If you don't want to be thought of as sexually available, make it clear that you don't drink alcohol, smoke cigarettes or chew qat (even if you do).

Most of Ethiopia is reasonably safe at night. The biggest risk in Addis Ababa is muggings. If you're concerned about getting home after dark, ask the restaurant, club or bar to ring or flag down a taxi for you. The NTO in Addis Ababa has a night taxi service (see Getting Around in the Addis Ababa section).

Many cheap hotels in Ethiopia double as brothels. If you've chosen to stay in these places, Ethiopian men will naturally wonder about your motives, particularly if you're alone; even hotel mangers have been known to come a-knocking on the door. While there's little need to feel alarmed, it's best to behave very conservatively – keep out of the hotel bar for example, and try and hook up with other travellers if you want to go out.

If there are no travellers around, one useful little wile is to pick a male Ethiopian companion, bemoan the problems you've been having with his compatriots and appeal to his sense of pride, patriotism and gallantry. Usually any ulterior plans he might have been harbouring himself are soon converted into sympathy or shame and a personal crusade to 'protect you'!

GAY & LESBIAN TRAVELLERS

Homosexuality has long been denounced in Africa as 'un-African'. At the end of 1999, leaders in Zimbabwe, Uganda and Kenya famously condemned the practice, culminating in President Mugabe's description of homosexuals as 'lower than pigs and dogs'.

In the Horn, homosexuality is severely condemned – traditionally, religiously and legally – and remains a topic of absolute taboo. Don't underestimate the strength of feeling. Reports of gays being beaten up are not uncommon. In Amharic, the word *bushti* (homosexual) is used as a very offensive insult, implying immorality and depravity.

The Ethiopian penal code officially prohibits homosexual acts, with penalties of between 10 days' and 10 years' imprisonment for various 'crimes'. Although gay locals obviously exist, they behave with extreme discretion and caution, and gay travellers are advised to do likewise.

Information on homosexuality in the Horn is very hard to come by, even in the well-known and comprehensive gay publications. Currently the best source of information is the International Lesbian and Gay Association (ILGA) Web site (www.ilga.org).

DISABLED TRAVELLERS

There is no reason why intrepid disabled travellers shouldn't visit Ethiopia. The recent civil war in the country left many soldiers disabled, so you should expect to find at least some degree of empathy and understanding.

Prostitution in Ethiopia

For male travellers, a word of caution. Almost 100% of the women encountered in the smaller bars, restaurants and nightclubs of the capital and towns are prostitutes. Often, it's very hard to distinguish them from 'ordinary' women: they're usually young, attractive and soberly dressed.

Most are found in the bars. Their mission is to extract from you as many drinks (for the bar or hotel) and as much money (for themselves) as possible. In exchange for your custom, they get a room at the bar/hotel. Be careful of being talked into buying a prostitute a drink. One is considered a sign of interest; two and you're as good as booking the girl's services. Bar girls charge as little as Birr20 to Birr30 for 'short', though it rises to Birr70 to Birr100 for the whole night. Be aware that the HIV infection rate is very high among prostitutes in Ethiopia (some estimate up to 50%), and is ever on the increase. See also Attitudes Towards Local Women and the boxed text 'AIDS in Africa' earlier in this section.

Some parts of Ethiopia are relatively accessible. All the sites on the historical route are easily reached by comfortable internal flights, and passengers in wheelchairs can be accommodated. To reach other areas of the country, you'll be relying on buses or 4WD vehicles. Car rental with driver is easily organised – though expensive in Addis Ababa. Roads can be rough in parts and journeys long, hot and hard, particularly on the back.

Taxis are widely available in the large towns and are good for getting around, though none have wheelchair access. In Addis Ababa at least two top-end hotels have facilities for wheelchair-users; a few other hotels have lifts. However, Addis Ababa's potholed streets and pavements aren't very wheelchair-friendly, and kerb ramps are nonexistent.

Outside the capital, facilities are lacking, but many hotels are bungalow affairs, so at least are easily accessible for wheelchair users.

Organisations

See the Access-Able Travel Source Web site (www.access-able.com) for general information for disabled travellers. Before leaving home, disabled visitors can get in touch with their national support organisation, listed here. Ask for the 'travel officer', who may have a list of travel agents that specialise in tours for the disabled.

Access – The Foundation for Accessibility by the Disabled (☎ 516-887 5798) PO Box 356, Malverne, NY 11565, USA

CNFLRH (☎ 01-53-80-66-66) 236 rue de Tolbiac, Paris

NICAN (☎ 02-6285 3713, fax 6285 3714) PO Box 407, Curtin, ACT 2605, Australia

Royal Association for Disability & Rehabilitation (☎ 020-7250 3222, fax 7250 0212) 12 City Forum, 250 City Rd, London EC1V 8AF, UK. Produces holiday 'fact packs' (UK£2), which cover planning, insurance, useful organisations, transport, equipment and specialised accommodation.

Society for the Advancement of Travel for the Handicapped (SATH) (☎ 212-447 7284) 347 Fifth Ave, No 610, New York, NY 10016, USA

SENIOR TRAVELLERS

Traditionally, older citizens are accorded great respect in the Horn, and in many tribal groups around Ethiopia, older men constitute the village 'council', acting as judges, mediators and negotiators in daily affairs. You'll be accorded a warm welcome.

One tip: bring some photos of your family with you. The family is the single most important thing in the lives of most Ethiopians, and the sharing of such details is also a gesture of friendship.

Older travellers interested in Ethiopia's culture have long formed the bulk of its tourism. Ethiopia is reasonably geared up to meet the requirements of this age group with adequate hotels, restaurants and medical care – at least in the capital and along the historical route. However, if you're dependent on special medication, don't forget to bring plenty of supplies with you.

Taxis are readily available in Addis Ababa, and comfortable cars can be hired for trips outside the capital. Travel by road

can be hard-going, particularly for those who suffer from back problems, so it's a good idea to opt for some internal flights where possible, and not try and do too much in too short a time – advice good for travellers of all ages!

TRAVEL WITH CHILDREN

Ethiopians are very welcoming and open towards children, and there are no particular reasons for not taking them with you. However, many useful facilities for babies – such as cots in hotels, safety seats in hired cars, highchairs in restaurants and nappy-changing facilities – are almost totally lacking outside the better hotels in Addis Ababa. There are no childcare agencies either.

Items such as disposable nappies, baby food, milk powder and toys are available in some of the expat supermarkets of Addis Ababa (albeit rather expensive), but don't forget to bring high-protection sunscreen. Medical facilities are good too, and in Addis Ababa there's a special 24-hour children's clinic with fully qualified paediatricians.

Diarrhoea and vomiting are the most common problems affecting children in the Horn; treatment is the same as for adults, but is given more intensively to children. Useful items for children and babies include antibiotic eardrops, eye baths and wet wipes.

The hottest months are probably best avoided, since toddlers and babies are more susceptible to the heat than adults.

Lonely Planet's *Travel with Children*, by Maureen Wheeler, contains detailed information about planning 'happy' family holidays.

DANGERS & ANNOYANCES

Compared with many African countries, Ethiopia – even Addis Ababa – is a very safe place. Serious or violent crime is rare. Outside the capital, the risk of petty crime drops still further. In order to avoid becoming the victim of petty crime, look always as if you know where you're going. Thieves and con artists get wind of an uncertain newcomer in a minute. Like anywhere in the world, you should avoid walking alone around Addis Ababa at night. Taxis are easy to find and are not too expensive.

The biggest source of complaint among travellers is the constant attention – shouting, comments and stares – that white skin seems to attract from some locals (see Mobbing & Faranji Frenzy following). However, this is almost always harmless, and is more than equalled by the continual kindness, generosity and hospitality shown you by the majority of Ethiopians.

Theft

In all the big towns, you should take care at the bus stations.

When camping out, security is not usually a problem, but in some parts of the Omo Valley region, where raiding is a tradition and a means of survival for the people, things can disappear in the night.

For information on carrying around money, see Security under Money earlier in this section. See also Dangers & Annoyances in the Addis Ababa section.

Shiftas

In some of the remoter areas, such as the Ogaden Desert in the south-east, and near some Sudanese border regions in the west, *shiftas* (bandits) are still reported – often ex-soldiers who have hung onto their weapons and mercenary lifestyle. In a few areas, government troops sometimes come into contact with local political opposition groups. However, the majority of such places lie far off the beaten track of most travellers.

In 1997, there were also reports of banditry on the train between Addis Ababa and Djibouti, and a few grenade attacks launched in public places in Addis Ababa and Harar. However, such incidents seem to be isolated and have not been repeated since.

If you're concerned, or are planning to visit more remote regions, your embassy in Addis Ababa is the best place for information on security in the country. The British embassy has a 'travellers advice' notice board that is updated regularly.

Scams & Rip-Offs

There are relatively few scams operating in Ethiopia (see the boxed text 'Siren Scam'

under Dangers & Annoyances in the Addis Ababa section).

Various hangers-on are found: 'friendly' Ethiopians will offer to take you to local bars or night spots, and once they have won your confidence, will ask you for a loan that will be 'repaid the following day'. Most such confidence tricks are pretty harmless and pretty transparent, but you should be aware of them.

Other common approaches are by those with 'hard luck' stories, or those soliciting sponsorship for education either in or outside Ethiopia – though some may be genuine. Women travellers may even get the odd marriage proposal if they're very lucky.

Look out for fake antiques in the shops (see Customs earlier in this section). Not only will you be charged high prices for them, but you're likely to have them denied export permission or confiscated at the airport!

At the Airport

At the airport in Addis Ababa, you will be greeted by a rabble of taxi touts, who will gather you up the minute you set foot out of the airport to feed you to one of the drivers. Taxis from the airport should cost no more than Birr20–30, but you may well be asked Birr100 or more. Make sure you negotiate the fare before you get in, and if the driver refuses to negotiate, just walk away; the price soon starts to fall.

There have been reports of airport taxi drivers 'hijacking' travellers and taking them to a hotel where commission is paid. Don't listen to any reports of 'fires', 'married couple restrictions' (dropped after the downfall of the Derg) or 'closed roads'. Always choose a hotel you want to stay in before you get into a taxi, and insist on it.

Most taxi drivers are very helpful, friendly and honest, though you'll certainly be seen as more lucrative custom than Ethiopian passengers.

Bribery & Bureaucracy

While some processes – such as changing money at banks, or waiting to make a telephone call or get a visa extension – can seem to take forever, bureaucracy in Ethiopia is not as bad as people make out. Sometimes, as a foreigner you may even be given priority or pushed to the front of the queue. Bribes are very rarely extracted from foreigners.

One tip: deference to figures of authority is an important part of Amhara cultural etiquette. If you're polite and deferential to policemen and officials in general, you'll be amazed how much more forthcoming passage or permission is. If you're a woman, a smile works wonders.

Don't confuse – as some travellers do – friendly questions such as 'What is your country?' with interrogation. In Ethiopia, such questions are a normal part of making an acquaintance.

Begging & Giving

Many travellers find begging one of the most distressing aspects of travel in Third World countries. After years of civil war, famine and population displacement, Ethiopia has its fair share of beggars.

In Addis Ababa particularly, there's an almost Goya-esque array of beggars: barefooted women with tiny babies, filthy street urchins, naked and raving madmen, cripples without crutches or wheelchairs, and badly maimed and mutilated war veterans.

In many countries, including Ethiopia, travellers often complain about being 'targeted' by beggars because they are foreign. However, after the high-profile aid efforts of such events as Live Aid, that's pretty inevitable. Unfortunately, the old Ethiopian pride, self-reliance, traditions and customs have all been greatly undermined by these (albeit well-meaning) efforts – foreigners are now seen as dispensers of charity and aid.

It's a difficult issue whether to give or not to give, to whom and how much. Not a bad rule of thumb is to give only to those who can't earn a living – such as the disabled, the ill, the elderly and the blind.

Most Ethiopians give small coins to beggars – doing so is thought to bestow a blessing on the giver. It is traditional to give, particularly outside churches or on special saints' days. If you don't want to donate money, say instead *exzabier yisteh/yistesh*

(m/f) (God bless you); this is a polite and accepted way of declining to give.

Never hand out pens or sweets to children. This only encourages the 'Santa Claus syndrome' in which all white people are seen as philanthropists of limitless resources. Hand-outs not only unfairly raise the expectations of the locals, but are likely to ruin the trips of travellers after you. Above all, it teaches children to beg, and if they start to profit by begging, parents may well begin to send their children out to beg rather than to school.

If your feelings of guilt are upsetting you, a much better idea is to give a donation to one of the local charities in Addis Ababa, or support the charitable gift shops. Many are excellent and most of the funds – unlike those of some international organisations – go straight to those in need. For the street children of Addis Ababa, meal tickets can be bought from Hope Enterprises (see the boxed text 'Hope Springs Eternal' under Shopping in the Addis Ababa section).

False Guides

Occasionally, a 'false guide' may offer his services. After latching on to you, he will bore you senseless, then expect you to pay a large fee for the privilege. Be suspicious of anyone who approaches you unasked, particularly at the exit of bus stations etc; there is almost always an ulterior motive. Be polite but firm. Laughter and humour is the most disarming and effective response to extortionate demands for fees.

If you do need directions, approach someone yourself. Most Ethiopians are exceptionally friendly and polite, and will bend over backwards to help you if appealed to.

Mobbing & Faranji Frenzy

The most notorious – and undoubtedly the most wearing – annoyance in Ethiopia is the locals' 'faranji frenzy' that greets most travellers to Ethiopia, particularly those travelling by bus, alone or in remoter parts. Travellers quite often find themselves surrounded by hoards of screaming, giggling or shouting children. For the new arrival as well as the old-timer, the phenomenon is in turns distressing, exhausting, infuriating and demoralising. Unfortunately you never quite get used to it.

There is no clear response either. Ignoring it or, even better, treating it with humour is probably the best answer. Anger only provokes children more. An Amharic *hid!* (clear off!) for a boy, *hiji!* for a girl or *hidu!* for a group is the Ethiopian response, and sends children scuttling, but it can have the reverse effect, and is considered rather harsh from a foreigner.

If you're a captive audience – such as when you're waiting for a bus – the best response is to break the 'animal in a zoo' feeling. Try and communicate with the children by asking their name: *semesh/semeh man no?* for a boy/girl, or with sign language. You'll soon transform the howling mob into delightful and charming individuals.

The shout of 'You, you!' from children as well as teenagers is the one that most raises the hackles of travellers. However, it's worth bearing in mind that the Amharic equivalent *(Ante!/Anchee!)* is a common – though not the politest – way of getting someone's attention. In other words, it's not as aggressive and rude as it sounds in English.

It's worth bearing in mind too that western travellers have only recently started to return to Ethiopia. Much attention results from the natural curiosity of children. Above all, it is almost *never* aggressive, or even hostile – unlike reactions to white people in many previously colonised African countries.

Most importantly, it may give you (in the author's opinion) a very useful insight into what it may be like for minority groups with different skin colours in your home country. The major difference is that in Ethiopia, the undue attention is motivated by curiosity, not, as in the West, by hostility or suspicion born from racism. It's a lesson you may never forget – perhaps everyone should spend a couple of weeks in Ethiopia.

Land Mines
Outside the capital, and after years of civil war, the biggest threat still is land mines.

Despite the government's best efforts – defusing more than 5000 mines – thousands still litter the countryside, and continue to sporadically kill and maim the population.

High-risk areas are confined to the sites of old battle fronts, but there is obviously some element of risk anywhere fighting has occurred. Areas such as the Ogaden region, the vicinity to the east and south of Harar and some of the roads leading north from Addis Ababa to the province of Tigray are known mined areas. Check with the local government or local village officials before travelling in remote areas. Keep where possible to paved routes, and never stray off the road.

If you're trekking, keep to well-trodden tracks, and avoid trekking in riverbeds. Avoid above all the area around bridges, water crossings and the approaches to villages. And forget about 'war souvenirs': you shouldn't touch anything. A useful phrase when out trekking is *Fenjy alle?* (Are there mines here?). The great majority of travellers should have nothing to fear from mines. Popular trekking area such as the Simien and Bale Mountains National Parks are perfectly safe. Trekkers keen to explore other areas should at least be aware of the risk.

Dangerous Animals
The best-known 'dangerous animals' such as the rhino, elephant and buffalo are confined to very restricted areas in Ethiopia such as the Omo Valley – you'd be very lucky to see one at all.

The hippopotamus is responsible for more deaths in Africa than any other animal. The rules are simple: stay away from any densely vegetated shore area. Hippos are not aggressive per se, but will trample anybody and anything that gets between them and the water – their refuge when threatened or frightened. If in a boat, steer well clear of mothers with young, who will attack if made to feel threatened.

Beware of the vervet monkeys and baboons in some of the camping grounds; they've become pretty deft thieves and will enter a tent or jump on a picnic after food.

The crocodile poses a danger on rivers and on riverbanks close to the water. Stay away

Smokers' Snub

Until quite recently, smoking was regarded as a grave sin in Ethiopia. The country's clergy and older generation still consider the habit as rather wicked. It is not known for sure why Ethiopians harbour this prejudice. Traditionally, it is said that on the day of the Crucifixion, all plants except the tobacco plant withered and died, and that the plant sprouted from the guts of the heretic Arius.

Even today, smokers never light up before a priest or before their parents, and confine their puffing to hotels and bars. Travellers are best advised to follow suit and to be similarly discreet.

from both, if crocodiles are known in the area.

The spotted hyaena is common in rural areas in the Horn and is a notorious scavenger. If camping, you should sleep inside a tent, or at least close to a campfire.

See also the Health section earlier for information on rabies and insect-borne medical problems, and Hazardous Marine Life in the special section 'Marine Life in the Red Sea'.

Snakes Apart from the python, snakes are not often seen in the Horn. But wearing boots, socks and long trousers will minimise the risk of being bitten when trekking in undergrowth where snakes may be present.

Be particularly careful when collecting firewood, or when climbing (and putting your hands into holes and crevices). Rocky crevices are the favoured habitat of Africa's most dangerous snake, the puff adder.

Even if you are bitten, most snakes are nonvenomous; those that are only dispense poison in about 50% of cases, and very few bites are capable of killing an adult human. Antivenins are usually available.

Immediately wrap the bitten limb tightly, as you would for a sprained ankle, and then attach a splint to immobilise it. Try and keep the bitten area below heart level, and the victim still, until medical help arrives. Avoid aspirin or alcohol, though paracetamol is

OK. Tourniquets and sucking out the poison are now comprehensively discredited.

The dead snake may help with identification, but don't attempt to catch it if there is a possibility of being bitten again.

LEGAL MATTERS

Foreign visitors are subject to the laws of the country in which they are travelling. If arrested, in theory you must be brought to court within 48 hours of apprehension. You have the right to talk to someone from your embassy as well as a lawyer or other professional adviser.

Drugs & Alcohol

Penalties for possession, use or trafficking of illegal drugs (including hashish) are strictly enforced in Ethiopia. Convicted offenders can expect long jail sentences, fines and possible confiscation of personal property.

Consumption of the mildly stimulating leaf qat is permitted in Ethiopia (see the boxed texts 'Chat Among the Pigeons' in the East of Addis Ababa section later in this chapter and 'Qat & Mouse' in the Djibouti chapter). It is particularly appreciated by the Muslim population in the east of the country, especially around the town of Harar, and also in Addis Ababa. Consumption is definitely on the increase.

Alcohol cannot be served to anyone under 18 years of age in Ethiopia. Disturbance caused by those under the influence of alcohol is punishable by three months' to one year's imprisonment. Driving while under the influence attracts a fine of Birr140.

BUSINESS HOURS

Government offices are open from 8.30 am to 12.30 pm (to 11.30 am Friday) and 1.30 to 5.30 pm weekdays. Private organisations and most NGOs are open from 8 am to 1 pm and 2 to 5 pm weekdays.

Most shops are open from 9 am to 1 pm and 3 to 6 pm Monday to Saturday. Restaurants in the capital and larger towns open generally between noon and around 2 pm and from 6.30 pm to around 10.30 pm daily except Sunday. In the rural areas, restaurants may stop serving – or just run out of food – as early as 8.30 pm.

For bank and post office hours, see Banks and Post & Communications earlier in this section.

PUBLIC HOLIDAYS & SPECIAL EVENTS

Many religious and secular festivals in Ethiopia are the occasion of much pageantry, feasting and dancing; if you get a chance to witness a public holiday or special event, don't miss it. Meskel and Timkat are probably the most colourful events.

Ethiopia's public holidays can be divided into three categories: national secular holidays, Christian Orthodox holidays, and Islamic holidays.

Because the country follows the Julian calendar of 13 months (see Calendar earlier in this section), some events trail those of the western Gregorian calendar by around one week. The following dates are correct on the Gregorian calendar.

National Holidays

National holidays include:

Victory of Adwa Commemoration Day 2 March
Ethiopian Patriots' Victory Day (also known as Liberation Day) 6 April
International Labour Day 1 May
Downfall of the Derg 28 May

Major Ethiopian Orthodox Festivals

Major Ethiopian Orthodox festivals include:

Leddet (also known as Genna or Christmas) 6–7 January. Less important than Timkat and Meskel, but still significant. The faithful attend all-night church services, often moving from one church to another. On Christmas day, the traditional games of *genna* (a kind of hockey) and sometimes *gugs* (a kind of polo) are played, along with horse racing. Priests don their full regalia. Lalibela is one of the best places to experience Leddet; Addis Ababa is also good.

Timkat (Epiphany, celebrating Christ's baptism) 19 January (three days). The most colourful festival of the year. The church *tabots* (replicas of the Ark of the Covenant) are taken to a nearby

---

Colourful Costumes

Don't miss the chance to attend one of the colourful local festivals.

During the major orthodox festivals large groups of Oromo horsemen – long famed for their skills on the battlefield – gather together attired in the traditional warrior outfit: a lion's mane or gelada baboon head-dress, hippopotamus hide shields, spears and brightly caparisoned horses.

Amharas dressed as noble warriors don richly embroidered capes over satin tunics and white jodhpurs.

At religious festivals, the colourful regalia of the priests can be seen. With them come a veritable sea of embroidered umbrellas and tall processional crosses. Some priests, framed in a kind of canopy, symbolise the sacred tabot or Ark of the Covenant.

《《《《《《《《《《《《《《《《《《《《《《《《《《《《《《《《《《《《《

---

body of water on the afternoon of the eve of Timkat. During the night, the priests and faithful participate in a kind of vigil around the tabots. The following morning, the crowds gather around the water, which is blessed, then splashed onto them; religious vows are renewed. The tabot is then paraded back to the church accompanied by much singing and dancing. Gonder is considered the best place to be on Timkat; Addis Ababa is also good.

Good Friday March/April. From Thursday evening before Good Friday, the faithful fast until the Easter service, which ends at 3 am on Easter Sunday.

Fasika (Orthodox Easter) March/April (one day). Fasika marks the end of a vegetarian fast of 55 days, in which no animal product is eaten. Officially, nothing should be eaten until the daily church service finishes around 3 pm. In the past, many of Ethiopia's enemies took advantage of the fasting period to inflict heavy casualties on its weakened armies.

Kiddus Yohannes (New Year's Day) 11 September. Ethiopian New Year (also known as Enkutatash) is an important family and social event. Traditionally, new clothes are bought and worn, particularly by children, and relatives and friends are visited. Special feasts are prepared. The traditional game of *gugs* can sometimes be seen.

Meskel (Finding of the True Cross) 27 September (two days). The most colourful festival after Timkat. Bonfires are built topped by a cross to which flowers are tied – most commonly the

ETHIOPIA

Meskel daisy. After the bonfires are blessed, they are lit, and dancing and singing begins around them. Priests don their full regalia. Addis Ababa, Gonder and Aksum are good places to experience Meskel.

Festival of Maryam Zion, date varies but is around the end of November. This festival is exclusive to Aksum, celebrating the namesake of the famous church St Maryam of Zion. The tabot of the church (believed by Ethiopians to be the original Ark of the Covenant) is brought out and there is much singing and dancing (see Aksum in the North of Addis Ababa section).

Kulubi Gabriel 28 December. Although not on the official religious holiday list, large numbers of Ethiopians make a pilgrimage to the venerated Kulubi Gabriel church near Dire Dawa in the east (see the boxed text 'Kulubi Gabriel' in the East of Addis Ababa section). If you're in the area, don't miss it.

Islamic Holidays

Islamic holidays follow a lunar cycle, so the dates change each year. See the table of Islamic holidays under Public Holidays & Special Events in the Facts for the Visitor section of the Djibouti chapter.

ACTIVITIES
Trekking

Trekking is the best-known and most developed activity in Ethiopia. The Simien Mountains are famous for their spectacular gorges, while the Bale Mountains are known for their excellent wildlife (birds and large mammals). For more information, see Flora & Fauna and National Parks in the Facts about Ethiopia section, and also the Simien and Bale Mountains sections later in this book.

White-Water Rafting & Kayaking

Rafting began in Ethiopia as early as the 1970s, when a Colorado expedition rafted a good part of the Omo River in southwestern Ethiopia. Since then, commercial rafting trips have made similar descents almost every year. See Organised Tours in the Getting Around section.

The Omo River season is from September to October, after the heavy rains. Tours most commonly last from one to three weeks, and their main attraction is not the white water (classed as a tame three or four on the US scale), but the exposure to wildlife (particularly birds) and the tribal groups (particularly those along the Omo River).

Kayaking is not yet developed in Ethiopia. In theory, excellent kayaking could be had on many of Ethiopia's rivers, including the Blue Nile, Omo and Awash Rivers, but it's certainly not for the inexperienced. A trip will need to be very well planned, well equipped and well backed up, as kayaking can be a very risky activity. Start with the ETC, which will put you in touch with experienced expat kayakers in Ethiopia.

Bird-Watching

Various tour agencies both inside and outside Ethiopia offer birding tours. See Organised Tours in the Getting Around section as well as the special section 'Birds in Ethiopia'.

Fishing

Ethiopia's lakes and rivers are home to over 200 species of freshwater fish including very large catfish (up to 18kg), tilapia, large barbus, tigerfish, the brown and rainbow trout and the Nile perch (known for their 'fight').

Fly-fishing, bait fishing with float and leger, freelining, threadline spinning and trolling are all permitted fishing practices, but you'll need to be totally self-sufficient as far as equipment is concerned.

Popular fishing spots include Lake Tana and around the Blue Nile Falls in the north of the country, the Rift Valley lakes in the south, and the Baro River in the west. Fishing is permitted everywhere in Ethiopia, with the exception of rivers in the Bale Mountains National Park, where endemic species are found.

COURSES

Amharic language and dance classes are available in the capital. Unless you're spending long periods there, classes will need to be scheduled with a private tutor, which can be expensive (see Courses in the Addis Ababa section).

WORK

Travellers in Ethiopia on tourist visas are not allowed to seek or take up employment.

If you're planning to work officially, you have to apply to the Ministry of Labour and Social Affairs for a work permit, and to the Department of Immigration in the Ministry of the Interior for a residence permit. Both ministries are found in Addis Ababa.

ACCOMMODATION

Tourism is still relatively undeveloped in Ethiopia, and accommodation is fairly limited outside the major towns. There are not yet any hostels, homestays, or university or rental accommodation available to travellers.

Camping

Unless you're planning to explore the very remote regions, or to do quite a bit of trekking, camping equipment is probably more of a hassle than a help in Ethiopia. Cheap hotels are available almost everywhere, and tents can be hired in the capital. In theory, if you have your own tent, you are free to camp anywhere, apart from near the obvious off-limits sites, such as military installations. There are a few 'established' camping grounds around the country, such as in some of the national parks, but most lack any kind of facilities and consist of little more than a clearing beside a river. It is essential to treat drinking water at the sites.

Some of the tour agencies based in Addis Ababa offer fully equipped camping trips (including a guide, cook, vehicle and driver), and also hire out camping equipment (see Organised Tours in the Getting Around section).

When camping out, security is not usually a problem, except for some parts of the Omo Valley region, where raiding is a tradition and a means of survival for the people, and things can disappear in the night.

Remember to ensure that the area in which you wish to camp is free of land mines, and beware of dangerous animals (see Dangers & Annoyances earlier in this section). Take care also that you don't start fires, and that all litter leaves with you (see Responsible Tourism earlier in this section).

Popular places for camping trips include the Bale and Simien Mountains, Lake Langano, and the Omo Valley, where there are very few hotels. In the future, it is hoped that the excellent, 'ecofriendly', NGO Farm Africa camp on Lake Langano in the south will reopen under private ownership.

Hotels

Hotels are plentiful and cheap at all levels, though facilities are lacking outside the larger towns. Maintenance is not usually a high priority, and the best hotels in the budget and mid-range categories are often those that have just opened. If you hear of a new hotel in town, it may well be the best place to head. Note that in Ethiopia a 'hotel' is more often than not only a restaurant.

Faranjis (foreigners) are often charged a different rate to Ethiopians. This isn't as inequitable as it sounds. Ethiopians could never afford to pay similar rates, you'll always get the best rooms, facilities and service, and prices are still incredibly reasonable. Some hotels charge tax (up to 20%) on top of room prices; check in advance.

In Ethiopia, a room with a double bed is usually called a 'single', and a room with twin beds a 'double'. Prices for one and two people are often the same. In this book, the usual single and double definitions apply.

Hotels vary hugely in standard. Always take a peek at the room (and bathroom) before accepting it. Unfortunately, few owners of the budget hotels speak much English; the LP phrasebook really is a good investment. A simple phrase is *alga/shawer alle?* – Do you have a bed/shower?

During the high season (October to January) and particularly over the major festivals in towns such as Lalibela and Aksum, some of the mid-range to top-end hotels quickly fill up with tour groups. Reservations should be made as far in advance as possible – six months is not too long!

There are no left-luggage facilities currently in Addis Ababa, though most of the hotels catering to foreign travellers provide a pretty safe and reliable service for no extra charge.

Budget Cheap hotels make up around 90% of hotels in Ethiopia and usually consist of spartan rooms, little or no furniture and a communal toilet and shower. Many invariably double as brothels, but in light of Ethiopia's permissive society, they are less seedy and surreptitious than similar hotels in other countries. Conversely, a few of the Muslim-run hotels permit only married or single-sex couples to share rooms. Most budget hotels cost US$1–2; sometimes there is a small extra charge for the use of the communal shower.

In rural areas, 'hotel' accommodation consists sometimes of little more than a bed in a hut, without running water, electricity or even facilities for washing.

Mid-Range Many of the so-called 'tourist class' hotels around the country were nationalised in the 1970s and '80s under the socialist Derg, and are run by government chains. In most of the government hotels, room rates are given in US dollars. You can pay in birr but the rate will be pegged to the daily dollar equivalent. Prices range from US$15 to US$40, and facilities usually include a room with private shower, a restaurant and parking. Though not bad and reasonably clean, many are rather run-down, soulless and lugubrious places, and very rarely offer good value for money. Currently, most are in the process of being sold off to the private sector, which should eventually see improvements.

Rooms can be booked through the NTO. The main government chains include the Ghion Hotel Group, the Ras Hotel Group, the Wabe Shebele Group and the Ethiopia Hotel Group. The Bekele Mola Hotel Group is a private chain that offers similar accommodation.

Most of the larger towns also have private hotels, which offer clean rooms with private bathrooms; many are much better value that the state-owned hotels, costing US$2–5 per night.

Top End The new, five-star 'Luxury Collection' Sheraton Hotel is Addis Ababa's pride and joy, and rivals almost anything in the world for facilities and comfort. In many of the larger towns, and along the historical route, private top-end hotels are mushrooming, and also offer good facilities.

FOOD
Restaurants

In Addis Ababa there is a wide selection of restaurants from Indian and Chinese to Italian and Armenian (see Places to Eat in the Addis Ababa section). These cater to quite a large expat community issuing from various countries, and the standard is often very high. The prices are very reasonable by western standards (but a 15% tax may be added to the bill – check in advance). Mains cost around Birr25–55 even in the most expensive restaurants. Wine normally costs from Birr50 for local varieties and from Birr120 for imported varieties..

Outside Addis Ababa, you'll find little more than local fare. If you just don't take to it – and short-stay visitors often don't – you can usually find an Italian-style dish somewhere on the menu: a simple spaghetti bolognese, for example, or lasagne. Prices are very

---

Edible Cutlery

However rude you are about injera, it does its job. Slightly bitter, it goes well with spicy food; like bread, it's filling; and like a kind of pancake, it's good for wrapping around small pieces of food and mopping up juices. It's also easier to manipulate than rice and doesn't fall apart like bread – quite a clever invention, really. And no need for plates or cutlery either (or tablecloths).

Although all injera may look to you like old grey kitchen flannel, grades and nuances exist. With a bit of time and perseverance, you may well become a bit of an injera connoisseur. Low-quality injera is traditionally dark, coarse and sometimes very thick, and made from millet or even sorghum. Good-quality injera is pale (the paler the better), regular in thickness, smooth (free of husks etc) and always, always made with the indigenous Ethiopian cereal *tef*. Because tef grows only in the highlands, the best injera is traditionally found there, and highlanders tend to be rather snooty about lesser lowland versions.

cheap: a meal for two rarely costs more than about US$1. In the large towns, the tourist-class hotels have a greater selection of faranji food. However, meat cutlet served with boiled potatoes and cabbage can get a bit wearisome after the 100th time, particularly as it wasn't outstanding in the first place.

For standard restaurant hours, see Business Hours earlier in this section. If you roll into town late, the budget hotels often have a *buna beat* (coffee house) attached to them, which can usually rustle up some sort of snack or meal.

In many of the towns, you will find a *keak beat* (cake shop), which serves an array of pastries and fresh fruit juices. Outside the large towns, the cakes can be a bit dry or bland, but the places aren't a bad bet for breakfast, serving coffee and tea. Many are open pretty early (from around 6 am).

Traditional Food

Like its wildlife, many of Ethiopia's dishes are 'endemic', and take a bit of getting to know. Ethiopia's food provokes strong reaction. Short-term visitors on the whole loathe it, longer-term visitors usually loathe it – then come to love it. Some loathe it – and go on loathing it.

Contrary to popular belief, Ethiopian cooking is quite varied. Though restaurants seem to offer exactly the same fare, other dishes are often available. It's worth experimenting too – prices are so cheap, you can afford to make the odd mistake!

In some of the smaller restaurants, menus are only available in Amharic. If you want to ask if something's on the menu, just add an *alle?* For example, *doro wat alle?* – Is there doro wat?

Vegetarian Ethiopians are rapacious carnivores and dishes usually consist of nothing but meat. If you're vegetarian you should order alternative dishes in advance. Cabbage and chickpea dishes are quite easily and quickly prepared.

On Wednesdays and Fridays, vegetarians can breathe easy, since these are the traditional fasting days, when no animal products are eaten. Vegetarian dishes most commonly consist of lentils, potatoes, cabbage, spinach and beetroot. Ask for *atkilt-b-dabbo* (vegetables with bread). A useful phrase for vegetarians is *sega albellam* (I don't eat meat).

You may even want to consider travelling during a fasting period, such as the one before Fasika (see Public Holidays & Special Events earlier in this section). By the same token, nonvegetarians may want to avoid this period, since vegetarian dishes are often all that's on offer, except in the fancier hotels that cater to foreigners.

Injera You're never likely to forget your first exposure to *injera*, the national bread-like staple. It serves as the base of every meal, spread out like a large, thin pancake. Food is simply heaped on top of it. An American tourist famously once mistook it for the tablecloth. Occasionally, injera is served rolled up, resembling remarkably those nice little hot towels served on the better airlines.

Would You Like Worms with That?

The big dilemma facing travellers is whether to eat raw meat, or give it a wide berth. There's no doubt that there's a risk of picking up a parasite (see Health earlier in this section), particularly outside Addis Ababa, where the meat is not 'certified'. However, unless you're part of a tour group, you're very likely to be invited to eat kitfo or raw meat with an Ethiopian, and it provides a great insight into Ethiopian etiquette and culture.

The author indulged voraciously throughout her many months of research in Ethiopia, and never had the least problem. But the risk is certainly there and is considered high outside Addis Ababa. The main thing is to be aware of parasite symptoms and swiftly swallow some medicine if you do suspect some unwelcome squatter within.

Food Glossary

Some terms, such as *arrosto* (roasted), *bistecca ai ferri* (grilled steak), *cabretto* (goat or kid), *costata* (chop), *cotoletta* (cutlet), *manzo* (beef), *scaloppina* (escalope) and *trippa* (tripe), are leftovers from the Italian Occupation.

All of the following are served with good-old injera unless indicated otherwise.

asa wat – freshwater fish served in a hot berbere sauce

atkilt-b-dabbo *(vegie)* – vegetables with bread

awazi – a kind of mustard sauce

berbere – as many as 16 spices or more go into making the famous berbere, the red powder responsible for giving much Ethiopian food its 'kick'. Many families prepare their own special recipe, often passed down from mother to daughter for generations, and proudly adhered to.

beyainatu – a small portion of everything on the menu (translates to 'of every type'), also known by its Italian name *secondo misto*

dabbo fir fir *(vegie)* – bits of bread with butter and berbere

derek tibs – meat (usually lamb) fried and served *derek* (without sauce)

doro wat – chicken drumstick or wing accompanied by a hard-boiled egg served in a hot sauce of butter, onion, chilli, cardamom and berbere; considered the most sophisticated of the wat dishes and almost the national dish of Ethiopia – the best are outstanding!

dulet – minced tripe, liver and lean beef fried in butter, onions, chilli, cardamom and pepper

enkulal tibs *(vegie)* – a kind of omelette made with eggs, green and red peppers, tomatoes and sometimes onions served with *dabbo* (bread) and great for breakfast

enset *(vegie)* – false-banana bread, a staple food (see the boxed text 'Enduring Enset' in the South of Addis Ababa section)

fatira – savoury pastries

Traditionally, injera is served on a communal tray on a *mesob* (a colourful, mushroom-shaped table, woven like a basket). You simply tear off a piece of injera with your right hand (see the boxed text 'Eating Etiquette' later in this section), and wrap it around the food served with it. Ask for more injera if you want it (there's no extra charge).

Wat Injera is most often accompanied by a *wat*, which resembles a kind of stew, though vegetables tend to be conspicuous by their absence. In most Ethiopian dishes – with the exception of fasting fare – you'll find little more than a few flakes of chopped onion, garlic and perhaps tomato, if you're very lucky. Meat is considered a luxury; vegetables are for poor households only.

Lamb is the most common meat constituent of wat in the highlands; beef wat is found in the large towns, and goat wat is most often encountered in the arid lowlands. Ethiopian Christians as well as Muslims do not eat pork. Just to confuse you, the word for beef is *lam*, the word for lamb is *beg*.

Much tourist literature describes Ethiopian food as hot. It's nothing compared to a good *vindaloo* or similar Indian dish, but it has a kick, and it may provoke a dab or two at your nostrils with a handkerchief. Most travellers take it in their stride. *Kai wat* tends to be spicier than other dishes. If you don't care for hot food, ask for *alicha* (mild) food, which is almost always available.

Tere Sega Considered something of a luxury in Ethiopia is *tere sega* (raw meat), which is traditionally served by the wealthy at weddings and other celebrations. Some

Food Glossary

genfo *(vegie)* – barley or wheat porridge served with butter and berbere

injera *(vegie)* – kind of large pancake (see the boxed text 'Edible Cutlery')

kai wat – lamb, goat or beef cooked in a hot berbere sauce

kekel – boiled meat

kitfo – minced beef or lamb like the French steak tartare, usually served warmed (but not cooked!) in butter, rosemary and berbere (see the boxed text 'Would You Like Worms with That?' earlier in this section)

kotcho *(vegie)* – like enset; served with kitfo

kwalima – sausage served on ceremonial occasions

kwanta – strips of beef rubbed in chilli, butter, salt and berbere then usually hung up and dried

mahabaroui – a mixture of dishes including half a roast chicken

melasena senber tibs – beef tongue and tripe fried with berbere and onion

messer *(vegie)* – a kind of lentil curry made with onions, chillies and various spices

minchet abesh – minced beef or lamb in a hot berbere sauce

shiro *(vegie)* – chickpea or bean puree lightly spiced, served on fasting days

tibs – sliced lamb, pan fried in butter, garlic, onion and sometimes tomato

tere sega – raw meat served with various spicy sauces

wat – stew (see Wat in this section)

ye som megeb *(vegie)* – a selection of different vegetable dishes, served on fasting days

yinjera fir fir *(vegie)* – torn-up bits of injera mixed with butter and berbere

zilzil tibs – strips of beef, fried and served slightly crunchy with *awazi* sauce

---

restaurants specialise in it, and resemble butcher shops with carcasses hung up close to the entrance, and men in bloodied overalls brandishing carving knives. The restaurants are not as gruesome as they sound: the carcass is to demonstrate that the meat is absolutely fresh, and the men in overalls are there to guarantee you get exactly the piece you fancy – two assurances you wouldn't necessarily get in the west.

Having selected your slab of meat, you're then handed a sharp, curved knife and a plate. *Awazi* and *berbere* powder are daubed on the plates; these make terrific dips. Served with a good hearty bottle of Ethiopian red, and enjoyed with Ethiopian friends, it's a ritual not to be missed – at least not for red-meat eaters.

Contrary to popular belief, Ethiopians do not and have never carved meat from a liv-ing animal. James Bruce, the famous 18th-century Scottish explorer, was responsible for perpetuating this myth.

Kitfo The next big 'treat' for the ordinary Ethiopian – akin to smoked salmon in the west – is *kitfo*. The best-quality and leanest meat is reserved for this dish, and is minced up then warmed in a pan with a little butter, berbere and sometimes *tosin* (rosemary). Like the French steak tartare which it greatly resembles, it can be bland and disgusting, or tasty and divine. If you're ravenous after a hard day's travelling, it's just the thing, as it's very filling.

Traditionally, it's just *leb leb* (warmed not cooked), though you can ask for it to be *betam leb leb* (well cooked). A *kitfo special* is served with *aib* (like a kind of dry cottage cheese) and *kosta* (minced spinach).

The Coffee Ceremony

The coffee ceremony is the best feature of Ethiopian hospitality, and an invitation to attend a ceremony is a mark of friendship or respect – though it's not for those in a hurry.

When you're replete after a meal, the ceremony begins. Scattered on the ground is freshly cut grass, 'to bring in the freshness and fragrance of nature', and nearby there's an incense burner smoking with *etan* (gum). The 'host' sits on a stool before a tiny charcoal stove.

Coffee beans are first of all roasted in a pan. As the smoke rises, it is considered polite to draw it towards you, inhale it deeply and express great pleasure at the delicious aroma by saying *betam tiru no* (lovely!). Next the beans are ground up with a pestle and mortar, then brewed up with water in a pan until it starts to bubble.

When it's finally ready, the coffee is served in tiny china cups with at least three spoons of sugar. At least three cups must be accepted. The third in particular is considered to bestow a blessing – it is the *berekha* (blessing) cup. Sometimes popcorn is passed around. It should be accepted with two hands extended and cupped together.

In offices, where time is more pressing, a cup of ready-prepared coffee is offered instead, but the gesture of welcome or respect is the same. Cups should always be accepted, even if you only have a sip.

In the Gurage region (where it's something of a speciality), it's often served with *kotcho* or *enset* (false-banana bread). Enset is best described as a very edible carpet liner. *Kitfo beats* (restaurants specialising in kitfo) are found in the larger towns.

Other Dishes Other meat dishes to look out for include the delicious *kwalima* (beef sausage), a speciality of the city of Harar. It's slightly like a Spanish *chorizo*, but is usually served on special occasions only.

Ethiopians are not great fish eaters, despite the number of lakes and rivers. You won't come across it very often, except in towns on the very edge of lakes. Some of the nomadic tribes (such as in the Ogaden) positively revile it. Desserts aren't commonly encountered either: usually just a bit of fruit is eaten, or yoghurt served with delicious local honey.

Fast Food & Snacks

In Addis Ababa, there are various fast-food restaurants, serving quite decent fare, usually at a slightly higher price than the local dishes. Outside town, fastfood is rarely found, though snacks such as *kolo* (roasted barley) and *bekolo* (popcorn) make great in-between-meal fillers.

Self-Catering

Supermarkets in the capital are reasonably well stocked; in those that cater to expats, familiar products such as cereals, tinned meat and vegies, jams and biscuits can be found. Campers and trekkers should have no problems stocking up, but Addis Ababa is the place to do it.

Outside the capital, provisions are very limited. Most groceries stock little more than sugar, coffee, packets of pasta and tomato puree, and pretty unimaginative biscuits. Good markets are found throughout the country, and a wide selection of fresh fruit and vegetables can be found. Saturday is the main market day throughout Ethiopia.

DRINKS
Coffee

Ethiopia claims to be the original home of coffee. The crop also represents the country's most important export by far. The famous 'coffee ceremony' is an integral part of Ethiopian culture and etiquette (see the boxed text 'The Coffee Ceremony'). Throughout the country, a buna beat is never far away. As a result of the Italian influence of the 1930s, macchiato, cappuccino and a kind of caffe latte known as a *buna bewetet* (coffee with milk) are also available in many of the towns.

Tea

In lowland Muslim areas, *shai* (tea) is often preferred, and is offered black, sometimes spiced with cloves or ginger. Ethiopians

Eating Etiquette

In Ethiopia, food is always shared from a single plate without the use of cutlery. The individual plate system of the west, with its individual meat and vegetable portions, strikes most Ethiopians as hilarious, as well as rather strange and wasteful. Sharing a meal with an Ethiopian is a great way of cementing a new friendship. But Amhara eating etiquette is refined and complex.

- If you're invited for a meal at an Ethiopian's house, it's customary to bring a small gift such as pastries or flowers in the town; sugar, coffee and fruit in the country.
- In households and many of the restaurants, a jug of water and a basin are brought out to wash the guests' outstretched hands before the meal. You remain seated throughout, and will be handed a towel afterwards.
- It's usual to invite those around you, even strangers, to join you, with an *Enebla!* (Please join us!) If you in turn are invited, it's polite to accept a tiny amount of food to show appreciation.
- Use just your right hand for eating. The left – as in Muslim countries – is reserved for personal hygiene only; keep it firmly tucked under the table.
- Avoid touching your mouth or licking your fingers.
- Don't put food back on the tray. It's better to discard it onto the table or floor, or keep it in your napkin.
- Take from your side of the tray only; reaching is considered impolite.
- However hungry you are, try not to guzzle. Greed is considered rather uncivilised.
- Filling your mouth too full, or on both sides of your cheeks, is also considered impolite.
- The tastiest morsels will often be laid in front of you; it is polite to accept them.
- The meat in dishes such as *doro wat* is usually saved until last, so don't hone in on it immediately.
- Don't be embarrassed or alarmed at the tradition of *gursha*, when someone – usually the host – picks a tasty morsel and feeds it directly into your mouth. The trick is to take it without letting your mouth come into contact with the person's fingers, or allowing the food to fall. It is a mark of great friendship or affection, and is usually given at least twice (once is considered unlucky). Refusing to take gursha is a terrible slight to the person offering it!
- It is considered good manners – and essential in the rural areas – to leave some leftovers on the plate after a meal. Failing to do so is sometimes seen as inviting famine, and may seriously upset the household.
- It is considered perfectly proper to pick your teeth after a meal with a toothpick (usually supplied in restaurants).

seem to get a fix from large amounts of sugar – it is copiously applied to all hot drinks and even fresh fruit juices. If you don't want sugar, you'll have to make that clear when you order. Ask for the drink *yale sukkar* (without sugar). If you want milk with your coffee or tea, ask for *betinnish wetet* (with a little milk). Decaffeinated coffee is not available except in the smartest hotels in Addis Ababa.

Water

The water in Addis Ababa is considered safe to drink, but as in many places, new arrivals may experience problems. Ambo is the most famous brand of mineral water, and its name has become synonymous with it. It's so fizzy that it keeps its sparkle even in a glass left overnight! It costs Birr2 for a 750ml bottle and is quite widely available.

Fruit Juice & Fizzy Drinks

In most towns, you'll find a *jus beat* (juice bar), which serves delicious, freshly squeezed juices such as papaya, orange and pineapple and sometimes banana, mango and guava too. A *spris* is a mixture – usually avocado, mango and papaya. In eastern

Ethiopia, try a juice made from the fruit known locally as *ambashok*. Newcomers may react to the tap water used to mix the juice, but you can try asking for mineral water to be used instead. Most travellers seem to experience no ill consequences at all, and fruit juices are a delicious way of getting those vital vits.

Widely available are various fizzy soft drinks, including the ubiquitous Coca Cola.

Alcoholic Drinks

In the bars, nightclubs and buna beats of the capital and towns, all the usual faves are available including whisky, gin, vodka and beer. As most are imports, they tend to be more expensive than local liquor. An Addis Ababa Piazza speciality is a *gin fir fir* – a concoction of gin and beer! If you want to raise an eyebrow or two in smart Addis Ababa society, try ordering it. Drunkenness is considered rather uncivilised in Ethiopia; if you've had one too many, try at least to pretend that you haven't (see Legal Matters earlier in this section).

Beer There are various varieties of local beer available, including the well-known Bedele beer manufactured near Bahar Dar. Ethiopian beer is generally mild, quite

smooth and perfectly drinkable. It's also cheap at Birr3–4.

Home-brews are also worth tasting. *Tella*, made from finger millet, maize or barley, is available across the country. Every village and every monastery makes it. Slightly bitter, often unfiltered, it's nevertheless amazingly refreshing if you're thirsty. Although it's made with local water, most travellers don't seem to suffer ill consequences from drinking it.

A variety of non-alcoholic beer is made in the Muslim town of Harar in the east.

Wine Local wine, though no huge cause for celebration, isn't at all bad, particularly the red Gudar and, second-best, Dukam wines. Of the whites, the dry Crystal is about the best bet. Unless you're a great aficionado of sweet red, avoid Axumite at all costs. Wine is also very reasonably priced in restaurants (Birr6–50). Imported plonk costs from Birr50.

Araki If you're not catching an early bus out of town the next morning, try the local *araki*, a grain spirit, which will make you rasp. A dash in a hot cup of tea on a freezing morning in the Bale Mountains seems to work wonders for morale. The Ethiopians believe it's good for high blood pressure! *Dagem araki* is 'twice-filtered' and is finer. A 1.5L bottle costs just Birr12.

Tej One drink not to be missed is tej, a delicious – and pretty powerful – local mead made from honey and from a local shrub known as *gesho*. It can also be flavoured with coffee and even qat! It comes in varying degrees of sweetness – the dryer it is, the more alcoholic. *Derek* is dry, *mahakalenya* is medium sweet, and *laslasa* or *bers* is sweet and pretty mild.

ENTERTAINMENT

Most of the country's facilities for leisure and entertainment are found in Addis Ababa. Here, decent cinemas (showing films in English), nightclubs, and various bars can all be found. There's also a number of theatres, though plays are almost wholly in Amharic.

Tej Beats

Once *tej* was the drink of kings, but today, many of the larger towns have tej beats, equivalent to pubs in the west. Tej (honey wine) is served up in delightful flasks known as *birille*, and costs Birr1–3, depending on the quality. The local men congregate to gossip, cogitate and commiserate. As in pubs, most people gather together at weekends, from around 3 pm. This is definitely men's territory, and unless it's in Addis Ababa or on the historical route, where the locals are used to seeing foreign women, it's best for women to steer clear.

Women traditionally drink tej at market days from glasses. It is also available in many restaurants.

A few of the larger hotels in the capital occasionally stage shows with folk musicians and dancers. Music in the town bars is for the most part Amharic pop, which, like the food, takes a bit of getting used to. But Western pop, jazz, reggae and various other types of music are also heard in Addis Ababa. Most bars close around 10 or 11 pm on weeknights, but open until at least 2 am on Friday and Saturday.

Ethiopians love to dance, and in the smaller bars such as in the Piazza in Addis Ababa, you'll get plenty of chances to see it. Traditional dancing is quite unique in style, with lots of variations on shaking body parts, but if you can give it a go, you'll win a lot of friends.

Nightclubs in Addis Ababa tend to be more 'westernised' in ambience and music. They are expensive by Ethiopian standards (Birr10–15 for entrance and per drink), and attract a wealthier crowd, many of them 'returnees'. They don't really get going until the weekend; some don't close until 5 am or later.

Outside the capital, entertainment is limited to a few bars and cafes; some of them have *biliardo* (Italian billiards) tables, which are rented by the half-hour or hour. In many of the larger towns, bicycle races are organised. Streets are cordoned off, everyone comes to watch, and it's all taken very seriously.

For more information, see Entertainment in the Addis Ababa section; see also Arts in the Facts about Ethiopia section.

SPECTATOR SPORTS

See also Spectator Sports in the Addis Ababa section.

Running

Ethiopia is known for its extraordinary pantheon of long-distance runners. One of the most famous, and still breaking records today, is Haile Gebreselassie, arguably the greatest long-distance runner in the world, and one of the best of all time. Many people know Ethiopia only through this man.

At just 1.6m (5 feet 3 inches) tall, Haile Gebreselassie has no fewer than 14 world records to his name, and three remain unbeaten – the 3000m, 5000m and 10,000m.

Other great athletes include Abebe Bikila, the marathon runner of the 1960s, who took gold medals at both the Tokyo and Rome Olympics (famously running barefoot at the latter). The legendary Belayneh Densamo held the world record for the marathon for close on one decade (1989–1998), with a time of 2:06:50.

Ethiopian women in recent years are causing no less of a sensation. At the Barcelona Olympics, Derartu Tulu became Ethiopia's first woman gold medallist in the 10,000m event. Fatuma Roba and Gete Wami are other remarkable long-distance and marathon runners. The latter took a bronze in the Atlanta Olympics, and in early 2000 was consistently beating the best European competitors.

Other Sports

By far the most popular national sport is football, played all over the country with balls made from an ingenious assortment of things. Other popular sports include volleyball, tennis, basketball and table tennis.

Ethiopia also has its own peculiar sports. Genna is a kind of hockey without boundaries, played traditionally at Christmas.

Gugs is also a festival event, typically seen at New Year (September 11) or Meskel (September 27). Riders take turns either pursuing or fleeing from one another. The idea is to get as close as possible to your adversary then hurl a wooden club at him. If you're fleeing, then you fend off such missiles with a traditional hippopotamus-hide shield. In the meantime, there's lots of war cries, goading, insulting, challenging and boasting. In the past, the games prepared young warriors for war. If you're in Addis Ababa during one of the festivals, don't miss it. The Jan Meda Race Ground normally hosts the event.

SHOPPING

Ethiopia has a terrific selection of souvenirs. To get a good idea of the range and quality of potential purchases, a trip to the excellent Institute of Ethiopian Studies in Addis Ababa is useful (see Libraries under Information in the Addis Ababa section).

The capital and some of the towns along the historical route have a good selection of souvenir shops, many selling items inspired by Ethiopia's Christian heritage, ranging from well-carved wooden crosses and rather garish animal-skin paintings to thick rugs woven with grumpy-looking lions of Juddah. Some shops sell the colourful baskets from the Muslim town of Harar, and intricate jewellery. Larger souvenirs such as wooden furniture are also available in the capital.

Quality and artistry ranges from poor to very high, so it's always worth taking a peek around and comparing wares. Prices largely depend on your skills of negotiation. Don't forget that strict rules apply as to what you can and cannot export as souvenirs. In some shops in Addis Ababa, ivory carvings and, less frequently, turtle shells are found. Apart from the environmental argument against buying these, it is also illegal to import them into most western countries (see Customs earlier in this section).

The *gabi*, the white, light cotton toga worn by the local men, is widely available, and makes a great, though rather bulky, travelling companion. They can be turned into blankets, pillows, mattresses, cushions (on long bus journeys) and warm wraps. Smaller versions include the men's *shamma* and the women's *natala*, with a beautiful *tibeb* (embroidered border).

Outside the capital, simple pottery, calabashes, basketware and woodcarvings can be found in many local markets. These are often Ethiopia's most authentic souvenirs, since they are designed to be functional as well as beautiful.

See the boxed text 'Arts & Crafts' under Gambela in the West of Addis Ababa section for more ideas on souvenirs.

Shipping stuff home isn't difficult to organise and is reasonably priced (see Post & Communications earlier in this section).

Getting There & Away

Warning

The information in this chapter is particularly vulnerable to change: prices for international travel are volatile, routes are introduced and cancelled, schedules change, special deals come and go, and rules and visa requirements are amended.

Airlines and governments seem to take a perverse pleasure in making price structures and regulations as complicated as possible. You should check directly with the airline or a travel agent to make sure you understand how a fare (and the ticket you may buy) works. In addition, the travel industry is highly competitive and there are many lurks and perks.

The upshot of this is that you should get opinions, quotes and advice from as many airlines and travel agents as possible before you part with your hard-earned cash. The details given in this chapter should be regarded as pointers and are not a substitute for your own careful, up-to-date research.

AIR

Travel during the month of August, and over Easter, Christmas and New Year, should be booked well in advance. Ethiopians living abroad tend to visit their families during this time, and tour groups often try and coincide with the major festivals. Prices of flights go up during this period too.

All fares quoted are for travel outside the high season (the high season is from 1 July to 15 September, and from 16 December to 15 January) and are valid for a period of between three and six months.

Buying Tickets

An air ticket alone can gouge a great slice out of anyone's budget, but you can reduce the cost by finding discounted fares. Stiff competition has resulted in widespread discounting – good news for travellers! The only people likely to be paying full fare these days are travellers flying in 1st or business class. Passengers flying in economy can usually manage some sort of discount. But unless you buy carefully and flexibly, it is still possible to end up paying exorbitant amounts for a journey.

For long-term travel there are discount tickets which are valid for 12 months, allowing multiple stopovers with open dates. For short-term travel cheaper fares are available by travelling mid-week, staying away at least one Saturday night or taking advantage of short-lived promotional offers.

When you're looking for bargain air fares, go to a travel agent rather than directly to the airline. From time to time, airlines do have promotional fares and special offers, but generally they only sell fares at the official listed price. One exception to this rule is the expanding number of 'no-frills' carriers operating in the United States and north-west Europe, which mostly sell direct to travellers. Unlike the 'full service' airlines, no-frills carriers often make one-way tickets available at around half the return fare, meaning that it is easy to put together a return ticket when you fly to one place but leave from another.

Airports & Airlines

Bole International Airport at Addis Ababa is currently the only international airport in

Shopping on the Internet

Although airlines occasionally have promotional fares and special offers, on the whole they only sell flights at the official listed price.

The one exception, however, is fares on the Internet. Many airlines offer some fantastic fares to Web surfers. Seats are sold either by auction or simply at cut prices to reflect the reduced cost of electronic selling.

Even better, many travel agents also have Web sites, which can make the Internet a quick and easy way to compare prices. Shopping for bargain fares has never been easier.

Air Travel Glossary

Cancellation Penalties

If you have to cancel or change a discounted ticket, there are often heavy penalties involved; insurance can sometimes be taken out against these penalties. Some airlines impose penalties on regular tickets as well, particularly against 'no-show' passengers.

Full Fares

Airlines traditionally offer 1st class (coded F), business class (coded J) and economy class (coded Y) tickets. These days there are so many promotional and discounted fares available that few passengers pay full economy fare.

Lost Tickets

If you lose your airline ticket an airline will usually treat it like a travellers cheque and, after inquiries, issue you with another one. Legally, however, an airline is entitled to treat it like cash, when if you lose it, it's gone forever. Take good care of your tickets.

Onward Tickets

An entry requirement for many countries is that you have a ticket out of the country. If you're unsure of your next move, the easiest solution is to buy the cheapest onward ticket to a neighbouring country or a ticket from a reliable airline that can later be refunded if you do not use it.

Open-Jaw Tickets

These are return tickets where you fly out to one place but return from another. If available, this can save you backtracking to your arrival point.

Overbooking

Since every flight has some passengers who fail to show up, airlines often book more passengers than they have seats. Usually excess passengers make up for the no-shows, but occasionally somebody gets 'bumped' onto the next available flight. Guess who it is most likely to be? The passengers who check in late.

Ethiopia. It has a bank, post office, Ethiopian Tourism Commission office, souvenir shops, restaurant and free trolleys!

The Commercial Bank is open daily from 6 am until around 1 pm (when flights finish) and from 9.30 pm to midnight. On Wednesday and Sunday, it's open only in the morning. Travellers cheques and major currencies are accepted. Porters expect Birr2 per bag.

The Ethiopian Tourism Commission office can make reservations for you at hotels free of charge, and can advise with any immigration/visa problems.

A new runway and terminal building at Bole International Airport should be completed by the end of 2000.

Ethiopian Airlines, the country's only international and national carrier, is considered one of the best airlines in Africa with a very good record for both safety and efficiency; it is also one of the largest, with a modern fleet of 737s, 757s and 767s.

Other major airlines serving Ethiopia include Lufthansa, Saudi Arabian Airways, Kenya Airways, EgyptAir and Djibouti Airlines. Bear in mind that choosing Ethiopian Airlines will give you priority on the domestic circuit if you're planning to take some internal flights.

When catching a flight out of Ethiopia, you should get to the airport well in advance of your departure (at least two hours is advised) to allow for the security and foreign currency checks, baggage inspection and departure tax payment.

Travellers with Special Needs

Ethiopian Airlines caters to various needs, which should be indicated when you make

Air Travel Glossary

Promotional Fares
These are officially discounted fares, widely available from travel agencies or direct from the airline's offices.

Reconfirmation
If you don't reconfirm your flight at least 72 hours prior to departure, the airline may delete your name from the passenger list. Ring to find out if your airline requires reconfirmation.

Restrictions
Discounted tickets often have various restrictions on them – such as needing to be paid for in advance and incurring a penalty to be altered. Others have restrictions on the minimum and maximum period you must be away.

Round-the-World Tickets
RTW tickets give you a limited period (usually a year) in which to circumnavigate the globe. You can go anywhere the carrying airlines go, as long as you don't backtrack. The number of stopovers or total number of separate flights is decided before you set off and they usually cost a bit more than a basic return flight.

Transferred Tickets
Airline tickets cannot be transferred from one person to another. Travellers sometimes try to sell the return half of their ticket, but officials can ask you to prove that you are the person named on the ticket. On an international flight, tickets are compared with passports.

Travel Periods
Ticket prices vary with the time of year. There is a low (off-peak) season and a high (peak) season, and often a low-shoulder season and a high-shoulder season as well. Usually the fare depends on your outward flight – if you depart in the high season and return in the low season, you pay the high-season fare.

---

a reservation. Among the special meals offered are those for Muslims, Jews (Kosher), Hindus, vegetarians, diabetics and the blind. Special meals for babies and children are also available.

A wheelchair service is available, and there is an escort service for children over two years of age.

Departure Tax

The international departure tax is US$20, which must be paid at the airport. Travellers should note that all foreign nationals except those with residence permits are charged in US dollars. It's a very good idea to keep dollars set aside especially for this; other currencies including Ethiopian birr are *not* accepted, and it can be both a hassle and time-consuming to change birr back into dollars. The bank at the airport is not always

open either. Travellers cheques in US dollars are accepted, but there's an extra commission payable for this.

The USA

Coming from the US, Ethiopian Airlines offers among the cheapest of those fares on offer. It flies direct to both Washington and New York. Flying from Addis Ababa, the airlines has 'special fare agreements' with US airlines to many other cities in the US, including Atlanta, Boston, Chicago, Dallas, Denver, Detroit, Houston, Los Angeles, Miami, Minneapolis/St Paul, New Orleans, New York, Pittsburgh, Portland, St Louis, San Francisco, Seattle, Tampa and Washington.

Examples of good-value fares include the direct flight from New York (Newark) to Addis Ababa (out on a Saturday and back on a Friday) for US$1200 return.

For the west coast, both Ethiopian Airlines and United Airlines currently offer the most competitive fares with flights from San Francisco to Addis Ababa for US$1600 return.

The UK

Lufthansa offers the most competitive flight from the UK to Ethiopia. It flies three times a week via Frankfurt from US$692 return.

Second-cheapest is Kenya Airlines, flying four times a week via Nairobi for US$699. EgyptAir flies once a week to Addis Ababa (with an overnight in Cairo) for US$726. Alitalia offers two flights a week via Rome or Milan for US$750.

Ethiopian Airlines connects Glasgow and London (Heathrow) to Addis Ababa.

The major attraction of flights from the UK is the remarkably generous 50kg luggage allowance.

Europe

Lufthansa and Alitalia offer the most competitive flights to Ethiopia from continental Europe, at prices similar to those offered from the UK.

Ethiopian Airlines connects Ethiopia to many European cities, including Amsterdam, Athens, Berlin, Brussels, Bucharest, Budapest, Cologne, Copenhagen, Dusseldorf, Frankfurt, Geneva, Hamburg, Madrid, Milan, Munich, Oslo, Paris, Prague, Rome, Stockholm, Stuttgart, Vienna, Warsaw and Zurich.

The Middle East

Ethiopian Airlines flies to Bahrain, Lebanon, Israel, Oman, Qatar, Saudi Arabia (Dhahran, Jeddah and Riyadh), the United Arab Emirates and Yemen.

Prices include: Jeddah from US$315/409 one way/return; Riyadh from US$430/547; and Sana'a from US$225/297.

Yemenia Yemen Airways flies to Sana'a from Addis Ababa twice a week for US$230/303 one way/return. Saudi Arabian Airlines flies from Addis Ababa to Riyadh for US$434 one way.

Africa

Ethiopian Airlines has the most extensive network of routes across Africa of any airline, and offers daily flights to West Africa – still the only airline to do so. It flies either directly or in conjunction with other carriers to the following African countries: Angola, Benin, Botswana, Burkina Faso, Burundi, Chad, Congo (Zaïre), Côte d'Ivoire, Djibouti, Egypt, The Gambia, Ghana, Guinea, Kenya, Libya, Madagascar, Malawi (Blantyre and Lilongwe), Mali, Mozambique, Niger, Nigeria (Kano and Lagos), Rwanda, Senegal, Sierra Leone, South Africa, Sudan, Tanzania (Dar es Salaam and Kilimanjaro), Togo, Tunisia, Uganda, Zambia and Zimbabwe.

Until 1998, flights went twice daily to Asmara, Eritrea, for US$118/236 one way/return. However, until the border conflict is resolved between the two countries, services will remain suspended.

Ethiopian Airlines flies daily to Djibouti from Addis Ababa (sometimes via Dire Dawa) for US$136/272 one way/return. Sometimes special fares for as little as US$56 (one way) are offered; check when you get there.

Djibouti Airlines departs Djibouti town every day to Addis Ababa for from US$200/300 one way/return, and four times a week to Dire Dawa for from US$95/150.

Other fares offered by Ethiopian Airlines include: Egypt from US$493/776 one way/return; Kenya from US$291/497; and (if operating) Sudan from US$275/352 (all departing from Addis Ababa).

Kenya Airlines flies between Addis Ababa and Nairobi for US$290/580 one way/return; special one-month excursion fares are sometimes available for US$446 return. At the time of writing, two small private companies, Arban Agency and Al Karim, were offering one-way flights three or four times weekly from Moyale to Nairobi for KSh5000.

EgyptAir flies between Addis Ababa and Cairo for US$521/670 one way/return.

LAND
Your Own Vehicle

If you're taking your own car or motorcycle into Ethiopia, you should always carry with you and be ready to show:

- Your passport
- A permit for your vehicle (available from the Transport and Communications Bureau)
- The vehicle's registration papers
- Proof of insurance (third-party is mandatory) covering all the countries you are visiting

A carnet de passage is also a good idea. It is effectively a passport for the vehicle and acts as a temporary waiver of import duty. Cars can be imported into Ethiopia for a period of four months duty free. The carnet should list any expensive spare parts that you're planning to carry with you, such as a gearbox. This is designed to prevent car-import rackets. Contact your local automobile association for details about all documentation.

Anyone planning to take their own vehicle with them needs to check in advance what spare parts are likely to be available for the vehicle in question.

Ethiopian law currently recognises international driving licences for a period of seven days only. To get an Ethiopian-endorsed licence, you'll need to do the following:

- Take your domestic licence to your embassy. If it's in English, get a photocopy certified; if it's in any other language, a full translation must be certified by your embassy.
- Take this copy of your licence to the Ministry of Foreign Affairs (☎ 51-73-45), Office No 1, opposite the Hilton Hotel in Addis Ababa, and pay Birr300 for an official stamp.
- Take the copy and stamp, along with two passport photos, to the Driving Licence and Issuing Department of the Transport and Communications Bureau (☎ 61-46-90 ext 503) on the Asmara road, where you fill out further forms, pay Birr25 and wait around two hours until the licence is ready. It's then valid for two years.

Border Crossings

There are six official points of entry by land into Ethiopia from neighbouring countries: at Rama and Zela Anbessa coming from Eritrea; at Doualé coming (by train) from Djibouti; at Moyale from Kenya; and at Humera and Metema from Sudan. All have full customs and immigration checks.

The overland route from South Africa to Ethiopia via Zimbabwe, Zambia, Tanzania and Kenya is quite well trodden, and should present few problems.

Djibouti

Bus There are no direct buses from Addis Ababa to Djibouti. The only way of getting to Djibouti by bus is in short hops (see the Getting There & Away information under Awash to Asaita in the East of Addis Ababa section). Taking the train or flying are better options.

Car & Motorcycle Since the outbreak of the conflict with Eritrea, Ethiopia has diverted its commerce through Djibouti's port. Every day, countless trucks and vans rattle along the roads connecting the two countries, and road communication has improved. If you're desperate to hitch, getting a ride shouldn't be a problem (see the Getting Around section of this chapter for a warning on hitching).

The quickest road to Djibouti is via Awash, Mille and Galafi in Ethiopia, and Yoboki and Dikhil in Djibouti. In the next ten years, there are plans (using private investment and EEC funds) to build a major highway linking the two countries. In the meantime, travel on the generally poorly maintained roads remains slow.

The border at Galafi sees very few tourists, and customs and immigration are not yet established there. If you want to travel this route, be sure to visit the immigration office in Addis Ababa for advice, and for a letter if you plan to come back into Ethiopia (see Visas in the Facts for the Visitor section of this chapter).

If coming from Djibouti, get a letter from the Ethiopian embassy there explaining your route, then go and see immigration in Addis Ababa after your arrival. Without entry/exit stamps on your passport, you could face real problems when you try to leave or re-enter Ethiopia: some travellers have been detained for several days or even weeks. See also under Land in the Getting There & Away section of the Djibouti chapter.

Train The old Addis Ababa–Djibouti town train still trundles along the old French-built tracks, passing through various small towns before finishing the first leg at Dire Dawa, 453km east of Addis Ababa (but this leg isn't recommended, see following). There, travellers can rest up overnight and continue on to Djibouti town by train the following morning.

There's not much to be said for taking the train from Addis Ababa to Dire Dawa, since sleepers are no longer available and the journey is slow, long and tiring. This leg takes place overnight, when the whole reason for the journey – the views – are not visible. A better bet is to do this leg by bus. For fares see Getting There & Away under Dire Dawa in the East of Addis Ababa section.

The second leg of the journey between Dire Dawa and Djibouti town is still worth it, both to enjoy a transport relic of the past and the changing landscape (but keep a sharp eye at all times on your possessions). When Evelyn Waugh made the journey in the 1930s he described the landscape as 'that intolerable desolation of French Somaliland'. Be your own judge. See the boxed text 'The Railway' under Dire Dawa in the East of Addis Ababa section later in this chapter for the story of the construction of the 785km-long railway.

For more information on train travel, see the Getting Around section later in this chapter.

Classes & Reservations There are three classes: 1st, 2nd and 3rd. Third is little more than a bench – or standing, as it gets very overcrowded. The 1st-class carriage is limited to just 14 people; a ticket should guarantee you a seat and it is reasonably comfortable, but it's essential to get there early (1½ hours before departure is advised), particularly if you've got lots of luggage. The train is often overbooked. Second-class carriages carry 20 people, 3rd-class 300! Tickets officially are sold from 8 am the day of departure, and usually sell out very quickly.

You can also do what the locals do: pay a porter to take your luggage to the train,

find a seat for you and guard both while you have a cup of coffee or breakfast. Make sure you pay the guard fee afterwards rather than before, and obviously keep valuable items with you. Get a seat on the left side of the train if you want to look out. On the right, the blinds are drawn against the sun.

Soft drinks and small snacks (including qat!) are available on the train, but it's a good idea to bring your own, particularly water. There are (nonflushing) 'flushing' toilets aboard.

Costs Train travel is pretty light on the wallet. Tickets from Addis Ababa to Dire Dawa in 1st/2nd/3rd class cost Birr75/47/24; trains leave daily at 4.30 pm and the journey takes around 13½ hours. From Dire Dawa to Djibouti it costs Birr58/39/19 and trains leave on Tuesday, Thursday and Saturday at 5.45 am. The journey takes around 10 hours.

Eritrea

Since the outbreak of the conflict with Eritrea, all roads connecting the two countries have been closed. Once diplomatic relations are established again, the roads should re-open.

There are three sealed roads connecting Ethiopia to Eritrea. The first goes from Aksum in Ethiopia to Asmara in Eritrea via Adi Quala and Mendefera, and is the best choice if you want to take in Eritrea's 'historical route', including the sites of Metera and Qohaito (see the South of Asmara section of the Eritrea chapter).

The second route goes from Adigrat in Ethiopia to Asmara via Adi Keyh and Dekemhare in Eritrea. Though the journey is faster and more comfortable, it's less interesting.

The third route connects Addis Ababa to Assab, which lies on the southernmost tip of Eritrea. From there, you can fly to Asmara. The only alternative is a three- or four-day (or even longer) bus journey along desert tracks to Massawa (see the Dankalia section of the Eritrea chapter).

Border crossings on both sides close at sunset (around 6.30 pm). At the Ethiopian frontier, you may be questioned about your itinerary and will have to fill in a currency declaration form (see Customs in the Facts for the Visitor section earlier in this chapter).

Bus Previously, buses ran three times a week between Addis Ababa and Asmara via Dessie and Mekele (Birr84, three days). Buses to Asmara could also be caught from Shire (60km from Aksum), departing every day at 5 am except Sunday (Birr16, eight hours). From Mekele, a bus left four times a week for Asmara (Birr25, nine hours) via Adigrat (Birr15, seven hours to Asmara). For information on routes via Assab in Eritrea, see the Assab section of the Eritrea chapter.

These services should eventually resume once relations between the two countries have sufficiently improved.

Sudan

Formerly, it was possible to take a bus from Gambela into Sudan. However, because of the current security situation in Sudan, the border is closed to foreigners. At the beginning of 2000, border relations had improved, and the border promised to reopen. Check the current situation when you get there.

There are no direct buses from Addis Ababa; the more usual route into Sudan was via Eritrea, but that's currently impossible.

Kenya

Moyale, in southern Ethiopia, serves as the frontier town for Kenya. There are usually few problems travelling between the two countries.

The Ethiopian and Kenyan borders are open daily from 6 am to 6 pm but, in theory, tourists can cross anytime. It takes around 30 minutes to clear customs and immigration on the Ethiopian side; it's a good idea to do this the night before you intend to travel, so that you don't miss the early morning buses or trucks from the other side.

If you're hitching, trucks over the border normally travel in convoys to deter bandits, so you may end up waiting a few days while they assemble.

By bus, you'll need to go to Agara Maryam first and change. There's one bus

daily from the long-distance bus terminal in Addis Ababa at 6.30 am (Birr28,10 hours).

For more information on trucks and buses to and from Moyale, see Moyale in the South of Addis Ababa section of this chapter.

Somalia

Travel between Ethiopia and Somalia is currently considered unsafe. Check out the situation very carefully before considering a trip to Somalia. There are currently no direct buses from Addis Ababa to Somalia (see Jijiga in the East of Addis Ababa section). If you're desperate to get to Somalia, overland access from Djibouti is easier.

Europe

The overland route from southern Europe to Ethiopia is known as the 'Nile Route', and passes through Egypt, Sudan and Eritrea. With the current Eritrea-Ethiopia conflict, the last leg is obviously impossible, and travellers are presently obliged to travel from Eritrea to Ethiopia via Sudan, though even Sudan was posing problems at the time of research.

You should check out the current security situation along each leg before travelling, as there have been serious problems in the past – such as Muslim fundamentalist attacks on tourists in Egypt.

RIVER

In the past, it was possible to take a boat from Gambela in southern Ethiopia to Sudan via the Baro River. Services are not currently operational, but there are plans to re-establish them in the future. If you're in Gambela, it might be worth checking out the current situation.

ORGANISED TOURS

Organised tours in Ethiopia are useful for three things: for a specialist activity that can't be organised in Ethiopia itself (unless it's tailor-made and very expensive), such as white-water rafting; for those interested in specialist subjects, such as history or birds (see the special section 'Birds of Ethiopia'); and for those with limited time.

Another possibility is to combine independent travel with a tour, but you'll have to be reasonably flexible with dates.

From the UK
In the UK, around a dozen travel agencies offer trips to Ethiopia, mainly around the so-called historical route in the north, trekking in the Bale and Simien Mountains, and to some of the parks; a few, such as Dragoman, offer an encounter with the tribal peoples of the south-west.

Naturetrek (☎ 01962-733051, ☻ sales@nature trek.co.uk) offers bird and botanical tours to Ethiopia.
Web site: www.naturetrek.co.uk

The British Museum Traveller (☎ 020-7323 8895, ☻ traveller@bmcompany.co.uk) sometimes offers history/art/archaeology tours to Ethiopia; sometimes they're led by Dr David Phillipson, the leader of recent excavations at Aksum.
Web site: www.britishmuseum.co.uk

Adrift (☎ 01488-684509, ☻ raft@adrift.co.uk) specialises in white-water rafting trips down the Omo River. It's based in New Zealand, with an office in the UK. Check that your tour has a satellite navigational system.
Web site: www.adrift.co.uk

Gane & Marshall (☎ 020-8441 9592, ☻ 101630.533@compuserve.com) offers trekking trips to Ethiopia.
Web site: www.GaneandMarshall.co.uk

Footprint Adventures (☎ 01522-804929, ☻ sales@footventure.co.uk) offers treks as well as birding tours.
Web site: www.footprint-adventures.co.uk

Yumo Tours (☎ 020-7631 5337, ☻ yumo@ dial.pipex.com) specialises in customised tours of Ethiopia, including fishing, photo safaris and birdwatching.
Web site: www.xgt17.dial.pipex.com

Dragoman (☎ 01728-861133, ☻ info@ dragoman.co.uk) caters to both campers ('who like to get off the beaten track') and an older market who prefer four firm walls.
Web site: www.dragoman.co.uk

Silk Steps (☎ 0117-940 2800, ☻ Info@Silk steps.co.uk) offers treks and historical tours 'for the independent-minded'.
Web site: www.silksteps.co.uk

Abercrombie & Kent (☎ 020-7730 9600, ☻ info@abercrombiekent.co.uk)
Web site: www.abercrombiekent.co.uk

Exodus (☎ 020-7673 0859, ☻ sales@exodus travels.co.uk)
Web site: www.exodustravels.co.uk

Encounter Overland (☎ 020-7370 6845, ☻ ad venture@encounter.co.uk)
Web site: www.encounter.co.uk

From the USA
The following agencies offer trips to Ethiopia:

Journeys (☎ 734-665 4407, ☻ travel@jour neys.com) specialises in wildlife safaris, water-water rafting on the Omo and a photo safari of the tribal groups of the south-west.
Web site: www.journeys.com

Mountain Travel Sobek (fax 510-525 7710, ☻ info@mtsobek.com) specialises in white-water rafting trips as well as trekking.
Web site: www.mtsobek.com

Adventure Center (fax 510-654 4200) specialises in camping trips in both Ethiopia and Eritrea.

Far Horizons (☎ 505-343 8076, ☻ journey@ farhorizon.com) specialises in archaeological and cultural trips and offers the historical route led by an American archaeologist.
Web site: www.farhorizon.com

Distant Horizons (☎ 562-983 8828, fax 983 8833, ☻ disthoriz@aol.com) also offers the historical route.

Getting Around

AIR

Domestic Air Service

The only regular domestic air service is provided by the national carrier, Ethiopian Airlines (see the Getting There & Away section earlier in this chapter for more details of the airline). Its 58 offices worldwide can give you information on the extensive network of domestic flights as well as international ones. Most flights leave from Addis Ababa; there are a very few that connect other towns to one another. The north and west of the country are particularly well served; for the more popular routes, there are departures at least three times a week, if not daily.

It's well worth considering a flight or two, even if you're travelling on a budget. Most flights are quite reasonably priced, and cut out days spent on the road. A good compromise between cost and time is to take the bus one way, and the plane to other.

In the usually clear, blue Ethiopian skies and lower-altitude flying of the smaller domestic planes, you'll still see some landscape, too. The views – such as when you cross the Simien Mountains between Gonder and Lalibela – are stunning. If you want a window seat, check in early.

Unfortunately, photos will be difficult since batteries for cameras (and any other items such as for personal stereos) are confiscated before you board, and returned when you arrive. Cigarette lighters, matches, cables and pocketknives suffer the same fate. It's a good idea to tuck such things away in your hold baggage before you check in.

A pretty thorough body and luggage search are a routine part of air travel, too. Carrying as little hand luggage as possible cuts down on the latter. Don't forget the restrictions on antiquities (see Customs in the Facts for the Visitor section) when buying souvenirs. At Aksum airport, suspect items – even rocks and stones – are sometimes confiscated (and not returned).

The baggage limit is 20kg on domestic flights for international travellers. Don't bring bulky hand luggage: many of the planes are small (twin otters, ATR42s and Fokkers).

Reservations

In theory you can buy a ticket and fly on the same day, but in practice, flights should be booked well in advance. A week is the minimum to be sure of a place, two weeks is better, particularly over the major festivals (see Public Holidays & Special Events in the Facts for the Visitor section), when some towns of the north, such as Aksum and Gonder, become very popular destinations.

Don't worry if you need to change the dates; they can be altered as many times as you like for no extra charge at any Ethiopian Airlines office. Domestic flights can be purchased at Ethiopian Airlines offices around the world before you even arrive in Ethiopia.

It's essential to reconfirm all flights the day before. If you don't, you may find that you've either missed the flight or forfeited your place. Schedules do quite frequently change, or can even be cancelled at the last minute, because of weather conditions, mechanical faults etc. Beware of planning an itinerary that's so tight that it doesn't make allowances for changes.

Costs

Though not the bargain they once were, domestic flights still represent good value. There are no discounts available for students or senior citizens.

Currently only the Ethiopian Airlines offices in Addis Ababa and Dire Dawa accept credit cards (Visa, MasterCard, Diners Club and American Express – AmEx), though there are plans to introduce the facilities in the other offices around the country in the near future. Some offices accept Ethiopian birr as well as other currencies for payment; others accept only US dollars. Travellers cheques are not accepted in any offices.

Air passes are not yet offered, and discounts are available only to tour operators for groups of 10 or more.

The following prices are for standard one-way economy fares (domestic fares do not vary seasonally). Flights leave Addis Ababa for Dessie (US$54), Bahar Dar (US$72), Arba Minch (US$75), Jinka (US$89), Dire Dawa (US$94), Gambela (US$95), Gonder (US$97), Lalibela (US$97), Mekele (US$122), Aksum (US$127) and Jijiga (US$142). See also Getting There & Away in the Addis Ababa section for international airline offices and more domestic flight details.

Flights between the different legs on the historic route in the north can save you many days on buses (and your back!). Flights depart from Aksum for Mekele (US$32), Lalibela (US$65), Gonder (US$68) and Bahar Dar (US$80) (although flights in and out of Aksum were suspended during the conflict with Eritrea, check the current situation). Flights leave from Bahar Dar for Gonder (US$29), Dessie (US$52), Lalibela (US$54) and Mekele (US$74). Flights leave from Dessie for Gonder (US$48); flights leave from Gonder for Lalibela (US$43).

Domestic Departure Tax

A charge of US$10 is made for domestic departure tax, which must be paid in US dollars, cash only; make sure you have set some aside for this. At the Ethiopian Airlines office near the National Theatre in Addis Ababa, you can pay for the tax in advance when your ticket is issued.

BUS

There are over 10,000km of gravel and dry-weather roads in Ethiopia, but under 4000km of asphalt road. Many of the asphalt roads are in a sorry state of repair after the years of civil war. Most roads serve to connect the capital, Addis Ababa, to the provinces.

A good network of buses connects all the major towns of Ethiopia. For the smaller towns and villages, you can normally find some kind of light transport service (see Minibus, Share-Taxi & Truck following).

Buses are dirt cheap, reasonably safe and comfortable, but slow going. On sealed roads you can expect to cover around 45km an hour, but on dirt roads, 30km or less.

Unlike in most African countries, standing in the aisles on buses is illegal in Ethiopia, making them both a safer and more comfortable way to travel. On the longer journeys, there are usually scheduled breakfast and lunch stops for between 20 and 30 minutes. There are no toilets aboard.

The major drawback with bus travel is the size of the country. For the historical route alone, you're looking to cover over 2000km – about ten days spent just sitting on a bus.

Most long-distance buses set off early. Although scheduled to 'leave' at 6.30 am or earlier, they don't actually get going for at least another hour. But don't think you can roll up late: even if you already have your ticket, you still have to put in an appearance at this time.

You should check schedules the day before too, as they're often subject to change. Remember that the Ethiopian clock is almost always used (see Time in the Facts for the Visitor section).

On longer journeys, there may be one or even two overnight stops at cheap hotels en route. There are no night buses; Ethiopian law stipulates that all long-distances buses must stop for the night by 6 pm.

For details of bus trips out of Addis Ababa see Getting There & Away in the Addis Ababa section.

Reservations & Costs

One government bus association and eight private ones operate in Ethiopia. The private buses tend to be less afflicted by bureaucracy – you buy your ticket on the bus from the conductor and the bus leaves when it's full.

For government buses (Walia buses, formerly Anbessa), you have to buy your ticket in advance then wait outside the bus until it's ready to depart. Once the bus is loaded with luggage, passengers board, tickets are again checked and the bus eventually sets off.

Prices are pretty much the same among private companies; government buses are a few birr cheaper, but tend to be older and less comfortable. At the time of writing, the company Africa was considered one of the best, but other, new, companies are sprouting up.

Tickets for most long-distance journeys (over 150km) can be bought in advance. This is a good idea both to guarantee a seat and also to cut out the touts who occasionally snap up the remaining tickets to resell for double the price to latecomers. Most ticket offices are open daily from 5.30 am to 5.30 pm.

For short distances (less than 150km), tickets can only be bought on the day. In some towns, such as Addis Ababa, there are different terminals for long- and short-distance buses.

Buses are very cheap in Ethiopia, and work out at around US$1 per 100km. There is just one class of travel.

MINIBUS, TRUCK & SHARE-TAXI

Light vehicles such as minibuses, Land-cruisers and pick-up trucks usually connect neighbouring towns, or serve the smaller towns and villages where there is no bus service, particularly on market days (usually Saturday, and sometimes an additional day of the week too).

The vehicles are privately owned, slightly more expensive than the buses, but have the advantage of being faster. Sometimes they're crammed to the gunnels with livestock and poultry as well as people!

Schedules are often erratic, and some services are infrequent, so if you're planning on depending on this form of transport in the remoter regions, you'll need both flexibility and time on your side.

You'll need to ask the locals where to find the light transport, as each town differs. Petrol stations or market areas are quite common collection points. Taxis are not marked and vehicles vary according to the terrain.

TRAIN

The old Addis Ababa–Djibouti train passes through various small towns in the east including Nazret and Awash before finishing the first leg at Dire Dawa, 453km from Addis Ababa. It's dilapidated, overcrowded and slow, but if you can spare the time, you

The Joys of Bus Travel

In the rural areas, you may discover that your ticket actually counts for two places: your seat and the seat on your lap. So apart from sitting next to someone, and someone else's shopping, chicken or baby, you may find yourself holding someone else's shopping, chicken or baby.

All those extra lungs can make the bus seem a bit steamy. But never ever try to open a window. A riot is likely to erupt at the slightest crack, and the window will be slammed shut. Ethiopians are convinced that an airflow of any sort will prove almost certainly fatal to them.

Windows are reserved for 'emergencies' only. According to one Ethiopian, you can tell where a bus has come from by the amount of vomit down its sides. Unfortunately, some Ethiopians may not be so well travelled as you, and find the narrow, winding roads of the Highlands just a little unsettling.

Fortunately, more serious accidents tend to be rare. For extra safety, many drivers dangle garish plastic virgins or one of an array of Ethiopian saints from mirrors, dashboards or windscreens. Protection is the important thing, rather like the Muslim belief in fate, no matter how bad the driving.

Additionally, some drivers may rely on qat, the mild narcotic, to keep them vigilant, or, more commonly, Amharic music – played at full blast. Not much chance of the driver falling asleep at the wheel – or of the passenger getting a nap.

may want to give it a go. Departures are quite often delayed. Buses are faster.

In the past – including an isolated incident in 1997 – the train was targeted a bit by bandits and particularly thieves. Security has greatly improved: there are grills on the windows and at least two armed guards aboard the train. Few problems are now reported.

The train passes through, among other places, Nazret (2½ hours) and Awash (six hours), but ticket prices are the same as for Djibouti.

Taxi Terminology

In the towns, villages and countryside of the Horn, taxis offer two kinds of service: 'contract taxis' and 'share-taxis'. Contract taxis are considered the luxury of the wealthy. In the towns, share-taxis ply fixed routes, stop and pick people up when hailed and work to all intents like little buses. The contract fare is divided between each passenger.

Though not really 'taxis' at all, minibuses, trucks, 4WDs and various makes of cars all work as taxis in the country. Contracting a large minibus for yourself is seen as perfectly normal if you should want to. Otherwise, the vehicles operate as share-taxis, departing for their destination when they are full.

For detailed information on classes, reservations and costs, see the Getting There & Away section earlier in this chapter.

CAR & MOTORCYCLE

For information on the documentation required to take your own car or motorcycle into Ethiopia, see Your Own Vehicle in the Getting There & Away section earlier in this chapter.

Road Rules & Advice

Driving in Ethiopia is on the right-hand side of the road. The standard of driving is not terribly high, and few people attach much importance to the use of such devices as mirrors or even indicators.

The speed limit for cars and motorcycles is 60km/h in the towns and villages and 100km/h outside the towns.

Some highland roads in Ethiopia are quite precipitous; you should drive defensively and keep a lookout for trucks coming fast the other way.

In the outskirts of the towns or villages, look out for people, particularly children playing on the road or kerbside. In some towns a kind of curfew comes into effect, particularly in the west, where you have to be off the roads by 6 pm. If in doubt, check with the local authorities.

At night, *shiftas* (bandits) still operate in the remoter areas. Additionally, some trucks just park overnight in the middle of the road without lights.

In the country, livestock is the main hazard; camels wandering onto the road can cause major accidents in the lowlands. Many animals – including donkeys – are unaccustomed to vehicles and are very carshy, so always approach with caution. The few tractors on the state-owned farms tend to pull out without warning.

Land mines throughout the country still pose a threat; drivers should stay on sealed roads or existing dirt tracks, particularly on the approach to villages and towns, airstrips and bridges and other places of obvious strategic importance.

During the rainy season, some roads, particularly in the west and south-west, become impassable. During the war, many bridges were destroyed and some roads now ford riverbeds. Before setting out into remoter areas, you should check road conditions in advance with the local authorities in the towns, who are always well informed and helpful.

Fuel (both petrol and diesel) is quite widely available, apart from the more remote regions such as the south-west. For travel in these places, it's essential to carry plenty of extra fuel. Unleaded petrol is not available in Ethiopia.

Rental

Cars and 4WDs are easily hired from agencies in Addis Ababa, though they don't come cheap, even by Western standards. A car is only viable in the capital; elsewhere you'll need a 4WD. Motorcycles of any sort cannot be rented. For listings of agencies that rent vehicles, see Organised Tours later in this section.

Outside the capital, cars are very rarely available. Some Addis agencies have branch offices in some of the towns along the historical route. You may be able to arrange for a car to meet you there, but you'll have to organise this through Addis first.

Though expensive, rental vehicles are sometimes the best means of reaching some regions, since you don't have to rely on erratic bus services and schedules. The most obvious candidate for travel by private vehicle is the Omo Valley.

On long distances, cars can cut by half the journey times of buses. If you're trying to calculate journey times by car, see the bus journey durations under Getting There & Away after specific destinations, and cut the time given by between a third for short journeys and a half for long journeys.

If you're travelling solo, or as a couple, you can reduce the cost of vehicle rental by joining up with other travellers and hiring a car plus driver-guide. Most vehicles accommodate around five passengers, though some have extra benches in the back and can take about ten. Or take an all-inclusive tour (see Organised Tours later in this section).

To hire a car, you must have a valid international driver's licence and be between 25 and 70 years old. Vehicles can't be taken outside Ethiopia.

Rental prices vary and are usually open to quite a bit of negotiation, so it's worth shopping around. You should also ask for a discount if hiring for more than a week. A deposit of at least Birr2000 is required for the rental of a 4WD; Birr1000 for a car.

Drivers are often supplied and are usually obligatory on a 4WD. In fact, they make very useful additions, acting as guides as well as interpreters.

Sometimes there's an additional charge if the driver clocks up more than eight hours in a day – check in advance. Make sure it's clear also who pays for the driver's food and accommodation. Normally drivers get a daily allowance, though it's usually pretty paltry, and it's a nice gesture at least to share food together, which costs very little.

Many drivers are very reluctant to drive at night. This is in part a leftover from the Derg (former socialist military junta) curfews, but is also a sensible precaution against shiftas, which still operate in some of the remoter regions. If you expect to do any night driving, make sure you discuss this with the agency in advance.

Cars cost from US$40 per day. The first 50km are usually free, then it's from

Drive Safe

Sensible precautions before setting out in remote regions include the following:

- Check the current condition and security of the roads you want to travel on with the local administration or police office as sometimes areas become off-limits. (In Djibouti town, all tour operators are required to know this information.)
- Give the car a quick maintenance check (including tyres, oil and water levels etc) and don't forget a proper breakdown kit: shovel, jack, rope, winch etc.
- Bring food, lots of drinking water, and spare fuel (150–200L for more remote travelling, and fill up with fuel at every opportunity).
- Tell your hotel or vehicle hire agency where you are going and roughly when you expect to get back. If you do break down somewhere remote, and have previously informed people where you were going, stick with your vehicle. You will have a much better chance of being found, and you'll fare better against the heat and sun.
- Never park in the *wadis* (dry river beds). When it does rain, these can fill up incredibly quickly. Don't try crossing them during this time, either!
- Drive during the day only to avoid various hazards (see Road Rules & Advice previous).

Expedition Equipment

If you're planning any forays into very remote regions – such as the Omo Valley – the following extra equipment is strongly advised:

- compass (or satellite navigational system)
- spare parts: extra fan belts and filters
- at least one shovel and towrope – getting stuck in mud or sand is common
- at least two spare tyres

A useful guide to travelling through Africa with your own vehicle, including suggested spares and supplies, is *Africa Overland* by David Brydon.

US$0.20 per kilometre. A 4WD costs from US$155 to US$200 per day including unlimited kilometres, a driver, fuel, third-party insurance and a collision damage waiver. Make sure you check if all government taxes and service charges are included, or you may end up paying up to 25% more.

Given Ethiopia's size, a deal with unlimited kilometres is the best bet. Car hire is always a lot cheaper if you organise it yourself in Ethiopia (particularly if you shop around) rather than through an agency outside the country.

Purchase

If you're looking to buy a second-hand vehicle, expect to pay a minimum of US$10,000 to US$15,000. With the large expat community resident in Addis Ababa, vehicles are not hard to find; one of the local English-language newspapers is the best place to start.

BICYCLE

Ethiopia's irregular terrain and rough roads are not ideally suited to cycling. However, if you're totally self-sufficient with all the spare parts you can possibly cram into your repair kit, as well as a capacity to carry sufficient amounts of water, there's nothing to stop you.

Quite decent cycles can be hired in some of the larger towns of Ethiopia and are very cheap (Birr3 per hour). Though they're really rented by the hour or day and for use inside town, you can usually persuade someone to rent you one for a longer period as well as for use outside the town.

Usually a cycle repair shop of some sort can be found in the larger towns. Punctures are easily repaired – just head for any *gommista* (tyre repairer) or garage. Many mechanics are more than happy to help with cycle problems, and often turn out to be ingenious improvisers.

Cyclists should show the usual caution when travelling around the country: never travel after dark, be wary of thieves and keep the bicycle well maintained. Brakes need to be in good order on some of the mountainous highland roads.

Be particularly wary of dogs and the risk of rabies; sometimes it's best to dismount and walk slowly away. Cycling in the rainy season can be very hard going.

The only regulation regarding the importation of a bicycle concerns customs. You must leave a deposit amounting to the cycle's worth at customs at the port of entry on arrival. When you leave, this will be returned to you. As in the case of electronic goods, this is to deter black market trading.

Cycles are accepted aboard Ethiopian Airlines international flights. On domestic flights, you'll need to clear your cycle first when you come to make a reservation: some planes are pretty tiny.

Cycles new and second-hand can be bought in Addis Ababa, but prices are rarely much cheaper than elsewhere.

HITCHING

If someone asks for a ride in Ethiopia, it's usually assumed that it's because they can't afford a bus fare; little sympathy is spared for them. Many Ethiopians, in the good highland way, traditionally suspect hitchers of hidden motives such as robbery (see the boxed text 'Xenophobia' in the Gonder section of this chapter). This used to be a genuine hazard on the roads during and immediately after the war. However, attitudes to foreigners in this respect are usually different, and most Ethiopians are accommodating and helpful.

For some towns not readily served by buses, hitching is even normal, and you will be expected to contribute something towards the ride, as if for a taxi service. The

Hitching

Hitching is never entirely safe in any country in the world, and we don't recommend it. Travellers who decide to hitch should understand that they are taking a small but potentially serious risk. People who do choose to hitch will be safer if they travel in pairs and let someone know where they're planning to go. Women should never hitch alone.

best places to look for a lift are the hotels, bars and cafes.

BOAT
The only domestic boat service available is that on Lake Tana, where a limited ferry service operates (see the North of Addis Ababa section of this chapter).

LOCAL TRANSPORT
Minibus
In many of the larger towns, a minibus service provides a quick, convenient and cheap way of hopping about town (around 50 ¢ for short journeys). 'Conductors' generally shout out the destination of the bus; if in doubt, ask.

Taxis
Taxis operate in many of the larger towns including Addis Ababa. Prices are reasonable, but foreigners are always charged more than locals, so be prepared to bargain. In the smaller towns, short trips cost around Birr1; in the capital, fares are usually between Birr10 and Birr15 depending on the distance. If in doubt, ask your hotel for an estimate of your fare.

In Addis Ababa, the private blue-and-white taxis run standard routes and pick up and let off passengers like little buses. They're fast, run regularly and fares are cheap (usually around Birr1 for a short hop), but you'll need to know the routes – ask your hotel.

Also in Addis Ababa, the state-owned National Tour Operation (NTO) has a fleet of Mercedes which can be booked (see Taxis in the Addis Ababa section).

Garis
Garis, horse-drawn carts, can be hired in some of the towns and are even cheaper than taxis – Birr0.50 at most. They're great for a sightseeing trip around town on a nice day or for getting to places of interest just outside town. Most drivers speak little or no English; you may have to enlist a local to act as interpreter.

ORGANISED TOURS
The National Tour Operation or NTO is a government-owned travel agency which

Travellers Lore
Once there was a dog, a goat and a donkey. They wanted to go on a journey together, and decided to take a taxi. The donkey paid and got out, the dog paid, got out but never got his change, and the goat got out but never paid.

To this day, and whenever a vehicle passes, the dog still chases his change, the goat still scatters at the first approach, and the donkey just plods tranquilly on.

Ethiopian folk tale

once had a monopoly. A spate of private operators has sprung up in the past seven years, all based in Addis Ababa, some with branch offices outside the capital. Most offer the usual services: car hire, camping trips, trekking in the Bale and Simien Mountains, the historical route, trips to the Rift Valley lakes etc. A five-day tour of the historical route and Rift Valley lakes comes to around Birr800 per person without fuel and extra kilometres.

If you're interested in taking a tour, the best thing is to contact the agencies in advance, compare itineraries and prices (which change frequently) and make it clear that you're looking for the best deal. Though prices are officially fixed, most are very open to negotiation.

Bahir Dar Tour & Travel Agency (☎ 12-38-02, fax 55-35-79, ✉ bahardar.tour@telecom.net.et) can be recommended, and has various branch offices in the north. The agency also owns a big new hotel in Bahar Dar. Ask for the efficient manager, Wondwossen.

Caravan Travel & Tour Agency (☎ 12-01-51, fax 55-36-56, ✉ caravan.tt@telecom.net.et) can combine tours with visits to neighbouring countries including Eritrea, Djibouti and Yemen.

Ethiopian Rift Valley Safaris (☎ 55-21-28, fax 55-02-98, ✉ ervs@telecom.net.et) originally began as a hunting outfit, but now offers various upmarket tours. Its speciality, however, is still the Omo Valley, where it offers photo safaris, wildlife viewing and visits to ethnic groups. Nassos Roussos' experience of animal tracking is unsurpassed; his wife, Susan, runs the agency with American efficiency and attention to detail. Still the only agency with a camp in the region and its own airstrip, it's a great choice if you're interested in this area, and can afford the prices.

Experience Ethiopia (☎ 15-23-36, fax 51-99-82, ✆ eet@padis.gn.apc.org), in the National Theatre in the centre of Addis Ababa, operates tours similar to Village Ethiopia's.

Four Seasons Travel & Tours (☎ 61-31-21, fax 61-36-16, ✆ fsta@telecom.net.et) also offers good trips to the Omo Valley.

Galaxy Express Services (☎ 51-03-55, fax 51-12-36, ✆ galaxyexpress@telecom.net.et) at the Ras Hotel in central Addis Ababa is the only Avis car hire representative.

Green Land Travel & Tours Agency (☎ 51-79-72, fax 51-79-72, ✆ etgreend@yahoo.com) is Italian run.

Hess Travel Ethiopia (☎ 51-58-20, fax 51-26-75, ✆ hesstravel@telcom.net.et) is run by an efficient and energetic German-Ethiopian. Camping equipment can be hired (tents cost US$6 per day; a gas stove with cooking equipment costs US$5 per day). In the future, the agency might establish camp sites in the south-western region. German and French are spoken.

National Tour Operation or NTO (☎ 15-92-74) is the government-owned travel agency. It's the largest agency and its drivers and guides have excellent reputations, but its prices remain uncompetitive and high.

Nile Touring Co (☎ 51-38-60, fax 51-35-53, ✆ nile.tours@telecom.net.et)

Rocky Valley Safaris (☎ 15-24-62, fax 51-64-08) at the Ras Hotel in central Addis Ababa offers good Omo Valley safaris.

Travel Ethiopia (☎ 15-00-36, fax 51-02-00, ✆ travelethiopia@telecom.net.et) is another excellent agency with many years' experience of the country. It's run by a joint Ethiopian-European team. The agency is also eco-minded. French, Italian and German are spoken.

T-Tam Travel & Tours (☎ 51-40-55, fax 51-45-29, ✆ T-TAM@telecom.net.et)

Village Ethiopia (☎ 55-22-69, fax 55-08-97, ✆ village.ethiopia@telecom.net.et) is run by an enterprising Brit, Tony Hickey, who knows Ethiopia very well. He was once a Tigrayan People's Liberation Front (TPLF) fighter, and previously ran Experience Ethiopia. He's also a strong advocate of ecotourism. He runs the usual tours, plus bird-watching and fishing trips, 'nature tours', white-water rafting and boat trips on the Omo River and Lake Tana. All budgets are catered for, from guided tours using public buses to fully equipped safaris.

Yumo Tours (☎ 51-88-78, fax 51-34-51, ✆ yumo@telecom.net.et)

The Dorze people live in beehive-shaped huts.

The rock-hewn church of Abuna Yemata Guh

Beta Giorgis, a monastery of Lake Tana

The Lion of Judah, Addis Ababa railway station

Karo house of straw in the Omo Valley

The Sheraton's 'singing fountain', Addis Ababa

FRANCES LINZEE GORDON

FRANCES LINZEE GORDON

Narga Selassie – a must-see island monastery on Lake Tana

FRANCES LINZEE GORDON

Emperor Fasiladas' castle

FRANCES LINZEE GORDON

The Queen of Sheba's Palace

FRANCES LINZEE GORDON

Yeha's 3000-year-old ruins

FRANCES LINZEE GORDON

Emperor Fasiladas' 17th-century castle is a highlight of Gonder

Addis Ababa

☎ 01

Addis Ababa in Amharic means 'New Flower'. Founded little more than a century ago, new it certainly is; flower it certainly is not. On first impression, Addis Ababa is noisy, dusty, sprawling and shambolic. But it's also a colourful and vibrant city that grows on you surprisingly quickly – helped undoubtedly by its gorgeous climate of seemingly perpetual blue skies and cool highland air.

Despite its huge size – it is the third largest city in Africa, with an estimated population of five million – it retains a kind of small-town feel. The donkeys trotting intrepidly through the red lights and snarling traffic of Meskel Square, and the goats grazing on the neat verges of the high-rise buildings, are a reminder that Ethiopia is still a firmly rural, agricultural society.

Addis Ababa is a strange mix of the past and the present: the old imperial statues and emblems coexist alongside the hammer and sickle placards of the former Marxist regime, as well as the slick advertisements of the new private-sector banks. Wattle-and-daub huts stand not far from austere Fascist buildings and luxurious high-rise hotels. On the streets, priests in medieval-looking robes mix with African bureaucrats, Western aid workers and young Ethiopian women with cell phones.

Though most travellers can't wait to hurry out of the capital the moment they hurry in, it's worth giving the city at least a day or two. The Merkato is one of the largest outdoor markets on the continent, and some of the museums are among the most important in sub-Saharan Africa.

There are plenty of 'cultural experiences' worth investigating too, such as Ethiopian folk dancing and singing, the age-old entertainment provided by the *azmaris* (wandering minstrels), and even a trip to a *tej beat* (a kind of Ethiopian pub). Also in the capital, you'll find some of the best Ethiopian cooking in the country.

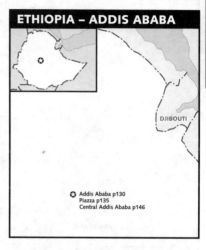

ETHIOPIA – ADDIS ABABA

DJIBOUTI

✪ Addis Ababa p130
Piazza p135
Central Addis Ababa p146

Addis Ababa, though capital of one of the ten poorest countries in the world, is hardly lacking in facilities. The new Sheraton Hotel is among the most luxurious hotels in Africa. International restaurants range from Armenian to Middle Eastern and Korean, with excellent Italian, French and Swiss restaurants in-between. Little pastry shops, cafes and bars line the streets everywhere, and the town provides a great hunting ground for souvenirs.

Ever the small town, it is also friendly, laid-back and amazingly safe compared with many African – and Western – capitals. Colourful, cheap and cheerful, it's a pretty easy city in which to settle.

HISTORY

Throughout Ethiopia's history her capitals have been transient – shifting like giant camps according to the political, economic and strategic demands of her rulers. Addis Ababa was no exception.

At the end of the 19th century Menelik II moved his capital first from Ankober in the region of Shoa to a site on Wuchacha Mountain, and finally to Entoto, to the north of the present-day city. There, the capital

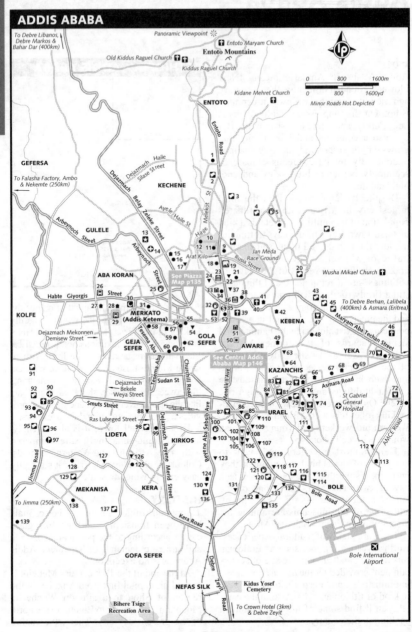

ADDIS ABABA

Panoramic Viewpoint

To Debre Libanos,
Debre Markos &
Bahar Dar (400km)

Entoto Maryam Church

Entoto Mountains

Old Kiddus Raguel Church

Kiddus Raguel Church

Kidane Mehret Church

ENTOTO

0   800   1600m

0   800   1600yd

Minor Roads Not Depicted

GEFERSA

To Falasha Factory, Ambo
& Nekemte (250km)

Entoto Road

Dejazmach Haile
Silase Street

KECHENE

Haile Melekot St

Ayele Haile St

Arbeynoch
Street

GULELE

Belay Zeleke Street

Dejazmach

13

14

ABA KORAN

15

16

17

Arat Kilo

Haile

Melekot St

18

Jan Meda
Race Ground

Ras Mekonnen Street

Wusha Mikael Church

Habte Giyorgis Street

26

27   28   29

30   31

25

MERKATO
(Addis Ketema)

KOLFE

Dejazmach Mekonnen
Demisew Street

1

2

3

4   5

7

6

8

10

12   11   9

19

23   21

24   22

33   34   37   38

32   35   36   40   41

52   53   39   42

51

50

**GOLA
SEFER**

AWARE

KEBENA

43

44

45

To Debre Berhan, Lalibela
(400km) & Asmara (Eritrea)

47

46

48

YEKA

Maryam Aba Techan Street

49

**GEJA
SEFER**

56   55

57

58

59   54

60   61   62

KAZANCHIS

63

64

65   66   67   68   69   70   71

91

Tesema Aba

Dejazmach
Bekele
Weya Street

Sudan St

Churchill Road

Menelik II Ave

83   82   81   80   79   78   77   76   75   74   72   73

84   85

Asmara Road

St Gabriel
General
Hospital

90

89

92

93

94

95   96

97

Smuts Street

Ras Lulseged Street

88

98   99

LIDETA

KIRKOS

100   101

102   103

104   105   106   107   108   109   110

111

87   86

URAEL

119

112

113

127   126

125

128

129

Jimma Road

MEKANISA

137   138

To Jimma (250km)

139

KERA

Dejazmach Beyene Merid Street

Beyene Aba Sebsib Ave

123

124

130   131

136

122   121   120   118   117   116   115   114

132   133   134   135

BOLE

Bole Road

Kera Road

GOFA SEFER

Debre Zeyit Road

NEFAS SILK

Kidus Yosef
Cemetery

**Bihere Tsige
Recreation Area**

To Crown Hotel (3km)
& Debre Zeyit

Bole International
Airport

See Piazza
Map p135

See Central Addis
Ababa Map p146

ADDIS ABABA

PLACES TO STAY
15 Semien Hotel
27 Aberash Tadesse Hotel
28 Kagnew Shaleka Hotel
41 Ras Amba Hotel
42 Bel Air Hotel
49 Gedera Hotel No 3
57 Extreme Hotel
65 Holiday Hotel
66 Axum Hotel; Debre Damo
    Hotel
68 Central Shoa Hotel
76 Classic Hotel
80 Plaza Hotel
113 Imperial Hotel
124 Hawi Hotel
132 Ibex Hotel

PLACES TO EAT
17 Addis Ababa Restaurant
22 Blue Tops Restaurant
24 Armenian Sporting Association
37 Forneria Italia (Bakery)
54 Oroscopo
63 La Canapé
74 Yohannis Gurage Kitfo Beat
75 Bekelech Kitfo Beat
81 Asni Pub (Kibnar Gurage
    Kitfo Beat)
84 Weizero Tsige Gayu (Nat
    Gwada Restaurant)
86 Rainbow Seoul Restaurant;
    Ram Jam Pub
88 Ras Restaurant
101 Pizza Deli Roma
102 Jeddah Restaurant; Taxi
    Stand; Mmmm My Flavour
104 Mulushoa Restaurant
105 Gazebo Pizza Bar & Restaurant
106 La Parisienne Hess Travel
    Ethiopia
107 Roby Pastry; Hard Luck Café;
    Hess Travel
108 Great Wall Chinese
    Restaurant; Purple Café
109 Burger Queen
110 Mendi Restaurant
112 Hill Belt
114 Saay Pastry
115 Tandoor Indian Restaurant
118 Habesha Restaurant; Peacock
    Restaurant; T-tram Travel &
    Tours
122 City Café & Pastry; Sangam
    Restaurant
123 Shanghai Restaurant; Mobil
    Petrol Station
126 B & B Kitfo

127 Le Petit Paris
130 Don Vito Pizzeria
131 Acropolis Greek Restaurant
133 Bonnie Cheese Shop
134 Karamara Restaurant

OTHER
1   Women's Fuelwood Carriers
    Project
2   Spanish Embassy
3   US Embassy
4   French Embassy
5   Total Petrol Station
6   Italian Embassy
7   Asni Gallery
8   Egyptian Embassy
9   Dibab Recreation Services
10 Addis Ababa University
    (Main Campus)
11 Institute of Language Studies
12 Institute of Ethiopian Studies;
    Ethnological Museum
13 Police Station
14 Ras Desta Hospital
16 Istituto Italiano di Cultura
18 Ministry of Finance
19 Lion House (Zoo)
20 German Embassy
21 Misrach Centre
23 National Museum
25 Shell Petrol Station
26 Autobus Terra (Long-distance
    Bus Station); Minibuses; Taxis
29 City Bus Station
30 Anwar Mosque (Great
    Mosque)
31 Alliance-Ethio Française
32 Mobil Petrol Station
33 Patriarch's Palace
34 Goethe Institut; Café Monique
35 Commercial Bank of Ethiopia
36 Natural History Museum
38 Mulugeta G. Yesus Garage
39 Trinity Cathedral & Museum
40 St Matthew's Anglican Church
43 Kenyan Embassy
44 Belgium Embassy
45 British Embassy
46 Kiddus Mikael Church
47 Mahoi Tej Beat
48 Balderas Calvary & Sports Club
50 Beta Maryam Mausoleum
51 Menelik Palace
52 Ministry of Education
53 Yegebawal Tej Beat
55 Shumeta Leda (Souvenir Shop)
56 Mokarar (Coffee Shop)
58 Caravan Travel & Tour Agency

59 Hope Enterprises
60 Immigration Office (Visas)
61 Shell Petrol Station
62 Haileselassie Alemayehu
    (Souvenir Shop)
64 Centre Français des Etudes
    Ethiopiennes
67 Ethiopian Tourism Trading
    Corporation (ETTC)
69 Shell Petrol Station
70 Beta Mengist Tej Beat
71 Transport & Communications
    Bureau
72 Kitaow Tej Beat No 2
73 Iveco AMCE Factory
77 Topia Tej Beat
78 Addis Tribune
79 Embassy of Bulgaria
82 My Pub
83 Behale Amba Cultural Evening
85 Shell Petrol Station
87 Memo Club
89 Church
90 Armed Forces Hospital
91 Dutch Embassy; Saudi
    Arabian Embassy
92 Ghanian Embassy
93 Afewerk Teklé's Home &
    Studio
94 Shell Petrol Station
95 Swiss Embassy; Irish Embassy
96 Yemeni Embassy
97 Addis Ababa Golf Club &
    Restaurant
98 Sudanese Embassy
99 Sheba's Daughter's Pillows &
    Treasures
100 Shell Petrol Station
103 Embuay Mesk Recreation
    Centre
111 Goshu Art Gallery
116 La Gazelle Piano Bar (Steak
    House); Four Seasons Travel &
    Tours
117 Djiboutian Embassy
119 Agip Petrol Station
120 Ugandan Embassy
121 Mobil Petrol Station
125 Novis Supermarket
128 Ato Basket Shop
129 Austrian Embassy
135 Torero Club; Barn Nightclub
136 Concord Hotel (Dome
    Nightclub); La Caverne
    Nightclub; Mobil Petrol Station
137 Somali Embassy
138 International Tennis Club
139 Alert Handicraft Shop

could easily be defended against rebellion from within as well as attacks from without. Later, as Menelik tightened his grip on the country, Entoto began to lose its strategic value, and its inconveniences – such as an inclement climate and difficulties of supply – began to outweigh its advantages.

In the meantime, Menelik's consort, Taitu, had her eye on a different site. Known as Filwoha or 'Boiling Water', after the hot springs found there, the spot lay amid the fertile foothills of the Entoto Mountains and benefited from a pleasant temperate climate.

In 1886, Menelik granted some land to Taitu on which to build. The queen named the new site Addis Ababa, and a settlement was quickly established. Soon the royal court began to spend more time here than at Menelik's sterile old capital at Entoto. Tents turned into *tukuls* (cone-shaped huts), wooden shacks became stone structures, the population grew and commerce flourished.

Addis Ababa's future was only briefly threatened in 1900, when the usual resource crisis (which had afflicted so many of Ethiopia's capitals in the past) arose. Menelik briefly contemplated establishing yet another capital at Addis Alem. However, the city was saved by an unlikely hero: the eucalyptus tree.

Recently introduced, the exotic species was known as the *bahar zaf* .(tree from beyond the water). With its rapid growth, and modest demands it soon became clear that the tree could meet the demands for wood of the ever-increasing population. (Later a Georgian resident called the new town 'Eucalyptopolis' – a name still rather appropriate.)

Today Addis Ababa is very much at the centre of things. Since 1958, it has been the headquarters of the United Nations Economic Commission for Africa (ECA) and, since 1963, the secretariat of the Organisation of African Unity (OAU). Many regard the city as 'Africa's diplomatic capital'.

For the traveller, too, Addis Ababa is centrally placed, geographically and practically, standing at the crossroads of the country's air, rail and road transportation network. The city makes an ideal springboard for travel to the surrounding regions,

which are otherwise as good as separated from one another.

CLIMATE

See also When to Go in the Facts for the Visitor section and Climate in the Facts about Ethiopia section. Lying on the southern slopes of the Entoto Mountains at an altitude of between 2300–2500m above sea level, Addis Ababa is the third highest capital in the world, and despite its proximity to the equator–just 8° north–enjoys a temperate climate with an average temperature of just 16°C.

Between late October and mid-January, the temperature can drop by almost 20°C to just above freezing at night. From July to mid-September, be prepared for almost daily rainstorms.

ORIENTATION

Until very recently there was no urban planning in the capital; Addis Ababa sprawls over 250 sq km.

Although there is no city centre per se, the city can be divided up into different sections. Churchill road (officially known as Churchill Ave) marks the central part of town and runs north to south. La Gare (train station) marks the southern end; St George's Cathedral, lying to the north of the road, marks the northern end. Many government and commercial buildings can be found here including Ethiopian Airlines, the main post office, telecommunications building and (a major landmark) the National Theatre.

The area known as the Piazza at the northern end of Churchill road is a legacy of the brief Italian Occupation, and still has a slightly Italian feel. It's here that many of the budget hotels can be found, as well as a rash of little cafes and bars, tailors, electronic shops and silversmiths and goldsmiths. The Piazza is centred roughly around De Gaulle Square.

Running almost parallel to Churchill Road in the east, the Entoto Road, which at its southern end becomes Menelik II Ave, is a kind of 'state and education' zone, with the Addis Ababa University and the museums in the north, and the National Palace in the south. The huge and ugly Meskel

Square in the centre, rebuilt and enlarged by the Derg as a kind of parade ground, is another landmark. The Ethiopian Tourism Commission (ETC) is found here.

To the west, the famous open-air market, Merkato, can be found. To the south-east, most of the embassies, as well as the city's international airport, are located.

Maps

The ETC map of the country (1987, 1:2,000,000) has a useful map of Addis Ababa on the back. The scale is small, but includes some of the main landmarks and is good for getting general bearings. It's available from some of the larger hotels as well as the Meskal gift shop beside the commission on Meskel Square.

The same map, but at its normal scale (1:15,000), is produced by the Ethiopian Mapping Authority (EMA), which is situated opposite the Hilton Hotel on Menelik II Ave in the centre. The office is open from 8.30 am to 12.30 pm and 1.30 to 5.30 pm weekdays. The map costs Birr21.

INFORMATION
Tourist Offices

For more general information see also this heading in the Facts for the Visitor chapter. The Tourist Information Centre (☎ 51-23-10, fax 51-38-99) in the ground floor of the ETC in Meskel Square is open from 8.30 am to 12.30 pm (until 11.30 am Friday) and 1.30 to 5.30 pm weekdays. In the peak season (December to April) it's also open from 8.30 am to 12.30 pm and 2 to 5 pm weekends. Though staff do their best, don't expect much more than the usual brochures (some of which are useful).

If you're looking for advice on travel itineraries, your best bet is the National Tour Operation (NTO) or one of the private travel agencies (see Organised Tours in the Getting Around Chapter earlier in this chapter), whose staff have a much greater knowledge and experience of travel in Ethiopia.

Money

See also this heading in the Facts for the Visitor chapter. Both government and private

Navigating around the City

If you're trying to navigate Addis Ababa with a map, be aware that few streets are sign-posted, and that few residents know the names of the streets anyway. Some streets may also have a variety of names depending on the map you use.

Instead, much of Addis Ababa is known by the main roads that lead to and from it, such as the Bole road (after the airport) or the Jimma road (which leads to Jimma) etc. Most residents go by local landmarks (usually large buildings) instead of street names. Major intersections also form important landmarks, such as Arat Kilo, a name derived from the number of kilometres (four) that it lies from the centre of town.

banks operate in Addis Ababa, and their exchange rates amount to pretty much the same. However, private banks usually have shorter queues. Ethiopian law does not currently allow foreign banks to operate in Ethiopia, though that will probably change shortly.

The branch of the Commercial Bank at the Hilton Hotel, on Menelik II Ave in the centre, keeps longer hours than normal: it's open from 6 to 11.30 am, 12.30 to 6.30 pm and 7 to 10.30 pm daily. Even more centrally located is the branch at the Ghion Hotel, which is open from 7 am to 9.30 pm daily.

A good private bank, not far from the ETC on Meskel Square, is the Wegagen Bank (☎ 65-50-15, fax 65-48-70). It's open from 8 to 11.30 am and 1 to 4.30 pm weekdays (and Saturday mornings).

If you need a money transfer, the Western Union (☎ 53-38-01, fax 53-32-29) on Ras Makonnen Ave is open from 8 to 11 am and 1 to 3 pm weekdays (and Saturday mornings).

Post & Courier Services

The main post office is on Churchill Road and is open 8 am to 6 pm weekdays, 8 am to 4 pm Saturday and 10 am to noon Sunday. The courier service DHL (☎ 61-49-85) has 11 offices about town; in the centre there's one on Ras Makonnen Ave. For more details see Post & Communications in the Facts for the Visitor chapter.

Telephone & Fax

The main telecommunications building is at the southern end of Churchill Road. It's open from 8 am to 12.30 pm and 1 to 10 pm Monday to Saturday (until 9 pm Sunday). Both phone and fax services are available.

The yellow public phoneboxes around town take two 10¢ coins; some accept phonecards.

Email & Internet Access

The Business Centre (☎ 51-84-00 ext 987, @ hilton.addis@telecom.net.et) at the Hilton Hotel provides access to the Internet. For guests, costs are calculated per three minutes (Birr10 for the first three minutes). Nonguests must buy 30/60/120 minute cards, which cost Birr50/85/150 and are valid for three months. The centre is open from 7 am to 11 pm daily, and also has a fax/secretarial service.

The country's national server is found at the Ethio Internet Centre (☎ 51-47-05, fax 51-57-77, @ internet-mark@telecom.net.et) beside the main post office on Churchill Road. At the time of research, Internet access was available to Addis Ababa residents only, for a minimum subscription of three months. In the next few years, the company hopes to open six cyber cafes in the city, including one at the airport.

Travel Agencies

For information on travel agencies, see Organised Tours in the Getting Around section earlier in this chapter; for day tours of Addis Ababa see Organised Tours later in this section.

Bookshops

Mega Bookshop (☎ 51-88-96), next to the Shell station off Meskel Square, has a selection of books including the textbook *Amharic for Foreigners* and David Phillipson's *The Monuments of Aksum*.

Bookworld (☎ 11-63-23) on Wavel St in the Piazza, is straight out of Europe, complete with thick carpets and pan-pipe background music. It's the best place for books in English (plus some in French), but because books are imported, prices are a bit higher than at home. There's a small section on Ethiopia, a children's section and an excellent fiction section. The shop also stocks around 45 European and US magazines from *National Geographic* to *Cosmo* and *Interiors* and has a good selection of postcards (Birr2.50 to Birr7). It's open from 9 am to 8 pm Monday to Saturday.

The African's Bookshop, diagonally opposite the British Council in the Piazza, is one of the best places for second-hand books on Ethiopia, particularly those currently out of print. For a very small commission, the helpful manager, Yohannes Bitowelign, can get you most things within a couple of days if you give him a list. It's also a good place for cheap holiday reads: second-hand fiction costs between Birr15 to Birr20.

Another great place for out-of-print second-hand books on Ethiopia and general fiction is the row of stalls behind the National Theatre, across the road from the ABC Stationery.

For newspapers, the big hotels such as the Ghion and the Hilton sell a selection of magazines including the *Economist, Time* and *Newsweek*, and newspapers such as the *International Herald Tribune, Le Monde* and *La Republica*. The Hilton also usually stocks Lonely Planet's *Ethiopian Amharic phrasebook*.

Libraries

The library of the excellent Institute of Ethiopian Studies (IES; ☎ 11-00-86, @ IES. AAU@telecom.net.et), north of the Piazza, boasts the best collection of books in English on Ethiopia in the world, including early works of explorers such as James Bruce (see the boxed text 'James Bruce: In Search of the Source' in the North of Addis Ababa chapter). It's free for a half-day's casual use by the general public and it's also open to researchers (US$50 for three months' access, with a letter of introduction). Regular lectures on Ethiopian culture are open to anyone interested. A program of events is posted up outside the library.

The collection of 20,000 books on Ethiopia housed in the National Library (☎ 51-22-41), west of Churchill Road in the centre, includes quite a good English-language section. It also boasts an important collection of maps, engravings and manuscripts, including a very rare 14th-century illuminated manuscript, which is thought to be the oldest-surviving manuscript in the country. The library is open from 8.30 am to 5 pm weekdays, until 4 pm Saturday and until noon Sunday; the English-language section is open weekdays only and closes for lunch between 12.30 and 1.30 pm.

Cultural Centres

Alliance-Ethio Français (☎ 12-95-46, fax 55-36-81), west of the Piazza, puts on French films once a week (Birr4), plus exhibitions of both Ethiopian and international artists once a month, as well as the occasional concert. The library is open to members only, but there's a cafe open to all, which serves good bistro-type food.

Centre Français des Etudes Ethiopiennes (☎/fax 51-32-09) was inaugurated officially in 1998 and is a centre of research specialising in archaeology and social and human sciences. It has a respectable library containing around 3000 books on Ethiopia and the Horn, which is open from 8 am to 5 pm weekdays.

Istituto Italiano di Cultura (☎ 11-36-55, fax 55-22-86), north of the Piazza, organises various Italian cultural events including concerts, exhibitions and dance and drama shows. It has a good library with over 10,000 books, which is open from 9 am to 2 pm weekdays and additionally from 4 to 6.30 pm on Tuesday and Thursday.

The British Council (☎ 55-00-22, fax 55-25-44, ✉ britcoun.di@telecom.net.et), in the Piazza, shows 16mm films on Tuesday and Friday at 5 pm. Talks on Ethiopia are also periodically held. It has a library, an information centre with various week-old English-language newspapers, a cafe and a very pleasant roof terrace. The library (with around two shelves on Ethiopia) is open from 10 am to 6 pm Tuesday to Saturday. Borrowing rights as well Internet access are limited to members only. To become a member, you'll need to be resident in Addis Ababa for a minimum of six months, with an address and sponsor in Ethiopia.

The Goethe Institut (☎ 55-28-88, fax 55-12-99, ✉ gci@telecom.net.et), east of the Piazza, puts on German films on Friday at 5.30 pm, as well as occasional concerts, theatres and workshops in collaboration with Addis Ababa University. It also has a reading room with week-old German magazines and newspapers. It's open from 9 am to 6 pm weekdays. There's no cafe, but the Café Monique next door is a good substitute.

Medical Services

The centrally located Ghion Pharmacy (☎ 51-86-06), north-west of Meskel Square, is well stocked with supplies including antigiardiasis, tapeworm, malaria and diarrhoea

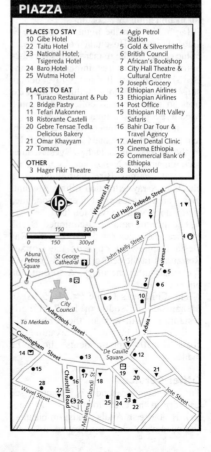

PIAZZA

PLACES TO STAY	
10	Gibe Hotel
22	Taitu Hotel
23	National Hotel; Tsigereda Hotel
24	Baro Hotel
25	Wutma Hotel

PLACES TO EAT	
1	Turaco Restaurant & Pub
2	Bridge Pastry
11	Tefari Makonnen
18	Ristorante Castelli
20	Gebre Tensae Tedla Delicious Bakery
21	Omar Khayyam
27	Tomaca

OTHER	
3	Hager Fikir Theatre

4	Agip Petrol Station
5	Gold & Silversmiths
6	British Council
7	African's Bookshop
8	City Hall Theatre & Cultural Centre
9	Joseph Grocery
12	Ethiopian Airlines
13	Ethiopian Airlines
14	Post Office
15	Ethiopian Rift Valley Safaris
16	Bahir Dar Tour & Travel Agency
17	Alem Dental Clinic
19	Cinema Ethiopia
26	Commercial Bank of Ethiopia
28	Bookworld

medication. It also stocks suntan cream, condoms, nappies and tampons. The pharmacist, Ato Habte Selassie, is helpful and knowledgeable and speaks good English. It's open from 8.30 am to 1 pm and from 2.30 to 8.30 pm Monday to Saturday and from 9 am to 1 pm Sunday.

If you need a doctor or want some tests done, head for the nearby Universal Clinic (☎ 51-57-94), which has a fully equipped lab; appointments aren't necessary. Blood/stool tests cost Birr5/4 and take from 2 to 30 minutes for an emergency/normal test. The clinic is open from 8 am to 7 pm Monday to Saturday, and until 5 pm Sunday. You'll be charged Birr10 for registration, but nothing for examination by a doctor.

If you're ill in the night, the private St Gabriel General Hospital (☎ 61-36-22) east of the centre off the Asmara road, is open 24 hours and comes recommended by the British embassy. It has X-ray, dental, surgery and laboratory facilities. Don't expect an ambulance to collect you; you'll need to get yourself there.

If it's the old snappers that are the problem, head for Alem Dental Clinic (☎ 11-16-15) in the Piazza. Dr Getachew (yes!) comes recommended by NGOs, speaks good English and charges Birr10/30/40/60 for a check up/X-ray/extraction/filling. Appointments aren't necessary, but are a good idea if you don't want to wait too long.

The private and well-equipped Brook Medical Services (☎ 51-51-15), on Ras Desta Damtew St opposite the Cottage Restaurant in the centre, has well-qualified specialists in gynaecology. A consultation only costs Birr20.

The Children's Clinic (☎ 71-15-15) in Mekanisa, just south of Le Petit Paris restaurant south-west of the centre, is a well-equipped hospital. An examination costs Birr50. Appointments should be made.

Other Services

The best place for laundry is your hotel (see Laundry in the Facts for the Visitor chapter). If you're in Addis Ababa on business and need a suit/skirt dry-cleaned, there are plenty of dry-cleaners who charge between Birr20 to Birr30.

If the old shoes or sandals need a bit of TLC, there are various wizard cobblers in the Piazza. The replacement of an entire leather sole costs Birr55.

If it's the hair, try Natalina at the Etsegenet Hairdresser (☎ 51-62-48) near Meskel Square, which is popular with expats. Women are charged Birr43 for a wash, cut and blow dry. Barbers can be found throughout the city including at the Addisu Filwoha Hotel and Hot Springs in the centre, which charges Birr25 for a haircut.

If it's the car that needs TLC, head for Mulugeta G. Yesus garage east of the Piazza (☎ 11-76-91), which is open from 8 am to 12.30 pm and 1.30 to 6 pm Monday to Saturday. All types of car or 4WD can be repaired; a good supply of spare parts is available. Mechanics can be dispatched to you if necessary, and cost a maximum of Birr100, including work plus minor spare parts.

Foto Batti (☎ 51-55-03) on Ras Makonnen Ave is one of the best photo shops in town, both for film (print and slide) and film developing. It stocks Fuji film such as Superbia 100 for Birr21 (36 exp) and Fujichrome Sensia for Birr35. Film (but not slides) can be developed in 45 minutes and costs Birr51.

Emergency

Emergency 24-hour numbers include the police (☎ 91), the fire brigade (☎ 93), and the Red Cross service (☎ 92).

Dangers & Annoyances

Violent crime in Addis Ababa is fortunately rare, particularly where the visitor is concerned. However, petty theft and confidence tricks are a problem and though there's no cause for alarm, travellers should always be vigilent.

The Merkato has the worst reputation for petty theft and pickpockets abound – targeting not just *faranjis* (foreigners) but Ethiopians, too. Angelic-looking boys often work in groups – one 'bumps' into you or distracts you in some way, while the others do out your pockets. In such areas, travellers are advised to leave expensive watches and all jewellery in their hotel. See also Dangers & Annoyances and Money in the Facts for the Visitor chapter.

Other spots where you should be vigilant include the theatre area of downtown, outside some of the larger hotels (most snatch-thieving occurs in a kind of circle linking the Ghion, Ethiopia and Ras Hotels at the southern end of Churchill road), the Piazza and at the minibus stands. In the city, particularly around the National Theatre, adult gangs sometimes operate. Common ploys are to feign a fight or argument and, when one man appeals to you for help, the other frisks your pockets.

NATIONAL MUSEUM

The National Museum (☎ 55-31-88) east of the Piazza off the Entoto road must rank among the most important sub-Saharan museums in Africa. Its collection was gathered in the 20th century, mainly by French archaeologists working in the north (and Eritrea). Though it contains some very important and interesting exhibits, the layout and display of some of the items is pretty lacklustre and unimaginative.

There are plans to build a purpose-built, more 'interactive' museum in the future, which will include a separate fine-art collection, an ethnographical exhibition and a souvenir shop. In the meantime, you'll just need to use your imagination.

The museum is divided into chronological sections starting with a prehistoric room (containing the cast of Lucy), then the pre-Aksumite, Aksumite, Solomonic and Gonder rooms.

Entrance to the museum currently costs Birr10 (though it may well go up shortly); student discounts are not available. The museum is open daily from 8.30 am (9 am on the weekend) to 5.30 pm, but is closed on national holidays (see Public Holidays & Special Events in the Facts for the Visitor chapter). English-speaking guides are available for no charge (but should be tipped afterwards). All photography is forbidden.

Siren Scam

One scam that seems to be on the increase in Addis Ababa is the 'siren scam'. Most commonly, a single male traveller is approached by a young, well-dressed Ethiopian male, often claiming to be a student.

The student may appeal for help – to practise English before an exam, with the deciphering of a letter from a faranji friend abroad, or to read a medical prescription, and will suggest visiting a coffee house, market or museum. The place turns out to be a small room in a private house, where a hostess will promptly dish copious quantities of *tej* (honey wine), and perhaps dancers and singers will perform. An invitation to 'rest' amid soothing company often follows.

Suddenly, the entertainment comes to a halt and a bill of US$50 to US$200 will be slapped on the table in front of you. The least query or protest provokes a barrage of hysterics, screams and shouts, as only an Ethiopian hostess can do. Most travellers pay up, thankful just to escape. The area around the hotels in the Piazza, along Churchill Road and around the telecommunications building in the centre seem to be the most common hunting ground for potential victims.

The little tukul set in the gardens outside is a good place for a drink or a cheap lunch after a walk around the museum. Dishes cost between Birr4 and Birr8.

The Department of Inventory and Inspection of the CRCCH is next door to the museum. This is where you bring souvenirs for inspection in order to obtain an export permit (see under Customs in the Facts for the Visitor chapter).

Things to See

The star of the present exhibition is undoubtedly **Lucy**, the fossilised hominid discovered in 1974 (see the boxed text 'Lucy in the Sky' under History in the Facts about Ethiopia chapter). The exhibit is in fact a plaster cast (albeit a good one); the real bones are preserved in the archives of the museum.

One of the highlights is the **pre-Aksumite room**. The solid, seated female figures in limestone are believed to be fertility icons and are remarkable for their great age (dating from the 5th century BC), their sculptural refinement, and for the inscriptions they bear in the ancient southern Arabic language. Look out for the beautiful, pre-1st century AD bronze oil lamp showing a dog chasing an ibex. There's also a charming cooing dove in terracotta, thought to have served as a pot for holy water. The scarab beetles in glass and bronze testify to very early contacts with Pharaonic Egypt. Keep an eye out also for the pre-Aksumite sacrificial altar with two sphinxes and a hole to let the blood escape.

In the **Aksumite room** a model of the Dongur edifice (popularly known as the Queen of Sheba's Palace) at Aksum gives an idea of how grandiose ancient Aksum must have looked. Look out also for the terracotta offerings found in a temple at Hawalti, including one showing yoked oxen thought to date to the 5th century BC, which suggests a very early use of the plough.

Upstairs, there's a good display of Ethiopian **art** ranging from early (possibly 14th century) parchment, to 17th and 18th century triptychs and 20th century canvas oil paintings by the leading modern artists such as Gebre Kristos Desta, Teshome Bekele and Afewerk Tekle (see the boxed text 'Afewerk Tekle' later in this section).

Another room contains a collection of secular **arts and crafts** including traditional weapons, jewellery, clothing and musical instruments. Look out for the *gabeta* board game, and the delightful wooden clogs with four 'legs', perhaps for walking through mud.

Other rooms contain lavish **royal paraphernalia**: ceremonial, royal and courtly robes and a good collection of crowns. Look out for the robes of Kaffa nobles, richly embroidered with silver buttons, buckles and tassels, which must have made a lovely jangling sound when worn. The enormous and rather hideous carved wooden throne is Indian-made and was a coronation gift from the Indian community to Emperor Haile Selassie in 1935.

ETHNOLOGICAL MUSEUM

Haile Selassie's former palace and grounds is now home to Addis Ababa University's main campus north of the centre off the Entoto road. The grounds were previously known as *Genete Le'ul* or 'Princely Garden' after the impressive formal gardens that are kept up to this day.

The palace building itself now houses the library of the Institute of Ethiopian Studies (see Libraries earlier in this section) and, upstairs, the Ethnological Museum, undoubtedly the best museum in Ethiopia.

The exhibits have been carefully selected and represent some of the finest arts and crafts of the country. Benefiting from all the space and light of the palace, the items are additionally well displayed and backed up with good captions in English and French, and evocative black and white photos.

The museum gives a great insight into the many different peoples of Ethiopia and their rich cultures. If you're not travelling to the remoter parts, this will give you a glimpse of them – like a quick trot around the country. See also the boxed texts 'Peoples of Ethiopia' in the Facts about Ethiopia section, and 'Peoples of the Lower Omo Valley' in the South of Addis Ababa section.

Entrance costs Birr20 (Birr1 for students). The museum is open from 8 am to noon and 1 to 5 pm Tuesday to Thursday; from 8 to 11.30 am and 1.30 to 5 pm Friday; and from 10 am to 5 pm weekends. English - and Italian-speaking guides are available for no charge (they should be tipped afterwards).

Things to See

The **first room** displays the different economies of the people, from highland ploughing to lowland crop cultivation, fishing, weaving and even trapping. Look out for the delightful 'rain capes' made entirely from reeds, and the *agelgil*, the leather lunch 'boxes' still used by Ethiopian travellers in the country today. The 'medical charms' from the regions of Shoa and Wolega worn to cure sicknesses such as eye infections and nose bleeds are evidence of the widespread belief in Ethiopia that art has the power to heal.

The **second room** deals with the daily life and customs of the different groups; each section deals with a different province. In the Afar section, take a peak at the traditional *daboyta* (hut), the wonderful hide sandals and a black-and-white photo of a stunningly beautiful Afar girl. There's also outstanding examples of basketry and some attractive coffee pots. There's a *tankwa* (traditional papyrus boat) from Lake Tana in the north; a traditional beehive from Gofam made from bark, bamboo and cow dung; examples of the famous chairs from Ilubador province in the west carved from a single piece of wood; and the famous and rather sinister *waga* or funeral sculptures from Konso (see the boxed text 'The People of Konso' in the South of Addis Ababa section).

In the **passageway** leading to further rooms, there are panels displaying 'impressions of Ethiopia' – paintings and drawings by famous travellers such as Henry Salt and Richard Burton.

In the **Kaffa room**, there's a display of royal regalia from the ancient kingdom of Kaffa (which dates from medieval times). The extraordinary and very oriental-looking crown was returned recently to Ethiopia by the family of Alfred Ilg, Menelik's Swiss adviser.

Other rooms show the preserved bedroom and bathroom of Emperor Haile Selassie, and an excellent selection of Ethiopian coins. Look out for the *amole*, the salt bars used from the 15th to the 19th century as a form of currency (see the boxed text 'Salt for Gold' under Danakil Desert in the North of Addis Ababa section).

Art & Craft Displays Upstairs, there's an exceptional overview of Ethiopian art starting from the 2nd millennium BC right up to the present day. The museum's collection of painted religious icons is the largest and most representative in the world (around 332), dating from the 15th to the 20th centuries. About 95% of the icon artists are unknown, since works were traditionally unsigned. The icons were cut from a single piece of wood, made into a triptych and bound skilfully so that they opened and closed perfectly. They

differ from their Byzantine counterparts in that the artist carved the wood as well as painted it. Look out for the Italian influence in the Renaissance clothing.

There's also a small but good section on the often neglected Islamic contribution to Ethiopian art, and a section on secular art including the tradition of animal skin painting. The Queen of Sheba legend is a common theme (see the boxed text 'The Legendary Queen of Sheba' under Aksum in the North of Addis Ababa section). The secular paintings show all the wit, humanity and charm of traditional Ethiopian painting. Look out for the picture showing a banquet given by Emperor Menelik, attended by very pink-faced *faranjis* (foreigners) with faranji food and faranji knives and forks.

Look out for the fascinating magic scrolls which, like the Roman lead scrolls, cast curses on people or appealed to the gods for divine assistance. Made from animal parchment, many are delightfully illustrated.

The lengthy Genealogy of the Prophets display looks like rolls and rolls of loo paper and starts right from the beginning with Adam. It's written in Ge'ez: the ancient ecclesiastical language of Aksum and ancestor of modern-day Amharic.

There's also an excellent collection of wooden and metal crosses in every imaginable shape, size and design. Traditionally, there are three types of crosses in Ethiopia: hand, neck and processional.

ADDIS ABABA MUSEUM

The Addis Ababa Museum (☎ 15-31-80), founded in 1986 on the centenary of the city as the capital, is housed in one of the oldest residential buildings in town on the southern edge of Meskel Square. It belonged formerly to one of Menelik's warlords, Ras Biru Woldegabriel.

Entrance is Birr2. The museum is open from 8.30 am to 12.30 pm and 1.30 to 5.30 pm weekdays, and from 8.30 am to noon weekends; photography is not allowed.

Things to See

The museum purportedly deals with the 'political, cultural and architectural history of the city'. The most interesting thing is the excellent collection of old photos, including candid portraits of the portly and redoubtable Empress Taitu, rakish Lej Iyassu, and the very beautiful Empress Zewditu as a young woman. The photo of Menelik's old capital at Entoto shows just a hill dotted with little, round huts.

There's also a **'first-in-Ethiopia room'**, which is more interesting than it sounds and which includes a picture of Menelik sitting proudly in Ethiopia's 'first plane' and another of the 'first pharmacy' – a man at the counter with his horse!

Upstairs, there's a small display of **crafts**; look out for the photos of the Ethiopian 'warlords' in their magnificent traditional warrior garb: lion's mane head-dresses, sheepskin shawls and hippopotamus-hide shields.

NATURAL HISTORY MUSEUM

The Natural History Museum (☎ 11-23-43) east of the Piazza, dates from the 1930s, when an Italian collected examples of Ethiopian mammals and birds. The collection has been greatly increased in the last five years (with international assistance) and now includes bats, rodents, insects, reptiles (including snakes) and amphibians.

The museum is probably of most interest to birders, with ten good bird cabinets showing 450 species including the country's endemics, displayed against painted dioramas.

Entrance is Birr5 (students Birr2.50). The museum is open from 10 am to 4 pm Tuesday, Thursday, Saturday, Sunday and holidays.

RAILWAY MUSEUM

The railway 'museum' (☎ 51-29-61) near La Gare consists of four decrepit carriages that once belonged to Emperor Haile Selassie (two apparently came from Queen Elizabeth of England). The museum (also known as Musée du Chemin de Fer) is probably of interest to train buffs only. In the future, the carriages may be used for short excursions.

The museum is open from 8.30 am to noon and 1 to 3 pm weekdays, as well as Saturday morning. For tickets (Birr30) go to the 'direction personnel' office.

NATIONAL POSTAL MUSEUM

The postal museum next to the main post office houses a complete collection of Ethiopian stamps, starting from the very first ones minted by Menelik in 1894, to the present day. There are also stamps from 182 other 'Universal Postal Union countries', but it is the Ethiopian ones that are the most interesting. Subjects range from Ethiopian trees to beetles, medicinal plants and lakes; many stamps have won international awards. The original drawings and designs can also be seen.

Stamps can't be bought here; if you're interested in buying collectables, try the main post office, which sometimes sells old stamps to travellers, as well as first day covers.

This museum is more interesting than it sounds, and is worth a peak if you're in the vicinity; it costs less than a postage stamp to get in (Birr0.25). The museum is open from 9 am to 12.30 pm (to 11.30 am on Friday) and from 1.30 to 5.30 pm weekdays.

ST GEORGE CATHEDRAL & MUSEUM

The present cathedral, in the Piazza, was as good as rebuilt by Emperor Menelik in 1896 following the victory at Adwa (see the boxed text 'The Battle of Adwa' under Adwa in the North of Addis Ababa Chapter) and in thanks to St George (Ethiopia's patron saint), whose icon was carried into battle. Greek, Armenian and Indian artists worked on the church. The Empress Zewditu (in 1916) and Emperor Haile Selassie (in 1930) were both crowned here and their coronation garb can be seen in the museum.

Cathedral

The cathedral is traditional in form: octagonal, but Neoclassical and rather severe in style. It's not outstandingly beautiful, but the guided tour provides an interesting and useful explanation of the Orthodox church layout and peculiarities.

Also of interest are some of the interior paintings, particularly those by Afewerk Tekle (see the boxed text 'Afewerk Tekle' later in this section) commissioned by the emperor when the artist was still a very young man. On the northern side can be found a painting of the coronation of the Virgin. On the eastern side is a depiction of Emperor Haile Selassie's coronation and the well-known Queen of Sheba and King Solomon painting. High up is quite a striking mosaic of Christ, with his arms held wide open. Look out for the signatures – the artist broke with Ethiopian tradition and caused a minor uproar at the time by daring to sign his name on the painting, traditionally considered almost sacrilegious in Ethiopian religious painting.

Museum

The museum is well presented and laid out and probably contains the best collection of ecclesiastical paraphernalia in the country outside St Mary of Zion in Aksum, including some beautiful hand crosses, prayer sticks and ceremonial umbrellas.

It's also a very good introduction to the Ethiopian Orthodox church, which still carries enormous influence in Ethiopia, explaining its traditions and ceremonies. Look out for the delightful, and very Ethiopian, versions of traditional Christian regalia, such as the lion and elephant incense burner, and the beautiful miniature *mesob* (woven table) used to hold Holy Communion, which is made from traditional reeds, blue velvet and silver.

Entrance is Birr10 and includes quite a good guided tour of the church and museum. The museum is open from 8 to 11 and 2 to 5 pm daily except Monday; flash photography is not permitted.

TRINITY CATHEDRAL & MUSEUM

Trinity Cathedral, north of the centre off the Entoto Road, is the biggest Orthodox church in the country. With its large dome and spindly pinnacles, it's one of the landmarks of the city and is a strange mishmash of international styles. It's well worth a visit, and provides an interesting and sometimes poignant glimpse into many historical episodes of Ethiopia's history. The museum was built by Emperor Haile Selassie in memory of the Ethiopian patriots who fought against the Italians.

Entrance is free unless you want a guided tour with a deacon (Birr20), which is recommended. The cathedral is open from 8.30 am to noon and 2.30 to 5 pm daily.

Things to See

Inside, the most notable features are the two beautifully carved thrones for the emperor and empress, made of white ebony, ivory and marble. Perpendicular are the four smaller thrones for the princes and princesses.

To the north of the Holy of Holies are the tombs of the emperor and empress, which borrow in their design from the ancient Aksumite tradition. The emperor's tomb currently lies empty; it is hoped that one day his body will be transferred here from Beta Maryam Mausoleum (see following). This issue – along with many others surrounding the emperor – remains a very touchy and controversial subject in Ethiopia.

Look out for the murals on the south wall depicting the emperor making his famous speech to the League of Nations (see Italian Occupation under History in the Facts about Ethiopia section). In the underground crypts are buried some of the emperor's children (including the crown prince, who died in the US in 1997).

Around the Cathedral

The churchyard outside is the burial place of many patriots who lost their lives during the Fascist Occupation, including Ras Imru, one of the great resistance fighters. In front of the cathedral is the tomb of British suffragette Sylvia Pankhurst, daughter of the famous Emmeline Pankhurst. Sylvia was one of the very few people outside of Ethiopia who protested against the Italian Occupation; she later lived in Ethiopia.

To the south of the cathedral is a memorial to the ministers and officials killed at a stroke by the Derg in 1974 and buried in a common grave (see History in the Facts about Ethiopia chapter).

MENELIK PALACE

Surrounded by a stone wall, the old Menelik Palace, north of the centre off the Entoto road (also known as 'the Gibbi') is now the

A Quick Key to 'Africa: Past, Present and Future'

Inside Africa Hall is a monumental stained-glass window by the artist Afewerk Tekle. The following interpretation of the work comes from the artist himself.

The first 'panel' represents 'Africa: Past'. Red is the predominant colour, symbolic of Africa's struggle against both ignorance (symbolised by the heavy shadow) and colonialism (the smug-looking dragon). The disintegrating state of Africa is represented by the disunited family and the lost child in the middle foreground. The skeleton with the whip shows evil driving the African continent – carried by a group of Africans – further and further into backwardness. The black chain framing the picture symbolises slavery.

The panel on the left represents 'Africa: Present'. The predominant colour is green, and Africa, symbolised by the man wielding a heavy double-handed sword, is struggling to slay the dragon of colonialism. In the background, a new sun rises; from it emerges all the peoples, religions and races of Africa. Above, the powers of evil represented again by the skeleton is taking flight, banished at last.

The middle panel shows 'Africa: Future'. Yellow is the predominant colour. In the foreground a family advance forward bearing torches, symbolic of a reawakening and the illumination brought by knowledge. Rallying behind are the other African countries, united and resolute in their aim for advancement. On the right, the knight in armour represents the United Nations holding out the scale of justice. In the background, a more serene landscape depicts a kind of African arcadia, in which peace and harmony reign on the continent at last.

government's main headquarters and is not open to the public.

BETA MARYAM MAUSOLEUM

Lying to the south of the old Menelik Palace is the Beta Maryam Mausoleum (also known as Menelik's Mausoleum), where among others, Emperor Haile Selassie, Empresses Taitu and Zewditu and Emperor Menelik lie buried. Built in 1911, the mausoleum is made of grey stone surmounted by a large gilt crown with four small cupolas on each corner. It's not outstandingly interesting either inside or out.

Entrance is Birr10; it's open from 6 to 11 am and 3 to 5 pm daily.

NATIONAL PALACE

Formerly known as the Jubilee Palace, the National Palace, in the centre on Menelik II Ave, was built in 1955 to commemorate the first 25 years of Emperor Haile Selassie's reign. Currently the palace is the state residence of the president and is not open to the public. In the future, it is hoped that a new museum will be built to house the stored contents of Haile Selassie's National Palace. Exhibits will include the royal carriages, gifts made to the emperor, his wardrobe, dinner services etc.

AFRICA HALL

Built in 1961 by Emperor Haile Selassie, Africa Hall, near Meskel Square, is the seat of the ECA. The Italian-designed building is not very interesting, barring the frieze-like motifs that represent traditional Ethiopian *shamma* (shawl) borders.

Far more interesting is the monumental stained-glass window inside, by the artist Afewerk Tekle, entitled 'Africa: Past, Present and Future' (see the boxed text following and also the boxed text 'Afewerk Tekle' later in this section). Measuring 150 sq m, it fills one entire wall and is one of the biggest stained-glass windows in the world. It's well worth a visit; during some hours of the day, the white marble floor of the foyer is flooded with colour.

To visit, you need to make an appointment through the ECA (☎ 51-72-00, fax 51-31-55), PO Box 3001, Addis Ababa.

LION HOUSE

If you're not keen on zoos, avoid this one. Opposite the ministry of finance, north of the centre off the Entoto road, the 19 resident Abyssinian lions are descendants of those belonging to Emperor Haile Selassie. He used them as a kind of royal signature, often travelling with them and making gifts of them. The Abyssinian lion has a darker mane than other African lions and is smaller. The cages are minute and the animals pathetically thin. Feeding time is at noon.

Entrance costs Birr1; if you want to take photos/video, you pay a further Birr10/100. It's open from 8.30 am to 5.30 pm daily.

MERKATO

Also known as Addis Ketema (New Town), Merkato is the largest market in eastern Africa. At first sight it appears to be an impenetrable mass of stalls, produce and people; on closer inspection the market reveals a careful organisation with different sections for different products – rather like the layout of a traditional Muslim market.

It's said that you can buy anything here, from a Kalashnikov or camel to the most precious incense. The locals say that you can even bargain for a new soul! Some of the most interesting sections include the spice market (which is so pungent it may make you sneeze), and the 'recycling market', where locals in open-air workshops turn old tyres into sandals, decrepit corrugated iron into metal buckets and olive oil tins from Italy into coffee pots and tiny scoopers. It's a veritable lesson in waste management.

The two large covered buildings next door to the city bus station are known as the Addis Gebeya (New Market). Here the cloth shops, tailors and curio stalls can be found. Don't forget that bargaining is the order of the day; some dealers are master salesmen and have been known to fleece gullible tourists. The best thing is to come with a guide, who can also act as interpreter; ask your hotel to provide one.

The market has a terrific reputation for thieves and pickpockets but as long as you're vigilant and sensible (a money belt is a great idea), there's no cause for alarm. Beware also of the *delalla* (commission agents), who will want to 'show you a shop'.

The market takes place from 8.30 am to 7 pm every morning (except Sunday), but the best time to visit is early on Saturday, when people from all over the country come in. See also Shopping in the Facts for the Visitor chapter.

THE ASNI GALLERY

The excellent Asni Gallery (☎ 11-73-60) near the French embassy, about 4km northeast of the centre, is housed in the century-old villa of Menelik's minister of justice, and hosts various changing events including art exhibitions, slide lectures and sometimes traditional music. Events are advertised in the *Addis Tribune*.

It also sells a small selection of more unusual, useful and quite attractive gift items such as traditional child carriers, back-packs, pencil cases, and pillows and cushions designed like the saddle cloths of the highlands.

For details on its vegetarian buffet lunches (which can be eaten on the very attractive and peaceful veranda) see Buffets under Places to Eat later in this section.

It's open 10 am to 5.30 pm on Thursday and Saturday and 1.30 to 5.30 pm on Monday, Tuesday, Wednesday and Friday. To get there, take a taxi from Arat Kilo or a minibus.

See also Shopping in the Facts for the Visitor chapter.

AFEWERK TEKLE'S HOME & STUDIO

A member of five international academies (including the French one) and with a drawer full of international decorations – 91 at the last count, including the British Order of Merit – Afewerk Tekle is considered among Africa's greatest artists (see the boxed text).

A tour of Afewerk's home and studio (☎/fax 71-59-41, ✉ hmal.afewerk.tekle@ telecom.net.et) is offered by the artist himself (by appointment only). The tours takes one hour and includes the artist's most famous paintings such as *The Meskel Flower*, *Mother Ethiopia* and *The Simien Mountains*. The tour costs US$10 (US$5 for students), payable in dollars or birr. From July 1 to September 15, the house is closed. Photography is permitted in the compound, but not in the house.

If you're thinking of souvenirs, bring your credit card: a painting costs anything from

Afewerk Tekle

Born in 1932, Afewerk Tekle is one of Ethiopia's most distinguished and colourful artistic figures. Educated at the Slade School of Art in London, he later toured and studied in continental Europe, before returning to work under the patronage of Emperor Haile Selassie. A painter as well as a sculptor and designer, he is also a master fencer, dancer and toastmaster.

Proud to have 'survived three regimes' (when friends and peers did not), his life has hardly been without incident. In almost cinematic style, a 'friendly' fencing match turned into an attempt on his life, and a tussle over (yet another!) woman, led to his challenging his rival to a dawn duel. In the royal court of the emperor, he only just survived an assassination attempt by poisoned cocktail.

The artist famously makes his own terms and his own conditions: if he doesn't like the purchaser he won't sell, and his best-known paintings must be returned to Ethiopia within a lifetime. In 1998, he was offered no less than US$10 million for the work considered his masterpiece, *The Meskel Flower*.

US$10,000 to US$975,000. Signed and numbered reproductions are a snip at US$200 to US$300. The artist is particular about being addressed by his formal title 'Maître Artiste Laureat', though 'Maître' will do for short!

The house and studio is west of the centre near the Ghanian embassy, off the Jimma road.

WATER ACTIVITIES & MASSAGE

If you're grubby, tired and stiff, you might fancy a trip to the Addisu Filwoha Hotel and Hot Springs (☎ 51-91-00), also known as the New Filwoha Hotel, where Addis Ababa's original *raison d'être*, its natural hot mineral water, is piped into the complex. A full massage with oil costs Birr50 and is performed by two blind men; a normal or 'hydromassage' costs Birr17. A sauna bath costs Birr24 for first class, Birr15/18 for second class in the morning/afternoon. A straightforward hot bath costs between Birr5 and Birr10. It's open every day from 6 am to 10 pm.

A sauna or massage (Birr50) is also possible at the Hilton or Sheraton Hotels (see Places to Stay – Top End later in this section). The Sheraton's Aqua Club is designed like a Roman bath complete with stunning Italian mosaics.

If you fancy a dip in the thermal waters of a swimming pool in the centre of town, the Hilton charges Birr65. The Sheraton, with the best pool in town, charges Birr65/85 for weekdays/weekends. The Ghion Hotel is way cheaper at Birr14/8 for a swim for adults/children. There's also a high diving board, children's pool and playground. It's open from 6 am to 5.30 pm daily, but gets very crowded at the weekend.

BALL SPORTS

The Hilton has a gym (Birr60 per day), table tennis, minigolf, ground tennis and squash costing between Birr16 and Birr60 per hour or game; rackets and balls can be hired (Birr25).

Tennis is cheaper at the International Tennis Club (☎ 20-01-45) south-west of the centre (Birr10 per hour). It's open daily from 6 am to 9 pm. To get there, catch a minibus from the stadium (Birr2); ask for 'St Gabriel church, near the old airport'.

You can play golf at the newly restored nine-hole Addis Ababa Golf Club & Restaurant (☎ 71-30-62) off the Jimma road in the south-west. Daily green fees are Birr200/150 during the week/weekend. A thwack on the driving range costs Birr20 plus Birr20/35 for 50/100 balls. It's also got a good restaurant; every Sunday there's a BBQ lunch from 1 to 3 pm for Birr60.

There's a tenpin bowling alley at the Embuay Mesk Recreation Centre (☎ 16-21-80) south of the centre, which is open daily from 8 am to 10 pm. It costs Birr3.40 per game; Birr1.10 for shoe hire.

HORSE RIDING

If you fancy a ride on the emperor's horses (or their descendants at least), the Balderas Cavalry & Sports Club (☎ 18-15-11) northeast of the centre, offers horse riding for Birr30/20 for adults/children per hour including a teacher. A hack in the country surrounding the club costs Birr40 for two hours. The club is open Thursday, Friday and Sunday only; reservations aren't necessary.

LANGUAGE COURSES

The Institute of Language Studies (☎ 11-90-43) at Addis Ababa University, north-east of the Piazza off the Entoto Road, teaches three Ethiopian languages (Amharic, Tigrinya and Orominya) and charges Birr60 per hour for scheduled classes. Private tuition is easy to arrange with any of the 17 teachers (who will travel to you); rates are negotiable. The building is immediately to the left of the main university gates. Head for room 210 on the second floor. See also Language in the Facts about Ethiopia section and the Language chapter at the end of the book.

DANCE CLASSES

If you fancy learning to shake your shoulders (see the boxed text 'Dancing the Iskista' under Arts in the Facts for the Visitor section), you can enrol for dance classes at the Ethio Traditional Desta Gebre Dance School (☎ 61-05-04) in the centre of town. It costs Birr300 per month, but travellers are welcome to join one class only and leave a gratuity at the end. Classes are from 4 to 5 pm and 5 to 6 pm from Monday to Saturday. The feisty and enterprising Weizero Desta speaks Amharic only.

ORGANISED TOURS

For contact details of travel agents in Addis Ababa, see Organised Tours in the Getting Around section earlier in this chapter. Four Seasons Travel & Tours (next to La Gazelle Piano Bar south-east of the centre on the airport road) offers walking tours of Addis Ababa for around US$33 per person. Nile Touring Co, east of Meskel Square, does half-day tours of Merkato for US$26 per person (minimum two).

For day excursions out of the capital see Around Addis Ababa at the end of this section.

PLACES TO STAY – BUDGET

Many of the cheapest hotels are found in the Piazza. Inevitably some may double as

To Chew or Not to Chew?

If you want to try chat, you could head for the Mendi Restaurant (see Other International under Places to Eat later in this section), which has designated chat-chewing rooms. Chat sellers lurk outside (Birr15 for ½kg or Birr5 for a portion). You can also buy chat (a little more cheaply) at the chat market in the centre. It costs Birr5 per person to use the room; most people come from 3 to 10 pm on the weekend. Women should be very discreet and suitably attired. See also the boxed text 'Chat Among the Pigeons' in the East of Addis Ababa section later in this chapter.

brothels. Many rooms cost the same for one/two people.

Near the two bus stations in the Merkato area, west of the Piazza and rock-bottom is the *Aberash Tadesse Hotel* (☎ 75-20-26) with 14 basic rooms for Birr14. The *Gibe Hotel* (☎ 11-03-06) in the Piazza, has 10 rooms for Birr15/10 depending on size. Though hotels are reasonably clean, they're small and lugubrious and only for travellers on their last cent. Showers are cold.

The best value is offered by the *Kagnew Shaleka Hotel* (☎ 13-42-66) west of the Piazza, which is clean, well run and good value with 46 rooms with communal/private bathroom from Birr15/40. Those with student cards can usually get a discount. The *National* and *Tsigereda Hotels*, in the Piazza, have adequate rooms for Birr25 but are unabashed brothels.

The *Baro Hotel* (☎ 11-55-90, fax 55-14-47, ✉ Baro@telecom.net.et) in the Piazza has long been a favourite with budget travellers. Although it's clean and quite comfortable and set in an attractive and leafy compound (with car parking), it's not the bargain it used to be. Ask to see a few rooms; some are pretty dark, damp and decaying. Rooms range from Birr50/70 for one/two people with communal bathroom to Birr60/80 for one/two people with private bathroom. Staff are friendly, and there's a cafe serving snacks.

ETHIOPIA

CENTRAL ADDIS ABABA

PLACES TO STAY
8   Sheraton
13   Hilton Hotel
15   Addisu Filwoha Hotel &
     Hot Springs
16   Harambee Hotel
21   Lido Hotel
22   Tropical Hotel
25   Ethiopia Hotel
28   Finfine Adarash Hotel &
     Restaurant
37   National Hotel
39   Ghion Hotel
46   Ras Hotel
50   Wabe Shebele
57   Blue Nile Ras Hotel
69   Yordanos Hotel
75   Buffet de la Gare

PLACES TO EAT
2   Le Jardin
26   Cottage Restaurant
40   China Bar & Restaurant
42   Beijing Restaurant;
     Stars Night Club
49   Lombardia

53   Legehar Minit Snack
62   Connection Pastry;
     Wegagen Bank
66   Shoa Restaurant
67   Tiru Restaurant
70   Girma Kitfo Beat
72   Great Burger House;
     Falcon Club
74   Juventus Club

OTHER
1   EgyptAir
3   Ethio Internet Centre
4   Yemen Yemenia Airways
5   Main Post Office;
     National Postal Museum
6   Ethio Traditional Desta
     Gebre Dance School
7   St George Interior
     Decoration & Art Gallery
9   Ethiopian Mapping
     Authority
10 Yewedale Azmari Beat
11 Bar Pisa Azmari Beat
12 East African Art Collection
14 Ministry of Foreign Affairs

17   Ambassador Cinema
18   Commercial Bank of
     Ethiopia (Main Branch)
19   Swedish Embassy
20   National Library
23   Second-hand Book Stalls
24   Shi Solomon Hailu
     Supermarket; Canadian
     Embassy
27   Universal Clinic
29   Commercial Bank of
     Ethiopia; Addis Fana
     General Merchandise
30   Reggae Bar
31   Ethiopian Heritage Trust
32   Shell Petrol Station
33   Police Station
34   Total Petrol Station
35   Wera Bar & Restaurant;
     Chilota Studio
36   Dutch Milk House
38   Travel Ethiopia; Village
     Ethiopia (Travel Agency)
41   Ghion Pharmacy; National
     Tour Operation (NTO)
43   Bike Hire

44   Ethiopian Airlines
45   National Theatre; Tunnel
     Nightclub
47   SRBH Craft Shop
48   Qat Market
51   Post Office
52   Short-distance Bus Station
54   Western Union; DHL;
     Foto Batti
55   Lufthansa
56   Telecommunications Office
58   Etsegenet (Hairdresser)
59   Yumo Tours
60   Eritrean Embassy
61   Air France; Ethiopian Wildlife
     Conservation Organisation
63   Ethiopian Tourism Commission
     (Tourist Information Centre);
     Meskal Gift Shop
64   Shell Petrol Station;
     Mega Bookshop
65   Commercial Bank; Post Office
71   Japanese Embassy
73   Addis Ababa Museum
76   Railway Museum

The ***Wutma Hotel*** (☎ 12-53-60) opposite the Baro represents better value, though it lacks the attractive compound of the latter. It has 15 small but very clean rooms for Birr53 for one/two people with a hot shower.

The ***Taitu Hotel*** (☎ 55-32-40, fax 55-34-67) also in the Piazza was built by Menelik's wife, Empress Taitu, in 1907, and was the country's first government hotel. It was such a novelty at the time that it had to be made clear that people had to pay for what they consumed. It's a wonderful old place with period furniture, high ceilings and

creaking floors. It costs US$12/18 for a room for one/two people with communal bathroom and US$18/20 with private bathroom. There's also a garden, parking, restaurant and an old tennis court. Discounts of up to 30% are often available. Ask for room 101, which is very spacious and has a nice balcony.

The more central ***Tropical Hotel*** (☎ 51-21-80), near the National Theatre, is another clean cheapie. Some rooms are better than others and cost between Birr20 and Birr30 depending on the shower. The bar can be a bit noisy.

In the centre, one of the best-kept secrets are the rooms of the *Finfine Adarash Hotel & Restaurant* (☎ 51-47-11) (also known as Finfine National Hotel). It's currently better known for its restaurant. Rooms with bathroom cost US$20; around the back are 12 pleasant and clean rooms with common bathroom (shared between two rooms) for Birr50 to Birr60 (open to negotiation). It's a pleasant, peaceful place with a garden.

Though a little way out, east of the Piazza, a good cheapie popular with tour agencies is the *Bel Air Hotel* (☎ 11-46-55), which has clean, quite spacious rooms with communal/private shower for Birr35/50.

Similar is the *Debre Damo* (☎ 61-26-30), east of the centre near the Axum Hotel, with very small but clean and well-furnished doubles without/with shower for Birr48/72. It's a peaceful place with a courtyard.

PLACES TO STAY – MID-RANGE

By far the best value in this category is that offered by the mass of private new hotels that have sprung up outside the city centre. Most lie along major roads and are well connected by the city's minibus service. Most hotels have private parking.

Centre

Most of the old government-run hotels are overpriced, run-down and depressing. The *Harambee Hotel* (☎ 51-40-00, fax 51-08-71) in the centre does have an enormous 'suite' (US$72) with two twin-bedded rooms, bathroom, a large dining room, three receptions and a kitchen (sink only), and might be just the ticket for a family or group. The *Ghion Hotel* (☎ 51-32-22, fax 51-02-78), though it has the advantage of a very central location near Meskel Square, now seems a bit overpriced compared with some of the private hotels. Adequate singles/doubles cost from US$44/54, bungalows from US$65 and apartments from US$67. It's a popular place with tour groups and is often booked up from October to January; reservations are advised. The Western-style restaurant gets my worst-restaurant-in-Addis award, though breakfast is OK, but check out the traditional restaurant (see

Places to Eat following). Most credit cards are accepted.

The *Buffet de la Gare* (☎ 51-78-88, fax 51-59-59), near La Gare, is one of the best-value hotels in town. It's an atmospheric place with quite well furnished and spacious rooms with private bathroom for Birr90 for one person and Birr120/160 for double/twin beds; prices include breakfast. There's also a good restaurant, parking and a pleasant, peaceful garden. Nearby, the government-run *Blue Nile Ras Hotel* (☎ 51-13-55) has 21 rooms with private bathroom for Birr100 for singles/doubles; they're a bit on the small side.

The *Lido Hotel* (☎ 51-44-88, fax 53-32-47), near the ministry of health, has smallish but adequate rooms (with shower and telephone) around a pleasant courtyard for Birr100/140 without/with breakfast.

The three-star *Yordanos Hotel* (☎ 51-57-11, fax 51-66-55) east of Meskel Square is very central. It has 36 singles/doubles with telephone and TV for US$20/30; the singles are on the small side. Credit cards are accepted.

Outside the Centre

The *Extreme Hotel* (☎ 55-37-77, fax 55-10-77) just south of the Piazza has doubles/twins (with telephone and TV) for Birr160/240. It is a simple but very adequate and peaceful place. Credit cards are accepted.

Outside the centre to the north-east and probably the best value in this category is the *Gedera Hotel No 3* (☎ 53-19-00, fax 53-38-93). It's a new and well-run place with well-furnished rooms with satellite TV for Birr99/132 (credit cards should be accepted soon). It's a popular place with ECA people, so reservations are a good idea.

The newish *Hawi Hotel* (☎ 65-44-99) south of the centre has small but modern and comfortable rooms with telephone for Birr100/130; discounts are usually available for longer stays.

The *Semien Hotel* (☎ 55-00-67, fax 55-14-10) north of the Piazza is a new hotel offering good value. Rooms with satellite TV and telephone cost Birr170/193 for one/two people. A gym, sauna and nightclub are planned.

The newish **Ras Amba Hotel** (☎ 12-27-37, fax 55-15-87) east of the Piazza has rooms that cost US$36/38/60 for one/two/three people. It's in a quiet, tucked-away location and is modern and comfortable. Singles are on the small side.

Out east on the Asmara road is a stretch of modern mid-range hotels. Good value is the **Holiday Hotel** (☎ 61-20-81, fax 61-26-27) with modern singles/doubles/twins with satellite TV, telephone, small balcony and private bathroom for Birr128/140/164. Similar is the **Classic Hotel** (☎ 61-35-98, fax 61-09-46) opposite, with singles/doubles with satellite TV and telephone for Birr132/150. The well-run **Central Shoa Hotel** (☎ 61-14-54, fax 61-00-63) offers small but comfortable rooms with satellite TV, fridge and telephone for Birr158 for one/two people. The **Plaza Hotel** (☎ 61-22-00, fax 61-30-44), has very comfortable first/second-class rooms (for one or two people) for Birr174/204. All rooms have telephones (satellite TV in first class). The smart **Axum Hotel** (☎ 61-39-16, fax 61-42-65) has comfortable rooms with telephone and satellite TV for Birr250/300 for one/two people.

Five minutes from the airport, south-east of the centre, is the **Ibex Hotel** (☎ 65-44-00, fax 65-37-37) with singles/doubles with TV for US$40/50, and good facilities including ground tennis, gym, sauna, restaurant, nightclub, and airport pick-up service. Credit cards are accepted.

PLACES TO STAY – TOP END

The central but rather overpriced **Wabe Shebelle** (☎ 51-71-87, fax 51-84-77) has comfortable well-furnished singles/doubles for US$64/78 with telephone (some with TV). There's also a small but pleasant garden. AmEx is accepted.

The excellent and well-run **Imperial Hotel** (☎ 61-44-90, fax 61-44-93, @ imperial hotel@telecom.net.et), 2km from Bole airport, is a new place with good facilities, including a sauna and steam room, good restaurant, conference room, gym and nightclub. It also has jacuzzis in the suites. Small-

ish but comfortable singles/double/suites cost US$66/84/114 and rooms have satellite TV and video, phone, balcony and even orthopaedic beds. Credit cards are accepted.

Built in 1969, and 12 storeys high, the **Hilton Hotel** (☎ 51-84-00, fax 51-00-64, @ hilton.addis@telecom.net.et) in the centre wouldn't win a beauty contest. Nevertheless, its 402 rooms are comfortable, with satellite TV, air-con, a minibar and balcony. There are facilities for visitors in wheelchairs. Rooms range from US$150 for one/two people to US$600 for a state suite. It has a swimming pool, a health club, sauna and massage service, four tennis courts, squash court and minigolf.

Top of the heap is the **Sheraton Hotel** (☎ 17-17-17, fax 17-27-27) in the centre. In 1998, it became the first 'luxury collection' hotel in Africa. Though rising like a lotus flower rather incongruously from the shacks around, it looks beautifully designed. Neoclassical in style, it also incorporates lots of Ethiopian traditional designs, architectural features and building materials (90% of its marble is Ethiopian). No expense has been spared: from Persian carpets and original Ethiopian paintings, to furnishings plated with 24-carat Ethiopian gold. Its 328 rooms start from US$200 for one/two people to US$2500 for a deluxe suite, and US$4200 for a villa with all the bells and whistles. Four rooms are specially designed for people in wheelchairs.

PLACES TO EAT

For a Food Glossary and tips on eating etiquette see Food in the Facts for the Visitor section. Most restaurants in Addis Ababa open from around noon to 3 pm and from 7 to 10 pm. If you roll into town late and ravenous, the Hilton has a 24-hour and reasonably priced 'night kitchen'.

Many restaurants – particularly the European ones – add a tax of up to 15% to bills; check in advance.

Ethiopian

Ethiopian restaurants can be split into two categories: the fast, cheap-and-cheerful (with dishes between Birr4 and Birr10), and those catering to Ethiopian office workers and professionals as well as to tourists (with dishes for Birr10 and Birr15). Many of the latter offer a kind of 'traditional experience': traditional food in traditional surrounding with traditional music. Prices tend to go up at night (by around Birr5) to subsidise the entertainment. Beer/tej/spirits cost Birr10/15/15. There's a mass of these places set into the base of the stadium near Meskel Square; though basic and a bit limited in choice, the food is perfectly good.

The *Tiru Restaurant* (☎ 15-95-51) east of Meskel Square, does reliable Ethiopian fare for Birr14 and 15. It's popular with local bureaucrats; open daily (except Tuesday).

South-east of the centre on the Bole road are two good 'traditional experience' restaurants. One of the most popular is the *Habesha Restaurant* (☎ 51-16-33) with music and sometimes dancing from 8 pm. The *Karamara Restaurant* (☎ 51-89-67) is one of the best traditional places, with music from 8.30 pm to midnight nightly. If you fancy it, you can try the Ethiopian specialities *tere sega* (raw meat) and *tej* (honey wine) here.

Similar, more central and a little cheaper (Birr10 to Birr15) is the *Shoa Restaurant* (☎ 51-00-16) east of Meskel Square (also known as the Yeshewaget Hotel), with dancing at the weekends from 8 pm until 3 am.

The excellent *Addis Ababa Restaurant* (☎ 12-87-33) is housed in a former aristocrat's residence just north of the Piazza. In the 1960s, the Women's Association took it over with the aim of 'promoting Ethiopian culinary culture'. The food is excellent as is the restaurant's tej (it has its own brewery).

The central *Finfine Adarash Hotel & Restaurant* (see Places to Stay – Budget earlier in this section) is also well known for its food and offers a more extensive menu than many, including a special vegetarian or 'fasting' menu. The restaurant is housed in the former home of a nobleman; there are also tables in little niches outside in the garden. There's traditional music and dancing in the garden every Sunday from 4 to 7.30 pm.

The traditional restaurant at the central *Ghion Hotel* (see Places to Stay – Mid-Range earlier in this section) is a good place to see traditional dancing, but the dancers voraciously extract tips from customers (Birr10 a go is expected). Dancing takes place on Tuesday, Thursday and Saturday from 7 pm until around 11 pm. Reservations are a good idea. *Araki* (local grain spirit) and *tef* (an indigenous grain used to make *injera*, Ethiopia's ubiquitous pancake) are also available. After a meal, you can enjoy a traditional coffee ceremony in the gallery above (see the boxed text 'The Coffee Ceremony' under Drinks in the Facts for the Visitor section).

The *Weizero Tsige Gayu* just east of the centre (officially known as the Nat Gwada Restaurant) is known for its excellent fish dishes (Birr25) served on fasting days. An azmari also performs here every night from 9 pm for a couple of hours.

For *kitfo* (raw mince warmed in butter and herbs) probably the best place in town is the *Yohannis Gurage Kitfo Beat*, lying just south of the Asmara road east of the centre. It's a large but unpretentious place with seating indoors and outdoors, but sometimes it's hard to find a free table. Kitfo/special kitfo costs Birr10/13. The smarter *Bekelech Kitfo Beat* nearby is probably second best, with kitfo/special kitfo for Birr12/15. *Girma Kitfo Beat* east of Meskel Square is more central. The new *Kibnar Gurage Kitfo Beat* (also known as 'Asni Pub') east of the centre on the Asmara road and the *B & B Kitfo* south-west of the centre are also good.

If you're game to try the Ethiopian delicacy, tere sega, head for the *Mulushoa Restaurant* (marked only in Amharic) diagonally opposite La Parisienne Café, south of the centre off the airport road. Though very simple, just wooden tables and benches, it's known for its high-quality meat (Birr24 for 1kg). You're unlikely to find many tour groups here.

Buffet

For a splurge, some of the larger hotels do good all-you-can-eat buffets serving both local and international food – a great way of tasting local food, without going hungry if you don't take to it.

The *Wabe Shebelle* hotel in the centre, does a great buffet breakfast (Birr15) from 6 to 10 am. Also good value is the *Ibex Lalibela Restaurant* in the Ibex Hotel 2km south of the centre, with a buffet lunch (Birr20) on Monday, Thursday and Saturday, and dinner (Birr30) on Saturday.

The excellent *Asni Gallery* (see earlier in this section) has a simple but tasty vegetarian buffet lunch of around eight dishes (Birr25) served from 12.30 to 1.30 pm (get there sharp) on Thursday and Saturday.

The Sheraton *Summerfields Restaurant* does a sumptuous daily lunch/dinner buffet, including around 14 different deserts, for Birr139. The *Hilton* has a popular poolside brunch (Birr98) from 11 am to 3 pm every Sunday with a live Ethiopian band.

For an Asian buffet lunch see Rainbow Seoul Restaurant under Other International following. See Activities earlier in this section for details of the barbecue lunch at the Addis Ababa Golf Club & Restaurant.

Italian

For those who don't take to local food, there's no shortage of Western fare, reflecting the influence of the city's immigrant populations; much of it is excellent. The largest influence is the Italian one.

In the Piazza, and long considered the best restaurant in Addis Ababa, is the Italian-run *Ristorante Castelli* (☎ 11-10-58), usually known just as 'Castellis'. Founded (albeit in a different location) in 1948, it's run by a Piedmontese family, and all dishes are home-made. It's open daily except Sunday; reservations are advised in the evening and at weekends. Mains cost from Birr35 to Birr80. Dishes are made to order; so don't come in a hurry. Local/imported wine costs from Birr50 to Birr120.

The *Juventus Club* (☎ 51-64-64) on the southern side of Meskel Square is an expat Italian club, but its restaurant, serving home-made Italian food (Birr30 for mains), is open to all. It's open daily except Sunday.

The well-known *Blue Tops Restaurant* (☎ 55-09-34), north of the centre on the Entoto road, is a favourite haunt of expats and has two restaurants, one for lunch and

snacks (open all day) and a more formal, Italian restaurant for dinner (roughly the same menu but twice the price). Mains include fillet steak, Nile perch and shish kebab (Birr22 to Birr27 for lunch). Ice cream, milkshakes, pizza and toasted sandwiches (Birr6 to Birr11) are also available.

The *Gazebo Pizza Bar & Restaurant* (☎ 15-07-66) off the Bole road, specialises in pizza cooked in traditional Italian ovens (Birr21), which can be eaten in the garden. The Italian-run *Bar Ristorante Pizzeria Don Vito* (☎ 65-38-09) south of the centre on the Debre Zeyit road lacks any atmosphere, but does excellent authentic, thin-crust pizzas (as well as home-made pasta dishes) for Birr25 to Birr30. It's open daily except Tuesday.

The simple but pleasant *Pizza Deli Roma* (☎ 51-12-04) on the Bole road does a selection of 40 quite decent pizzas for Birr14 to Birr32. More central is *Le Jardin* (☎ 55-31-72) with not bad pizzas for Birr28 to Birr35 served either in the garden, tukul or restaurant. It's open daily except Wednesday. Just south of the Piazza and a much cheaper bet is the *Oroscopo*, a simple but good place, serving pizzas for Birr10 to Birr15.

Lombardia (☎ 51-99-60) in the centre is simple but very popular locally, with Italian mains for Birr10 to Birr15. It's open daily until 10 pm.

Other European

Mmmm My Flavour (☎ 51-23-87) south of the centre near Jeddah Restaurant is known as the place for a romantic evening, but also as 'Mmmm My Wallet' for its prices (mains cost around Birr30 to Birr40 plus 5% tax). But the food is good (a mixture of European cuisines) and more imaginative than some places, including lots of vegie dishes.

The *Acropolis Greek Restaurant* (☎ 16-36-11) is a very upmarket place south of the centre, which offers a good selection of traditional Greek dishes including vegie options. Mains cost around Birr26 to Birr40 (plus 15% tax). It's open daily except Tuesday.

La Canapé (☎ 51-93-14) north-east of the centre is another popular place for quite good Italian and French food – it looks a like an Italian country church. Mains cost around Birr25 to Birr45. It's open daily except Sunday lunchtime.

The **Steak House** (☎ 51-89-00), inside La Gazelle Piano Bar south-east of the centre, is known for its (surprise!) steaks, which cost from Birr20; the fillet steak is the best choice; others can be tough. It's open daily except Sunday.

Le Petit Paris (☎ 20-48-80), south-west of the centre, is considered the best place in town for French food, serving everything from *foie gras* (paté) to *escargot* (snail) and has an attractive enclosed veranda. Mains cost on average Birr30 to Birr40 plus 10% tax. It's open daily except Monday.

The cosy **Cottage Restaurant** (☎ 51-63-59) in the centre is designed like a Swiss chalet and has a good and varied menu and an excellent (imported) wine list. Mains cost around Birr25 to Birr30; credit cards should be accepted soon. The pepper and mushroom steak and Irish coffee are something of a speciality.

Cheaper restaurants serving 'faranji food' include the simple but ever-popular **Peacock Restaurant** (☎ 53-09-51) near Habesha Restaurant on the Bole road. Fillet steak costs Birr15; a hamburger with fries costs Birr8; soups cost Birr6 to Birr7.

The **Hill Belt** (☎ 61-21-60) 3km south-east of the centre, has won various local awards and serves good and varied food (such as Singapore noodles), it does good fast food (Birr10 to Birr12).

Great value is the central **Legehar Minit Snack**, a basic but very popular local joint serving cheap-and-cheerful fare such as burgers for just Birr3 or cheese/tuna sandwiches for Birr3. Spaghetti costs Birr6.

In the Piazza, **Tefari Makonnen** (formerly Bar Torino) is an old and popular place with the locals which does good, very cheap fare. Lasagne and pasta dishes cost Birr4. It's also known for its *baklava* (sweet Turkish pastry), which costs Birr2.

The **Ras Restaurant** near Mexico Square, just south-east of the centre, offers a four-course lunch menu for just Birr14 (buffet lunch on Tuesday costs Birr 21).

Other International

The new **Great Wall Chinese Restaurant** (☎ 51-88-86) on the Bole road offers an extensive menu including soup, rice, noodle and vegetarian dishes (all around Birr25 to Birr30). On weekends, there's a special three-course set menu for Birr60 (plus 15% tax).

Cheaper and more central is the cosy **Beijing Restaurant** (☎ 51-56-73) near the stadium, with good mains for Birr12 to Birr28. The nearby **China Bar & Restaurant** (☎ 51-37-72) and the **Shanghai Restaurant** (☎ 65-52-90) on the Debre Zeyit road (open daily except Wednesdays) are popular with expats.

Sangam Restaurant (☎ 51-89-76) near City Café & Pastry on the Bole road is considered one of the best Indian restaurants in town. Curries and tandooris (including vegie dishes) are prepared by an Indian chef, and cost around Birr28. It also does children's portions (Birr18). It's open daily except Monday. A bit cheaper but less atmospheric is the **Tandoor Indian Restaurant** (☎ 18-74-50) nearer the airport, with mains for around Birr23 to Birr25.

The very elegant **Shaheen Indian Restaurant** (☎ 17-17-17 ext 3633) in the Sheraton serves excellent and imaginative Indian dishes for Birr25 to Birr58. It's open daily except Monday; reservations are advised and credit cards are accepted.

Rainbow Seoul Restaurant (☎ 51-23-11) on the Bole Road serves Korean, Japanese and Chinese food; mains average around Birr20 to Birr40. There's an excellent all-you-can-eat buffet (Birr33) served from noon to 2.30 pm Sunday, with at least 25 imaginative dishes, including vegie ones.

The excellent **Omar Khayyam** (☎ 11-22-59) in the Piazza does great-value and tasty Middle Eastern food in simple but attractive surroundings. Soups cost from Birr5, mains from Birr8.50. The **Jeddah Restaurant** (☎ 20-36-30) south-east of the centre also serves decent fare at decent prices (Birr10 to Birr15), including tasty snacks such as *shwarma* (meat and salad in pita bread) and hamburgers for Birr8. The **Mendi Restaurant** (☎ 51-21-43) nearby, serves good dishes (Birr17 to Birr30) with a Yemeni slant.

The *Armenian Sporting Association* *(☎ 11-35-72)* just north-east of the Piazza is good for those in search of something different, such as mint soup and delicious spicy sausages for around Birr20. It's open daily except Sunday.

Cafes & Pastry Shops

Most cafes are open from around 7 am to 6 pm daily, and are great for breakfast. Most cakes cost from Birr1 to Birr5, fruit juices cost around Birr3.50.

The *Tomaca* cafe in the Piazza is a great old Italian place, which serves delicious coffee. It also sells five types of coffee (ground or beans) for Birr34 for 1kg, as well as traditional coffee pots for Birr12, and even entire DIY coffee ceremony sets for Birr230 (see the boxed text 'The Coffee Ceremony' under Drinks in the Facts for the Visitor chapter). A simple but good choice in the Piazza is *Gebre Tensae Tedla Delicious Bakery*; a speciality is the baklava (Birr2).

Near the Ghion Hotel in the centre, *Connection Pastry* has a good selection of cakes, fruit juices and milkshakes. Try the 'fruit punch', in fact a fruit salad (Birr3.50).

The *Forneria Italia* east of the Piazza on the Entoto road bakes a good selection of Italian breads. It's open from 6.30 am to 8 pm daily.

There are a good many places along and nearby the Bole road south-east of the centre. The *City Café & Pastry* is one of the best pastry shops in town, opened recently by a returnee from America who brought with him many of his recipes; try the famous apple strudel. Ice cream and mini-pizzas are also available. Nearby, the unmistakably purple *Purple Café* is also good; the delicious *millefeuilles* (jam and cream pastries) are a speciality. Hot chocolate, juices and ice cream are also available. The *Roby Pastry* and *Saay Pastry* are also good. Designed like a rural French cafe, *La Parisienne* is a great place for breakfast, specialising in delicious croissants (chocolate, cheese, cream etc) fresh from the oven. It also sells a good variety of wholemeal bread, as well as herb/spice teas (Birr1.50) and more unusual fruit juices (ginger, mandarin, cranberry etc). If you're craving cheese,

the little *Bonnie Cheese Shop* has a small selection of delicious home-made cheeses produced from Jersey cattle milk (for around Birr10 for 100g), as well as yoghurt and milk.

The *Hilton* has an excellent pastry shop open from 7.30 am to 8 pm daily, selling everything from strawberry tarts and black forest gateau, to cheesecake and carrot cake (Birr5 to Birr10); freshly baked croissants cost Birr4 to Birr8.

Top of the heap is the aptly named *Temptations* pastry shop in the Sheraton, whose Swiss chef makes everything from pralines to candied fruit and cherry pie, plus an excellent variety of bread (Birr1 for a roll). Most cakes cost Birr6.

Fast Food

Burger Queen on the Bole road was pronounced 'the best fast-food place in Africa' by one traveller. Burgers are good but expensive by local standards (Birr12 to Birr20); they come in a basket along with a giant portion of thin-cut and crunchy fries. Fries alone cost Birr4.

The best value is the fast-food cafe on the ground floor of *My Pub* (see Pubs & Bars); fries/burgers cost just Birr3/7.

The 24-hour *Great Burger House* at the Falcon Club on Meskel Square is great for those out on the town or those feeling peckish after hours; fries/burgers cost Birr6/10.

Self-Catering

Shi Solomon Hailu Supermarket near the National Theatre in the centre is quite well stocked with Western 'faves', from cereals and bikkies to mineral water and tomato ketchup. It's great for stocking up for a camping/trekking expedition, or for preparing a picnic (there's a cheese and cold-meat counter). It's open from 7 am to 8 pm Monday to Saturday and 8 am to 6 pm Sunday.

Novis Supermarket, south-west of the centre, is a favourite with the expat community and stocks everything from smoked salmon to Italian chocolates and cheeses. It's also known for its high quality fruit. It's open from 9 am to 7.30 pm Monday to Saturday and from 9.30 am to 1 pm Sundays.

ENTERTAINMENT
Pubs & Bars
Most places charge around Birr5/15 for local/imported beer, and are open until 2 am during the week, and 5 am at the weekend.

The cluster of *bars* in the Piazza around the National and Taitu Hotels are simple and cheap but very atmospheric places, where locals come for a beer and for a dance to their favourite Amharic tunes. It's a great area for bar-hopping and is safe for women: follow the music.

Still in the Piazza, the *Turaco Restaurant & Pub* is designed rather like a Western pub and is a popular place with the younger local crowd (happy hour is from 5 to 6 pm Monday to Wednesday). Beer costs just Birr3; spirits Birr4. It's open daily to midnight.

For reggae, head for the *Ram Jam Pub* opposite the entrance to Memo club near the Rainbow Seoul Restaurant on the Bole road. It's a pretty lugubrious place with a small but loyal following, playing a mixture of reggae, soul and pop. The central *Reggae Bar* is a simple but fun place open from 6 pm to 1 am daily, 3 am on the weekend. The bar at the *Buffet de la Gare* hotel near La Gare in the centre is also a good place; on Sundays at 6 pm there's a live reggae band.

The oddly named, French-Djiboutian-run *Hard Luck Café* on the Bole road near Roby Pastry has a lively bar and dance floor designed a bit like a beach bar, and is very popular with a younger expat crowd. There's a happy hour from 5 to 7 pm daily except Sunday. It also serves good, homemade nosh from barbecued hamburgers (Birr15 to Birr20) to chocolate mousse.

The 'pub' in the back of the *Cottage Restaurant* (see Other European under Places to Eat previous) is straight out of London, complete with darts, ale mugs and an old telephone box. It's open from 5.30 pm to midnight daily. *My Pub (☎ 61-43-98),* east of the centre on the Asmara road, is like an American bar and English pub rolled into one, with pool table, darts and juke box.

The *Dutch Milk House* in the centre is a laid-back Dutch-owned bar in a pleasant shady courtyard. It also does good snacks; the sausages and pizzas are a speciality.

Wera Bar & Restaurant (☎ 53-31-36), in the centre, is little more than a room with a few stools, but it belongs to the famous pop singer, Mohammud Ahmed, who usually makes an appearance each night (usually after midnight). His songs are some of the 'easiest' on a Western ear – sort of Sinatra style. You can request his famous song *Tisita* (Remembrances). It's open from 10.30 pm to 3.30 am nightly except Monday. Entrance is charged only on Thursdays (Birr20), when there's a live band. Drinks cost Birr15.

A great place for a drink at sunset is the outdoor terrace of the *Ras Amba Hotel* east of the Piazza. For a 'sundowner' in the centre of town, the veranda of the traditional restaurant of the *Ghion Hotel* looks on to the garden; it's another early-evening place. The balcony of the top-floor restaurant of the *Wabe Shebelle* hotel affords a terrific 360° panoramic view of the city. (For all of these hotels see Places to Stay previous).

For a civilised drink, *La Gazelle Piano Bar* on the Bole road has live piano music from 8.30 pm to around midnight Tuesday to Saturday, and jazz on Sunday. The *Imperial Hotel* (see Places to Stay – Top End previous) has a jazz night in its diminutive but civilised top-floor bar on Friday from 9.30 pm to midnight. Entrance is fee.

The central *Hilton* has a happy hour from 5 to 6 pm in all of its bars (the second drink comes free); cocktails normally cost Birr24. At the *Sheraton* nearby, you may want to visit the popular spectacle of the 'singing fountain', in which 92 tracts of music and coloured floodlights are synchronised with jets of water. This takes place 7.30 to 8.30 pm on Tuesday, Thursday and Friday. Coffee/beer/spirits in the Sheraton Fountain Court cost from Birr13/15/25. Happy hour in all the bars of the Sheraton is from 5.30 to 7 pm (50% off, but make sure you *pay* before 7 pm; credit cards are accepted).

Tej Beats
A tej beat is a kind of Ethiopian pub, serving tej instead of beer. A flask of tej costs around Birr1.50. Most are open to around

10 pm, but are busiest in the evening. Women should be aware that these places are the traditional haunt of men and should always keep a low profile (see the boxed text 'Tej Beats' under Drinks in the Facts for the Visitor section).

Kitaow Tej Beat No 2 (literally meaning 'punisher' or 'killer' in Amharic) lies off the Asmara road near the Iveco, and is one of the most authentic tej beats in Addis Ababa. Punters sit on long benches in a courtyard, though there's also seating inside. To reach it, follow the 'JVC Japan International Volunteer Centre' signs until you come to an opening in the road; it's through the gates on your right.

The *Beta Mengist Tej Beat* nearby is like a huge beer hall. It's not signposted, but you can't miss it for the noise. It's a pretty rowdy place, but good fun. Note that it's for men only.

The *Yegebawal* tej beat is a good place east of the Piazza. *Topia Tej Beat* is known for its high-quality tej.

Nightclubs

Most clubs get going about 11 pm, and stay open to around 2 am during the week and 5 am on the weekend. Entrance generally costs Birr15/20 for a weekday/weekend (but is sometimes free). Beer costs Birr10, spirits from Birr12 to Birr15. If you fancy a big night out, it's not a bad idea to hire a taxi for the night (around Birr20 per hour).

Memo Club south of Meskel Square is a cosy little place with the usual silver mirror balls. It plays a mixture of African and Western music; on Sunday there's usually a live band. Sometimes there's a bar and grill outside.

Very popular with young European expats is the *Torero Club* near the Ibex Hotel south-east of the centre. It's more a pub than a club, but has a small dance floor near the front; music is entirely Western. There's no entrance fee. Nearby is the *Barn* nightclub (at the time of writing the most fashionable club in town) with live bands at the weekend. Designed like a barn, it feels more like a private party. The best nights are on Thursday and Saturday; Tuesday night is 'Ethiopian night'.

The *Tunnel Nightclub* just down from the National Theatre in the centre is open Friday and Saturday only. Designed like a tunnel, it's got a not-bad sound-and-light system, but the huge population of adolescent males could do with a bit of diluting.

The aptly named *La Caverne* next door to the Concorde Hotel south of the centre on the Debre Zeyit road is a new cavernous place with a large dance floor, which plays a wide variety of music. The *Dome Nightclub*, next door and better known as the *Concorde* after the hotel that houses it, is a good place for live music. There's usually a band playing Ethiopian music (sometimes modern) from 9 to 11.30 pm nightly except Monday.

Stars Night Club, near the Ghion Hotel, is crammed with bar girls and isn't a first choice, but it's very central if you fancy a drink and a dance. The *Falcon Club* (see Great Burger House under Fast Food in the Places to Eat section previous) in the centre is a more Ethiopian place with live Ethiopian bands every night (closed Monday).

The *Gaslight* nightclub in the Sheraton is *the* place to be seen in Addis Ababa. There's live entertainment from 10 pm to 3 am Monday to Thursday, until 4 am on Friday and Saturday, closed Sunday.

Azmari Beats

The azmari is a kind of Ethiopian equivalent to a stand-up comedian, and is a very ancient tradition. Though performances are always in Amharic, it's still a fun thing to watch. Entrance to the azmari beats is free; drinks cost Birr10 (even for mineral water).

The *Bar Pisa* azmari beat in the centre on Zewditu St is a tiny but attractive little place designed like a tent with bamboo walls. To find it, look out for the little twin-peaked roofs. *Yewedale* (He likes it) nearby is one of the best azmari beats in town; it's often hard to find a seat. Some of the best Addis Ababa azmaris perform here; look out for well-known azmari, Adane.

Traditional Music, Dance & Theatre

For general information on Ethiopian music and dance see Arts in the Facts about

Ethiopia chapter. Many of the hotels and restaurants put on traditional shows (see Ethiopian under Places to Eat earlier in this section, see also Azmari Beats previous).

Though lying 12km south of the centre on the Debre Zeyit road, the *Crown Hotel* (☎ 34-14-44) probably puts on the best traditional dancing show in town in its giant tukul, and is popular among Ethiopians as much as among foreigners. The dancing (of about 13 different ethnic groups) takes place every evening from 7 pm to around midnight. Friday, Saturday and Sunday are the best nights, but don't leave it too late as some of the best dancing takes place early evening. Food (Birr15) and drink (from Birr5) is served, and photos and videos can be taken.

A great local place is *Behale Amba Cultural Evening* east of the centre. It's a kind of rough and ready singing hall, with just a bar, a stone floor, and some wooden tables and benches, but the atmosphere's great, and you won't find a tour group in sight. It's best at the weekend. Entrance is free but you'll be expected to down a drink or two (Birr10 even for mineral water). The singing is very traditional and usually by strident and emotive female performers.

Currently almost all theatrical productions are staged in Amharic (see Theatre under Arts in the Facts about Ethiopia chapter). If you still fancy catching Shakespeare in Amharic, there are shows at the *National Theatre* (☎ 15-82-25) in the centre on Wednesday, Thursday and Friday. Performances start at 5.30 pm and last around two hours; on the weekend, shows start at 2.30 pm and last around 3 hours. Tickets cost between Birr6 and Birr10. There are around 20 musical shows a year too, usually staged on public holidays; ring for details, or check in the *Ethiopian Herald*.

Productions are also shown at the plush 1000-seat *City Hall Theatre & Cultural Centre* (☎ 11-25-26) in the Piazza Friday to Sunday for Birr10; sometimes there is traditional Ethiopian music during public holidays. Theatre, musicals and dancing

---

Mincing Minstrels

An ancient entertainment that continues to this day is that provided by the azmari, or wandering minstrel, and his *masenko* (single-stringed fiddle). In the past, the azmari accompanied caravans of highland traders to make the journey more amusing.

At court, resident azmaris, like the European jesters, were permitted great freedom of expression – so long as their verses were witty, eloquent and clever.

During the Italian Occupation, the azmaris kept up morale with their stirring renditions of Ethiopian victories and resistance. So successfully, in fact, that many were executed by the Italians.

Today, azmaris can be found at weddings and special occasions furnishing eulogies or poetic ballads in honour of their hosts.

In certain bars (azmari beats) of the larger towns, some have become celebrities in their own right

and, like stand-up comics, attract a loyal following. The cleverest can compose their rhyming verses spontaneously, and may even use the audience as the butt of their jokes. Current affairs, such as the affair between Clinton and Monica, can also feature large. Sometimes the humour is light and whimsical, sometimes bitingly satirical, and more often than not often extremely vulgar. It revolves on clever puns, complex double meaning and learned allusion. Don't miss the chance to see them.

DAWIT ABEBE

are also staged nearby at the *Hager Fikir Theatre* (☎ 12-07-41).

Cinema

The *Ambassador Cinema* (☎ 15-77-33) in the centre is one of the better cinemas in town and puts on the usual diet of action-packed and slightly dépassé Hollywood films (in English). Occasionally, French films are shown with English subtitles. Bollywood and Middle Eastern films are also shown. Films are shown daily in three sessions; seats cost Birr4 and Birr5.

In the Piazza, the *Cinema Ethiopia* (☎ 12-94-20) puts on four films a day and charges between Birr 1.50 and Birr3 depending on the class of seat and the film.

SPECTATOR SPORTS

At Jan Meda Race Ground (☎ 11-25-40) north-east of the Piazza there's horse racing from mid-November to mid-June on weekend mornings. Entrance is free. If you're in Addis Ababa for Ethiopian Christmas (January 7th), don't miss the festivities here (including the traditional game of *genna* – see Public Holidays & Special Events in the Facts for the Visitor chapter).

If you fancy watching a bit of the nation's favourite sport, it costs Birr3 Birr20 for a ticket in the 27,000 seat football stadium (☎ 51-43-21). The National League games begin at 2 and 4 pm every Sunday and attract big crowds. Around once a month, there's a pan-African international match. Sometimes athletics, cycling and boxing events are held here, as well as pop concerts. Events are advertised in the *Ethiopian Herald*.

SHOPPING

See also Business Hours, Shopping and Post & Communications (for shipping information) in the Facts for the Visitor chapter.

Souvenirs

Addis Ababa is a great place for souvenir shopping. If you're short of time, there's quite a good souvenir shop in the Hilton. It's a branch of the Ethiopian Tourism Trading Corporation so prices are no higher than elsewhere.

Along Churchill Road there's a string of souvenir shops. Take a good look around as quality and prices vary hugely. Shumeta Leda (☎ 12-65-41) just south of the Piazza is good, with Harari baskets from Birr5 and Birr15, wall rugs from Birr6 per 'panel', head rests from Birr30, and Afar knives from Birr80. It's also got a good selection of jewellery. Haileselassie Alemayehu (☎ 12-95-03), just north of the centre, is also good, with a popular mix-and-match bead counter, and traditional clothing (Birr180 to Birr220).

The Meskal Gift Shop beside the ETC on Meskal Square is particularly good for books on Ethiopia, including the ETC pamphlets, such as *Endemic Birds*. It's also got one of the best selections of postcards in town (Birr1).

The Ethiopian Tourism Trading Corporation (ETTC; ☎ 18-10-55) east of the centre on the Asmara road has some good furniture such as stools, lamps and blinds. The St George Interior Decoration & Art Gallery (☎ 51-09-83) in the centre has some beautiful (but not cheap) traditionally inspired modern furniture. Other items include well-designed jewellery, crosses and cushions.

The Goshu Art Gallery (☎ 61-47-47) south-east of the centre just off the Bole road has some more unusual items including *washint* (traditional flutes) for Birr25, as well as skin and canvas paintings (from Birr250).

Sheba's Daughter's Pillows & Treasures (☎ 51-24-30), south of the centre near the Sudanese Embassy, has one of the best and most interesting selections of high-quality souvenirs in Addis Ababa. It stocks cushion covers in traditional fabric, *dula* (walking sticks), Jimma wooden stools, a beautiful selection of silver jewellery and old shields. But it's not for the impecunious.

The excellent Chilota Studio (☎ 53-33-29) in the centre near Wera Bar & Restaurant sells good souvenirs such as baskets, pots, head rests and cushion covers; many items are attractively framed.

If you fancy a painting, the East African Art Collection (☎ 51-85-92), also in the centre, sells diverse works from around 30 artists for between Birr700 and Birr2000. The studio of the talented artist, Lulseged Retta (☎ 55-23-02), known for his wide-eyed people, can also be visited; paintings cost from Birr2000; posters from Birr50.

On the Ambo road, 9km north-west of Addis Ababa, is Ato Worku Saboka shop known as the 'Falasha Factory' (around 500m after the Gullele soap factory). It's probably the best place in the country for traditional (but fired in modern kilns) Falasha red pottery, and prices are very reasonable. Items range from little hen vases (Birr6) and *doro wat* (a chicken, egg and sauce meal) plates (Birr12), to large sculptures (Birr45).

For baskets, the best place in town is Ato Basket (Mr Basket) shop (☎ 20-10-49) south-west of the centre, which sells everything from hats and pots to mesob, chairs and huge laundry baskets (great for getting excess luggage home). Prices are negotiable.

Charity Shopping

Many first-timers in Addis Ababa are disturbed by the sight of the city's poor. If you want to contribute something a great way is through these excellent shops.

The award-winning Women's Fuelwood Carriers Project (☎ 11-71-94) north of the centre on the Entoto road, just beyond the Spanish embassy (look out for the signposts 'WFC project'), is a charity shop selling a small selection of well-made souvenirs including hand-woven shawls (Birr40), straw hats, and poufs (Birr70). You can also see traditional spinners and weavers at work.

The Misrach Centre (☎ 12-04-65) north-east of the Piazza is a rehabilitation centre for the disabled with a gift shop selling attractive greeting cards, toys and small gifts. It's good for last-minute pressies for the family back home.

The SRBH Craft Shop (☎ 15-06-17), in the centre, sells a small selection of embroidered traditional clothing (Birr25 to Birr60); proceeds go towards the blind.

Alert Handicraft Shop (☎ 15-81-71), north-east of the centre off the Jimma road, sells a good range of crafts including wall hangings, tea cosies, embroidered cushion covers, table cloths and matching napkins; many are made by ex-lepers.

Provisions

For coffee (beans or ground), head for the Mokarar coffee shop on Churchill Road, just south of the Piazza, which sells coffee ground to your taste (Birr32 to Birr35 per kg) or, for a complete coffee ceremony set, head to the excellent Tomaca cafe in the Piazza (see Cafes & Pastry shops under Places to Eat earlier in this section).

For typical Ethiopian spices, including *berbere* (see Food in the Facts for the Visitor chapter), try the Joseph Grocery in the Piazza.

For a tailor-made suit for men or women (Birr250 to Birr300), head for the tailors in the covered building known as 'New Market' in Merkato (west of the Piazza and close to the city bus station); suits take two or three days to make.

For camping gear, try the Addis Fana General Merchandise (known as the Baro supermarket) opposite the trade entrance to the Hilton Hotel and close to the Commercial Bank. It sells basic sleeping bags for Birr253 and blankets for Birr109.

In the Piazza are found most of the city's goldsmiths and silversmiths. Gold goes for Birr65 to Birr100 per gram depending on the carat; silver costs Birr5 per gram (a simple pair of silver earrings cost around Birr24).

GETTING THERE & AWAY
Air
All airlines accept credit cards, though Saudi Arabian Airlines and Kenya Airways take AmEx only. Most airlines are dotted on or around Churchill Road (Alitalia, Saudi Arabian Airlines and Kenya Airways are near the Harambee Hotel in the centre) within a stone's throw from one another and include:

Air France (☎ 51-90-44)
Alitalia (☎ 51-44-00, fax 51-03-79)
EgyptAir (☎ 12-11-20, fax 55-22-03)
Kenya Airways (☎ 51-30-18, fax 51-15-48)
Lufthansa (☎ 51-56-66, fax 51-29-88)
Saudi Arabian Airlines (☎ 51-26-37, fax 51-43-99)
Yemenia Yemen Airways (☎ 51-18-09, fax 51-44-04)

Ethiopian Airlines Ethiopian Airlines has various offices dotted around town including at the Hilton Hotel and near the National Theatre in the centre, and on De Gaulle Square in the Piazza. The branch at the Hilton (☎ 51-15-40) generally has far shorter queues. It's open from 6 am to 9 pm Monday to Saturday. Schedules change frequently and flight duration depends on the type of plane, so check details carefully in advance. Flight duration includes stopover ground time. For prices on some of the following domestic routes see also the Getting Around chapter earlier. The following flights leave from Addis Ababa.

Aksum via Mekele (two hours) daily
Arba Minch (1½ hours) twice weekly
Bahar Dar (Lake Tana) (35 minutes) three times a day
Dessie (one hour) daily
Dire Dawa (one hour) twice daily
Gambela via Jimma (two hours) three times a week
Goba (one hour) three times a week
Gonder via Bahar Dar (one hour)

Gonder via Debre Markos and Debre Tabor (2¼ hours) three times a week
Jijiga via Dire Dawa (three hours) twice weekly
Jimma (one hour) once or twice daily
Jinka via Arba Minch (two hours, 10 minutes) once a week
Lalibela via Bahar Dar (one hour, 50 minutes) daily
Mekele (1½ hours) daily
Mizan Tefari via Jimma (one hour, 40 minutes) twice weekly
Shir (2½ hours) twice weekly

Bus
There are two bus stations in Addis Ababa: the long-distance station (for any journey over 150km) known as Autobus Terra, which is found at Merkato, west of the Piazza; and the short-distance station, found near La Gare on Ras Makonnen Ave in the centre. (See also Bus in the Getting Around chapter earlier).

Long-Distance Station For information on departures call ☎ 13-59-03. All buses leave officially at 6.30 am.

Aksum (Birr72, 2½ days) via Shire, Dessie and Mekele
Arba Minch (Birr32, 12 hours)
Awash via Dire Dawa (Birr34, 11½ hours) or via Harar (Birr35, 12 hours)
Bahar Dar (Birr37, 1½ days) via Debre Markos or Dangala
Dessie (Birr24, nine hours)
Gambela (Birr50, two days) via Jimma
Goba (Birr31, 12 hours)
Gonder (Birr50, two days) via Debre Markos or Dangala
Jijiga (Birr42, two days) via Hirna Jimma, west of Dire Dawa (Birr21, 9½ hours)
Nekemte (Birr20, 8½ hours)

Short-Distance Station For information on departures call ☎ 15-03-40. Buses leave regularly for the following destinations from 6.30 am to around 6 pm.

Akaki (Birr2, 30 minutes)
Debre Zeyit (Birr3, 45 minutes)
Lake Langano, go first to Shashemene and ask to be dropped off en route (Birr 16, five hours)
Nazret (Birr6.50, two hours)
Shashemene (Birr16, five hours)

Train

Addis Ababa's La Gare (train station) is officially known as Chemin de Fer Djibouto-Ethiopien. The only railway line in the country is between Addis Ababa and Djibouti town; for information on trains to Djibouti call (☎ 51-72-50, ext 214). See also Train in the Getting There & Away and Getting Around chapters earlier.

The ticket office is open from 7 am to noon and from 2 to 4.30 pm (or later depending on trains) daily.

Car & Motorcycle

See this heading and Organised Tours in the Getting Around chapter earlier for details of car rental.

GETTING AROUND
To/From the Airport

Bole International Airport lies just 5km south-east of the city; both international and domestic flights depart from here.

Minibuses serve the airport daily from 6 am to 8 pm. To the airport from the Piazza/Mexico Square/Meskel Square costs up to Birr1.20. Some charge an additional Birr2 or Birr3 for luggage (see Minibus following).

Taxis to the airport should cost between Birr30 to Birr40, or Birr50 at night or early in the morning. From the airport, it costs around Birr30, though you'll be asked for at least double or triple this (see Dangers & Annoyances in the Facts for the Visitor chapter). A taxi association has set up a little office at the exit of the airport and charges a 'fixed rate' (negotiable) of Birr30 and Birr40, which at least cuts out the touts.

You can make the airport dash in a Mercedes-Benz NTO taxi (see Taxi following) from the Hilton for Birr40 to Birr50 during the day (Birr85 to Birr100 after midnight).

Bus

Buses in Addis are considered the poor man's transport. They are cheap but slow, run less regularly than the minibuses and are notoriously targeted by pickpockets – the minibuses are a much better bet.

Minibus

Addis Ababa is served by an extensive network of little blue and white minibuses, which are fast, efficient, cheap and a great way of getting around.

Minibuses operate from around 5.30 am to 8.30 pm every day. Short journeys (up to 2.5km) such as from Arat Kilo to the Piazza cost 50¢; medium journeys (up to 7km) cost 75¢. For every additional 2.5km, another 45¢ is charged.

Minibus stops can be found around town. Some major ones include that on Ras Makonnen Ave; in front of La Gare; at Merkato; on De Gaulle Square in the Piazza; and in front of the main post office on Churchill Road in the centre. If in doubt, ask at the stop as people are always willing to help.

There are two principal minibus stations: Meskel Square in the centre and Arat Kilo north-east of the Piazza. Roads around these intersections branch out spider-like, and minibuses ply the routes back and forth; to catch a minibus, check out the road on which your destination lies, and hop on at the start of the road that leads there. The conductors shout out the names of the main destination of the bus.

Car & Motorcycle

Parking is not usually too much of a problem in Addis Ababa. Most of the larger hotels and restaurants have parking spaces – often guarded – and don't usually mind your leaving your car there. In other places, it's worth paying for a guard; thieves work incredibly quickly.

Taxi

Most taxis operate from 6 am to 11 pm. Short journeys (up to 3km) usually cost foreigners Birr10 (Birr15 at night). Medium/long journeys cost Birr15/20. If you share a taxi, the normal fare is split between each person.

If you want to visit a lot of places in Addis Ababa, it's a good idea to hire a taxi for a half or full day; negotiate the rate (Birr75 to Birr150 is pretty reasonable). A 'city tour' lasting a couple of hours should cost around Birr40 to Birr50.

Taxis can be found outside many of the larger hotels in the centre, as well as the National Theatre, stadium, and on De Gaulle Square in the Piazza. At night, many line up outside the nightclubs.

The NTO (☎ 15-17-22) at the Hilton Hotel has a fleet of yellow Mercedes-Benz, but prices are about thrice that of local taxis (and six times at night). They're only useful for trips to the airport (prices are about the same as local taxis) or, as a last resort, at night – the service is 24 hours. During the day journeys cost around Birr40 to Birr50 (Birr85 to Birr100 after midnight).

Bicycle
Bicycles can be hired from beside the stadium in the centre for Birr3 per hour or Birr20/40 per half/full day. They are available from 7 am to 6 pm weekdays (until 5.30 pm on the weekends). Make sure you get one with a lock.

Around Addis Ababa

There are a mass of interesting and pleasant places within a day's trip of Addis Ababa. Places include Mt Yerer, Mt Zuqualla, the crater lakes of Debre Zeyit, the hot-spring resorts of Sodore (see the East of Addis Ababa chapter for all of these) or Ambo (West of Addis Ababa) and the stelae field at Tiya (South of Addis Ababa chapter). The Akaki wetlands (East of Addis Ababa chapter) is a very good place for birders.

For those spending any time in the city, the booklets *Twenty One Day Trips from Addis Ababa*, available from The Ethiopian Heritage Trust (☎ 15-88-02) in the centre, or *Ethiopia: One to Two Days from Addis Ababa* published by the ETC, are recommended.

ENTOTO MOUNTAINS
The Entoto road leads north past the university and the US embassy, to the top of the Entoto Mountains, the site of Menelik's former capital. There's a terrific but windy panoramic view of Addis Ababa below.

Near the summit is the octagonal church of Entoto Maryam, which contains mural paintings. The church is only open Sundays.

Next to the church is a museum (Birr10), which contains a large collection of religious garb mostly dating from Emperor Menelik's time. The museum is open daily except Monday.

About 1km west of Entoto Maryam is Kiddus Raguel Church. Nearby is the old rock-hewn Kiddus Raguel Church.

A new 'natural park' measuring 13 sq km is being established by the Ethiopian Heritage Trust above the Kidane Mehret Church. It's currently a pleasant place to ramble and a good spot for birders.

To get to Entoto, take minibus No 17 to its terminus from Arat Kilo; it's then around 3km on foot to Entoto.

WUSHA MIKAEL CHURCH
Wusha Mikael Church is a 30-minute walk up a hill behind the new Kiddus Mikael's church (both east of the British embassy). Though local priests date it to the 3rd century AD, it most probably dates to the 12th century. If you're not planning to visit the churches at Lalibela or Tigray in the north, it's definitely worth a peek as an example of this extraordinary building tradition. Unfortunately, for four months of the year (July to October), the church is often flooded with rainwater. Entrance is Birr20.

BIHERE TSIGE RECREATION CENTRE
The large and wooded Bihere Tsige Recreation Centre is the closest thing Addis Ababa has to a park. Covering an area of over 400 sq km, the gardens contain more than 6000 varieties of flowers, shrubs and trees. It's a very pleasant place for a walk in the late afternoon or for a picnic. If you're a birder, several species of endemics are found here. The park lies 5km south-west of the centre off the Debre Zeyit road. Entrance costs Birr1; it's open from 8.30 am to 12.30 pm and 1.30 to 5.30 pm daily. A minibus from Meskel Square will drop you off around a 20-minute walk from the park.

Taking in the Simien Mountains from Geech camp

Sof Omar caves in the south

The Abay River, en route to the Blue Nile Falls

The standing stones of Tiya

The majestic Blue Nile Falls are the second-largest falls in Africa.

Orthodox church near Gonder

Heading home from Nazret, in Ethiopia's east

Aksum's skyline is dominated by the 1960s church in the St Mary of Zion compound.

Bale Mountains National Park is a trekker's heaven.

North of Addis Ababa

I weary of writing more about these buildings, because it seems to me that I shall not be believed if I write more ... but swear I by God in Whose power I am, that all that is written is the truth, and there is much more than what I have written, and I have left it that they may not tax me with its being falsehood.

The early-16th-century Portuguese writer Francisco Alvares

Since the 16th century, European travellers have returned from northern Ethiopia with incredible stories of ancient civilisations, extravagant courts and marvellous buildings. Today's travellers are no less amazed at the sites they find here.

Known as the historical route, a trip north takes in all of Ethiopia's most famous monuments, including the ancient stelae of Aksum, the medieval rock-hewn churches of Tigray and Lalibela, and the 16th-century castles of Gonder.

The region is also exceptional for its landscape. Once the centre of tremendous volcanic activity, the landscape is riven by great canyons and chasms and gorges. At the highest point sits Ras Dashen (4543m), the fourth-highest mountain in Africa, forming part of the very beautiful Simien Mountains. At the lowest point lies the Danakil Depression, 100m below sea level, and one of the lowest, hottest and most inhospitable places on Earth.

In between, and in complete contrast again, are the spectacular Blue Nile Falls and Blue Nile Gorge. Lake Tana, Ethiopia's largest lake, is home to a group of remote island monasteries, sanctuaries for centuries of Ethiopian ecclesiastical tradition; the Ark of the Covenant itself was supposed to have resided here for a time. Nearby lies the source of the Blue Nile, the location of which puzzled and preoccupied humans for millennia.

Providing a tremendous insight into Ethiopian history, religion, geography and culture, a trip north is an absolute must for every traveller to Ethiopia. Well served by both the national airline and the bus companies, the area has the added advantage of

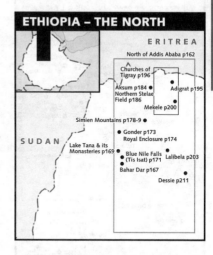

ETHIOPIA – THE NORTH

ERITREA

North of Addis Ababa p162

Churches of Tigray p196

Aksum p184
Northern Stelae Field p186

Adigrat p195

Mekele p200

Simien Mountains p178-9

SUDAN

Lake Tana & its Monasteries p169

Gonder p173
Royal Enclosure p174

Blue Nile Falls (Tis Isat) p171

Lalibela p203

Bahar Dar p167

Dessie p211

ease of access. Most travellers work northward starting with Bahar Dar and ending with Lalibela. A trip to the Simien Mountains makes a terrific break in between.

For those really keen on their history, it's possible to do the sites in chronological order, flying first to Aksum, then continuing by bus or plane to Tigray, then on to Lalibela. You can then fly from Lalibela to Gonder, bussing back to Addis Ababa via Bahar Dar and the Blue Nile Gorge. This cuts out a lot of road travel, but still takes you through some spectacular landscape.

To get the most out of the sites, it's worth having a quick flick through the History section of the Facts about Ethiopia section. The historical route covers a distance of over 2000km – you should have plenty of time to do so!

ADDIS ABABA TO DEBRE MARKOS

Debre Markos, a day's drive from Addis Ababa, serves simply as a convenient staging point on the way north. There are, however, a few places en route that might be worth a detour if you have the time.

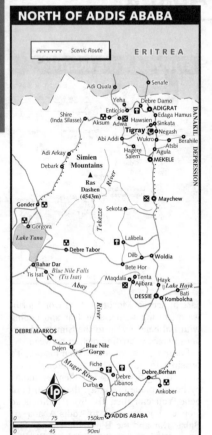

NORTH OF ADDIS ABABA

Scenic Route

ERITREA

Adi Quala
Senafe
Yeha
Enticcio
Debre Damo
ADIGRAT
Shire
(Inda Silasse)
Aksum
Adwa
Hawsien
Edaga Hamus
Sinkata
Abi Addi
Wukro
Negash
Atsbi
Berahile
Adi Arkay
Hagere
Salem
Agula
MEKELE
Simien
Mountains
Debark
Ras
Dashen
(4543m)
Tigray
Gonder
Sekota
Maychew
Gorgora
Lake Tana
Lalibela
Debre Tabor
Dilb
Woldia
Bahar Dar
Blue Nile Falls
(Tis Isat)
Tis Isat
Bete Hor
Abay
Maqdala
Tenta
Ajibara
Hayk
Lake Hayk
Bati
DESSIE
Kombolcha
DEBRE MARKOS
Dejen
Blue Nile
Gorge
Fiche
Debre Berhan
Debre
Libanos
Durba
Ankober
Chancho
ADDIS ABABA

DANAKIL DEPRESSION

River

Tekeze

Abay

River

Muger River

0   75   150km
0   45   90mi

On the way north, look out for the road-side vendors selling various regional specialities such as well-made and very cheap basketware, and the *araki* (liquor that is sold in White Horse whisky bottles). If you can stop, they're both worth investigating; a little glass of the latter will set you back 30¢.

Keep an eye out also for the shepherds or goatherds in their delightful reed 'rain-coats', the Amhara women in their pleated highland skirts, and the men carrying their indispensable *dula* (see the boxed text 'The Deadly Dula').

Muger River Gorge

The Muger River Gorge, accessible from the village of Durba, 22km from Chancho, is a great spot for a bit of rambling and wildlife. The endemic gelada baboon is often seen here, as well as a fair number of endemic birds.

From Chancho (45km north of Addis Ababa), two Ford share-taxis run to Durba every morning (Birr2, 45 mins). To continue on to Debre Markos (Birr27, 6–7 hours) or Addis Ababa (Birr3, one hour), buses stop en route between the two towns.

Debre Libanos

Lying 115km north of Addis Ababa is one of Ethiopia's most holy sites. The monastery of Debre Libanos was founded in the 13th century by a priest credited not only with the spread of Christianity throughout the highlands, but also the restoration of the Solomonic line of kings. That priest was Tekla Haimanot, today one of Ethiopia's most revered saints.

Although no trace of the ancient monastery remains – it was yet another casualty of the Muslim-Christian wars – the site is beautifully set beneath a cliff on the edge of a gorge and is a peaceful place to wander. It's also a very good place to break the journey to Bahar Dar.

The Deadly Dula

The *dula* is the chosen travelling companion of almost every Amhara man. A kind of hardwood staff, measuring about 1m long, it serves a variety of purposes. It is used to carry loads to and from market, to brace the shoulders on long treks, to lean on during the never-ending church services, and to defend oneself in times of need.

In the past, every Amhara was skilled in its use. The *gabi* (toga) was spun around the left arm to make a quick shield, and the right arm used to bring the stick crashing down on the adversary's cranium – sometimes with fatal consequences. Today it's used most commonly for fending off dogs.

Death at Debre Libanos

During the Italian Occupation, Debre Libanos was the scene of some of the worst excesses of Fascist brutality. Following the attempt on the life of the infamous viceroy Graziani, the monastery, long suspected as a hotbed of rebel activity, was singled out for reprisal.

On 20 May 1937, 267 monks – said to be 'all without distinction' – were executed; a week later, Graziani ordered the execution of all of the 129 young deacons. Satisfied at last, he wrote to Mussolini 'The monastery is closed – definitively'.

Debre Libanos has great significance for Ethiopians. Since the saint's time, it has served as the principal monastery of the Shoa region, and remains one of the largest and most important in the country. Five religious schools are found in the premises; look out for the little novices in white gabis.

Today, many Ethiopians continue to make pilgrimages to the monastery and some still seek the curative holy waters – said to be particularly good for evil spirits and stomach disorders!

The present **church**, the latest in a succession of structures, was built in 1961 by Haile Selassie. A priest apparently prophesied that the construction of a new church would ensure a long reign. The old church was replaced with one apparently in the emperor's seemingly peculiar style: monumental, hybrid and hideous.

The church interior doesn't contain a great deal of interest, beyond what is supposed to be a tomb of the saint. The stained-glass windows and mural paintings are not in fact by Afewerk Tekle, as the other guidebooks and church literature like to make out.

Five minutes up the hill from the monastery is Tekla Haimanot's **cave**, where the saint is said to have done all his praying (see the boxed text 'Know Your Saints'). It's also the source of the monastery's holy water.

If you continue up the hill from the cave, there's a marvellous **view** of the monastery in its dramatic setting. The cross-shaped tomb next to the carpark is dedicated to those executed by the Fascists.

Near the turn-off to the monastery is the so-called **16th-century Portuguese Bridge**, in fact built at the end of the 19th century by the Emperor Menelik's uncle, Ras Darge. However, like all of Debre Libanos, the scenery and atmosphere make up for the lack of tangible historical remains. Look out for the gelada baboons.

Tickets (bought from the little office near the main gate) cost Birr15 (Birr50 for video cameras) and include a guided tour. Ask for the excellent Belete Negash – himself cured from stomach ailments!

Travelling by bus from Addis Ababa, the closest village to Debre Libanos is the 'junction town' (as opposed to the main town) of Fiche (Birr8, three hours). From there, you can take a minibus to the monastery, 15km to the north (Birr2, 25 mins). The minibuses leave every hour.

Blue Nile Gorge

North of Fiche, around 100km from Addis Ababa, begins one of the most dramatic stretches of road in Ethiopia. Dropping over 1000m, the road gradually winds down the escarpment to the bottom of the Blue Nile Gorge.

For centuries, the Blue Nile River separated the old provinces of Shoa and Gojam, running south of Lake Tana all the way to Sudan. The present road and bridge were built by the Italians, who demonstrated their usual flair for civil engineering with beautiful construction. Keep an eye out for the huge lammergeyer birds.

If you're looking for a place to stay, the *Tizale Dejen Hotel* in Dejen, 118km from Fiche at the bottom of the gorge, is the best bet. Rooms cost from Birr20 (Birr30 with private shower).

Debre Markos & Fiche

There not much of interest in Debre Markos, but as the capital of Gojam, it's well furnished with hotels and restaurants. Most buses from Addis Ababa overnight here. If you're filling time, the 19th-century Church of Markos with its well-

Know Your Ethiopian Saints

There's hardly a church in Ethiopia not adorned with colourful, vibrant and sometimes very beautiful wall paintings. At first sight, the subjects depicted look more like mythological characters than biblical ones; for the non-Orthodox onlooker, they can be difficult to interpret. In fact, the paintings usually follow a set pattern, depicting again and again the key personalities of Ethiopia's peculiar pantheon of saints. See Painting under Arts in the Facts about Ethiopia section. Here's a quick key:

St George

The patron saint of Ethiopia features in almost every church. He is depicted either as the king of saints, with St Bula – who at first refused to recognise his kingship – looking on petulantly in the background, or as the great dragon slayer on his horse. In Ethiopia, the archetypal damsel in distress has a name: she's known as Brutawit, the girl from Beirut.

St Tekla Haimanot

According to legend, the saint prayed for seven years standing on just one leg, until the other finally withered and fell off! Throughout, a bird brought him just one seed once a year for sustenance. For his devotion, God awarded him no fewer than three sets of wings. The saint is normally depicted in his bishop's attire, surrounded by bells; sometimes the detached leg is shown flapping off to heaven, or else brandished by an angel.

Abuna Aregawi

One day, while wandering at the foot of a cliff, Abuna Aregawi spotted a large plateau high above him. Deciding it was the ideal spot for a nice, quiet, hermit's life, he prayed to God for assistance. Immediately, a large python stretched down from the plateau and lifted him up. The famous monastery of Debre Damo was founded then. The saint is usually depicted riding up the snake – like a kind of snakes and ladders game in reverse.

St Gebre Manfus Kiddus

One day, while preaching peace to the wild animals in the desert, this Ethiopian St Francis of Assisi came across a bird dying of thirst. Lifting it up, he allowed the bird to drink the water from his eye. The saint is usually depicted clad in furs and girded with a hempen rope. Leopards and lions lie at his feet, and the bird flaps near his head.

St Eostateos

St Eostateos (or St Thaddeus) is said to have arrived in Ethiopia borne up the Nile from Egypt on three large stones. Apparently water continued to obey him: whenever the saint chose to cross a river or a lake, the waters parted conveniently before him.

Abuna Samuel

Abuna Samuel lived near the Takezze River, where he preached and performed many miracles, accompanied by a devoted lion. He is usually depicted astride his lion.

executed paintings is worth a peek, as is the market, which has a good selection of basketware.

Decent hotels include the basic *Nehasie 30 Hotel* with rooms for Birr7–12 (Birr10–12 with private shower). Up a notch, the *Menkorer Hotel* (☎ 71-27-25) has rooms for Birr10 (Birr30 with shower).

If you get stuck in Fiche, you could try the simple *Hamer Hotel* (☎ 29) which has rooms for Birr6 to Birr12. The *Alem Hotel* (☎ 3) has adequate rooms with shower for Birr30. Both hotels have a restaurant and parking.

One bus leaves daily for Addis Ababa (Birr19, nine hours), and Bahar Dar (Birr20, 7½ hours).

Know Your Ethiopian Saints

St Yared
Ethiopia's patron saint of music is sometimes shown standing before his king with an orchestra of monks along with their sistrums, drums and prayer sticks. In the background, little birds in trees learn the magic of music.

St Mikael
The judge of souls and the leader of the celestial army, St Mikael evicted Lucifer from heaven. In most churches, the portals to the Holy of Holies are guarded by a glowering Mikael, accompanied by Gabriel and Raphael, fiercely brandishing their swords.

Belai the Cannibal
Belai the Cannibal is a favourite theme in religious art. Devouring anyone who approached him including his own family, Belai yet took pity one day on a leper begging for water in the Virgin's name. After Belai died – some 72 human meals later – Satan claimed his soul. St Mikael, the judge, balanced Belai's victims on one side, the water on the other. However, the Virgin cast her shadow on the side of the scales containing the water, and caused them to tip. Belai's soul was saved.

St Gabriel
God's messenger is usually represented cooling the flames of a fiery furnace or cauldron containing three youths condemned by Nebuchadnezzar: Meshach, Shadrach and Abed-nego.

St Raphael
Raphael apparently once rescued an Egyptian church from the tail of a thrashing whale beached on the land. He's usually depicted killing the hapless whale with his spear.

St Gebre Kristos
This Ethiopian prince sacrificed all his belongings to lead a life of chastity, and ended up a leprous beggar. He's usually depicted outside his palace where only his dogs now recognise him.

Equestrian Saints
They are usually depicted on the north wall of the Holy of Holies and may include Fasiladas, Claudius, Mercurius, Menas, Theodorus and George.

Mary
Very popular and little known outside Ethiopia are the numerous and charming legends and miracles concerning Mary, as well as the childhood of Jesus and the flight to Egypt. A tree is often depicted hiding the holy family – and the donkey – from Herod's soldiers during the flight to Egypt; the soldiers hear only the braying of the donkey. Sometimes a furious Mary is shown scolding Jesus who's managed to break a clay water jug. He later redeems himself a bit by fixing it.

From Fiche, buses run almost every hour to Debre Markos (Birr20, six hours) and Addis Ababa.

BAHAR DAR
☎ 08

With its wide avenues of palms and flamboyant trees, and its scenic location on the southern shore of Lake Tana, Bahar Dar is one of Ethiopia's most attractive towns. It makes a pleasant base from which to explore the area's main sites: the Blue Nile Falls and the island monasteries of Lake Tana.

Though more geared up to tourism than most other towns in Ethiopia, Bahar Dar miraculously still retains a semblance of a soul. For centuries right up to the present day, Bahar Dar has been an important commercial centre, symbolised by its famous *tankwa*, the open-ended papyrus canoe that continues to be used on Lake Tana for trade today.

In the 16th and 17th centuries, various temporary Ethiopian capitals were established in the vicinity of Lake Tana. It was also here that the Jesuits attempted – with disastrous consequences – to impose Catholicism on the Ethiopian people. One Jesuit building that was built by the well-known Spanish missionary, Pero Pais, can still be seen today in the compound of St George's church.

In the 1960s, Haile Selassie briefly toyed with the idea of moving his capital to Bahar Dar.

Information

A little tourist office (☎ 20-11-12) can be found in the centre of town.

Ironically, despite its proximity to the falls, the town suffers from water shortages; try not to waste it.

Malaria is endemic in Bahar Dar. According to a local doctor, an average of six people daily die of malaria. Make sure you take adequate preventative measures.

Things to See

The bustling **markets** of the town are well worth exploring, particularly on Saturday, the main market day. Look out for the colourful, striped, woven cloth, and the delightful *agelgil*, a kind of leather-bound lunch box, still used by local travellers for transporting their *injera* (bread-like staple) and *wat* (sauce-like stew). The Bahar Dar version of the *agelgil* is furry, being made from goatskin. Good coffee can also be bought here.

The famous **source of the Blue Nile** lies a couple of kilometres outside the town near

---

James Bruce: In Search of the Source

Half undressed as I was by the loss of my sash, and throwing my shoes off, I ran down the hill towards the little island of green sods, which was about two hundred yards distant.

…It is easier to guess than to describe the situation of my mind at that moment – standing in the spot which had baffled the genius, industry and enquiry of both ancients and moderns, for the course of near three thousand years.

From *Travels to Discover the Source of the Nile* by James Bruce, 1790, published by Gregg, Godstone, 1971

One of the first European explorers in Africa was a Scot, James Bruce, who had a passionate interest in unknown lands.

After serving as consul general in Algiers, he set off in 1768 in search of the source of the Nile – a puzzle that had preoccupied people since the time of the Egyptian Pharaohs.

After landing in Massawa, Eritrea, he made his way to the powerful and splendid court of Gonder, where he became a close friend of the Empress Mentewab.

In 1770, he reached the source of the Abay, the main river that feeds Lake Tana, above the Blue Nile Falls. There he declared that the mystery of the source of the Nile had been solved, dedicated his discovery to King George III, and returned home to national acclaim.

In fact, Bruce had traced only the source of the *Blue* Nile River, the main tributary of the Nile. Not only that, but he had been beaten to his 'discovery' – as he very well knew – over 150 years earlier by a Spanish Jesuit, Pero Pais.

Of greater interest was the account of his journey, *Travels to Discover the Source of the Nile*, published in 1790. It remains a very useful source of information on the history of the country and customs of the people. At the time, his contemporaries considered much of it to be gross exaggeration, or even pure fiction. Given his earlier claims, no wonder.

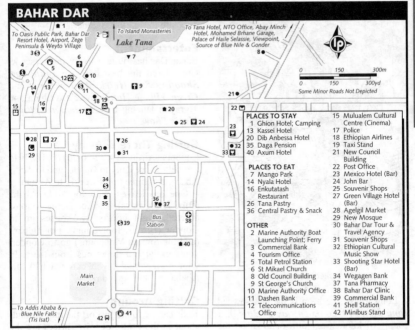

BAHAR DAR

Lake Tana

To Oasis Public Park, Bahar Dar Resort Hotel, Airport, Zege Peninsula & Weyto Village

To Island Monasteries

To Tana Hotel, NTO Office, Abay Minch Hotel, Mohamed Brhane Garage, Palace of Haile Selassie, Viewpoint, Source of Blue Nile & Gonder

0   150   300m
0   150   300yd

Some Minor Roads Not Depicted

Bus Station

Main Market

To Addis Ababa & Blue Nile Falls (Tis Isat)

PLACES TO STAY
1 Ghion Hotel; Camping
13 Kassei Hotel
20 Dib Anbessa Hotel
35 Daga Pension
40 Axum Hotel

PLACES TO EAT
7 Mango Park
14 Nyala Hotel
16 Enkutatash Restaurant
26 Tana Pastry
36 Central Pastry & Snack

OTHER
2 Marine Authority Boat Launching Point; Ferry
3 Commercial Bank
4 Tourism Office
5 Total Petrol Station
6 St Mikael Church
8 Old Council Building
9 St George's Church
10 Marine Authority Office
11 Dashen Bank
12 Telecommunications Office
15 Mulualem Cultural Centre (Cinema)
17 Police
18 Ethiopian Airlines
19 Taxi Stand
21 New Council Building
22 Post Office
23 Mexico Hotel (Bar)
24 John Bar
25 Souvenir Shops
27 Green Village Hotel (Bar)
28 Agelgil Market
29 New Mosque
30 Bahar Dar Tour & Travel Agency
31 Souvenir Shops
32 Ethiopian Cultural Music Show
33 Shooting Star Hotel (Bar)
34 Wegagen Bank
37 Tana Pharmacy
38 Bahar Dar Clinic
39 Commercial Bank
41 Shell Station
42 Minibus Stand

the Blue Nile bridge. Along the river, keep an eye out for hippos and crocodiles.

The former **Palace of Haile Selassie** lies on a hill 5km north-east of town. It's approached via a long avenue of jacaranda trees. Though it's not currently open to visitors, there's a wonderful, panoramic view from in front of the entrance gates – over the Blue Nile River, Lake Tana and the town.

Around 2km west of town, beyond the Ghion Hotel, is a **Weyto village**. The Weyto people are known for their production of tankwa boats; you can watch the skilled artists at work. Though the tankwas look as flimsy as paper – in fact they are made from papyrus – they can take huge loads, including firewood and even oxen.

Good souvenir shops are marked on the Bahar Dar map.

Places to Stay

Campers can find a spot in the lovely grounds of the otherwise overpriced **Ghion Hotel** (☎ 20-07-40). Camping costs Birr44 per person including the use of a hot shower.

Bahar Dar's budget hotels vie with one another for awfulness. Though basic, the **Kassei Hotel** (☎ 20-07-67) stands head and shoulders above the rest, with rooms with a sink for Birr8. The sign is in Amharic only.

Grubby and basic, but central and cheap, is the **Daga Pension** (☎ 20-00-70) with singles/doubles with cold shower for Birr20/40. Beware the 'guides' who hang about outside. The **Axum Hotel** (☎ 20-09-75) near the bus station is less grubby, but noisy, with rooms for Birr35.

Offering the best value in the middle range is the peaceful **Abay Minch Hotel** (☎ 20-00-38) on the Gonder road beyond the Tana Hotel, with rooms with bathroom for Birr50/80.

A new hotel is the **Dib Anbessa Hotel** (☎ 20-14-36, fax 20-18-18) offering good-value double/twin rooms for Birr120/150.

DAWIT ABEBE

A typical market scene in Ethiopia.

Long top of the heap is the state-owned *Tana Hotel* (☎ 20-05-54, fax 20-20-42), a couple of kilometres north of town on the Gonder road. Singles/doubles/suites attractively decorated in the traditional style cost US$36/48/72. Though furnished with fewer facilities than the private hotels, the place has an unbeatable location at the very edge of the lake. If you can't afford to stay here, come for a drink at dusk. Its gardens are considered one of the best spots for bird-goggling.

About to open at the time of writing is the huge and modern *Bahar Dar Resort Hotel*. Rooms with fridge and TV should cost around US$50.

Places to Eat

Very popular locally are the simple *Enkutatash Restaurant* and *Nyala Hotel*, which offer the usual Ethiopian dishes for Birr4–8. *Mango Park* on the edge of the lake is a shady spot for a snack.

For *faranji* (western) food, the *Tana Hotel* restaurant has a good reputation. The *Dib Anbessa Hotel's* restaurant isn't bad.

A good place for a pastry, fruit juice or breakfast is the new *Tana Pastry*. If you're waiting for a bus, *Central Pastry & Snack* opposite the station is good.

Entertainment

Bahar Dar has quite a lively music scene. Considered the best bars are *John Bar*, *Shooting Star Hotel*, *Mexico Hotel* and *Green Village Hotel*. There's Amhara and Tigrayan dancing at the *Ethiopian Cultural Music Show*.

Getting There & Away

Ethiopian Airlines (☎ 20-00-20) flies daily to Lalibela, twice daily to Gonder and to Addis Ababa, and three times weekly to Aksum.

One bus leaves daily for Addis Ababa (Birr37, 1½ days), and for Debre Markos (Birr20, eight hours); two buses go to Gonder (Birr13, four hours). For Debark (and the Simien Mountains) go to Gonder; you can catch a direct bus from there. In your own vehicle, you can reach Addis Ababa (578km) in a day.

Getting Around

Taxis can be found just off the main roundabout in the centre of town; prices are the same as in Addis Ababa. Taxis are not allowed outside the town (eg, to Tis Isat village or the Blue Nile Falls). Minibuses also whiz about the town, and cost and function as they do in Addis Ababa. For the airport, taxis ask Birr50 and minibuses cost Birr10.

For car hire, Bahir Dar Tour & Travel Agency (☎ 20-01-75) offers competitive rates. Tours and cars should be booked in advance at the company's head office in Addis Ababa (see Organised Tours in the main Getting Around section earlier in this chapter).

Bicycles can be hired from next door to the Central Pastry & Snack, and cost Birr2 for one hour, Birr4 for half a day, Birr8 for one day, and Birr24 for three days.

The NTO (☎ 20-05-37), based at the Tana Hotel, rents cars, offers city tours (Birr70 per person for one or two people, or Birr40 per person for three people), and organises trips to the falls (Birr120 per person for one to three people). It can also arrange visits to the island churches on Lake Tana, and even birdwatching tours.

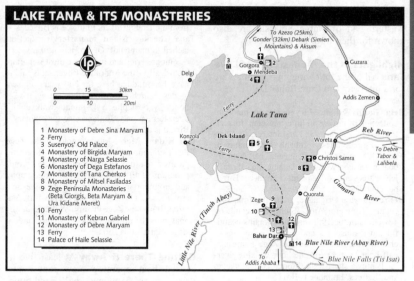

LAKE TANA & ITS MONASTERIES

1 Monastery of Debre Sina Maryam
2 Ferry
3 Susenyos' Old Palace
4 Monastery of Birgida Maryam
5 Monastery of Narga Selassie
6 Monastery of Dega Estefanos
7 Monastery of Tana Cherkos
8 Monastery of Mitsel Fasiladas
9 Zege Peninsula Monasteries
   (Beta Giorgis, Beta Maryam &
   Ura Kidane Meret)
10 Ferry
11 Monastery of Kebran Gabriel
12 Monastery of Debre Maryam
13 Ferry
14 Palace of Haile Selassie

AROUND BAHAR DAR
Lake Tana & its Monasteries

Covering over 3500 sq km, Lake Tana is
Ethiopia's largest lake and has long been
known to the outside world – the Egyptians
called it Choloe Palus, the Greeks knew it
as Pseboe. Today, the lake is most famous
as the home of the monasteries established
on some 20 of its 37 islands.

Many of the monasteries date from the
late-16th or early-17th century, though most
were founded much earlier and may even
have been the site of pre-Christian shrines.
Many have long provided a safe sanctuary
for royal treasures and tombs, and are still
tremendous havens of peace. Visiting them
really is like stepping back several hundred
years into the past.

Information Unfortunately, women
can visit only certain monasteries; however, some of these are among the most
interesting!

The cost of boat hire and entrance fees
soon adds up. To reduce the cost, it's a good
idea to try and find other travellers and form
a small group. Boat excursions are worthwhile; the arrival by boat is certainly part of

the charm of these remote and sometimes
very beautiful islands.

To visit some of the more remote islands
(via those closer to home), you're looking
at a full day's excursion. Bring lots of Birr1
and Birr10 notes for tips and entrance fees
– the priests never have change. Be aware
that a fee of between Birr50 and Birr100 is
charged for video cameras.

Allow enough time for the keeper priests
to be located; sometimes you can wait up to
20 minutes. Beautiful little silver crosses
are sold by children on the most popularly
visited islands on the Zege Peninsula for as
little as Birr25, but remember the antiquity
prohibition on exports (see Customs in the
Facts for the Visitor chapter). For information on appropriate behaviour, see the
boxed text 'Church Etiquette' under Responsible Tourism in the Facts for the Visitor
chapter.

Camping is permitted on the islands,
but be aware that islanders may be very
suspicious of foreigners in light of recent
church robberies.

If you're keen on birds, you may want to
consider a trip to Mitsel Fasiladas Island, a
breeding ground for wetland birds. The

eastern shore of Lake Tana and the southwestern end of Narga Selassie are also known for their birdlife.

Highlights of the Monasteries of Lake Tana

All of the following journey times are for a one-way trip from Bahar Dar.

Beta Giorgis & Beta Maryam Has an important collection of crowns in little 'museum' (one attributed to Yohannes IV) and interesting paintings in monasteries – probably 19th century or later. It's on the Zege Peninsula, half hour by boat and a short walk from landing stage through lemon trees and coffee plants. Entrance is Birr15 per church.

Debre Maryam Original church dates from 14th century (Emperor Amda Sion), but rebuilt by Tewodros in the 19th century; contains beautiful old manuscripts and a good collection of church treasures. It's on the Zege Peninsula; half hour by boat (or one hour walking overland) plus a short walk through coffee, mango and fig trees. Entrance is Birr15.

Dega Estefanos island monastery One of the most sacred monasteries; rebuilt mid-19th century. Houses 16th-century painting of Madonna, and mummified remains in glass coffins of five former emperors of Ethiopia (13–17th centuries). Set on a hill nearly 100m above the lake; 30–45 minute walk one way; lies beside Narga Selassie (see following). Open to men only. Entrance is Birr35.

Kebran Gabriel island monastery One of the most beautiful and atmospheric of the lake monasteries; dates from the 17th century; 12-columned portico; good paintings on *maqdas* (inner sanctuary); look out for depiction of Iyasu before Christ. Half hour by boat and a short walk from the landing stage. Open to men only. Entrance is Birr20.

Mitsel Fasiladas island monastery Most of its treasures were robbed in the early 1990s but it's still worth visiting if you're in the vicinity. It has an attractive setting; the foundations remain of the old church. It's around two hours by boat and a short walk from the landing stage. Entrance is Birr15.

Narga Selassie (Dek) island monastery This place is a 'must' – it was built in the mid-18th century in the style of Gonder castles in a very beautiful location. Has effigies of Mentewab and James Bruce engraved on the exterior of the church plus fine 18th-century paintings and crosses. Little visited, peaceful and atmos-

pheric; 2½ hours by boat and a two-minute walk from the landing stage. Entrance is Birr20.

Tana Cherkos 'island' monastery (in fact attached to mainland). One of the most mysterious monasteries and one of the most important historically – the Ark of the Covenant is said to have been hidden here for 800 years. Present modest church dates from 19th century. It's 2½ hours by boat plus a 45-minute walk uphill; open to men only. Entrance fee is voluntary – Birr20 is advised.

Ura Kidane Meret Most famous of the Zege Peninsula monasteries with a very beautiful painted *maqdas* that is practically a compendium of Ethiopian religious iconography and an important collection of old crosses and crowns, said to date from the 16th to 18th centuries. It's on the Zege Peninsula; 30 minutes by boat plus 10-minute walk from the landing stage. Entrance is Birr15.

Getting There & Away

At least five licensed boat operators now rent boats. Prices are not fixed, and you'll need to negotiate hard; in the wet season, you should be able to get good discounts.

Boat 'agents' can be found hanging around the Ghion and Tana Hotels (see Places to Stay in the Bahar Dar section earlier). Boats (with captain, guide and fuel included) cost from Birr100-150 for one to four people, depending on the monastery you want to visit. A visit to, say, four monasteries on the Zege Peninsula costs from Birr250. A whole day to Narga Selassie via the Zege Peninsula, plus church entrance fees, costs from Birr600.

The Marine Authority charges Birr250 for a trip to two Zege monasteries in a small boat (up to six people), or Birr170 per hour for one to five people. The office keeps normal government office hours (see Business Hours in the Facts for the Visitor section).

Check that the boats have life jackets and spare fuel, and bring a raincoat or umbrella and something warm.

The Zege Peninsula can also be reached by road. It lies around 23km from Bahar Dar. To get there, you can hire a car or bicycle from Bahar Dar. You'll need two days to visit all the islands.

A ferry service connects Bahar Dar to Gorgora on the northern shore of the lake, via the Zege Peninsula (see Gorgora under Around Gonder later in this section). However, it operates just once a week and is really intended to pick up passengers from Zege, and not transport them there.

Blue Nile Falls (Tis Isat)

Known locally by the more evocative names of Tis Isat (Smoking Fire) or Tis Abay (Smoking Nile), the Blue Nile Falls is one of the most spectacular falls in Africa. When in full flood, it is as impressive for its incredible width (measuring over 400m) as for its depth (45m). Dropping over a sheer chasm, the thunderous noise can be heard long before arrival, and the spray that is thrown up can be felt up to a kilometre away.

James Bruce, the 18th-century Scottish traveller and one of the first Europeans to describe it, called it: 'a magnificent sight, that ages, added to the greatest length of human life, would not efface or eradicate from my memory'.

The falls creates its own microclimate, and a perennial mini-rainforest has grown up beside it. The luscious vegetation teems with birds – including parrots, bee-eaters, lovebirds and turacos. Look out for the vervet monkeys too.

The falls lies 32km south-east of Bahar Dar, just beyond the village of Tis Isat. It's 1km from the car park to the village. Entrance tickets must be bought from the ticket office in the village (open daily from 6.30 am to 6.30 pm). Tickets cost Birr15,

or Birr5 for students; Birr100 for video cameras.

You'll get plenty of offers to guide you; engaging a guide (around Birr30) will deter the others. From the village, it's a 30-minute walk down into a gorge, across an old 17th-century Portuguese bridge and up to the falls. Make sure you have good walking shoes.

You can also get right down beside the falls (following the so-called western route) by crossing the river just above the falls in a tankwa (Birr60 return) – quite hair-raising if the river is running strongly! Then it's a straightforward 20-minute hike down to the base, where you'll get a compulsory shower from the spray. The whole trip takes around 1½ hours, not including stops or the walk from the road. In the dry season, you can walk from a point near the car park (45 minutes one way) to the foot of the falls. It's a great place for a picnic.

The falls are at their most spectacular immediately after the rainy season (from mid-September to mid-October), when the volume of falling water can reach 8000 cubic metres a second. Try and get here early in the morning.

If you need accommodation in Tis Isat because you missed the last bus, the very basic and none-too-clean *Zeyin Hotel* (Birr5) is the best bet.

Camping is permitted near the falls; there are no facilities and it's free.

Getting There & Away From Bahar Dar, buses leave every hour (from 6 am to 4 pm) for Tis Isat village (Birr3, one hour).

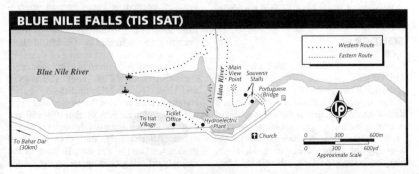

Damming the Blue Nile

Sweeping down from the high plateaus of Ethiopia, the Blue Nile carries with it hundreds of tonnes of highland soil. Dispersing it on the desert banks of Egypt, the river accounts for 85% of Egypt's fertilising lime. No wonder talk of damming the Blue Nile causes Egyptian hackles to rise. For Ethiopia, the river is seen as a vast, untapped source of both water (to feed thousands of kilometres of irrigation schemes) and of hydroelectricity. It is even believed that the river is the key to Ethiopia feeding itself.

From Tis Isat, four to six buses run daily to Bahar Dar, the last between 3 pm and 4 pm; if you miss the last bus, you may be able to hitch with one of the returning Bahar Dar tour operators or hotel vehicles.

Various tour operators in Bahar Dar run half-day excursions to the falls for around Birr200 per person.

Debre Tabor

Lying around 100km by road north-west of Bahar Dar is the town of Debre Tabor. Though not so illustrious now, it was formerly the site of an important Ethiopian capital during the 18th and 19th centuries, including that of the ill-fated Emperor Tewodros II (see Emperor Tewodros under History in the Facts about Ethiopia section).

Today just ruins of the old palace remain, along with the old churches of Debre Tabor and the 19th-century Heruy Giyorgis. However, if you're passing through on your way to Woldia, it's worth a leg-stretch. Buses run daily between Bahar Dar and Debre Tabor.

GONDER
☎ 08

Gonder has been called Africa's Camelot, and with its series of castles and churches is one of the major attractions of the historical route.

Surrounded on all sides by fertile and well-watered land, and at the intersection of three major caravan routes, Gonder was the perfect place for a capital. To the south-west lay the rich sources of gold, civet, ivory and slaves; to the north-east lay Mas-sawa and access to the Red Sea, and to the north-west lay Sudan and Egypt.

The Emperor Fasiladas founded Gonder in 1636. The city became the country's first permanent capital, and flourished for the next 200 years. By the time of the emperor's death in 1667, Gonder's population exceeded 65,000 and its wealth and splendour had become a local legend.

The Gonderine period is one of the most colourful in Ethiopia's history, and drifting through the old palaces, banqueting halls and former gardens, it's not difficult to imagine the courtly pageantry, ceremony and intrigue that went on here.

It is still not certain who built the castles. Scholars currently believe that Portuguese craftsmen who remained after the expulsion of the Jesuits were probably responsible.

Though extensively looted in the 1880s by the Sudanese Dervishes and damaged by British bombs during the liberation campaign of 1941, most of Gonder remains amazingly well preserved.

Look out for the fascinating and outstanding examples of Italian Fascist Art Deco architecture, such as the cinema, the telecommunications building, and the Quara and Ethiopia Hotels. If you wander some of the streets on the outskirts of town, you may come across some beautiful old Italian villa.

For more information on the city's history see The Rise of Gonder under History in the Facts about Ethiopia section.

Information

A little tourist information centre (☎ 11-00-22) has just opened; it keeps normal government office hours (see Business Hours in the Facts for the Visitor section). An interpretative centre funded by the World Bank should open in the next couple of years.

Particularly good times to visit Gonder are during the festivals of Leddet (Christmas) and Timkat (see Public Holidays & Special Events in the Facts for the Visitor section).

Guides charge fees of Birr100–150 per day, and can be organised through the tourist office. Alternatively, the NTO has good guides for Birr150 per day. Beware of the many unofficial guides operating in Gonder.

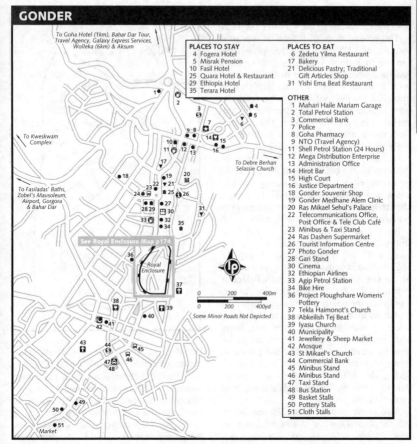

GONDER

To Goha Hotel (1km), Bahar Dar Tour, Travel Agency, Galaxy Express Services, Wolleka (6km) & Aksum

To Kweskwam Complex

To Fasiladas' Baths, Zobel's Mausoleum, Airport, Gorgora & Bahar Dar

To Debre Berhan Selassie Church

See Royal Enclosure Map p174

Royal Enclosure

0   200   400m
0   200   400yd
Some Minor Roads Not Depicted

Market

PLACES TO STAY
4 Fogera Hotel
5 Misrak Pension
10 Fasil Hotel
25 Quara Hotel & Restaurant
29 Ethiopia Hotel
35 Terara Hotel

PLACES TO EAT
6 Zedecu Yilma Restaurant
17 Bakery
21 Delicious Pastry; Traditional Gift Articles Shop
31 Yishi Ema Beat Restaurant

OTHER
1 Mahari Haile Mariam Garage
2 Total Petrol Station
3 Commercial Bank
7 Police
8 Goha Pharmacy
9 NTO (Travel Agency)
11 Shell Petrol Station (24 Hours)
12 Mega Distribution Enterprise
13 Administration Office
14 Hirot Bar
15 High Court
16 Justice Department
18 Gonder Souvenir Shop
19 Gonder Medhane Alem Clinic
20 Ras Mikael Sehul's Palace
22 Telecommunications Office, Post Office & Tele Club Café
23 Minibus & Taxi Stand
24 Ras Dashen Supermarket
26 Tourist Information Centre
27 Photo Gonder
28 Gari Stand
30 Cinema
32 Ethiopian Airlines
33 Agip Petrol Station
34 Bike Hire
36 Project Ploughshare Womens' Pottery
37 Tekla Haimonot's Church
38 Abkeilish Tej Beat
39 Iyasu Church
40 Municipality
41 Jewellery & Sheep Market
42 Mosque
43 St Mikael's Church
44 Commercial Bank
45 Minibus Stand
46 Minibus Stand
47 Taxi Stand
48 Bus Station
49 Basket Stalls
50 Pottery Stalls
51 Cloth Stalls

Good souvenir shops (including the charitable Project Ploughshare for women potters) are marked on the map.

Unless otherwise indicated, the sights in Gonder keep the same opening hours as the Royal Enclosure: from 8.30 am to 12.30 pm and 1.30 to 5.30 pm daily. All sites except the Royal Enclosure charge Birr15 entrance and Birr50–75 for a video camera.

Royal Enclosure

Gonder's Royal Enclosure is pretty large: it covers an area of over 75,000 sq m and contains castles, palaces and various houses and outbuildings. Surrounded by high stone walls, the enclosure is connected by a series of tunnels and raised walkways. A ticket for the enclosure (Birr50, Birr75 for a video camera) is valid for the duration of your stay.

Fasiladas' Palace is the oldest and perhaps most impressive of the castles. It stands two storeys high, has a crenellated parapet and four small, domed towers. Made of roughly hewn brown basalt stones, it is reputedly the work of an Indian architect, and shows an unusual synthesis of Indian, Portuguese and Moorish as well as Aksumite influences. From the rectangular tower in the south-west corner, there's a terrific view over the enclosure all the way to Lake Tana.

The ground floor of the castle was used as a dining hall and formal reception area. On the first floor, Fasiladas' prayer room has four windows in four directions, each with a view of one of the city's many churches. On the roof, religious ceremonies were held, and it was from here that the emperor addressed his people. The second-floor rooms contain Fasiladas' bedroom.

Behind the castle are various ruined buildings including what is thought to be the remains of a **bathing pool**. Nearby is the two-storeyed quadrangular **library** of Fasiladas' son, Yohannes I (r. 1667–82), and a **chancellery**, topped by a tower, once an impressive palace decorated with ivory.

Next door to the palace is the two-storeyed saddle-shaped palace of Iyasu I. The son of Yohannes I, Iyasu (r. 1682–1706) is considered the greatest ruler of the Gonderine period. **Iyasu's Palace** is unusual today for its vaulted ceiling. In former times, the palace was sumptuously decorated. Gilded venetian mirrors and chairs made up the furnishings; gold leaf, ivory and beautiful paintings adorned the walls. Visiting travellers described the palace as 'more beautiful than Solomon's house'. Sadly, the 1704 earthquake as well as British bombing in the 1940s have done away with the interior.

Also in the compound are the remains of the Emperor Dawit's **House of Song**, in which many religious and secular ceremonies and lavish entertainment took place.

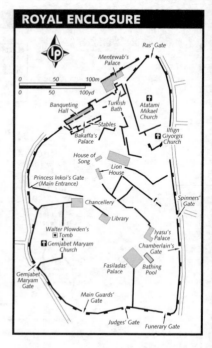

ROYAL ENCLOSURE

Ras' Gate
Mentewab's Palace
Banqueting Hall
Turkish Bath
Atatami Mikael Church
Stables
Ilfign Giyorgis Church
Bakaffa's Palace
House of Song
Lion House
Princess Inkoi's Gate (Main Entrance)
Spinners' Gate
Chancellery
Library
Walter Plowden's Tomb
Gemjabet Maryam Church
Iyasu's Palace
Chamberlain's Gate
Fasiladas' Palace
Bathing Pool
Gemjabet Maryam Gate
Main Guards' Gate
Judges' Gate
Funerary Gate
0 50 100m
0 50 100yd

The Foundation of Gonder

The Archangel Raphael one day appeared to the Emperor Lebna Dangal. 'Seek out and find', the angel said, 'the site of the new capital, whose name shall begin with the letter G'.

Obediently, the emperor and his successors subsequently founded Guzara and Gorgora. It wasn't until the mid-17th century and the foundation of Gonder that the archangel's name game was finally cracked.

Dawit (r. 1716–21) also built the **Lion House**, where until recently Abyssinian lions were kept. Other buildings in the compound included a House of Assembly, a House of Mourning and two public squares used for proclamations and public executions.

When Dawit came to a sticky end (he was poisoned in 1721), the Emperor Bakaffa (r. 1721–30) took up the reins of power, and built the huge **banqueting hall**, the scene of vast feasts and banquets. He also built the nearby **stables**. Next door was a *wesheba* (Turkish bath), which operated in the same way as Roman baths, and which apparently worked wonders for those suffering from syphilis!

Bakaffa's consort was responsible for the last castle, known as **Mentewab's Castle**, a two-storeyed structure that is now used as a public library. The Gonder cross is used as a decorative motif.

Also in the enclosure is **Walter Plowden's Tomb**; Plowden served for a time as

British consul and became a close friend of the Emperor Tewodros, before he was murdered journeying to the coast.

Fasiladas' Baths

Around 2km north-west of the city centre lies Fasiladas' Baths (in fact attributed to both Fasiladas and Iyasu I). A large, rectangular sunken pool is overlooked by a small but charming two-storeyed tower, surrounded by a stone wall. It's a peaceful, shady and beautiful spot, and is well worth a visit.

Although the complex is popularly known as a bathing palace, or as baths, most probably it was constructed for important religious celebrations, the likes of which still go on today. Once a year, Fasiladas' Baths are filled with water for the important *Timkat* ceremony. After being blessed by a priest, the pool becomes a riot of spraying water, shouts and laughter as the crowd jumps in. The ceremony replicates Christ's baptism in the Jordan River, and is seen as an important renewal of faith.

Just beyond the wall of the compound is a small pavilion known as **Zobel's Mausoleum**, after a horse which, Nero-style, was honoured by Fasiladas or Iyasu.

If you can't be bothered to walk to the baths, you can hop on one of the town minibuses (75¢) that leave from near the Ras Dashen Supermarket in the centre. Entrance to the compound is included in the Royal Enclosure ticket; note that tickets can't be bought at the baths themselves.

Kweskwam Complex

Lying in the hills about 3.5km north-west of town is the royal compound known as Kweskwam, which was built by the Empress Mentewab, redoubtable wife of the Emperor Bakaffa.

Though less well preserved than the Royal Enclosure, it too is made up of a series of buildings including a long, two-storeyed, castellated palace used for state receptions and also for housing the royal garrison. Like the empress' other palace, its exterior is decorated with red volcanic tuff. Look out for the figures of crosses and Ethiopian characters and animals, such as St

Samuel riding his lion, all said to have belonged to a bishop of the time.

The nearby smaller building is said to have been the empress' private residence. To the west of the palace, there was once a fine church, which was rebuilt after damage by British bombs. A tiny crypt contains the mummified bodies of the empress, her son and her grandson, the Emperors Iyasu II and Iyo'as.

The complex is a wild, overgrown place, and there's a good view of the town if you can battle your way through the undergrowth.

Ras Mikael Sehul's Palace

Located outside the Royal Enclosure, this palace is like a small version of Fasiladas' castle, but has a slightly foreboding air. Perhaps it's because it was the residence of Ras Mikael, the dictator who usurped power at the end of the 18th century, as the monarchy became increasingly impotent and ineffectual. Later, the building was used – more chillingly – as a prison during the Derg, and is said to have been the site of untold brutality and torture. It's currently closed to visitors.

Debre Berhan Selassie Church

Lying around 2km to the north-east of Gonder is probably the country's most famous church, one of the highlights of Gonder – and Ethiopia. Debre Berhan Selassie, meaning 'Trinity at the Mount of Light', is familiar to many long before they arrive, from the endlessly reproduced photographs of its ceiling. The winged heads of 80 Ethiopian cherubs entirely cover the ceiling; all have slightly different expressions.

No less impressive than the ceiling are the paintings on the walls attributed to the same artist, Haile Meskel. Full of all the colour, life, wit and humanity of Ethiopian art at its best, they provide practically a compendium of Ethiopian saints, martyrs and lore.

Look out for the 'portrait' of Emperor Iyasu I, the church's founder; the depiction of the Prophet Mohammed on a camel being led by a devil; and the almost Bosch-like depiction of Hell.

The building itself is rectangular in design and dates from the reign of Yohannes I. According to local tradition, the church was saved from the sacking of the Dervishes by a timely swarm of bees.

Some have claimed that the emperor planned to bring the Ark of the Covenant here from its reputed resting place at Aksum, and that the church was in effect especially designed to house such a prestigious relic.

The church is open daily from 5 am to 8 pm. Flash photography inside the church is no longer permitted.

Places to Stay
Camping is possible in the grounds of the **Terara Hotel** for Birr44 per tent including access to a hot shower.

One of the best-value budget hotels is the **Ethiopia Hotel** with clean rooms with common shower for Birr12. One step up and best in its range is the **Fasil Hotel** (☎ 11-02-21) with small doubles/twins (with common hot shower) for Birr20/30.

The quiet **Misrak Pension** (☎ 11-00-69) with rooms with private cold shower for Birr40 has long been a popular mid-range choice.

The Italian-built **Quara Hotel** (☎ 11-00-40) has adequate rooms with hot shower for Birr60. The *tukuls* (conical thatched huts) in the **Fogera Hotel** are quite pleasant (Birr160); the rooms are overpriced.

Top of the range is the **Goha Hotel** (☎ 11-06-34, fax 11-19-20). Designed by the same architect responsible for the Tana Hotel in Bahar Dar, rooms cost US$36/48/72 for singles/doubles/suites. Like the Tana, its greatest asset is its location. Perched on a high natural balcony overlooking the town and castles, it lies around 2km north of Gonder. If there's one hotel worth splurging on in Ethiopia, this is the one, particularly after a hard trek in the Simien Mountains. If you can't afford a room, a sunset drink (beer costs Birr5) or dawn stroll on the lovely terrace is almost as good. Camping in the grounds costs US$15 for a small tent ($US20 for large) and use of shower.

Places to Eat & Drink
Considered the best place by the locals is the **Yishi Ema Beat Restaurant** (look out for the sign saying 'Culture Restaurant'). Another excellent place is the **Zedetu Yilma Restaurant** next door to the Misrak Pension.

For faranji food, the **Fogera Hotel** has a good reputation.

A great place for breakfast is the new **Tele Club Café** below the telecommunications office.

Decent pastry shops are marked on the map; the **Delicious Pastry** is quite delicious. The **Ras Dashen Supermarket** is probably the best place for stocking up for treks in the Simien Mountains.

A lively local bar is the **Hirot Bar**. A well-known *tej beat* (mead house) is the **Abkeilish Tej Beat**.

Getting There & Away
Ethiopian Airlines (☎ 11-01-29) flies twice daily to Addis Ababa, and daily to Lalibela, Aksum and Bahar Dar (see the main Getting Around section earlier in this chapter). If you're flying to Aksum, try and get a seat on the right-hand side of the aircraft, which gets the best views.

Buses leave daily from Gonder for Bahar Dar (Birr13, four hours), Addis Ababa (Birr50, 1½ days via Debre Markos) and Debre Tabor (Birr12, four hours). Two buses go daily to Debark (Birr8, 3–4 hours) for the Simien Mountains.

For Woldia and Lalibela (Birr31, two days), take the bus towards Dessie. For Aksum, you should go to Shire (Birr27, 12 hours), then change for Aksum (2½ hours).

Getting Around
The airport lies around 20km from the town. A taxi one-way in either direction should cost no more than Birr40. A taxi for the whole day including airport pick-up should cost around Birr130 for half a day (Birr200 for a full day). If you want to organise a taxi driver in advance, call Daniel Tsegaye (☎ 11-05-01). Taxis between the Goha Hotel and the town centre cost Birr10. *Garis* (horse-drawn carts) can also be hired (Birr3 for a short journey).

You can rent a 4WD through the Goha Hotel or the NTO for around Birr800–950 per day (including driver). Bahir Dar Tour & Travel Agency (☎ 11-19-66) and Galaxy Express Service (☎ 11-15-46) rent cars; the latter rents camping equipment too.

Bicycles can be hired from in front of the public library for Birr3 per hour.

The NTO (☎ 11-03-79) offers city tours (Birr190 per person), as well as various tours of one to eight days in the Simien Mountains (a three-day tour costs Birr5500 for one or two people all-inclusive), and to Gorgora (Birr700 for one day – also for one or two people).

AROUND GONDER
Gorgora
The little town of Gorgora, 67km from Gonder on the northern shore of Lake Tana, makes a pleasant excursion from Gonder for those with time. It's also a particularly good spot for birds.

The most interesting relic of its former days as capital is the attractive round church of Debre Sina, built in 1608 by the Emperor Susenyos' son. It's decorated with fine frescoes from the same period. Entrance costs Birr15.

Nearby, the ruins of Susenyos' old palace can be visited by boat or car (1½ hours from Gorgora), as can various churches, such as Birgida Maryam (closed to women) and the monastery at Mendaba (also closed to women), an hour from Gorgora. A speedboat can be hired from the nearby Lake Tana Transport Enterprise office and costs Birr100 per hour for one to six people, including captain and fuel.

The 1970s-style but comfortable *Tana Lake Hotel* (☎ 7) has doubles/twins for Birr165/220. The huge three-bedroom suite (Birr420), with its own little terrace jutting into the lake, once accommodated Colonel Mengistu Haile Mariam.

Both buses and minibuses ply the Gonder-Gorgora route (Birr10, three hours). There's also a weekly ferry service from Bahar Dar to Gorgora (Birr123 for first-class, one-way, two days) via Zege village

Xenophobia

Ethiopian Highlanders are notoriously xenophobic – not just towards foreigners, but towards fellow Ethiopians, even from neighbouring villages. Centuries of war, civil strife and courtly intrigue are believed to lie at the root of such suspicion.

When travelling, some Highlanders still take with them their own horn cup. In the past this was to prevent poisoned drinks being served to them.

In the tej beats of the rural areas, the host still sometimes pours out the drink onto his hand first and takes it to his mouth to demonstrate that it is safe for his guests to drink.

on the peninsula, with an overnight stop at Konzola. It leaves Bahar Dar every Sunday at 7 am. From Gorgora to Bahar Dar, the ferry leaves between 6 and 7 am on Thursday. You should bring food and water with you, as there's no restaurant or cafe on board. In Konzola, where passengers stay overnight, the *Getahun Abay Hotel* is the best bet (Birr10 for singles or doubles).

Wolleka (Falasha Village)
Around 6km north of Gonder is the little village of Wolleka, once the home of a thriving population of Falashas or Ethiopian Jews. Before the coming of Christianity, Judaism was for centuries the dominant religion of most of north-western Ethiopia.

After the adoption of Christianity as the state religion, the Falashas were continually persecuted. The punishment for refusing to convert was the confiscation of land. Many Falashas then became skilled craftsmen. Recent research suggests that it was the Falashas who provided the labour for the construction and decoration of the castles.

From 1985 to 1991, many Falashas were airlifted to Israel, and today, none but a handful remain (see the boxed text 'Passports to the Promised Land' under Religion in the Facts about Ethiopia section). Sadly, the pottery for which they were famous has degenerated into clumsy, half-hearted affairs, produced to feed the demand from tourists.

ETHIOPIA

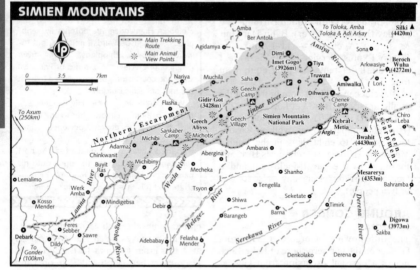

SIMIEN MOUNTAINS

The old synagogue and Falasha homes can be visited, but a special trip to the village can't be called very worthwhile. To get here from Gonder, you can catch a taxi (Birr25), a minibus (Birr1.50, 30 mins, just three a day), or a gari (Birr4 one-way).

SIMIEN MOUNTAINS

According to Homer, the Simien Mountains were the playground of the Greek gods, who came here to play chess.

The traveller Rosita Forbes, travelling in Ethiopia in 1925, described the mountains as 'the most marvellous of all Abyssinian landscapes'. By any standards – Ethiopian or African – the scenery is spectacular; in places it's breathtaking.

The Simien Mountains, which lie north of Gonder and east of the main road to Aksum, make a terrific break from the monument-bashing on the historical route. They'll also give you a taste of Ethiopia's remarkable wildlife. Home to a variety of endemic plants, mammals and birds, including the beautiful walia ibex found only here, the park has been declared a World Heritage Site by Unesco.

Although facilities for trekkers are few – the undeveloped state of the park is one of its attractions – the mountains are nevertheless easily accessible and treks can be quickly organised. Most demands can be catered to, from casual strolls after a picnic, to hard-core rock climbing.

For anyone remotely interested in walking, wildlife or scenery, the Simien Mountains are not to be missed; they are undoubtedly among the most beautiful mountain ranges in Africa.

See also the boxed text 'Considerations for Responsible Trekking' under Responsible Tourism in the Ethiopia Facts for the Visitor section. Lonely Planet's *Trekking in East Africa* includes a chapter on the Simien Mountains.

Geography & Geology

Comprising one of the principal mountain massifs of Africa, the Simien Mountains are made up of several plateaus, separated by broad river valleys. A number of peaks rise above 4000m, including Ras Dashen.

The dramatic landscape of the Simien Mountains is the result of massive seismic activity in the area about 40 million years ago. Molten lava poured out of the Earth's core reaching a thickness of 3000m. Subse-

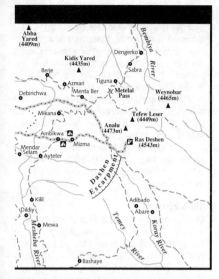

quent erosion over the millennia has left behind the jagged landscape of the Simien Mountains: the gorges, chasms and precipices. The famous pinnacles – the sharp spires that rise abruptly from the surrounding land – are volcanic necks: the solidified lava and last remnant of ancient volcanoes.

The park itself stretches over 179 sq km and lies at an altitude of between 1900m and 4430m, in the 'Afro-Alpine' zone. A typical trek takes you through tiny villages and fields of barley in the lower valleys to the steep gorges and sheer escarpments of the lower slopes. Beyond lies the wild and sometimes bleak landscape of the upper slopes including those around Ras Dashen.

Climate

The average daily temperature of the Simien Mountains ranges between 11.5°C and 18°C. At night, the temperature drops to around 3°C; during the coldest period from October to December, it can dip several degrees below freezing point.

Flora & Fauna

The mountains are home to three of Ethiopia's larger endemic mammals: the walia ibex (around 600 are estimated to remain, though groups of 60 were being reported at a time in 2000), the more common gelada baboons, and the very rarely seen Ethiopian wolves. Other mammals sometimes seen are the jackal, bushbucks, rock hydras and klipspringers.

Endemic bird species include the commonly seen thick-billed raven, and the less common black-headed siskin, white-collared dove, white-billed starling, wattled ibis, spot-breasted plover and white-backed tit. One of the most memorable sights is the huge and soaring lammergeyer – quite easily seen in the Simien Mountains.

For more information, see Flora & Fauna in the Facts about Ethiopia section.

Planning

All treks begin and end in Debark, where the park headquarters and the nearest medical assistance are located, and this is where all trekking is organised.

In Gonder itself, there are more and more freelance 'agents' offering to organise things for you. If you're in a hurry, this may save you some time; they charge only a nominal commission. The agents can organise car and equipment rental (tents cost Birr25 to rent; sleeping bags cost Birr10) and can even buy food for you. One agent to be particularly recommended is the efficient and obliging Habteselassie Asemare (☎ 11-12-13, fax 11-07-05).

Nevertheless, it's perfectly straightforward organising the trekking yourself in Debark, and you'll have more control over your choice of guide, mules etc.

Maps Almost the only map currently available is the *Simen* [sic] *Mountains Trekking Map* (see Maps under Planning in the Facts for the Visitor section). Occasionally it's available at the Simien Park Hotel in Debark for Birr120, but you're best advised to get it before leaving home.

When to Go December to March is the driest time, but October, after the rainy season, is when the scenery is greenest and the wildflowers are out.

Vanishing Wolves

Though it takes its name from the mountains, the Ethiopian wolf (also known as the Simien fox) is close to extinction in the area. Officially, the population is estimated at 100, yet in 1999, a local journalist, using recent records from the park authorities, put the number at just four.

Many wolves have died from diseases caught from local dogs. Other have died after eating rats poisoned by villagers to protect their crops. Hybridisation with dogs is another threat. Fortunately, the endemic animal is faring far better in the Bale Mountains to the south (see the boxed text 'The Ethiopian Wolf' under Bale Mountains in the South of Addis Ababa section).

During the main rainy season, between June and September, mist often obscures the views and the trails can be slippery underfoot. Even in the wet season, however, you are assured of several hours of clear, dry weather for walking; the rain tends to come in short, sharp downpours.

Park Fees Entrance to the park costs Birr70 per 48 hours (plus Birr10 for a vehicle) and is payable at the park headquarters.

It takes at least two hours to arrange everything; the best plan is to arrive in the afternoon and arrange everything for an early start the following morning.

The park headquarters is open from 8.30 am to 12.30 pm and 1.30 to 5.30 pm weekdays. If you arrive over the weekend, you can normally dig out the cashier.

Supplies Outside Debark, there are no shops, although you can buy eggs (Birr1 for three eggs), chickens (Birr7) or sheep (Birr60) from villages on the mountain. Your guide will negotiate prices, and mule handlers will gladly kill, skin and roast a sheep if they get to tuck in too. If you leave the carcass a little way outside camp, it may well attract a lammergeyer.

Debark's shop supplies are limited to a few tin cans, plus some fresh fruit and veg-

etables from the market and fresh bread. Gonder is a better place for stocking up. You can also find stoves, lanterns and kerosene (paraffin) in Gonder. Anything 'specialised', such as packet soups, porridge oats and imported tinned food should be bought in Addis Ababa (where it's also cheaper).

Water is available in various places on the mountain but should be treated. Make sure the cook, if you have one, boils the water sufficiently, rather than just warming it up.

If you're worried about warmth, do as the locals do: buy a gabi (Birr80) at Debark, which makes a great blanket/shawl/pillow/cushion.

Trekking

Only part of the park can be reached by 4WD vehicle. The rest is crisscrossed by paths that for centuries have connected villages and pasture lands. These make terrific trekking routes. The walking itself is generally not challenging and gradients are not too steep.

Don't forget to allow time for acclimatisation when planning your routes, particularly if you're aiming to reach Ras Dashen, which is best done in no less than five days including a rest day at one of the high camps such as Chenek.

The most popular trekking routes are along the western side of the massif; these take in the most impressive sections of the famous escarpment. The park 'camps' of Sankaber, Chenek and Geech make convenient spots at which to overnight.

With two days you could walk from Debark to Sankaber and back. With four days you could reach Geech; with five you could get to Chenek, taking in Mt Bwahit; and with seven days you could bag Ras Dashen. All times include the return journey to Debark.

The foot that is restless, will tread on a turd.
Ethiopian proverb

Guides, Cooks & Mules Guides (Birr50 per day) are compulsory in the park. Though they are freelancers, the guides are trained at the national park headquarters on a course established by an Austrian team. Most are excellent, a few are lousy.

Guides now work by rota, so there's little point recommending any by name. However, don't be afraid to ask for another guide if you're not happy with the one assigned to you (see also the boxed text 'Guidelines for Guides' in the Facts for the Visitor section).

'Scouts' (armed park rangers) are also compulsory (Birr30 per day). They don't usually speak English, but what they lack in conversation they more than make up for in willingness to help. Some scouts, though fit, are quite old; a tip at the end is particularly appreciated.

Cooks can also be hired for Birr30 per day, a welcome but not-too-costly luxury.

Porters are not available in the Simien Mountains, but mules with handlers can be hired to carry both you (if you want to ride) and your gear. Mules cost Birr20 per day, and handlers the same amount. The guide and scout will expect at least one mule for carrying their blankets and provisions.

When you hire mules, make sure you check them carefully. Ask the handler to walk them up and down for any signs of tender feet. Lift up the saddle and blanket and check for saddle sores along the mule's back, or girth sores on its belly. If there are any sinister signs, ask for another mule; there are plenty of good mules in Debark.

Guides, cooks and mule handlers are expected to provide food for themselves. Many bring token offerings or nothing at all and will then look to you for sustenance. Either check that they have enough or bring extra packets of rice etc.

At the end of the trek, staff will expect a tip. A rule of thumb is that if the service has been good might be an extra day's pay for every three days' work.

Cooks, mules and guides are all organised at the park headquarters (☎ 16 through the operator) in Debark (about ten minutes' walk from the Simien Hotel), though a guide will probably find you long before you get there.

Choosing a Trekking Route

In a nutshell, if it's spectacular scenery you're after, head for Geech. If it's the walia ibex, Chenek is good. If it's the gelada baboon, try Sankaber, Chenek and particularly Geech. If it's good walking, from Geech to Chenek is a good stretch.

Ras Dashen frankly doesn't offer a great deal, beyond the satisfaction of 'bagging it'. The going can be tedious, and gradients are steep in parts.

Debark to Chinkwanit (12km, 4 to 5 hours) Sankaber can be reached in a single day, but many trekkers prefer to break the first day at Chinkwanit, where there's a good camp with a stream. About 100m to the north of Chinkwanit, and hidden by a slight incline, is a fabulous viewpoint from the top of the main Simien escarpment. Get there at sunset for the best view. Early in the morning, you may see klipspringers here. If you do want to push on to Sankaber, it's another 5km (around two hours).

Chinkwanit to Geech Camp via Sankaber (15km, 7 to 8 hours) The dirt road and your guide will take you straight to Sankaber, but a more scenic route is to follow the narrow path that keeps close to the escarpment edge. There are particularly good views between Michibi and Sankaber. During the civil war, this area was the scene of fierce fighting – look out for spent cartridges.

Towards Sankaber, the escarpment narrows to a ridge with gorgeous views on both sides. You may well meet your first troop of gelada baboons.

At Sankaber camp, water is available from a rather vegetated well. Fill up here, as there's no more water available for several hours.

From Sankaber, you can either follow the escarpment edge again or keep to the dirt road, before descending into a valley known as Michotis. The often-dry Wazla River (called the Koba River on some maps) runs along the valley floor.

At the top of the other side of the valley, to the north-east, are the waterfalls of the Jinbar River, which plummet into the spectacular Geech Abyss, a vast canyon cut into the main wall of the escarpment.

From Sankaber to Geech it's between 4–5 hours' walk. At Geech, there's a long-drop

Monkey Trouble

Now the focus of international scientific studies including a BBC documentary by David Attenborough, the extraordinary endemic gelada baboon is yet little appreciated by the locals. Resented for its alleged damage to village crops and pasture, it has become the scapegoat for more sinister goings-on too. According to local police reports in Sankaber, gelada baboons are responsible for local thefts, burglaries, rapes and even murders – in one case bursting into a house to drag an adult man 1.5km before shoving him off a cliff face! If in doubt blame the gelada! See also the boxed text 'The Gelada Baboon' in the Facts about Ethiopia section.

toilet and a convenient nearby waterfall for washing in.

Geech Camp to Chenek via Imet Gogo (20km, 7 to 9 hours)
Geech to Chenek takes about 5–6 hours, but a very worthwhile diversion is the promontory of Imet Gogo, around 5km north-east of Geech. It takes 1½–2 hours one-way.

The promontory, at 3926m, affords some of the most spectacular views of the Simien Mountains, north and east over the rock spires and mesas of the lowlands. If you want to make a day of it, another detour will take you to the viewpoint known as Saha.

From Imet Gogo you have two choices: the first is to return to Geech by your outward route, then head directly south, back across the Jinbar River and up to an area called Ambaras where you meet the dirt road and follow it all the way to Chenek. The alternative, which is harder but more scenic, is to follow the escarpment edge south by way of another promontory viewpoint called Gedadere.

Whichever route you choose, just before arrival at Chenek, you will pass a spot known as Kebrat Metia, which provides stunning views of the lowlands below and the escarpment edge to the west. Lammergeyers are often seen here.

There is a fast-running stream about five minutes' walk south of Chenek camp. Chenek is probably the best spot in the Simien Mountains for wildlife.

Chenek to Bwahit (6km, 3 hours)
The summit of Bwahit (4430m) lies to the south-east of the camp; the landscape on the ascent changes dramatically from coarse moorland to barren scree slopes. From the top, you can see a tiny piece of Ras Dashen.

Around 20 minutes from the camp towards Bwahit, there's a spot that affords one of the best opportunities for glimpsing, at long range (around 300–400m), the walia ibex. The animal, a member of the wild goat family, lives on the crags of the steep escarpment above 3000m. Don't miss it, but come very early in the morning with binoculars.

Chenek to Ambikwa (11km, 8 to 9 hours)
From Chenek, a track leads eastward then south-eastward up towards a good viewpoint on the eastern escarpment, to the north of Bwahit. To the east, across the vast valley of the Mesheha River, you can see the bulk of Ras Dashen.

Near the village of Ambikwa, there's a camping spot and a river.

Ambikwa to Ras Dashen and Return (17km, 8 to 10 hours)
Most trekkers stay two nights at Ambikwa and go up to the summit of Ras Dashen on the day in between. It's a good idea to start at first light.

At Ras Dashen, there are three distinct points, and most people head for the one on the left. Whichever peak you go for, the total walk from Ambikwa to reach one summit is about 5–6 hours. If you want to knock off the others, add 2–3 hours for each one. Returning by the same route takes about 3–4 hours.

Ambikwa to Debark (55km, 3 days)
Most trekkers return from Ambikwa to Debark along the same route via Chenek and Sankaber.

There are, however, a number of other options that take you through some of the more remote and interesting villages of the southern Simien Mountains. Your guide will be able to suggest routes depending on the time available.

Ambikwa to Adi Arkay (about 65km, 3 to 5 days) One interesting alternative return route is to trek from Ambikwa to Arkwasiye, to the north-east of Chenek, taking in the nearby peaks of Beroch Wuha (4272m) and Silki (4420m).

From Arkwasiye to Adi Arkay will take another two to three days of strenuous walking, via Sona (three hours from Arkwasiye) and Mekarebya (seven hours from Sona).

From Adi Arkay, which lies about 75km north of Debark, you can continue northward to Aksum.

Other Routes There are endless alternatives for keen trekkers or rock climbers, such as a return route from Ras Dashen back to Ambikwa and Chenek, via the east and north sides of the Mesheha River.

A very few travellers have even managed to trek south-east from Ras Dashen all the way to Lalibela (16 days), following the Tekezze River southward for part of the way to a point about 20km west of Lalibela. Since Lalibela is an important religious centre, the paths are quite well-trodden and usually easy to follow. However, the going is hot, dusty and dry with lots of ups and downs. Water is not always available.

Places to Stay
Debark Most trekkers stay at the *Simen Hotel*, a block back from the main street and a short walk from the bus stop and market. Basic but clean rooms with a communal shower cost Birr15. The restaurant is quite good.

Newer, well-run and a little quieter is the *Simien Park Hotel* (☎ 55), on the right as you come in from Gonder, past the park headquarters. The 12 rooms have double/twin beds for Birr25/45; showers (hot) are communal.

On the Mountains Unfortunately, the excellent stone huts at Sankaber, Geech

and Chenek were destroyed during the war. Those that have been repaired are currently reserved for the park rangers.

Camping is the next best alternative, but you'll need to be fully self-contained with tent, sleeping bag and cooking gear (all of which can be hired in Addis Ababa and sometimes in Gonder).

The park camps provide flat ground, water, and simple shelters that can be used by the guides, scouts and mule handlers.

If you don't have camping equipment you can do as the guides do: stay in the local huts. You'll be made to feel welcome, but should contribute about US$1 per night to the household. Don't expect too many luxuries. A floor or wooden platform covered with a goatskin serves as your bedroom; any number and combination of goats, children, chickens and especially fleas serve as your roommates.

Getting There & Away
Two buses run daily between Gonder and Debark (Birr8, 3–4 hours).

Another option from Gonder to Debark is to hire a local taxi (Birr450–500 for one to four people, 2½ hours).

A 4WD vehicle can be hired through the Goha Hotel or the NTO in Gonder for around Birr800–950 per day. To continue on to Sankaber from Debark will cost around another Birr500. Or you might be able to find a 4WD in Debark to drop you off at Sankaber or Ambaras (Birr340–500). Ask your guide, or at the hotels in Debark. As this book goes to print, the new dirt road is being pushed beyond Ambaras towards Chenek, so eventually nonwalkers will be able to visit the park too. During July and August, the road can be difficult.

To return from Debark to Gonder, arrange for your driver to come and collect you, or simply take the Gonder bus. There are no taxis in Debark.

Coming from Aksum, you'll need to get to Shire first, then catch a bus going towards Gonder, which will drop you at Debark en route. Going to Aksum, it's easier to go back to Gonder and go from there.

SHIRE

Shire, marked on maps as Inda Selassie, is a large town, but is of interest to travellers only as providing a link with Aksum, 60km to the east. Buses from the north and south stop here.

The plains on the outskirts of Shire were the scene of fighting between the Tigrayans and advancing Italians in the 1930s, and later against Mengistu's army in the civil war.

AKSUM
☎ 04

Tiny, dusty, rural: Aksum is modest almost to a fault. On first sight, it's hard to imagine that the town was ever the site of a great civilisation. See Kingdom of Aksum under History in the Facts about Ethiopia chapter.

Yet Aksum is one of Ethiopia's star attractions. The little town is littered with the ruins of palaces, underground tombs, stelae and inscriptions. The ancient Aksumite kingdom has been described by Dr Neville Chittick as 'the last of the great civilisations of Antiquity to be revealed to modern knowledge'. Aksum is to sub-Saharan Africa what the pyramids are to North Africa.

Incredibly, 98% of Aksum remains unexcavated; what has been excavated has

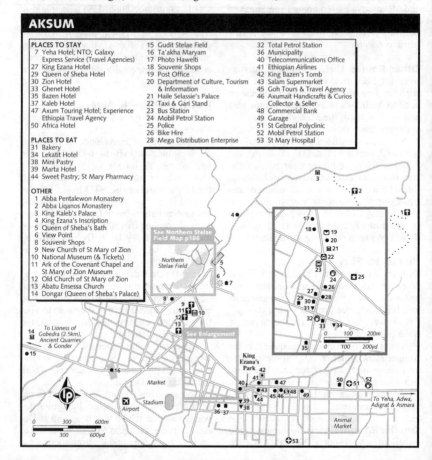

AKSUM

PLACES TO STAY
- 7 Yeha Hotel; NTO; Galaxy Express Service (Travel Agencies)
- 27 King Ezana Hotel
- 29 Queen of Sheba Hotel
- 30 Zion Hotel
- 33 Ghenet Hotel
- 35 Bazen Hotel
- 37 Kaleb Hotel
- 47 Axum Touring Hotel; Experience Ethiopia Travel Agency
- 50 Africa Hotel

PLACES TO EAT
- 31 Bakery
- 34 Lekatit Hotel
- 38 Mini Pastry
- 39 Marta Hotel
- 44 Sweet Pastry; St Mary Pharmacy

OTHER
- 1 Abba Pentalewon Monastery
- 2 Abba Liqanos Monastery
- 3 King Kaleb's Palace
- 4 King Ezana's Inscription
- 5 Queen of Sheba's Bath
- 6 View Point
- 8 Souvenir Shops
- 9 New Church of St Mary of Zion
- 10 National Museum (& Tickets)
- 11 Ark of the Covenant Chapel and St Mary of Zion Museum
- 12 Old Church of St Mary of Zion
- 13 Abatu Ensessa Church
- 14 Dongar (Queen of Sheba's Palace)
- 15 Gudit Stelae Field
- 16 Ta'akha Maryam
- 17 Photo Hawelti
- 18 Souvenir Shops
- 19 Post Office
- 20 Department of Culture, Tourism & Information
- 21 Haile Selassie's Palace
- 22 Taxi & Gari Stand
- 23 Bus Station
- 24 Mobil Petrol Station
- 25 Police
- 26 Bike Hire
- 28 Mega Distribution Enterprise
- 32 Total Petrol Station
- 36 Municipality
- 40 Telecommunications Office
- 41 Ethiopian Airlines
- 42 King Bazen's Tomb
- 43 Salam Supermarket
- 45 Goh Tours & Travel Agency
- 46 Axumait Handicrafts & Curios Collector & Seller
- 48 Commercial Bank
- 49 Garage
- 51 St Gebreal Polyclinic
- 52 Mobil Petrol Station
- 53 St Mary Hospital

See Northern Stelae Field Map p186

Northern Stelae Field

See Enlargement

To Lioness of Gobedra (2.5km), Ancient Quarries & Gonder

Market

Stadium

Airport

King Ezana's Park

To Yeha, Adwa, Adigrat & Asmara

Animal Market

0   300   600m
0   300   600yd

0   100   200m
0   100   200yd

suffered at the hands of looters and stone robbers, or from overbuilding. In addition, the museum is a nonstarter, there is no written information available, and the standard of the guides is not high, so you'll need to bring your imagination.

Perhaps this is part of Aksum's charm. Though no longer a wealthy metropolis, the town continues to flourish as a centre of local trade; life continues as it has for millennia. Around the crumbling palaces, farmers go on ploughing their land, village boys splash in the Queen of Sheba's Bath, and hurrying past the towering stelae are the market-goers and their donkeys. You won't find pyramid-parking coaches or sound-and-light shows here.

A particularly good time to visit is during one of the major religious festivals or for the festivities of Maryam Zion in late November (see Public Holidays & Special Events in the Facts for the Visitor chapter). To do the town justice, you should schedule the barest minimum of one full day if you have a vehicle, or two days if you're on foot.

History

According to the Kebra Negast, Ethiopia's great national epic, Aksum was the Queen of Sheba's capital in the 10th century BC (see the boxed text 'Kebra Negast' under Arts in the Facts about Ethiopia chapter). More fantasy than fact that may be, but what is certain is that a high civilisation had arisen here several centuries before the birth of Christ.

By the first century AD, Greek merchants knew Aksum as a great city and the powerful capital of an extensive empire. For close to 1000 years, Aksum dominated the vital sea-borne trade between Africa and Asia. The kingdom numbered among the greatest states of the ancient world.

Even after its dramatic and somewhat mysterious decline, the town retained considerable prestige and status. Today, Aksum serves as a kind of unofficial religious capital and many kings have been crowned here.

Pilgrims still journey to Aksum and important festivals are celebrated here. The great majority of Ethiopians believe passionately that the Ark of the Covenant resides within the town. Aksum is to Ethiopians what Mecca is to Saudi Arabians.

Aksum has a vibrancy, life and continuing national importance very rarely found on ancient sites.

Information

There is no tourist office in Aksum. Tickets, which can be bought from the National Museum, cover all the historical sites within the immediate vicinity of Aksum (except the St Mary of Zion church compound) and are valid for the duration of your stay. They cost Birr50 (Birr25 for students).

Guides are best hired from the National Museum, since this cuts out the unofficial ones. Though they are provided free, they will expect a tip – as good as a fee – which should be negotiated in advance. The Department of Culture, Tourism and Information office recommends Birr10–20, but guides may well expect five times that. Be aware also that many get commission from your purchases in shops.

The standard of guides, as usual in Ethiopia, is not high (some are much better than others), but they do know their way around and will point out things you might otherwise miss. They're also good on the local tradition and legends. Bring a torch.

Tombs

Aksumite tombs were first dug out from under the ground, then lined with very large, beautifully worked blocks of granite.

To the east of the largest obelisk in the Northern Stelae Field is the remarkable Tomb of King Ramha, known more officially as the **Tomb of the Brick Arches**. Though it dates from the late 3rd century, it is incredibly well preserved. Every feature is Aksumite, and its architecture is considered exceptionally fine. Comprising four rock-cut chambers, it is subdivided by a series of brick arches.

The tomb is just one of two so far excavated that have avoided wholesale robbery. The remains of at least two skeletons were discovered, along with pots, glass vessels and metalwork including a 69cm-long spearhead.

Discovered in 1972, the **Tomb of the False Door**, also in the Northern Stelae Field, is

A Quick Guide to Aksum's Stelae

For perhaps as long as 5000 years, monoliths (stelae) have been used in north-east Africa as a kind of tombstone-cum-monument to local rulers. In Aksum, this tradition reached its apogee. Like Egypt's pyramids, Aksum's stelae were like great billboards announcing to the world the authority, power and greatness of the ruling families. The more finely carved the stele, the most splendid and complex the tomb underneath. Aksum's astonishing stelae are striking for their huge size, their incredible, almost pristine, state of preservation, and their curiously modern look. Sculpted from single pieces of granite to look like multistoreyed buildings, they more closely resemble Manhattan skyscrapers than 2000-year-old obelisks. Though the stone is famously hard, Aksum's masons worked it superbly, often following a set design.

Six of the stelae imitate multistoreyed buildings complete with little windows, doors and sometimes even door handles or locks. The architectural style mirrors the traditional Aksumite style of the time, used to construct the city's houses and palaces (see Architecture in the Facts about Ethiopia chapter).

In former times, metal plates, perhaps in the form of a crescent moon and disc, are thought to have been riveted to the top of the stelae both at the front and back. The crescent is an ancient pagan symbol, originating from southern Arabia. In 1996, a broken plate that matched perfectly the rivet holes at the top of the stelae was excavated. It bore the effigy of a face, perhaps the ruler to whom the plate's stele was dedicated.

At the base of the stelae is a stone platform thought to have served as an altar. The little carved cavities probably held sacrificial offerings. In King Ezana's stele, look out also for the *gabeta* board game, carved into the platform by bored ancients clearly unimpressed by what towered above them!

Many aspects of the stelae are still shrouded in mystery. It is uncertain why they were designed in this way. And no one has yet figured out how the massive blocks of granite were transported at least 4km from the quarries, then stood upright; the largest weighed no less than 517 tonnes. Traditionally it is believed that the celestial powers of the Ark of the Covenant were harnessed for the feat; archaeologists believe that the earthly forces of elephants, rollers and winches were probably used.

Northern Stelae Field

The Northern Stelae Field contains over 120 extant monoliths. The biggest stele here, the Great Stele, measures a massive 33m. It is the largest single block of stone that humans have ever attempted to erect, and overshadows even the Egyptian obelisks in its ambitiousness and conception (see following).

NORTHERN STELAE FIELD

Queen of Sheba's Bath
Enda Iyesus Church
Tomb of the Brick Arches
0 100 200m
0 100 200yd
King Ezana's Stele
Former Location of Rome Stele
Main Entrance
Great Stele
Tomb of Nefas Mawcha
Mausoleum
Tomb of the False Door

The stele near the entrance, attributed to King Ezana, is now the biggest, measuring 24m high. Henry Salt, the British traveller and first foreigner to describe it in 1805, proclaimed it 'the most admirable and perfect monument of its kind'.

In 1997, another huge stele (18m) was discovered near the church of Enda Iyesus. It is unusual for the circle carved in relief at the top.

thought to date from the 4th or 5th century AD. It was totally robbed in antiquity and is thought to have contained objects of great value, judging from the lengths to which the robbers went to gain access. Look out for the metal clamps – like a kind of giant staple used to fix blocks firmly together. Scientists have not to his day been able to identify the iron ore used for this 'miracle metal', which is apparently astonishingly strong. The tomb

A Quick Guide to Aksum's Stelae

Among the various other monoliths is one measuring 8m long, which depicts near its top end a box-like object formed by a rectangle surmounted by a triangle. It has been suggested that this might represent the Ark of the Covenant.

The Great Stele

Once this stele was believed to have stood, but following further investigations in 1998, scholars now believe that the monolith never stood; that it toppled over as it was being erected sometime in the second quarter of the 4th century. It now lies like a broken soldier. Look out for the unworked 'root', which contrasts dramatically with the sleek, carved base; it gives you a vivid idea of the precision, finesse and technical competence of the Aksumite stone workers.

When the great stele crashed to the ground sometime around the turn of the first millennium, it sounded the knell not only on the long tradition of obelisk erection in Aksum, but also on the old religion.

Some scholars have suggested that the disastrous collapse of the massive stele may actually have contributed to the people's conversion to Christianity – like a kind of Ethiopian Tower of Babel – or even that it was sabotaged deliberately to feign a sign of God. Whatever the origin of its downfall, the stele remains exactly where it fell 1600 years ago, a permanent reminder of the defeat of paganism by Christianity.

The Rome Stele

The second-largest stele, at 25m high, was shipped to Italy in 1937 during the Italian Occupation, on the personal orders of Mussolini. It stands to this day in the Piazza di Porta Capena in Rome, and is sometimes known as the Rome stele. After decades of negotiation, it should be returned to Ethiopia in the near future.

But that's easier said than done. The stele will have to be lowered onto its side, cut into two pieces, then flown back in a special plane – probably US-supplied – large enough to take it. Then there's the problem of road transportation and re-erection when it arrives; archaeologists believe that the proposed site, which marks underground tombs, may not be stable enough to hold it.

While all the head-scratching continues, the achievement of the ancient Aksumites is rather thrown into perspective: the stele was transported and erected at Aksum in the first place – without chopping it up, without US planes and without archaeologists – around 2000 years ago.

Gudit Stele Field

Though less immediately arresting than those found in town, the stelae in the Gudit Stelae Field, opposite Dongar (the Queen of Sheba's Palace), are thought to be older, dating perhaps to the first half of the first millennium AD.

Roughly and irregularly hewn, they slightly resemble the menhirs that Asterix and Obelix used to toss around; they may mark the graves of lesser nobles. Look out for the sole decorated stele: four horizontal bands are incised, topped by a row of circles in relief. According to local tradition, the stone marks the grave of the Queen of Sheba herself. No excavation work has yet been carried out here.

The walk to the complex makes a lovely walk at dusk; you'll meet the farmers and their animals returning home before nightfall.

also contains sarcophagi, absent in many other tombs. Look out for the ancient 'yardstick' used by the masons.

Other tombs include the huge and well-constructed **Tomb of Nefas Mawcha** and the so-called **Mausoleum**, partly disfigured at some unknown date by robbers who managed to dig through 1.5m of solid masonry. If, as is thought, the other stelae also mark graves, then the whole area may be a mass

Aksumite Coins

Aksumite coinage provides a vital and fascinating source of information on the ancient kingdom. The coins bears the names, effigies and sometimes lineage of no fewer than 20 different kings.

Beautifully struck, the coins depict the royal crowns, clothing and jewellery of the kings – even the large earrings worn by some monarchs. A curiosity still unexplained by historians is the fact that almost all the coins are double-headed: on one side the king is depicted with his crown, on the other, he dons a modest head-cloth.

In the mid-1990s, a find near the little town of Hastings in southern England caused a mild sensation: an original Aksumite bronze coin was unearthed. In fact, the coin almost certainly arrived on English shores not through ancient trade with Britain, but rather through modern tourism.

of underground tombs. In some places, you can hear the sound of an unopened tomb echoing below your feet. This is part of Aksum's appeal – the thought that untold treasures lie waiting to be discovered. The temptation to return in the night with a shovel is almost unbearable!

Most other tombs so far excavated have been pillaged by robbers, so very little is yet understood about Aksumite burial customs. In the meantime, we'll just have to wait for the Ethiopian Tutankhamen.

St Mary of Zion Churches

Opposite the Northern Stelae Field in a walled compound lie the two churches of St Mary of Zion.

The rectangular **old church** was built by the Emperor Fasiladas, the founder of Gonder, in 1665. Look out for the old podium on which it sits – it may well belong to the original church erected by King Ezana or King Kaleb in the 4th or 6th centuries after the adoption of Christianity. This would have been the very first church on African soil. Unfortunately, the building was destroyed during the incursions of Mohammed

Gragn in 1535 (see The Muslim–Christian Wars under History in the Facts about Ethiopia chapter).

Inside there are some fine murals including a painting of the Nine Saints, and a collection of musical instruments used in church ceremonies.

The little **'museum'** in the compound contains an unsurpassed collection of crowns belonging to former Ethiopian rulers. Neither the church nor the museum is open to women, but some of the crowns can be brought out by obliging priests; you should tip them afterwards.

A carefully guarded building in the church compound is said to contain the famous **Ark of the Covenant**. Don't think you can take a peek: just one specially chosen guardian has access to the Ark. And many unfortunate onlookers 'burst into fire' just for getting close!

The huge **new church**, which now dominates the Aksum skyline, gets the 'hideous carbuncle' prize. Haile Selassie, displaying his usual fine taste, had it erected it in the 1960s. It sits like a bloated onion gone to seed – with a disproportionately tall bell tower sprouting heavenwards.

In the church courtyard, look out for the remains of the **old thrones** upon which generations of monarchs were crowned.

Entrance to the whole church compound costs Birr60 (Birr100 for video cameras).

National Museum

Poor National Museum: it's dusty, decrepit and badly neglected. However, it's still worth a wander, even if the labels are often missing, and the exhibits are so crammed into cabinets, they resemble someone's top drawer. Hiring a guide is a good idea.

The museum contains some fine ancient Sabaean and early Ge'ez **inscriptions** and an interesting variety of objects found in tombs, including ordinary household objects such as drinking cups, lamps and incense burners. Look out particularly for the collection of **Aksumite coins** dating from the 4th to 6th centuries AD (though those housed in the Ethnological Museum in Addis Ababa are finer). The museum is open from 8 am to noon and 2 to 6 pm daily.

In the next five years, a new museum should be built, partly funded by the World Bank.

King Ezana's Park

Lying in a little shelter in the park in the centre of town is the famous stone of the 4th-century King Ezana. Ezana's kingdom stretched from eastern Sudan all the way to modern-day Yemen across the Red Sea.

It may not look much, but the stone is of immense historic importance. The inscription records the many victories achieved by the king over his 'enemies and rebels' – rather as the Roman emperors liked to do.

However, the stone's significance lies in the fact that the inscription is written in three ancient scripts (Sabaean, Ge'ez and Greek) like a kind of Ethiopian Rosetta stone. The inscribed stone is actually one of many in Aksum.

King Bazen's Tomb

In contrast to the dressed blocks used to construct the tombs of the kings in the stelae fields, King Bazen's tomb is hewn out of solid rock. Perhaps it is older; the king is thought to have reigned at the time of the birth of Christ. The tomb may also have contained the king's family. Look out for the numerous other graves carved into the rock face.

Queen of Sheba's Bath

This huge water reservoir, hewn out of solid rock, is thought to post-date the queen by at least a millennium! Still, it remains a great piece of ancient engineering. Today, local women who come to wash clothes here claim that the waters are cursed. At least one boy every year drowns in the water apparently.

Ta'akha Maryam

Unfortunately Ta'akha Maryam was as good as obliterated during the Italian Occupation, when a road was cut straight though it. Nevertheless, the refinement and sophistication of the building is still very evident from the ruins. Ta'akha Maryam was undoubtedly a magnificent palace, dating from the 4th or 5th century AD.

The Legendary Queen of Sheba

Ethiopia's most famous legend concerns the Queen of Sheba. According to the Kebra Negast, the Ethiopian queen once undertook a long journey to visit the wise King Solomon of Israel.

At the great palace, Solomon assured the queen that he would take nothing from her so long as she took nothing from him. However, the crafty king had placed at her bedside a glass of water. During the night, awaking thirsty after the spicy food served to her, the queen reached for a drink.

Solomon wasted no time demanding his side of the deal, and the queen returned to Ethiopia carrying his child, the future king Menelik.

Menelik later visited his father in Jerusalem, but as he left the Holy Land, he made off with the Ark of the Covenant (it seems Solomon got his comeuppance after all). Returning with it to Ethiopia, he later established a dynasty that would reign for the next 3000 years.

Though there are serious anachronisms in the legend – the queen is thought to have lived a thousand years before this period – many Ethiopians believe it passionately, at least in parts. Haile Selassie himself, the last Ethiopian emperor, claimed direct descent from King Solomon, and therefore the divine right to rule.

The palace, which covered a vast area of some 120m by 80m, was far larger than medieval European palaces, and contained at least 50 rooms. It also benefited from a very sophisticated drainage system. The building was approached by grand monumental stairs on the north and south sides, and the whole complex was enclosed by huge walls and towers in the corners. The ruins stand on the outskirts of town on the Gonder road.

Dongar (Queen of Sheba's Palace)

Strangely, and very sadly, the excavational work carried out at Dongar (popularly known as the Queen of Sheba's Palace) nearly 50 years ago by a French team of archaeologists has never been fully published and information is not forthcoming. The architectural style – the small undressed stones set in a timber framework with the walls recessed at intervals and tapering with height – are typically Aksumite.

The **stairwells** suggest the existence of at least one upper storey. The well-preserved **flagstone floor** is thought to have belonged to a throne room. The palace also contains a private bathing area and a kitchen, where two large **brick ovens** can still be seen.

Despite the colourful legends, archaeologists now date the palace to some 1500 years after the Queen of Sheba's time in the 10th century BC, to around the 5th or 6th century AD.

King Kaleb's Palace Lying on a small hill 1.8km from town is the so-called palace of the 6th-century King Kaleb. Kaleb was one of Aksum's most important rulers; he succeeded in bringing southern Arabia under Aksumite rule.

Measuring a roomy 60m by 60m, the square building is thought to have been topped by four corner towers. Perhaps this was the building the 6th-century writer Kosmos described as adorned with 'four brazen figures' of unicorns. Local tradition has it that the building was the treasury of King Kaleb, and the tomb of his son Gebre Meskel.

A stairway leads down to a number of **underground chambers**. The massive dressed granite blocks used to construct the chamber fit perfectly against one another without a trace of mortar. The tomb is roofed with a single huge monolith. Look out for the **Byzantine cross** carved on one of the tombs. If you're not a bat fan, it may be best to steer clear.

The tomb is a great example of the sheer sophistication of Aksumite architecture and building techniques. The 19th-century British traveller Theodore Bent exclaimed magnanimously that the palace was 'built with a regularity which if found in Greece would at once make one assign it to a good period'! According to local sources, 5000 elephants were used to transport the great blocks.

The coffers are said once to have contained unimaginable wealth, Egyptian-tomb-style: overflowing with pearls, gold and precious stones. One chamber contains three stone **sarcophagi**. Blocked off behind deep granite walls, other rooms extend tantalisingly into the hillside.

A visit is well worthwhile and makes a lovely walk through the *tef* (cereal grass) fields that have been cultivated here for millennia. The walk will also take you through the other side of Aksum, where the 'other half' lived: the workers, farmers and craftsmen. Just as important and as fascinating as the great palaces and tombs, the area only now is receiving attention from archaeologists.

King Ezana's Inscription On your way up to King Kaleb's palace, you'll pass a little shack containing a remarkable find stumbled upon by a farmer in the 1980s: another trilingual inscription dating from King Ezana's time and giving thanks to God for conquests in Saudi Arabia. The inscription contains a curse: 'the person who should dare to move the tablet will meet an untimely death'. The tablet remains exactly where it was found! You should tip the guardian something small for opening the hut.

Abba Pentalewon & Abba Liqanos Monasteries Around 2km from King Kaleb's Palace lies the Abba Pentalewon Monastery, with a church thought to date from the 6th century. It's open to men only, but some fine **manuscripts** and **church regalia** can be brought out by the priests. Entrance costs Birr20.

From Abba Pentalewon, it's around 20 minutes on foot to the Abba Liqanos Monastery, which contains similar religious paraphernalia. The church is open to men only. It boasts excellent views.

Neither churches are must-sees, but they make pleasant walks. Look out for the jagged blue hills of Adwa in the distance to the east.

Abatu Ensessa Church The little church of Abatu Ensessa boasts some interesting **murals** and church regalia.

Lioness of Gobedra Though often overlooked by visitors, the mysterious lioness, 3km west of the city on the Gonder road, should not be missed. It is etched in relief on a large fallen rock, and measures over 3m long. It is not known who is responsible for the art, nor why a lioness is depicted in this spot.

Ancient Quarries Near the lioness, at a site known as Wuchate Golo, have a look for the ancient quarries, where granite for the **stelae** was cut. In one area, you can see clearly the process used by the workers to cut the hard stone from the rock – a row of little holes. It is thought that wooden or metal wedges were driven into the rock, or that holes were filled with water and left to fracture.

In another place, there's a kind of ruler, with regularly spaced notches, and elsewhere, a stele almost completely free of the rock. It's a fascinating place.

Places to Stay

Aksum's cheapies leave a lot to be desired. The *Queen of Sheba Hotel*, with rooms for Birr10–15, is about the cleanest, but your best bet is to head for the *Ghenet Hotel* (☎ 75-02-17), look like a budget traveller and ask for a discount. Clean, adequate rooms cost Birr25–30 (Birr50 with private shower). Discounts to Birr15 can usually be negotiated for the smaller rooms.

Avoid particularly the *King Ezana Hotel* and the *Zion Hotel*.

The best mid-range joint is the peaceful *Kaleb Hotel* (☎ 75-02-22), set around a grassy courtyard and garden, which has rooms for Birr35 (Birr50 with private bathroom). A Birr10 discount is given to students. It's a fave with archaeologists, so it's sometimes booked out. The *Bazen Hotel* (☎ 75-02-98) with rooms for Birr30–40 is also good.

A longtime favourite with travellers (and Italian archaeologists) is the *Africa Hotel* (☎ 75-17-00), a little further from the centre. Rooms cost Birr25 (Birr50 with shower).

The *Axum Touring Hotel* (☎ 75-02-05, fax 75-02-78), an old Italian *albergo* (hotel) is a popular place with tour groups. It has adequate singles/doubles with bathroom, set around a flowering garden, for Birr150/225.

Top of the heap is the *Yeha Hotel* (☎ 75-03-77, fax 75-03-82) with rooms for US$36/48; suites cost US$72. Like its 'brothers', the Tana Hotel in Bahar Dar and the Goha Hotel in Gonder, the hotel boasts the best location in town – on a hill overlooking Aksum (around eight minutes' walk up a steep hill). Low season and empty, it can be a weeny bit depressing.

Places to Eat & Drink

The evening draws to a close early in Aksum. Make sure you eat before 7.30 or 8 pm. Quite a good idea is to ask your hotel to prepare a picnic lunch for you, and have it among the ruins (don't forget that what arrives with you should leave with you).

The *Lekatit Hotel* is a local favourite, as is the *Marta Hotel*. The *Axum Touring Hotel* has a good reputation for faranji food and offers three-course menus for Birr25; the garden is a great place for breakfast. A bit more expensive is the restaurant in the *Yeha Hotel*, which offers mains such as steak or shish kebab for Birr13 (plus tax). Its terrace is also good for brekky (Birr12 for continental, Birr18 for American) or – even better – a drink at sunset; a beer costs Birr5.50. See Places to Stay previous for both of these.

The *Mini Pastry* probably has the best selection of goodies and fruit juices, and there's a dear little garden at the back. At night it transforms itself into a respectable bar. *Sweet Pastry* is also good.

Seek out the *tella beat* (local beer houses) in the tiny streets around town; they're great places for Tigrayan dancing. You'll probably need an Ethiopian friend to help you find them.

Getting There & Away

Ethiopian Airlines (☎ 300) flies to Aksum from Addis Ababa, Gonder and Lalibela (see the main Getting Around section earlier in this chapter). You would be advised to check in early for a pretty rigorous luggage search.

By bus, for Gonder, Debark and the Simien Mountains, you'll need to go to Shire first (Birr8, two hours, around six buses daily). Two buses run daily to Mekele

(Birr21, nine hours), and around six buses go to Adigrat (Birr20, five hours).

For Asmara in Eritrea – when the border reopens – two buses run daily (Birr21.50, six hours). For Adwa, buses and minibus leave every 15 minutes between 5.30 am and 6 pm (Birr4, 45 mins). For Debre Damo, two buses leave daily (Birr15, three hours).

Getting Around

To get to the airport, a taxi costs Birr40 or Birr5 'shared'. Wait under the tree at the bus station square. Garis to the airport cost Birr20.

Taxis for elsewhere charge foreigners from Birr10 for short journeys (up to 3km), medium journeys cost Birr15, longer ones cost Birr20. To hire a taxi for a full day, negotiate the rate; Birr150 is pretty reasonable.

Garis cost Birr5 for short journeys, Birr15 per hour, or Birr30 for half a day. For Dongar they cost Birr10; for the Lioness of Gobedra they cost Birr15.

If you're short of time and want to make day trips to Yeha, cars can be hired from the local travel agencies if you make arrangements in advance in Addis Ababa (see the Aksum map for their locations). A couple of private vehicles are sometimes available for hire (Birr700–800 all-inclusive for a 4WD); ask at the Department of Culture, Tourism and Information, or at your hotel.

Bicycles can be hired from a street near the bus station and cost Birr6 per hour.

ADWA
☎ 04

Like Aksum, tiny little Adwa belies its status. For Ethiopians, the town holds huge significance. It was in the hills surrounding Adwa that the Emperor Menelik II inflicted the biggest defeat ever on a colonial army in Africa (see the boxed text 'The Battle of Adwa'). Ethiopia was saved from colonisation.

Though an attractive enough town, there's not much to see besides a couple of churches (the Selassie Church contains some good murals). But you may want to use the town as a base from which to visit Yeha.

About 11km east of Adwa is the **monastery of Abba Garima**, said to have been founded by one of the Nine Saints in

The Battle of Adwa

In September 1895, as the rains began to dwindle, the Emperor Menelik II issued a decree: All the able-bodied men of his empire should gather together and await his arrival at fixed points across the country. Once assembled, the vast army began its march north; behind it trundled 40 cannons, as well as mules with 100,000 rifles on their backs. In the north, the Italians were ready.

In the initial skirmishes that followed, the Ethiopians succeeded in capturing the Italian strongholds at Amba Alage and Enda Iyasus. However, because of the serious shortage of food, the two sides agreed to sue for peace. But the Italians continued to insist on Italy's protectorate claim, and an agreement could not be reached.

In February 1896, Crispi, the Italian prime minister, sent his famous telegram to General Baratieri. In it, he declared the motherland was 'ready for any sacrifice to save the honour of the army and the prestige of the monarchy'.

Four days later, at dawn, the Italians made a surprise attack. Stumbling in the darkness over difficult terrain, with inaccurate maps and with no communication between the three offensive brigades, the attack was a disaster. Menelik, whose spies had long before informed him of the forthcoming attack, was ready to meet the Italians on every front. A thunderous artillery duel followed, then a bout of fierce fighting.

Nearly half the Italian fighting force was wiped out – over 6000 soldiers – and of the five Italian field commanders, three were killed, one was wounded, and another was captured. Finally, laying down their arms, the Italians ran. Though the Ethiopians had lost almost equal numbers, the day was clearly theirs.

To this day, the battle of Adwa is celebrated annually, and like the Battle of Hastings in Britain or the War of Independence in America, it is the one date every Ethiopian child can quote.

the 6th century. It is known for its collection of religious artefacts including three illuminated gospels from the 10th century, thought to number among the oldest extant manuscripts in the country. It makes a great day's hike (around six hours' walk), but bring lots of water and food.

If you get stuck in Adwa the *Tourist Hotel* is the best bet with rooms with common shower for Birr10.

Buses and minibuses run throughout the day to Aksum (Birr4, 30 mins). For Yeha, catch a bus to Enticcio, and ask to be dropped in Yeha village (Birr5, 40 mins). From the main street of the village, it's a 5km walk. Contract taxis cost Birr200 to Yeha and Birr400 to Debre Damo.

YEHA

Yeha, 58km north-east of Adwa, is a little-visited but very peaceful and evocative spot. Of all Ethiopia's historical sites, Yeha is perhaps the most enigmatic. The journey there takes you through some attractive highland scenery. If you have the time, it's a must.

Yeha was Ethiopia's first known capital, and is considered the birthplace of the country's earliest civilisation. It is believed to have been established by colonists from southern Arabia. The immense, windowless, sandstone walls of the ruins look like something straight out of Yemen, and in the late afternoon light, the fawn-coloured temple could easily feature in a David Roberts painting.

Entrance to the site costs Birr20.

Things to See

Apart from the massive walls of a pre-Christian so-called **temple**, little remains at the old capital. Yet Yeha's ruins are impressive for their sheer age, dating from around the 5th century BC – though some experts have dated them as early as the 8th century BC – and for their stunning construction. Some of the sandstone building blocks of the temple measure over 3m long and are so perfectly dressed and fitted together – without a trace of mortar – that it's impossible to insert so much as a 5¢ coin between them. The whole temple is a grid of perfect lines and geometry.

Near the temple is the modern **Church of Abuna Aftse**, which replaced a church dating from the 6th century. Inside, there is an outstanding collection of beautifully incised ancient Sabaean inscriptions, believed to come from the temple, as well as some good **manuscripts** and crosses. Incorporated into the walls of the church are stones removed from the original temple. In the west wall, look out for the famous and exceptional **relief of ibexes**, stylised and with lowered horns; the ibex was a sacred animal of southern Arabia. The National Museum in Addis Ababa contains many other important finds unearthed at Yeha.

Nearby lie various other ruins including, 200m to the north-east, the remains of a monumental structure known as **Grat Beal Gebri**, distinguished for its unusual, square-sectioned, monolithic pillars (such features are also found in the Temple of the Moon in Ma'rib in Yemen). Important rock-hewn tombs have also been found in the vicinity.

Getting There & Away

Buses, minibuses and pick-up trucks run daily from Aksum to the main street in Yeha village (Birr4–15, two hours). From the village it's around 5km to the ruins. A contract taxi from Aksum costs Birr350.

From Adwa, you can hop on a minibus running to Enticcio and ask to be dropped at the turn-off to the ruins (signposted). From there it's around 5km (about an hour's walk).

Go early to be sure of return transport, and bring water – the walk is very hot and dusty.

DEBRE DAMO

Around 86km north-east of Aksum lies one of the most important religious sites in Ethiopia. The monastery of Debre Damo dates back to Aksumite times and the reign of King Gebre Meskel, successor to King Kaleb. It boasts the oldest standing church in the country. The monastery's exact age, however, is the subject of endless debate, since the buildings have been repeatedly rebuilt.

The monastery is equally famous for its position, perched on a 2800m-high *amba* or flat-topped mountain surrounded on all

Rope Tricks

Access up the 24m-high rock face to the monastery is by rope – in fact two ropes. One is tied around your waist and is used by the monks above to try and hoist you up; the second is fixed to the rock, and you use it in combination with the footholds to scramble up. The priests use just the second rope and flash up like spiders. See also the boxed text 'Toeholds in Tigray' later in this section.

The ascent is not difficult, but requires some nerves and a bit of bicep. Women are not allowed to visit the monastery, but the priests will let you have a dangle on the rope if you really want to. Shouts of 'Becka, becka!' (Enough!) will soon make it clear you've come far enough!

sides by vertical cliffs. How the solid stones of the monastery were carted up has also been the subject of much speculation.

According to local tradition, the monastery was founded by Abuna Aregawi, one of the Nine Saints of the 6th century, with a little help from a snake (see the boxed text 'Know Your Ethiopian Saints' earlier in this section).

During Aksumite times, the place was used – in the Ethiopian way – to coop up excess male members of the royal families, who might have posed a threat to the reigning monarch.

During the Mohammed Gragn incursions, the Emperor Lebna Dengel took refuge here, before giving up the ghost in 1540.

Some 80 monks live in the monastery, which comprises a total area of around half a square kilometre. The inhabitants are entirely self-sufficient (though gifts of coffee, sugar or honey are greatly appreciated), and even have their own livestock (males only) and reservoirs of water hewn deep into the cliff.

For male travellers, a visit to Debre Damo is very well worthwhile, and gives you an idea of the extraordinary artistic heritage Ethiopia might have had, had it not been for the devastation of the Muslim–Christian wars.

If you get stuck here, men can spend the night at the monastery, and women can find accommodation with the nuns at the foot of the monastery.

Things to See

From the top, there are great **views** over the countryside all the way to Eritrea. The largest of the two **churches**, located in the easternmost part of the amba, is remarkable as an almost prototypical example of Aksumite architecture. One window, with its wooden tracery, is almost a replica of the one depicted in stone on the largest of the Aksumite stelae. Look out for the famous Aksumite **'frieze'** – a row of false window openings constructed of wood. Also notable are the beams and ceiling, famously decorated with carved **wooden panels** depicting Ethiopian wild animals: elephants, lions, gazelles, rhinos, giraffes and snakes etc. Various recent **paintings** can be seen too.

The monastery has long been used as a safeguard for religious treasures. It now has an outstanding collection of at least 50 **illuminated manuscripts**, among them the oldest surviving fragments in the country.

At the base of the cliff, look out for the minute **caves** still inhabited by seven hermits (two of them women). They rely entirely on the food and water brought to them from the monastery and the village.

Getting There & Away

From Aksum, two buses leave daily for Debre Damo (Birr15, three hours). The alternative is to take a bus from either Adwa or Mekele along the main Adwa-Mekele road, and ask to be dropped at the junction for Debre Damo (5km south-east of the village of Bizet if you're travelling from Adwa to Mekele). From there it's a 9km walk to Debre Damo (around two hours).

ADIGRAT
☎ 04

Adigrat is the largest town in Tigray after Mekele, and the last sizeable town in the north. Though not endowed with any must-see attractions, it lies on an important junction linking Ethiopia with Eritrea, and with its many hotels and restaurants it makes a useful stop-off point. The town also makes

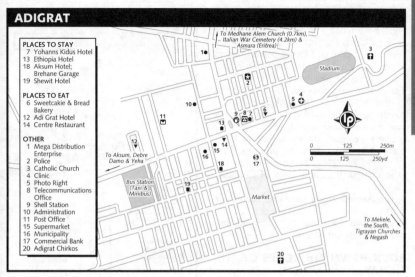

ADIGRAT

PLACES TO STAY
7 Yohanns Kidus Hotel
13 Ethiopia Hotel
18 Aksum Hotel;
     Brehane Garage
19 Shewit Hotel

PLACES TO EAT
6 Sweetcakie & Bread
     Bakery
12 Adi Grat Hotel
14 Centre Restaurant

OTHER
1 Mega Distribution
     Enterprise
2 Police
3 Catholic Church
4 Clinic
5 Photo Right
8 Telecommunications
     Office
9 Shell Station
10 Administration
11 Post Office
15 Supermarket
16 Municipality
17 Commercial Bank
20 Adigrat Chirkos

To Medhane Alem Church (0.7km),
Italian War Cemetery (4.2km) &
Asmara (Eritrea)

Stadium

To Aksum, Debre
Damo & Yeha

Bus Station
(Taxi &
Minibus)

Market

To Mekele,
the South,
Tigrayan Churches
& Negash

0   125   250m
0   125   250yd

---

a good base from which to explore some of the northern rock-hewn churches of Tigray.

Things to See
If you're filling in time, two churches are worth a peek: the 19th-century **Adigrat Chirkos**, and the 20th-century **Medhane Alem**. There's also a peaceful **Italian war cemetery**, 4km outside town on the Asmara road. It commemorates some 765 Italian soldiers, many of them *caduti ignoti* (the unknown fallen) of 1935–38.

The **market** is also worth a wander. Look out for the locally produced pale honey, and the *beles* (prickly pears), which cost just Birr1 for 10; they're deliciously refreshing.

Travelling south from Adigrat, look out for the attractive Tigrayan stone farmsteads with their **dry-stone walls** – the country can look almost Tuscan. The houses have few windows and those they do have are kept small in order to keep the interior cool.

Places to Stay & Eat
The best budget hotel by far is the **Yohanns Kidus Hotel** (☎ 45-02-84), with simple but spotless rooms for Birr7. It's often full. The **Aksum Hotel** (☎ 45-03-56) makes a good sec-

ond choice with rooms at the same price. It's not signposted in English; look out for the sign with the stelae. Both have shared cold showers.

A step up is the **Shewit Hotel** (☎ 45-00-28), where singles/doubles cost Birr35/40 (Birr50/60 with hot shower). It has a small space for parking.

A popular restaurant locally is the **Adi Grat Hotel**; good for a local breakfast is the **Centre Restaurant** opposite the Ethiopia Hotel. **Sweetcakie & Bread Bakery** is one of the best pastry shops in town.

Getting There & Away
When the border with Eritrea was open, two buses ran daily to Asmara (Birr23, seven hours). At least 10 buses run daily to Mekele (Birr8, around 2½ hours); one bus goes daily to Shire (Birr25, six hours). For Addis Ababa, go to Mekele and change; for Aksum, take the bus towards Shire. Seven minibuses run daily to Wukro (Birr7, one hour). Minibuses and pick-up trucks connect the nearby villages with the town.

NEGASH
Situated on a small hill around 10km north of Wukro is the tiny town of Negash,

which – like Aksum and Adwa – belies its prestigious past.

Negash was the first site of Muslim settlement in Ethiopia. Fleeing persecution in Saudi Arabia in Mohammed's own lifetime, a community of Muslims took refuge here. The current mosque is said to lie on the site of the 7th-century original. An ancient cemetery, also believed to date from the 7th century, was found recently.

Every year, an important festival takes place at Negash, attracting pilgrims from all around. Just 3% of Tigray is Muslim; the little mosque sits amid a sea of Christian churches.

The *Negash Hotel* has basic rooms for Birr6.

Minibuses and taxis ply the route between Wukro and Negash.

ROCK-HEWN CHURCHES OF TIGRAY

Far less famous that their prestigious cousins in Lalibela, the rock-hewn churches of Tigray are nevertheless a vital part of Ethiopia's historical heritage.

Many of the churches almost certainly predate those at Lalibela, and may represent a crucial link between Aksum and Lalibela, chronologically, artistically and technically. The architectural features, though less perfect than at Lalibela, where the rock-hewing tradition reached its zenith, are just as remarkable and intriguing.

Between the Tigrayan towns of Adigrat and Mekele lie a veritable rash of churches. It is still unknown exactly how many exist – at least 120 at the last count. Unlike many of the churches of Lalibela, which were carved out of the ground, the Tigrayan churches are generally sculpted into cliff faces or into pre-existing caves.

Many are pretty inaccessible; it's thought that security was the major concern. In other words, the more remote the church was, the better its chance of survival. Some churches require quite steep climbs; others require scrambles up almost sheer rock faces using just footholds in the rock.

But somehow this adds to the churches' attraction. To come across an absolute

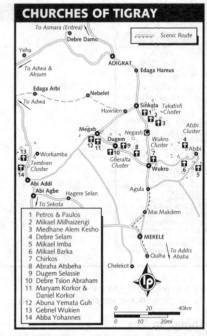

CHURCHES OF TIGRAY

1 Petros & Paulos
2 Mikael Milhaizengi
3 Medhane Alem Kesho
4 Debre Selam
5 Mikael Imba
6 Mikael Barka
7 Chirkos
8 Abraha Atsbeha
9 Dugem Selassie
10 Debre Tsion Abraham
11 Maryam Korkor & Daniel Korkor
12 Abuna Yemata Guh
13 Gebriel Wukien
14 Abba Yohannes

jewel hidden for centuries in the mountains, after a long and arduous toil through the arid and rocky landscape of Tigray, makes for a very rewarding excursion. For those who want to combine trekking with terrific art and history, this may be just the ticket. The Tigrayan churches may well prove to be Orthodox Ethiopia's best-kept secret.

History

Right up until the mid-1960s, the churches were almost unknown outside Tigray – even to fellow Ethiopians. Still almost nothing is known about their origin, history and architects.

Local tradition attributes most of the churches to the 4th-century Aksumite kings, Ezana and Atsbeha. This attribution was long laughed out of court by historians, who dated the churches to the 14th century or even later.

However, it now appears that some churches may indeed date to the 4th century (though from the 6th to the 10th centuries seems the most likely time bracket for most), and that they do predate their prestigious cousins at Lalibela.

Much work remains to be done on the churches. Sadly, many are in a very sorry state of repair and are rapidly deteriorating further; in places, seepage is ruining the frescoes. Funds for restoration are funnelled to the country's better-known attractions such as Lalibela.

Orientation & Information

Mekele makes the best base from which to explore the churches, and a trip to the excellent Tigray Culture, Tourism and Information Bureau in Mekele is a good place to begin (see Mekele following). The staff are very knowledgeable and helpful, can advise on itineraries and routes and should be able to find you a decent guide.

Guides are essential, not only to locate the remoter churches, but also to act as interpreters for tracking down the often elusive priests, keepers of the all-important church keys. The tourist centre recommends a daily fee of Birr50–100 for guides. Ask also for the useful brochure *Tigre: The Open-Air Museum*, which has a small map on the back and a brief description of the churches.

The only other current information on the churches is in papers written for journals by two Brits, Ivy Pearce, and David R. Buxton. The tourist centre can give you references if you're interested.

Many of the churches are located in groups, referred to as 'clusters'. The most famous clusters are Gheralta, Takatisfi, Tembien and Atsbi (see the Churches of Tigray map). The Gheralta cluster is considered the most important (with the highest number of churches), and the Takatisfi cluster is the most accessible (around 3km east of the Mekele-Adigrat road).

Since 1994, all churches have been supposed to charge Birr20 for entrance. If you're asked for more, simply hand over Birr20, firmly and politely. Don't forget, however, that a small tip or donation after a trip is usual and greatly appreciated; the tourist office recommends Birr5–10.

Heavenly Visions

One day, St Gabriel appeared in a dream to a farmer. The saint commanded the man to build a new church that would replace the old one, and gave his messenger careful instructions as to its location and construction.

Yet another Ethiopian religious tale? Yes, only the day in question was in 1982, and the 'new church' replaces the current one of Petros & Paulos, near Sinkata. The old farmer can be seen chipping away at this very minute. In Ethiopia, traditions, legends and myths live on.

Be sure to bring good walking shoes, a torch, lots of small notes for tips and entrance fees, and water.

Highlights of the Rock-Hewn Churches of Tigray

Abraha Atsbeha (Gheralta) Said to date from the 10th century; large cruciform church with interesting architectural features such as cruciform pillars and step capitals plus well-preserved 17th- and 18th-century murals. One of most accessible churches, just off the road. Lies roughly halfway between Dugem and Wukro.

Abuna Yemata Guh (Gheralta) One of the most impressive churches; known for very beautiful 15th-century frescoes. Stunning views from the top. Well worth the climb – probably the most exciting church to visit south of Megab. Climb considered most challenging (one hour up, using footholds for the last 20 minutes).

Debre Tsion Abraham (Gheralta) Probably dates from the 14th century; known for diverse architectural features. Like a workshop of design, with beautiful, though faded, 16th-century murals. Unusual, large 15th-century ceremonial fan. Situated like a fortress on a hill; one hour's quite steep walk from Dugem.

Maryam Korkor (Gheralta) Large impressive church, known for rich decoration: carving, architectural features and fine 13th-century paintings. The smaller Daniel Korkor Church, a few minutes away, can also be visited. Near Megab; 50-minute reasonably steep ascent.

Dugem Selassie (Gheralta) Tiny older church lies within the newer one. Large double-tomb chamber with three 'shelves'; look out for the beautifully carved ceiling above the maqdas. Probably converted to a church later. In the village of Dugem, just off the road.

Medhane Alem Kesho (Takatisfi) Also known as Adi Kesho. One of the oldest and finest churches in Tigray; known for its architectural features, particularly the very elaborately carved coffered ceiling. Found 40–60 minutes walk from Mikael Milhaizengi.

Mikael Milhaizengi (Takatisfi) Tiny church but known for carved ceiling and dome nearly 3m high; thought to date from the 8th century. Around 15–20 minutes walk from Petros & Paulos (see following).

Petros & Paulos (Takatisfi) Only partly hewn; built on a ledge with only a sanctuary within the rock; delightful old murals, but very rapidly deteriorating. From Wukro, or Adigrat, take a minibus to Teka Tesfay and walk about 3km from the junction. Five-minute climb to the church using footholds up one part.

Chirkos (Wukro) Three-quarter sandstone monolith, dates possibly to 8th century; very unusual and interesting architecture, with cubical capitals, outstanding Aksumite frieze and barrel-vaulted ceiling. Lies around 500m from Wukro; most easily accessible church.

Abba Yohannes (Tembien) Very impressive location set in a 300m-high sheer cliff face; three-aisled and four-bayed interior; finely hewn arches and high domes. Lies 15km from Abi Addi, including 1km walk and short climb.

Gebriel Wukien (Tembien) Said to be the finest church in this cluster; three-aisled, four-bayed church; well-carved, interesting details; eight massive, finely hewn freestanding pillars. Lies 16km north-west of Abi Addi, including a 15-minute easy walk then a 10-minute climb up the mountain.

Mikael Barka (Atsbi) Small church shaped like a cross; probably dates from 13th century. Lies 17km from Wukro, including short 10-minute climb.

Mikael Imba (Atsbi) Many Aksumite features; lovely barrel vaulting; good view from the top. Lies 9km south of Atsbi; quite easy 20-minute ascent with a ladder.

Debre Selam (Atsbi) 'Church within a church'; exceptional architecture and paintings; look out for the beautiful carved arch leading into the maqdas. Lovely setting and good views from top. Close to Atsbi; quite easy 20-minute ascent.

Places to Stay & Eat

Accommodation in the nearby villages is spartan to put it mildly; many have only limited supplies of water and don't have electricity. Many hotels double as noisy bars or brothels, and are infested with fleas.

> ### Toeholds in Tigray
>
> Though daunting at first sight, the ascents up the rock faces required to reach some of the Tigrayan churches are not difficult if taken carefully. Just focus on the footholds, get a good grip, don't stop and don't look down. If you're having trouble, or finding that your nerves are getting the better of you, get someone to climb in front showing you the footholds. Sometimes the holds are very small, hewn by the bare feet of generations of priests, in which case do as they do and take off your shoes. It's amazing the grip a toe can get!

Most serve only Ethiopian food. It's a good idea to bring extra provisions with you.

In Wukro, the Muslim-run **Selam Hotel**, with rooms for Birr5–10, is the best bet for men, but women can't stay there. The second-best (women and men allowed) is the **Beheresege Hotel**, with rooms for Birr7. The smarter-looking **Fasika Hotel** is not recommended unless you're after a noisy, flea-ridden brothel. The **Fikra Selam** has a good restaurant.

In Hawsien, the **Hawsien Hotel** has over-priced rooms without shower for Birr20–25.

Megab has no hotels.

In Sinkata, the **Walwalu Hotel** is the best joint, with rooms for Birr6.

In Abi Addi, the **Brhane Reda Pension** has rooms for Birr8; there's just a bucket shower.

Getting There & Around

Many of the churches lie in remote places – between 20km and 30km off the main road. A private vehicle is much the easiest way of reaching them, and cuts travel time between them. However, if you have camping equipment and lots of time, an exploration by foot is perfectly possible.

A whole new network of sealed roads is being cut to connect the churches and village in a complete circle; access should become easier and easier.

The other alternative is to take a tour, which solves two problems: transport and guides. Village Ethiopia and Experience

Ethiopia, in Addis Ababa, are good for this area (see Organised Tours in the main Getting Around section earlier in this chapter). A few tour operators can also be found in Mekele. Goh Tours (☎ 40-21-25, fax 40-26-48) has the best reputation; cars can be hired for Birr1200 per day, all-inclusive.

You can rent 4WDs in Mekele, but not in Adigrat. However, Addis Ababa–based travel agents can arrange for a vehicle to meet you in either town.

If you can't afford either a tour or a vehicle, there are still around a dozen churches that can be easily reached with a combination of public transport and walking. Adigrat, Mekele, Hawsien, Wukro, Atsbi, Abi Addi and Sinkata are all served by minibuses.

Although a 4WD will take you close to the churches, there's almost always a climb to the top of a hill or rock. Though the climbing is not especially difficult, the gradients can be a little steep. Access to some churches requires ascents up almost sheer rock faces, using just footholds in the rock. Obviously those who suffer in the least from vertigo should avoid these ascents (see the boxed text 'Toeholds in Tigray').

MEKELE
☎ 04

Mekele, Tigray's capital, owes its importance to the Emperor Yohannes IV, who made it his capital in the late 19th century.

Today, some accuse the current prime minister, Tigrayan-born Meles Zenawi, of making it his capital too. Over 150 million birr has been poured into the region. Tempting private investment incentives have been dangled like carrots and hotels are appearing everywhere.

The excellent Tigray Culture, Tourism and Information Bureau (☎ 40-10-32) is open from 8.30 am to 12.30 pm and 1.30 to 5.30 pm weekdays.

Things to See

Like Adigrat, Mekele boasts little major sightseeing, but is nevertheless a pleasant town with good facilities and hotels.

The very lively **market** is definitely worth a stroll, particularly on Saturday, the

Salt for Gold

Since earliest times right up to the present day, salt has been used as a kind of currency in Ethiopia. Salt, in demand for both people and animals, circulated instead of money for hundreds of years throughout the Ethiopian highlands. According to Kosmos, a 6th-century Egyptian writing in Greek, the kings of Aksum sent expeditions west to barter salt, among other things, for hunks of gold.

Mined in the Danakil Depression, the mineral was transported hundreds of kilometres west across the country to the Ethiopian court in Shoa. Later, the salt was cut into small, rectangular blocks, which came to be known as *amole*; their value grew with every kilometre that they travelled further from the mine. Local lords often demanded extortionate payments for the right of passage across their territory.

To this day, Afar nomads and their camels continue to follow this ancient salt route. Cutting the bars by hand from the salt lakes in western Ethiopia and Djibouti, they spend weeks travelling by caravan in order to barter the bars at Ethiopian markets.

main market day – get there by 10 am. Look out for the salt bars brought in by camel from the Danakil Desert, and sawn into little blocks; the market is the largest market for salt in the country. The **spice market** is also interesting: a huge variety of roots, bark and herbs is used in traditional medicine. Notice that many Tigrayan women don blue or orange *insosela* (the plant source of the dye) 'tattoo' patterns on their hands and feet.

The **Yohannes IV museum** is also worth a peek for those with time to fill. It was built for the emperor in 1873 by two Frenchmen, and gives a good overview of the sites and points of interest in the region. It also houses some furniture and manuscripts that date from the days of the emperor. From the roof, there's quite a good view of Mekele.

Places to Stay

The *Wolwalo Hotel* is basic but very clean. More peaceful and reasonably clean is the

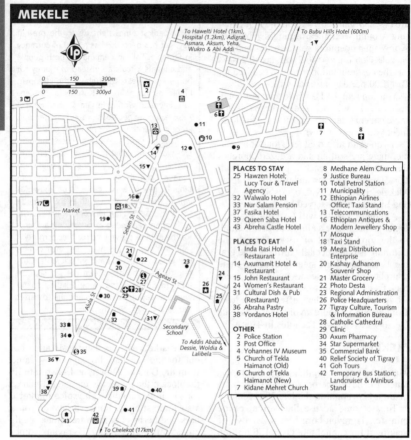

MEKELE

PLACES TO STAY	
25	Hawzen Hotel; Lucy Tour & Travel Agency
32	Walwalo Hotel
33	Nur Salam Pension
37	Fasika Hotel
39	Queen Saba Hotel
43	Abreha Castle Hotel

PLACES TO EAT	
1	Inda Rasi Hotel & Restaurant
14	Axumamit Hotel & Restaurant
15	John Restaurant
24	Women's Restaurant
31	Cultural Dish & Pub (Restaurant)
36	Abraha Pastry
38	Yordanos Hotel

OTHER	
2	Police Station
3	Post Office
4	Yohannes IV Museum
5	Church of Tekla Haimanot (Old)
6	Church of Tekla Haimanot (New)
7	Kidane Mehret Church
8	Medhane Alem Church
9	Justice Bureau
10	Total Petrol Station
11	Municipality
12	Ethiopian Airlines Office; Taxi Stand
13	Telecommunications
16	Ethiopian Antiques & Modern Jewellery Shop
17	Mosque
18	Taxi Stand
19	Mega Distribution Enterprise
20	Kashay Adhanom Souvenir Shop
21	Master Grocery
22	Photo Desta
23	Regional Administration
26	Police Headquarters
27	Tigray Culture, Tourism & Information Bureau
28	Catholic Cathedral
29	Clinic
30	Axum Pharmacy
34	Star Supermarket
35	Commercial Bank
40	Relief Society of Tigray
41	Goh Tours
42	Temporary Bus Station; Landcruiser & Minibus Stand

Nur Salam Pension. Both have rooms with shared cold shower for Birr10. The new *Fasika Hotel* is probably the best place in the budget category, with singles/doubles for Birr12/15. The *Queen Saba Hotel* has not-bad rooms for Birr20/25.

Best in the middle range is the new *Hawelti Hotel* (☎ 40-10-86), with comfortable rooms for Birr30 (Birr50–60 with hot shower); it has two pleasant terraces. The well-known *Abreha Castle Hotel* is now looking a bit shabby for the price, but its terrace overlooking the town is a great place for an evening drink.

The new *Hawzen Hotel* (☎ 40-43-33, fax 40-43-49) has singles/doubles for US$36/42; it also has a nightclub. Top of the top-end range is the well-designed *Bubu Hills Hotel* (☎ 40-44-00, fax 40-44-10), set on a hill above town. It has rooms with fridge, telephone and satellite TV for Birr240/360. There's a swimming pool, tennis court and children's playgrounds. The terrace with its views over town is a good place for a drink.

Places to Eat

Two restaurants very popular locally are the *John Restaurant* and *Cultural Dish & Pub* (also known as the Lion Pub); the latter is also a good place for a beer.

The traditional restaurant in the huge 100-year-old tukul in the **Inda Rasi Hotel** should reopen soon. The **Abraha Pastry** is a good place for a spot of breakfast.

The **Yordanos Hotel** has pleasant tukuls around a courtyard and serves good local and faranji food. The rooftop terrace of the **Axumamit Hotel & Restaurant** is also good for faranji food. The **Women's Restaurant** is run for and by unemployed widows; the food is excellent and everyone is welcome.

Getting There & Around
Ethiopian Airlines (☎ 40-00-55) flies from Mekele daily to Addis Ababa; five times a week to Bahar Dar; three or four times a week to Aksum and Lalibela; and three times weekly to Shire (see the main Getting Around section earlier in this chapter). A share-taxi to the airport, 7km out of town, costs Birr30. A new international airport is under construction in Mekele.

Five or six buses run daily between Mekele and Adigrat (Birr8, 2½ hours); one bus goes to Aksum (Birr21, nine hours); three or four buses go to Addis Ababa (Birr50, two days). For Woldia and Lalibela, take the Addis Ababa bus. A new bus station is being planned, check the situation out when you get there.

Short hops in a share-taxi cost Birr5.

DANAKIL DESERT
With several points lying more than 100m below sea level, the Danakil Desert has acquired a reputation as one of the hottest, most inhospitable places on Earth; temperatures can soar to 50°C. The region, due east of Mekele, is nevertheless home to the fascinating Afar people, a nomadic ethnic group known in the past for their legendary ferocity (see the boxed texts 'Peoples of Ethiopia' under Population & People in the Facts about Ethiopia section and 'The Dreaded Danakils' in the East of Addis Ababa section).

For centuries the Afars have mined and transported salt from the great Danakil salt lakes to highland markets in Ethiopia (see the boxed text 'Salt for Gold').

Though little more than a wasteland, the area is strangely beautiful in parts, and more surprisingly, is home to some interesting wildlife including gazelles, zebras and the now extremely rare wild ass.

An excursion into the region is best organised through tour operators in Addis Ababa (see Organised Tours in the main Getting Around section earlier in this chapter). Otherwise, you'll need to treat a journey here in full expedition style: people have perished within a matter of hours here.

The region is cooler from December to February. Berahile, east of the Adigrat-Mekele road, is the most usual jumping-off point; currently a new road is being constructed. Check security in advance too.

WOLDIA
The town of Woldia provides a springboard for visits to its famous neighbour, Lalibela, 120km to the west. Don't forget to stock up here on petrol, camera batteries, birr (at the bank), snacks and drinks (if you're planning on long treks), and anything you might need from a pharmacy. Lalibela, despite its fame, is still the back of beyond.

Offering about the best value in town is the **Genet Hotel** on the main Dessie–Addis Ababa road, which has simple but very clean rooms for Birr12. The rather depressing **Lal Hotel** has singles/doubles for Birr45/90 with private bathroom. Ask to see several rooms as they vary hugely.

The **Manen Restaurant** is a local favourite and lies – unnamed – on the main Dessie–Addis Ababa road, next door to the Photo Addis film store. For faranji food, the **Lal Hotel Woldia** is the best bet.

Getting There & Away
Four buses run daily to Dessie (Birr7.50, four hours) and to Addis Ababa (12 hours). For Lalibela, there's at least one bus daily (Birr20, seven hours) and one 4WD share taxi daily (Birr25, four hours).

Buses coming from Dessie stop in Woldia at around 10 am on their way to Mekele, Gonder (Birr31, two days) and Bahar Dar (Birr26, 1½ days).

If there are several of you, you can consider taking a 4WD contract taxi to Lalibela. Officially it costs Birr1000 one-way for the whole vehicle, but you can usually negotiate a price of around Birr750. Aid trucks also make the journey around two or three times a week and charge Birr20 (11 hours). Ask at the Mobil station in Woldia.

LALIBELA
☎ 03

Also known as 'Africa's Petra', Lalibela and its rock-hewn churches are arguably Ethiopia's top attraction. Though it has drawn 'tourists' since the 16th century, the town remains incredibly undeveloped. Until recently, there was no electricity; there are still no petrol stations, no pharmacies and no banks. In 1998, the tiny tourist office unceremoniously opened.

Lalibela also remains a very isolated place, lying in the rugged Lasta Mountains at an altitude of 2630m. Right up until 1997, the main road leading to the town was impassable during the wet season. Today, the journey overland is still quite long and arduous – the sense of arrival at the little town is rather like that after making a great pilgrimage.

And in fact Lalibela is a centre of pilgrimage. Among the dimly lit passageways and tunnels of the medieval churches, robed priests and monks still float; from hidden crypts and grottoes comes the sound of chanting, and in the deep, cool recesses of the interiors, the smell of incense and beeswax candles still pervades.

Lalibela undoubtedly ranks among the greatest historical sites not only on the African continent, but even in the Christian world. Just as remarkable, however, is its seeming total disregard for its status. Medieval Lalibela just gets on with going about its business. More than anywhere in Ethiopia – perhaps in the world – one has the impression of landing in a kingdom at least seven centuries behind our own.

History
Lalibela was the capital of the Zagwe dynasty in the 12th century, but was known initially as Roha. On the death of King Lalibela,

the ruler credited with the construction of the churches, the town was named after him.

The churches are thought, in accordance with local tradition, to date from the 12th or 13th centuries – during King Lalibela's reign. An interesting popular legend has is that King Lalibela was exiled to Jerusalem. There he wondered at the buildings he found there, and vowed to build a new holy city when he returned to his own kingdom in Ethiopia.

Perhaps King Lalibela was making a deliberate attempt to create a 'new Jerusalem' on African soil, far from Muslim usurpers, and accessible to all Ethiopians. Even the names of Lalibela's features echo those of Jerusalem: the River Jordan, Calvary, and the Tomb of Adam, for example.

In fact the buildings are so different in style, craftsmanship and state of preservation that they may well span a much longer period than Lalibela's reign.

Lalibela's churches are remarkable for three main reasons: because many are not carved into the rock, but freed entirely from it; because the buildings are so refined; and because there are so many and within such a very short distance of one another. Alvares, the early-16th-century Portuguese writer, described them as 'edifices, the like of which – and so many – cannot be found anywhere else in the world'.

During construction, first a large area was marked out. Trenches were then cut on all four sides until a solid rock remained. This was then chiselled out from inside. The relatively soft red volcanic tuff was quite conducive to the hewing.

Who built them remains unclear. Some scholars have estimated that it would have taken a workforce of some 40,000 (see the boxed text 'Legends of Lalibela').

However, foreign intervention, whether celestial or mortal, can almost certainly be ruled out. Long a victim of the usual 'It can't be African' chauvinism, Lalibela in fact represents the pinnacle of a very long-standing Ethiopian building tradition.

Exceptional masonry skills had long been in existence during the days of Aksum, and indeed most of the churches show clear characteristics of the ancient Aksumite

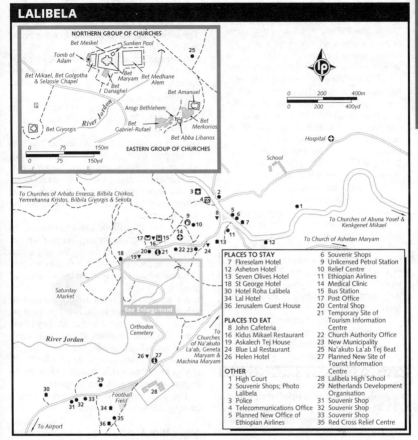

LALIBELA

NORTHERN GROUP OF CHURCHES

Bet Meskel — Sunken Pool

Tomb of Adam

Bet Mikael, Bet Golgotha & Selassie Chapel — Bet Maryam — Bet Medhane Alem

Bet Danaghel

Bet Amanuel

Arogi Bethlehem

River Jordan

Bet Giyorgis — Bet Gabriel-Rufael — Bet Merkorios

Bet Abba Libanos

EASTERN GROUP OF CHURCHES

Hospital

School

To Churches of Arbatu Ensessa, Bilbila Chirkos, Yemrehanna Kristos, Bilbila Giyorgis & Sekota

To Churches of Abuna Yosef & Kenkenet Mikael

To Church of Ashetan Maryam

Saturday Market

See Enlargement

Orthodox Cemetery

River Jordan

To Churches of Na'akuto La'ab, Geneta Maryam & Machina Maryam

Football Field

To Airport

PLACES TO STAY
7 Fkreselam Hotel
12 Asheton Hotel
13 Seven Olives Hotel
18 St George Hotel
30 Hotel Roha Lalibela
34 Lal Hotel
36 Jerusalem Guest House

PLACES TO EAT
8 John Cafeteria
16 Kidus Mikael Restaurant
19 Askalech Tej House
24 Blue Lal Restaurant
26 Helen Hotel

OTHER
1 High Court
2 Souvenir Shops; Photo Lalibela
3 Police
4 Telecommunications Office
5 Planned New Office of Ethiopian Airlines
6 Souvenir Shops
9 Unlicensed Petrol Station
10 Relief Centre
11 Ethiopian Airlines
14 Medical Clinic
15 Bus Station
17 Post Office
20 Central Shop
21 Temporary Site of Tourism Information Centre
22 Church Authority Office
23 New Municipality
25 Na'akuto La'ab Tej Beat
27 Planned New Site of Tourist Information Centre
28 Lalibela High School
29 Netherlands Development Organisation
31 Souvenir Shop
32 Souvenir Shop
33 Souvenir Shop
35 Red Cross Relief Centre

style. If angels did build the churches, they were most certainly Ethiopian angels!

Many travellers are shocked by the rather unflattering corrugated-iron roofs donned by many of the churches. During the 1990s, seepage had become a major problem and the only way of protecting the churches from further damage was with the construction of temporary shelters. An EU-funded competition to design more sympathetic shelters is being launched. These should be in place by 2002, to protect the churches until the huge funds required for their proper restoration can be found.

Orientation

The churches can be divided into three main groups. The first two groups lie within a short distance of the town centre, one to the north of the canalised watercourse known as the 'River Jordan', and another to the east. The third group lies outside town.

Information

Tourist Office There is a kind of privately operated tourist office (☎ 205) close to the church of Bet Maryam; it will be relocated soon to a site near the high school. The 'director' isn't adverse to offering his services

Legends of Lalibela

Shortly after the king was born, a thick cloud of bees surrounded him in his cradle. His mother, seeing the bees as symbolic of the soldiers who would one day serve her son, called him 'Lalibela', meaning 'the bees recognise his sovereignty'. However, Lalibela soon began to arouse the jealousy of his elder brother and incumbent ruler, King Harbay.

Harbay's various attempts to get rid of Lalibela culminated in a poisoned potion that cast the young prince into a mortal sleep. During the next three days, Lalibela was transported by angels to heaven.

There, God instructed him to build churches the likes of which had never been seen before. Lalibela then returned to Earth equipped with detailed instructions as to the churches' location, design, and construction.

After Harbay had been reconciled with his brother and had abdicated in his favour, Lalibela was proclaimed king. Soon, all the world's greatest artists and craftsmen had been gathered together, and work on the great project began.

Toiling all the hours of daylight, the earthly workforce was then replaced by a celestial one, who toiled all the hours of darkness; the churches rose at a miraculous speed.

as a guide. The centre is open from 8.30 am to 12.30 pm and 1.30 to 5.30 pm daily.

The Ethiopian Tourism Commission (ETC) does a useful publication on Lalibela; it's sometimes available in souvenir shops in Lalibela for Birr30–50. *Lalibela: World Wonder Heritage* by Tilahun Assefa is sometimes available at the Hotel Roha Lalibela.

Money Since there are not yet any banks in Lalibela, you should come prepared. The Hotel Roha Lalibela and the Seven Olives Hotel do change money, but only travellers cheques and cash in US dollars, and only for guests. If you're desperate, a black market operates in some of the souvenir shops.

Tickets Tickets are bought from the Church Authority office. They cost Birr100 and give access to all churches inside town (but not to those outside) for the duration of your stay. The office is open from 6 am to noon and 2 to 5 pm daily.

Entrance to each of the churches outside town costs Birr20 (unless otherwise indicated); for these, you should pay at the churches.

The fee for video cameras is Birr150 inside town and Birr50 per church outside town.

Guides A guide is a good idea, as much as for keeping others at bay as for finding your way around, but as elsewhere in Ethiopia, the standard is pretty low, despite recent attempts at training (see also the boxed text 'Guidelines for Guides' in the Facts for the Visitor section).

The price for official guides is now fixed at Birr50 per person per day, but you'll probably be asked Birr100 during the major festivals. The tourist office can find you one.

Some children offer their services as guides. Though they charge less, using them encourages them to play truant at school, and money earned is often spent on booze and cigarettes. Neither do they know much about the churches. If you really can't afford an official guide, the tourist office will offer to find you a guide for Birr10–20 if you are a bona fide student. There is no excuse for using children as guides.

The self-appointed shoe bearers should be tipped Birr1–2 per church.

Mule Hire Mules can be a welcome addition to the longer or steeper treks, and can be hired for Birr25 (for Asheta Maryam and Na'akuto La'ab) and Birr50 (for churches further afield) per mule and driver, per day. The tourist office advises the following tips: Birr15 per mule driver per day for shorter distances, and Birr30 for longer distances, or Birr100–200 at the end of, say, three days. The mule drivers are obliging and work hard – far harder than the petulant and well-fed guides; they also earn a lot less, and tipping is greatly appreciated.

When to Visit A good time to visit Lalibela is during the country's major religious festivals, though the tourist office recommends flight and hotel reservations six months in advance for Timkat and Leddet, and three or four months in advance for Fasika (Easter).Outside these periods, find out from the tourist office if any of the local churches are celebrating their saint's day; these are well worth attending. You'll need at least three days to do the churches justice.

Northern Group of Churches

Bet Medhane Alem This church, whose name means 'Saviour of the World', is said to be the largest rock-hewn church in the world, measuring 33.5m by 23.5m. It's as impressive for its size as for its majesty – the building resembles far more a Greek temple than an Ethiopian church.

Scholars have suggested that the church may even have been a copy in rock of the original St Mary of Zion church in Aksum.

The building is supported by 36 large, square columns on the outside (many actually replicas of the originals), and a further 36 inside which support the gabled roof.

The interior of the church consists of a barrel-vaulted nave and four aisles. In one corner, three empty graves are said to have been prepared symbolically for Abraham, Isaac and Jacob. Look out for the pierced stone 'panels' filling the window, each of which is decorated with different central crosses. It was from this church that the Lalibela Cross was stolen in 1997 (see the boxed text 'The Lalibela Cross').

Bet Maryam Connected to Bet Medhane Alem by a tunnel is a large courtyard containing three churches. The first, Bet Maryam, is small, yet designed and decorated to an exceptionally high standard. It's also unusual for its three projected porches, which lead into a triple aisle. The ceilings and upper walls are painted with very early frescoes, and the columns, capital and arches are covered in beautifully carved details such as birds, animals and foliage, including a curious two-headed eagle and two fighting bulls, one white, one black (thought to represent good and evil). Look out also for the 'Aksumite frieze' (row of false windows).

Donkey Lore

Ever wondered why donkeys nuzzle and sniff one another when they meet?

Once upon a time, long ago, the donkeys became tired of their role as beasts of burden. So they called a big meeting and decided to send a representative to God to plead their cause, and to end their suffering at the hands of people.

But though years have passed, their representative has not yet returned. The donkeys go on waiting patiently and submissively, but every time they meet one another, they put their heads together to ask 'Has our envoy returned yet?'

For so it is that all living things yearn for freedom.

A traditional Ethiopian tale

At the eastern end of the nave is a column that is kept permanently wrapped in cloth. It is said that Christ leant against it as he appeared in a vision to King Lalibela. On it is said to be inscribed the 'past and future of the world' (you can't sneak a peek – a priest keeps up a vigilant guard). Above the western porch, look for the rare and beautifully carved bas-relief of St George fighting the dragon.

The church is dedicated to the Virgin, who is particularly venerated in Ethiopia, and to this day remains one of the most popular churches among pilgrims. Some believe it may have been the first church built by Lalibela.

In the courtyard there is a deep sunken pool; the water is said to have miraculous properties, and on certain days, infertile women come here to bathe.

Bet Meskel Carved into the northern wall of the courtyard of Bet Maryam is the tiny chapel of Bet Meskel. Four pillars divide the gallery into two aisles spanned by arcades.

Keep an eye out for the cross carved in relief beneath stylised foliage on one of the spandrels of the arches.

Some of the large caves in the chapel are still inhabited by hermits.

The Lalibela Cross

Said to have been the personal property of King Lalibela himself, the 800-year-old Lalibela Cross is one of Ethiopia's most revered national treasures. No doubt this made the artefact particularly alluring to the thieves who, in 1997, stole it from the rock-hewn church in which it was housed. Fortunately, eagle-eyed Belgian customs officers identified it in the luggage of an art collector returning from an Ethiopian trip. The collector, who had purchased the cross from an Ethiopian antiques dealer for US$25,000, was recompensed by the Ethiopian government and to the great delight of the Ethiopian Orthodox Church and all Ethiopians, the cross returned to its home in May 1999.

Bet Danaghel To the south of the Bet Maryam courtyard is the chapel of Bet Danaghel, said to have been constructed in memory of the 50 maiden nuns martyred on the orders of the 4th-century Roman emperor Julian in Edessa (modern-day Turkey). Many of its features – the cruciform pillars and bracket capitals – are typical architectural features of the churches.

Bet Golgotha & Bet Mikael A tunnel at the southern end of the Bet Maryam courtyard connects it to the twin churches of Bet Golgotha and Bet Mikael (also known as Bet Debre Sina).

Bet Mikael serves as an anteroom to the Selassie Chapel, one of the holiest sanctuaries in Lalibela. It contains three monolithic altars. One is decorated with a beautiful relief of four winged creatures with their hands held up in prayer; it is thought to represent the four evangelists. Unfortunately, the chapel is very rarely open to the public.

Bet Golgotha is known for containing some of the best early examples of Christian art in Ethiopia. On the so-called Tomb of Christ – an arched recess in the northeast of the church – a recumbent figure is carved in high relief; above it, in low relief, hovers an angel. Look out for the exceptional, life-sized depiction of seven saints carved into the niches of the walls.

The two churches also boast among the most important religious treasures in Lalibela, such as some fine processional crosses. You may be shown a blackened but richly decorated metal cross, thought to have belonged to the founding king.

Close to the Tomb of Christ is a moveable slab of stone, said to cover the most secret place in the holy city, the tomb of King Lalibela himself. Such is the importance and sanctity of Golgotha that a visit is said to assure your place in heaven!

Standing in a deep trench in front of the western facade of Bet Golgotha is the so-called Tomb of Adam. It consists of a giant, hollowed-out block of stone. On the upper floor there's a hermit's cell; the ground floor serves as an entrance to the nearby churches.

Bet Giyorgis Lying slightly apart from the main northern cluster – towards the southwest of town – is the church of Bet Giyorgis. The most famous and photographed of all Lalibela's churches, it represents the apogee of the rock-hewn tradition: it is the most visually perfect of all. It is also exceptionally well preserved.

The church is constructed on a three-tiered plinth and is shaped like a Greek cross. Though considered the most recent church, it still incorporates many features of Aksumite architecture.

Inside, an old box carved from olive wood is said to have been carved by King Lalibela himself, and used by him for storing his famous tools.

Eastern Group of Churches

Bet Amanuel The freestanding, monolithic church of Bet Amanuel is considered one of the most finely carved churches in Lalibela; some have suggested that it was used by the royal family as their private chapel.

In style, it is typically Aksumite, perhaps more than any other church in Lalibela, with its projecting and recessed walls, monkey heads, and carved windows and doorways. A spiral staircase connects the four-pillared walls to an upper gallery.

The most striking feature of the rather elegant interior is the double Aksumite frieze in the nave. In the southern aisle, a hole in the floor leads to a long, subterranean tunnel (one of three) which connects the church to Bet Merkorios.

In the courtyard outside, look out for the little cavities hewn in the wall to attract the sacred bees. Throughout Ethiopia, the honey produced in churches is believed to be endowed with special healing properties.

The chambers in the walls are the old graves of pilgrims who requested to be buried here.

Bet Merkorios Bet Merkorios may not in fact have served as a church at all. The discovery of ankle shackles among other things has led scholars to believe that the building may once have served as the town's prison, or house of justice. It was not until much later that the building was converted to a church.

On the north-eastern wall, there's a fading but beautiful fresco thought to represent the three wise men. With their little flipper hands and eyes that look askance, the painting is delightful, and it may date from the 15th century. The Twelve Apostles are also depicted; this less attractive fresco is probably of a later date.

The painting on cotton fabric is believed to date from the 16th century. Formerly, such paintings were plastered to the church walls with a mixture of straw, ox blood and mud.

Bet Abba Libanos Bet Abba Libanos is unique among the town-based churches in that it's a hypogeous church – that is, only the roof remains attached to the overhead rock.

Like Bet Amanuel, many of its architectural features, such as the friezes, are Aksumite. Curiously, the interior, which looks large from the outside, is actually very small.

The church is said to have been constructed in a single night by Lalibela's wife, Meskel Kebra – with a little help from the angels. Three-quarter cut, the church seems to grow from the rock; it gives you a vivid idea of the feat required to hew out one of these churches.

A tunnel leads off the church to the tiny chapel of Bet Lehem.

St George

Just as King Lalibela was finishing off his series of churches, he was suddenly paid an unexpected visit. Astride a white horse and decked out in full armour came the country's patron saint, George. However, the saint turned out to be severely piqued: not one of the churches had been dedicated to him.

Lalibela – profusely apologetic – promised to make amends immediately by building him the most beautiful church of all.

Today, the priests of Bet Giyorgis (meaning 'Place of George') point out the hoof prints left behind by the saint's horse, permanently imprinted in stone on the side of the trench.

Near the church is the so-called monastery-village of Lalibela, where 12 monks and six nuns continue to live in tiny caves (4m by 3m) hewn out of the rock. You can visit them, but you should leave something for the community.

Bet Gabriel-Rufael Because of its curious, irregular plan, it is thought that Bet Gabriel-Rufael also served another function before its conversion to a church – perhaps as a residence of the royal family.

The complex is made up of three halls and two courtyards. King Lalibela is said to have addressed his people from the top. Its monumental facade is its most interesting feature; look out for the very unusual Aksumite windows with little pointed arches. Inside, the decoration is quite plain – just three Latin crosses.

A tunnel leads to the so-called Arogi Bethlehem, a bakery for making the holy bread.

Churches Outside Town

There are various other churches within a day's journey of Lalibela. Many of them require quite long walks, or rides by mule. They are well worth a visit; they vary greatly in style, age and design, and the journey to them will take you through some beautiful countryside. Many churches are quite tucked away. None are currently listed on any maps, so you'll definitely need a guide to find them; ask at the tourist office.

Yemrehanna Kristos Lying 20km northeast of Lalibela, Yemrehanna Kristos is undoubtedly the finest church outside the town.

The hideous brick wall, built in 1985 to improve the church's security, conceals the jewel within. Unusually, the church is built – rather than excavated – within a cave. Very much in the Aksumite style, it may well predate Lalibela.

There are surprises everywhere. The exterior of the church is decorated with white marble panels (whitewashed), and the whole church sits on a foundation of carefully laid olive-wood panels, which 'float' it perfectly above the marshy ground below. Look out for the elaborate nave ceiling; everywhere the carving and decoration are exceptional.

At the back of the church, under an overhanging rock, are the bones of countless pilgrims who chose to be buried here. Tombs, also at the back, are said to contain the remains of Yemrehanna Kristos.

Entrance to the church is Birr50. It takes about five hours to get here by foot or mule from Lalibela. If the road is passable, you can also drive to within about 15 minutes of the church. Around 95% of tourists never get here; don't be one of them.

Arbatu Ensessa To the south-west of Yemrehanna Kristos is Arbatu Entsessa, a three-quarter monolith in a wild, overgrown, but rather beautiful state.

Though one of the most easily accessible churches, its interior is open only one day a month. An amble around the exterior is free, but you should tip the solitary caretaker Birr5.

Bilbila Chirkos Lying close to Arbatu Ensessa, Bilbila Chirkos is well designed, but it's particularly known for its frescoes. It's a three-minute walk from the road.

Bilbila Giyorgis Bilbila Giyorgis lies to the west of Arbatu Ensessa, and resembles Bet Abba Libanos in design. According to

tradition, five swarms of bees are always in residence here; their honey is said to have curative properties, particularly for psychological disorders and skin problems! The priest will let you taste it. There's a 15-minute walk up the hill to the church from the road.

Ashetan Maryam The church of Ashetan Maryam sits atop a mountain that rises above Lalibela to an altitude of nearly 4000m. There are commanding views in all directions. The local priests believe they are 'closer to heaven and to God' here, and it's easy to see why.

The monastery is believed to have been started during King Lalibela's reign, but finished under King Na'akuto La'ab; some claim the latter lies buried in the chapel.

The architecture of much of the complex compares pretty poorly with what lies below in Lalibela; it even looks strangely like imitation. However, the journey takes you through lovely country. Listen out for the witchlike cackle of the francolins resounding around the valley.

The 1½-hour climb to reach it is quite steep; many travellers take mules, though you'll still need to walk on the rockiest parts.

Na'akuto La'ab Lying 6km from Lalibela, Na'akuto La'ab was built by King Lalibela's nephew and successor. It is a simple but attractive little church (apart from the outer security wall), built around a cave. It was almost certainly the site of a much older shrine.

Empress Zewditu built the ugly inner red-brick building. Some very old stone receptacles collect the precious holy water as it drips from the cave roof.

The church boasts various treasures said to have belonged to its founder, including crosses, crowns and an illuminated Bible. It's just a 10- to 15-minute walk from the village of the same name.

Geneta Maryam Geneta Maryam lies near the source of the Tekezze River. It is known for the 24 massive rectangular pillars that support it, and for its remarkable 13th-century paintings.

On the western wall, look out for the face of Christ, shaped like a moon, and on the southern side, the very grumpy-looking elephants. Architecturally, it resembles a little the church of Medhane Alem in Lalibela. It lies about four hours by foot from Lalibela, or 1½ hours by vehicle, with a two-minute walk from the road.

Machina Maryam Two hours' walk from Geneta Maryam is the remote church of Machina Maryam, said traditionally to have been constructed by King Gebre Meskel in the 4th century.

The church is constructed under an overhanging rock in a natural cave; to the north, there used to be a monastery. It rather resembles Yemrehanna Kristos in design, and many features are Aksumite, but its beautiful frescoes are the main attraction – look out for the hunting scenes with the many one-eyed lions.

The church also contains many bricked-up tombs. Bodies buried under the rock are said to be preserved forever. The church is very little visited, but is well worth the long – and in parts steep – ascent; mules are probably a good idea.

Abuna Yosef It's an eight-hour walk (one-way) to reach Abuna Yosef from Lalibela. Little more than a cave, albeit an old one, it is devoid of both paintings and architectural details. But it does make a great trek through beautiful country, and Ethiopian wolves have been seen here in the past couple of years.

Nearby is a holy spring, said to have sprung up from the blood of Abuna Yosef, who cut his leg when the devil pushed him over.

It's possible to overnight in a nearby mountain village (don't expect more than a goatskin on an earthen floor). Otherwise you'll need to bring camping equipment; two day's food should be brought too.

Kenkgenet Mikael Lying not far from Abuna Yosef, the rock-hewn church of Kenkgenet Mikael is much more interesting architecturally. Many of its features are similar to those found in the Tigrayan rock-hewn churches, and it would appear to be quite old.

Places to Stay

Lalibela, including its hotels, still suffers from water shortages; you have to shower at a certain time or may be given a bucket of warm water, even in the smarter hotels. Don't waste it.

If you want to camp, tents (Birr300 per tent) and cooking equipment are available for rental from the Church Authority office. You can pitch a tent at the *Hotel Roha Lalibela* (see their listing following).

Budget hotels are not Lalibela's strong point: most are flea-ridden brothels and are really only for those on their last cent. The least awful are the *St George Hotel* with cells for Birr10 (two rooms have rather beautiful views), and the *Fkreselam Hotel* with rooms in a green courtyard behind the hotel for Birr15–20. Both have common cold showers.

The *Asheton Hotel (☎ 230)* has character, is clean and quite well run, and is a longtime favourite with travellers. It charges Birr30–35 for rooms (Birr60 with private bathroom). Seven rooms have hot water. In the low season, discounts are possible.

A brand-new place is the pleasant and very peaceful *Jerusalem Guest House (☎ 240)*, which has rooms with private bathroom and attractive balconies for US$23 (discounts of up to 30% are available in the low season).

The government-run *Seven Olives Hotel (☎ 220)* has over-priced singles/doubles for US$24/36.

Offering much the best value in the top-end category is the *Hotel Roha Lalibela (☎ 209)*, around 2km out of town. It belongs to the same government chain as the Goha in Gonder, and charges US$36/48/72 for singles/doubles/suites. Reservations should be made through the Ghion Hotel in Addis Ababa (see Places to Stay – Mid-Range in the Addis Ababa section). Camping is possible in the grounds for US$6 per person, including the use of a hotel room for a hot shower.

The private *Lal Hotel (☎ 208)* has singles for US$126–210 and doubles for US$196–280, depending on the season; though reasonably comfortable, the rooms are wildly overpriced.

Ethiopian Magic

Despite the deep roots of Christianity, a surprising amount of magic and superstition still pervades Ethiopia.

The *lelafa sedeq*, a magic charm made from a parchment scroll, is still sometimes attached to the body of the deceased to guide them to heaven. Many children wear charms or talismans around their neck, attached to the *matab* (cord given at baptism) and used to deter evil spirits and terrible diseases.

In the country, many people believe in the *zar* (spirits or genies), both good and bad. The *buda* is the evil eye, who by night can transform a person into an evil-doing hyaena – like the European werewolf.

Places to Eat & Drink

A good idea is to ask your hotel (or failing that, a restaurant) to prepare a picnic lunch for you, which you can have while exploring the churches.

The **Kidus Mikael Restaurant** is supposed to be the best restaurant in town for local fare; the **Tisita Hotel** is also good. The simple **Helen Hotel** also has a good reputation (try the home-brewed *tej* or mead).

The **Blue Lal Restaurant** is a very pleasant place designed like a tent, and is much the best place for faranji food. Pizza and quiche can be ordered with advance notice. The **John Cafeteria** is considered the best cafe in town.

Don't leave Lalibela without tasting the excellent tej. A little flask costs Birr2. Considered one of the best watering holes in town is **Askalech Tej House**, open daily until 10 pm. It's the thatched, whitewashed building through the church compound wall.

Getting There & Away

Contrary to what guidebooks or tourist literature may tell you, the town (since 1997) *is* accessible throughout the year. However, unless you have your own vehicle, getting to and from Lalibela is still simpler by air.

Ethiopian Airlines flies daily from Lalibela to Addis Ababa (via Bahar Dar) and Gonder; it flies three times a week to Aksum (see the main Getting Around section earlier in this chapter). At the time of writing the Ethiopian Airlines office is near the Seven Olives Hotel, but will move soon to a new site in town.

Overland, the best approach currently is via Woldia. There are two routes from Woldia, one via Dilb (120km) and another along the new road via Gashema (170km). The old road is still quicker, but is not always passable in the wet season.

From Lalibela, buses and other vehicles run erratically to Woldia. In theory, they leave every day; in practice, they leave only when there's enough demand. The best thing is to check at the bus station around 4 or 5 pm the day before you want to leave. If there's a bus, the driver will sell you a ticket (Birr16, or Birr25 in a 4WD share taxi). It takes seven hours by bus, and five hours by taxi or private vehicle, depending on the route.

Coming from the west, buses also run between Debre Tabor and Dilb, 83km from Lalibela. In Dilb, you can sometimes hop on buses going to Lalibela from Woldia. There are no hotels in Dilb, so if you arrive late, you should continue on to Woldia.

Two new roads are being built to connect Lalibela to Addis Ababa, and Lalibela to Aksum via Sekota; they are scheduled to be completed by 2003.

Getting Around

The airport lies around 13km from town; a new, sealed road is being built. The NTO, which has an office in the Seven Olives Hotel, runs a taxi service for Birr70 return (it collects you and takes you back to the airport).

There are currently no petrol stations in Lalibela, though there are plans to open one in the future, so stock up in Woldia. Currently an unlicensed 'station' operates. It's all rather under the table, and prices are high. Don't rely on it unless you're desperate!

At the time of writing, the Church Authority office had three vehicles for hire: the 4WD pick-ups cost Birr500 per day including driver and fuel; the Landrover costs Birr800 per day.

The NTO also has vehicles for hire. It also offers short trips for one to three people, such as to Geneta Maryam (Birr275 per person, three hours return) and to Na'akuto La'ab (Birr45 per person, two hours return). Prices include fuel and driver, but not guide or church entrance fees. 'City tours' cost US$25 for one person or US$12 per person for two people. The Lal Hotel also does excursions, but they're expensive.

DESSIE
☎ 03

Though it's quite attractively set amid eucalyptus-forested hills, Wolo's capital wouldn't win a beauty contest. However, it's a major transport hub, makes a good stopover point on your way to or from Lalibela, Hayk or Maqdala, and has a good range of reasonably priced hotels and restaurants.

In 1998, a **museum** opened in the curious, Indian-built old governor's palace. It's open daily (mornings only on Saturday and Sunday); entrance costs Birr7. Exhibits include musical instruments, local arts and crafts, and regal and religious regalia. The captions are in Amharic only, but it's not a bad time-filler.

Places to Stay & Eat
The *Menafasha Restaurant*, close to the bus station, has good-value rooms for Birr10–12. It's also a local favourite for food. The *Admas Restaurant* also serves good food. You'll need to ask for both, as signs are in Amharic only. A smarter place for local and faranji food is the *Ambaras Hotel*.

The *Fasika Hotel* (☎ 11-29-30) is much the best-value hotel in town, with good rooms for Birr17 (Birr22 with telephone and hot shower). It's often full; you should make a reservation. The *Royal Pension* (☎ 11-11-40) has adequate rooms for Birr30 (Birr50 with shower).

The *Ambaras Hotel* (☎ 11-28-20) has small but comfortable singles for Birr48–60 and doubles for Birr72, both with hot shower. It's better value than the old *Ghion Ambassel Hotel*.

The *Ras Pastry* is good for breakfast. The *Tiruneh Alemu Hotel* is the best tej beat in town.

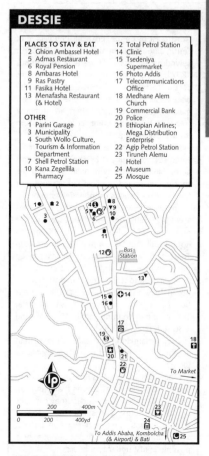

DESSIE

PLACES TO STAY & EAT
2 Ghion Ambassel Hotel
5 Admas Restaurant
6 Royal Pension
8 Ambaras Hotel
9 Ras Pastry
11 Fasika Hotel
13 Menafasha Restaurant (& Hotel)

OTHER
1 Parini Garage
3 Municipality
4 South Wollo Culture, Tourism & Information Department
7 Shell Petrol Station
10 Kana Zegellila Pharmacy
12 Total Petrol Station
14 Clinic
15 Tsedeniya Supermarket
16 Photo Addis
17 Telecommunications Office
18 Medhane Alem Church
19 Commercial Bank
20 Police
21 Ethiopian Airlines; Mega Distribution Enterprise
22 Agip Petrol Station
23 Tiruneh Alemu Hotel
24 Museum
25 Mosque

Getting There & Away
Ethiopian Airlines flies daily to Addis Ababa, and once a week to Gonder via Bahar Dar (see the main Getting Around section earlier in this chapter). Flights depart from the airport at Kombolcha; taxis to the airport cost Birr50.

At least five buses run daily to Addis Ababa (Birr24, 10 hours) via Debre Berhan; one bus leaves daily for Mekele (Birr26, 12 hours). Minibuses run every 15 minutes to Kombolcha (Birr3, 45 mins). Three buses leave daily for Woldia (Birr7.50, four hours). For Lalibela, go first to Woldia.

ETHIOPIA

Battle of Maqdala

North-east of Dessie, near the tiny village of Tenta, are the remains of the Emperor Tewodros' fortress and the site of the famous 1867 battle of Maqdala. Though little remains of the fortress – it lies strewn across the plateau since the British flattened it – a visit makes a terrific walk, and there are stunning views of the surrounding countryside from the windswept top.

Maqdala is rather a sad, mournful place – some say still haunted by the unhappy emperor. Find a villager who will show you the spot where Tewodros killed himself and, not far away, his famous cannon, Sebastopol.

The walk to Maqdala involves a 700m descent from Tenta before a steep ascent up the mountain, which lies at around 3000m. It's not difficult, but takes around 3½ hours from Tenta to Tewodros' fortress. Mules can be hired, and are advised for the last ascent.

You'll need to stop at the administration office in Ajibara (10km before Tenta) to get papers giving you permission to visit Maqdala. The office is open from 8 am to 12.30 pm and 1.30 to 5 pm weekdays.

The **Roman Hotel** in Ajibara is better than anything Tenta has to offer, and has rooms for Birr10.

One 4WD and one bus runs from Dessie to Tenta each morning at around 8 am (Birr25). Though it's only 140km, the journey can take up to five hours. The service will stop at Ajibara so you can get permission papers. With your own vehicle, the same journey is possible in just under two hours.

For Djibouti, buses run every day to Diciotto near Galafi (Birr18.50, 10 hours).

HAYK

Lying 28km north of Dessie on a well-wooded peninsula is the little town of Hayk, known for its monastery and lake.

The monastery dates from the mid-13th century and was founded by Abba Iyasus Moa. Between the 13th and 15th centuries, it was among the most important monasteries in the country, and contains the oldest known manuscript to record its own date: the book of the four gospels produced for the monastery in 1280–81. It is open to men only.

The lake and its environs, 2km from town, is an excellent spot for birders.

Minibuses and buses run to Hayk every 15 minutes from Dessie (Birr4, one hour).

KOMBOLCHA

Dessie's twin town, Kombolcha, lies 25km from Dessie. Like Dessie, it has quite good facilities, and is closer to the airport (2km).

If you want to stay here, the **Lem Hotel** off the main Kombolcha–Addis Ababa road has adequate rooms for Birr10. The **Rose Pension** on the same street offers very clean rooms with cold shower for Birr25. The **Tekle Hotel** off the main Kombolcha road has good rooms with hot shower for Birr50–70.

One traveller wrote to declare the **Kingo Pastry** 'the best pastry shop in Africa'. The hotels mentioned all offer adequate food.

Most intercity transport leaves from Dessie; minibuses connect the two towns (Birr3, 45 mins). One bus leaves daily for Addis Ababa (Birr22, 11 hours).

AROUND KOMBOLCHA

The little town of **Bati**, 41km east of Kombolcha, is known for its large, colourful Monday market, which attracts up to 10,000 Afars and Oromos from all around. It's not as spectacular as the tourist literature makes out, but if you're in the area, it's worth a peek. Bati is the largest market in the country after Merkato in Addis Ababa. At least 10 minibuses leave daily from Kombolcha (Birr3–4, one hour).

Along the road stretching south of Kombolcha to Debre Berhan are **wetlands** that attract good numbers of birds (particularly the stretch around 45km and 55km south of Kombolcha). Look out for the endemic blue-winged goose.

DEBRE BERHAN

☎ 01

Lying 130km north of Addis Ababa, the town of Debre Berhan makes another useful stopping point on the road to or from the north. It does boast one church thought to date from the 15th century. It is known for its woven wool rugs, which can be bought here, though a better selection can be found in Addis Ababa.

All the following places to stay and eat in Debre Berhan lie on the Dessie–Addis Ababa road. The *Girma Hotel* has simple but very clean rooms for Birr6–8. The *Helen Hotel* has rooms for Birr10 (Birr30 with hot shower). Its restaurant is considered one of the best places in town. Most comfortable is the *Akalu Hotel* (☎ 81-11-15) with rooms for Birr24 (Birr40 with shower). The *Tekelle Tafach Pastry* has cakes and fruit juices.

At least 10 buses run daily between Debre Berhan and Addis Ababa (Birr8, three hours). For Dessie, buses pass through from Addis Ababa between 10 and 10.30 am.

ANKOBER

The little town of Ankober lies 40km southeast of Debre Berhan. Right up until the late 19th century, when Addis Ababa was founded, it was the capital of the Shoan princes.

The 2km ascent up to the ruins of the old fort perched on a hill above town makes for a great walk. The area is also a very good place for birding and is the official home of a very rare endemic, the Ankober serin. A guide can be found at the little cafe *Shibirey Kursbeat* in the village. On the way, several historic churches and their treasures can also be visited (Ankober Mikael, St Maryam and Medhane Alem). With your own vehicle, you can drive to the foot of the fort.

One bus runs every morning to Ankober (Birr4, two hours). The churches are usually open just from 6 to 8 am, so you'll have to make an early start from Debre Berhan.

South of Addis Ababa

If the north is known for its historical attractions, then the south is known for its natural attractions. Combining scenic landscapes with excellent wildlife and some of the most diverse and fascinating peoples of the country, the south represents the other side of Ethiopia – almost the antithesis of the Amhara north. In some ways, it is also the most 'African' region of Ethiopia.

The African Rift Valley dominates the south. Africa's largest and most famous geographical feature, it runs from Djibouti all the way down to Mozambique, and is home to a string of lakes known for their birdlife. The national parks, also running in a string from north to south, are quite different from each other, offering different scenery, different birds and different mammals.

Quite distinct from one another too are the vast numbers of ethnic groups inhabiting the area; no less than 45 languages are spoken. The Omo region in the south-west has been called the last great wilderness on the African continent, and is home not just to Ethiopia's few remaining rhinos, giraffes, buffaloes and elephants, but also to its last 'untouched' peoples, including the famous Mursi lip-stretchers and body-painting Karo.

Travellers planning a trip to the south-west should note that the main rains occur from March to May or June, and the light rains from October to December. In the wet season, many roads in the Omo Valley become impassable.

To the south-east of Addis Ababa, the Bale Mountains rise high above the surrounding pastures of the Oromo people, dominating the landscape for miles around. Contained within the mountains is a very beautiful national park, one of the largest mountain parks in Africa, boasting the most extensive area of Afro-alpine habitat on the continent. Though less well known than the Simien Mountains, the Bale Mountains provide some of the most scenic walking in the country. In the rain and among the heather, the Bale Mountains can resemble Scotland.

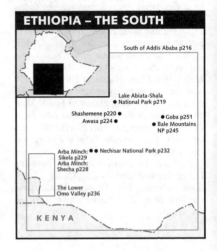

ETHIOPIA – THE SOUTH

South of Addis Ababa p216

Lake Abiata-Shala
National Park p219

Shashemene p220 ●
Awasa p224 ●

● Goba p251
● Bale Mountains
NP p245

Arba Minch: ● ● Nechisar National Park p232
Sikela p229
Arba Minch:
Shecha p228

The Lower
Omo Valley p236

KENYA

Without a doubt, the Bale Mountains National Park is the best place in the country to see endemic wildlife. The Ethiopian wolf, the rarest canid in the world and as good as extinct in most other areas of Ethiopia, is quite easily spotted here. The park is also home to no fewer than 16 endemic bird species; sightings are so common that there is a saying in the park that 'in Bale, every bird is endemic'.

In the south-east, look out for the Arsi Oromo women, who adorn themselves with lavish bead necklaces and heavy copper and brass bangles. Many of the Muslim Oromo women wear long, black headscarves known as *shash*, and the men wear heavy, cotton shawls known as *buluko* to insulate themselves against the cold.

Cattle rearing is the mainstay of the south-east's economy, and the cow is greatly prized by the local people. The animal supplies not just meat, milk, butter and blood for food, but dung for fuel and for building houses. Ownership of cattle confers great social status on Oromo men: if a herdsman has more than 1000, he is entitled to wear a crown.

The typical Oromo dwelling is a round, thatched hut; its roof is either domed or flat with an overhang, and is often topped with an ostrich shell or pot at the apex. Euphorbia is commonly used as a kind of living fence to keep the animals off the crops.

The great majority of Oromos in the south-east are Muslim. Two very important Muslim shrines can be found in the region: Sheikh Hussein, the centre of the most important annual Muslim pilgrimage in Ethiopia; and the Sof Omar Caves, which are also an important natural attraction.

SOUTH TO LAKE ZIWAY
Via Meki
Of the two routes south to Lake Ziway, the quickest is via Debre Zeyit and Meki, and the great majority of buses heading south come this way.

Along the road, about 20km south of Mojo, the **Koko Dam** is worth a brief stop for those with their own vehicle. Part of an hydroelectric power station, the dam supplies most of Addis Ababa with its electricity, and attracts many birds. Hippos also can sometimes be seen.

Continuing southwards, keep an eye out for the **Oromo tombs**, decorated with bright murals including elephants and warriors on horses.

Via Butajira
The second route south via Butajira is slower, but more interesting, and takes you past several important historical sites. The area can also be visited as a day trip or, better, a weekend trip from Addis Ababa. Access is easy. Just hop on a bus to Butajira from the Autobus Terra in Merkato, and ask to be dropped off at the sites.

Melka Kunture, 1.5km from the little town of Melka Awash, is famous for the remarkable prehistoric stone-tool factory discovered in the 1960s. It is difficult to visit (you need a special letter of permission from the Oromo Investment Bureau in Addis Ababa) and there is not much to see as the site has become pretty overgrown. If you do stop off, accommodation can be found in Melka Awash. The *Mane Nyaato Awash*

Enduring Enset

When travelling in the south, look out for the false banana (Musa ensete), which as the name suggests, resembles a single-stemmed banana plant. Known locally as enset, this ancient plant has been cultivated in Ethiopia for millennia and is eaten by over a third of the population.

The preparation of enset for cooking is a laborious process. After the plant is cut, it must be scraped to remove all excess fibre, then chopped and beaten into a white pulp (often seen for sale at markets). Finally, the plant is buried in an underground pit and allowed to ferment for at least a month.

The end product? A kind of sticky, unleavened bread that closely resembles a fibrous type of carpet liner. It also makes a very chewy porridge.

Despite its appearance, texture and rather lowly status as a food staple, enset may well provide the solution to an age-old Ethiopian problem: the threat of famine. Enset can be stored for up to 20 years, providing its cultivators with an emergency ration in times of hardship. The plant is also famously resistant to drought. An American team of scientists has been enthusiastic about its potential.

Hotel, with rooms for Birr6, is probably your best bet.

A five-minute walk from the village of Adadi will take you to the impressive rock-hewn church of **Adadi Maryam**. Dating from the 12th or 13th century, the church is a three-quarter monolith.

A place well worth a stop is Tiya, the site of around 40 ancient **stelae**, the largest of which stands up to 2m high. They are as fascinating and as mysterious as any of the standing stones found in Europe, but are only one cluster among many that dot the countryside all the way down to Dila, south of Awash. Almost nothing is known about the monoliths' carvers or their purpose. Most of the stones are engraved with enigmatic symbols, notably swords. French excavations have revealed that the stelae mark mass graves of individuals aged between 18

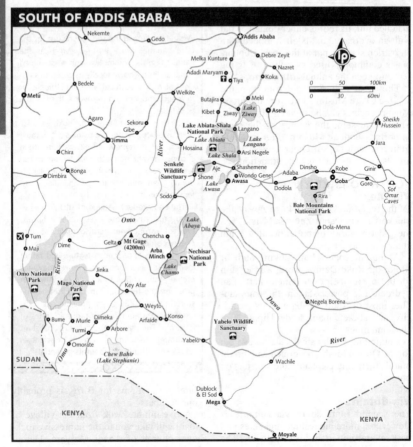

SOUTH OF ADDIS ABABA

and 30. The stelae lie 500m from the village of Tiya.

Close to the village of Kibet, south of Butajira, is the so-called **Silti stele**. From Kibet, it's a 9km drive, followed by a seven-minute walk south-east of the road up a hill. A few minutes south of the stone is the village of Bazoso, where the 'head' of the stone can be found. Like the Tiya monoliths, very little is known about this large and ancient stone. Its engravings appear to depict female sexual features and it is thought that the stone may mark an ancient and important grave, perhaps of an ancient princess.

Also in the area, 1km off the Addis Ababa road, 2.8km from Kibet, is the strange crater lake of **Hare Shetan**, which means 'Place of the Devil' in the local Silti language. The lake is known for its extraordinary colour – like a fluorescent, cloudy emerald, which according to the locals changes colour from green to yellow and white depending on the season. The place is surrounded in local myth and superstition. It's a five-minute walk from the road to the rim of the crater, and you can pick up a guide in the Woreda Council Administration Office in Kibet.

If you get stuck in Butajira, the pleasant *Mateus Baka Hotel* has rooms with cold shower for Birr12 (Birr20 with hot shower). It also has a good restaurant. From Butajira, five or six buses leave daily for Ziway (Birr4, two hours); eight or nine buses leave for Addis Ababa (Birr10, four hours); four buses go to Hosaina (Birr8, three hours); and six buses run to Kibet (Birr1, 30 minutes).

LAKE ZIWAY

Measuring 400 sq m, Lake Ziway is the largest of the northern group of Rift Valley lakes and makes a good introduction to them. Surrounded by blue volcanic hills, it's a scenic enough place, but is known particularly for its **birdlife**, attracted by the teeming tilapia population. White pelicans, knob-billed geese and sometimes saddlebill and yellowbill storks are all seen here, as well as kingfishers and waterfowl. The lake lies about 1.5km east of the town of Ziway.

One of the best and most accessible spots to see birds is the earthen 'jetty' to the east of town, which serves as a departure and arrival point for many of Ziway's fishermen. It's known locally as the 'Cafeteria'. If you're coming from Addis Ababa, take the side road immediately after the Bekele Mola Hotel; it's around 2km from the main road. The birds are particularly numerous after 5.30 pm, when they gather to pick at the fishermen's cast-offs. You can also take a local punt (Birr10–20 per hour after hefty negotiation) to see the **hippo pods**, about 15 minutes from the jetty.

The lake is also home to five little volcanic islands. At least three of these islands once boasted medieval churches. Tullu Gudo, 14km from Ziway and the largest of the islands, is still the site of three monasteries. **Debre Sion**, the most famous, has a long and very enigmatic history. According to local tradition, the church once housed the Ark of the Covenant, when it was brought here by Aksumite priests fleeing the destruction of the city at the hands of Queen Gudit in the 9th century. The Ark apparently remained at the monastery for the next 70 years. The original church now lies in ruins and a new one has been built. Unfortunately, the church's treasures are in a sad state of repair. Curiously, the oldest written documents on Aksum were discovered here and the inhabitants speak a language thought to relate to Ge'ez and use boats which greatly resemble the papyrus *tankwas* of Lake Tana.

Tullo Gudo is a beautiful, little-visited place and is definitely worth an excursion. The walk to the church through the *tef* (indigenous cereal), wheat and barley fields is pleasant and there are very good views from the top of the hill, where the church is perched. There are also hot springs; you can bathe in the little tub created by the islanders near the shore front. A brief exploration of the island takes around two hours.

Boats can be hired from private operators in Ziway. A boat for up to six people costs Birr250–300. Journey times vary according to the power of the boat, taking from 20 minutes to 1½ hours. One operator to be recommended at the time of writing was Fitsum Yohannes (☎ 41-02-07), who provides life jackets and waterproofs, and can also lend you fishing gear, if you fancy a fish on your plate for dinner. Be sure that extra fuel is brought along. Fitsum can be also be contacted through the Perfect Laundry, next door to the Firehiwot Pastry on the main street (near the bus station) in Ziway. If Fitsum's not around, Gemechu Argo, a waiter in the Bekele Mola Hotel, can help you find a boat. If you want to be sure of a boat, call him at the hotel in advance.

Camping is possible on Tullo Gudo and fishing is allowed on the lake.

ZIWAY
☎ 06

The town of Ziway, 162km from Addis Ababa, is home to an important fishery centre as well as some horticultural gardens, which export fruit and vegetables to countries as far flung as Belgium and Germany. It's a pleasant, laid-back little place, with good hotels, restaurants and cafes.

The Commercial Bank does not have foreign exchange facilities; for these you should go to Shashemene.

Places to Stay & Eat

The *Lulaa Hotel* off the main street, around 200m north of the Ziway Tourist Hotel, has spotless rooms for Birr10 (Birr15 with shower).

The *Park Hotel* (☎ 41-06-11) at the northern end of town past the Mobil petrol station, is probably the best value in town, with rooms with cold shower for Birr17 (Birr33–44 with hot shower). The *Bekele Mola Hotel* (☎ 41-00-21) has adequate rooms with hot shower for Birr25–30; its restaurant serves the usual *faranji* (Western) food.

A very popular local restaurant is the *Brothers' Hotel*. A pleasant and popular place for a drink in the evening is the *Ziway Tourist Hotel*. The *Firehiwot Pastry* is good for cakes and fruit juices.

Getting There & Away

Six buses leave daily for Shashemene (Birr6, two hours); five or six buses leave for Butajira (Birr4, two hours); and three depart for Addis Ababa (Birr11, 3½ hours). For Debre Zeyit or Nazret, go to Mojo first (Birr6, two hours).

There are no taxis in Ziway, only minibuses. To take you to the Bekele Mola Hotel, or the Wabe Shebele Hotel on Lake Langano, they charge Birr300 (for up to 12 people one way). Bikes can be hired in Ziway for Birr0.50 per hour.

LAKE LANGANO

Set against the blue Arsi Mountains, which rise to 4000m above the lake, Lake Langano is an attractive sort of place. However, as it is not far from Addis Ababa, it is overrun at weekends when accommodation is often booked up. During the week, Langano is a quieter, more peaceful place, and not a bad spot to rest up for an afternoon after some hard travelling in the south. There's little to do here besides swimming and sunbathing on the sandy shores.

Although its curious colour resembles a cup of strong English tea – with a dash of milk – the lake's waters are very clean. Along with Lake Shala, it is one of the only lakes in the country that is thought to be bilharzia-free. It also makes a convenient base for a visit to the Lake Abiata-Shala National Park.

Boats on the lake are privately owned; there are no longer any water sports facilities for visitors.

Places to Stay & Eat

Right opposite one of the Abiata-Shala park entrances, on the main Addis Ababa–Shashemene road, is the 3km road leading to the *Bekele Mola Hotel* (☎ Langano 3). Older rooms with private shower cost Birr60 (newer rooms cost Birr150). Pleasant, Italian-designed bungalows containing two double bedrooms and a single bed in the sitting room cost between Birr150 and Birr250, depending on their age and location. The bungalows have terraces; young Ethiopian weekenders like to have *chat* (mildly narcotic plant) parties here. Camping is possible on the lakeshore and costs Birr15 per small tent. The hotel's restaurant serves the usual faranji food, plus fresh fish.

A more interesting place for food – and the only alternative in the area – is the *Jangle Bar*, found in the two little *tukuls* (cone-shaped huts) about 50m down the road from the Bekele Mola. Pizzas cost Birr15; local dishes cost Birr5 to Birr10.

The *Langano Resort Hotel* (☎ Bulbula 24), better known as the *Wabe Shebele Hotel*, lies 16km from the Abiata-Shala park, 10.3km from the village of Bulbula (including the 3km walk down the track off the main road). Bungalows with two/three rooms cost Birr243/337 during the week and Birr298/420 at the weekend. Prices include breakfast. Camping costs Birr24 for a two-person tent and Birr12 per person for more than two people. A couple of bungalows are available for Birr170 for one or two people. This hotel is less attractively set and designed than the Bekele Mola, but it's quieter and more peaceful, particularly at the weekend. If they're in working order, motorboats can be hired for lake tours and visits to the hot springs. Boat hire costs Birr200 for up to six people.

Getting There & Away

To get to Lake Langano, take any bus plying the Addis Ababa–Shashemene road, and ask to be dropped off at the turn-off to your hotel; it's then a 3km walk to either hotel.

LAKE ABIATA-SHALA NATIONAL PARK

Of much greater interest than Lake Langano are the twin lakes of Abiata and Shala, which form part of the 887-sq-km Lake Abiata-Shala National Park. Mt Fike, which sits on the 3km-wide strip of land separating the two lakes, dominates the landscape at 2075m.

Unfortunately, the park has suffered greatly at the hands of humans. Large numbers of people have settled in the park (even though this is officially 'illegal'). Their domestic animals and plantations have taken over the place and much of the surrounding acacia woodland has been cut down for charcoal. Also, the factory close by continues to pollute the lake (for more information, see Ecology & Environment in the Facts about Ethiopia Chapter).

Despite all these disturbances, however, the park is still well worth a visit. Some of the scenery is very beautiful; the sight of pelican colonies on the silver water of Lake Abiata at dusk is an unforgettable one.

Information

Entrance to the park costs Birr50 per person per 48 hours, plus Birr10 per vehicle with up to five seats. Armed scouts, who also act as guides, cost Birr50; the park advises you to hire one, as robberies have occurred here. It is essential to keep all car doors locked and possessions out of sight; a guard for the car is a good idea. Gangs of thieves are so adept at breaking in that the park authorities are convinced that they have a master key.

Things to See

Though they are 'twin' lakes, Abiata and Shala could not be more different. Lake Abiata is a shallow, brackish pan, just 14m deep. Curiously, its natural level fluctuates periodically; it is still uncertain why. The changing levels have left exposed mud

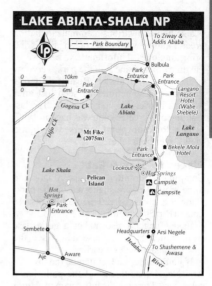

banks and grass flats, which attract many birds, including vast colonies of **flamingos**.

Lake Shala, on the other hand, is a crater lake; with a depth around 260m, it is the deepest in the Ethiopian Rift Valley. A few volcanic islands dot its surface, and around it bubble up several **sulphurous springs**. A kind of local resort has grown up to the north-east of the lake. Amid the steaming springs, the local people come to bathe, wash clothes and seek cures for rheumatic ailments. Vendors sell maize cobs that have been boiled in the spring water. The water of the lake has a high saline content; fish are not found here.

The islands on Lake Shala provide valuable nesting sites and are home to the most important breeding colony of **great white pelicans** in Africa. Because of the lack of fish in the lake, the birds are obliged to feed on Lake Abiata. The islands are protected sanctuaries and can't be visited.

Other birds seen on the lake include African fish eagles, Egyptian geese, plovers, herons, coots, waders and various species of duck. In the surrounding acacia woodland, look out for the various species of weaver bird, the red-billed hornbill, Didric's cuckoo, the Abyssinian roller and the superb starling.

According to the park literature, the park is also home to various mammals including greater kudus, warthogs, golden jackals and oribi antelopes. Unfortunately, because of the many disturbances to the park, very few of these are in evidence. Beautiful **Grant's gazelles** can sometimes be seen just after the park barrier – keep an eye out. The last sighting of a greater kudu was back in 1997.

The **lookout point** offers very good views over both lakes.

Places to Stay & Eat

Camping is permitted on Lake Abiata, and three main sites are suggested by the park. Camping costs Birr20 per adult per 48 hours (Birr5 per child).

Lake Langano also makes a good base from which to visit these lakes (see the Lake Langano section earlier).

If you're after budget hotels, the town of Arsi Negele, south-east of the park, has a selection. The wonderfully named *Mana Buna Gaara Guuroo Hotel* near the police station has basic but clean rooms for Birr7.

Getting There & Around

The main entrance to the park lies directly opposite the turn-off to the Bekele Mola Hotel to the west of the Addis Ababa–Moyale road. It's conspicuous because of the ostriches stalking around in an enclosure near the edge of the road. Any bus doing the run from the capital to Shashemene will drop you off at the entrance gate.

If you're without a vehicle, you can walk to most of the places of interest in the park (about a 12km round trip). It's a good idea to go early in the morning or later in the afternoon. The wildlife is better and you'll avoid the heat of the day.

With your own vehicle, road conditions usually make 4WD compulsory. Cars should not be left unattended anywhere at either of the lakes.

SHASHEMENE
☎ 06

Shashemene, which lies at an important crossroads connecting the north to the south and the east to the west, bustles with traffic

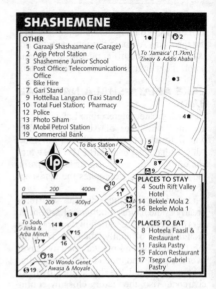

SHASHEMENE

OTHER
1 Garaaji Shashaamane (Garage)
2 Agip Petrol Station
3 Shashemene Junior School
5 Post Office; Telecommunications Office
6 Bike Hire
7 Gari Stand
9 Hottellaa Langano (Taxi Stand)
10 Total Fuel Station; Pharmacy
12 Police
13 Photo Siham
18 Mobil Petrol Station
19 Commercial Bank

To 'Jamaica' (1.7km), Ziway & Addis Ababa

To Bus Station

To Sodo, Jinka & Arba Minch

To Wondo Genet, Awasa & Moyale

PLACES TO STAY
4 South Rift Valley Hotel
14 Bekele Mola 2
16 Bekele Mola 1

PLACES TO EAT
8 Hoteela Faasil & Restaurant
11 Fasika Pastry
15 Falcon Restaurant
17 Tsega Gabriel Pastry

and trade. Like all crossroad towns, it's grubby, noisy and shambolic: bars are cheek by jowl with brothels, blaring music shops and truckers' cafes. Shashemene is a strong contender for the least-attractive-town-in-Ethiopia award. Both Wondo Genet and Awasa are far more pleasant places to stop over.

In the town, keep an eye out for petty thieves, who aren't averse to trying to remove an appendage or two, such as lights or mirrors, from vehicles. Deft pickpockets also roam the streets and markets.

Shashemene can boast one claim: it is the unofficial capital of the Ethiopian Rastafarian community, which inhabits a locality to the north of town known appropriately as Jamaica. It lies on the main Addis Ababa road, 1.7km from the Agip petrol station. Though usually hospitable and welcoming, the community is understandably a little tired of being viewed as either a tourist attraction or as a source of marijuana (illegal anyway in Ethiopia and the cause of recent police raids). Unless you're genuinely interested in the movement, understand that the community prefers to be left in peace.

Places to Stay & Eat

Of the two Bekele Mola chain hotels in Shashemene, the older one known as *Bekele Mola 1* (☎ 10-00-50) offers better value, with reasonable rooms for Birr10 (Birr15 with shower). Its restaurant serves quite adequate faranji food, including fresh fish. The *Bekele Mola 2* (☎ 10-05-99) offers smarter rooms for Birr35.

Top of the range of hotels and restaurants is the new *South Rift Valley Hotel* (☎ 10-14-58) on the outskirts of town. Rooms with private bathroom go for Birr30–60. The hotel's best features are its extensive and well-designed gardens. The restaurant serves good Ethiopian and faranji food.

For local fare, Shashemenites rate highly the *Hoteela Faasil & Restaurant* and the *Falcon Restaurant*, better known as the 'Tef Restaurant' after the old owner.

Getting There & Away

Shashemene is the principal transport hub of the south, and you can catch buses in any direction from it.

Three buses leave daily for Arba Minch (Birr15, six hours) and for Addis Ababa (Birr15, five hours); two buses run daily to Goba (Birr20, eight hours) and to Ziway (Birr6, two hours). One bus leaves daily for Moyale (Birr40, with an overnight stop at Yabelo). Minibuses as well as buses run daily to Dila (Birr10, three hours) and to Awasa (Birr2, 30 mins).

Tickets can't be bought the day before; if you're planning an early start, get the ticket by 5.30 am, or you may find yourself stuck in Shashemene for another day.

Getting Around

Garis can be hired for Birr1, from the bus station or from the stand north of the main street. Bikes can be hired for Birr10 for half a day or Birr20 for a full day. Taxis can be found outside the Hottellaa Langano in the town centre.

AROUND SHASHEMENE
Wondo Genet

A very worthwhile excursion off the main north-south route is to the hot-springs resort

Rastafarians

When the Emperor Haile Selassie was crowned in 1930, he assumed subjects who lived far beyond the confines of his own 'kingdom'. In Jamaica, where Marcus Garvey's 'return to Africa' movement had been established, many saw the emperor's coronation as fulfilment of the ancient biblical prophesy that 'Kings will come out of Africa'.

Identifying themselves passionately with the new Ethiopian monarch, as well as with Ethiopia's status as an independent African state, they rejected European Christianity and created a new religion all of their own.

In it, they accorded the emperor the rank of divinity – the Messiah of African redemption. The new faith's name derived from the emperor's name before he assumed the crown: Ras Tafari. The emperor, meanwhile, is said to have been somewhat embarrassed by all this unexpected adulation.

Rastafarians follow strict dietary taboos: pork, milk and coffee are forbidden. Ganga (marijuana) is held to be a sacrament.

Today, the Rastas patiently await the restoration of the Ethiopian monarchy. The current Ethiopian-Eritrean War is seen as a punishment visited on the country for having killed its king – the chosen one of God.

of Wondo Genet, around 15km south-east of Shashemene. Surrounded by dense forest and filled with bird song, it's like an oasis. If you've spent too much time in Addis Ababa, if you've taken one bus too far or if you're after some peace and quiet, Wondo Genet is just the ticket. It's also rather a romantic place, and may provide a timely panacea for road-weary and bickering couples! Be aware that the resort can get crowded at the weekends; choose a weekday if you can.

The resort hotel (see Places to Stay & Eat), set amid old shady trees, citrus orchards and flowering gardens, is on a natural balcony overlooking the Rift Valley. In the hotel grounds there are a couple of **swimming pools** fed with natural hot-spring water; you can use them any time of day or night. Next to the pools, the spring water is piped over the cliff face to make a fabulous waterfall-type shower.

There's also great **hiking** to be had in the surrounding forest. Birdlife in the forest is abundant, and bushbucks, hyaenas and Anubis baboons are also found here. In the gardens, colobus and vervet monkeys are easily seen.

Travellers can also visit the nearby **Wondo Genet Agricultural College** (☎/fax 20-14-90) with its beautiful forests where many indigenous tree species (such as *Cordia africana* and *Podocarpus gracilia*) have been replanted. Parts of the ancient forest also remain, and give a great insight into how most of Ethiopia must once have looked. Six endemic birds are found in the forest. There's also an **arboretum** with over 124 species of trees. The college keeps normal government business hours (see Business Hours in the Facts for the Visitor chapter).

The entrance gate to the hot springs and pools lies 300m from the hotel. Entrance fees are no longer charged, but use of either the natural 'showers' or the constructed cubicle baths costs Birr3.30–5.50.

The main pool is cleaned (and so emptied) every Wednesday. If you're with children, there's a toddlers' area, and near the hotel, a small children's playground.

Guides to the surrounding forests can be organised by the hotel (Birr30 for half a day or Birr50 for a full day). Walks to consider might be to the local villages in the hills, to see the birds or wildlife in the forest or to the local plantations. A 10-minute walk immediately above the springs will take you to their source, where you can also see the cooling system in action. In the boiling water upstream, local cowherds cook their lunch: 17 minutes for potatoes, 35 minutes for maize!

If you've forgotten your swimming kit, costumes and trunks can be bought at the shop near the entrance to the springs.

Places to Stay & Eat The *Wondo Genet Resort Hotel* (☎ 20-15-76) provides the only accommodation in Wondo Genet. Prices are high for what you get: the usual 1970s lino floor, brown decor and run-down bathroom,

typical of Ethiopian government hotels. You're definitely paying for the location here. Rooms cost Birr140 (Birr175 on weekends). Three-bed bungalows cost Birr281 (Birr350 on weekends), and the once lavish tukul known as the 'Menelik Suite', built by one of the daughters of Haile Selassie, costs Birr263 (Birr349 on weekends).

Camping in the hotel grounds costs a mere Birr36 per person, but includes access to showers and swimming pools. A campfire and a whole roasted sheep (for up to 10 people) can be arranged for between Birr230 and Birr345.

The restaurant – which uncannily resembles a space rocket – serves both faranji and Ethiopian food. Tasty snacks such as steak sandwiches and hamburgers are also available. Mains and snacks cost about Birr12 plus tax.

If you're coming on a weekend, it's a good idea to make a reservation. You can contact the hotel directly or ring the Wabe Shebele head office in Addis Ababa on (☎ 01-51-71-87); the hotel is part of the Wabe Shebele chain.

If you can't afford the hotel at Wondo Genet, you can stay in a budget hotel in the nearby village of Washa. The *Absiniya Hotel* is about the best bet but is also a bit overpriced with basic rooms with communal shower for Birr15. Camping costs Birr10.

Getting There & Away The resort lies off the main Shashemene–Wondo Genet road, 5km before it reaches the village of Wondo Genet. The turn-off is on the left near the village of Washa.

From Shashemene, seven buses and 10 minibuses run daily to the village of Wondo Genet (Birr2.50). They start at around 7.30 am and the last leaves at around 5.30 pm. The buses can drop you off at the turn-off to the springs (at the village of Washa) from where it's a 3km walk. To catch a bus back, wait on the Shashemene road opposite the junction to the springs.

A contract taxi from Shashemene to the springs costs Birr60/150 one way/return (including waiting time). Bikes – a great way of reaching the springs – can also be hired in Shashemene.

From Awasa, a contract taxi will cost Birr170 return.

Senkele Wildlife Sanctuary

The Senkele Wildlife Sanctuary, west of Shashemene, stretches over 36 sq km and was originally established to protect the endemic Swayne's hartebeest.

Other mammals found in the park include Bohor reedbucks, greater kudus, striped and spotted hyaenas, serval and civet cats, caracals, warthogs, common jackals and oribi antelopes, as well as 91 species of bird.

The open acacia woodland of the park is quite scenic and many of the animals are fairly easily seen, particularly the Swayne's hartebeest, whose population is estimated currently at between 250 and 300 individuals. You can approach quite close to them.

The park is well worth a visit if you have your own vehicle. There's a 65km track around the park, but not all of it is maintained. There's a gorgeous view over the plain from the Borana Hill, around 6km east of the park office. But count the cattle! Unfortunately, the park is overrun with livestock, and epitomises, perhaps more than any other park in Ethiopia, the clash of interests between conservationists and local people (see also Ecology & Environment in the Facts about Ethiopia chapter). When first established in the 1960s, the park covered 54 sq km; one-third has been lost to settlement. The trees are being cut down, watering holes are being dug, houses built and crops cultivated.

Visitors should contact the administration office in Aje before visiting the park; a guide can be provided. Entrance to the park costs Birr50 per person plus Birr3 for a vehicle, and Birr10 for a driver. The best time to visit Senkele is early in the morning or after 4 pm.

If you get stuck in Aje, the **Hoteela Abdii Rabbi** is about the best bet for accommodation, with basic rooms for Birr6. The **Lam-lam Hotel** is not a bad place for food.

The road leading to the park lies 5km beyond the town of Aje, 28km west of Shashemene. From the turn-off to the park

Hateful Hyaena

Contrary to popular belief, the striped hyaena is a friend not a foe. It very rarely makes a killing itself, preferring to scavenge from the leftovers of others, and provides a very useful and efficient waste-disposal service. Cleaning the environment of carcasses, it limits the spread of disease, and by crunching up the bones, it promotes the recycling of vital minerals.

However, the animal's predilection for carcasses has led to much superstition growing up around it. In many parts of the Horn, the animal is a kind of equivalent to the European werewolf – certain men are said to turn into hyaenas at night. The animal is universally disliked and persecuted.

gate, it's another 17.5km to the park headquarters.

If you're continuing on towards Arba Minch, you'll pass through some of the most fertile land in Ethiopia, where abundant fruit plantations are found. If you can stop, don't miss the bananas – no bigger than your middle finger, but as sweet as nectar. Around 50km south of Sodo, boys on the road sell papaya, *gishta* fruit (worth tasting), and – more bananas. Look out for the Wolaita 'haircut houses' too, with neatly trimmed eaves that look like fringes.

AWASA
☎ 06

Capital of the old Sidamo province, Awasa is an attractive town in a beautiful setting, poised at the very edge of Lake Awasa. It is a pleasant place to break a journey to or from the south and is well equipped with hotels, little pastry shops and restaurants. The Commercial Bank changes travellers cheques as well as major foreign currency. A small tourist office operates in the grounds of the Wabe Shebele Hotel 1 and can give information on local sites of interest.

Things to See & Do

Though there isn't a great deal to see or do in Awasa, a boat trip on the lake in the late

ETHIOPIA

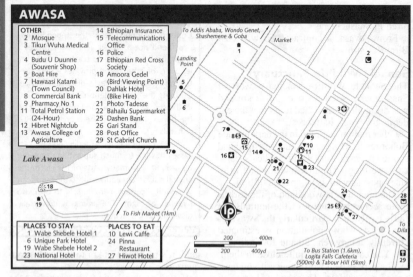

AWASA

OTHER
2 Mosque
3 Tikur Wuha Medical
   Centre
4 Budu U Duunne
   (Souvenir Shop)
5 Boat Hire
7 Hawaasi Katami
   (Town Council)
8 Commercial Bank
9 Pharmacy No 1
11 Total Petrol Station
    (24-Hour)
12 Hibret Nightclub
13 Awasa College of
    Agriculture
14 Ethiopian Insurance
15 Telecommunications
    Office
16 Police
17 Ethiopian Red Cross
    Society
18 Amoora Gedel
    (Bird Viewing Point)
20 Dahlak Hotel
    (Bike Hire)
21 Photo Tadesse
22 Bahailu Supermarket
25 Dashen Bank
28 Gari Stand
29 Post Office
29 St Gabriel Church

To Addis Ababa, Wondo Genet,
Shashemene & Goba

Market

Landing
Point

Lake Awasa

To Fish Market (1km)

0   200   400m
0   200   400yd

To Bus Station (1.6km),
Logita Falls Cafeteria
(500m) & Tabour Hill (5km)

To
Dila

PLACES TO STAY
1 Wabe Shebele Hotel 1
6 Unique Park Hotel
19 Wabe Shebele Hotel 2
23 National Hotel

PLACES TO EAT
10 Lewi Caffe
24 Pinna
    Restaurant
27 Hiwot Hotel

afternoon or early evening makes a very pleasant excursion. The little rowing boats (and rower) can be hired at the small pier just beyond the Unique Park Hotel, and cost Birr24 per hour for up to 10 people (these are better value than the ones available at the Wabe Shebele Hotel 2). A trip to Tikur Wuha (Black Water) to see the hippos will take three hours return.

A trip to Amoora Gedel (Crow Valley), behind the Wabe Shebele Hotel 2, is good if you're keen on birds.

You can also walk along the edge of much of the lake, following the footpath that leads southward from Wabe Shebele Hotel 1. For a very good view of the lake, you can climb Tabour Hill, around 5km from town.

The waters of the lake teem with fish, including tilapia, catfish and barbus, which in turn attract good birds. Kingfishers, herons, storks, crakes, darters and plovers are among the species commonly seen on the waters' edge. The fig forest and scrub around parts of the lake attract weavers and hornbills, as well as the endemic black-winged lovebird. Hook fishing is permitted, but you'll need your own equipment.

The town market (on Monday and Thursday) and the fish market (every morning near the Wabe Shebele Hotel 2) are worth wandering through. Both Oromo and Sidama people come in from all around. Straw hats, baskets and mats are all typical Sidama products.

Places to Stay

The *National Hotel* has small but very clean rooms with shared cold shower for Birr11. Its restaurant is popular locally.

One of the best-value hotels in town is the *Unique Park Hotel* (☎ 20-13-18), situated very close to the lakefront. Rooms cost Birr15 with cold shower (Birr25 with hot shower and mosquito nets). The attractive garden teems with birds and is a cool, pleasant place for a drink in the evening. In theory, the music goes off at 9 pm.

The *Wabe Shebele Hotel 2* (☎ 20-04-15) has very overpriced rooms for Birr75–90. A better reason for visiting the hotel is the outdoor pool, which is filled at weekends; nonguests are charged Birr3. Camping is permitted in the grounds and costs Birr30 for a small tent (Birr40 for a large one). The lakeside terrace is a pleasant place for a drink in the evening; the spot is known for its water birds. A beer costs Birr4.25 and a coffee costs Birr1.75, including tax.

The *Wabe Shebele Hotel 1* (☎ 20-00-04) is even poorer value, with a range of adequate bungalows and villas for around Birr160–263.

Places to Eat

A favourite with the Awasa bourgeoisie is the *Pinna Restaurant*, half pastry shop (on the ground floor), half restaurant (on the first floor). The cakes are home-baked and pretty tasty, and the restaurant serves a good selection of western dishes; mains cost Birr10–14. The restaurant is open from 6.30 am to 10 pm daily. At the time of writing, a new, large hotel was being built by the same family next door. It should offer upper-range accommodation once completed.

The *Lewi Caffe* is a good place for breakfast. The *Hiwot Hotel* is known for its *kitfo* (raw minced meat) and on fasting days for its fish dishes. A new place in a giant tukul is the *Logita Falls Cafeteria*.

Getting There & Away

The main bus station lies 1.6km from the town, but you can ask buses to drop you off in the centre. Otherwise, garis are available at the station.

One bus runs daily to Addis Ababa (Birr16, seven to eight hours), Arba Minch (Birr18.50, eight hours) and Moyale (Birr38, 1½ days). Buses run every 30 minutes to Shashemene (Birr2.50, 30 minutes). For Ziway (Birr8, two hours), take the bus towards Addis Ababa. For Goba and Wondo Genet, change at Shashemene. Minibuses run every half hour to Dila (Birr10, two hours).

Getting Around

Garis charge Birr1.50 for short journeys and Birr2 for longer ones. They can also be hired by the hour for Birr3, or by the day for Birr20. Taxis should charge around Birr25 per hour.

Bikes can be hired in front of the Dahlak Hotel and cost Birr7.50 for half a day or Birr12.50 for a full day. Better bikes are

Sidama Style

The Sidama people are particularly known for their beautifully constructed woven huts, which take the form of beehives. A framework of bamboo is first covered with grass then waterproofed with enset leaves. A little front porch is the only opening.

Inside, the hut is divided into two parts. The animals have the left side; the family has the right. Nearby, a euphorbia hedge or bamboo fence protects the vegetable plot.

available for Birr15 for half a day or Birr25 for a full day.

DILA

Dila, south of Awasa, represents a kind of epicentre of the southern Ethiopian tradition of **stelae** erection. Before visiting any of the monoliths, however, travellers must first get permission papers from the Gedeo Culture & Information Office in Dila, where you can also pick up a guide.

Tutu Fella is probably one of the most impressive sites. It lies near the village of Wonago, 13km from Dila, along a track up a hill. Around 80 stones are variously carved with facial features, phalluses etc. The 'sex' of the stone is thought by locals to denote the sex of the person buried underneath.

Tutiti, the second major site in the area, lies on a hill 2.3km from the village of Chalba and consists of some very large, tapering, generally uncarved standing stones, again marking graves.

Also worth a stroll is Dila's large **market**; parasols made from enset leaves shelter the abundant agricultural produce. The locally made straw boaters make great sunhats if you're planning on some trekking in the Bale Mountains.

The new *Zeleke Hotel* has decent rooms for Birr12 (Birr20 with private hot shower). The bizarrely named *Get Smart Restaurant* is considered a smart place to eat. The *Delight Pasty* is good for cakes, fruit juices and breakfast.

One bus leaves daily for Yabelo (Birr20, four hours) and for Moyale (Birr30, seven hours). Four or five buses run daily to Shashemene (Birr10, three hours) via Awasa (Birr8, 2½ hours). For Addis Ababa, go first to Shashemene. You should get to the ticket office early (around 5.30 am).

YABELO

Yabelo lies around halfway between Dila and Moyale on the road to Jinka, about 4km off the main road. If you have your own vehicle, it makes a convenient base for a visit to both Yabelo Wildlife Sanctuary and a couple of places situated close to the town.

If you get here on a Saturday, the local Borena market is worth a peek.

If you haven't already stocked up for a trip in the Omo Valley, Yabelo's your last chance. A couple of local groceries stock tins of sardines, biscuits, cheese, coffee powder, soft drinks etc, as well as 'usefuls'

such as batteries, candles, matches and loo paper. Electricity is very erratic in Yabelo.

Yabelo boasts few sumptuous hotels. About the best bet is the *Hoteela Waggaa Haaraa*, which has clean rooms with shared shower for Birr10.

The *Salam Restaurant* does quite good local food. The *Kokeb Restaurant* is also good, and serves freshly baked rolls for breakfast.

If arriving by bus, ask to be dropped at the junction to Yabelo on the main Dila-Moyale road. One bus leaves daily for Moyale (Birr20, three hours) and one for Dila (Birr25–30, four hours). Only trucks run to Konso (Birr20, three hours).

AROUND YABELO

A foray into Borena territory is worthwhile and makes a great day trip with your own vehicle. The famous 'singing wells' (see the boxed text 'The Singing Wells of the Borena' following) are dotted around the nearby

Oromo farmers off to market – weekly markets play an important role in social life.

The Singing Wells of the Borena

Inhabiting the dry, hot plains to the east of Konso, the Borena people are semi-nomadic pastoralists whose lives revolve entirely around their cattle. During the long dry season, they struggle to keep their vast herds alive. To combat the problem, the Borena have developed their own peculiar solution: a series of wells dug deep into the earth, carefully assigned to the different Borena families and clans.

A series of water troughs is constructed close to each well's mouth, approached by a kind of long 'street' that drops to about 10m below the ground and acts as a funnel, guiding the cattle to the troughs. It is just wide enough to allow two single columns of cattle to pass one another.

When it is time to water the cattle, the men make a kind of human ladder down the well (which can be up to 30m deep), tossing buckets of water between each other from the bottom up to the top where the troughs are gradually filled. The work is incredibly hard and the men often sing in harmony to encourage one another as well as to reassure the cattle. Several hundred or even thousand cattle come to drink at a time; it's a memorable sight.

---

village of Dublock, 70km south of Yabelo. There are nine wells currently operating in the region, and some have been used for over a century. To find them, you can pick up a guide from Dublock. Some Borena chieftains now demand a kind of entrance fee from tourists: Birr2 per man working in the well.

The village of El Sod, around 12km south of Dublock, is one of the largest salt deposits in Ethiopia. Known as the **'House of Salt'**, it is famous for its 100m-deep crater lake, one of four in the region. The lake measures around 800m across and is so dark, it looks like an oil slick. Valuable, muddy, black salt has been extracted from the lake for centuries. Today, donkeys laden with the heavy black mud continue to toil up the steep sides of the crater. The processed salt is transported across the country. From the village, it's a 30-minute walk down to the water.

Near the village of Borena, 6km outside Yabelo, there are some small but interesting **cave paintings**; giraffe, hyaenas, lions and ostriches are among the animals depicted. It's a one-hour walk to the caves from Borena, through an attractive landscape of sorghum fields and crops. You'll need a guide from the village.

YABELO WILDLIFE SANCTUARY

Covering an area of 2496 sq km, the Yabelo Wildlife Sanctuary was created originally to protect the endemic Swayne's hartebeest. It has now become better known for its birds,

and contains some 194 species including the endemic white-tailed swallow and Stresemann's bush crow, which were first described only in the 1930s and 1940s. One of Africa's rarest birds, the Prince Ruspoli turaco (see the boxed text 'The Strange Case of the Vanishing Turaco' in the special section 'Birds in Ethiopia'), has been reported in the juniper forest.

The park is made up of acacia woodland and savanna grass as well as some juniper forest. The 25 mammal species inhabiting the acacia woodland and savanna grass include Burchell's zebra, the greater and lesser kudus and the gerenuk.

The town of Yabelo provides the nearest accommodation. Travellers are advised to report to Yabelo Administration before a visit to the park. Guides can be provided.

MOYALE

Moyale serves as the frontier town between Ethiopia and Kenya, and both countries share the town. If you have to spend the night here, the Ethiopian side is the more pleasant of the two. Its hotels offer much better value and there's a decent selection of different types of places to eat. Fuel is also cheaper in Ethiopia. The Commercial Bank here can change travellers cheques.

Places to Stay & Eat

On the Ethiopian side, the *Africa Hotel* just off the main road is a simple but peaceful and clean place with rooms with shared shower for Birr6–10. The **Ysosadayo Borena Moyale Hotel** has rooms with private bathroom for Birr25.

The **Mana Ciiraa Mana Cuuniffaa** is a favourite local restaurant; the **Fekadu Hotel** is popular with local officials.

On the Kenyan side, the **Hotel Madina** is about the best budget bet, with basic, small but clean singles/doubles with shared shower for KSh120/200. The similarly priced **Liban** isn't bad and has a restaurant.

Getting There & Away

At the time of writing, two small private companies, Arban Agency and Al Karim, were offering one-way flights three or four times weekly from Moyale to Nairobi for KSh5000.

For crossing into Kenya by land, there are no buses, but trucks leave daily for Nairobi (KSh1000 for back seats and KSh1500 for front seats, two days). If you miss the Nairobi bus, you can hitch a ride with a truck to Marsabit (KSh700 for back seats and KSh1000 in the front, five to six hours) or Isiolo (KSh900 in back, KSh1200 in front, 1½ days). Most trucks leave from outside the police station at the police barrier on the Kenyan side. During the wet season (from March to May and from October to December), trucks don't leave so frequently.

From Moyale, minibuses leave daily for Yabelo (Birr20, three hours) and one bus leaves daily for Shashemene (Birr40, 10 hours).

ARBA MINCH
☎ 06

Arba Minch, the capital of the old Gamo-Gofa province and the largest town in southern Ethiopia, lies 252km by road south-west of Shashemene. On an escarpment overlooking Lake Abaya to the north, Lake Chamo to the south, and the Rift Valley to the west, the town boasts a lovely position and is a pleasant and friendly place. Arba Minch also makes a good base from which to explore the nearby Rift Valley lakes, the very beautiful Nechisar

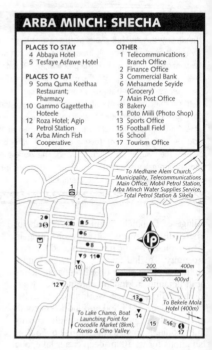

ARBA MINCH: SHECHA

PLACES TO STAY		OTHER	
4	Abbaya Hotel	1	Telecommunications
5	Tesfaye Asfawe Hotel		Branch Office
		2	Finance Office
PLACES TO EAT		3	Commercial Bank
9	Soma Quma Keethaa	6	Mehaamede Seyide
	Restaurant;		(Grocery)
	Pharmacy	7	Main Post Office
10	Gammo Gagettetha	8	Bakery
	Hoteele	11	Poto Miili (Photo Shop)
12	Roza Hotel; Agip	13	Sports Office
	Petrol Station	15	Football Field
14	Arba Minch Fish	16	School
	Cooperative	17	Tourism Office

To Medhane Alem Church, Municipality, Telecommunications Main Office, Mobil Petrol Station, Arba Minch Water Supplies Service, Total Petrol Station & Sikela

0   200   400m
0   200   400yd

To Bekele Mola Hotel (400m)

To Lake Chamo, Boat Launching Point for Crocodile Market (8km), Konso & Omo Valley

National Park, and the highland town of Chencha.

If you've come from the Omo Valley, Arba Minch will seem like a place of incredible sophistication, with its electricity, showers, real loos, coffee with milk, and pastries. Even so, at first sight – and after all the guidebook hype and tourist literature – Arba Minch disappoints. Your arrival is greeted by a line of pylons and the streets are grubby and chaotic. But Arba Minch will soon start to work its charm. A bit of advice? Head straight for the terrace of the Bekele Mola Hotel near the southern entrance to the town; you'll soon see why.

Orientation & Information

The town actually consists of two settlements connected by a 4km stretch of asphalt. Sikela, on the plain to the north, is the commercial and residential centre; Shecha, perched on the hill overlooking the lakes to the south, is where most of the government

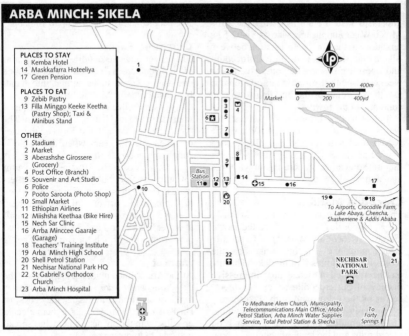

ARBA MINCH: SIKELA

PLACES TO STAY
8 Kemba Hotel
14 Maskkafarra Hoteeliya
17 Green Pension

PLACES TO EAT
9 Zebib Pastry
13 Filla Minggo Keeke Keetha
    (Pastry Shop); Taxi &
    Minibus Stand

OTHER
1 Stadium
2 Market
3 Aberashshe Girossere
    (Grocery)
4 Post Office (Branch)
5 Souvenir and Art Studio
6 Police
7 Pooto Saroota (Photo Shop)
10 Small Market
11 Ethiopian Airlines
12 Miishsha Keethaa (Bike Hire)
15 Nech Sar Clinic
16 Arrba Minccee Gaaraje
    (Garage)
18 Teachers' Training Institute
19 Arba Minch High School
20 Shell Petrol Station
21 Nechisar National Park HQ
22 St Gabriel's Orthodox
    Church
23 Arba Minch Hospital

Market

Bus Station

To Airports, Crocodile Farm,
Lake Abaya, Chencha,
Shashemene & Addis Ababa

NECHISAR
NATIONAL
PARK

To Medhane Alem Church, Municipality,
Telecommunications Main Office, Mobil
Petrol Station, Arba Minch Water Supplies
Service, Total Petrol Station & Shecha

To
Forty
Springs

buildings are found, as well as most of the
'smart' tourist hotels.

The tourism office (☎ 81-01-86) has enthusiastic staff and keeps the usual business
hours. It can provide guides (Birr50) to the
town, suggest walks and bike rides and give
information on the region. The office can
also help organise boats to Lakes Chamo
and Abaya.

The Commercial Bank exchanges travellers cheques.

Lakes Abaya & Chamo
Measuring 1160 sq km, Lake Abaya is the
longest and the largest of the Rift Valley
lakes. Its peculiar dark red colour is caused
by suspended hydroxide in its waters. The
smaller Lake Chamo (551 sq km) lies to
the south. Both are ringed by savanna
plains, and are considered by many to be
the most beautiful of the Rift Valley lakes.
The ridge of land that divides the two lakes
is known as 'Bridge of God' or 'Heaven'

for the commanding and beautiful views
from it.

On the waters of the lake, look out for the
Guji people in their high-prowed *ambatch*
boats. These boats are constructed of very
thin wooden poles bound together like reeds
and, despite their fragile appearance, they are
capable of carrying several cows at a time.

Forty Springs
Arba Minch (Forty Springs) derives its
name from the innumerable little springs
that bubble up in the evergreen forest covering the flats below the town, at the base of
the escarpment. The forest is the only
ground-water forest in East Africa, and the
semipluvial vegetation provides a good
home for birds and mammals. You can
bathe in the pools around the springs. The
guardian likes to collect the crystal water in
a leaf to show you the pure silver streaks.

For as long as the current conflict with
Eritrea continues and security is seen as

under threat, you'll need to get permission papers to visit the springs from the Arba Minch Water Supplies Service (☎ 81-02-52), next door to the Total petrol station between Sikela and Shecha. It's a simple procedure and doesn't take long. If you arrive at the weekend when the office is closed, you can ask the guardian of the building to dig up someone in the town.

To get to the springs, take the road towards Nechisar National Park. Where the road forks, 1.6km from Sikela, take the road that bears right. The springs are a further 2.8km. You can camp here if you wish; it's also a great place for a picnic.

Crocodile Market

The place to see Lake Chamo's famously large crocodiles is the so-called Azzo Gabaya (Crocodile Market) – Crocodile Beach more like – at the point where the Kolfo River empties into the lake. The site has been called Africa's most impressive display of big crocodiles; they sun themselves on the warm sand of the lakeshore.

Normally the spot can be reached with a 15 to 20 minute boat ride, but it depends on recent rains and the level of water. The boat launching point is down a track to the east off the Konso road, 8km south of the roundabout in Shecha. The best time to go is in the late afternoon, around 4.30 pm, when it's cooler and the crocodiles and birds are feeding. Hippos can also be seen but they are shy, since the local Guji people hunt and eat them. Twitchers may want to take the trip just for the birdlife.

The crocodile market can also be approached by land through the park. However, be very careful when approaching the spot. Fishermen continue to be taken by crocodiles, and increasingly use nets from boats, rather than fishing from the shore. It's a very good idea to bring one of the armed scouts from Nechisar National Park.

Boats can be hired from the Marine Authority (☎ 81-01-97), in the unmarked building opposite the Sports Office, next to the Fish Cooperative, in Shecha. It keeps normal government hours, but if you arrive at the weekend, a local boy can extract an official

from the town. Boats cost Birr300 for up to five people, and Birr600 for up to 10 people.

Crocodile Farm

The government crocodile farm contains around 9000 crocs (living in rather cramped enclosures), soon to be turned into handbags and belts for Middle Eastern markets.

Eggs are collected from the lakeshores, then incubated and hatched at the farm. The crocodiles are slaughtered between the ages of seven and 12 years when their skin is supple but not too soft.

Entrance costs Birr10; the guided tour (30 mins) is free, but you should tip afterwards. The farm is open daily from 8.30 am to 4 pm. It lies off the Addis Ababa road past the old airport 10km from the roundabout at Sikela. You can get a contract taxi here from Arba Minch for Birr20–40.

Market

At the Arba Minch markets, look out for the delightful bamboo *doro beat*, tiny hen houses that look like miniature tukuls; they cost just Birr8. Around town, you'll see them erected on stilts, with thorny acacia branches spread underneath to deter predators.

Fishing

Fishing on the lakes is permitted, but you'll need your own equipment as it can't be hired. Tilapia, catfish and barbus are all found in Lake Chamo, as are the famously large Nile perch (which can weigh more than 100kg). Tigerfish are also found here.

Places to Stay

One of the best budget hotels is the *Kemba Hotel*, which has basic but clean rooms for Birr5. The *Maskkafarra Hoteeliya* has clean rooms for Birr12.

The *Abbaya Hotel* (☎ 81-01-81) has simple but very clean rooms with private bathroom for Birr30. It also does reasonable faranji food, and its garden is a good place for a drink. It's often booked up, and it can be noisy. If it is, the *Green Pension* (☎ 81-04-46) has rooms for Birr15 (Birr20 with bathroom) and makes a peaceful alternative with its large, green area. With rooms at the same price, the *Tesfaye Asfawe Hotel* (☎ 81-00-53), unmarked but opposite the Abbaya Hotel, is adequate.

The *Bekele Mola Hotel* (☎ 81-00-46), just 2.8km from town, has a spectacular position on the edge of a bluff overlooking the lakes and the national park. The panorama must rank among the most spectacular in Ethiopia. Rooms in the little bungalows with private bathroom cost Birr50–70; they're nothing special, but are very clean and peaceful. The restaurant serves quite good faranji food; mains cost Birr12. Camping is permitted in the grounds for Birr20 (including cold shower). It's the perfect place for a beer at sunset. A taxi here costs about Birr20–30.

Places to Eat

The *Soma Quma Keethaa* restaurant, though simple, serves very good local fare. Try the *goden* fish – fried fish in batter. The best fish restaurant in town is considered – appropriately – to be that run by the *Arba Minch Fish Cooperative*, next door to the Marine Authority in Shecha. The fish (Birr5) is very fresh and helpings are generous.

The *Gammo Gagettetha Hoteele*, better known as the 'Asham Hotel', is a local favourite. The *Roza Hotel* does good fish cutlets served with chips and veg and is a pleasant restaurant, half-covered in bougainvillea. The restaurant now charges faranjis more than Ethiopians.

The *Filla Minggo Keeke Keetha* in Sikela is probably the best pastry place in town. Try the speciality, the Turkish-style baklava, dripping in honey (Birr2). Good fruit juices are available too (Birr1.25). The *Zebib Pastry* is also worth a visit.

Getting There & Away

Ethiopian Airlines (☎ 81-06-49) flies from Arba Minch twice a week to Jinka and Addis Ababa. The airport lies 3km out of town, but the airline office is inside the bus station. Sometimes flights are cancelled after rain, since the runway is just a track. A new international airport is currently under construction.

All buses leave from the bus station in Sikela. Buses depart daily for Addis Ababa

(Birr32, 12 hours), Awasa (Birr18, 7½ hours), Chencha (Birr10, two hours), Konso (Birr10, four hours) and Shashemene (Birr17, five hours). Buses go three times a week to Jinka (Birr40, nine hours) via Weyto (Birr30, six hours).

Trucks also go to all of these destinations and cost about Birr5–10 more; they depart from outside the Agip and Shell petrol stations.

Getting Around

Contract taxis (blue minibuses or 4WDs) can be hired in front of the Filla Minggo Keeke Keetha pastry shop in Sikela. Trips to and from the airport cost Birr30 (there's no public transport to or from the airport). They should charge around Birr50 per hour, but you'll need to negotiate.

Frequent minibuses connect Shecha and Sikela and cost Birr1; you just hop on.

The Arrba Minccee Gaaraje (☎ 81-03-62) has three 4WD vehicles for hire for Birr400 per day (all-inclusive, with driver) within the region; for travel outside the region, such as to the Omo Valley, prices go up. Discounts for weekly and low-season rentals – to say Birr350 per day – are negotiable. Make sure that your agreement is clear, and that you extract a promise from the garage that they will send a replacement if you have problems with your vehicle; there have been 'misunderstandings' in the past.

Bikes can be hired in Sikela near the bus station, outside the Miishsha Keethaa general store, and cost Birr40 per day, but prices are negotiable.

NECHISAR NATIONAL PARK

Nechisar means 'White Grass' in Amharic, in reference to the pale savanna plains that stretch over much of the park's 514 sq km. In the early morning and at dusk the grass looks golden, but in the shimmering heat of the midday sun it does seem to turn a kind of white.

Nechisar's name, though evocative, conceals the diversity of the park, which has an incredible range of habitats. The road around the park winds through wide-open savanna, thick bush, acacia woodland and riparian

ETHIOPIA

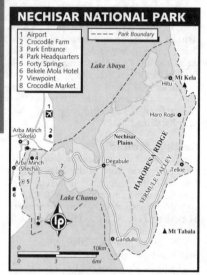

NECHISAR NATIONAL PARK

1 Airport
2 Crocodile Farm
3 Park Entrance
4 Park Headquarters
5 Forty Springs
6 Bekele Mola Hotel
7 Viewpoint
8 Crocodile Market

– – – – Park Boundary

Lake Abaya

Mt Kela
Hitu

Haro Ropi

Arba Minch (Sikela)
Arba Minch (Shecha)

Nechisar Plains

Degabule

Telkie

Lake Chamo

Gandullo

Mt Tabala

0   5   10km
0   3   6mi

forest. Occasionally, lovely views of Lakes Abaya and Chamo open out. With the blue Sidamo hills providing a backdrop, the park is very beautiful; it ranks among the most scenic – yet least visited – in East Africa.

In the forest bushpigs, warthogs, Anubis baboons, genets, bushbucks and vervet monkeys are found. On the savanna plains where animals are most easily seen, the Burchell's zebra is the most conspicuous animal, sometimes seen in herds of 100 or more. You can get close to them and they are a beautiful sight, bucking defiantly or baying as they lope off before the car. The most commonly seen antelopes are the greater kudu, with its beautiful spiralling horns, and the tiny Guenther's dik-dik, which is often seen in pairs, since it is a monogamous animal. The Grant's gazelle, with its horns pointing forward, is also easily seen, as is the endemic Swayne's hartebeest. If you're very lucky you may get to see African hunting dogs and black-backed jackals. Around 70 mammal species are found in the park. Six Abyssinian lions are said to inhabit Nechisar. In the eastern area of the park, keep an eye out for colobus monkeys lurking in the trees.

Like mammals, birds are diverse, reflecting the wide range of habitats; 350 species have been counted including hornbills and bustards. At the edge of the lakes, kingfishers and African fish eagles can be seen.

The local Guji and Koira people inhabit parts of the park; look out for their huts, which resemble haystacks with doors. The neat piles of pebbles that look like round cheeses are burial mounds.

Officially, cattle should not be kept in the park, but you'll see plenty. The people are apprehended only if they kill the wildlife, receiving a prison sentence of between three months and one year. Still, wildlife is killed both for food and to make crafts such as shields. Fierce local disputes continue to flare up between the Guji and the Koira.

The altitude of the park ranges from just 1108m to 1650m. On the plain, it can seem very hot and dusty.

Orientation & Information

The park headquarters lies 1.9km from the roundabout in Sikela, near the entrance to the park. Information and a map are available at the headquarters.

The park is large: a complete circuit covers 120km, while a shortened version covers 85km and takes around 6½ hours to complete, including stops.

Entrance costs Birr50 per person per 48 hours (Birr25 for children up to 12 years old), and a one-off charge of Birr10 is made for vehicles with up to five seats.

Scouts, who act as guides, can be hired for Birr20 per day, but they're not compulsory.

Places to Stay

Though most people stay at Arba Minch, it's possible to camp anywhere in the park. There are two official camping grounds, including one beside the Kulfo River, around 5km from the park headquarters. A fee of Birr20 per person is charged.

Getting Around

A 4WD vehicle is a must for exploration of the park as parts of the road are steep and rocky; in the wet season, mud is the main problem. If a 4WD is beyond your budget, you can still explore the hot springs and dense forests surrounding the Forty Springs. Although these form part of the park, they remain accessible (and free).

DORZE & CHENCHA

Lying 36km to the north of Arba Minch, high up in the Guge Mountains, is the cold, cloudy territory of the Dorze people. Belonging to one of the numerous branches of the Omotic peoples of the south-west, they have become famous for their huge **beehive huts**. The first Dorze huts can be seen around 30km from Arba Minch at the settlement known as Dorze. The Dorze are also skilled farmers who prevent soil erosion of the mountainside with ingenuous terracing.

Some of the country's best woven cotton is reputed to come from Chencha, and some fine cotton *shammas* and *gabis* (togas) can be bought here. Traditionally, it is the men who weave and the women who spin. You can visit the **weaving cooperative** at the village of Gambela Dokko, 1.2km from Chencha, though you'll be expected to pay at least Birr10 if you want to take photos. Gabis cost Birr25–60, depending on the size. The cooperative is open every day except Sunday, from 8 am to 5 pm.

There's a very colourful **market** at Chencha on Tuesday and Saturday, and at Dorze on Monday and Thursday. Woven blankets (Birr80–90), honey (Birr5), traditional woven Dorze trousers (Birr30–60) and decorated gourds (Birr15) can all be bought. The piles of white, mushy dough wrapped in green leaves are enset (see the boxed text 'Enduring Enset' earlier in this section).

Getting There & Away

The journey up to Chencha is worthwhile in itself, and affords some spectacular views over Arba Minch and the Rift Valley lakes. Trucks and 4WDs travel each morning between Chencha and Arba Minch (Birr10, two hours). If you're driving, check the conditions of the road in advance. After rain, the roads becomes a steep and slippery quagmire – even in a 4WD.

> ### Dorze Huts
>
> The famous Dorze hut stands up to 12m high and rises from the landscape like a giant beehive. Constructed with vertical hardwood poles and woven bamboo, it is then topped with a thatched dome of enset leaves. When the fire is lit in the spacious interior, the house appears to smoke. On the outside, a kind of aristocratic nose juts out, serving as a small reception room.
>
> Though fragile-looking, the hut normally lasts up to 60 years. If the roofing gives out, the hut is simply moved and reroofed. Thanks to the vertical poles that make up the structure, the hut is easily transported to a new location. Eventually, rot or termites will get the better of the structure, and the hut will be abandoned.
>
> Each Dorze hut boasts its own little garden containing vegetables, spices and tobacco, as well as enset plantations.

KONSO

The little village of Konso, 90km south of Arba Minch, is well worth a stop. Apart from serving as a base from which to visit the Yabelo Wildlife Sanctuary (see that section earlier), and as a kind of frontier and gateway to the Omo Valley beyond, it also has an ancient, complex and fascinating culture all of its own. Travellers who want to find out more about the Konso people should consult the library of the Institute of Ethiopian Studies (IES) in Addis Ababa (see Libraries in the Addis Ababa section).

At the Monday and Thursday **markets**, look out for the colourful woven cotton 'shorts' (Birr20) and blankets (Birr30). You'll also find tea, millet, tobacco, raw cotton, sweet potatoes, butter, incense and cassava. The giant two-handled pots are for making *tella* (home-brewed beer). If you're lucky, you may come across some lovely old Konso glass beads.

A large Ethio-Japanese archaeological venture known as the Konso Gardula Project is currently underway just outside Konso. Human fossils dating from between 1.3 and

ETHIOPIA

The People of Konso

Until quite recently, outside influence was almost unknown to the people of Konso. A pagan society with a complex age-grading system similar to that of the Oromos, these people boast a rich culture and a highly specialised and successful agricultural economy.

The beautifully constructed, buttressed stone terraces have allowed the Konso to eke out a living from the dry, unyielding land around them. Surrounding the Konso villages and fields are sturdy stone walls, which serve as a defence against straying cattle and flash flooding, as well as against unwelcome visitors. Visitors are compelled to enter a Konso house, via a wooden tunnel, on hands and knees – a compromising position should the intruder turn out to be a foe.

When Konso warriors die, they are honoured with the erection of a series of carved wooden sculptures – the famous Konso *waga*. The waga is designed according to a strict formula. The 'hero' is usually distinguishable by the phallic ornamental *khalasha* worn on his forehead (traditionally denoting the chief) or by his slightly larger size. Placed on either side of the hero are between two and four of his wives (identifiable by necklaces and breasts) and the hero's slain enemies (usually smaller and without phallic symbols), or animals (such as leopards) that the hero has killed. Occasionally a monkey-like figure stands at the feet of the hero, and sometimes his spears and shields are included too. The eyes of the figures are usually represented with shells or ostrich eggshells, the teeth with the bones of goats.

Unfortunately, waga erection is dying out. The widespread theft and removal of the statues to Addis Ababa for sale to diplomats and tourists (for between Birr15,000 and Birr20,000), as well as the work of missionaries who are against ancestor worship, has discouraged the continuance of the ancient tradition.

1.9 million years ago have already been unearthed. The site may well be declared a Unesco World Heritage Site in the future, and

there are plans eventually to build a museum to exhibit the finds.

On arrival in Konso, visitors are supposed to report to the Culture, Information & Tourism Office to pay an obligatory Birr30 camera fee. With the permit issued, you are then free to photograph any village in the vicinity of Konso; you may well be asked for proof of the permit. Video cameras are – strangely – not allowed since it's thought that they 'kill tourism' by removing the need for travel. There's no bank in Konso.

Places to Stay & Eat

The *Kiddus Maryam Hotel* (also known as the St Mary Hotel) is considered the best hotel in town and has rooms for Birr15; there's a shared shower. The *Konso Wubet Hotel* and the *Arbera Hotel* have the best restaurants. The *Nice Hotel* is a good place for a drink in the evening.

Getting There & Away

Trucks and 4WDs run to Yabelo (Birr3, six hours) on Monday and Thursday (tying in with market days) at 1 pm. One bus and various trucks leave daily for Arba Minch (Birr10, three hours) and for Weyto (Birr10, two hours). For Jinka, you can sometimes hop on the Jinka bus coming from Arba Minch (if there are any seats left). It passes through Konso on Monday and Wednesday. Occasionally, private vehicles go to Turmi.

AROUND KONSO

With your own vehicle, a popular excursion from Konso is to the village of Gesergio (pronounced gas-**ag**-ee-yo), popularly known as 'New York'. According to local tradition, thieves once stole some sacred drums and buried them at Gesergio temporarily. All the people of the village prayed for help to get them back, and God himself came down to retrieve them, excavating them with his own hands from the soil. New York was left – an extraordinary landscape of sand pinnacles formed by the wind and rain. New York lies 16km from Konso. It's possible to walk down from the village among the pinnacles.

Around Konso, you can also visit various Konso villages where the famous wagas can be seen (see the boxed text 'The People of Konso'), including Machekie (9km from Gesergio) and Arfaide (19km from Konso). In 1997, local thieves working with antique dealers in Addis Ababa stole around 60 of the villages' best statues. A French team from the Centre Français des Etudes Ethiopiennes is currently carrying out an inventory of the statues, and nailing metal tags to their reverse sides. If you don't have a vehicle, but want to see the statues, the Culture, Information & Tourism Office in Konso has some in a locked shed for safekeeping.

JINKA

Jinka, at 1490m, feels like a breath of fresh air after the close, steamy and muddy confines of the lowlands. It is the nearest town to the Omo and Mago National Parks and lies 138km from Konso. After a foray into the Omo, Jinka can seem like Paris.

Though it serves as the administrative centre of the South Omo Zone, Jinka still retains a very small-town feel. Its grassy airstrip is situated in the very centre of the village. It doubles as the town's football pitch and as tasty pasture for the local cows in the evening; both players and cows are cleared from the airstrip on the arrival or departure of a plane.

Although the town boasts a bank, its services are rather erratic, depending on the reliability of electricity (in theory, there's electricity in town from 6.30 am to midnight) and the photocopy machines. Sometimes it's not possible to change either cash or travellers cheques.

Jinka has a couple of petrol stations (although supplies are sometimes erratic), a good garage (John Garage opposite the South Omo Transport & Communication Office to the south-west of town) and an Ethiopian Airlines office (opposite the Orit Hotel in the 'airport area').

The large and very colourful Saturday market is well worth a visit. You can expect to come across a number of different ethnic groups, among them the Ari, Hamer, Banna, Karo, Koygu and Bodi (see the boxed text 'Peoples of the Lower Omo Valley' later in this section). From Jinka, you can do a day trip to Mursi territory, around 60km from the town.

Places to Stay & Eat

Rocky Recreation Campsite on the edge of town charges Birr10 per person and per car, and has a couple of showers.

The **Omo Hotel**, opposite the Orit Hotel, is about the cleanest of the budget hotels with rooms with private cold shower for Birr10.

The **Orit Hotel** (☎ 45) is one of the best hotels in town, with clean rooms with private cold shower for Birr20; there's also quite a good restaurant serving both local and faranji food. You can camp in the pleasant grounds with use of a shower for Birr10. The hotel can provide a guide to the surrounding area for around Birr40–50 per day. Cars can be hired here for Birr800–900 per day, all-inclusive. In the future, the hotel will also rent out camping equipment. The friendly owner is also happy to give local information on the area, including advice on itineraries, current road conditions and distances between places.

The **Goh Hotel** (☎ 33) is another good place, with similar rooms and prices. It's also considered one of the best places to eat.

For local food, the **Hirut Hotel** (also known as Busca) is good; it lies not far from the South Omo Transport & Communication Office. There are several small **grocery stores**, including one opposite the Orit Hotel. If you haven't already stocked up for a camping trip, Jinka is your last chance.

For music and dancing, the **Dejene Hotel and Restaurant**, diagonally opposite the Commercial Bank, is a popular place.

Getting There & Away

Ethiopian Airlines flies to Jinka via Arba Minch three times weekly. Sometimes flights are cancelled in the wet season because of the weather. In the future, a new airport will be built 5km from town.

A weekly bus does the run between Jinka and Kako (Birr3, 50 mins), Key Afar (Birr6, 1½ hours), Weyto (Birr20, 2½ hours), Konso (Birr30, 4½ hours) and Arba Minch (Birr40, 6½ hours).

Trucks also leave Jinka for Konso (Birr30, daily) and Key Afar (Birr5, every Thursday). After Jinka's main market on Saturday, they leave for Turmi (Birr25, seven hours) via Dimeka (Birr20, six hours).

Various government and missionary cars also circulate in the region; they will usually give you lifts, but you should make a contribution for fuel. The Mobil and Agip petrol stations are good places for looking for lifts. Many trucks leave from in front of the Orit and Omo Hotels, and in front of the large *warka* (sycamore fig) tree in the village.

Bob Travel (☎ 58), located in the same building as the post office, rents 4WDs for US$175 per day, all-inclusive. To be sure of having transport you should contact the owner, Fikre Markos Desta, in advance (Bob Travel, PO Box 14, Jinka, South Omo Region). He sometimes works as a guide and has an excellent knowledge of the region, as well as useful contacts.

LOWER OMO VALLEY

The vast Omo River meanders for nearly 1000km from south-west of Addis Ababa, all the way to Lake Turkana in Kenya;

Body Decoration

Though the people of the Omo lack any form of advanced material culture, they have nevertheless developed art forms that allow them great artistic expression, as well as serving important social and cosmetic purposes. The practice of body painting and scarification developed by the tribes is among the most ornate and extravagant seen anywhere in the world.

For most of the Omo tribes, scarification serves as a distinction for brave warriors; the men are not allowed to scarify themselves until after they have killed at least one foe. For the women, the raised texture of the skin is considered highly desirable, and is said to hold great sensual value for the men.

Scarification is achieved using a stone, knife, simple hook or razor blade. Ash is then rubbed into the wound, creating a small infection and promoting scar tissue growth. As the wound heals, the raised scar creates the desired knobbly effect on the surface of the skin.

there, it is the sole feeder of East Africa's fourth-largest lake.

Before it reaches Turkana, the Omo carves out the border between the old provinces of Kafa and Gamo-Gofa. Here lie Ethiopia's largest, wildest and most inaccessible parks: the Omo National Park on the west bank, and Mago National Park on the east.

Wild, undisturbed and little visited, the parks boast not only remarkable wildlife, but also remarkable peoples. It is here that some of the most fascinating and colourful ethnic groups of the country are to be found (see the boxed text 'Peoples of the Lower Omo Valley').

Many of the peoples' ancient customs and traditions have remained almost entirely intact. Animism is still the peoples' religion, and some still practise a purely pastoral economy. Hostility between neighbouring tribes is still high and internecine warfare is common.

The Lower Omo Valley landscape is diverse, ranging from the dry, open savanna plains to the riverine forest that borders the Omo and Mago Rivers. Mammals that

THE LOWER OMO VALLEY

make their home here include giraffes, zebras, oryx, greater and lesser kudus, tiangs, hartebeests, elands, waterbucks, gazelles and gerenuks. Lions, buffalos and elephants also inhabit the area. Primates include colobus, vervet, De Brazza's and patas monkeys, as well as Anubis baboons.

Unfortunately, after years of hunting and continued poaching, the animals are shy and are not often seen. Visitors hoping for a Kenya- or Tanzania-type safari will be disappointed, but the parks do offer something unique: an unforgettable glimpse into the pre-colonial, pre-tourism days of Africa.

When visiting the villages of the Lower Omo Valley, try and coincide with at least one market day (see the boxed text 'Market Day in the Omo Valley'); the markets are not to be missed.

Dangers & Annoyances

The whole Lower Omo Valley is still an incredibly remote place – one of the reasons it has remained so 'unchanged', and undoubtedly one of its attractions. Road conditions are rough. Annual rainfall at 500mm to 800mm is quite high and quickly turns the tracks into quagmires. There is nothing in the world quite like the thick, black, oozing Omo mud, and a journey after even light rain can result in your vehicle getting stuck again and again on a single journey.

Tsetse flies are a big problem in some areas, particularly in the wet season or after rain. Mago National Park is probably the worst area, along with village of Makki in Mursi country. Malaria is endemic in some parts of the region, particularly south of Key Afar; precautions are essential (see Health in the Ethiopia Facts for the Visitor chapter). A doctor is available in Jinka, but the nearest hospital is in Arba Minch.

For many ethnic groups, raiding is a part of life – a means of survival in a very harsh environment. In the Karo language, the word for 'thief' doesn't exist, and children are encouraged to pilfer from a young age – they're only beaten if they're caught out. Belongings disappearing from visitors' tents has been a problem in the past. Some of the peoples are master thieves: things can disappear before

Market Day in the Omo Valley

A terrific way of seeing some of the colourful Omo people is at the local markets. Try to get there between 10.30 am and 2 pm; some of the peoples have long journeys to or from the markets. The most interesting ones include:

Dimeka	Tuesday & Saturday
Jinka	Saturday
Key Afar	Thursday
Konso	Monday & Saturday
Turmi	Monday
Yabelo	Saturday

your very eyes in broad daylight. Camps should never be left unattended, and all jewellery including watches is best removed before you mingle with some groups such as the Mursi. It's not just faranjis who are targeted either (see the boxed text 'A Trip to Visit the Mursi' later in this section).

Some travellers may be disappointed or even shocked by the seemingly mercenary nature of the different peoples. However, the local people have a right to benefit from the 'encounter' as much as you do, and should benefit, like Ethiopians elsewhere, from tourism. In fact, business goes on as always, only it's money bargained for photos instead of money bargained for crops. Tourism may even help to sustain the groups economically and preserve their traditions.

Many tribes now demand at least Birr2 for photos, and you'll probably be asked for more. Some people, particularly the Mursi, have got very good at intimidating tourists – by throwing hysterics, shouting, or even grabbing your hands and not letting go. Just be firm and polite, stay calm and keep smiling. Ideally, get your guide, if you have one, to negotiate for all photos in advance. The following tips may also help ease your visit:

- Give practical gifts instead of money: coffee, razor blades, soap, salt and beads are all very appreciated.
- Bring with you a good stash of *new* Birr1 notes; noses are often turned up at old ones.
- Remember that however much you want to see a dance, the request is a pretty unnatural one for

ETHIOPIA

Peoples of the Lower Omo Valley

The Lower Omo Valley is almost unique in the world in that so many different peoples inhabit such a tiny area. Historians believe that the south served for millennia as a kind of cultural crossroads, where quite different ethnic peoples – Cushitic, Nilotic, Omotic and Semitic – met as they migrated from the north, west, south and east. The peoples of the Lower Omo Valley are considered among the most fascinating on the African continent.

The Ari

The Ari inhabit the northern border of Mago National Park and have a population of around 100,000 people. They keep large numbers of livestock and produce large amounts of honey, often used for trade. The women wear skirts made from the enset tree.

The Banna

The Banna are believed to number around 35,000; they inhabit the higher ground to the east of Mago National Park. Most practise agriculture, though their diet is supplemented by hunting. If they manage to kill a buffalo, they decorate themselves with clay and put on a special celebration and feast for the whole village.

The Bodi

Numbering around 2500, the Bodi are agro-pastoralists and their language is Nilo-Saharan in origin. They inhabit the north-east edge of Omo National Park.

The Bumi

The Bumi, numbering around 6000, inhabit the land south of the Omo National Park, but sometimes invade the southern plains when grazing or water is scarce.

Like the Bodi, the Bumi are agro-pastoralists, growing sorghum by the Omo and Kibish Rivers as well as fishing and rearing cattle. They also hunt in the park and smoke bees out of their hives. They are known as great warmongers, at war with almost everyone, particularly the Karo, the Hamer and the Surma.

The Bumi use scarification for cosmetic purposes, tribal identification and as indications of prowess in battle. Both men and women use little *pointilles* or dots to highlight their eyes and cheekbones. The women also scarify their torsos with curvilinear and geometrical designs.

The Dizi

Inhabiting the north-west edge of Omo National Park, the Dizi are sedentary agriculturists, cultivating sorghum, root crops and coffee. They also practise terracing on the mountain slopes.

The Hamer

The Hamer, who number around 30,000, are subsistence agro-pastoralists. They cultivate sorghum, vegetables, millet, tobacco and cotton, as well as rearing cattle and goats. Wild honey is an important part of their diet.

The people are known both for their fine pottery and their remarkable hairstyling. The women mix animal fat with ochre and rub the mixture into their hair to create coppery-coloured strands.

If they have recently killed an enemy or a dangerous animal, the men are permitted to don clay hair buns that often support magnificent ostrich feathers. The buns – with the help of a special headrest for sleeping – last from three to six months, and can be redone for up to one year.

The Hamer are also considered the masters of body decoration. Every adornment has an important symbolic significance, eg, earrings denote the number of wives a man possesses.

Peoples of the Lower Omo Valley

The women wear bead necklaces, iron coils around their arms and skins decorated with cowry shells. The iron torques around their necks are known as *ensente* and are worn by married or engaged women only. They indicate the wealth and prestige of a woman's husband. Young, unmarried girls wear a metal plate in their hair that looks a bit like a platypus's bill.

The Hamer territory stretches across the plains of the Lower Omo to Chew Bahir in the east, almost to the Kenyan border in the south, and to the territory of the Banna in the north.

The Karo

The Karo people are thought to be one of the most endangered groups of the Omo, with a population of about 1000 people. They inhabit the eastern bank of the Omo. They were formerly pastoralists, but many of their cattle have been wiped out by disease, and many have turned to agriculture.

In appearance, language and tradition, they slightly resemble the Hamer, to whom they are related. The Karo are considered the masters of body painting, in which they engage when preparing for a dance, feast or celebration. Most famously, chalk is used to imitate the spotted plumage of the guinea fowl.

The Karo are also great improvisers: Bic Biros, nails, sweets wrappers and cartridges are all incorporated into jewellery and decoration. Yellow mineral rock, black charcoal and pulverised red iron ore are traditionally used.

The Koygu

The Koygu (also known as the Muguji) inhabit the junction of the Omo and Mago Rivers. They commonly grow sorghum, and collect wild fruit, berries and honey. The Koygu are known for fishing and for hunting the hippo, which they eat. They use both guns and traps for hunting.

The Mursi

Perhaps the best known of the Omo peoples are the Mursi, the subject of a number of recent TV documentaries. The Mursi, thought to number around 5000, are mainly pastoralists who move according to the seasons between the lower Tama Steppe and the Mursi Hills in Mago National Park.

Some Mursi practise flood retreat cultivation, particularly in the areas where the tsetse fly prohibits cattle rearing. Honey is collected from beehives made with bark and dung. The Mursi language is Nilo-Saharan in origin.

The most famous Mursi traditions include the lip plate worn by the women, and the fierce stick fighting between the men.

The Surma

Formerly nomadic pastoralists, the Surma now largely depend upon the subsistence cultivation of sorghum and maize. The Surma have a fearsome reputation as warriors, in part inspired by their continual search for grazing lands. Fights against the Bumi, their sworn enemies, still occur.

It is believed that the Surma once dominated the area, but their territory has been reduced to an area stretching along the western edges of the Omo National Park, in the hills around Maji and along the Kibish River. They are believed to number around 40,000, and are split into three subgroups: the Chai, Tirma and Bale. The Surma hunt in the park and make beehive huts. Like the Mursi, the Surma men are famous for their stick fighting, the Surma women for their lip plates.

The Surma are known for their white, almost ghostlike body painting. White chalk is mixed with water to create a kind of wash. The painting is much less ornamental than that found in other tribes and is intended to intimidate enemies in battle. Sometimes snake and wavelike patterns are painted across the torso and thighs.

the peoples. Most dances celebrate special occasions, such as a harvest, or the death of an elder; don't insist, and be sensitive when taking photos. Around Birr300 is usually asked, which is not excessive when you consider that it will be shared among the whole village.

Omo Valley Villages

A good itinerary which gives you a glimpse of some of the ethnic groups, as well as diverse scenery, begins in Konso and takes you through the little villages of Weyto, Arbore, Turmi, Dimeka and Jinka, and Mago National Park.

The little village of **Weyto** lies halfway between Konso and Key Afar. The Tsemay, part farmers, part pastoralists, inhabit the region. Just after Weyto, there's a junction; take the road that branches south-west towards the village of **Arbore**.

The Arbore people resemble the Borena people, with their bead and aluminium jewellery. The people sleep on 5m-high platforms to try and escape the mosquitoes, which are notorious here; locals outside the village know it as 'mosquito town'.

South of Arbore, off the main Arbore-Turmi road, tracks lead to the strange saline lake of **Chew Bahir** (also known as Lake Stephanie). From Arbore to the junction of the main track, it's a 35km drive. From the junction to the lake it's a further 60km. Oryx and gazelles are sometimes found near the lake, though they are not as numerous as they once were. The ground around the lake is notoriously unstable – in fact the 'lake' is more of a flooded marsh, so a guide is essential for approaching the lake or walking around it. You should take a policeman-guide from Arbore (Birr50 per day). When it is totally dried out, you can drive on the lake's surface. January to December is the best time for a visit.

After the Weyto Valley, the road enters Hamer territory. Just over 3km outside the town of Turmi, look out for the pump and well at the side of the road, close to the Wadi Kaske. Local Hamer women come from miles around to fetch water from the well.

Nearby, on the other side of the road, there's a pleasant spot to *camp*, though the trees that once provided shade are being cut down fast. If you do camp here, watch all your possessions – things have been known to disappear. It's a very good idea to employ a Hamer guard from Turmi (Birr30 per 24 hours). The camp site is also a very good spot for **birds**, which populate the acacia trees and tamarinds lining the wadi.

At **Turmi** itself, the main town of the Hamer, the Monday market is a must. The main square fills with Hamer market-goers, selling vegetables, spices, butter and milk. It's a great place for picking up the beautiful incised gourds, which are used by the local women as shopping baskets and as a sort of handbag for stashing cash. If you spot one you like, you can probably negotiate for it. Make sure you check inside; sometimes they still contain money, little photos or other items women keep in their bags!

Also worth a peek is the excellent Hamer Traditional Goods, a souvenir shop next door to the Gulilat Haile Hotel in Turmi. There's a good selection of high quality and authentic souvenirs at not bad prices. You can buy yourself a traditional – and fantastically smelly – goatskin decorated with beads and cowry shells, if you fancy. Incised gourds, *dola* (milk containers) and jewellery are also for sale.

South-west of Turmi, the road continues to **Omorate**, marked on some maps as Kelem, where there is a small but lively daily market. This is Mursi territory. Here you could cross the Omo River by car ferry and enter the Omo National Park, until the ferry fell into disuse.

A worthwhile detour is to the camp of **Murle**. Here Ethiopian Rift Valley Safaris has established a beautiful, shady camp on the banks of the Omo. Facilities include a restaurant (usually for clients only), safari cars and boats. There are also rather pricey but very comfortable bungalows (with private bathroom). Camping costs US$8 per person (no charge for Ethiopian drivers and guides). Reservations in Addis Ababa are essential; you can't just roll up (see Organised Tours in the Getting Around section earlier in this chapter).

Close by, there are a couple of Karo villages, such as **Kolcho**, just north of Murle. There's a lovely camp site on the plateau overlooking the Omo River and Valley, but hiring a guard from the local village (Birr50 per 24 hours) is essential, as theft is big problem here.

Around 1km from Kolcho is a lake which is a great spot for birdwatching or fishing. The Bumi village of **Kanga** can also be visited from Murle; it's around half an hour's drive from the camp. You should take a guide from Murle for all these places.

At the village of **Dus**, around 20km from Murle, you can arrange to see traditional dancing, though it'll cost you at least Birr500.

The road from Murle back to Turmi traverses a beautiful savanna plain where oryx and Grant's gazelles are frequently seen. This whole area is known as the **Murle Controlled Hunting Area**, and is the one area where wildlife reaches more normal density levels; there are far more animals reported here than at Mago National Park (it says much for the role controlled hunting now has in conservation). It is hoped that other species, such as giraffes, black rhinos and zebras, will be reintroduced in the future.

There are also 340 bird species in the region. Look out for the delightful carmine bee-eaters, which fly alongside your car and snap up the insects stirred up by the wheels. Honey guides are also quite a common sight, trying to lure you off to a nearby beehive. The clouds of little quail-like birds are red-billed queleas; they explode like popcorn from the grass as your car passes.

Mago National Park

Mago National Park measures 2162 sq km. Parts of the park lie at just 450m, and temperatures can reach 41°C. The park was originally created to protect the plains animals, and boasts, in theory, an exotic collection, including buffalos, lions, leopards, elephants and giraffes. In practice, widespread poaching in the area keeps populations down, so animal viewing is not what it might be – or what it's made out to be in the tourist literature.

Mammals more commonly seen are Burchell's zebra, the greater and lesser kudus and the gerenuk. Topis and Lelwel hartebeest are also sometimes seen. Occasionally, very large herds of buffalo are reported, usually close to sources of water.

The tiny visitors' centre at the park headquarters contains some information panels, maps and the usual dead animals – skulls and skins.

Park entrance costs Birr50 per person and Birr20 per tent, per day. Vehicle entrance costs Birr10 (once only). Hang onto your ticket; you will be asked to show it at the park barrier, 26km from the park headquarters. The headquarters also provides day and night guards (Birr40 per 24 hours); they're essential if you're leaving your belongings and tents unattended, and they will also collect water and dead firewood, if you want it. You can also find a guide to take you looking for wildlife such as buffalo.

The 'camping grounds' at Mago National Park consist of little more than clearings. The so-called Buffalo Camp, beside the Neri River, is considered the most pleasant.

Mago National Park can be reached via a track from Jinka. No public transport runs here, and almost no trucks. You really need your own vehicle to reach the park.

Mursi Territory

About 6km from the headquarters of Mago National Park, a track to the left used to cross a bridge over the Mago River and lead to the Mursi Hills (shown on some maps as the Ngalibong Mountains) and into Mursi territory. The bridge was broken in 1997 and the local government has yet to fix it. In the meantime, the Mursi settlements such as Omo Mursi remain inaccessible to vehicles. The village of Haile Woha lies 35km from the river; from this village, which lies at a junction, it's a further 37km to Omo Mursi and 45km to Hana Mursi.

From Mago National Park, you can get to the edge of the Mago River (around two hours' drive) and close to the Mursi settlement across the river. You can either wade across (sometimes it can be quite deep and strongly flowing) or wait for the locals to

A Trip to Visit the Mursi

'OK, 10 minutes and then we're out of there', Abraha the driver said with great authority.

'Ten minutes? But why?' I asked.

'You don't know the Mursi. They are thieves', he said, 'Thieves!' raising his voice for extra effect.

'Oh come on, Abraha, opportunists maybe… '

'They would even take the shoes from your feet, I tell you', Abraha continued.

'You mean the shirt from your back? Well, no matter…but 10 minutes?' Abraha's attitude seemed typical of the Ethiopians' innate xenophobia – even towards fellow Ethiopians from a different ethnic group.

We were off that day to the Lower Omo River in southern Ethiopia, home to several Nilotic-Omotic peoples including the Mursi, considered among the most fascinating and colourful tribes on earth.

'Of all of them, the Mursi, they are the bad ones', Abraha went on. 'And you know what?' Abraha looked away, deeply embarrassed. 'They don't wear any clothing! They are savages, savages!' he said, raising his voice again.

I had seen photos of the Mursi; they were magnificent: unusually tall and dark, and quite naked except for a long spear or an AK-47 rifle slung over a shoulder. Scarification of the body was common, not just for ornamentation, but also to indicate prowess in battle and the number of enemies killed. Internecine warfare was still rife in this part of the world; just two months ago, Galeb warriors (from Old Omo, 20km north of Omorate) had made incursions into Hamer territory to steal cattle; the Hamer then retaliated by invading Galeb territory. Around a dozen warriors were killed.

'And the women!' Abraha went on, 'Plates…plates', he said, pulling at his lower lip.

Clay lip plates – often quite large – are a distinguishing feature of the Mursi women, inserted into slits in their lower lips. Anthropologists offer several theories to explain the practice: the lip plates are to deter slavers looking for unblemished girls; to prevent evil from entering the body by way of the mouth; or to indicate social status by showing the number of cattle required by the wearer's family for her hand in marriage.

find you; word of dollar-clutching tourists soon gets around. The road even to this point is very variable and is often impassable. Check conditions at the park headquarters before setting out.

Omo National Park

In terms of habitat and the animals that make their home here, Omo National Park is very similar to Mago National Park, though its wildlife is almost certainly more prolific.

Currently, the only access to Omo National Park is by plane, from Addis Ababa to Tum. There are no vehicles for hire in Tum, so walking is the only option. You'll need to be totally self sufficient. Guides and mules can be found in Tum. You should register upon your arrival at the police station in Tum and check out the security situation in the region.

In the past, the park was accessible by car ferry, which forded the Omo River from Omorate, outside the park. Unfortunately, the ferry has fallen into disuse in recent years, but you can inquire about its status at the National Tour Operation or NTO (☎ 01-15-17-22) in Addis Ababa. In the future, roads will be built to make the park more accessible.

On the western side, a new road to the park from Maji is currently under construction. In the future, the road will also provide access to the Surma region in the western valley of the Omo River.

Places to Stay & Eat

Most of the villages of the Lower Omo Valley are without electricity and have only very basic hotels: rooms with dirt floors, no showers and sometimes earth 'beds'. Camping is the best bet. If you don't have

A Trip to Visit the Mursi

Tradition remained remarkably intact here; undoubtedly because of the inaccessibility of the region. The journey had certainly been a long and arduous one. From the outset, our party of two 4WDs had taken it in turns to tow each other out of the thick, glutinous mud. It covered everything – the cars, our clothing, faces, hair. Our knuckles and fingertips bled from the constant digging. The heat was stifling too and swarms of tsetse flies bit mercilessly. Radiators boiled over, cooling pipes exploded and tyres punctured.

As we pulled into the first Mursi village at last, Abraha gave some final words of warning: 'So remember, we take off all watches, we lock all doors, and we stay awake. Ten minutes', he added firmly.

We left 3½ hours later. Our car had got stuck in the mud again. But the Mursi had proved to be a sociable, entertaining and resourceful people, with a fabulous sense of humour.

As we left, Abraha in a dismal voice started to make an inventory of 'Things Missed'.

'One car aerial', he began.

'One lens cover', I joined in.

'One shovel.'

'One Bic Biro.'

'Nearly one spare tyre.'

'Nearly one bra' (curious Mursi women).

'Some rope.'

'Some hairs from my head' (curious Mursi men).

'Some shoes from the driver's feet.'

'What?' I inquired.

It seemed Abraha's shoes had disappeared from right under his nose as he lay them out to dry on the bonnet of the car.

'You see?' he said resignedly. 'They take even the shoes from your feet.'

From the Author's Diary

tents, some of the following villages have hotels, and can usually rustle up something to eat as well.

In Weyto, there are no hotels, but you can *camp* opposite the Breiley Hotel (in fact a restaurant).

In Key Afar, the *Abebe Hotel* is the best bet (Birr5).

At Turmi, the *Gulilat Haile Hotel* is the best choice. Rooms cost Birr5 and there's a shared shower and restaurant. Because of the heat, some travellers hire a room in which to leave their belongings, and take their bed outside into the compound (Birr10 per tent). You can also camp near Wadi Kaske, 3km outside of Turmi (see Omo Valley Villages earlier).

At Omorate, the best choice is the *National Hotel* with rooms for Birr10 with mosquito net; buckets of water are available for washing. Quite good food is also avail-

able. You can camp in the compound of the *Tourist Hotel* or *Adama Hotel*.

At Dimeka, the *Ashabir Hotel* is the largest hotel, with rooms for Birr5; there's no communal shower.

Getting There & Around

The best time to visit the Lower Omo Valley is during the dry season, from July to August and December to January, because roads can become impassable in the wet season. In recent years, however, the rains have been very erratic and unpredictable. No public transport goes to Mago or Omo National Parks.

Bus & Truck A small amount of public transport (mainly pick-up trucks) connects the villages in the Omo Valley. The best thing is to use the local transport connecting towns on market days. If you're planning to use local transport for travel, you'll need weeks on your hands.

From Addis Ababa, one bus usually runs three times a week to Arba Minch and Jinka then back again, depending on the weather. From Arba Minch a bus runs once a week to Konso, Key Afar and Jinka and back again.

Pick-up trucks, however, do link the villages a bit more frequently. Interconnected villages include Weyto, Key Afar, Arbore, Turmi, Omorate and Dimeka.

Organised Tours If you're alone or in a couple, the cheapest alternative to public transport is to try and tag onto a tour group. These are not regularly scheduled, so you're best advised to check as far in advance as possible with the travel agencies in Addis Ababa, and organise your itinerary around that (see Organised Tours in the Getting Around chapter). Tours are not cheap compared with 'safaris' offered in other East African countries, but if you can afford one, the opportunity is not to be missed. Most tours last a minimum of 10 days, but also take in the Rift Valley lakes, Awasa and Arba Minch.

4WD Rental Hiring a 4WD and driver in Addis Ababa is tantamount to organising a tailor-made tour. It's a very good idea to try and hook up with another car party and arrange to travel in convoy. If one member of the expedition gets stuck in the mud, then at least the other can attempt to extract you. All the usual equipment for a full expedition applies (see the boxed text 'Expedition Equipment' in the Getting Around chapter).

Make very sure that your vehicle is adequately equipped before you leave Addis Ababa. A guide – or at least a knowledgeable driver – is essential. Sometimes the roads are little more than mule tracks that lose themselves in the savanna or clearings through the jungle. If you do get stuck, and you're within a 10km radius of Mago National Park, a tractor can help pull you out, or one of the 4WDs that are equipped with winches and ropes.

Extra fuel is essential – at least 150–200L (for some 500km). The last sure sources of petrol are Konso and Jinka. After Konso and Jinka, you should depend on your own water, and your own food is useful outside the villages.

A local guide who knows the area quite well is Dinote Kusia Shenkere, who can be located at the Culture, Information & Tourism Office in Konso. He doesn't come cheap, and now charges Birr100 per day. The ETC 1:2,000,000 map is barely adequate but there's no other available.

SOUTH-EAST TO THE BALE MOUNTAINS

The agricultural town of **Asela** makes a convenient overnight stop en route to the Bale Mountains, but if you can bus straight through to Dinsho or Goba, do. Most of Asela's hotels are fleapits. The best bet is the newish *Hooteela Bezaa* off the main road down from the Ras Hotel, which has clean rooms for Birr10 (Birr15 with hot shower). The *Reesstoorantii Fellaqach* opposite the bus station is a local favourite for food.

If, on the other hand, you should get stuck in **Dodola**, the large *Bale Mountain Hotel* on the approach to town (from Nazret) has decent rooms for Birr15–30.

Buses travel from Asela to Nazret (Birr5, two hours, six to 10 daily), Addis Ababa (Birr11.50, five hours, one daily) and Dodola (Birr13, six hours, two daily). For Dinsho, change at Dodola.

From Dodola, over 20 buses run daily to Shashemene (Birr8, three hours). For Dinsho, buses run according to demand, but 15 buses run daily to Adaba (Birr3, 30 mins), about halfway to Dinsho. At both Dodola and Adaba, you can sometimes hop on one of the four daily buses running from Addis Ababa or Nazret to Goba, if there's space.

BALE MOUNTAINS NATIONAL PARK

More than any other park in Ethiopia, the Bale Mountains are known for their wildlife. Over 60 mammal species have been recorded, and over 260 bird species.

The scenery, though less spectacular than in the Simien Mountains, is no less beautiful. Rivers cut deep gorges through the plateaus, and streams, waterfalls and alpine lakes are quite common features of the landscape. In the lower hills, Highlanders canter along century-old paths on their richly caparisoned horses, and the noise of shepherd boys cracking their whips echoes around the valley. Among the abundant wildflowers, beautiful birds such as the malachite and Tacazze sunbirds flit about.

If the Simiens with their spectacular gorges are a trekker's paradise, the Bale Mountains with their gentle, rolling hills are a walker's heaven.

Geography
The national park stretches over 2400 sq km and ranges in altitude from 1500m to 4377m.

The Harenna Escarpment splits the park in two, running fracture-like from east to west. To the north-east of the escarpment lies the high-altitude plateau known as the Sanetti Plateau. Lying at 4000m, it is broken by a series of volcanic plugs and small peaks, including Tullu Deemtu, which at 4377m is the highest point in southern Ethiopia.

To the south, the land gradually falls away from the plateau, and a thick heather belt gives way to heavily forested areas known collectively as the Harenna Forest.

Climate
On the plateau, temperatures range from 10° to 26°C depending on the time of year. The dry season has the highest range of temperatures: it can get quite hot in the daytime, while at night, frost and even snow are sometimes reported.

The wet season has more moderate temperatures. Most rain falls between March and October, and the annual rainfall is high: an average of 1150mm.

Flora
The park can be divided into three main zones. The northern area of the park, around

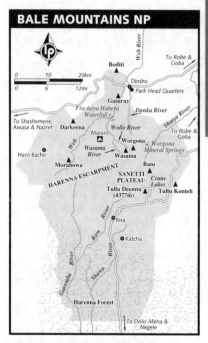

the park headquarters at Dinsho, consists of grassy, riverine plains and bushland, most commonly sagebrush and St John's wort. From 2500m to 3300m, woodland is found, most often *Hagenia abyssinica* and *Juniperus procera*. The abundant wildflowers in the area include geranium, lobelias and alchemilla.

Higher up, montane grassland gives way to heather. Here the plant can be found not only as little bushes, but as large and mature trees.

The second zone, the Sanetti Plateau, is home to typical Afro-alpine plants, some of which have adapted to the extreme conditions by either remaining very small or becoming very large. The best known is the curious-looking giant lobelia (*Lobelia rhynchopetalum*), which can reach 5m in height. The *Helichrysum* or 'everlasting' flowers are the dominant wildflowers. Keep an eye out for the indigenous Abyssinian rose, with its lovely subtle scent.

ETHIOPIA

The Ethiopian Wolf

The Ethiopian wolf *(Canis simensis)* is the rarest canid (dog family member) in the world. Found only in the Ethiopian highlands, it is thought to be on the verge of extinction. Only 700 wolves are believed to remain in the whole country.

Wolves are found on both sides of the Rift Valley, in the old provinces of Gonder, Wolo, Menz, Arsi and Bale. The Bale Mountains are home to by far the largest number. In Amharic, the wolf is known as *Ky Kebero* or 'red jackal'. Though the wolf does look like a kind of jackal, its connection to the wolf family has recently been established.

Living in family groups of around 13 animals, the wolves are highly territorial and family orientated. When the dominant female in the pack gives birth to her annual litter of between two and six pups, all members chip in, taking it in turns to feed, look after and play with the young. When it comes to hunting, however, the wolves forage alone. Any of the 19 rodent species found in Bale provide snacks. The giant molerats provide a feast and are the favourite food of the wolves.

The main threats to the wolves are rabies and distemper caught from the dog population, and cross-breeding (male wolves with female dogs). In the Bale Mountains, the 1991–92 outbreak of rabies reduced the population from around 400 animals to 120. In 1995, distemper also took its toll.

Encroachment on the wolves' territory and local superstition are other obstacles to be overcome. Locals believe that the antirabies vaccine changes the character of their dogs, or renders them less efficient as guard dogs. It is also considered very bad luck if a wolf crosses your path; many of them in the past were deliberately run over or shot by truck drivers.

Current measures to try and save the animal from extinction include an antirabies vaccination and a sterilisation program for the local dog population. There are also plans to start a captive breeding program. Though it is still threatened, the Bale population of wolves now looks healthier than it has in decades.

The third habitat, the moist, tropical Harenna Forest, is home to tree species such as *Hagenia*, *Rapanea*, *Celtis* and *Podocarpus*.

Fauna

The Bale Mountains are known particularly for their endemic wildlife. The park was created initially to provide a stronghold for two endemic animals: the Ethiopian wolf and the mountain nyala.

The sighting of an Ethiopian wolf, the world's rarest canid, is a highlight of a trip to the Bale Mountains, and is almost guaranteed on the Sanetti Plateau. But there are plenty of other no-less-remarkable endemics to be seen, including Menelik's bushbuck and the giant molerat.

Other large mammals commonly seen in the northern area include grey duikers, Bohor reedbucks and warthogs. Serval cats and Anubis baboons are occasionally seen.

In the Harenna Forest, giant forest hogs, bushpigs, warthogs, colobus monkeys and spotted hyaenas are all found, as well as leopards, lions and African hunting dogs. The last three are rarely seen.

Though most travellers can't wait to get trekking, the area around the park headquarters at Dinsho is, ironically, the one place where many of the larger mammals are easily seen. The park grounds are fenced, keeping most of the animals in and the people out. The best times for spotting wildlife and for photos are from 6.30 to 9 am and 4 to 6 pm.

Bale is also famous for its incredible number of endemic birds – 16 at the last count, though in 1998, an entirely new species of falcon may have been recorded by American researchers. Unusually, the endemics are very easily seen. No self-respecting twitcher should leave the mountains off their itinerary! On the plateau, sightings of the blue-winged goose, wattled ibis, thick-billed raven, black-headed siskin and spot-breasted plover are almost guaranteed. The birdlife in the juniper forests around the park headquarters is outstanding too. Ask for Daniel Ejigu ('Danny'), a guide who is good at locating birds.

Near the park headquarters, a 1km nature trail leads up to Dinsho Hill, from where there are quite good views of the surrounding park. The little museum is also worth a peek. Though tiny, it's crammed with various local stuffed animals including the honey badger, civet cat and aardvark. Some look a bit like overly loved teddy bears, with squinty eyes, limbs at funny angles and stuffing coming out. Look out for the flattened giant molerats, which look just like children's animal bedroom slippers.

Planning

All treks begin and end in the little highland town of Dinsho, which lies at the entrance to the park, around 30km north-west of Goba. There's no electricity in town.

Maps The only map of the park currently available is the very basic sketch map on offer at the park headquarters at Dinsho Lodge. If you want to trek off the beaten track, you'll have to rely on local guides and knowledge.

When to Go December to March is the driest time, but late September to December, after the rainy season, is when the scenery is greenest and the wildflowers are out.

During the main rainy season – between June and September – mist often obscures the views and the trails can be slippery underfoot. Even in the wet season, however, you are assured of several hours daily of clear, dry weather for walking; the rain tends to come in short, sharp downpours.

Park Fees & Regulations Entrance to the park costs Birr50 for tourists and Birr30 for residents, per 48 hours. Fee are paid at the park headquarters at Dinsho Lodge. The headquarters are open Monday to Friday from 8.30 am to 12.30 pm and 1.30 to 5.30 pm, and on Saturday mornings. Vehicle fees are Birr10–20 (depending on vehicle size) per 24 hours.

Fires are permitted only at camp sites. However, deforestation is a major problem here as in other parts of Ethiopia (see the boxed text 'Considerations for Responsible Trekking' in the Facts for the Visitor chapter). Cheap kerosene stoves can be bought in Addis Ababa. Many guides and scouts like to make fires in the evening to keep warm. Try at least to use the dead erica (heather) wood.

Supplies There's just one store in Dinsho, selling little more than the basics. If you're planning more elaborate menus, you should stock up in Addis Ababa. You can usually barter for eggs (Birr1 for three) and chickens (Birr5–7) at the nearby villages.

Water is available in various places on the mountain but should be treated (see Water under Health in the Facts for the Visitor chapter).

If you don't have your own tent, you can usually hire one from the park headquarters (Birr20 per 24 hours). As a last resort you could rely on the caves and tukuls in the area; ask your guide. A three- or four-season sleeping bag is essential. Sleeping bags can't be hired, but if you're desperate, warm Dinsho blankets can be bought in the town (Birr85–120).

Sunscreen and lip balm are vital for the high altitude and the sometimes strong winds on the plateau. Bring plenty of warm clothing; it can feel very cold and damp, even in Dinsho. Waterproofs are a very good idea, and are essential in the rainy season.

Binoculars greatly assist with wildlife spotting.

Trekking

Organising the 'team' (guide, scout, horses) inevitably takes time. The best plan is to arrive in Dinsho in the early afternoon, sort out your trek for the following morning, then spend the rest of the day exploring the wooded land immediately surrounding the park headquarters. A night spent in Dinsho is also a good start towards acclimatisation.

Most trekking in the Bale Mountains is fairly gentle and undemanding, following good, well-trodden paths or sheep tracks. But don't forget that the effects of altitude can make easy-looking terrain quite heavy going.

Trekking in Bale lacks the variety of trails and the drama of the high escarpments of the Simiens, and the most beautiful

ETHIOPIA

Under Threat

Like many national parks in Ethiopia, the Bale Mountains National Park is under threat. Locals continue to fell the hygenia trees (known locally as *kosso*) for fuel, and large numbers of livestock are taking over wildlife habitat. The Ethiopian wolf has become so used to cattle that it now uses the cows to conceal itself when hunting for rodents. Goats are causing rain erosion by stripping off the plant cover on the steepest slopes.

Heather burning, traditionally practised by the locals to improve grazing, is causing soil erosion and loss of plant diversity. Thatching for local huts demands large quantities of reeds from the swamps. The marshes are vital for holding and slowly releasing rainwater in the region.

On the Sanetti Plateau, vehicles are the biggest threat to wildlife.

scenery is found among the hills immediately below the plateau. The plateau, itself at 4000m, can be very bleak and monotonous, though there are some scenic lakes in places. The birds and wildlife, however, more than compensate for the landscape.

Guides, Scouts & Horses According to park regulations, all trekkers must be accompanied by a guide and a park ranger (known as a 'scout').

Guides work as freelancers. Perhaps because the park receives fewer visitors than the Simiens, the guides are much less 'spoilt' and on the whole are good. Few scouts speak English, but they make willing additions to the team. Guides cost Birr50 per day; scouts Birr30.

Porters are not available, but horses can be hired to carry both you and your gear, and cost Birr15 per day. The scouts usually look after them, unless you're in a big group, in which case you'll be expected to hire a horse driver as well (Birr15 per day). The guide and scout will expect at least one horse to carry their blankets and provisions.

Guides, cooks and handlers are expected to provide food for themselves. Many bring

token offerings or nothing at all and will then look to you for sustenance. Either check they have enough or bring extra. As compensation, the guide is often happy to act as cook, and the scout to collect dead wood.

At the end of the trek, staff will expect a tip. A rule of thumb – if the service has been good – might be an extra day's pay for every three days of work.

Guides, scouts and horses are all organised at the park headquarters at Dinsho Lodge. A scout is always posted at the lodge. He can call up the lodge manager, who lives nearby, outside opening hours. Guides tend to hang around outside; those who can be recommended include Danny, Idriss and Hussein.

Standard Route The park covers a relatively small area, and most treks last just four days with a vehicle or six days without a vehicle, though longer excursions can be planned. The four- or six-day standard trek begins at the park headquarters in Dinsho and works its way south-east up the Web and Wollo Valleys to the Finchaya Habera Waterfall (two or three hours from the park headquarters). You can either camp here or continue on to Mararo, where there's a pleasant camp site beside a stream at 3750m.

Day two is spent walking up the Wasama Valley (six hours). A good stop on the way is the mineral springs at Worgona; the water tastes slightly salty, and cowherds bring their cattle to drink here. Keep an eye out for the giant molerats, which are easily seen in the area. The steep ascent to the Sanetti Plateau then begins. A good camp site is beneath the crags of Mt Batu in the Shaiya Valley.

Mt Batu can be climbed on day three, before you walk to the very picturesque camp site situated in the Tegona Valley under the sheer cliffs beside the Garba Guracha Lake (six hours). The camp site is a terrific spot for birds of prey. Lammergeyers, buzzards and eagles are all commonly seen here. Look out also for the short-eared and Cape eagle owls, which roost in the clump of erica growing around the stream to the south of camp.

Day four is spent walking to the Crane Lakes (six hours), known for their water birds including the crane, and as one of the best spots to see the Ethiopian wolf. A detour can be made to visit Tullu Deemtu. Your vehicle can then meet you on the Goba–Dola-Mena road. Without a vehicle, it'll take you another day's trekking back to Dinsho.

Tullu Deemtu is probably best done in a vehicle if you have one, as it's little more than a very monotonous scree slope, with a pretty unattractive observatory planted on the top. However, it affords good views from the summit, over the Harenna Forest to the south, the Sanetti Plateau to the north and the town of Goba to the north-east. From the main Goba–Dola-Mena road, it's around 4km to the mountain.

Alternative Routes Alternative walks are to the Worgona Valley from the Shaiya Gorge or the Wasama Valley. From there, you could continue on to the Danka Valley via the Kara Worgona Pass, camping beneath the so-called 'balancing rocks'.

You could also follow the Web Valley all the way to its source near Morabowa Mountain, before turning east and back onto the Sanetti Plateau.

For those very short on time, one-day excursions might include walks up the Web Valley to Gasuray Peak (3325m) and Adelay Ridge. The Web Gorge takes around 1½ hours to reach, and is good for seeing colobus monkeys. Go early in the morning.

A great overnight excursion is to the spot known locally as Kotera. It is the site of an old observation post for the Ethiopian wolf, and the animal is still often seen here. It's a good choice if you're keen to see a wolf, but haven't got a vehicle. The walk takes five hours one way.

For a very pretty walk that includes birds and a good chance of seeing the Ethiopian wolf, the Finchaya Habera Waterfall, followed by a night at the so-called 'French Camp' close by, makes a good excursion. Leopards are seen very occasionally near the waterfall.

With your own vehicle, you could walk in a morning or afternoon from the plateau road up to the summits of Tullu Konteh (around 20 minutes from the main road),

Potent Plants

While trekking in the Bale Mountains, look out for the endemic plant *Kniphofia foliosa*, a member of the red-hot poker family, found quite commonly in the hills between 2050m and 4000m. Growing in clumps, it's easy to spot because of its yellow, orange or red flowers, which spread along much of the upper stalk and give it the appearance of a sort of milk-bottle cleaner. The plant flowers from May to October and also from December to January, and is found in central, northern and south-eastern Ethiopia.

The local Bale people have long valued the plant for its medicinal properties, using it to relieve stomach aches and cramps. Recently, a scientific investigation revealed that the plant does in fact contain several anthraquinones including islandicin, which is found in fungi such *Penicillium islandicum*.

Tullu Deemtu (around 1½ hours from the road) or Mt Batu (six to eight hours from the main road).

For those who want to spend longer periods in the mountains, the almost totally unexplored Harenna Forest offers great hiking potential. Recent scientific expeditions here have discovered many new endemic species.

Nontrekkers

If you've got only limited time, or can't walk far, you can still see a great deal of wildlife with your own vehicle. The top of Tullu Deemtu can be reached by 4WD, via the Sanetti Plateau.

If you get to the plateau early enough (between 6.30 and 9 am), you are almost guaranteed a sighting of the Ethiopian wolf. The afternoon between 3.30 and 5.30 pm is also good. The animal wakes up ravenous after a cold night and spends the early hours of the morning intently searching for food. If you get out of the car and approach from downwind, you can get very close indeed.

A pleasant, short stroll from the road is to the Crane Lakes, an excellent spot for birds (though in the dry season, some of the lakes evaporate). Wattled cranes often nest here, migrating to the lowlands during the dry season. June and September are the best months to see them.

Places to Stay & Eat

Dinsho Most trekkers stay at the pleasant *Dinsho Lodge* (where the park headquarters is also found). Accommodation is dorm-style and prices depend on the number of beds in each room. Rooms with two/three/six/eight beds cost Birr50/20/15/10 per person. The two communal showers are cold. There's also a pleasant communal area that acts as a sitting room-cum-museum, with several stuffed animals for company, and a large open fireplace. If you want to make up a fire (there's no other form of heating in the lodge), bundles of firewood cost Birr15. The lodge has a generator, but it's only used when there are enough guests staying. Bring candles and torches. If you fancy easing those weary limbs, there's also a sauna you can fire up. It costs Birr10 for one person, but decreases by Birr2 per additional person.

There's no restaurant or cafe in the lodge, but you can use the lodge kitchen, which lies in a separate block. It costs Birr4 per person per day including, in theory, gas stoves. Willing cooks are available from the village. In the wet season, you may well find that you have the lodge to yourself; over Christmas, you may be hard pushed to get a bed. Reservations can be made through the Ethiopian Wildlife Conservation Organisation (☎ 01-44-44-17) in Addis Ababa.

Camping is possible on Dinsho Hill behind the lodge.

The only alternatives to the lodge are the budget hotels in Dinsho town. None are especially inviting. The *Hotel Tsahayi* was undergoing maintenance at the time of writing, but used to be the best bet. Rooms cost Birr10. *Hotel Genat* is adequate, with rooms for Birr10. In both places, buckets of hot water can be brought to the 'showers' (toilets) for Birr0.50.

The hotels serve a limited selection of local dishes. Dinsho also has its own *tej beat* (mead house), open to around 9.30

pm. A bottle of *araki* (local spirit) is not a bad accompaniment to a trek. A little nip in the morning cuppa or before going to bed at night can work wonders for troop morale!

On the Mountains The national park has established various sites for camping, chosen for their proximity to water, ready grazing for horses and their position about a day's walk from one another (four to six hours). You'd be forgiven for walking right past them as there are no huts, shelters or other facilities established on the sites. In other words, you'll need to be fully self-contained with tent, sleeping bag and cooking gear. Camping costs Birr20 per 48 hours for tourists and Birr10 for residents, payable at park headquarters.

Getting There & Away

Ethiopian Airlines flies from Addis Ababa to Goba.

Regular buses run between Addis Ababa and Goba, 30km from Dinsho. From Goba, the nearest large town to Dinsho, you can take a bus or hitch a ride with a truck to Dinsho, from where it's a 2km walk to Dinsho Lodge.

Buses also run from Shashemene, Dola-Mena and Dodola to Goba. From Asela, buses run to Dodola and Goba.

It's 425km from Addis Ababa to Dinsho; by private vehicle, you can get there in a single day if you make a dawn start.

Getting Around

If you don't have your own vehicle, you can catch one of the buses or trucks that ply the Dinsho–Dola-Mena road. The road takes you right through the park, up over the Sanetti Plateau and down into the Harenna Forest. You can explore the area from the road, then hitch back, which isn't too difficult, but don't leave it too late.

GOBA & ROBE

The twin towns of Goba and Robe, 32km east of Dinsho, lie 14km from one another. Goba, the old capital of the Bale region, is still the most convenient of the two. The town is larger than Robe and is the terminus of most bus travel. It also has an Ethiopian Airlines office and a Commercial Bank. The bank changes travellers cheques in US dollars only.

At the town markets, look out for the delicious local acacia honey, the attractive basketry and the heavy cotton buluko. Both the honey and the shawls make a great accompaniment to a Bale Mountains trek. Gobe's market (the largest) is on Wednesday, Robe's is on Thursday.

Beyond the colourful markets, there's little to see in either town, but you may well be obliged to spend the night here on your way to or from the Bale Mountains.

Places to Stay & Eat
One of the best budget hotels is the **Hooteela Goobbaa Roobee** with basic but clean rooms with shared shower for Birr7.

The **Yilma Hotel** (signposted in Orominya as 'Yimaa Amossaa') has a pleasant garden. Rooms with private hot shower cost Birr15.

One step up is the peaceful **Goba Wabe Shebele Hotel** (☎ 61-00-24) with twin/double rooms with hot shower for Birr148/119. It lies 1.7km from the Commercial Bank in the north of the town.

The **Baltena Hotel & Restaurant** is one of the best restaurants in town, with local food. The **Mana Kitifoo Zariihuun** is a great kitfo house. The **Goba Wabe Shebele Hotel** does good faranji food, including breakfast. The **Nyala Pastry** is considered the 'best pastry shop in Bale', and the **Siitii Kaafee** (City Cafe) is good for fruit juices, fresh bread and a local breakfast.

Getting There & Away
Ethiopian Airlines flies about twice a week to Goba from Addis Ababa via Dire Dawa. The airport lies 7km from Robe and 21km from Goba.

One bus runs daily to Shashemene (Birr15, five to six hours) and to Addis Ababa (Birr31, 12 hours). For Dola-Mena, four or five Land Cruiser taxis depart daily (Birr20, four to five hours); trucks also travel to Dola-Mena for the same price.

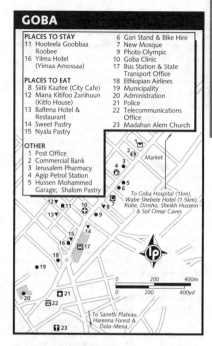

GOBA

PLACES TO STAY
11 Hooteela Goobbaa Roobee
16 Yilma Hotel (Yimaa Amossaa)

PLACES TO EAT
8 Siitii Kaafee (City Cafe)
12 Mana Kitifoo Zariihuun (Kitfo House)
13 Baltena Hotel & Restaurant
14 Sweet Pastry
15 Nyala Pastry

OTHER
1 Post Office
2 Commercial Bank
3 Jerusalem Pharmacy
4 Agip Petrol Station
5 Hussen Mohammed Garage; Shalom Pastry
6 Gari Stand & Bike Hire
7 New Mosque
9 Photo Olympic
10 Goba Clinic
17 Bus Station & State Transport Office
18 Ethiopian Airlines
19 Municipality
20 Administration
21 Police
22 Telecommunications Office
23 Madahan Alem Church

To Goba Hospital (1km), Wabe Shebele Hotel (1.5km), Robe, Dinsho, Sheikh Hussein & Sof Omar Caves

To Sanetti Plateau, Harenna Forest & Dola-Mena

Getting Around
Regular transport connects the two towns (Birr1.50, 15 mins).

A couple of privately owned vehicles plus driver are usually available for rental in Goba. Head for the State Transport Office inside the bus station at Goba and ask for the manager. The office is open daily from 6 am to 12.30 pm and 1.30 to 6 pm. Vehicles cost around Birr700 per day including fuel and driver. You can also hire the car (with driver) for a trip to the Sanetti Plateau (Birr200), Sof Omar Caves (Birr380) or Sheikh Hussein (Birr700).

Bicycles can be hired in both Goba and Robe for Birr3 per hour or Birr15 per day. You can also hire them for several days at a time, but you'll probably have to leave ID at the local police station.

SOF OMAR CAVES
The Sof Omar Caves, 120km east of Goba, are thought to be among the largest

underground caverns in the world. Winding down the Bale Mountains, the Web River has, over the millennia, carved a 16km course through the limestone hills.

The huge caves, with their vaulted chambers, flying buttresses, massive pillars and fluted archways, resemble a cathedral; in fact, Sof Omar has long been an important religious site. Sheikh Sof Omar reportedly took refuge here in the very early days of Islam. The caves are still greatly venerated by Muslims in the area, although, curiously, many pagan rites and ceremonies seem to have carried over from the ancient past.

The highlights of the caves are the so-called Chamber of Columns or Conference Hall, the dome and the balcony not far from the entrance to the cave; the balcony affords very good views of parts of the front of the cave and the river flowing though it. In an antechamber, little strips of hide are hung up, remnants of the visits made by pilgrims who came here to sacrifice animals in order to offer thanks for the fulfilment of a wish.

The normal 'tour' takes around 20 minutes. If you have swimming gear with you, you can even swim in the river to explore the chambers and caverns beyond. You can also hire a boat from Sof Omar village.

A good guide and torches are essential. One who can be recommended is Abdul Jabar in Sof Omar village; you should bring torches with you. During the rainy season, the cave can become flooded and impenetrable. People who are afraid of bats are advised to steer clear of the caves.

The villagers at Sof Omar now demand an 'entrance fee' of up to Birr100, but Birr15, including a guide, ought to be adequate.

A visit to the caves takes a full day; they're probably only worth a visit if you're planning a full exploration or want to visit the Sof Omar market too. The market is a colourful event, held every Saturday.

Getting There & Away
By public transport, you'll have to go first to Goro, 40km east of Goba. One bus travels there daily from Goba (Birr7, two hours). From Robe, one bus (Birr7) and around seven minibuses (Birr10) run daily to Goro.

From Goro, you should catch a bus or pick-up truck to Sof Omar (Birr10, 1½ hours, 45 km). The best time to do the last leg is on Saturday (market day at Sof Omar). During the rest of the week, you'll have to rely on lifts, which can be difficult to come by.

SHEIKH HUSSEIN
North of Sof Omar, and 78km north of Ginir, Sheikh Hussein is Ethiopia's most important centre of Muslim pilgrimage. Attracting thousands of pilgrims every year, the complex is made up of an attractive little mosque and various tombs within a wall. Various shrines and caves are found within an hour's walk east of the complex. The centre's namesake, Sheikh Hussein himself, used to visit them to seek some peace and quiet from the village for praying. The complex is at least 500 years old, and is dedicated to the 13th-century holy man, who was responsible for the conversion of many Bale and Arsi Oromos to Islam. Many pilgrims come here in thanks for wishes fulfilled, and make gifts of camels, money and meat to the villagers. Others come to make wishes – for a child, for good health, for prosperity etc. Feast days take place during May and October, with minor ones during February and September; the exact dates depend on the lunar calendar.

The *danke* (walking stick with a forked end) carried by many travellers along the road is a mark that they have made the pilgrimage. Look out also for the evergreen shrub *Salvadora persica* along the roadside; it's used by the locals as a kind of toothbrush (see the boxed text 'A Nomad's Toothbrush' in the South to Ali Sabieh section in the Djibouti chapter).

Sheikh Hussein is a peaceful, very atmospheric place and Christians as well as Muslims are welcome to visit the site. Local religious leaders will give you a tour. It's customary to leave a small contribution of Birr10–20 after a visit.

If you get stuck in Jara to the south, the *Golocha Hotel* is the largest hotel with very basic rooms for Birr4 (plus Birr0.75 for a cold, shared shower).

The drive to the site takes you through some very beautiful scenery, and birdlife is abundant – a reason for going in itself. Bring a picnic.

Getting There & Away

Unless you visit the shrine during a major pilgrimage (when local transport is laid on from surrounding towns, including Robe), you'll need you own vehicle to visit Sheikh Hussein. A contract Land Cruiser taxi from Goba there and back would set you back Birr1200–1500 (for up to six people).

A bus runs daily between Robe and Jara (Birr14, five to six hours); on Saturday two minibuses make the journey. From Jara, you'll have to try and hitch a lift with private local transport to Sheikh Hussein (57km, two hours).

If you have your own vehicle, you should bring extra fuel.

DOLA-MENA

Dreary Dola-Mena. But the drive to the town, 110km south of Goba, is a terrific one.

Traversing the eastern part of the Bale Mountains National Park, crossing the Harenna Escarpment and winding up onto the lofty Sanetti Plateau itself, the route is the highest all-weather road in Africa. It ranks among the continent's most spectacular. Mengistu, the socialist dictator, was responsible for the road's construction. It was designed to move his troops south in a hurry.

The drive takes you through the extraordinary *Podocarpus* woodland known as the **Harenna Forest**. With its twisted trunks draped in 'old man beard' lichens, mosses and ferns, and with cloud swirling all around, the forest is like something straight out of a Grimm brothers fairy tale.

Wild coffee is found in the forest, as well as a whole host of endemic plants, amphibians and insects. The forest really is like an enchanted place, and undoubtedly ranks among the most remarkable woodlands in Ethiopia. It begs further exploration. Unfortunately the local demand for firewood is

Injera is a large, pancake-type food used as a base on which to serve most Ethiopian dishes.

DAWIT ABEBE

seriously threatening the forest. In the meantime, a Dutch World Wide Fund for Nature project awaits the signature of both the local and federal authorities.

Further south near Rira, bamboo thickets are found; it is here that lions are most commonly seen – or rather heard. At Katcha, around 9km from Rira, a clearing has been made for a *camp site*, though you'll need a guide to find it; it lies around 10 minutes' walk off the Goba–Dola-Mena road. There's a small waterfall nearby, and the whole place is a jungle of vegetation and reverberating animal and bird noises. Butterflies abound too.

From the camp site, it's a further 31km to Dola-Mena, where the very basic *Mulu Hotel* has rooms for Birr5, and a restaurant.

Two or three pick-up trucks connect Goba and Dola-Mena (Birr20 for back seats, Birr25 in the front). On market days at Dola-Mena (Wednesday and Saturday), around seven trucks make the journey.

From Dola-Mena, at least one pick-up truck leaves daily for Negele Borena, 179km to the south (Birr30, six to eight hours).

There is no fuel available in Dola-Mena.

NEGELE BORENA

Continuing south from Dola-Mena, the town of Negele Borena is the south-eastern equivalent of Shashemene. Sitting at an important crossroads of the region, it serves as a useful transport hub, but not much else.

The journey south is pleasant enough. On the way, look out for the oblong-shaped beehives, made from cow dung, bark and mud, high up in the trees. The little children standing on the large platforms in the middle of the fields are human scarecrows, there to keep the birds off the maize.

Birds and wildlife abound. You may well see jackals and grey duikers. Hornbills, vulturine guinea fowls, bustards, hoopoes and white-billed go-away birds are common sights. Soon *foutahs* (sarong-like wrap) replace shammas, camels replace cows, and the region becomes more and more arid.

At Negele Borena, the *Tourist Hotel* has clean but basic rooms for Birr7–11. The *Green Hotel* has rooms for Birr20 (Birr30–50with private shower).

Getting There & Away

From Negele Borena, you can continue by truck 300km south-west to Mega (one day); very occasionally some trucks follow the rough track all the way to Moyale on the Kenyan border.

Most trucks turn westward from Negele towards Yabelo (Birr30, six to nine hours); one truck leaves daily for Dola-Mena (Birr30, 11 hours).

A bus runs daily to Shashemene (Birr25, eight hours). One bus leaves daily for Addis Ababa (Birr40, 1½ days), and one for Moyale (Birr40, eight to 10 hours).

With your own vehicle, the Negele Borena–Moyale route, which winds through thick acacia bushland, is at times very difficult to make out. You'll need a guide. Giving lifts to locals from village to village is not only polite and friendly, but solves the problem of guides. The route makes for some great off-track exploration, and wildlife is abundant.

West of Addis Ababa

The Anuak people in western Ethiopia believe that if you keep walking, you will eventually fall off the end of the world. In western Ethiopia, if you keep walking, you fall into another world. Where the province of Wolega ends and Ilubador begins, the landscape changes abruptly. The highland plateau gives way to lowland plains, fields of yellow *tef* (an indigenous grass) to plantations of verdant banana and mango, Semitic people to dark Nilotic people, and a bracing climate to the torrid humidity of the tropics. Geographically, climatically and ethnically, the far west has much more to do with Sudan than with Ethiopia.

Of all of Ethiopia's regions, the west remains the least known and the least explored by travellers. Though lacking the historical monuments of the north and east, and the wildlife of the south, the region is still rich in both culture and natural beauty. Gentle hills, fertile valleys, montane forest and little streams make up most of the area; birdlife and wildlife abound and fruit, crops and vegetables seem to grow in every corner. Even the donkeys and horses look quite sleek and happy. As you wind through the west, the region seems like a kind of Ethiopian Arcadia.

The region, specifically Kafa, is also said to be the original home of coffee. When visiting the province, it is easy to see why; much coffee still grows wild. Curiously, it is this plant that was responsible for opening up the once almost impenetrable region: quite good roads now ford the great rivers and gorges, which for so long isolated the area from the rest of Ethiopia.

The west is quite well served by public transport, and a road connects all the major towns in a convenient loop which begins and ends in Addis Ababa. However, the torrential rain during the wet season can still quickly change all that.

The best time to visit the region is between mid-November and mid-January, when the weather is driest. A tour of the west

ETHIOPIA – THE WEST

West of Addis Ababa p256

Nekemte p260 ●

● Gambela p262

Jimma p275 ●

SUDAN

comprising a loop to Gambela, Nekemte and Jimma takes at least a week; 10 days is better.

ADDIS ABABA TO NEKEMTE

If you're a birder, keep an eye out for the Gefersa Reservoir, which lies 18km west of Addis Ababa. The reservoir, which is fed by the Akaki River, supplies the capital with its water and attracts a good number of birds including Egyptian geese, cormorants and sometimes pelicans.

Coming into view not far after the reservoir is Mt Menagesha. According to local tradition, the mountain was the site of an ancient coronation place for many of Ethiopia's kings. If you fancy a hike there from the main road, it will take you around an hour one way.

Menagesha Forest

With your own vehicle, you may want to make a special detour to the very beautiful Menagesha Forest, which lies around 20km from the village of Menagesha (29km from Addis Ababa) at the base of Mt Wuchacha. Here, on the western slopes of the crater,

ETHIOPIA

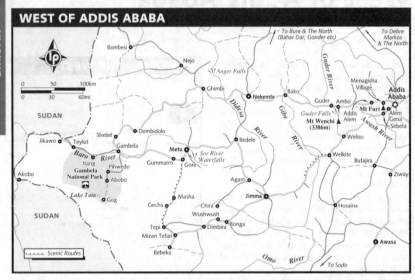

you can get a good idea of how Ethiopia's ancient, indigenous forest looked before the arrival of local settlements and the eucalyptus: giant juniper and *wanza (Podocarpus)*. Some trees are over 400 years old.

The forest forms part of a state park; the land, along with the vegetation, birds and animals that inhabit it, are protected. Look out for colobus monkeys. The endemic Menelik's bushbuck is also found here as well as duikers and, higher up near the crater rim, klipspringer, though the last three animals are rarely seen.

Addis Alem

Another place worth investigating is the town of Addis Alem, lying 55km west of Addis Ababa. It was here, at this unprepossessing little spot, that the Emperor Menelik II once thought of establishing a new capital at the end of the 19th century. Addis Ababa at this time was as good as crippled by fuel shortages and Menelik went as far as sending engineers and builders to Addis Alem to start construction on this 'new world'.

The result, after some three years' sawing and hammering, was a cluster of buildings situated on a small hill 1km to the south of the present-day village. Among the structures, the **St Maryam Church** stands out for its lavish decoration. The exterior of the basilica church, as well as the *maqdas* (inner sanctuary), is entirely covered with murals, depicting not just biblical scenes but a pantheon of Ethiopian rulers, landscapes, plants and various wild animals too, including some very grumpy-looking lions of Judah. It is said that Menelik wished to create here a kind of western equivalent of St Mary of Aksum.

If you haven't yet seen any examples of Ethiopian painting, the church is well worth a visit. Unfortunately, a fire in 1988 destroyed many of the old treasures of the church which were housed in an adjacent building. The remains of the buildings that served as the royal dining room and kitchen can still be seen, though there's nothing very regal about them now. Entrance to the church costs Birr10.

Addis Alem today is a typical western Ethiopian agricultural town. At the time of writing, bright blue and green Wellington boots seemed all the rage. Come in the rainy season and you'll see why.

Outside the village, look out for the shepherd boys selling delightful and amazingly complex models of St Maryam Church, Ethiopian houses and sometimes even aeroplanes and cars, made from the local river reeds, which are abundant here. The basins of no fewer than three of Ethiopia's major rivers converge on the area: the Omo, the Awash and the Guder.

Getting There & Away At least 10 buses run every day between Addis Alem and Addis Ababa (Birr4, 1½ hour). Buses also connect Addis Alem to Ambo (Birr6, two hours).

Ambo
☎ 01

Lacking the facilities of Sodore in the east or the scenic beauty of Wondo Genet in the south, Ambo does, however, boast a naturally heated mineral water pool and attracts Addis Ababan weekenders in their hordes. It's nothing special, but if you're desperate for a dip, it's worth a stop. There's also a children's pool and a common 'hot bath'; all are set in a pleasant garden area and there's a snack bar nearby. Note that the main pool is only filled from Friday to Sunday; entrance costs Birr2.

In Ambo itself, look out for the fine Italian 1930s architecture, such as the post office, police headquarters and some of the hotels. If you come to Ambo on a Saturday, the market is worth a stroll; you can pick up the brightly coloured Ambo baskets here.

The famous Ambo mineral water factory can also be visited. It lies 5km west of town and is open for visits from 8 am to noon and from 1 to 4pm Monday to Friday; entrance is free and guided tours are available. Ambo mineral water, which accounts for Ethiopia's principal bottled mineral water, actually comes from the nearby springs at Senkele.

Places to Stay & Eat The old, colonial *Ambo Ethiopia Hotel* (☎ 36-00-09) has rooms for Birr48 (Birr66 with shower) and suites for Birr84. Though not great value, the rooms are pleasant and peaceful enough and are set around a leafy garden. The

Ethiopian Traditional Dress

Perhaps because Ethiopia was never colonised, its traditional dress has largely survived. Most young women don their best finery for religious festivals, and markets give a good glimpse of different regional or ethnic preferences.

Highland women traditionally wear white cotton dresses *(kemis)* decorated with coloured embroidery. The *natala*, white shawls, have matching beautifully woven borders. Highland men wear white cotton jodhpurs and tunics *(shamma)*, also decorated with borders, but less ornate.

Border designs are usually based on traditional motifs such as stylised Ethiopian crosses, but flowers, birds, aeroplanes and even cars have in the past crept into fashion.

Muslim Harari women wear a cotton dress over a full, embroidered underskirt *(gorgora)* and snugly fitting velvet trousers.

Sidamo women favour black, yellow, red and white striped cloth; the Gurage wear off-white cotton and a black headscarf. The peoples of the Omo wear animal skins embroidered with beads, cowry shells, even rifle cartridges and metal rings.

The Afar and Somali people of the torrid lowlands wear a simple cotton *shirit* or sarong, along with their famous curved knives.

restaurant serves both national food and *faranji* (foreigner) food, including a good full/continental breakfast for Birr10/5 plus 10% service charge.

Offering better-value rooms is the new *Abeba Hotel* (☎ 36-11-40) with rooms for Birr15 (Birr40 with shower).

The *Hoteela Wanddimuu Shiree* is considered the best place in town for Ethiopian food.

Getting There & Away Between Ambo and Addis Ababa, eight buses run daily (Birr8, 3 hours). Some minibuses also ply the route. One bus leaves daily for Nekemte (Birr16, six hours). Around four pick-up trucks run each week south to Weliso (Birr6, two hours); for Guder, minibuses run around every half hour from Ambo (Birr1, 15 mins). The same minibus can also drop you off at the Ambo mineral water factory (Birr1).

For Mt Wenchi, privately owned 4WDs can often be hired and cost Birr400 for the return journey including driver. Ask around at the bus station.

Mt Wenchi

Mt Wenchi, 36km south of Ambo, rises 3386m high and consists of a steep-sided crater, with a lake lying at the bottom, several caldera and mineral springs. A small village has grown up beside the lake, and its inhabitants cultivate the surrounding fields inside the crater. A day trip from Addis Ababa is a picnic lunch in this beautiful crater, followed by an afternoon swim in Ambo.

To get to Mt Wenchi you can either make a day's hike of it from Ambo, or you can take one of the Landrover taxis that run between Ambo and Weliso. From the turn-off to Mt Wenchi, it's a 3km walk to the crater rim. It can be a problem finding space in a taxi on the return journey, so make sure you don't return too late in the day. Alternatively, you can bring camping equipment with you.

At the weekend, you may be able to hitch a lift with a private vehicle coming from Ambo; ask around at the Ambo Ethiopia Hotel. The top of the crater can usually be reached with a 4WD (around one hour from Ambo); the last bit of road is only difficult after rain. With your own vehicle, a guide from Ambo is essential; you can normally find one in the Jibat and Mecha Hotel at the town crossroads.

From the little village near the top of the crater rim, horses (Birr10 each, one way) can be hired for the steep descent. You'll need to negotiate the price; the 'guide' who arranges the horses (this may take an hour) and accompanies you will expect at least Birr5. Even if you prefer to walk down, you may be grateful for the horses on the way back up. It takes 30 minutes to descend and about one hour to ascend.

At the lakeside, you can hire a dugout canoe (Birr5 per person) for the five-minute journey to the island church of Cherkos.

Ethiopian Houses

Ethiopian houses are famously diverse; each ethnic group has developed its own design according to its own lifestyle and own resources.

In general, the round *tukul* (hut) with a cone-shaped roof forms the basis of most designs. Circular structures and conical thatched roofs better resist the wind and heavy rain. The one major exception is the *hidmo*, the rectangular, stone, flat-roofed house found in arid Tigray (see the boxed text 'Heavy Hidmos' in the Facts about Eritrea section).

In the smaller huts, the roof is usually held up with one central pole, while larger buildings have an inner concentric circle of supports.

The walls of the huts are usually constructed by burying poles in the ground. The gaps are then filled with branches and bundles of straw tied together. Finally, this skeleton is plastered over with a daub of dung, mud and straw.

Windows are usually absent, as are chimneys. The smoke, which escapes through the thatch, serves to fumigate the building, protecting it against insect infestations such as termites. Entry is through a single, low doorway.

Inside, furniture is usually very sparse. Beds, placed around the walls, are made of raised platforms of beaten earth covered with goat skins or blankets. Other furnishings typically include a couple of stools, a large stone, which serves as a table, and a few basic kitchen utensils.

Hooks are found all over the hut and are used to hang up clothes, water receptacles, knives and animal skins, and anything else that need not occupy the limited floor space.

Sometimes the huts are shared: the right side for the family, the left for the animals. In this way, livestock are not only protected from predators, but in some regions, they also provide a kind of central heating.

Particularly colourful examples of Ethiopian houses include the Sidama bamboo and enset leaf house, the very tall, woven 'beehive' of the Dorze people (see the boxed text 'Dorze Houses' in the South of Addis Ababa section), the geometrically patterned Anuak hut of Gambela, and the dry-stone two-storeyed 'tower-houses' of Lalibela.

There's little to see in the church, but the boat journey and the attractive and peaceful island setting make a visit worthwhile. Entrance to the church costs Birr10.

Waterbirds float on the lake, raptors soar above the crater. On the paths up and down, look out for the monkeys and baboons. The lakeside makes a great spot for a picnic.

Guder River Falls

Located 12km outside Ambo are the modest but pretty Guder Falls. It's a good place for a picnic. There's a great view of them from the main Ambo-Nekemte road as it winds up onto the hill past the falls.

To get to the falls, hop on any of the minibuses that ply between Ambo and Guder. The turn-off for the falls lies 1km beyond Guder, on the left side of the road (look for the corrugated iron gates).

The falls themselves measure around 8m by 20m wide, though in the dry season, they can be reduced to little more than a trickle. It's a three-minute walk to the falls from the parking compound.

The Guder River is an important tributary of the Blue Nile. The ubiquitous Ethiopian red plonk, Guder wine, was named after the river, and a few **vineyards** can still be seen covering the surrounding area.

Vineyards soon give way to **coffee plantations**, particularly after the village of Bako, which marks the boundary of the old provinces of Wolega and Shoa. Wolega is also known as the home of Ethiopia's frankincense and some of its gold reserves. Ethiopian frankincense still fetches high prices in the Middle East and Egypt.

The stretch of road between Guder and Nekemte is an attractive one, with good views across the surrounding hills, valleys and streams. Monkeys including colobus are often seen on the approach to Nekemte.

NEKEMTE
☎ 07

Lying some 187km beyond Guder is the large, sprawling commercial centre of Nekemte. The town serves not just as the regional capital, but also as an important coffee forwarding centre. In the town, look out for the many star and sickle emblems, leftovers of the Marxist Derg.

The town boasts a well put-together museum (see following), which is worth a visit if you're spending the night in the town. After the Ethnological Museum in Addis Ababa, it rates as the second best in the country.

Though not beautiful, Nekemte is easygoing and friendly. The markets bustle most on Wednesday, Thursday and Saturday. The old palace is not open to visitors at present. The Commercial Bank can change travellers cheques, but not cash.

Museum

The museum was entirely financed from contributions from the people of Wolega. The exhibits give a very good insight into the Wolega Oromo life and culture; the people of the region mostly belong to the larger Mecha Oromo group, who practice both pastoralism and agriculture.

Items on display include a good collection of musical instruments and an Ethnographic Room dealing with traditional local industries such as spinning, weaving, leather, wood, basketware and metalwork. The baskets are waterproofed by using very fine weaving followed by an application of the waxy sap of the candelabra euphorbia tree (known locally as the *qulqual*).

Keep an eye out for the decorated leather bed-sheet, still in the shape of a cow complete with tail; the ivory or bone cups in leather cases that travellers carried with them to avoid being poisoned (see the boxed text 'Xenophobia' in the North of Addis Ababa section); the marvellous *berchuma* (high-backed chair) carved from a single piece of wanza; and the wooden coffin. According to traditional Oromo culture, men must prepare their own coffins.

Other exhibits include a reconstruction of an Oromo hut, a smithies' workshop, and a good collection of arms including a massive spear measuring 2.5m long and a traditional (and immensely tough) hippo- and buffalo-hide shield. Look out also for the collection of delightful gourd pipes and incense burners. Five different sorts of incense are on display.

ETHIOPIA

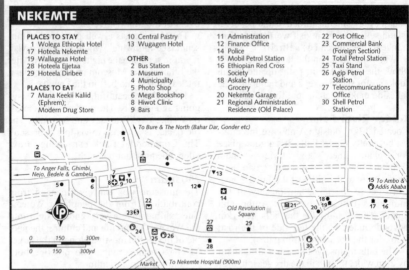

NEKEMTE

PLACES TO STAY	10 Central Pastry	11 Administration	22 Post Office
1 Wolega Ethiopia Hotel	13 Wugagen Hotel	12 Finance Office	23 Commercial Bank
17 Hoteela Nekemte		14 Police	(Foreign Section)
19 Wallaggaa Hotel	OTHER	15 Mobil Petrol Station	24 Total Petrol Station
28 Hoteela Ejjetaa	2 Bus Station	16 Ethiopian Red Cross	25 Taxi Stand
29 Hoteela Diribee	3 Museum	Society	26 Agip Petrol
	4 Municipality	18 Askale Hunde	Station
PLACES TO EAT	5 Photo Shop	Grocery	27 Telecommunications
7 Mana Keekii Kaliid	6 Mega Bookshop	20 Nekemte Garage	Office
(Ephrem);	8 Hiwot Clinic	21 Regional Administration	30 Shell Petrol
Modern Drug Store	9 Bars	Residence (Old Palace)	Station

To Bure & The North (Bahar Dar, Gonder etc)

To Anger Falls, Ghimbi,
Nejo, Bedele & Gambela

15 To Ambo &
Addis Ababa

Old Revolution
Square

0   150   300m
0   150   300yd

Market   To Nekemte Hospital (900m)

The museum is open from 9 am to noon and 3 to 6 pm Tuesday to Sunday. Guided tours are available.

Places to Stay & Eat

The *Hoteela Nekemte* is scraping the bottom of the budget barrel with cell-like but reasonably clean rooms and common shower for Birr5. A much better bet is the *Hoteela Diribee* with rooms for Birr10.

The *Wallaggaa Hotel* (☎ 17-61-09) offers by far the best upper-budget deal with rooms for Birr12 for one or two people. Its restaurant is also considered the best place in town for local fare. *Hoteela Ejjetaa* is also a good place for Ethiopian food. Some of its rooms (Birr7) have great views, but are a bit grubby and noisy.

The *Wolega Ethiopia Hotel* (☎ 61-10-88) has slightly overpriced rooms with hot shower for Birr60, but it's the best in its range.

The *Wugagen Hotel* offers about the best range of faranji food.

The *Mana Keekii Kaliid*, known locally as 'Ephrem', is the best cake shop in town and also does good fruit juices. The fresh mango juice served with a squeeze of lemon

is exquisite. It's also a great place for a local breakfast. Try the famous enset porridge *(enset bula)*, which resembles wallpaper paste. (See the boxed text 'Enduring Enset' in the South of Addis Ababa section.) The spicy, tomato-based *sils* and chickpea *ful* are delicious. For the less adventurous, sandwiches and omelettes are also served.

Getting There & Away

One bus leaves daily for Addis Ababa (Birr20, nine hours); for Ambo (Birr13, six hours); to Dembidolo (Birr24, 10 hours); and to Jimma (Birr25, eight hours). For Gambela, go to Jimma or Dembidolo first. One or two small buses go to Bedele (Birr15, four hours).

After Nekemte, the asphalt ends and the bumpy, hard-surfaced road begins.

Getting Around

Contract taxis can be hired and cost Birr5 for short hops about town. To Ambo, a taxi costs Birr200.

AROUND NEKEMTE

With your own vehicle, the **Anger Falls** on the Didesa River provide the most interesting of the natural attractions in the area.

In the region, look out for the *gotera*, granaries with little thatched roofs. The typical Oromo hut in this area is made from *chika* (mud mixed with straw). The eaves are extended downwards and supported on poles to form small verandas. Young animals and firewood are sheltered here from the frequent rain.

After Nekemte, the vegetation seems to get denser and denser until it begins almost to smell rank; elephant grass is increasingly found. Birds are abundant in the area; look out for the elegant widow birds. The delightful and ubiquitous little red and black 'finches' are black-winged bishops. Monkeys are also much in evidence.

Along the road, mango, papaya and banana grow wild. If you want to buy bananas, an entire bough will set you back Birr6.

On the brow of a hill or under an ancient wanza tree, the Oromo elders meet to ponder the affairs of the village. In the wet season, you'll see travellers and shepherds wrapped in the delightful traditional reed raincoats.

Close to the little town of Nejo, around 170km north-west of Ghimbi, is said to lie the oldest gold mine in the world. According to some, it was the source of the legendary King Solomon's mines.

DEMBIDOLO

Situated around 215km west of Ghimbi is the pleasant commercial town of Dembidolo. The town is known for two things above all: its goldsmiths and its *tej* or honey wine. The former can be seen at work, the latter can be tasted in any of Dembidolo's numerous *tej beats* (wine places).

If you get stuck here en route to or from Gambela, the new **Berhane Hotel** is the best bet in town and offers rooms for Birr12 (Birr25 with hot shower). The hotel lies near the end of the town, if you're driving west to Gambela. The central **Hoteela Yaadannoo** has adequate rooms with common shower for Birr8.50.

From Dembidolo, one bus leaves daily for Nekemte (Birr24, two hours). Only trucks run to Gambela (Birr30, five hours).

After Dembidolo, look out for the diverse Mecha Oromo houses, all designed slightly differently to stand up to the torrential rain during the wet season. Some don a woven bamboo grille on the facade; some have elongated eaves which stretch almost to the ground; others are rectangular and incorporate on one side a generous veranda which protects the walls.

GAMBELA

Muggy, swampy, sweaty, lying at an altitude of 450m, Gambela is unlike any other town in Ethiopia. Its history is also unlike any other in the country; it has more to do with the town's western neighbour, Sudan.

Situated on the banks of the Baro River, just a few kilometres upstream from Sudan, Gambela's strategic and commercial importance began to be noticed only at the end of the 19th century.

At this time, Menelik II – ever the innovator, and in conjunction with the British – dreamt of linking Ethiopia with both Egypt to the north and Sudan to the west. An inland shipping service was to be formed connecting the Baro with Sudan's capital, Khartoum.

The British rubbed their hands at the thought of access to the rich resources of western Ethiopia; the Emperor Menelik rubbed his hands at the thought of asserting

Shifty Shiftas

The stretch of road between the little town of Shebel and Gambela has, in the past, been targeted by *shiftas* (bandits). If coming this way, check the situation in Nekemte in advance.

It's pretty unlikely, but if you should be unlucky enough to encounter a gun-toting shifta on the road, stop at once, stay very calm, hand over a respectable wad of money as calmly and quickly as possible (it may even be a good idea to keep an easily accessible stash somewhere nearby) and don't attempt to move until the man or men have quite disappeared back into the bush. Accidents only happen when drivers panic and try and do a runner. If you have a driver, make sure he understands the plan of action!

ETHIOPIA

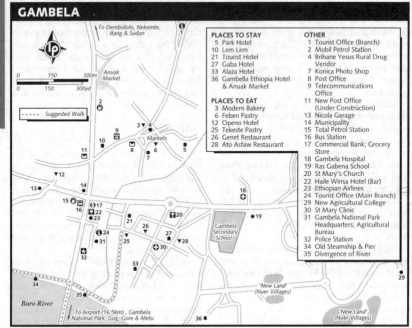

GAMBELA

To Dembidolo, Nekemte, Itang & Sudan

Anuak Market

0   150   300m
0   150   300yd

····· Suggested Walk

Markets

Gambela Secondary School

Gambela National Park Headquarters; Agricultural Bureau

Gambela Secondary School

Baro River

To Airport (16.5km), Gambela National Park, Gog, Gore & Metu

'New Land' (Nuer Villages)

'New Land' (Nuer Villages)

PLACES TO STAY
5   Park Hotel
10 Lem Lem
21 Tourist Hotel
27 Gaba Hotel
33 Alaza Hotel
36 Gambella Ethiopia Hotel & Anuak Market

PLACES TO EAT
3   Modern Bakery
6   Feben Pastry
12 Openo Hotel
25 Tekeste Pastry
26 Genet Restaurant
28 Ato Asfaw Restaurant

OTHER
1   Tourist Office (Branch)
2   Mobil Petrol Station
4   Brihane Yesus Rural Drug Vendor
7   Konica Photo Shop
8   Post Office
9   Telecommunications Office
11 New Post Office (Under Construction)
13 Nicola Garage
14 Municipality
15 Total Petrol Station
16 Bus Station
17 Commercial Bank; Grocery Store
18 Gambela Hospital
19 Ras Gabena School
20 St Mary's Church
22 Haile Winsa Hotel (Bar)
23 Ethiopian Airlines
24 Tourist Office (Main Branch)
29 New Agricultural College
30 St Mary Clinic
31 Gambela National Park Headquarters; Agricultural Bureau
32 Police Station
34 Old Steamship & Pier
35 Divergence of River

his independence from the French colonial government of Djibouti, which then owned and controlled the valuable Djibouti–Addis Ababa railway.

And so it was that Menelik agreed to grant the British an enclave on the Baro River and, in 1902, the contract was formally signed between the two parties in Addis Ababa. The original agreement cited Itang as the intended site of the station. However, further investigation quickly revealed a better location, one that would allow boats to operate for more months of the year: the site was called Gambela.

In 1907, Gambela was formally inaugurated as a port and customs station. Gambela was 'not to exceed 400 hectares' and was to be administered and occupied as a commercial station so long as Sudan remained under Anglo-Egyptian rule.

Soon steamers were chugging up and down the wide Baro River, laden with valuable ranging from coffee, salt and beeswax

to skins, liquors and cotton. Commerce flourished and Gambela boomed. The journey from Khartoum to Gambela took exactly seven days; from Gambela upstream to Khartoum, it took 11 days.

The Italians briefly captured Gambela in 1936, during which time a fort was built; it now lies in ruins. In 1941, the British won the river port back again and in 1951, it became part of Sudan. When Sudan gained its independence, the enclave reverted to Ethiopian ownership and, in 1955, the old shipping service to Khartoum that had operated for almost half a century, formally ceased to be. During the Mengistu regime, the port's fortunes further dwindled.

Currently, the Ethiopian government is entertaining plans to revive the river port and the region's economic fortunes. In the meantime, Gambela seems to stand still in time; slumbering until its hour of reawakening.

Today Gambela, with its huge old brick warehouses, colonial-style bungalows, mer-

The Ethiopian Slave Trade

Ethiopia's slave trade was a lucrative one. From the 16th century right up to the 19th century, the country's main source of foreign revenue was from slaves. At the height of the trade, it is estimated that 25,000 Ethiopian slaves were sold every year for markets across the world.

chants' villas, old wharves and neat grid street pattern, retains an unmistakably colonial air. In the old, fading buildings, colonial fans still churn the thick air.

Yet the town also manages to retain its native identity, too. Along the vast, meandering and sluggish Baro River, the local people go about their lives as they have always done. Women collect water, children paddle in the shallows and men spend the days fishing for the abundant Nile perch, tigerfish or catfish from dugout canoes.

The Baro is the only truly navigable river in Ethiopia. It was along this watercourse that the raiding slave parties transported thousands of captured men.

Wildlife in the area, though not as prolific as it once was, is still good. Birdlife is particularly impressive and includes a large number of waterbirds as well as raptors. Gambela town also serves as a base from which to visit the Gambela National Park.

Orientation & Information

Gambela is rather amorphous in shape and spills out disobediently around the old, colonial grid imposed upon it. A roundabout marks the colonial area; the heart of the town lies between the main road and the river.

Both the Tourist Office and Branch Tourist Office can provide information on the town as well as the national park. Of the two, the Branch Office is more helpful; ask for Berhaneselassie Lemma. Town guides are not available; it's best to ask at your hotel. Both offices are open from 8 am to noon and from 3 to 6 pm Monday to Friday.

The Commercial Bank can change travellers cheques (in dollars only), but not cash.

Dangers & Annoyances

Malaria is a major problem in Gambela, dispensing with an extraordinarily high percentage of the population. Adequate precautions are essential. If you don't have a mosquito net, make sure you stay in a hotel that supplies one. The Mobil antimosquito sprays are very effective and can be bought in the grocery near the Commercial Bank. Cover up at night; if not, you'll be eaten alive.

Swimming is possible in the Baro River, but keep to the places frequented by the locals. The crocs are a problem and the well-known case of the US Peace Corps volunteer who was eaten by a crocodile in the Baro after ignoring the warnings of the locals is still cited.

Photographers should show even more sensitivity and caution than normal in Gambela. It is strictly forbidden to take photos of or from the bridge and you're likely to seriously upset even ordinary citizens if you try to.

The Anuak and Nuer people are also notoriously camera-shy. Always ask permission first; if you don't, you may provoke real

The Anuak

The Anuak people survive mainly through fishing, though some grow crops such as sorghum. Most Anuak choose to live in extended family groups, rather than villages, which are made up of around five or six huts in a small compound.

The little huts are characterised by very low doorways and thickly thatched roofs with eaves that stretch almost to the ground to keep out the torrential rain and baking sun. The walls of the houses are often decorated with engraved designs including animals, magical symbols and geometrical patterns.

Widespread among many Nilotic peoples of Ethiopia and Sudan, including the Anuak, is the practice of extracting the front six teeth of the lower jaw at around the age of 12. This is said to have served originally as a precaution against the effects of tetanus or 'lockjaw'.

The Nuer

The Nuer people, forming the largest ethnic group in Gambela, are largely cattle herders, though like the Anuak, they also fish. The people's love of their cattle is legendary and much Nuer oral literature, including traditional songs and poetry, celebrates their beasts.

Unlike the Anuak, the people like to live together in large villages on the banks of the Baro River. Very tall and dark, the Nuer women are fond of ornamentation, including bright bead necklaces, heavy bangles of ivory or bone and, particularly, a spike of brass or ivory which pierces the lower lip and extends over the chin. Cicatrizing is also widely practised; the skin is raised in patterns used to decorate the face, chest and stomach, and rows of dots, in particular, are often traced on the face.

upset, anger and aggression. You should even ask permission from locals before photographing the local houses or animals.

Try and communicate with the local people; though at first they may seem reticent and deeply suspicious of you, they soon reveal themselves as a warm, gentle and friendly people. *Daricho* or *male*, the Anuak or Nuer 'hello', makes a very useful greeting. It's a good idea to find an Anuak or a Nuer guide for visits to the nearby villages.

Things to See & Do

The best way to take in Gambela is to stroll around it – no cars are available for hire and there are no taxis. The riverside, the bridge, the old steamship and pier visible from the riverbank, and the markets are all worth a wander.

The point where the river diverges is a great place at sunset, when many people come here to bathe, walk or catch up with other news. See the map for a suggested walk. You can also visit the Nuer villages on the outskirts of town which are known as 'New Land'.

Daily markets serve the different peoples. An Anuak market can be found near the Gambella Ethiopia Hotel from around 9 am to 6 pm (though from 2 to 6 pm is the best time to visit). Sometimes little Gambela clay pots and baskets can be bought here.

The Anuak vendors sit in the shade of the trees selling their products: cereals, wood, large Nile perch and tobacco; at the same time many indulge in *nargile* (water pipe) smoking. You can sometimes taste the traditional 'beer' *borde*, served to thirsty market-goers from metal buckets.

Places to Stay

Decent budget hotels are not Gambela's forte. The very basic *Gaba Hotel* has rooms with common shower for Birr7 and is about the best of the dirt-cheap hotels.

Of the budget to mid-range joints, the *Park Hotel* (☎ 2153) is much the best bet with reasonable rooms with common shower around a large courtyard for Birr12. Unfortunately, it's often booked up.

The *Tourist Hotel* (☎ 81) makes an adequate second choice with clean rooms and common, grubby shower for Birr10. In third place is the *Alaza Hotel* (☎ 2065) with rooms for Birr10. The *Lem Lem* (☎ 2089) is centrally placed and comes in a lame fourth with rooms for Birr12.

The *Gambella Ethiopia Hotel* (☎ 2044) is the biggest hotel in town. Rooms with private bathroom, ventilator fans and mosquito nets cost Birr144. It's clean, but like the majority of government hotels in Ethiopia, is run-down and very overpriced.

Places to Eat

The *Ato Asfaw Restaurant*, diagonally opposite the Gaba Hotel, is a favourite place locally. Also popular is the unmarked *Genet Restaurant* (look for the pink and blue-washed building). The owner, Genet, is reassuringly ample. The *Openo Hotel* is very good for fresh fish dishes, as well as some Sudanese-influenced dishes served with rice.

The *Gambella Ethiopia Hotel* serves good local food inside a pleasant and cool traditional tukul with a fan. It's also about the best place for faranji food, with grilled steak, shish kebabs etc for Birr10 (plus 15% tax). The *Park Hotel* does great *kitfo* (raw mince) and raw meat, if you've developed a carnivorous penchant for either.

The new *Feben Pastry* has the best selection of cakes in town, in a peaceful, sandy garden. It's a good place for breakfast.

Considered the best bar is the *Haile Winsa Hotel*, which uniquely in town boasts a CD player. It's open daily until 11pm. The sign is in Amharic only; if in doubt, ask.

Getting There & Away

From Gambela, one bus leaves daily for Addis Ababa (Birr50, 2½ days) via Nekemte (same price, 1½ days), overnighting at Bedele (Birr30, 12 hours) or, six times a week, at Metu (Birr25, 6½ hours), and Welkite. Two buses leave daily to Gore (Birr25, six hours), and to Itang (Birr5, two hours). One truck leaves daily for Dembidolo (Birr15, seven hours). During the wet season (July to end of September), some of these services run very erratically.

From Nekemte to Gambela, the route via Dembidolo is often impassable during the wet season; check conditions in advance during this time. If it is, you can get to Gambela via Bedele to the south. By bus, the journey from Nekemte to Gambela takes about three days.

Ethiopian Airlines (☎ 2099) flies four times a week from Gambela to Addis Ababa via Jimma. Payment for tickets is in Ethiopian birr (cash) only. The airport lies 16.5km outside town. Note that there are no taxis in Gambela. To get to the airport, Ethiopian Airlines puts on special transport; you should get to the office no later than two hours before the flight is due to leave.

During the wet season, cargo boats occasionally run on the Baro River from Gambela all the way to Akobo on the Sudanese border (330km). A few passenger boats also run from Gambela to Itang (Birr6, 45km), Teylut (Birr15, 100km) and Jikawo (Birr20, 130km). In the future, a regular passenger service should run again. Check current operations at the tourist office, which can put you in touch with tour operators.

AROUND GAMBELA
Gambela National Park

Gambela National Park was originally created for the protection of the swampy habitat that spreads over the vast area – over 5060 sq km – around the town. Less than 50 years ago, the area was one of the richest places for large mammals in the country, including elephants, lions, leopards, giraffes, buffaloes, topis, tiangs, roan antelopes, white-eared kob, hartebeests and waterbucks. The park was also unusual for representing species not found elsewhere in Ethiopia. The Nile lechwe, for example, is more typical of neighbouring Sudan.

Today, however, the huge influx of refugees from Sudan, as well as the ever-growing need for shelter and firewood, has dramatically reduced the wildlife's habitat and numbers. A few years ago, the Alwero dam project was constructed bang in the middle of the park, 45km from Gambela; at Pihwedo, 90km from Gambela, there's a very large refugee centre. In the meantime, thousands of people continue to burn down the forest for the cultivation of crops and to feed the continual demand for building houses and for firewood.

Fire is another problem; many locals prefer open land around their camps in order to protect against raids from other tribes. Fire, used to smoke out bees, is also used in the collection of honey and sometimes gets out of control.

The lack of funds is a serious obstacle to the park, too. With the transfer of responsibility from the central government to the regional government, the park's budget has been slashed to almost nothing; regional authorities are rarely interested in conservation. Recently, the skeleton staff of five scouts was reduced to just one. Gambela is one of the most neglected and most threatened parks in Ethiopia.

Travellers are best advised not to come here in search of animals. Birdlife, however, is outstanding, both in the forest and around the swamps. Gog is particularly good for woodland birds, and Itang and Jor for waterbirds. Considered a highlight is the odd-looking whale-headed stork that frequents the swamps.

With an altitude ranging from a mere 400m to 768m, temperatures are high here, as is rainfall: 1500mm falls annually, mostly

ETHIOPIA

Arts & Crafts

Ethiopia is home to a particularly rich tradition of arts and crafts. The reasons behind this include the wide range of raw materials available, from gold to fine highland wool; the number and diversity of the country's ethnic groups, 64 at the last count; and the differing needs arising from the different environments, such as the papyrus *tankwas* (traditional boats) developed for getting about on Lake Tana.

Basketware

Harar is traditionally the centre of basketware. Baskets come in a large variety of bright colours and patterns and serve diverse functions. The largest are the *mesob*, the 'tables' on which traditional Ethiopian meals are served.

Traditional Paintings

Animal skins provide the traditional canvas for paintings, and sometimes the hairy hide forms a kind of frame around the picture. Subjects are traditionally religious or depict popular legends such as that of the Queen of Sheba and Solomon. Paintings on finer parchment are sometimes used to make lampshades.

Musical Instruments

Traditional Ethiopian musical instruments, many with very ancient histories (see Music under Arts in the Facts about Ethiopia section), are quite widely available in Addis Ababa. Sometimes miniature versions, such as drum sets, are made also.

Pottery

Ethiopian red pottery was traditionally made by the Falasha (Ethiopian Jews) in particular. Although the numbers of these people have greatly declined in recent years, tiny pockets of local pottery production are still found in the Falasha villages outside Gonder.

Other pottery can be found throughout the country and ranges from simple pots and bowls to figurines and sculptures. The firing process is simple, however, and the pottery is very fragile. In Addis Ababa, electric kilns are used, so souvenirs, though less authentic, are more sturdy.

Woodcarving

Ethiopia's best woodcarving traditionally comes from Jimma in western Ethiopia, where large forests of tropical and temperate hardwoods once flourished. Though less furniture is now produced because of the gradual disappearance of the forest, the famous Jimma curved-back chairs and three-legged stools can still be found. Other woodcarving includes the decorated meat dishes, bowls and spoons of the Gurage people and the tella basins of the Sidamo.

between April and October. The vegetation is largely made up of woodland and grassland, with large areas of swamp in between.

The park headquarters are found in the Agricultural Bureau building in Gambela. If you want a guide, you can hire a park scout (Birr50 per day), but few speak any English.

Places to Stay Camping is permitted in the park, but you should take a scout. Fighting between the Anuak and Nuer is still quite common in the forest. The month before the author visited, four men were killed in ethnic skirmishes around Itang. Tourists are not targeted, though you should steer well clear of the border areas. Without camping equipment, you can stay in the village of Gog (see following).

Gog

The main reason for a trip to Abobo, 40.5km from Gambela, and Gog, 96km south of Gambela, is for the journey through the

Arts & Crafts

Metalwork

Ethiopia has an ancient tradition of metalwork, ranging from the famous and diverse Ethiopian crosses to the intricate earpicks and the beautifully crafted silver jewellery and ornaments from Harar. Many other ethnic groups also fashion metal jewellery, including the Oromo as well as the tribes of the Omo River. Material ranges from gold and silver to brass, copper and iron.

Weaving

Konso in south-western Ethiopia is particularly known for its woollen products including the famous and very heavy blankets known as *buluko* and the colourful and unusual Konso shorts. While spinning is women's work, weaving is traditionally regarded as the domain of men.

The Gurage and Dorze weavers are known for their high-quality cotton products, which make up the *kemis* (traditional women's dresses) and men's *shamma* (togas). Special skills are particularly required for making the ornate and beautifully coloured *tibeb* (borders) of the women's *natala* (shawls).

Debre Berhan, north of Addis Ababa, is considered the capital of rug making. Using highland wool, thick-pile carpets as well as flat-weave mats are produced. Colours are usually natural – brown, black and cream – and designs are stylised, with simple, geometrical designs or the popular Lion of Judah motif. The size of the rugs varies from huge wall-hangings to tiny mats measuring no more than 50cm.

Leatherwork

Ethiopia has more cattle than any other country in Africa; they outnumber the people by two to one in some areas. Although most hides are exported, accounting for the second-biggest foreign-exchange earner, some leather is processed, and cheap leather belts, sandals and bags are available, particularly in Addis Ababa. Other items include traditional hippopotamus-skin shields and water jugs made from sheepskin.

Outside the capital, the attractive *agelgil* can be found, particularly in the markets of Bahar Dar. Made of two baskets – a base and a lid, covered in leather and bound together with leather thongs – the agelgil is used by highlanders as a kind of picnic basket when travelling.

Hornwork

Not wishing to waste other cattle products, artists skilfully make horn into a variety of practical and ornamental items including drinking vessels, shoehorns, sculptures, vases, combs and household decorations.

Painting

Continuing the ancient tradition of painting (see Painting under Arts in the Facts about Ethiopia section), Ethiopian artists go on producing paintings on parchment, wood and canvas.

---

middle of Gambela National Park. However, you will see little wildlife, just piles of park firewood for sale – illegally – along the road. Occasionally, lions are sighted.

Gog was once the best place to see elephants, and some sightings have been made in recent years. The best time to see them is from January to March, when they cross from the southern areas of the park to the east in search of food. However, sightings are rarer and rarer, and you'd be extremely lucky to see one. Poaching is the main problem.

From Gog, with your own vehicle, you can drive to the nearby Lake Tata, 9.3km north-west of Gog. The spot is outstanding for waterbirds, with 230 species recorded here or in the vicinity, including saddle-billed, whale-headed, open-billed and woolly-necked storks, and many varieties of heron, ibis and kingfisher, as well as abundant raptors. You can pick up a guide at the village of Gog; it's a good idea to make your presence known at the local police station, where police will also help you find a guide.

Ethiopian Hairstyles

Hairstyles in all societies form an important part of tribal identification. Reflecting the huge number of ethnic groups, Ethiopian hairstyles are particularly diverse and colourful. Hair is shaved, trimmed, plaited, sculpted, brushed and tied in countless different styles.

The Tigray and Amhara women braid their hair from the scalp, but allow the ends to splay out over the shoulders; Arsi women don fringes and bobbed cuts; Harari women part their hair in the middle and arrange two large buns behind their ears.

The Hamer and Karo women of the Omo Valley rub animal fat and ochre into their hair to form strands or balls. The Bume men sculpt a ridge with fat and coloured mud in which to plant ostrich feathers.

Hairstyles are sometimes so elaborate and valued that special wooden head-rests are used as pillows to preserve them.

Rural children, on the other hand, often have their heads shaved, except for a single topknot or tail plait. Serving practically to discourage lice, this is traditionally left so that 'God should have a handle with which to lift them unto Heaven', should he call them.

If you want to stay the night at Gog, the **Brehane Hotel** has clean rooms for Birr8. The road to Abobo and Gog is good, and a truck leaves daily from Gambela to Abobo (Birr5, one hour) and Gog (Birr15, three hours).

Itang

It's also possible to continue due west from Gambela to the village of Itang and beyond. The area is incredibly remote, populated by sparse groups of Anuak and Nuer people.

At the time of writing, the area was closed because of security problems along the Sudanese border. Check out the situation first in Gambela. Because of the problems, no public transport currently runs here; in the rainy season, the roads west can be impassable.

Like in Gambela, life revolves around the river and markets. The remains of the old British wharves can still also be seen.

GAMBELA TO BEDELE

As you leave Gambela on the road to Gore, the road takes you across the Baro River via the longest single-spanned bridge in the country, built by Mengistu in the 1970s. There's a great view from the bridge over the town and the river. Don't forget, however, that photography is strictly prohibited around any bridge in Ethiopia.

The road then gradually wind its way a thousand metres up onto the escarpment. Around 10km before Gore, look out for the tea plantations lining the road. The Gummarro plantation is the biggest in Ethiopia, with 800 hectares given over to the little plants. Colobus monkeys are also seen here.

Gore

The old town of Gore, lying 146km east of Gambela, is set on the edge of the escarpment 1500m above the lowlands below, and is known for its market.

The town rose to importance in the 19th century when it became the base of one of the Emperor Menelik's main commanders, Ras Tessema Nadew. In the town, the ras' old palace can still be seen, as can two little churches. Gore was also an important collecting point for the region's coffee, linking the lowlands with the Baro River and British Sudan to the west.

If you have a chance, try and taste the local honey (for sale at the market), for which the little town is famous locally.

If you're obliged to spend the night here, the new **Tewodros Hotel** has rooms (with bucket shower) for Birr10. There's a good restaurant and parking.

Minibuses from Gore run to Metu (Birr5, 30 mins). For Gambela (Birr13, four hours), the Addis Ababa bus stops here daily; you can normally hop on it if it's not full.

Metu

Situated 25km beyond Gore, and spreading over the slope of a small hill, is the town of Metu, the capital of Ilubador province. Metu has an interesting market where everything from coffee and berries to wild honey can be found. Metu has a petrol station, but the

Commercial Bank does not have foreign currency exchange facilities.

If you want to overnight at Metu, the *Hotela Lusii* (☎ 41-17-75), also known as the Luci Hotel, is the best bet, with rooms for Birr12 (Birr20 with shower). There's also parking and a good restaurant.

Getting There & Away One bus departs daily for Gambela (Birr13, five hours), for Bedele (Birr15, three hours), for Addis Ababa (Birr40, 1½ days, overnight at Jimma), and for Jimma (Birr25, eight hours). Minibuses run to Gore (Birr5, around 20 mins). For Nekemte, go to Bedele first.

To reach Mizan Tefari from Metu, there are no direct buses or trucks; you'll have to hop in stages via Masha (75km), Gecha (35km) and Tepi (45km) and on to Mizan Tefari (56km). If you start early enough, you can reach Mizan Tefari in a day.

Sor River Waterfalls

A very worthwhile excursion from Metu is to the Sor River Waterfalls, one of the most beautiful falls in Ethiopia. It lies close to the village of Bechu, 13km south of Metu. The one-hour walk to the falls takes you for 30 minutes along a path, for 15 minutes through cultivated fields and for 15 minutes through some dense forest that absolutely teems with birds and monkeys. Suddenly, in a small opening, the Sor River drops 100m over the lip of a wide chasm.

The falls, which are surrounded by a kind of natural amphitheatre, create their own microclimate. With the giant ferns, twisting tendrils, fronds and creepers, dripping undergrowth and the barking of baboons echoing in the forest, it's like walking straight into a South American rainforest.

To get to the falls, you'll need a guide from the village. Birr10 is a reasonable tip for the excursion. If you have a vehicle, you should pay someone to watch it.

Getting There & Away A Land Cruiser leaves Metu every morning for Bechu (Birr10, 40 mins) at between 8 and 9 am. From Bechu, the Land Cruiser leaves at between 11 am and noon; you may have to

walk back to Metu. In your own vehicle, you can pick up a guide (Birr5 to Birr10) to take you to Bechu. At Bechu, it's best to enlist the help of a villager (Birr10).

Between Metu and Bedele, the road is lined with thick forest; look out for the colobus monkeys which are often seen here, often in quite large troupes.

BEDELE
☎ 07

Lying 115km east of Metu, Bedele is little more than a grubby roadside town; additionally, faranji frenzy registers pretty high here. The town is famous for its beer. The beer factory (☎ 61-20-04) is the largest, newest and most 'high tech' in the country, churning out an average of 36,000 little brown bottles a day. The equipment and 'know-how' are Czech.

The factory can be visited if you're interested in beer breweries – or rather free samples – and lies around 3km from the town centre. The factory is open Monday to Friday from 8 am to 4 pm; entrance is free.

Bedele lies at an important crossroads linking the towns of Nekemte in the north, with Metu in the west, and Jimma and the famous Kafa region in the south. The town is furnished with various hotels and restaurants; the best bet is probably the *Hoteela Ka'umsaa Fi Ga'umsaa* with rooms for Birr10 (Birr12 with hot shower). It also has a good restaurant.

From Bedele, four buses go daily to Jimma (Birr15, 3½ hours), two buses to Nekemte (Birr15, two hours), two buses to Metu (Birr25, four hours) and one bus to Addis Ababa (Birr30, via Welkite, arriving 10 am the next morning).

SOUTH OF METU

An excellent alternative to the usual Gambela-Jimma route via Bedele is to make a short deviation via the little towns of Tepi and Mizan Tefari. The route will take you through perhaps the wildest, most beautiful scenery in the whole of the west, characterised by densely forested hills, some so luscious and verdant that they resemble rainforest. After Gore, you'll see many

A Scream So Strong, It Would Shake the Earth

The practice of female genital mutilation (FGM), or female genital cutting as it is now officially known, is practised in 30 countries worldwide. In Africa and parts of Asia, it is believed that two million women are circumcised each year; in other words, 6000 women every day.

In the West and in other cultures unfamiliar with the practice, the custom is seen as outrageous and barbaric. But female genital mutilation is neither a modern phenomenon nor one restricted to Africa and Asia. According to modern sociology, the practice is just the 'natural continuation of the ancient patriarchal repression of female sexuality'. The Romans tried to keep tabs on their slave girls by the insertion of genital rings. The Crusaders in the 12th century introduced the chastity belt to Europe in order to keep their wives literally under lock and key, while they campaigned abroad.

In 19th-century Europe and America, doctors counselled operations on the female genitalia to treat a variety of antisocial conditions, including nymphomania, insanity, hysteria and depression. A London practitioner by the name of Dr Isaac Baker Brown advocated genital mutilation with a pair of scissors in order to treat 'insomnia' and 'unhappy marriages'. In New York, in the 1950s, a young girl underwent a clitoridectomy (the removal of the clitoris), because her well-to-do family suspected her of masturbation. Prostitutes were encouraged to undergo similar operations by church evangelists trying to 'rehabilitate' them.

In no other continent, however, has female genital mutilation taken such hold as on the continent of Africa. Although it appears to occur in some countries more than others (particularly in the Horn), the practice is more tied up with individual ethnic groups than national or religious boundaries. The type and severity of the mutilation also depends to a large degree on the particular traditions of the different groups.

In theory there are three types of mutilation. 'Circumcision' (the name often given confusingly to all types of mutilation) involves the removal of the prepuce or hood of the clitoris; it is the least severe but also the least practised form.

'Excision' involves the removal of all or some of the clitoris and all or part of the inner genitals (labia minora). It is the commonest form of mutilation, accounting for 80% of cases.

'Infibulation' is the severest form of circumcision and requires the removal of the clitoris, the inner genitals and most or all of the outer genitals (labia majora). The two sides of the vulva are then stitched together with catgut, thread, reed or thorns. A tiny opening is preserved by the insertion of some small object such as a twig, allowing for the passing of urine. The girl's legs are then bound together from hip to ankle and she is kept immobile for a period of up to 40 days to allow the formation of scar tissue.

Operations are carried out with a variety of instruments including special knives, scissors, pieces of glass or, as they become more available, razor blades. Sometimes sharp stones have been used or, in Ethiopia, cauterisation (burning). The operation is normally the special responsibility of one woman in the group, who may also be credited with special powers such as knowledge of the occult. Except for very rich families in the hospitals of big cities, no anaesthesia is ever employed.

The area known as the Horn of Africa, encompassing Ethiopia, Eritrea, Djibouti and Somalia, is home to a particularly rampant tradition of female circumcision. In Djibouti, 95% of women are estimated to be infibulated.

Many westerners are quick to express outrage and incomprehension at female circumcision and a desire to see it banned immediately. However, these customs are deeply entrenched and are inextricably tied up with the cultural, religious and social lives of the inhabitants who practise them.

One reason given for the practice is hygiene. In hot climates, where water for washing is not readily available, removal of the genitals is supposed to facilitate cleanliness. Aesthetics is another con-

A Scream So Strong, It Would Shake the Earth

sideration. Genitals are considered ugly and dirty: a flat, smooth area of skin is considered more pleasing to the sight and touch.

Superstition also plays a part. In Ethiopia, some groups believe that if the female genitals are not removed, they will continue to grow, as a man's do, into puberty. Some believe that an uncircumcised woman cannot conceive; others believe that if she does, the unexcised clitoris is capable of killing the first-born child just by coming into contact with it.

The practice also contributes to maintaining social cohesion within groups. By conforming to a community's rules and regulations, members expect to reap the benefits of group protection and interaction. This sense of belonging and identification plays an extremely important part in the lives of most Africans (and is the issue probably least understood by non-Africans). Just as male circumcision is seen as crucial to Jewish tradition, so female circumcision is seen as crucial to some African traditions.

Another common defence for circumcision is the claim that it prevents female promiscuity. After genital mutilation, the female is said to have her libido lessened for life. In Muslim African countries such as Djibouti, where polygamy is permitted, circumcision is said to lessen the demands that wives make on a single husband.

Circumcision is also seen as a means of guaranteeing the virginity of a future bride. In nomadic cultures such as exist in Djibouti, it is a young girl's duty to tend the herds, obliging her to spend long hours alone. Circumcision is designed to 'protect' her and to discourage the roving eye of nomadic men (if a girl was raped the evidence would be obvious and the perpetrator would be punished).

Virginity in all traditional African societies is a prerequisite for marriage. It reflects the moral prestige of the girl's family, ensures a good 'market value' for the bride and establishes the paternity of future children.

There is no doubt that female genital mutilation brings enormous physical and psychological pain and suffering. Postoperative complications include haemorrhage, damage to other organs or bones from badly performed operations or struggling patients, and septicaemia as a result of using unsterilised instruments. Doctors have estimated that 15% of girls die postoperatively of infections or bleeding.

Those who survive often suffer ongoing complications such as infections or abscesses, or even, after infibulation, an inability to empty the bladder fully because of the narrowness of the opening left after the operation. The next chapters in a girl's life, the marriage night and childbirth, bring repeat experiences of unbearable pain and sometimes life-threatening danger.

Though little studied to date, the psychological damage of the operation is considered no less serious. Cases of severe depression, frigidity, anxiety and very low self-worth have often been reported. As one doctor put it: 'These women are holding back a scream so strong, it would shake the earth'.

Most of the arguments for the defence of female genital mutilation are, as outlined above, based entirely on superstition, myth or the perpetuation of tradition. However, if elimination of the practice is to be brought about, it will not be through the edicts of governments proclaiming 'this is illegal', nor the lectures of aid organisations claiming 'this is barbaric'. A grassroots campaign is required that seeks to understand as well as to confront the deeply ingrained traditions of the local people. Above all, it will depend on the will and the courage of the victims themselves. As Captain Thomas Sankara, the late president of Burkino Faso, put it:

... the liberation of women of our country, the women of Africa, of women as a whole, will not come about as an act of charity. It will depend on their will and their determination to struggle ...

colobus monkeys lining the road. The road is in quite good condition.

Lying close to both Tepi and Mizan Tefari are huge coffee plantations. These can be visited and give a great insight into Ethiopia's most important export (see Economy in the Facts about Ethiopia section). The plantations are also very beautiful, and good walking and bird-watching are possible in some. Bebeka is the oldest and largest; Tepi is much more accessible.

Though visitors are welcome to turn up, it's probably a good idea to arrange for a proper tour of either estate in advance. You can do this by contacting the head office in Jimma first (☎ 07-11-02-02). The coffee harvest, from May to October, is a particularly good time to visit.

Tepi

At Tepi the main occupation seems to be the consumption of qat. The main attraction is the nearby coffee plantation, the second-largest in Ethiopia, stretching over a huge 6205 hectares. The plantation headquarters can be found in a complex around 600m

Traditional coffee ceremony.

from the second roundabout at the edge of Tepi town if you're heading towards Mizan Tefari. You'll need your own vehicle to explore it properly, though you can hike to some parts.

The farm, comprising the plantation itself, the pulping and processing stations, a crater lake and spice and fruit plantations, makes a very interesting visit, though it takes about seven hours by car to cover all the distances.

The plantation is state-run and produces 2500 tonnes of raw arabica coffee per year. Banana plantations line the coffee plantations and act as 'trap crops' to attract the elephants and keep them from trampling the coffee seedlings or uprooting the plants to get at the roots. In fact, elephants in the area have greatly declined since 1986.

Because Ethiopia lies so near the equator, the coffee requires extra protection from the intense sunlight; tall *Gravilia robusta*, *Melia*, *Cordia africana Cuperessus* and rubber trees provide the plants with 70% shade.

The very beautiful and shady forest is brimful of birds and makes a lovely drive or walk. In the experimental spice plantations, cardamom, cinnamon and black pepper as well as fruit trees are all found, demonstrating Ethiopia's desire to diversify and break its dependency on coffee. Cardamom seems to offer most promise.

Places to Stay & Eat The *Felege-Ghion Hotel* (☎ 11-15-56) is the best of the hotels in Tepi town with simple but well-maintained rooms and a common shower from Birr7 to Birr12. Even better is the *Coffee Plantation Guesthouse* (☎ 11-05-58). Although it's normally reserved for the plantation workers, you can stay if there's space. Pleasant rooms with private cold shower set in a garden cost from Birr15 to Birr20 (prices are subsidised). It also has a good restaurant. The *Unique Cafeteria* in Tepi town is a good place for a coffee and a cake.

Getting There & Away From Tepi, one bus runs daily to Masha (Birr6, three hours). For Metu, go to Masha first. For

Mizan Tefari, buses and minibuses run daily (Birr10, one hour).

Mizan Tefari

Mizan Tefari, the capital of the Bench people, makes a good base for a visit to the nearby Bebeka coffee plantation. The Commercial Bank at Mizan Tefari does not offer foreign currency exchange facilities.

If you need a place to say, the best of the cheapies is the *Genet Hotel* with basic, small but clean rooms with common shower for Birr7. In the mid-range, the *Aden Hotel* is really the only option with overpriced rooms for Birr20 (Birr40 with private bathroom). Rooms are pretty basic but are clean and set around a peaceful garden. There's also parking. The restaurant is the best place in town for faranji food.

Minibuses and small buses run daily to Tepi (Birr10, one hour); for Metu go to Tepi and Masha first. For Bonga (Birr8, five hours), two buses leave daily. For Jimma (Birr16 to Birr23, eight hours), one bus runs daily. For Addis Ababa (Birr37, 1½ days, via Jimma), one bus leaves daily.

Around Mizan Tefari

Bebeka Coffee Plantation Bebeka, covering an area of 6537 hectares, is Ethiopia's largest and oldest coffee plantation. Around 240km of road winds around it and it takes about six hours to tour the plantation. But like a visit to the Tepi plantation, it's well worth it.

Around 15,000 quintals of arabica coffee are produced annually, and during the harvest, up to 7000 workers are employed. Beehives have also been established with the help of the German government and now produce up to 4500kg of forest honey a year. It's delicious and costs just Birr15 for a kilogram; pots can normally be provided. Bananas cost just Birr0.15 for a kilogram!

Experimental spice and fruit plantations have also been established (look out for the black pepper absolutely clambering up the trees and doing very well), as well as an organic coffee plantation and an interesting coffee arboretum, with around 40 different coffee species originating from all over the

Home of Coffee

The southern region of Kafa has a strong claim to be the original home of coffee. Consumed in Ethiopia as early as AD 1000, it is believed the coffee bean was introduced into Yemen from the 14th century, spreading from the Middle East to the rest of the world soon afterwards.

According to local legend, coffee was discovered by accident. Kaldi, a young goatherd from Kafa, noticed one day that his goats became even more troublesome than usual after grazing on certain berries. When he tried the berries himself, he began to empathise with his excited charges.

Later, a monk came across the merry band, joined them and discovered that the useful little berries also stopped him nodding off over his sacred texts during the night. The word got around the monastery and soon all the priests and monks in Ethiopia were happily munching away.

For many centuries after its discovery, coffee was chewed not drunk. Curiously, in some areas of Ethiopia, the tradition continues to this day: in parts of Kafa and Sidamo, coffee is crushed then mixed with *ghee* (Ethiopian butter). It was not until the 13th century that the hot drink was introduced. Nescafé has not yet made great inroads into Ethiopia ...

world including Brazil, Cuba and India. A wood workshop and brick factory have also been set up for the plantation workers.

Bebeka has a very attractive and comfortable *guesthouse* set in the thick of the plantations; it's a fantastic place for birds and you're free to explore the surrounding forests.

The two large bungalows have a sitting room and private bathroom with hot water and cost Birr50. This must be one of Ethiopia's best getaway secrets. If you can spend the night here, do. Temperatures are muggy, though; Bebeka lies at an altitude of between 920m and 1394m.

The eight semidetached bungalows cost Birr25/40 for one/two people. Reservations are advised, but not essential, through the

Commercial Department of the Coffee Development Commercial Enterprise (☎ 01-71-03-82) in Addis Ababa, who will radio the plantation. Food can be ordered in advance at the 'canteen'.

No public transport runs to Bebeka, lying around 30km from Mizan Tefari; your own vehicle is essential. It takes one hour to reach the plantation from Mizan Tefari, along quite a good road.

Wushwush

The 1240-hectare tea plantation, 5km from the village of Wushwush, lying 92km from Mizan Tefari, also makes an interesting excursion for those with time. A tour of the plantation and packaging factory can be arranged; harvesting takes place throughout the whole year.

The plantation lies 2.3km off the main Mizan Tefari–Jimma road and is open from 7.30 am to 12.30 pm and from 2 to 5 pm Monday to Friday and on Saturday morning only.

The *Wushwush Guest Lodge* lies 200m from the main Mizan Tefari–Jimma road, near the turn-off to the plantation. It's a comfortable place to stay and costs Birr10 (Birr20 with hot shower). You'll need to register with the Administration Office (☎ 11-29-79) in the factory complex itself before staying here. Sometime the lodge is full; you can make reservations through the office.

Near the lodge, there's a basic restaurant and bar, used by the plantation workers as a kind of 'club house' (open to 10 pm), or you can use the lodge kitchen. Camping in the lodge grounds is also possible; there's currently no charge.

Bonga
☎ 07

Though sprawling over quite a large area, the town of Bonga is an attractive place where the vegetation still keeps up a fierce fight for space with the conglomeration.

In the past, the area formed part of the great kingdom of Kafa. In the surrounding area are a number of unexcavated historical sites, including what is thought to be an an-

cient burial site for kings, defensive ditches believed to date from the 14th century, some churches possibly 500 years old and various old battle sites.

There's also terrific potential for hiking in the surrounding hills. Caves, waterfalls, natural bridges, hot springs, natural forest, wildlife and birdlife are all found not far from town.

For more information on this almost totally unexplored but fascinating and beautiful area, you can visit the little Bonga Tourist Office (☎ 78 through the operator) PO Box 6, Bonga, Kafa. Guides can be provided by the office.

In Bonga, the *Yimiseratch Hotel* has very basic, small but clean rooms with common shower for Birr10.

The best but not the cheapest bet is the pleasant *Supak Mission Guesthouse* (☎ 11-15-98) lying around 2km from the centre on the hill above town. Rooms in the guesthouse or in the tukuls (with common bathroom) cost US$10 per person. You can also use the kitchen, or camp in the pleasant grounds.

JIMMA
☎ 07

Jimma is the capital of the old province of Kafa and remains the most important coffee-collecting centre in the country. Wild coffee can still be seen growing in many parts of the region.

The largest town in western Ethiopia, Jimma can seem incredibly sophisticated, almost genteel, after a trip west. Cake shops, topiary hedges, neat roundabouts, manicured lawns and well-maintained public parks are among the city's proud attributes, and there's no shortage of decent hotels and restaurants. Jimma's inhabitants suddenly seem rather sleek and fat, too.

Kafa lies to the west of the Great Rift Valley and is characterised by gentle, rolling hills and valleys. Lying at an altitude of between 1300m and 2100m, with a temperate, frost-free climate that never exceeds 29°C, and an ample annual rainfall of 1600mm, Kafa provides the perfect conditions for growing not just coffee, but cereals, legumes

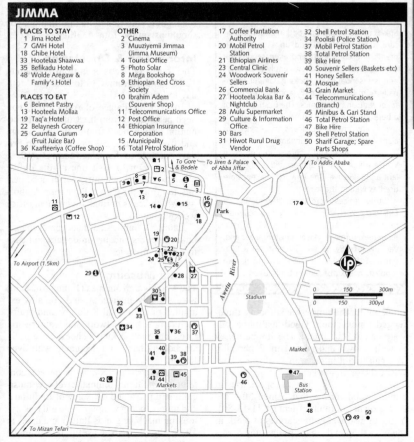

JIMMA

PLACES TO STAY
1   Jima Hotel
7   GMH Hotel
18 Ghibe Hotel
33 Hootelaa Shaawaa
35 Befikadu Hotel
48 Wolde Aregaw &
     Family's Hotel

PLACES TO EAT
6   Beimnet Pastry
13 Hooteela Mollaa
19 Taq'a Hotel
22 Belaynesh Grocery
25 Guunfaa Gurum
     (Fruit Juice Bar)
36 Kaafteeriya (Coffee Shop)

OTHER
2   Cinema
3   Muuziyemii Jimmaa
     (Jimma Museum)
4   Tourist Office
5   Photo Solar
8   Mega Bookshop
9   Ethiopian Red Cross
     Society
10 Ibrahim Adem
     (Souvenir Shop)
11 Telecommunications Office
12 Post Office
14 Ethiopian Insurance
     Corporation
15 Municipality
16 Total Petrol Station

17 Coffee Plantation
     Authority
20 Mobil Petrol
     Station
21 Ethiopian Airlines
23 Central Clinic
24 Woodwork Souvenir
     Sellers
26 Commercial Bank
27 Hooteela Jokaa Bar &
     Nightclub
28 Mulu Supermarket
29 Culture & Information
     Office
30 Bars
31 Hiwot Rurul Drug
     Vendor

32 Shell Petrol Station
34 Poolisii (Police Station)
37 Mobil Petrol Station
38 Total Petrol Station
39 Bike Hire
40 Souvenir Sellers (Baskets etc)
41 Honey Sellers
42 Mosque
43 Grain Market
44 Telecommunications
     (Branch)
45 Minibus & Gari Stand
46 Total Petrol Station
47 Bike Hire
49 Shell Petrol Station
50 Sharif Garage; Spare
     Parts Shops

and root crops as well. The whole region is like a kind of Garden of Eden: incredibly fertile where anything will grow, fertilisers are superfluous and insecticides unnecessary.

Kafa also has a distinguished history. For centuries, a powerful Oromo monarchy ruled the region from their capital at Jiren (part of present-day Jimma). The region owed its wealth to its situation at the crux of several major trade routes which passed from west to east and south to north. At its height, the Oromo court was filled with merchants, musicians, eunuchs, artists and concubines, and the kingdom stretched over 13,000 sq km. When Menelik came to power in the late 1800s, he required the region to pay high tribute.

Jimma boasts some good examples of 1930s Italian Fascist architecture. Take a peek at the cinema, post office, the old hotels, municipality and the old Banca d'Italia. In 1938, Jimma counted a third of its population as Italian. As the capital of the most fertile region in the country, the Italians had great hopes for the town and planned the construction of a great new city.

Jimma's markets are also well worth a wander; Thursday is the main market day.

Ethiopian Spices

Spices play an important part in Ethiopian culture, flavouring food and drink, curing ailments and complaints and even serving for beautification. Garlic grows easily in Ethiopia and is essential to its cooking. Ginger (originally from India) is greatly appreciated for its fever-reducing properties. The fresh leaves of a herb known as rhu are used to flavour coffee, as are cardamom, cloves and – since ancient Aksumite times – cinnamon.

Basil, smaller and more pungent than Western varieties, is appreciated as a stimulant and digestive. The flowers and seeds are used as well as the leaves.

Other spices sometimes found in an Ethiopian's kitchen include Bishop's weed, nutmeg, myrtle (also used as hair oil), pepper, fenugreek, turmeric, cloves, mustard seeds and, very importantly, cumin. Thyme grows wild in much of the highlands and is used to flavour food (such as kitfo) and for tea infusions.

Look out for the simple but attractive three-legged Jimma stools. Good-quality basketware can also be found. The Jimma honey is well known and costs Birr13 per kilo. You can find it in the warren of shacks opposite the grain market.

A good souvenir shop that specialises in Jimma woodwork is that named after the Adare owner, Ibrahim Adem (☎ 11-15-80). You can also watch the carvers at work in the workshop in the back of the shop. Items include Jimma stools, jewellery boxes, candlesticks and fruit bowls. You can specially order items; even, as an American tourist recently did, an exact copy of the king's toilet in the Jimma museum. A kind of woodwork market also exists near Ethiopian Airlines where prices are cheaper.

Well provided with hotels, restaurants and other facilities, the town makes a good overnight stop en route to or from Gambela (423km to the west) or Addis Ababa (335km to the east).

In the vicinity of Jimma, there are various caves, hot springs and a hippo pool (at the Boye Dam, 5km from Jimma) that can be visited. Access is currently difficult by road, but if you want more information, you should ask at the Tourist Office.

Information & Orientation

The Tourist Office is open from 7.30 am to 12.30 pm and from 1.30 to 5.30 pm Monday to Friday.

To visit the Palace of Abba Jiffar, you need permission from the Culture & Information Office, open from 8.30 to 11.30 am and from 1.30 to 5.30 pm Monday to Friday. Entrance to the palace costs Birr10.

If you want to visit one of the coffee plantations in the vicinity, you'll need permission from the Coffee Plantation Authority (which keeps normal government office working hours).

Jimma's Commercial Bank can exchange both travellers cheques in dollars and cash in major currencies.

Jimma Museum

The Muuziyemii Jimmaa (Jimma Museum) is reasonably interesting and contains examples of traditional Kafa arts and crafts, including fine woodwork and leatherwork. Look out for the king's shoes, beautifully stitched by hand and decorated with dyed leather.

Other objects include ox-horn water containers, traditional Jimma jewellery, musical instruments and a display of traditional and more modern weapons. The old rickety-looking machine gun is Italian and dates to 1936; there's also a useful Italian-made walking stick-come-gun! In another room, there are a delightful pair of wooden shoes with four 'legs', perhaps for tramping through Jimma's thick mud, and a good display of traditional clothing. Look out for the bark skirts and the reed raincoats, both still worn in the country today.

The museum also contains a collection of furniture, clothes and personal possessions belonging to the king, including a carved wooden throne, a bath and even the king's toilet – which looks like a frying pan with a hole in it.

Look out for the magnificent and massive wooden urn, used as a kind of clothes chest, with a circumference of 3.16m. The large drum was used to summon the people to war.

In the future, the collection will be transferred to the palace museum. The museum is open from 9 am to noon and from 2 to 5 pm Monday to Friday. On Saturday, Sunday and on holidays, it's open in the afternoon only. Entrance is Birr10. Captions are limited; a guide is recommended.

Palace of Abba Jiffar

The two-storey, 150-year-old Palace of Abba Jiffar lies 7km north of the town centre near the village of Jiren on a hill. King Jiffar (1852–1933) was one of the most important local lords of the Kafa kingdom, and ruled at the end of the 19th century.

Though the palace is rather decrepit, there are some interesting oriental architectural details, and it boasts a very pleasant location and attractive views west; come at dusk.

Making up the palace are the private family mosque, which is still in use and which once boasted a library, and the rooms said to have served as throne room, reception chamber, king's guard room, sentry tower, courthouse and guesthouses.

The house adjoining the palace is said to have belonged to the king's sultan grandson. From the balcony overlooking the courtyard, the royal family watched musicians, wrestlers, singers and poets. Nearby, 1.6km from the palace on the road back to Jimma, lies the tomb of the king.

After rain, the road can be difficult; you'll need a 4WD. City buses (Birr0.50) or contract taxis (Birr30) can take you as far as to the end of the asphalt; after that it's about a one-hour walk.

Places to Stay

Jimma boasts a handsome collection of squalid little hotels. About the best in the budget range is the *Hootelaa Shaawaa* (☎ 11-07-38) which has clean and adequate rooms for Birr10; choose those for Birr5/6/8 and you may be pushing it. Music in the bar doesn't shut down until 11.30, so don't come here for an early night.

The *Befikadu Hotel* (☎ 11-17-57) has quite good rooms for Birr18 (Birr25 with cold shower). The latter are on the small side. Ask for a room at the back.

The *GMH Hotel* (☎ 11-01-03) is an old, cavernous, colonial place with simple but clean, light and spacious rooms for Birr35 (Birr45 with shower).

Much the best mid-range to top-end place is the *Wolde Aregaw & Family's Hotel* (☎ 11-27-31) directly opposite the bus station. It has rooms with common shower for Birr33, and various different rooms with hot shower for between Birr44 and Birr88. For between Birr110 and Birr154, you additionally get a fridge, TV and telephone. There's also a good restaurant serving both Ethiopian and faranji food. It's a very good place for breakfast (Birr7/12 for continental/full). The hotel is set in large grounds, complete with cake shop, barber, parking and billiard room.

Both government hotels, the *Jima Hotel* and *Ghibe Hotel*, are dank, run-down and overpriced, when compared to the new privately run hotels; the former does have a garden which makes a pleasant place for a drink in the evening.

Places to Eat

The simple restaurant at the back of the *Belaynesh Grocery* is a favourite with the locals. It also does respectable faranji food including a vegetarian pasta dish. The *Hooteela Mollaa* is another simple but good place, which does a very good *doro arrosto* (roast chicken).

The *Taq'a Hotel* opposite the Agip station is actually a pastry shop. Despite its unpromising appearance, it does good, fresh cakes and fruit juices. The new *Beimnet Pastry* is popular with a younger crowd and has a good selection of cakes. The *Guunfaa Gurum* fruit juice bar is also good.

Try and taste the local *besso* drink, made from ground barley. Some of Jimma's swinging bars – or rather dinghy dives – are marked on the map.

Getting There & Away

Ethiopian Airlines (☎ 11-00-30) flies five times a week from Jimma to Addis Ababa;

twice a week to Tepi; four times a week to Gambela; and once a week to Gore, Dembidolo and to Mizan Tefari. Note that during the rainy season, flights are particularly subject to delays or cancellations. It is essential to reconfirm your flight at least 24 hours before departure.

One bus leaves daily for Addis Ababa (Birr21, eight hours); Tepi (Birr17, eight hours); Bedele (Birr10, five hours); Mizan Tefari (Birr16, seven hours); and Welkite (Birr12, five hours).

Getting Around

Garis (horse-drawn carts) are a great way of getting around town or to your hotel from the bus station. Short journeys (up to 1km) cost Birr1; a half/full day's hire costs Birr17.50/35. Bikes can be hired from close to the Total petrol station and cost Birr10/5 per full/half day.

No buses or minibuses go to the airport; to get there you'll need to take a contract taxi (Birr25).

JIMMA TO ADDIS ABABA

After Jimma, the road begins to wind back in a north-easterly direction towards Addis Ababa. Along the 144km stretch of road between Jimma and Abelti, the road descends to the Omo Valley and the scenery in places is spectacular. Look out also for the local handicrafts sold alongside the road.

Between Welkite and Indibir, there are terrific views of the highland plateau and surrounding valleys. If you get stuck at **Welkite** or are planning to catch an early bus south, the *Tefera Hotel* has simple but clean rooms for Birr10 (Birr12 with shower). The restaurant is also good. At least one bus runs daily to Jimma (Birr12, four hours), Addis Ababa (Birr10, three hours) and Hosaina (Birr13, three hours).

The little town of **Weliso**, 43km northeast of Welkite, is known for its hot springs. A naturally heated swimming pool can be found at the *Weliso Hotel* (☎ 41-00-02), as well as various cabins containing tubs piped with the naturally hot mineral water. The hotel rooms contain huge, sunken baths and make a fun stop en route to Addis Ababa if

you can afford the rather inflated prices. Rooms and bungalows cost Birr72–84. Camping is the best bet; the grounds are full of birds and vervet monkeys.

Those on a budget can stay at the *Refera Hotel* (with clean rooms for Birr15, or Birr25 with shower) and just use the facilities of the Weliso Hotel; nonguests are charged Birr7. The outdoor pool is filled from Friday morning to 4 pm Monday only; the indoor pool is open daily except Monday. The hotel lies 1.4km from the town centre; you can hop on a gari for Birr0.50. Regular buses and minibuses connect Weliso to Addis Ababa and Jimma.

Around Weliso is Gurage country (see the boxed text 'Peoples of Ethiopia' in the Facts about Ethiopia section). The Gurage huts have very low eaves to keep out the rain and many are topped with little spikes that make them look just like WWI German

---

The Bench

The Bench people, formerly known as the Gimirra, inhabit the province of Kafa alongside their numerically superior neighbours, the Oromo.

In the past, the Bench also formed a large ethnic group. 'Gimirra' means 'honey collector', or 'tree climber', and the Gimirra were known as great honey gatherers, industrious cultivators as well as brave warriors.

Living in semi-isolation in the thick forests of the Kafa highlands, they were, unfortunately, much persecuted for a period of several hundred years and were almost wiped out.

From the 15th century right up to the mid-20th century, the Gimirra were hunted like animals, sold into slavery by the tens of thousands, tortured and mutilated. The so-called 'progressive' Lej Iyasu himself (see History in the Facts about Ethiopia section) was rather partial to his Gimirra slave-hunting trips. Indeed, the Gimirra slaves provided a very significant source of revenue for the rich kingdom of Kafa, and were sold to markets across the world: to northern Africa, to Arabia and even to Europe.

soldier helmets. The Gurage villages stand in green meadows, amid plantations of enset, coffee, tobacco and qat. Horses and donkeys graze on the rich grass. Ethiopia here seems like a land of plenty; a far cry from its international image as a famine-wracked desert. A bag containing around 30 Gurage lemons sold on the roadside costs just Birr2.50.

From the nearby village of **Sebeta**, a good 3½ hour trek (one way) takes you up to the top of Mogli, one of the peaks of Wuchacha.

Turning left at the junction just beyond Alem Gena, not far from Sebeta, the road leads south to Butajira. Lying around 10km from the road, at a turn-off 1km from the Alem Gena junction, is **Mt Furi**. A narrow gravel road leads up the mountain; a 4WD can get you to the top. From the mountain, there are spectacular panoramic views in all directions, as well as some good hiking in the surrounding area, such as to the spur lying to the north of Furi. On the western side are a series of built caves, inhabited until quite recently. Continuing south, on the main Alem Gena–Butajira road are some falls near the bridge over the Awash River.

Just as you enter Addis Ababa on the Jimma road (7.5km from Meskel Square), there's a leprosarium, the All Africa Leprosy and Rehabilitation Training Center (ALERT), on the right, which sells various handicrafts such as cushion and bed covers produced by the patients. It's open from 8 am to 4 pm Monday to Friday and 8 am to noon on Saturday.

East of Addis Ababa

The east could be a different world. In stark contrast to the green, densely populated, Christian highlands, the east is largely arid, sparsely populated, low-lying and Muslim. In it lies one of Ethiopia's greatest and perhaps most underestimated attractions: the old walled town of Harar. A visit here is a must.

For centuries, the town existed as an independent state; situated at an important commercial crossroads, trade flourished. For a time, no Christian was allowed to set foot within the city on pain of death. The town still retains a rather exotic Oriental air. At night, with the ritual feeding of the hyaenas (something for which Harar is famous), the place becomes distinctly eerie.

Awash National Park is easily accessible from both Harar and Addis Ababa and is one of the highlights of this region. If you're not planning a trip to the parks in the south, an excursion here is highly recommended.

The road north-east to Eritrea penetrates a very sparsely populated, arid, often desolate area known as the Danakil region. There are no must-see attractions here, and wildlife in the so-called national park (Yangudi-Rassa) is barely visible. But the journey does take you through the heart of Afar territory. The Afars (formerly known as the Danakils), almost the only people capable of surviving in these harsh conditions, have long fascinated European travellers. For those with plenty of time and their own vehicle, an exploration of this very remote region could prove rewarding.

The east is also known as the home of some of the best coffee in the world; some believe that coffee originated here. Almost as famous is the notorious *chat*, the mildly intoxicating leaf (see the boxed text 'Chat Among the Pigeons' later in this section); if you want to try it – now's your chance!

For day trips from Addis Ababa to the east see Around Addis Ababa at the end of the Addis Ababa section.

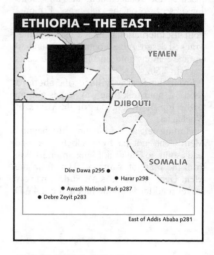

ETHIOPIA – THE EAST

YEMEN

DJIBOUTI

SOMALIA

Dire Dawa p295 ●
● Harar p298
● Awash National Park p287
● Debre Zeyit p283

East of Addis Ababa p281

AKAKI WETLANDS

The Akaki wetlands, 22km south-east of Addis Ababa, attract an abundant range of waterbirds. The birds are attracted to the wetlands' diverse range of habitats (dam, marsh, seasonal lakes and riverland), which spreads for around 13km west of the village of Akaki. The country is very attractive but is of most interest to birders. Note that much of the water is seasonal, and that the so-called lakes can dry up to nothing. With water, you can expect to see a good range of ducks, waders, raptors and herons. September/October is probably the best time for a visit.

Hotels in Akaki are much of a muchness. The **Dese Hotel** (☎ 34-00-84) has the edge with rooms for one/two people for Birr8; there's a common shower, and a restaurant. Take the first right (if approaching from Addis Ababa) before the Commercial Bank, then first right again, and follow the road for around 100m.

Getting Around

A *gari* (horse-drawn cart) is the only way of getting to the wetlands from the village (Birr5, one hour); they can be found around

EAST OF ADDIS ABABA

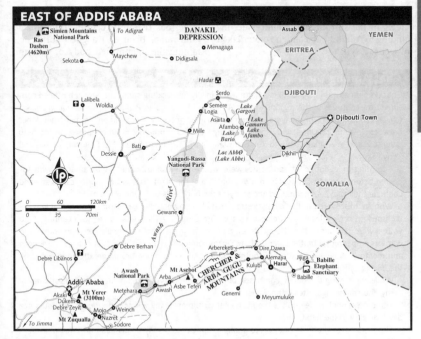

the marketplace. For the return journey, you can sometimes flag down farmers returning to town at the end of the day or arrange for the gari to come back and collect you. To hire a gari for a few hours will cost around Birr20, but you'll need to negotiate. Enlist the help of a local; few gari drivers speak English.

A charming – albeit rather down-and-out – guide is Ghirma, an ex-Derg fighter pilot, who charges a very reasonable Birr10 for a full day of guiding. His knowledge of birds is not great, but he knows the area very well and his English is good. He can usually be located in the Dese Hotel.

Getting There & Away
Minibuses and buses leave daily for Addis Ababa (Birr2, 30 mins). Minibuses leave for Dukem (Birr2, 50 mins), Debre Zeyit (Birr2, 45 mins) and Nazret (in the morning, Birr4, two hours). Akaki is on the Addis Ababa–Djibouti train line.

DUKEM
Dukem owes its existence to the volume of traffic rattling between Addis Ababa, the east and the south. It makes a useful base for a trip to nearby Mt Yerer.

If you get stuck in Dukem, the *Misrak Ber Hotel* is the best bet, with rooms with/without shower for Birr20/15 for one or two people. The restaurant's delicious *derek tibs* (deep fried lamb without sauce) is well known – during the weekend the place is packed with Addis Ababans. If the Misrak is full, the *Harar Meda Hotel* has basic rooms for Birr10/8 with/without shower.

Minibuses and buses run regularly between Dukem and Akaki (see previous) and Debre Zeyit (see following).

MT YERER
Just 10km north of Dukem, Mt Yerer (rising 3100m above the surrounding country) is an extinct volcano thought to be some three to four million years old. From the

top of the caldera, there are very good views of the surrounding countryside, including to Addis Ababa and the crater lakes of Debre Zeyit.

The caldera is partly collapsed and has a large rock rise in its centre. Unfortunately (and rather bizarrely) a glass coffin containing the mummified body of a hermit,

Chat Among the Pigeons

Chat (known as *qat* in Djibouti) is a natural and mildly intoxicating stimulant, which has been consumed for centuries in the regions of East Africa and the Arabian Peninsula. *Catha edulis Forskal* (chat) is an evergreen shrub, averaging around 2m in height, which is found on warm, humid slopes between 1500 to 2800m. It grows wild in many East and Southern African countries, on the Arab peninsula and in Afghanistan and Turkmenistan, but is actively cultivated in Ethiopia, Yemen and Kenya.

According to legend, chat's properties were revealed miraculously one day by an angel who appeared before two Muslim holy men. With the help of the plant, they were able to resist sleep and continue their prayers, meditation and study of the holy texts throughout the night.

Whoever discovered it, it is almost certain that chat originated in East Africa, and that it was established on both sides of the Red Sea by the 15th century. As far back as the 13th century, Arab writers were recommending the plant as a panacea for melancholia; they also recommended it to warriors preparing for battle. Later Arab historians commented on its ability to stimulate intelligence and memory, as well as to suppress both appetite and sleep; properties all greatly appreciated by the intellectuals of the day.

While masticating the leaves, consumers drink large amounts of liquid (water, tea, and soft drinks); many also smoke cigarettes or hookahs.

The professional, male adult is the main chat customer. Many will spend at least five hours in a day indulging in the habit.

The psychological effects of chat are multiple, but can generally be divided into three phases.

The first phase, which normally lasts around two hours, is known as the 'euphoric period'. Consumers quickly feel a sensation of wellbeing, optimism, excitement and a lack of inhibition or reserve.

The second phase is called the 'illusory period', and usually lasts for the next two hours. Intellectual activity seems to increase, the imagination becomes more active and attention becomes sharper. Later, consumers become more reflective and introverted, and gradually lose themselves in an imaginary world where anything seems possible. All kinds of projects and plans are dreamed up, and all problems are apparently resolved. Towards the fourth hour, an increase in libido is commonly felt.

The third phase, known as the 'depressive period', generally lasts from five to six hours. It is characterised by a physical and mental weariness and consumers inevitably become sullen and silent. However, the brain continues in its activities, and both insomnia and a loss of appetite commonly result. Individuals often feel uneasy, anxious and nervous, with a sudden desire to seek other diversion. Some consumers end up in nightclubs, bars or even in a curb-crawl of the city's red light district, and many resort to alcohol in an attempt to alleviate this 'come-down'. Sensations of guilt, remorse and worthlessness are also usually experienced.

After consumption male impotence or unsatisfactory sexual performance is the commonest complaint (eating cloves is said to alleviate the problem). The next day, many chat chewers experience a kind of hangover, in which sensations of dehydration, lethargy and tiredness are felt – often lasting right up until the next day or the next chat session.

Much more serious are the socio-economic consequences of excessive chat consumption (see the boxed text 'Qat & Mouse' in the Djibouti Facts for the Visitor section). Inspiration to poets, artists and musicians, companion to intellectuals and saviour of students, qat is also a ravager of the economy, catalyst of bankruptcy and provoker of divorce. The debate for and against the leaf rages on.

which had been housed in a nearby hermit's cave, was apparently stolen by thieves in 1996. Mt Zuqualla (see later in this section) probably makes a more interesting excursion.

Getting There & Away
Mt Yerer lies 35km from Addis Ababa. With your own vehicle, and depending on the road conditions, you can get a good way up the mountains, but you'll need to find a good guide in Dukem to show you the way. In the wet season, the road can become impassable. The mountain can also be approached from Debre Zeyit.

DEBRE ZEYIT
☎ 01

Known in the local Oromo language as Bishoftu, Debre Zeyit serves a divergent double function: it is both the base for the Ethiopian air force and a very popular weekend resort for Addis Ababans. On arrival, it looks suspiciously like yet another shabby little one-horse town, but this facade conceals an unusual and very special attribute: a position at the centre of no less than five crater lakes, and near another three.

With your own vehicle, most of the lakes can be visited within a half day. A good guide who knows the location of all the lakes as well as Mt Yerer and Mt Zuqualla is Melkamu, who can be usually be found at the Hotel Bishoftu.

Lake Bishoftu
Lake Bishoftu is the most central lake. Though almost denuded of trees, the lake still attracts quite good birdlife. The best place to admire the lake is probably from the Hotel Bishoftu, beer or gin and tonic in hand. The view overlooking the crater rim is impressive; you can also walk around the edge if you fancy it.

Lake Hora
Lake Hora lies 1½km north of the centre of Debre Zeyit; follow the signposts to the Hora Ras Hotel. Lake Hora boasts an attractive setting and its birdlife is outstanding. Storks, pelicans, shovellers, and grebes,

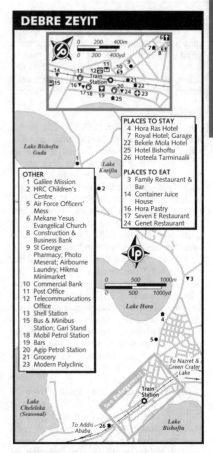

DEBRE ZEYIT

PLACES TO STAY
4 Hora Ras Hotel
7 Royal Hotel; Garage
22 Bekele Mola Hotel
25 Hotel Bishoftu
26 Hoteela Tarminaalii

PLACES TO EAT
3 Family Restaurant & Bar
14 Container Juice House
16 Hora Pastry
17 Seven E Restaurant
24 Genet Restaurant

OTHER
1 Galilee Mission
2 HRC Children's Centre
5 Air Force Officers' Mess
6 Mekane Yesus Evangelical Church
8 Construction & Business Bank
9 St George Pharmacy; Photo Meserat; Airbourne Laundry; Hikma Minimarket
10 Commercial Bank
11 Post Office
12 Telecommunications Office
13 Shell Station
15 Bus & Minibus Station; Gari Stand
18 Mobil Petrol Station
19 Bars
20 Agip Petrol Station
21 Grocery
23 Modern Polyclinic

Lake Bishoftu Guda
Lake Koriftu
Lake Hora
To Nazret & Green Crater Lake
Train Station
Lake Cheleleka (Seasonal)
To Addis Ababa
Lake Bishoftu
See Enlargement

as well as brightly coloured kingfishers and passerines, are among the species seen here.

At the weekend it can get a bit noisy. Along the shore, a kind of resort has grown up (with an entrance fee of Birr2). It's easy enough to escape the crowds, though: just follow the footpath around the lake as it winds through the pleasant forested slopes of the crater. A circumnavigation of the lake takes around 1½ hours. You should go accompanied, as thieves are said to lurk in the bush.

At the lakeside, boats can be hired. In the future, boat trips and watersports will be available and a cafe should open soon too.

The whole lakeshore, along with the Hora Ras Hotel (see Places to Stay following), may well undergo – or suffer – a general tarting-up. The lake is not bilharzia-free, so a dip is not advised. At the beginning of October, a big festival is held here that celebrates the beginning of the planting season.

Other Lakes

Just 3km north of Debre Zeyit is the scenic and peaceful **Lake Bishoftu Guda**. **Lake Koriftu**, nearby, is known particularly for its *tilapia* (a fish that is eaten locally), and is the site of a Protestant mission. You can stay at the guesthouse in the mission (rooms with bathroom cost Birr50–300 depending on the class), but it's a no-smoking no-alcohol zone. Birdlife at Lake Koriftu is quite good and the fishing is fine, but there is an 'entrance fee' of Birr2.50.

Around 14km north of town, beyond the Godino Soil Conservation and Forestry Development Nursery, are the so-called **Cuban lakes**. In fact, they are dams, but they provide one of the best places for spotting birds, including pelicans, cormorants and egrets.

Lake Chelelaka, 5km before town off the road to Addis Ababa, is in fact little more than seasonal floodwater, but the shallow mudflats usually attract excellent birdlife, including flamingos.

Green Crater Lake, 10km south of town off the Nazret road, beyond the air force camp, is both very large, and – as the name suggests – green (the result of algae). There is a very impressive view over the lake from the crater rim. At night, flamingos often converge on the water; for the best chance of seeing them, try and get here at sunset or at dawn.

Lake Hora Kiloli lies 20km from Debre Zeyit. A side road leaves the main road just past the Oromiya water mines and energy resources complex. The lake is 5km from the village of Kaliti; it's well worth a visit for those with time. The journey takes you through some beautiful landscape.

Place to Stay

Bottom of the range is the very basic but clean *Hoteela Tarminaalii*, with rooms with/without cold shower for Birr10/8.

The selling point of the *Hotel Bishoftu* (☎ 33-82-99) is its attractive location above Lake Bishoftu. The rooms (Birr30 or Birr40 with hot shower) are adequate. If it's full, the *Bekele Mola Hotel* (☎ 33-80-05), set back from the lake, offers similar rooms costing Birr30 for one/two people.

The new *Royal Hotel* (☎ 33-99-89), nearby, is top of the range, with comfortable and good-value rooms with/without shower for Birr40/20. The hotel has very pleasant gardens as well as parking.

The town's smartest hotel, the *Hora Ras Hotel*, is positioned on the rim of the largest crater, Lake Hora, just north of town. At the time of writing, Ethiopia's big business tycoon, Alamoudi (responsible for the Sheraton), had just bought the hotel and was planning to refurbish it. The terrace of the hotel used to be a terrific place for a drink in the evening. At the moment, it's possible to camp around Lake Hora as well as in the grounds of the hotel.

Places to Eat

The *Hotel Bishoftu* (see Places to Stay previous) is a great place for breakfast. The nearby *Hora Pastry*, which is opposite the Shell station, is a good place for a cake or breakfast. The *Container Juice House* offers a good variety of fruit juices for Birr3.

For Ethiopian food, *Seven E Restaurant*, just before the Mobil station as you come into town, is a local favourite; mains cost Birr6–10. A very simple but popular place is the *Genet Restaurant* nearby. The *Royal Hotel*, also in the centre of town, serves Ethiopian food in a traditional *tukul* (hut).

The *Family Restaurant & Bar* north of the centre on the outskirts of town resembles an American bar. It is supposed to be the best place for *faranji* (Western) food. The food is good but the prices are not the cheapest; most mains cost Birr20–28, and hamburgers and snacks cost Birr13–18. Cocktails (Birr12–16), ice cream and even chocolate cake are available.

Getting There & Away

Minibuses leave from the main bus station for Addis Ababa (Birr3, 45 mins), Nazret

(Birr4, 40 mins), Dukem (Birr2, ten mins) and Akaki (Birr2, 45 mins).

Trains on the Addis Ababa–Djibouti line also stop here daily for Dukem (Birr1, 15 mins), Akaki (Birr2, 40 mins), Nazret (Birr3, 1 hour 20 mins) and Addis Ababa (Birr3, 1½ hours). See also Getting There & Away under Dire Dawa later in this section. All prices are for third class (remember: travelling in third class can be very slow and carriages can get extremely crowded).

Getting Around

A gari is a great way of visiting the lakes and can be hired per half/full day for Birr20/40. They can be found just outside the bus station, and operate from 7 am to 6 pm. With a gari, you'll need around two days to see all the lakes. Short hops about the town cost Birr1–2. The blue and white minibuses are also a good way of hopping about town (50–75¢).

MT ZUQUALLA

Debre Zeyit also makes a good base from which to explore the extinct volcanic cone of Mt Zuqualla. Though rising to little more than 600m, the mountain dominates the landscape for miles around. The views from the top are stunning on a clear day – come early – and overlook the Rift Valley to the east and the lakes to the south; Addis Ababa and the Entoto Mountains are just discernible to the north-west.

The crater, measuring 2km across and over 60m deep, contains a lake that has long been held holy by the monks of the nearby monastery. According to the monks, the Holy Spirit changes the colour of the lake five times a day. Pilgrims come here to drink the water, which is said to have great healing properties. As is the case in many holy places in Ethiopia, women are not allowed to get too close to the water (50m is considered a 'safe' distance).

The monastery of **Mt Zuqualla Maryam**, set amid ancient and thick juniper forest, is traditionally thought to have been founded by Saint Gebre Manfus Kiddus (see the boxed text 'Know Your Ethiopian Saints' in the North of Addis Ababa section) in the 12th or 13th century. The site may actually date to the 4th century, when a hermit community may have been established here by Saint Mercurios.

Two churches are found in the monastery. The round basilica was built by the Emperor Menelik in 1880 (designed by the Italian architect Sebastiano Castagna). Higher up, the church of Kidane Meret was built during the reign of Haile Selassie. The monastery is entirely self-sufficient, with its own vegetable patches, weaving room, water cistern, bakery and so on.

In March and October, large festivities are held at the monastery, and pilgrims come from miles around. If your trip coincides with the festivities, you will be able to join the pilgrims on the toil up to the church and then on the circuit around the lake following the *tabot* (replica of the Ark of the Covenant, see the boxed text 'The Tabot' in the Facts about Ethiopia section). Later, a bonfire is lit and hymns are sung around the fire.

The whole complex, including the simple hermit caves (still used by the monks today) and the little graveyard overlooking a beautiful valley, has a very peaceful, serene and hallowed air. Because the trees populate a sacred place, they have been preserved, unlike the totally denuded landscape below the mountain.

A Birr50 entrance fee per vehicle is now levied by the monks. Monks are happy to act as guides, but because their English is limited, you're more likely to get a pointing tour than anything very instructive. Don't forget that smoking is considered a 'sinful act' by monks and priests in Ethiopia (see the boxed text 'Smokers' Snub' in the Ethiopia Facts for the Visitor section).

In the beautiful hills behind the monastery, you can walk to a place known as **Wednesday and Friday Mountain** (after the days of fasting). Here, there are two large rocks lying close to one another. Locals maintain that if you can't squeeze through them, you won't go to heaven, since you haven't done your fasting! In another place, it is believed that two rocks will clash together and crush you if you're an unrepentant sinner. If you want to take these tests, each place takes around one hour's walk there and back. The rocks are a great excuse for a ramble through the lovely forest, where it is possible to see plentiful birdlife and colobus monkeys. Beware, though: leopards (known by the priests as 'tigers') are said to be found here.

Places to Stay

You are welcome to spend the night at the monastery, but don't expect luxury accommodation. The 'guesthouse' resembles a stable – albeit a rather snug one – spread with straw. You can also camp in the church compound; there's no charge for either but remember that any gift, such as sugar or coffee, is greatly appreciated by the monks (see Church Etiquette under Responsible Tourism in the Ethiopia Facts for the Visitor section). You should bring your own food with you.

Getting There & Away

Mt Zuqualla lies south-west of Debre Zeyit and is approached via the tiny settlement of Wember Maryam (25km from Debre Zeyit, two hours by car), which lies at the foot of the mountain. Guides are essential. You can reach Wember Maryam from either Debre Zeyit or from Dukem.

A 4WD is essential, as the gradients up the cone are very steep in parts and rough. After rain, the road can be impassable. You can also walk up the mountain from its foot at Wember Maryam (three hours up, 2½ hours down). Look out for the indigenous Abyssinian rose on the way up, which sometimes lines the roadside. Without your own car, you can try catching a lift with one of the supply vehicles that run from Debre Zeyit to Wember Maryam; ask around at the main hotels in Debre Zeyit.

NAZRET
☎ 02

With no great churches, ancient monasteries or sacred relics, Nazret's name, derived from Christ's birthplace in Israel, seems a bit of a misnomer. Lying 100km from Addis Ababa, it is large, commercial and bustling. Surrounded by fields of crops and papaya plantations, it is an important agricultural

centre and one of the biggest cattle collecting points in the country. Nazret is a popular destination for Addis Ababans escaping the city and is thus well-endowed with hotels and restaurants. It makes a convenient and pleasant enough overnight stop on your way to or from the east. The banks here have foreign exchange facilities.

Garis are good for getting around town. From the bus station to your hotel costs a flat rate of Birr1.

Places to Stay & Eat

Of the rock-bottom budget places, the *Hoteela Afrikaa*, on a side road leading north of the Commercial Bank, is about the best bet; rooms with cold communal shower cost Birr7.

The *Canal Hotel* (☎ 11-25-45), not far from the bus station, is by far the best option in the budget to mid-range category; very good rooms with shower cost Birr25. The restaurant is popular locally.

The *Palace Hotel* (☎ 11-38-00, fax 11-10-87) opposite the bus station, just off the main Addis Ababa–Awash road, has recently renovated rooms with balcony for Birr60/78/84 depending on facilities. It has a large garden bar, the faranji food is not bad and there are vegetarian dishes.

The *Adama Makonnen Hotel* (☎ 11-08-88, fax 11-41-79) is a new hotel on the western approach to town from Addis Ababa. It has well-furnished rooms with balcony, telephone and satellite TV for Birr85/99, depending on their size. The nearby *Ras Hotel* (☎ 11-21-88), with rooms at Birr126, is rather overpriced but it has a reasonably well-maintained outdoor pool in a garden (Birr5.50 per day for nonguests).

If you're looking for a bite to eat, the *Rift Valley Hotel*, the first big hotel on the road into town from Addis Ababa, serves quite good faranji food.

The *Hoteela Firaanko*, which is around the corner from the Palace Hotel, was founded by its namesake, an Italian called Franco, and has a good reputation for its Italian dishes – announced on an Amharic-only menu! It's also a good place for breakfast.

BM Pastry across from the bus station is the best pastry shop in town.

Getting There & Away

Buses leave daily for Sodore (Birr2.50, 30 mins), Debre Zeyit (Birr4, one hour), Addis Ababa (Birr6.50, two hours) and Awash (Birr9, 2½ hours).

When heading south for Bale Mountains National Park, go to Asela first and change (Birr5, two hours). For Ziway and the Rift Valley lakes, go to Mojo (Birr2, 15 mins) and change.

Nazret is on the Addis Ababa–Djibouti train line (see Train in both the Ethiopia Getting There & Away and Getting Around sections, as well as Getting There & Away in the Dire Dawa section later in this chapter).

AROUND NAZRET
Sodore

The hot-springs resort of Sodore also attracts Addis Ababan weekenders – up to 2000 of them per day! During the week, it's a quieter place. It's not a patch on its hot-spring cousin, Wondo Genet (see under Around Shashemene in the South of Addis Ababa section). Unless you're filling time or are desperate for a dip in the Olympic-sized thermal pool (open from Friday to Sunday only), it's not worth a special excursion. Entrance to the resort costs Birr5.50.

The riverine forest that lines the nearby Awash River in the grounds of the resort is home to good birdlife and monkeys. In the river itself, crocodiles and (rarely now) hippos can be found. Beware of the crocodiles – they have taken children from the banks. There's good hiking in the hills behind the resort. You can ask for a guide at the hotel; the charming assistant manager, Getachew Tenagne, will help you find one.

Sodore Wabe Shebele Resort Hotel (☎ 11-34-00) is the only accommodation inside the resort. Various rooms, bungalows and huts are on offer. The A-shaped huts with twin beds and toilet but no shower (use those at the springs) cost Birr54 and represent the best value. Rooms for one or two people (all with bathroom) cost Birr72/

150/180 depending on facilities; bungalows with fridge cost Birr252. Camping is possible in the resort grounds (Birr15 per person). Tents can be hired for Birr15. Watch your possessions – theft is a problem.

Getting There & Away Sodore lies 24km south-east of Nazret, 7km off the main Nazret-Asela road. Minibuses run back and forth from Nazret (Birr2.50, 30 mins) past the resort gates. A contract taxi from Nazret costs Birr50 one way.

AWASH NATIONAL PARK

Awash National Park is one of the best-known and most visited of Ethiopia's parks. Easily accessible from Addis Ababa, the park offers good wildlife viewing and outstanding birdlife. It also contains an interesting range of volcanic landscapes. See also National Parks in the Facts about Ethiopia section.

The park takes its name from the Awash River, the longest river in Ethiopia. Marking the park's southern boundary, the river then veers north before disappearing into the remote and desolate confines of the Danakil region; the salt lakes around the Ethiopian-Djiboutian border are the river's last gesture.

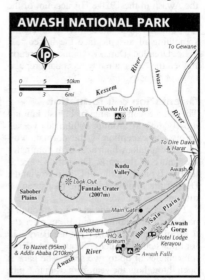

AWASH NATIONAL PARK

To Gewane

0   5   10km
0   3   6mi

Kessem River
Awash River

Filwoha Hot Springs

To Dire Dawa & Harar

Kudu Valley

Awash

Look Out
Fantale Crater (2007m)

Sabober Plains

Main Gate

Metehara

HQ & Museum

Illala Sala Plains

Awash Gorge

Hotel Lodge Kereyou

To Nazret (95km) & Addis Ababa (210km)

River
Awash

Awash Falls

The Dreaded Danakils

Every man wore, strapped across his stomach, a formidable curved dagger known as a *jile*, with a sixteen-inch blade sharp on each side. Nearly all these daggers had one or more brass-bound leather thongs dangling from the scabbard, each thong denoting a man killed...I was prepared to accept the fact that they would kill a man or boy with as little compunction as I would shoot a buck.

The Danakil invariably castrated any man or boy whom they killed or wounded, removing both the penis and the scrotum. An obvious trophy, it afforded irrefutable proof that the victim was male, and obtaining it gave the additional satisfaction of dishonouring the corpse...It is impossible to exaggerate the importance that the Danakil attached to this practice, rating as they did a man's prowess by the number of his kills.

From *The Life of My Choice* by Wilfred Thesiger, HarperCollins, 1992

Wilfred Thesiger, the well-known British explorer, set off in search of the source of the Awash in the 1920s. His account of the Afar peoples (then known as the Danakils) encountered along the way has become something of an epic (see the boxed text 'The Dreaded Danakils') and it greatly fuelled the Afars' already legendary reputation for ferocity.

Orientation & Information

The park covers an area of 827 sq km and mostly lies at around 1000m above sea level. The exception is the dormant volcano of Fantale, which at 2007m dominates the centre of the park. The park's vegetation is typical of the hot, arid lowlands. During the rainy season, the roads can be difficult.

The main gate to the park lies through a barrier on the right around 10km after the town of Metehara. Park fees are Birr50/25 for adults/children per 48 hours and Birr10 for vehicles of up to five seats. The park is open throughout the year from 6 am to 6 pm.

Because the park is so low-lying, it can get very hot. If you want to get the most from the park and see the greatest number of animals, it is essential to go either first thing in the morning or late in the afternoon as at midday, many animals retire to the shade of the trees. The speed limit for vehicles inside the park is 40km/h. The park headquarters lies 12km south-east of the main gate.

In the same complex as the park headquarters, there's a small museum filled with the usual stuffed animals, but with some quite interesting 'interpretative materials' on the area's flora, fauna and people and some useful animal locator maps. Both the viewpoint over the Awash Falls and the southern camping grounds are nearby. The falls are a good spot for birds; you can also walk down to the base of the falls and have a dip if you want.

Armed scouts (park rangers) can act as guides (Birr50 for the whole day) and are recommended (especially Adam Mohammed and Mamo Alemu). They are compulsory if you're planning to travel in the northern region of the park, where tribal conflicts between the Kereyu, Afar and Yetu pastoralist tribes are still common.

Dangers & Annoyances

Watch out for both the baboons and the grivet monkeys, which have become adept camp pillagers; they seem to have a particular penchant for packet food, and occasionally take cameras out of spite.

Malaria here is a problem; make sure that you take adequate precautions.

Don't drink the river water (even boiled) as the sugar factory lies upstream and uses the river to clean its equipment. You'll need to bring all drinking water with you.

A park guard (Birr25 per day) is a good idea if you're planning on leaving the camping ground during the day.

Recently, there have been moves to discourage walkers in the park. Robbery is apparently a real risk.

Fantale Crater

Towards the west of the park lies the Fantale Crater. There are terrific views down into the enormous elliptical caldera, which measures 3.5km in diameter. The local Kereyu people can be seen grazing their animals and growing crops far below (see the boxed text 'A Conflict of Interests' later in this section). On the lower slopes of the mountain, the remains of an extensive 16th-century settlement have been found.

On the southern flank, look out for the dark lava, evidence of the last volcanic flow in 1820. Steam can be seen issuing from the vent of the crater. Animals found on its steep slopes include klipspringers and mountain reedbucks. Keep an eye open for the huge lammergeyer soaring in the thermals above.

The crater rim lies around 25km from headquarters; it's a two-hour drive as the road – little more than a path – is very steep and rough in parts. With its terrific views, total quiet and cool air, it is a great place for a picnic. Hamadryas baboons are easily seen.

Filwoha Hot Springs
In the far north of the park, around 30km from the park headquarters, the Filwoha Hot Springs can be found. You can swim in the turquoise-blue pools, which aren't as refreshing as they look, with temperatures touching 36°C! In the cooler areas of the springs, as well as in the Awash River, crocodiles and hippos are found. Hippos are shy, choosing to feed at night (the locals kill them because they feed on their crops). Around the springs, look out for the doum palms, much appreciated by the Afar people who live in the area. After 5 pm, the area comes alive with birds.

Wildlife
In the south of the park can be found the grassy Illala Sala Plains, which attract most of the larger mammals. The spectacular Awash Gorge marks the southern border of the plains. Beisa oryx are easily see on the plains, as are Soemmering's gazelles. Swayne's hartebeests were introduced to the park, but their numbers have since declined.

In the bushland areas, particularly in the rocky valleys to the north, greater and lesser kudus and warthogs are found. Defassa wa-

---

Crunching Carnivores

The spotted hyaena (*Crocuta crocuta*) is by far the largest member of the hyaena family, and is known for its powerful build (the male hyaena can weigh up to 63kg), massive skull and robust teeth. The species is also the most carnivorous member of the hyaena family. Whereas other carnivores waste up to 40% of their kills, the spotted hyaena devours almost every scrap, including hooves, horn, bone and teeth. Bone fragments up to 9cm long are swallowed whole. Unlike its more peaceful cousin, the striped hyaena (see the boxed text 'Hateful Hyaena' in the South of Addis Ababa section), the spotted hyaena is a predator as well as a scavenger, sometimes forming packs in which to hunt.

In place of social cooperation common to the striped hyaena, the spotted hyaena has an openly competitive system. Access to kills and mates depends entirely on the power of the individual to dominate the rest of the clan. Clans are territorial and are led and dominated by the females, who lead the group into battle against rival clans.

---

terbucks are seen around the bushes near the river, as are Anubis and hamadryas baboons. The greater kudu is often also seen east of the Awash Falls, as well as on the way to the Filwoha Hot Springs.

The colobus monkey is found in the riverine forest. Salt's dik diks prefer to live in the acacia bushes. Leopards, lions, black-backed and golden jackals, caracals, servals and wildcats are also found in the park, but are seen pretty rarely. Striped and spotted hyaenas are often heard at night.

Birds
To date, over 400 bird species have been recorded in the park, among them six endemics: the banded barbet, golden-backed woodpecker, white-winged cliff chat, white-tailed starling, thick-billed raven and wattled ibis.

A good place to observe birds is around the camping grounds near the river, where doves, barbets and hoopoes are all seen.

A Conflict of Interests

Awash National Park epitomises the clash of interests between the local people and conservationists, and the difficulty of law enforcement in such situations. Though prohibited from grazing their animals inside the parameters of the park, the Kereyu are quite often spied there, particularly during times of drought. In 1993, the Kereyu even managed to establish villages close to Hotel Lodge Kerayou; they were forcibly evicted by the authorities in 1994.

Cattle found within the parameters of some parts of the park are rounded up by the park authorities, and are only released on the payment of a fine of Birr10 per animal.

Outright conflicts with the park authorities still occur. A few years ago, a park warden was shot and wounded by a local herdsman, whose cattle he was trying to pen. The locals have lived on the land for centuries and see it as their own; during times of hardship, they have no other means of survival.

Additionally, great prestige among the people still results from the killing of a lion. Local superstition has it that the hunter will assume some of the lion's strength and majesty in a kind of ritual power transferral: from the king of the beasts to king of the people.

The conflict will continue until the local people become actively involved in the park's conservation and benefit directly from its protection (see also Ecology & Environment in the Facts about Ethiopia section).

Near the river kingfishers and bee-eaters are found. On the plains, bustards are quite easily spotted, and sometimes secretary birds and ostriches are also found. The rich selection of raptors includes tawny and fish eagles, dark chanting goshawks and pygmy and lanner falcons.

Places to Stay & Eat

Camping Camping is the best option inside the park. The shady sites along the Awash River in the area known as 'Gotu', 400m from the park headquarters, are nice. Of the six spots, the *Gumarre* (hippo) site is considered the most pleasant. At night, you can often hear the noises of hippos, hyaenas and jackals who come to the river to drink. If you're lucky, you may hear the roar of a lion. Of all the camping grounds in Ethiopia, this has to rank among the most attractive. The area around the Filwoha Hot Springs in the northern extreme of the park, with its shady fig trees, is also good. Camping costs Birr20/10 per adult/child. Fees are payable at the park headquarters.

Caravans Lying at the edge of the gorge, a very decrepit caravan site, the *Hotel Lodge Kerayou*, 9km from the park headquarters, offers 20 caravans with cold 'showers' (in fact buckets) for Birr150/255 for one/two people. Both the plumbing and mosquito nets leave a lot to be desired; and when asked if the air-con worked, the caretaker hooted with laughter ... However, there is a restaurant with a terrace that boasts wonderful views over the Awash River and gorge. Set menus cost Birr28 for two courses plus fruit. If you're determined to boil alive in the caravans, make reservations through the Ras Hotel head office in Addis Ababa (☎ 51-60-70).

Getting There & Away

The park lies 95km from Nazret, 210km from Addis Ababa and 14km from the town of Awash. The main Addis Ababa–Assab highway runs through it.

Getting Around

Walkers are 'discouraged' (read not allowed) in the park (see Dangers & Annoyances earlier); the only alternative is to hire a vehicle or take a tour with one of the Addis Ababa–based tour operators. If there's enough of you, you can also try hiring a contract taxi in Awash. The only times you will need a 4WD are for the Fantale Crater or during the rainy season (July–September).

If you can't afford either of the above options, there's a simple solution: walk along the Awash-Metehara road. Many animals, including oryx and gazelles, can be seen on the plains from the road. You could even hop off a minibus near the main entrance gate and walk back to Awash (3½ hours). Remember to go early or late to maximise your chance of seeing wildlife.

AWASH

Though the little town of Awash also takes its name from the river, after the park, it appears rather a dismal, scruffy place. Its *raison d'être* (reason for being) is more to do with the railway; the town provides a halfway stop between Addis Ababa and Dire Dawa, and is the most important stop en route between the two capital cities.

On Monday, there is a very colourful market that attracts both Kereyu and Afar people. The Kereyu women wear skins and leather sandals and often braid their hair and the men don a kind of shaped Afro hairstyle, often ornamented with combs. Animal fat (like a kind of Ethiopian Brylcreem!) is rubbed into the hair to give it a chic gloss and keep it in fine condition. If you're in town on this day, don't miss it.

Around 600m behind the station lies the Awash Gorge. There's good hiking potential around here if you're filling time.

There's a bank in Awash, but it has no facilities for foreign exchange. Nazret or Dire Dawa are your best options.

Places to Stay & Eat

The *George Hotel* on the main road is the best budget bet, with rooms with/without cold shower for Birr15/10.

The old *Buffet d'Aouache* (also known as Buffet de la Gare), lies south of town, across the railway line. It's a great old relic of French railway days, and was built in 1904. Spacious rooms (with two double beds) complete with huge baths on legs cost Birr70 (Birr40 with shower only). It's also a great place to come for a drink or dinner. The garden is brimful with birds and the restaurant is good; Greek-Italian-style mains cost around Birr15. The hotel might be the place for a wee splurge, or a romantic 'Aren't we having a lovely holiday?' evening.

A cheap and reasonably cheerful local restaurant on the main road is the *Park*

Hotel, which offers good local and pasta dishes for Birr6.

Getting There & Away

At least one bus leaves daily for Addis Ababa (Birr15, four hours) and Dire Dawa (Birr35, eight hours). Going north, one bus leaves daily for Gewane (Birr10, two hours). When relations improve again with Eritrea, buses should resume the service all the way to Assab at the end of the road (see Border Crossings in the Ethiopia Getting There & Away section earlier).

One train runs daily to Debre Zeyit (Birr9–30 depending on the class, four hours), Akaki (Birr11–35, five hours), Dire Dawa (Birr13–38, eight hours) and Addis Ababa (Birr13–38, 5½ hours). Trains west to Addis Ababa often leave in the early hours. The train east to Dire Dawa departs at 10.30 pm.

AWASH TO ASAITA

The road north to Asaita takes you through the Yangudi-Rassa National Park via the town of Gewane. Don't expect to see much wildlife; there is probably less here than in any national park in Ethiopia. The road is of interest, however, as it takes you through the heart of Afar country (see the boxed texts 'Peoples of Ethiopia' under Population & People in Facts about Ethiopia and 'Ogling the Afars' over next page). In general the land is incredibly flat without so much as a mound in sight; the road just heads straight through it, like an American highway in the Midwest.

Drive for 666km and you'll come to the Red Sea port of Assab in Eritrea. En route are the salt lakes around Asaita and an archaeological dig, site of one of our 'missing links': Lucy, at Hadar.

Yangudi-Rassa National Park

The 4730 sq km Yangudi-Rassa National Park is a semidesert, and its vegetation consists of little more than semi-arid grasses, acacia trees and succulent scrub. The park was originally founded for the protection of the extremely rare wild ass (see the boxed text 'The Wild Ass' following). Other mammals that you're more likely to see (although

Ogling the Afars

On the journey north, look out for Afar women in long brown skirts, bright bead necklaces and brass anklets. The men – who often sport goatee beards – wear a kind of sarong along with a cotton cloth slung over a shoulder. Some carry gourds, which act as waterbottles. Keep an eye out for the famous *jile*, the curved knife described by the writer Wilfred Thesiger (see the boxed text 'The Dreaded Danakils' earlier in this section), which is still carried by many Afars. Today, the knives are often accompanied by AK47s. Inter-clan rivalry and conflict is still rife.

Many Afars still lead a nomadic existence, and when the herds are moved in search of new pasture, the huts in which the Afars live are simply packed onto the backs of camels; the wooden boughs used for the armature look like great ribs curving upwards from the camels' backs. In the relatively fertile plains around the river, some Afars have turned to cultivation, growing tobacco, cotton, maize and dates.

the chances are still remote) include Soemmering's gazelles, Grevy's zebras, hamadryas baboons, gerenuks and beisa oryx. Ostriches are quite often spotted here. Unfortunately, the park is so overrun with local herds, you will be lucky to see even one specimen of any species (if you do, it will probably be lying flattened on the road). It's certainly not worth a special visit.

There's no established entrance gate. The so-called park headquarters is found in Gewane, and you can hire a scout-cum-guide for around Birr25 per day. A few tracks crisscross the park, but these are used by herdsmen and their animals rather than by vehicles. Camping is the only option in the park.

If you want to overnight in the windswept, dusty little town of Gewane, 62km south, the *Agip Motel* has rooms with/without common shower for Birr20/10. It also has a restaurant that does a delicious *dabbo fir fir*: torn-up bread with butter and *berbere* (spice mixture).

Malaria is a big problem in this area; make sure you take adequate precautions.

Getting There & Away The main Awash-Assab highway runs right through the park. One bus departs Gewane daily for Awash (Birr10, two hours), as do several trucks (Birr15). Continuing north, only trucks travel to Mille (Birr15, 3½ hours) and Logia (Birr20, 4½ hours).

Mille

Not much goes on here; just sitting through the heat, with a bit of chat-chewing thrown in.

The *Ephrem Hotel* offers the most comfortable accommodation, with rooms with/without private cold shower for Birr20/10. The restaurant is also good.

The return trip to Addis Ababa can be made via Bati, the little town with the very big Monday market (see under Around Kombolcha in the North of Addis Ababa section).

From Mille, trucks run south to Gewane through Yangudi-Rassa National Park (see previous) and east to Djibouti town (Birr10, 2½ hours) via Dieciotto in Ethiopia and Galafi in Djibouti (see Border Crossings in the Ethiopia Getting There & Away section earlier).

One bus goes west to Dessie (Birr13, 4 to 5 hours – see the North of Addis Ababa section for Dessie), as does a truck (Birr20). For Asaita, you should take the truck to

Hadar – Lucy Woz 'Ere

Around 80km north-east of Mille, a track leads to the famous archaeological site of Hadar. It was here that the hominid Lucy was discovered (see the boxed text 'Lucy in the Sky' under History in the Facts about Ethiopia section). The site is still being excavated, and finds continue to be made. However, most discoveries are whisked straight off to Addis Ababa for examination, and there is little to be seen on the site itself. If you still want to visit, you should contact the Asaita tourist office, which is responsible for the region.

Galafi and ask to be dropped off at Logia, 45km from Mille. From Logia, you can hop on the daily bus to Asaita coming from Dessie (Birr5).

Asaita
☎ 03

Around 62km east of Logia is the town of Asaita, at the heart of Afar territory. It has been the region's capital, but it will soon be eclipsed by Semere, which is in the process of being developed as the new capital. Asaita makes a useful base from which to explore the 30 salt lakes in the area. Around the town are cotton and sesame plantations, as well as maize and millet.

Torrid, poor and dingy, and supporting a suffocating climate for nine months of the year, the town is little visited. The police will expect you to register with them on arrival, and you'll need permission to visit any of the surrounding attractions. Disputes over land ownership occur, sometimes resulting in outright conflict between the different clans; you should check the current security situation. The police office will also provide you with an armed guard.

There's also a helpful tourist office in Asaita just off the western side of the main square. Asaita's Commercial Bank is very proud to be able to change travellers cheques. Market day at Asaita is Tuesday, and is a must if you're in town.

Places to Stay & Eat The *Basha Hotel* is probably the most popular hotel in Asaita. Simple but clean rooms with ceiling fan and common shower cost Birr12. Some travellers prefer to sleep on the roof terrace (Birr5), where mosquito nets are supplied. At night, you can hear the hyaenas and the nomads' camels; the latter make a noise like a troublesome kitchen sink. You can see the Afar nomads camping below. The hotel also has a good restaurant.

If the Basha is full, the *Lem Lem* makes a good second choice, with rooms at the same price and an even better restaurant.

Getting There & Away To visit the lakes from Asaita, a contract taxi will take you as

The Wild Ass

The African wild ass *(Equus africanus)* is the most endangered equine in the world. It is found throughout the Horn, but is thinly spread, estimated in the mid-1990s at just 1 to 2 animals per 100 sq km. During the last 10–20 years, populations in the Horn have been reduced by at least 80%. Extinction is certain unless adequate measures to protect the animal are taken soon.

Very little is known about the animal's behaviour, reproductive biology and genetic make-up. It is thought that the female reaches sexual maturity at between 3–4 years, and that just one foal survives every two years. The ass is very susceptible to predation (particularly when young), in particular by hyaenas and people.

The three major threats to the animal are hunting (particularly in Ethiopia and Somalia, where the ass is used as a source of food and medicine); competition with livestock for limited water and grazing during drought periods; and interbreeding with the domestic donkey.

far as the old Italian fort overlooking Lake Gamarri for Birr50.

With your own vehicle, Dikhil (Djibouti) can be reached from Asaita in 3–4 hours. With public transport, you'll have to take a bus back to Logia, and from there take a truck to Dieciotto (Birr10, 1½ hours). At Dieciotto, minibuses, trucks and pick-ups go to Galafi (Birr100) in Djibouti. See Border Crossings in the Ethiopia Getting There & Away section earlier.

One bus leaves daily for Mille (Birr10, one hour) and Dessie (Birr19, 10 hours). At least 3–4 minibuses leave each day for Logia (Birr10, two hours).

Salt Lakes
The salt lakes around Asaita have a stark, desolate, almost surreal beauty, and birdlife is very good: storks, flamingos, ibises, egrets, vultures and raptors can be seen. The journey also takes you through very remote Afar country; the people are magnificent. However, it takes time to reach the lakes

Kulubi Gabriel

The little village of Kulubi is the site of a very important pilgrimage at the end of December (see Public Holidays & Special Events in the Ethiopia Facts for the Visitor section). Tens of thousands of pilgrims converge each year on the church of Saint Gabriel on the hill above the town. Traditionally, the truly pious walk the 64km here from Dire Dawa. Pilgrims come to express thanks after the fulfilment of a wish, or in the hope of a miraculous cure. If you're in the area during the festival, it's well worth a stop.

A little church was founded here by Ras Makonnen in thanks for the great victory over the Italians at Adwa. In 1962, the Emperor Haile Selassie, with his usual delicacy, erected the huge and hideous cathedral. Nevertheless, the church is one of the most significant churches in Orthodox Ethiopia. The bright mosaic on the facade represents St Gabriel cooling the flames of a cauldron containing the three boys condemned to death (see the boxed text 'Know Your Ethiopian Saints' under Addis Ababa to Debre Markos in the North of Addis Ababa section).

The **Ras Hotel** (no telephone) on the edge of town is the largest and best hotel; basic but clean rooms with communal shower cost Birr10.

and sometimes access is limited because of security concerns. At the time of writing, it was impossible to proceed further south than Lake Gamarri.

The reeds that grow along the streams are used by the Afars to make their famous mats (see the boxed text 'The Fabulous Fiddima' in the Around the Gulf of Tadjoura section in the Djibouti chapter).

Lakes in the region that can usually be visited include Lake Gamarri (around 30km from Asaita – known for its hundreds of flamingos); Lake Afambo and Lake Bario (both near the town of Afambo); and Lake Abbe (Lac Abbé). If you have the option, Lac Abbé approached from the Djibouti side is a far better choice, for accessibility as well as for natural beauty (see the South-West to Lac Abbé section in the Djibouti chapter).

See Getting There & Away under Asaita earlier.

AWASH TO DIRE DAWA

Going east, the landscape seems to get drier and drier, the temperature hotter and hotter. It's not too long, though, before the road once again starts to climb upwards from the arid lowlands.

This is the heart of Oromo country. The men gathered under ancient trees are attending the usual village assembly. Look out for the children on the roadside selling 'local Colgate' or the local version of a toothbrush (see the boxed text 'A Nomad's Toothbrush' in the South to Ali Sabieh section in the Djibouti chapter). The Oromo women wear very colourful skirts, headbands and waistbands. Saturday is market day for many villages in the region – if you can travel east on this day, do. This is also coffee country – stop and try a cup of the rich and bitter brew.

Around the Chercher Mountains, the very first signs of chat cultivation appear – look for the little bushes with shiny, dark-green leaves planted in neat rows. As the road begins to climb, you're taken through some very beautiful scenery with stunning views; the 126km stretch between Arbereketi and Dire Dawa is one of the prettiest in Ethiopia. The markets along this route, eg, the Thursday market at Asbe Tefaru, are amongst the most colourful in the country. Don't miss them.

DIRE DAWA
☎ 05

The great Addis Ababa–Djibouti railway was originally intended to pass through the old commercial town of Harar. But, in order to cut the ever-burgeoning costs, it was decided to bypass the Chercher Mountains and stick to the lowlands instead. In Harar's place, a new town was conceived, which Menelik chose to call New Harar. In 1902, Dire Dawa – as it was known locally – came into being.

Dire Dawa is now the second most populous town in Ethiopia, with nearly 100,000

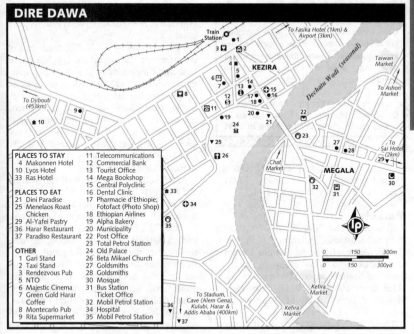

DIRE DAWA

To Fasika Hotel (1km) &
Airport (3km)

Train
Station

KEZIRA

Dechatu Wadi (seasonal)

Taiwan
Market

To Ashon
Market

To Djibouti
(453km)

Chat
Market

To
Sai Hotel
(2km)

MEGALA

To Stadium,
Cave (Alem Gena),
Kulubi, Harar &
Addis Ababa (400km)

Kefira
Market

Kefira
Market

0   150   300m
0   150   300yd

PLACES TO STAY	11 Telecommunications
4 Makonnen Hotel	12 Commercial Bank
10 Lyos Hotel	13 Tourist Office
33 Ras Hotel	14 Mega Bookshop
	15 Central Polyclinic
PLACES TO EAT	16 Dental Clinic
21 Dini Paradise	17 Pharmacie d'Ethiopie;
25 Menelaos Roast	Fotofact (Photo Shop)
Chicken	18 Ethiopian Airlines
29 Al-Yafei Pastry	19 Alpha Bakery
36 Harar Restaurant	20 Municipality
37 Paradiso Restaurant	22 Post Office
	23 Total Petrol Station
OTHER	24 Old Palace
1 Gari Stand	26 Beta Mikael Church
2 Taxi Stand	27 Goldsmiths
3 Rendezvous Pub	28 Goldsmiths
5 NTO	30 Mosque
6 Majestic Cinema	31 Bus Station
7 Green Gold Harar	32 Mobil Petrol Station
Coffee	34 Hospital
8 Montecarlo Pub	35 Mobil Petrol Station
9 Rita Supermarket	

inhabitants. Cement, textile and soft drink factories lie all around its periphery. Unlike almost all other Ethiopian towns, Dire Dawa boasts the unusual distinction of town planning: it features straight, tree-lined streets, neat squares and some interesting colonial architecture.

Foreign influence is still much in evidence in Dire Dawa. Look for the Italian in some of the architecture and the number of restaurants still serving Italian food; the French in the baguette bread and the hotel bidets.

Apart from the markets, there's not much to see in Dire Dawa. After – or in anticipation of – Harar, Dire Dawa invariably disappoints and can seem hot, dusty and dull. However, a 'city tour' in a gari is a pleasant way to while away a morning or afternoon.

The mosquitoes will form part of your less pleasant recollections of Dire Dawa; remember to take adequate precautions against malaria.

Orientation & Information

The town is made up of two distinct settlements, divided by the Dechatu wadi. Lying to the north and west of the stream is the 'new town' known as Kezira, planned and built in response to the railway.

On the southern and eastern side of the wadi is the 'old town' known as Megala, which, with its labyrinth-like streets and Arab-looking houses, has a distinctly Muslim feel. Here, Dire Dawa's enormous market, Kefira, is found (see Markets following).

The Commercial Bank in Kezira has foreign exchange facilities. The tourist office (☎ 11-36-73) is opposite. If you want to take home some Ethiopian coffee, the Green Gold Harar Coffee shop in Kezira sells 1kg packets for Birr22.50. Traditional coffee pots go for Birr6.

The National Tourist Organisation (NTO; ☎ 11-11-19) has an office in Kezira; cars can be rented here for the usual rates (see

ETHIOPIA

Remote People

I am constitutionally a martyr to boredom, but never have I been so desperately and degradingly bored as I was during the next four days...Most of the time I thought about how awful the next day would be.

From Evelyn Waugh's *Remote People*, Duckworth, London, 1931, about when he was stuck briefly in Dire Dawa in 1931

under Car & Motorcycle in the Getting Around Ethiopia section earlier). There's also a travel agency in the Sai Hotel.

Markets

Kefira market in Megala attracts people from miles around, including Afar herders, Somali pastoralists and Oromo farmers; sometimes large camel caravans march in from the Somali desert. The market takes place from 10 am to 1 pm daily except Sunday. A large variety of spices are sold here.

There is a thriving contraband market; stuff is brought in from Djibouti either by night caravans across the remote frontiers, or carefully concealed in trucks. Ashon Market on the outskirts of town sells everything from hair curlers and beard trimmers to Johnson's Baby Powder, fake designer watches and photo albums. The nearby Taiwan Market, as its name suggests, specialises in cheap electronic goods. Both are worth a peek.

A two-hour tour of the old markets by gari costs Birr10.

Places to Stay

The *Lyos Hotel* (☎ 11-04-72) is probably the best budget deal in town, although it's set a little way out, west of the town centre. Rooms with private shower cost from Birr12–20 and are arranged around a pleasant garden.

Makonnen Hotel (☎ 11-38-48) near the train station is an old Italian colonial hotel that has simple but very clean and quite pleasant rooms with communal shower for Birr20. The multilingual manager, Nigatu,

is friendly and helpful. It's often filled with Djiboutian merchants, so reservations are a good idea.

Fasika Hotel (☎ 11-12-60), north-east of the centre on the airport road, is one of the best mid-range places. Rooms set in quiet gardens with private bathroom for one/two people cost Birr50.

The *Ras Hotel*, with tired, over-priced rooms, is worth a visit for its outdoor pool and garden only (Birr4.40/6.60 for non-guests during weekdays/weekends). It also may be worth a visit for its pub (see Places to Eat & Drink following).

Much better value is the well-run Muslim *Sai Hotel* (☎ 11-22-85, fax 11-32-42), 2km east of the centre on the Megala side of town, with comfy rooms for one/two people for Birr125/150 (some with satellite TV and fridge). Officially, couples should be married – you may be asked for proof of this. Reservations are advised. The restaurant serves quite good faranji food; there's a good fixed menu (soup, pasta dish, main, salad, fruit and coffee) for Birr17 plus tax. Alcohol is not served in the hotel. An airport pick-up service is available and there's a travel agency here.

Places to Eat & Drink

Menelaos Roast Chicken in Kezira is the nearest thing Dire Dawa has to a fast-food joint. It does reasonably finger-lickin'-good roast chickens for Birr15.

The *Al-Yafei Pastry* in Megala is a good place for fruit juices (Birr2).

Dini Paradise is a cafe set in a garden near the bridge; if you're feeling out of touch, it's got a satellite TV showing CNN. Sandwiches/hamburgers go for around Birr5; the fruit juices here are good.

The *Paradiso Restaurant* on the Addis Ababa road south of the centre serves both Ethiopian and Italian food, and is considered one of the best places in town. It's an attractive place with a veranda as well as 'smarter' *salons* (little dining rooms). Diagonally opposite, the *Harar Restaurant* (signposted in Amharic only) is a large, lively, local place also serving traditional and Italian food inside and out.

Fragrant local honey for sale at a market

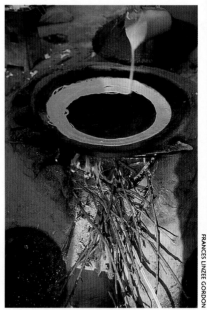

Making injera, traditional Ethiopian pancakes

A vendor and her wares at Nekemte market

Traditional skin cushions are stuffed with straw.

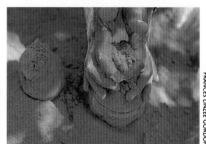

Berbere, a special Ethiopian blend of spices

Bahar Dar's market has all sorts of traditional and ceremonial clothing on offer.

Locally made sunhats can come in handy.

A bit of comfort, Ethiopian-style

Afewerk Terkle's Africa, depicted in stained glass

For a drink, you can try the ***Rendezvous*** or ***Montecarlo*** pubs, both in Kezira. The ***Ras Hotel*** (see Places to Stay previous) is a civilised place, where the town's big and little fish often gather together.

Getting There & Away

Trains head east for Djibouti town (Birr58/39/19 for 1st/2nd/3rd class) on Tuesday, Thursday and Saturday at 5.30 am, arriving around 5 pm. It's a very good idea to book your ticket early the previous day. 'Check in' is at 4 am.

Trains head west for Addis Ababa (Birr75/47/24, twelve hours) daily at 5.30 pm, via Awash (Birr38/25/13, eight hours), Nazret (Birr60/38/20, 10 hours), and Debre Zeyit (Birr6/42/21, 10½ hours).

Buses run daily to Addis Ababa (Birr34–50, 12 hours) via Awash (same price, six hours), Nazret (10 hours) and Debre Zeyit (11 hours). Minibuses run every 15 minutes to Harar (Birr6, one hour) and Kulubi (Birr7, one hour 20 mins). Note there are no buses to Djibouti; only trains run there.

Ethiopian Airlines flies twice daily to Addis Ababa, and twice weekly to Jijiga and to Djibouti town. Credit cards are accepted.

Getting Around

Garis are a great way of getting around town. Short journeys cost no more than Birr1; a full/half day costs Birr40/20. A contract taxi to the airport should cost Birr5–10.

HARAR
☎ 05

Lying just off the southern edge of the Chercher Mountains at an altitude of 1870m, Harar is the capital of the old Harerge province. Situated just a few hundred kilometres east of the staunchly Christian highlands, Harar, like an exotic bird, might have been blown off course – either from across the waters of the Red Sea or from the northern deserts of Muslim North Africa.

For centuries Harar spearheaded Islam's penetration into sub-Saharan Africa. It still holds very special significance for Ethiopia's Muslim population.

The Railway

In the 1890s, an ambitious project was dreamed up by Emperor Menelik's Swiss technical adviser, Alfred Ilg. Ilg imagined a railway running for nearly 800km, which would link Ethiopia's capital with French Somaliland (present-day Djibouti) on the Red Sea coast. Travelling though some of the most inhospitable terrain in Ethiopia, it was hoped that a railway would end for good the old isolation of the Ethiopian highlands.

Putting Ilg's vision into practice proved easier said than done. Each kilometre of line demanded no less than 70 tonnes of rails, sleepers and telegraph poles, as well as massive quantities of cement, sand and water, and food and provisions for the army of workers. Expensive iron sleepers were essential to protect against termites. But to keep the costs down, a narrow gauge of just one metre was used.

To cross the difficult terrain, several viaducts had to be built and 22 tunnels (one nearly 100m long) had to be constructed. Thirty four stations were built and extensive earthworks were needed to keep the track level.

Throughout the process, the local Afars, whose territory the 'iron monster' was penetrating, kept up an active opposition to the project. They ran horrific raids on the line at every opportunity, stealing building materials and killing workers.

The railway wasn't finally completed until some 20 years after it was begun. By this time the colonial powers in the region, France, Britain and Italy, had decided that the railway belonged to France, so long as it was not extended beyond Addis Ababa.

Today, the railway continues to play an extremely important role in the modern Ethiopian economy, particularly since the Eritrean-Ethiopian border dispute broke out in 1998. Now, the railway carries a large part of the country's imports and exports back and forth to the Red Sea port of Djibouti town.

A crossroads for every conceivable commerce, the town boomed, great dynasties of rich and powerful merchants grew up and

ETHIOPIA

HARAR

PLACES TO STAY	3 Officers' Training School	29 City Council & Oromo	48 Medersa
6 Dessie Hotel	4 Agip Petrol Station	Region Office	49 Fatuma Safir Ahmed's House
8 Ras Hotel	5 Ethiopian Red Cross Society	30 Bus Station	(Souvenir Shop)
17 Tourist Hotel	7 Mobil Petrol Station	31 Shell Petrol Station	50 Old Palace
24 Tewodros Hotel	9 Mega Bookshop	33 Christian Market	51 Rimbaud's House
32 Belayneh Hotel	10 Clinic	34 Berka Food Store	52 Medhane Alem Cathedral
41 Harar Academy Hotel	11 Tourism Office (Region 13)	35 Cottage Bar	54 Ras Tafari's House
	13 Regional Sports, Tourism &	36 Samsun Hotel & Bar	55 Magala Guddo Mosque
PLACES TO EAT	Culture Office	37 Photo Shop	56 Magala Guddo Market
12 Hirot Restaurant	14 Harar Military Academy	38 Hashim Pharmacy	(Muslim Market)
22 Medre Genet Hotel	15 Ras Makonnen Statue	39 Regional Police Office	57 Tomb of Abu Said Ali
23 Canal Cafeteria	16 National Hotel	40 Feres Magala;	58 Zeituna Yusuf
27 Andenya Menged Cake	18 Harar Laundry	City Taxi Stand	Grille's Shop
House	19 Post Office	42 Emir Nur's Tomb	59 Sheikh Abadir's Tomb
53 Cafeteria Ali Bal	20 Telecommunications	43 Hospital	60 Community Fountain
	21 Selassie Church	44 Al-Jami Mosque	61 Aounsar Shrine;
OTHER	25 Commercial Bank	45 Ay Abida Shrine	Hyaena Feeding
1 Babille Mineral	26 Region 13	46 St Mary's Catholic Church	62 Harar Clinic
Water Factory	Administration Office	47 Harari National Cultural	63 Mosque
2 Heymet Fana Hospital	28 Konika Photo Express	Centre & Museum	64 Old Leper Colony

the arts flourished. Harar became a kind of commercial meeting point of Africa, India and the Middle East. Right up until 1850, it was home to the most important market in the Horn.

Still something of an exotic bird in a country that prides itself above all on its ancient Christian heritage, this great city is perhaps Ethiopia's most undervalued attraction.

History

In 1520, a local emir, Abu Bakr, decided to relocate his capital. The site he chose was Harar, not far from the old capital of Dakar. Five years later, the sultan was overthrown and the new city was taken over by the legendary Ahmed Ibn Ibrahim al Ghazi, nicknamed Mohammed Gragn the Left-Handed (see under History in the Facts about Ethiopia section).

Decades of war against the Christian empire of the West followed, during which time the rich resources of the city were depleted.

By the time the great leader himself had been killed, the town had fallen upon hard times. A new threat then arose: the migrations northwards of the Oromo. In response, Gragn's successor, Nur Ibn al-Wazir Mujahid, erected thick 5m-high walls around the town, which stand to this day.

For the next three decades, Harar existed as a kind of independent city state, sometimes ruled by a strict Muslim theocracy. Commerce continued to flourish, however, and the town even issued its own currency. Harar's merchants travelled as far afield as India, Arabia and Egypt, and both coffee and chat were actively cultivated.

In the 17th and 18th centuries, Harar become known as an important centre of Islamic scholarship. Handicrafts flourished, in particular book-binding, weaving and basketry; the tradition continues to this day.

In 1875, Harar was again threatened, this time by the Egyptians, who dreamed of establishing an East African empire. Marching with 4000 men on a virtually defenceless city, they killed its ruler, Abd al-Shakur, and occupied the town for a decade. Though he met with fierce resistance, the emir Abdullahi eventually took over, only to be defeated (in 1887) by the Emperor Menelik, who sought to expand his highland empire. Menelik, considered the great unifier by the Amharas, is to this day greatly resented by many Hararis.

However, with the new government and the new federal constitution of 1995, Harar won back a kind of independence, being recognised legally as a city-state among the 14 regions comprising the Federal Republic of Ethiopia. It is a major landmark in the city's history.

For years, the city was closed to Christians. In 1854, Richard Burton, the famous British explorer, was the first non-Muslim to penetrate the city (see the boxed text 'Forbidden Footsteps'). Later, the bustling commercial town attracted many foreign merchants from India, Armenia, England and France. The famous French poet, Arthur Rimbaud, spent some of his last years here (see the boxed text 'Arthur Rimbaud – the Revolting Genius' later in this section).

Harar's economic fortunes suffered a serious blow at the end of the 19th century when the Addis Ababa–Djibouti railway was diverted to Dire Dawa. To this day, the city retains a somewhat isolated, inward-looking feel. The Hararis have their own ethnic identity, their own language and their own culture. As Dire Dawa continues to flourish and grow, Harar languishes somewhere in the past – for the traveller, this greatly contributes to the old city's charm.

Orientation & Information

The tourism office (☎ 66-18-14) on the main street is open from 8 am to 12.30 pm and 2 to 5.30 pm weekdays. The Commercial Bank, near Harar Gate, has foreign exchange facilities.

Water shortages are a major problem in Harar and can affect the city for three days or more. However, there are plans to pipe water from Dire Dawa (by 2004).

Although you can probably see the major attractions in a day, two days is better.

Forbidden Footsteps

The spectacle, materially speaking, was a disappointment: nothing conspicuous appeared but two grey minarets of rude shape: many would have grudged exposing three lives to win so paltry a prize. But of all that have attempted, none ever succeeded in entering that pile of stones: the through-bred traveller ... will understand my exultation.

From *First Footsteps in East Africa* by Richard Burton, who, in 1854, became the first European to enter the forbidden Muslim stronghold of Harar, published by Dover, New York, 1988

Harar's old town, with its 362 alleyways squeezed into just 1 sq km, is a fascinating place that begs exploration. Taxis cost Birr1 for a short hop about town.

Guides For your first foray into Harar, it's quite a good idea to hire a guide and take a turn round the town's main attractions. Later, it's well worth returning unaccompanied. Even if you get lost, Harar is so small you'll eventually come to a major street or wall that will lead you back to the main gate.

Unfortunately, the standard of guides in Harar is low even by Ethiopian standards. One, whose name appeared in another guidebook, has become so blase, he doesn't bother turning up for appointments; the other has made a speciality of howling like a Harar hyaena if his inflated expectations are not met. Sadly, some visitors have claimed that their trips to the city were ruined by such 'misunderstandings'. See the boxed text 'Guidelines for Guides' under Money in the Ethiopia Facts for the Visitor section. The tourism office suggests a fee of Birr25/50 per half/full day for a guide. If you have a major problem with a guide you should let the tourism office know.

Inside the Walls

The walled city of Harar covers an area of a little over 1 sq km. There are over 87 **mosques** in the old town alone, and these

ETHIOPIA

DAWIT ABEBE

Chewing the mildly intoxicating leaves of chat helps the users chat and chat and chat...

are said to form the largest concentration of any city in the world. **Shrines** devoted to local holy men or religious leaders are even more numerous; no one has yet managed to count them. Many are very peaceful, beautiful and well-kept places which can be visited by both men and women.

Look out for the Harari Adare women, known for their very colourful **traditional costumes**, which consists of dresses – usually black, yellow, red or purple – worn over velvet trousers. Many also wear orange head scarves and carry on their heads huge bundles of cloth or baskets. You should be sensitive when trying to photograph these women (see Photography & Video in the Ethiopia Facts for the Visitor section).

It's well worth visiting a traditional Adare house (see Traditional Adare Houses later) but you'll need a guide to find one.

Walking Tour A tour of the old town begins at the main gate, which is known as the **Harar Gate** or Duke's Gate after the first Duke of Harar, Ras Makonnen. There are seven gates in total; two were added by the Emperor Menelik in 1889 to the five original ones, which date from the 16th century. Streets lead from each gate and converge in the centre at a little square, known as *Feres Magala* (horse market). It is here that you can find a guide (or a guide will find you). Radiating out from the square are a maze of little alleyways and passages.

On and around the central square are many of the old town's attractions. **Medhane Alem Cathedral** was built by Emperor Menelik at the end of the 19th century. Constructed in the very heart of the city, the cathedral is typical of Menelik's arrogance and forcefulness when dealing with the peoples he conquered. Contrary to what the tourist literature tells you, the motley church treasures are not worth a special visit for those pushed for time.

On the south-east corner of the square is the seedy Harar Academy Hotel. This was one of four places where the great French

Arthur Rimbaud – The Revolting Genius

Arthur Rimbaud was born in 1854 in the Ardennes, north-eastern France. His upbringing in the little town of Charleville by his strict disciplinarian mother, was to instil in him a loathing for the rigid and conventional life of the provinces.

With a precocious and brilliant intellect, and encouraged by his rhetoric teacher, Rimbaud began to experiment with new forms of poetry. In 1871, he published his first major collection, *Le bateau ivre (The drunken boat)*. Later that year, Rimbaud sent some poems to the famous poet Paul Verlaine (of the school 'Art for art's sake'). 'Come, beloved great soul, you are called, you are awaited', was Verlaine's reply, and in September the young poet arrived in Paris.

Verlaine introduced Rimbaud to all the literary notables of the day. His reception in Paris was lukewarm: with his arrogance and charm, his obscenity and beauty, his ingenuity and boorishness, Rimbaud both repulsed and fascinated the society of the capital. Embarking upon a life of drink and debauchery, he began a homosexual affair with Verlaine that caused great scandal in the capital.

In 1872, Verlaine abandoned his wife to follow Rimbaud to England. The existence of the two poets was often precarious, and their relationship stormy. In July 1873, Verlaine fired two pistol shots at his lover, wounding Rimbaud in the wrist. He was sentenced to two years' imprisonment, and Rimbaud returned to France to write his *Une saison en enfer (A season in hell)*, an account of his affair with Verlaine and of his abject failure in art and love. After *Illuminations*, and discouraged both by the reception of his poetry in Paris and by increasing financial worries, Rimbaud decided to turn his back on poetry forever. He was just 21 years old.

In 1876, Rimbaud set out to see the world. By June 1879, he had joined – and deserted – the Dutch colonial army in the Indies, crossed the Alps by foot and (apparently) joined a German circus on its way to Scandinavia.

In the winter of 1879, in the service of a coffee trader in Aden (Yemen), Rimbaud became the first white man to travel into the Ogaden region of south-eastern Ethiopia. In October 1885, he risked all his savings on a venture to run guns to King Menelik of Shoa. It has been suggested that Rimbaud was also involved at this time in darker dealings, such as the trafficking of slaves.

While in Ethiopia, Rimbaud lived like a local in a small house in Harar (the exact house is unknown). His interest in the Ethiopian culture, languages and people made him popular with the locals, and his plain-speaking and integrity won the trust of the chiefs and the friendship of Menelik's nephew, the Governor of Harar. His home, which he shared with a local woman, became a popular destination for both Ethiopian and European visitors. In his letters to his mother written during this time, Rimbaud confesses to a longing for companionship, both intellectual and sentimental. This led him to plan a holiday home in order to look for a wife.

In 1891, Rimbaud developed a tumour on his right knee. Leaving Harar in early April, he endured the week's journey to the coast on a stretcher. Treatment at Aden was not a success, and Rimbaud continued on to France. Shortly after his arrival at Marseilles, his right leg was amputated, and he was diagnosed with cancer.

By the time of his return, Rimbaud was becoming increasingly known as a poet in a France. But he was indifferent to his fame and dreamed only of returning to Ethiopia. He died later that year at the young age of 37.

Rimbaud's poetry has won a huge popular following for its daring imagery, verbal eccentricities and beautiful and evocative language. Few poets have been the object of more passionate study or have exercised greater influence on modern poetry. Rimbaud, the man, may have repulsed; his poetry has enchanted.

poet **Rimbaud** is said to have lived (see the boxed text 'Arthur Rimbaud – the Revolting Genius'). **Rimbaud's House** in the middle of the square is (yet another) building in which the poet is said to have lived. Although he did live in the city, it was not here. The building houses a new **museum** dedicated to Rimbaud, containing a collection of books and writings about him and photos illustrating his life, as well as a selection of traditional **Adare arts and crafts**. The museum is open from 8 am to 12.30 pm and 2 to 5.30 pm daily. Entrance costs Birr5. From the rooftop, there's a good view over Harar to the blue Chercher Mountains.

Close to the museum is **Ras Tafari's House**, which has now been taken over by a local family including a holy man-cum-herbal-healer. A sign declares that the sheikh can fix anything from STDs to diabetes, mental illness and cancer. Past patients – apparently testifying to his success – return to look after the holy man, cooking and cleaning for him for the rest of their lives. The house was built by an Indian trader and many of its features, such as the Hindu figures on the door are Oriental. Haile Selassie spent some of his childhood here.

The **Al-Jami Mosque** just south of the square is Harar's great mosque. It was built in the 16th century, though according to local tradition, a mosque has stood on the site since the 12th century, long before the foundation of Harar.

Just north of the square is Magala Guddo (the so-called **Muslim market**); it's definitely worth a stroll by. Monday is the day that many Oromo and some Somali people come in from the surrounding areas (it's most busy from 2.30 to 5.30 pm).

The **Erer Gate** in the west was the one Richard Burton entered disguised as an Arab merchant (see the boxed text 'Forbidden Footsteps' earlier in this section). The **chat market** is found here.

Traditional Adare Houses Heading west towards Erer Gate, the **museum** of the Harari National Cultural Centre is designed like a typical Adare house and contains examples of traditional arts and crafts, typical

Adare Houses

The traditional Adare house, the *gegar*, is a rectangular, two-storey structure with a flat roof. Constructed with clay reinforced with wooden beams, then whitewashed, the house remains cool whatever the temperature and echoes the Arab coastal architecture of Eritrea and Djibouti. Sometimes the facades are adorned with bright green, blue or ochre murals. A small courtyard keeps the interior of the house out of the view of curious passersby. Just 100 years ago, nearly all the houses in Harar were constructed in this way; today they make up less than 25% of the total building stock.

The upstairs room is now used as a bedroom; in former times, it served as a storeroom. The main living room consists of five raised platforms of different levels, which are covered in rich rugs, cushions and stools. The platforms are used according to the status of guests or household members. The walls are usually painted bright red or ochre – said to symbolise the blood that every Harari was willing to shed during the resistance to Menelik's annexation of the city – and are then covered with woven cloth or hung with carpets. Eleven niches are carved into the wall, and these serve to display cups and pots. Every sort of pot, plate, receptacle or basket is made by the Adare women – all serve a strictly functional purpose.

The grills above the main entrance door are said to serve for hanging carpets, advertising that a girl of marriageable age resides within the household.

After marriage, newlyweds occupy a tiny, windowless, cell-like room to the side of the living quarters for one whole week, during which time relatives pass them food and water through the little hatch.

household objects and ornaments, traditional clothing, writing implements etc. Entrance costs Birr3. The museum is open from 8.30 to 11.30 am and 1.30 to 5 pm weekdays.

In some of the Adare houses in the old town, the ever-enterprising Adares have set up **souvenir shops** displaying beautifully made baskets and silver and amber jewellery. One such house that can be recommended is that belonging to **Fatuma Safir Ahmed**, just south of the Muslim market. Another is **Zeituna Yusuf Grille's shop**, just north of the market, which is as good as an antique shop. Amber necklaces cost around Birr550, baskets cost from Birr700–1500. Ask your guide to take you to the shops, and bring your sharpest bargaining skills. It's customary to tip the owner something after a tour around.

Shrines & Tombs To the north of the Muslim market lies the **Tomb of Abu Said Ali**, a former religious leader of the town. The tomb looks a little like a miniature mosque. Local tradition has it that below his tomb there lies a well that can sustain the whole city in times of siege.

Another tomb that can be visited is **Sheikh Abadir's Tomb** near the northernmost point of the old town. The sheikh was one of the most important preachers of Islam in the region and his tomb still attracts worshippers seeking answers or resolutions to their daily struggles in life: financial concerns, illnesses, family crises and infertility. If their prayers are answered, many devotees then return to make gifts to the shrine: usually rugs or expensive sandalwood.

Emir Nur's Tomb, south of square, is devoted to the ruler who built the city's walls. It resembles a spiky beehive. The **Ay Abida Shrine** nearby is visited by those who are desirous of seeing their daughter or son soon married, as well as by those praying for health. Harari families often send big pitchers of milk or tea there or food to feed the pilgrims or the city's poor seeking alms.

Outside the Walls

Outside the city's walls, Harar seems to go rather flat. Here the town is made up of once grandiose buildings (now falling apart) and a few shops and tourist hotels.

The **Christian Market** has been relegated outside the walls, near Shoa Gate, in the same way that Muslim markets are rele-

gated to a position outside the centre in many Christian Ethiopian towns. The market is at its peak of activity from 2.30 to 5.30 pm. Look out for the incense that comes from Jijiga in the far east of Ethiopia; it's sold for the Christian churches and coffee ceremonies. The spice market is filled with bark, roots and twigs used in the preparation of traditional medicine.

In the centre of **Ras Makonnen Square** stands a rather Italian-looking, equestrian statue of the *ras* (duke) cast in bronze by the well-known Amhara artist Afewerk Tekle (see the boxed text 'Afewerk Tekle' under Exhibitions & Galleries in the Addis Ababa section). The ras is said to look towards Somalia and the lands conquered there. Ras Makonnen was Emperor Menelik's cousin and was appointed first ruler of Harar after the emperor's occupation of the city. The ras is also known as the father of the Emperor Haile Selassie.

Also by Afewerk Tekle are the well-executed **stained glass windows** in Harar Military Academy facing the square. Unfortunately, the academy is currently closed to the general public; it will hopefully reopen soon. The windows depict different Ethiopian rulers of the past.

Hyaena Feeding

Possibly Harar's greatest attraction and certainly its most famous one (shown recently on a CNN clip of 'world culture'), are the hyaena men of Harar. As night falls (from around 7 pm), the last remaining hyaena man (see the boxed text 'The Hyaena Man of Harar' over the page) sets himself up just outside the city walls near Sanga Gate in the west of the old town. Sometimes the hyaena man risks feeding the animals from his own mouth – you can have a go at this, too, if you like!

Though the tradition of feeding spotted hyaenas like this has existed for no more that 35 years, the spectacle is less of a tourist show than some travellers imagine, or some guidebooks claim. The Hararis have long had a strange relationship with the hyaena, and some rituals remarkably similar to this one have existed for at least 700–800 years

ETHIOPIA

The Hyaena Man of Harar

Yusuf Ahmed is 43 years old, and is married with five children. By day, Yusuf is a farmer. He learnt the art of hyaena feeding from his uncle, who was also a hyaena feeder; now he's teaching his six-year-old son.

The hyaenas he knows by name. There's *Krincaiyo* (Grinder), *Cha'ala* (Big Girl), *Defkinater* (Not Fussy), *Gelaa* (Crooked – after his crooked leg) and so on. When called, they approach, a little slowly perhaps, but they know their names. Sometimes up to 30 come in a single night. The hyaenas take anything the town's butchers give Yusuf: gristle, bone, even hide, but they like the intestines the most.

Usually Yusuf feeds the hyaenas at 7 pm. But in summer, it's a little later – maybe 7.30 to 8 pm. The peasants are working in the fields and they return late; they are afraid. They ask Yusuf to feed the hyaenas later.

The young hyaenas are unpredictable and uneducated. The female hyaenas are the most daring; they are aggressive too and are the most dangerous; sometimes they are not polite. The babies they leave behind; baby sitters and guards look after them at home.

The hyaenas know him now, but he will never tame them. You can never tame a hyaena. The hyaenas fight sometimes among themselves – there are rival gangs – and always with the town dogs. But they are friends with the cats.

There is a King Hyaena. He lives in the Hakian hills, but he never comes. Yusuf saw him in April. He is a little bigger, and he is all white. The hyaenas protect Yusuf. If someone hurts Yusuf, the hyaenas will come in the night and destroy that person's house.

Sometimes Yusuf has an accident – they do not mean to bite him. The last time, two females came forward together; one jumped up, the other made a grab for the meat underneath. Yusuf's hand was caught. Yusuf's not afraid of the hyaenas; he's more afraid of the city's dogs.

Yusuf Ahmed was interviewed by the author

(see the boxed text 'Hyaena Porridge' later in this section).

If you want to see the feeding, just let your guide know. Be sure to establish the fee in advance; the tourism office advises paying a minimum of Birr50 per 'show', but if there's a few of you (say four) Birr25 per person is sufficient.

Places to Stay

Unfortunately, all the places on the square in the old town are rough, ready and probably charge by the hour rather than by the day. If you're desperate to stay on the square, the *Harar Academy Hotel* is at least clean, with a few rooms that look onto the square for Birr15 (other rooms for Birr10 are windowless cells).

A much better bet in the budget category is the *Tourist Hotel* in the new town, with clean rooms around a courtyard with/without bathrooms for Birr10/8.

The *Tewodros Hotel* (☎ 66-02-17) near Harar Gate has rooms with/without cold shower for Birr25/15. The Birr15 rooms are a bit basic, but those for Birr25 are jewels. You can watch the hyaenas stealing about in the shadows from the balconies of these rooms. In the early hours, when the town is quiet, the animals try and sneak into the city to scavenge. The city's dog population does its best to keep the intruders out in a kind of pitched street battle of advancing and retreating. It's your very own hyaena show, and is fascinating to watch – you will never forget the noises the hyaenas make. Rooms 12 and 13 have the best views; 14 and 15 are second best.

If the Tewodros is full, the peaceful *Dessie Hotel* (☎ 66-07-68) east of the new town has simple but clean rooms with/without bathroom for Birr15/10.

Probably the best mid-range place is the pleasant *Belayneh Hotel* (☎ 11-03-16), near the bus station and Shoa Gate. Very clean rooms cost Birr60/80/100 depending on facilities (see also Places to Eat & Drink following).

The *Ras Hotel* (☎ 66-02-88) east of the new town is currently the only top-end hotel in Harar. With its long, bare, white corridors and smocked, dour staff, it rather resembles a loony asylum. Even by Ras Hotel standards it's depressing, but there's a sense of humour there somewhere: it costs Birr188/227 (singles/doubles) for the pleasure to stay here.

Places to Eat & Drink
The *Ras Hotel* has a faranji menu that is more varied than most. The one at the *Tewodros Hotel* isn't bad; ask for the *mahabaroui*, a mixture of different dishes including half a roast chicken (see Places to Stay previous for both of these).

The *Canal Cafeteria* near Harar Gate serves freshly baked sponges each morning. It does the best fruit juices in town, as well as sweet spicy tea. Try the Harari speciality *hasher ka'ah*, a kind of tea made from coffee husks. The new *Andenya Menged Cake House* nearby has quite good cake as well as delicious samosas and *fatira* (savoury pastries).

Inside the old town, the *Cafeteria Ali Bar* is a local favourite. A room on the left serves as a boutique selling traditional arts and crafts.

The *Medre Genet Hotel* west of Ras Makonnen Square is a favourite place with the locals, and the large outdoor seating area is often crammed at night. It's also very reasonable: dinner plus beers and mineral water costs Birr15. The *zil zil tibs* (fried beef with sauce) is something of a speciality (Birr10 for two people). The service is a bit slow, but it's worth the wait.

The *Belayneh Hotel* near Shoa Gate is also good; it has a pleasant and cool roof terrace where you can have lunch. There's a good view over the town.

Beer Please

Harar is well known for its beer. The amber nectar known as Harar is light and very drinkable. Achim Stout is a stout that was apparently developed in consultation with German brewers. Another to try is Achim, a kind of lager. Sofi is a non-alcoholic beer specially developed for Harar's pious Muslims.

〈〈〈〈〈〈〈〈〈〈〈〈〈〈〈〈〈〈〈〈〈〈〈〈〈〈〈〈〈〈〈

WARNING

! The vicinity east and south of Harar is a known mined area (see Dangers & Annoyances in the Ethiopia Facts for the Visitor section). Trekkers beware!

The *Hirot Restaurant*, lying south of Ras Makonnen Square is a homy sort of place, which resembles someone's front room. The local dishes are very reasonably priced.

The best bars in town at the time of writing were the *Samsun Hotel & Bar* and the *Cottage Bar*, both inside the old town. The *National Hotel*, north of Ras Makonnen Square, is a kind of nightclub with live bands playing from around 8.30 pm to 2 or 3 am. The music is the usual cocktail of Western and Ethiopian pop.

Getting There & Away
Minibuses and buses run daily to Kombolcha (Birr4, 30 mins). Buses leave daily for Babille (see following) and Dire Dawa (Birr6, one hour), where connections can be made with the Addis Ababa–Djibouti train (see Getting There & Away under Dire Dawa earlier in this section). Buses also depart daily for Jijiga (Birr10, 2½ hours) and Addis Ababa – to ensure a seat, tickets to the capital should be bought the day before (Birr35, 12 hours).

All buses, minibuses and 4WD taxis leave from the bus station near Harar Gate. Driving in the area is not advised at night due to *shifta* (bandit) activity.

AROUND HARAR
When you're 2km out of Harar heading east, look out for the well-known **view of Harar** at Dekka village.

There are a number of important mosques and shrines around Harar, including that of the holy man and teacher, Sofi, who lived nearly 1000 years ago. **Sofi's Tomb**, an important centre of pilgrimage, is 7km from Harar. It's a simple and peaceful place.

Near the village of Kombolcha, 15km from Harar, are important **cave paintings**. It's a 25-minute easy walk to the caves; you'll need a guide from the village. Men and animals such as buffaloes, elephants and antelopes are depicted on the cave face, outside the actual cave. Unfortunately, they've been much scribbled over by the local children.

The nearby **Mosque of Umi-Koda** dates back a millennium, when it was erected by Nur Hussein, but was largely rebuilt in the 15th century by the Turks. The building is largely in ruins, but interesting architectural features remain, including flower friezes and the remains of columns that once supported the roof. Women who are infertile come here to pray for children. Food is left for the local hyaenas here (see the boxed text 'Hyaena Porridge').

See also the boxed text 'Valley of Marvels' later in this section for another excursion from Harar.

Hyaena Porridge

Once upon a time, many years back, there was a terrible famine in the city of Harar. Both people and animals went hungry. One day the hyaenas outside the town began to prey on the herds, and even the people. That night, a man 'pure of heart' had a dream. In it, he was instructed by God to make a pact with the hyaenas and feed them a special porridge. The man did so, and from that day on both man and beast remained in harmony, even during times of hardship.

To this day, the agreement is renewed annually by the people of Harar. On the seventh day of Muharram, during the religious festival of Al-Ashura, a special porridge is prepared with different cereals and served with abundant melted butter.

The hyaena king (actually the dominant female), the leader of the pack, always comes forward to taste the porridge first. If the hyaena eats more than half the bowl, the year will be plentiful and good. But if, on the other hand, the hyaena only picks at the porridge or refuses it, the omens augur ill: pestilence may be on the horizon. If the king devours the whole bowl, famine may be around the corner.

BABILLE

The little town of Babille is famous as the site of hot springs and is the source of the Babille bottled water distributed all over eastern Ethiopia. If you get stuck here, the **Bruk Hotel** has basic rooms with common shower for Birr8. It is located just after the regional commissioner's office (the sign is in Amharic only). The **Anwaar** restaurant serves good food.

Minibuses and buses leave daily for Harar (Birr5, 30 mins). For Jijiga, you can sometimes hop on a bus coming from Harar if there's space (Birr10, two hours).

Babille Elephant Sanctuary

The Babille Elephant Sanctuary was established originally for the protection of the endemic species of elephant, *Loxodonta africana orleansi*. Spreading over 6982 sq km, the park is also said to contain kudus, lions and wild asses.

Unfortunately, like many of Ethiopia's parks, the place has been taken over by the local people and their livestock as well as suffering at the hands of poachers and due to the influx of refugees from Somalia. It is unlikely that you will see any animals in the park; a special visit is not worthwhile. There is no formal park headquarters or entrance gate.

JIJIGA

☎ 05

Lying 60km north-east of Babille is the town of Jijiga, the last major Ethiopian town before Somalia. It is an important administrative and commercial centre and has been colonised by various large international aid organisations, but contains little of interest to the traveller.

If you find you have time to fill here, the large market is definitely worth a trot around. In it you may well find high-quality, intricately woven mats as well as silver jewellery and yellow amber necklaces. The rest is just masses and masses of contraband 'junk', though you can pick up T-shirts for Birr8 if you need some.

The Commercial Bank has no foreign exchange facilities; the nearest place is Harar.

If you're desperate, a black market always operates in the marketplace.

The ***Roman Hotel*** just east of town is a good budget choice; rooms with communal shower cost Birr13. By far the best mid-range bet is the ***Africa Hotel*** (☎ 75-05-03), which has very clean rooms with private cold shower for Birr25. There's also a good restaurant and parking.

Getting There & Away

Buses leave daily for Harar (Birr10, 2½ hours), Dire Dawa (Birr15, four hours) and Addis Ababa (Birr60, 12 hours) – book tickets to the capital the day before you want to leave.

One bus leaves daily for Hargeisa in Somalia (Birr50, four hours); check the security situation (see Border Crossings in the Ethiopia Getting There & Away section earlier).

Ethiopian Airlines flies from Jijiga to Addis Ababa via Dire Dawa twice a week. The airport is 2.5km out of town.

Valley of Marvels

Some 4km from Babille, the road passes through the Dakhata Valley, now better known as the Valley of Marvels. This was rechristened by the Italians after the strange volcanic formations found here, in which tall rocks have been sculpted into strange shapes by the elements. Many of these are topped by precariously balanced boulders, including the famous boulder that resembles a kind of celestial arch. The valley stretches for some 13km.

The birds also are particularly diverse and colourful in this area. Look out for the local beehives placed high up in the acacia trees; cylindrical in shape, they're made from bamboo and sweet-smelling grass. The black-headed sheep, creamy-coloured cattle and very tall people are all reminiscent of Somalia.

A contract taxi from Harar will cost in the region of Birr200 for the whole day.

ORAL LITERATURE IN THE HORN

Chaque vieux qui est mort, c'est comme une bibliothèque detruite.

Every time an old person passes away, it's as if a whole library were lost.

Djiboutian saying

In the West, culture is usually defined in terms of ancient monuments, works of art and sophisticated traditions. In some countries, however, and particularly where the climate dictates a nomadic existence for its people, culture manifests itself not in permanent buildings and great writings, but in the spoken word, passed down from generation to generation.

Many languages in Africa are in the process of disappearing along with the cultures that support them. And while vast amounts of time, effort and money continue to be invested in excavating tangible evidence of past civilisations, the intangible evidence – the oral patrimony, which is just as important and certainly as fragile – is allowed to disappear forever.

The oral tradition of many African societies is rich, and particularly so in the Horn, including Ethiopia, Eritrea and Djibouti. Here, literally thousands of proverbs, maxims and tales are in circulation, told and retold for centuries by nomads, cattle herders and traders.

Among the nomadic people of East Africa, the tale serves as a kind of bedside story. After the heat and work of the day, when the animals have been fed, watered and safely penned, families gather around the fire outside the tent. Storytellers are usually the older members of the family; among the Somalis in Djibouti, it is the grandmother who plays the part of narrator.

The tales are told to teach as well as to entertain. Children are taught not only morals and the difference between right and wrong, but useful lessons about the world they live in, and about human nature. The stories teach children to listen, to concentrate and to make judgements based on the dialogue of the characters, as the story unfolds. It encourages them to think and to analyse, and it develops their power of memory.

Tales also serve the adult population. Sometimes they are employed to clarify a situation, to offer advice tactfully to a friend, or to alert someone diplomatically to trouble or to wrongdoing. Like poetry, the tale can express a complex idea or situation economically and simply. The tale has also been used – and still is, particularly in Djibouti – to latently attack corrupt leaders or governments without fear of libel or persecution.

In Ethiopia, there is said to be a tale for every situation (see the boxed text 'Ethiopian Eloquence' in the Facts about Ethiopia section).

In Djibouti, travellers will be amazed how often the locals resort to proverbs, maxims or stories during the course of normal conversation. It is said that the first Somali proverb of all is: *Les Somalis peuvent mentir, mais ils ne font jamais des proverbes faux* (Somalis are allowed to tell fibs, but they never ever tell false proverbs).

Unlike Western tales, which are often sentimentalised, particularly where animals are involved, these stories are real, objective, often bloody and brutal. There are few Mickey Mouses and Bambis to be found in the tales of the Horn: the stories teach lessons of survival in a hostile, competitive environment where life is difficult and resources precarious.

The following tales were recorded and transcribed by the author during her travels around the Horn.

Ethiopia

Nuer

The Elephant and the Mouse

Once the lion went hunting. But times were bad, and all he managed to catch was a little mouse. But the mouse begged the lion to spare him:

'Oh lord lion, king of all beasts, do not eat me. If you let me go today, one day I may help you.' The lion laughed.

'How can you, little mouse, tiniest of all creatures, help me? But I will let you go.'

A few days later, the lion became trapped in a snare laid by the men of the village. The lion's roars could be heard throughout the forest. Many animals, summoned by their king, came, but none of them – neither the clever monkey nor the powerful elephant – could assist him.

As fast as he could, the little mouse scampered to the lion. When he saw the trap, he began to gnaw at the cord. After many hours of hard work, the rope at last snapped, and the lion sprang free.

'May creatures forthwith never underestimate the might of small things or the power of good deeds,' proclaimed the lion.

Oromo

The Golden Earth

Once there was a hard-working farmer who owned good land which produced much *tef* (an indigenous grain). His three sons, however, were lazy, and while the farmer toiled day and night and took the grain to market, they amused themselves all day in the fields.

The farmer was growing old, and one day he fell sick. He begged his sons to go out and continue his work, but they made excuses and lay around instead.

The farmer's condition grew worse.

'My sons', he began, 'God has given me this good land because I respected my father and mother and obeyed the Lord. If you do not

ORAL LITERATURE IN THE HORN

DAWIT ABEBE

also, we will be ruined.'

Still the sons did nothing, and soon their father's store of grain ran out. Finally, close to death, the farmer summoned the three sons to him.

'My sons, since my time is near, I will tell you a secret. Buried on my land is a treasure that will never run out. Since I can no longer show you where it is hidden, you must go out and dig until you find it. When you do, you will become rich.'

After their father had died, and now hungry with nothing to eat, the sons went out and desperately started to dig. But they found nothing. After several days, all their father's land had been ploughed up, but still they had not found the treasure.

Finally, one of the sons, the clever one, turned to his brothers to exclaim:

'But don't you see? This land is our father's treasure. If we use it, we will reap the rewards.'

So the sons sowed the seed in all the places they had ploughed, and soon they had a wonderful harvest and plenty to eat. Then the sons began to work hard, and over time, they grew very rich.

Top Left: Ethiopian farmers use tools and cultivation methods unchanged for centuries

Eritrea

Tigre

God Has Provided

Once upon a time in days gone by, when there was plenty of food and all the animals lived in harmony, the tortoise was without a shell. With nothing to fear from other beasts or from humans, the tortoise had neither long legs, nor sharp claws, nor pointed teeth with which to protect himself.

One day the jackal, the fox and the hare were sitting in the shade of an old acacia tree, taking refuge from the afternoon sun. Then the fox remarked to the jackal:

'Have you ever noticed, brother jackal, how plump and tender-looking is our brother tortoise?'.

'It is true', said the jackal. 'I bet he would feed a mouth or two ... in fact, I bet he'd do you, me and hare all put together.' The hare looked at his companions the jackal and the fox but said nothing.

'And why should we', the fox went on, 'exhaust ourselves day and night looking for food and water in this merciless heat, in this merciless land, when it's right there for the taking?'.

'That's right', said the jackal, 'meat on a platter right under our noses!'.

'But how stupid we have been!' cried the fox. 'Well, brother jackal, brother hare, from tomorrow, we shall eat the tortoise. And from tomorrow, we shall never have to go searching for food again. God has provided for us!'

'God has provided for us!' said the jackal, licking his lips.

During the night, the hare looked everywhere for the tortoise.

'Oh brother tortoise. The fox and the jackal have decided that tomorrow they will eat you. You must run far away like brother gazelle.'

'Oh brother hare, how can I run far away when I have just little legs to run on?'

'Then you must dig a hole in which to hide yourself, like brother mouse.'

'How can I hide myself when I have just little claws with which to dig?'

'Then you must build a big house in which to protect yourself, like brother termite.'

'How can I build a big house when there is just me to build?'

'But, brother tortoise, you can't just let them eat you!'

'Brother hare, there is nothing to be done. It is God's will', the tortoise said sadly, and he sat down on some grass to wait for the morning.

Early the following morning, the fox, the jackal and the hare found the tortoise. Spreading across his back, there was a huge armoured covering, and when they approached, the tortoise withdrew underneath it as if retreating into a house.

'You see', the hare said, turning to his brothers the fox and the jackal, 'God has provided'.

Djibouti

Afar

Camel in the Sky

Once there was an elderly woman who lived with her elderly donkey. As the days passed, their limbs grew heavier and their walk stiffer.

One morning the old woman set off with her donkey on the long journey to collect water. It was hot and the old woman soon became tired and clambered onto the donkey's back. But the donkey was weary too and its steps became slower and slower.

'Giddy-up, old donkey', said the old lady, 'or we shall never arrive at the well'. When the old couple finally arrived, night had already fallen.

As the old lady bent over the well, she noticed the reflection of the stars in the water. Looking up, she saw the constellation of the camel just above her head.

'How handsome you are, oh camel', she exclaimed. 'So big, so strong and so youthful; you would carry me and my water to the ends of the earth and back ...' Then the old lady looked at her donkey: 'And you ugly old donkey, with your crooked legs and bad breath, with your stooped gait and weary eyes, wretched good-for-nothing! You are a curse on me!' she said, and flying into a fit of rage, she hit the donkey on the head and killed it.

The next morning the old woman set off back to her village. But without either a beautiful camel or an old donkey, she had to walk the whole way, bent double with the load of the water.

A young goatherd near Sittona

Colour plays an important role in appearance.

Selling chillies in Adi Quala market in the south

Inspecting the produce at an animal market

Priests celebrating the festival of Meskel

FRANCES LINZEE GORDON

Eritrea

It tells like a story from the heroic past. For 30 years, a tiny nation struggled against giants, wicked baddies, and powerful outside forces to win its freedom. Every family fought; every family lost. But good prevailed in the end, and the goodies finally won. Then a legendary political tale begins, with the building of a Utopian nation in which corruption was unheard of and crime was unknown. Ministers rode bicycles, women walked free and everyone lived happily and in harmony. But one day, two old friends and fighting buddies had a squabble, and things began to turn nasty.

The bloody dispute which broke out in May 1998 between President Isaias of Eritrea and Prime Minister Meles Zenawi of Ethiopia over a tiny stretch of barren borderland has been likened to two bald men fighting over a comb. Tens of thousands of lives have been lost, the economy has been ruined and political credibility abroad has evaporated. Eritrea's fairy tale has turned into a horror story.

However, hopefully the tragic and wasteful conflict between the former allies will be resolved soon. And although the extraordinary – and highly infectious – mood of optimism, excitement and hope that once prevailed in Eritrea's streets has waned, the country is still a fascinating and rewarding place to visit.

The capital, Asmara, is like a film set from an early Italian movie. Old chrome espresso machines churn out cups of macchiato, Cinquecento taxis putt-putt about and all over town you can see outstanding examples of Art Deco architecture. Asmara is without doubt one of the safest, cleanest and most attractive capital cities on the continent.

Eritrea's landscape, though often stark and arid, can be very beautiful and has a peculiar draw. The Sahel Mountains in the north, for long the home of the guerilla fighters, have a wild and bleak quality. Stretching to the south, the apocalyptic wasteland of Dankalia is considered to be

Massawa p383
Massawa Island p385
Taulud Island p387
Asmara p357 ✪
Central Market p367
Central Asmara p369
Asmara Walking Tours p361
Dahlak Island National Park p392
SUDAN
ETHIOPIA

Highlights

- Admire Asmara's remarkable architecture and savour a coffee and cake in the capital's Italian cafes
- Strap on your snorkel or scuba-diving gear and view the unspoilt treasures around the Red Sea reefs
- Explore Eritrea's remarkable archaeological ruins and take a trip around the National Museum
- Take a tour of war-torn Nakfa, once the heart of Eritrean resistance
- Fuel up on Asmara gin and go dancing with the locals

ERITREA

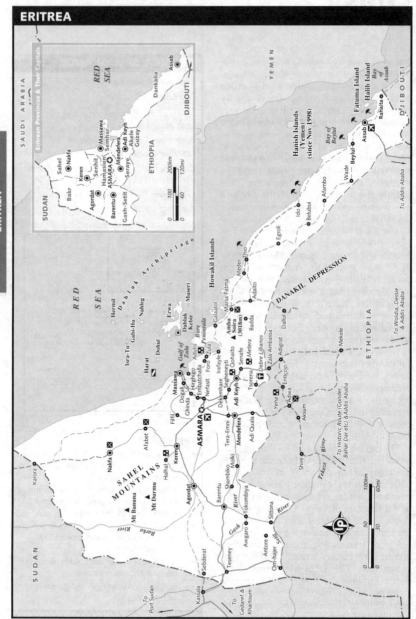

ERITREA

one of the most inhospitable places on earth.

Eritrea's nine colourful ethnic groups have had to adapt to these different environmental conditions and are correspondingly diverse and individual. Many have ancient and intriguing cultures. The Afars and Rashaida, in particular, have fascinated European travellers for centuries.

On the coast, the sultry town of Massawa epitomises Islamic influence. It is also the starting point for visits to the Dahlak Islands. Eritrea's coral reefs are considered among the richest, least spoilt and least known in the Red Sea.

Though less spectacular than Ethiopia's historical sites, those in Eritrea are no less important. With over 8000 sites at the last count, Eritrea has one of the highest densities of archaeological sites in Africa. New finds are unearthed almost every day, calling into question key aspects of the region's history.

Perhaps Eritrea's greatest resource is its people. Though impoverished, the nation has from the outset showed self-reliance, vigour, and independence. Eritrea is not about to become anyone's *vassal* (client), and this attitude has elicited both passionate admiration and furious exasperation from visitors, aid workers and international organisations alike. Towards the traveller, Eritreans show exceptional politeness, hospitality and friendliness. The inhospitality of the countryside in which most of the people live as nomads may contribute to this keen sense of the importance of hospitality.

In practical terms, the country has many attractions too. The cost of living is low, travel around the country is reasonably easy and cheap, hustling and hassling is practically unknown, and many people speak English. Above all, tourism is still almost unknown.

For the traveller, it is Eritrea's combination of dignity, self-respect and self-sufficiency, the very understated but impressive attractions, and the quiet but genuine hospitality of its people that make the country so remarkable. Many travellers fall passionately in love with Eritrea, and end up going back again and again.

Land of Punt

Since the dawn of history, the Horn of Africa has been known to the outside world. Lying on the African side of the Red Sea, the area provided a crucial trade link, connecting Egypt and the Mediterranean with India and the Far East.

But this wasn't the region's only asset. Known to the Egyptian Pharaohs as 'Land of the Gods' or 'Land of Punt' (together with what is now Djibouti), the area yielded a seemingly limitless supply of precious commodities. Gold, frankincense, myrrh, slaves, ostrich feathers, antelopes, ebony and ivory were all loaded onto foreign ships jostling in the region's ports.

Egyptian accounts of the Land – which accorded it almost legendary status – provide the earliest glimpse of the region. Expeditions are thought to date from the First or Second Dynasties (2920–2649 BC). At Queen Hatshepsut's famous Theban temple of Deir al-Bahri (built around 1490 BC), dramatic pictorial reliefs recount the departure of an entire fleet to the magical land.

For scholars today, the Land of Punt retains its legendary aura. Said to lie somewhere between the lands to the south of Nubia and those just north of present-day Somalia, no one knows for sure its exact location. Eritrea, Djibouti, Yemen, Somalia and even Kenya have all made claims to be Punt's location.

Facts about Eritrea

HISTORY
Prehistory

In 1995, several well-preserved hominid fossils were unearthed near Buya in the Debub region (around Adi Keyh in southern Eritrea), and are thought to date from around two million years ago. To date, 51 prehistoric sites have been found in Eritrea, including the Karora site in the north-east of the country and the Beylul site in the south-east.

Tools found in the Barka Valley dating from 8000 BC appear to offer the first concrete evidence of human settlement. Numerous rock paintings have been found throughout the country, particularly in the

ERITREA

southern Debub area. The latter date from at least 2000 BC, and appear to be the work of a nomadic or semi-nomadic people who bred cattle.

Eritrea's earliest inhabitants are thought to have been related to the Pygmies of Central Africa. Later, they intermingled with Nilotic, Hamitic and finally Semitic peoples migrating from across Africa and Arabia. By around 2000 BC, close contacts had been established with the people of the Nubian lowlands to the west and those from the Tihama coast of southern Arabia to the east. See also Pre-Aksumite Civilisation in the Facts about Ethiopia section earlier in this book – some ruins in Eritrea are thought to date from this period.

Aksumite Civilisation

Around the 1st century AD (or even earlier), the powerful kingdom of Aksum began to develop. Situated in Tigray, in the north of modern Ethiopia (around 50km from present-day Eritrea), Aksum lay just 170km from the sea. Much foreign trade – on which Aksum's prosperity depended – was seaborne, and came to be handled by the ancient port of Adulis in Eritrea.

On the way to Adulis (a 12- to 15-day journey from Aksum) many exports, including rhinoceros horn, hippopotamus hides, slaves and apes, passed through Eritrean towns, including Koloe (thought to be present-day Qohaito in the south).

Some of the goods exported were Eritrean in origin. Obsidian, a black volcanic rock, came from the waters of the Red

The Red Red Sea

Eritrea is said to derive its name from the Greek word *erythrea*, meaning red. It was coined from the famous *Periplus of the Erythrean Sea*, a trade or shipping manual written by a Greek-speaking Egyptian sailor or merchant around the 1st century AD. The Erythrean or 'Red' Sea comes from the fact that the water's colour turns a kind of vermilion as a result of newly spored algae during certain periods.

Sea, and was highly prized by the ancients for the manufacture of jewellery and votive offerings. Red Sea tortoiseshell was another export much valued by the ancients.

Arrival of Christianity

Christianity was undoubtedly the most significant 'import' into the region during the Aksumite period. According to the Byzantine ecclesiastical historian Rufinus, the religion was brought to the region by accident when Christian Syrian merchants travelling home from India were shipwrecked on the Red Sea coast. Whatever its origin, by the 4th century AD, Christianity had become the Aksumite state religion, and King Ezana began to mint coins bearing the cross of Christ.

The new religion had a profound impact on Eritrea's culture, influencing much of the country's art and literature, as well as shaping the spiritual and moral lives of the Christian population.

Islam & the Decline of Aksum

The other great influence on the region, and one coinciding with Christian Aksum's decline in the 7th century, was Islam. Though not directly responsible for the empire's collapse, the expansion of the religion was concomitant with the increasing power of the Arabs, who fast became the new masters of the Red Sea. Aksum's commercial domination of the region was over.

Islam made the greatest inroads in the Dahlak Islands, which later grew into a significant kingdom in its own right. Muslims traders also settled in nearby Massawa on the mainland.

Aksumite authority had long been challenged by other forces too, with incursions, attacks, rebellions and even mass migration by neighbouring tribes. The Beja tribe, a Cushitic people originating from present-day Sudan, were particularly active. From the 4th century onwards, most of the northern coast, the highlands and the north-west of Eritrea were settled by the Beja. Five kingdoms were established, and to this day their influence can be felt in the traditions and beliefs of the local people of the region.

After the settlement of the Beja in the interior of the country, and the Arabs on the coast, the Ethiopians were unable to recover the influence the Aksumites held over the region for another thousand years. Several attempts were made by later kings who tried to regain the vital access to the Red Sea – but all of them failed.

Turks & Egyptians
The Turks first arrived in Eritrea at the beginning of the 16th century. For the next 300 years (with a few short-lived intervals) the Eritrean coast, including the port of Massawa, belonged to the Ottomans.

By the middle of the 19th century, new powers were casting covetous eyes at the region. The Egyptians, under Ali Pasha, invaded Sudan and occupied parts of Ethiopia. Soon after, the western lowlands of Eritrea were also taken, including the port of Massawa.

Under threat, the Ethiopian King Yohannes eventually forced a battle. In 1875 at Ghundet, near Adi Quala in southern Eritrea, and later at Gura, near Dekemhare, resounding defeats were inflicted on the Egyptian armies. Although Egyptian influence lingered on along the coast and particularly in the region of Keren, the victories stamped out forever their designs on the territory.

At the same time, Egyptian rule in Sudan was overthrown by Mohammed Ahmed, known as the Mahdi. His successor Khalifa Abduhalli and his dervishes then threatened western Eritrea. The power vacuum left by the departing Egyptians was soon to be filled by yet another meddling foreign power – the Italians.

The Italians Arrive
During the 'Scramble for Africa' (see the boxed text following for more details) in the second half of the 19th century, France grabbed Djibouti (then known as French Somaliland) and Britain laid its hands on Aden in Yemen, as well as a stretch of Somali coastline. Though less industrialised than the other European powers, Italy wasn't going to miss out on a piece of the pie.

In November 1869, an Italian shipping company bought up a piece of land near Assab in southern Eritrea for 8100 Maria Theresa dollars. Ten years later, the Sultan of Rahaita in southern Eritrea was induced to part with further territory near the border between Eritrea and Djibouti.

In 1882, the Italian government arrived, buying out the shipping company, installing a local administration and setting up a permanent garrison. Colonisation had begun.

The new European power had a mixed reception. The Ethiopian emperor, Yohannes, reproached the British for failing to impede the Italian arrival in the region. By not doing so, they had contravened the Hewett Treaty, signed in 1884. Privately, the British welcomed the arrival, as a means of countering French influence in Djibouti and of deterring Turkish designs on the coast.

Alarmed by further expansion and the threat it posed to his kingdom, Yohannes eventually challenged the Italians. An Italian battalion was massacred at Dogali in 1887. As both sides rallied further forces, the dervishes (Muslim fraternities) raised their heads again, diverting Yohannes on the western front. Shortly afterwards, in 1889, the Ethiopian emperor was killed in battle.

As the Struggle for Independence preoccupied the Ethiopians, the Italians were left to get on with the realisation of their military ambitions. First the highland town of Keren was taken, followed by Asmara. Soon a march southwards began.

With the new Ethiopian emperor, Menelik, relations were at first good, and in 1889 the Treaty of Wechale was signed. In exchange for granting Italy the region that was to later become Eritrea, the Italians recognised Menelik's sovereignty and gave him the right to import alms freely though Ethiopia. However, a dispute over a discrepancy in the purportedly identical Amharic and Italian texts later led to its dissolution, and relations began to sour. In the meantime, Italian campaigns continued in the west.

Towards the end of 1889, the Italians turned their attention to the south. In 1890, Adwa and Mekele in Ethiopian territory were taken. Despite attempts to subvert the

ERITREA

local chiefs of Tigray, and in a rare act of unity, they sided with the Ethiopian emperor, Menelik.

The Italians managed to defeat Ras Mangasha and his Tigrayan forces at Adwa in 1894, and the Italians proceeded to annex further important Ethiopian towns, including Aksum, Adigrat and Mekele.

In 1896, battle lines were drawn up again. To international shock and amazement, the Italian armies were resoundingly defeated. The Battle of Adwa was one of the biggest and most significant in African history – one of the very few occasions when a colonial power was defeated by an African force (for more details, see the boxed text 'The Battle of Adwa' in the North of Addis Ababa section of the Ethiopia chapter).

In the months that followed new international boundaries were drawn up: Ethiopia remained independent and Eritrea became for the first time a separate territory – and an Italian colony.

Italian Colonial Rule

Of all Italy's colonies (which included Libya and Italian Somaliland), Eritrea was considered the jewel in the crown. Apart from providing a strategic base for imperial ambitions (particularly against Ethiopia), it boasted vital and lucrative access to the Red Sea, as well as potential for mineral and agricultural exploitation. For this reason, much investment was made in the little country, and major schemes began to be developed.

One of the most famous schemes was the building of the great railway between Massawa and Asmara in 1909, which was later extended to Keren. Other projects included the construction of a national network of roads, aqueducts, tunnels and bridges, a telecommunication system unique in the region, efficient irrigation systems, as well as much urban planning and construction. In 1935, a massive aerial tramway was built to transport goods from Massawa to Asmara. Larger than any other in the world, the tramway was later dismantled by the British, after the Italians departed.

By the end of the 1930s, Eritrea – albeit on a diminutive scale – was one of the most highly industrialised colonies in Africa. Plantations and orchards, factories and mines had all been established, and cotton, sisal, fruit and potash had begun to be exported. By 1930, Massawa had become the largest port on the East African coast. The population of the country numbered a staggering 760,000 in 1941.

Eritrea was initially governed by indirect rule through local chieftains. Later, a series of provinces were created, administered by a large body of Italian civil servants, headed by a governor.

During this period, much land was expropriated from Eritreans and handed over to private enterprise. This policy was deeply resented, and opposition to Italian rule simmered and sometimes erupted. In 1894, Batha Hagos led a rebellion in Akele Guzay, which was only crushed by the Italian superiority of weapons. His declaration on Italian colonial policy – 'When the white snake has bitten you, you will search in vain for a remedy' – has become famous.

Dispossession of the land also swelled the urban population, and was responsible for the eventual establishment of a substantial working class and an urban-based 'intelligentsia'.

British Administration

In May 1935, Italy avenged itself of Adwa and defeated the Ethiopians. In 1940, with the outbreak of WWII, Italy declared war on Britain, and soon became embroiled in conflicts in what was then British Sudan. Though initially successful, Italian campaigns in this area were soon repulsed by reinforced British armies.

Soon British forces were giving chase to the Italians, pursuing them into Eritrea, and capturing Agordat. In 1941, the strategically important town of Keren was captured, and the Italian general Lorenzini was killed. On 1 April 1941, Asmara surrendered, and the colony became a British mandate.

Although the British attempted (largely from practical constraints) to maintain the status quo in the territory by leaving in place the old Italian administration, the

The Scramble for Africa

At the beginning of the 19th century, European maps of Africa showed little more than huge, blank spaces. Fifty years later, these gaps began to be filled with the continent's major physical features: the great African lakes, mountains and rivers. European explorers, keen to win kudos for themselves, their religion and their country, fell over one another in the rush to 'discover' them. Within a decade, more than 10 million sq miles of Africa and over 100 million Africans had been swallowed up by the European powers. The 'Scramble for Africa', as the Partition is more luridly known, was the most dramatic instance of the carving up of the world by foreign powers in the history of mankind.

There are various 'explanations' for the Partition. Commercially, Africa was seen as a vast tropical treasure house that would yield huge quantities of food, precious metals, and valuable commodities such as ivory and slaves. The development of new markets abroad was seen as essential to the newly industrialised, all-consuming, capitalist states of Europe. Also, ignorance about the continent of Africa was seen as rather shameful, and many Europeans became increasingly fascinated by the natural sciences as a whole, and in particular by the new and fashionable research on ethnology, the study of races and peoples.

In political and diplomatic terms, the Partition was seen as a kind of grand power play between the competing European countries. Statesmen could use overseas territories as bargaining counters in a ruthless game of global diplomacy. Others have suggested that colonial policies were used to distract attention from irksome tensions at home. Italy, for example, was encouraged to dream of re-creating the great Roman Empire. In Germany, Bismarck is said to have staged colonial advances in Africa in 1884 purely as an electioneering stunt. Missionaries, convinced of their divine mission to save souls and convert the world, were another important influence. New technologies such as the train and the steamship, and the discovery of the antimalarial quinine facilitated European invasion of the deep, dark African continent.

Although the causes of the Partition can be debated, the results are more transparent. It sent out political, economic and social shock waves that are felt in Africa to this day. As Dr WEB Dubois put it:

There came to Africa an end of industry...Cheap European goods pushed in and threw the native products out of competition...Methods of work were lost and forgotten. The authority of the family was broken up; the authority and tradition of the clan disappeared; the power of the chief was transmuted into the rule of the white district commissioner...The old religion was held up to ridicule, the old culture and ethical standards were degraded or disappeared, and gradually all over Africa spread the inferiority complex, the fear of colour, the worship of white skin, the imitation of white ways of doing and thinking, whether good, bad or indifferent. By the end of the 19th century the degradation of Africa was as complete as organised human means could make it.

Dr WEB DuBois, *The World and Africa,* International Publishers, New York, 1965

The old imperial chauvinism seems to have been replaced by a new cultural one. And, with the proliferation of aid and financial packages, many would argue an economic one, too.

---

colony inevitably sank into a state of demoralisation and decline.

However, the loss of Italian state subsidies eventually forced the colony towards a more self-reliant stance. For a short period in the early 1940s, the economy experienced a brief revival. The ports of Massawa and Assab became important imperial staging posts and many of the big industrial names known today established themselves – Melotti beer, Tabacchi cement, Sava glass and Maderni matches.

However, the fortunes of the colony were pinned to larger events unfolding beyond it.

When the course of WWII changed, the territory lost its strategic importance and in 1945 the British began a slow withdrawal.

Unfortunately, the British decided to take most of the colony with them, cleaning the place out lock, stock and barrel. Valued at nearly US$90 million, everything – from the cement factories and dry docks of Massawa, to the airport and aerial tramway – was dismantled and removed. With the British went Eritrea's carefully constructed infrastructure.

By 1946, the country was in trouble. The economy was floundering, unemployment was soaring with two-thirds of the workforce without jobs, and unrest was brewing.

Federation with Ethiopia

In 1948, Eritrea's fate was pondered by a four-power commission consisting of the UK, the USA, France and the Soviet Union. Unable to reach a decision, the commission passed the issue on to the United Nation's General Assembly.

In 1947, a Commission of Enquiry found the population divided into three main factions: the pro-Ethiopian Unionists (mainly Christian), the anti-unionists (mainly Muslims in favour of a Muslim League) and members of a Pro-Italia party (many of them Italian pensioners). The commissioners, whose findings reflected the political interests of their respective governments, produced totally different conclusions and recommendations.

In 1950, the very contentious Resolution 390 A (V) was passed. Eritrea became Ethiopia's fourteenth province and disappeared from the map of Africa.

Annexation to Ethiopia

This 'shotgun wedding', as it has been described, between Eritrea and Ethiopia was never a happy one. Little by little, Ethiopia began to exert ever-tighter control over Eritrea, and both industry and power were moved to Ethiopia's capital, Addis Ababa. The Eritrean economy stagnated, and the province's autonomy dwindled. Eritrean politicians and leaders were soon ousted, Ethiopian Amharic replaced Tigrinya as the official language in schools, and protests against the regime were suppressed with brutality. During the General Strike of 1958, several protesters were killed or wounded.

The repeated appeals by the Eritrean people to the UN fell on deaf ears. With the start of the Cold War in the 1950s, the Americans had set their sights on establishing a communications centre in Asmara. When in the early 1960s Ethiopia formally annexed Eritrea in violation of international law, Cold War politics ensured that both the US and the UN kept silent.

With no recourse to the international community, the frustration of the people grew. In 1961, the inevitable happened. In the little town of Amba Adal in the western lowlands, a small group of men led by Hamid Idriss Awate assailed one of the much-resented police stations and stole some pistols. The fight for independence had begun.

Eritrean Resistance

The Struggle, as resistance to Ethiopian rule became popularly known, was an extraordinary event in the history of the Horn. Lasting for 30 years, it shaped, physically and psychologically, the new nation and its people. For the first time, a real sense of national identity was forged. For more details, see the boxed text 'A Super Struggle' following.

The first resistance movements on the scene included the ELM (Eritrean Liberation Movement), the (Christian) People's Liberation Front (PLF), and the (Muslim) Eritrean Liberation Front (ELF). From the latter two, a splinter group emerged, the Eritrean People's Liberation Front (EPLF), which called for social revolution as well as national independence. Continual conflict between the various groups, particularly the ELF and the EPLF considerably undermined the nationalist movement throughout its history. It was only after periods of bloody civil war and the defeat of the ELF towards the end of the war in 1981, that the EPLF emerged as the leader of unified forces.

Nevertheless, the resistance continued to make progress, and in 1978, the Eritreans were on the brink of winning back their country. However, just on the point of victory, yet another foreign power decided to intervene.

A Super Struggle

The price of Eritrea's freedom was high. Africa's longest war this century, the Struggle for Freedom lasted 30 years, wrecked the country's infrastructure and economy, cost 65,000 lives, and drove at least a third of the population into exile to live as refugees or displaced persons.

The war was not a story of vast armies, brilliant leadership and sweeping conquests, but one of resilience, determination and valiance in the face of all odds. For three decades, a tiny guerilla force (which numbered at most 40,000 during its last days), was able to thwart the might of a country 10 time its size, backed by two superpowers and with all the modern weaponry of the 20th century.

Initially a ragbag bandit force, the resistance fighters were gradually converted into what was described by a BBC journalist in the 1980s as 'the best guerilla army in the world'. The fighters operated in tightly organised cells, taught their soldiers reading and writing, history, philosophy and political economy, as well as guerilla tactics. Equality of all people was advocated; soldiers had to respect the gender (many soldiers were women), ethnic group, religion and race of their fellow fighters.

In response to the devastating blanket bombing inflicted by the Ethiopians, whole villages were constructed underground, with schools, hospitals, factories, printing presses, mills, pharmacies, workshops and entertainment halls. The remains of these 'towns' can be seen today in the village of Nakfa in the north of Eritrea.

The workshops became places of incredible ingenuity and resourcefulness. Everything was put to use or recycled. Tin cans were turned into water buckets, sterilising dishes, cooking utensils and oil lamps. Even the labels were peeled off and scrawled with verses of poetry. Fighters learnt to repair captured weapons, then to replace small parts, and even to manufacture equipment. Live land mines were dug up and relocated.

Outside the country, expatriates were no less resolute and self-sacrificing. They raised funds, trained themselves in useful disciplines and contributed up to half of their salaries towards the effort. Some funds also came from the Middle East, Cuba and China. In contrast, the Ethiopians benefited from the backing of two superpowers – first the Americans and later, in 1977, the Russians. The latter contributed what has been estimated as US$12 billion in military aid, including 72 MIG-21 and 23 fighter planes.

During the most intense onslaught against the fighters, the famous 'Strategic Withdrawal' removed them to what is now known as the Sahel province in the north-east. There, they dug themselves into the mountainside, living for years in narrow, filthy and vermin-infested trenches. Reminiscent of WWI, the Ethiopian lines were in places so close that grenades could be caught and thrown back, giving the name 'volleyball courts' to some of the lines on the front. Today many Eritreans hold special regard for those who were 'in Sahel'.

The Eritrean Struggle for freedom is without doubt one of the most remarkable in modern history.

In 1974, Colonel Mengistu Haile Mariam, a communist dictator, had come to power in Ethiopia. Three years later, the Soviet Union began to arm his troops. In the face of massive aerial bombardment and an army bristling with modern weaponry, the EPLF was obliged to retreat. The famous 'Strategic Withdrawal', as it is known, later proved to be crucial to the movement's survival.

Eight major offensives were carried out against the Eritrean fighters from 1978 to 1986, all of which were repulsed. From 1988, the EPLF began to inflict major losses on the Ethiopian army, capturing first its northern headquarters in Afabet, then the large highland town of Keren. In 1990, amid some of the fiercest fighting of the war, the EPLF took the strategically important port of Massawa.

By this time, however, Mengistu Haile Mariam's regime was threatened from within, and civil war had broken out in

Attitude Problem?

Obliterated politically, ignored internationally and isolated economically for over 30 years, the Eritreans won their sovereignty through their own efforts and on their own terms. Naturally the source of much pride, this achievement has bred a 'we-do-it-our-way' and a 'we'll-go-it-alone' philosophy .

Attitude, some would say. Used to more deferential and grateful recipients, international aid organisations were astonished and infuriated when Eritrea snubbed their offers for aid because the conditions 'infringed upon their sovereignty'.

From 1994, nongovernmental organisations were required to file financial reports, with no more than 10% of their expenditure used for 'administration'. In 1995, four officials from the World Food Programme and USAID were actually expelled for contravening such regulations.

Nor are the niceties, complicated procedures and strict protocol surrounding many international organisations much appreciated. When Eritrea was formally admitted to the Organization of African Union, President Isaias told the assembled heads of state that the organisation had done too little for Africa, spent too much money on itself and met far too often.

Ethiopia. In 1991, Mengistu was overthrown and fled to Zimbabwe. His 140,000 Ethiopian troops laid down their weapons and ran. The EPLF walked into Asmara without having to fire a single bullet.

The New State

In April 1993, the Provisional Government of Eritrea held a referendum on Eritrean independence. More than 99.81% of voters opted for full Eritrean sovereignty, and on 24 May 1993, independence was declared. Eritrea was back on the African map.

In early 1994, the EPLF dissolved itself and re-formed as the People's Front for Democracy and Justice (PFDJ) under the chairmanship of the head of state, President Isaias Afewerki. Some members of the old ELF were also invited to join the team.

After the war, the country showed the same determination, discipline and self-reliance that had helped it win the Struggle for Independence. The little nation worked hard to rebuild its infrastructure, repair the economy and improve conditions for its people.

Wide-ranging laws, policies and constitutional rights were drawn up, from protection of the environment and positive discrimination towards disabled people at work to the rights of women and the fight against AIDS.

Eritrea was also at pains to establish good international relations with, among others, Ethiopia, the Gulf States, Asia, the USA and Europe. Soon the Eritrean leadership was hailed, in US president Bill Clinton's words, as belonging to a 'new generation of African leaders'.

However, this progress was seriously undermined at the end of 1997. For a detailed discussion of the war with Ethiopia that broke out in May to June 1998, see History in the Ethiopia chapter.

A long-standing dispute with Yemen over the Hanish archipelago was resolved finally in 1998. An international jury ruled against Eritrea, and it was obliged to hand the islands back. Relations with neighbouring Djibouti have also been stormy, after President Isaias accused it of supporting Ethiopia in the dispute with Eritrea. Relations with Sudan improved marginally after the signing of a reconciliation pact in May 1999.

GEOGRAPHY

With a land area of 124,320 sq km, Eritrea measures about the size of England or the state of Pennsylvania in the US. The coastline measures around 1000km and off it there are over 350 islands.

Eritrea has three main geographical zones: the eastern escarpment and coastal plains, the central highland region, and the western lowlands.

The eastern zone consists of desert or semidesert, with little arable land. The people inhabiting the region are generally nomadic pastoralists or fishing communities.

The northern end of the East African Rift Valley opens into the infamous Dankalia region in the east, one of the hottest places on earth. This semidesert lies in a depression up to 120m below sea level, and is home to several salt lakes.

The central highland region is more fertile, and it is intensively cultivated by sedentary farming communities.

The western lowlands, lying between Keren and the Sudanese border, are watered by the Gash and Barka Rivers. Farming is practised, but less intensively than in the highlands; future agricultural projects are planned in the area.

CLIMATE

The country's climate corresponds to its geography.

The low, eastern zone is by far the hottest area. Temperatures range from a torrid 30° to 39°C during the hot season (June to August) and from 25° to 32°C during the cooler season (October to May).

Rainfall on the coast is less than 200mm per year, and occurs mostly from December to February. The high humidity in the coastal region can make temperatures seem much higher than further inland.

In the Dankalia region, temperatures can reach 50°C in the shade! Rainfall is practically zero.

In the highland zone, the average annual temperature is 18°C (17°C in Asmara). May is the hottest month, when daily temperatures can reach around 30°C. The coldest months are from December to February when lows can approach freezing point. Day and night temperatures can vary by up to 20°C. Mists are also prevalent at this time. Light rains fall from March to April, with heavy rains from the end of June to the beginning of September. Average annual rainfall is 540mm.

In the western zone, temperatures range from 30° to 41°C in the hot season (April to June). December is the coolest month (13° to 25°C). Rainfall mirrors that in the highland zone.

ECOLOGY & ENVIRONMENT

Like many sub-Saharan African countries, three factors have had the greatest impact

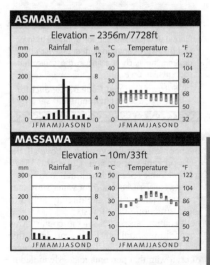

on Eritrea's environment: war, famine and demographic pressure. When the new government came to power in 1994, it was faced with the huge task of rebuilding the shattered country. Surprisingly, conservation not only featured on the agenda but was attributed substantial importance.

As the government was quick to realise, Eritrea's economic future is inextricably linked to its environment. In most developing countries, people and their environment are much more mutually dependent than in more developed, industrialised countries. Much of Eritrea's farming is still subsistent or semi-subsistent, so land productivity is vital to the population's survival. For this reason, a wide-ranging program of projects, legislation and research has been initiated, motivated as much by pragmatic, economic motives as by ideological ones.

In the mid-1990s, various international conventions were also signed, including the 1973 Convention on International Trade in Endangered Species (Cites) and the 1992 Convention on Biological Diversity (CBD).

The Forests

Eritrea's forests supply wood for firewood and construction, traditional rural medicine and products such as gum. In times of

ERITREA

Environmental Code

[show] A deep respect for all living things, and the natural environment upon which they depend, for each is a link in the chain that supports life on earth.

Eritrean National Code of Conduct for Environmental Security

<<<<<<<<<<<<<<<<<<<<<<<<<<<<<<<<<<<<<

famine, trees provide emergency rations for the people and their livestock. Above all, the trees prevent soil erosion. Currently, 35–70 million tonnes of soil are estimated to be lost every year. Eritrea's current water shortages and low-yielding land are directly linked to the destruction of the forests.

A century ago, 30% of the country was covered by woodland. Fifty years later, this had fallen to just 11%. Today, after 30 years of civil war, that percentage has dwindled to less than 1%. Various factors have contributed to the destruction. During colonial times, 300,000 hectares of forest was cleared by Italian colonialists for farming. During the war with Ethiopia, troops on both sides cleared forests for the construction of shelters, trenches and other fortifications.

Today, the demand for firewood is the biggest threat, with 4.4 million cubic metres of firewood consumed per year. The traditional *hidmo* hut also requires large quantities of wood (see the boxed text 'Heavy Hidmos' following).

Traditional attitudes are also seen as an obstacle to reform. Trees are regarded as permanent features of the landscape, part of God's bounty and hence freely available to all.

Measures to combat deforestation include a nationwide program of tree planting and the establishment of nearly 100 nurseries nationwide. In the 1990s, a policy of 'hillside closure' was introduced. In these areas, all logging, grazing, and crop cultivation is banned. Currently, around 100,000 hectares are protected in this way.

The Land

The old land tenure system of *diessa*, enforced by the Italians, was directly in opposition to long-term land development. In response to land shortages resulting from their own expropriations, land was divided equally among villagers, and rotated every seven years. Incentives for farmers to carry out permanent improvements were lost. Most farmers exploited the land to the maximum during their term, resulting in huge land degradation. In 1994, a new land law was introduced, which did away with the old *diessa* system.

Today, population growth is the biggest problem, placing increased demands on the land and leading to overgrazing and overcropping. The practice of 'shifting cultivation' in the south-western lowlands (in which whole areas of vegetation are burnt before planting) is also seriously detrimental to the region's flora.

FLORA

The eastern landscape is characterised by acacia woodland (several species), brushland and thicket, semidesert vegetation, riverine vegetation and mangrove swamp. Around Massawa, small plantations of *Conocarpus lancifolius* exist, and along the roadsides of major towns, kassod tree *(Cassia siamea)* and flame tree *(Delonix regia)*.

The highland region is dominated by an indigenous species of juniper (*Juniperus procera*) and wild olive (*Olea africana*). Various species of acacia are also found. In degraded areas, various pioneer species have been introduced including East African laburnum *(Calpurnia aurea)* and native hops *(Dodonaea viscosa)*. Various eucalyptus plantations have also been established.

The Semenawi Bahri or Green Belt area is found to the north-east of Asmara, around the village and valleys of Filfil. It contains the last remnant of mixed, evergreen, tropical woodland in Eritrea. At an elevation of between 900m and 2400m, it stretches north to south for about 20km. During the colonial era, large tracts of the forest were cleared for coffee plantations and agriculture.

The landscape to the west is made up mainly of woodland savanna, brushland, thicket and grasslands *(Aristida)*. Around 50% of the firewood needed for the population of Asmara is collected from this area,

Heavy Hidmos

The large rectangular *hidmo*, dotted among the hills, is the traditional house of the highlanders. The heavy, earthen roof is supported by a crisscrossing of poles and, both inside and out, pillars made of juniper and wild olive are used to provide support.

This method of construction, as well as the size of the house, demands much wood, and at least 100 trees are felled for a single house. Wastage is high in the selection of poles of the right size and shape. Renovation is also periodically required to replace poles damaged by insects.

Because of these demands, the hidmo is considered one of the main threats to the country's surviving forest.

resulting in serious deforestation. Species include the doum palm (*Hyphaenea thebaica;* see the boxed text 'Palmy Purposes' under Teseney in the West of Asmara section), found particularly along the Barka River, eucalypts and various acacia species. Other species include baobab *(Adansonia digitata)*, toothbrush tree *(Salvadora persica)* and tamarisk *(Tamarix aphylla)*.

FAUNA
Mammals & Reptiles

In the past, Eritrea was home to a large range of animals, including buffaloes, cheetahs, colobus monkeys, elephants, giraffes, hippos, Nubian ibexes, leopards, lions and waterbucks. With the loss of the forests and the decades of civil war, many of these animals have disappeared.

Mammals commonly seen today include the Abyssinian hare, African wild cat, black-backed jackal, common jackal, genet, ground squirrel, pale fox, Soemmering's gazelle and warthog. Primates include the vervet monkey and hamadryas baboon.

Lions, greater kudus and Tora hartebeests are said to occur in the mountains of Gash-Setit province, north of Barentu. In the Bure peninsula, dik-diks and dorcas gazelles can be seen. Less common sightings include bushbucks, duikers, greater

kudus, klipspringers, leopards, oryxs and crocodiles. In the area between Awgaro and Antore, Eritrea's last population of elephants is said to roam.

Birds

Eritrea's range of habitats is surprisingly diverse, and its birdlife is correspondingly rich. A total of 537 species of birds have been recorded, including the rare blue saw-wing.

The isolated and uninhabited Dahlak Islands, and the rich feeding grounds which surround them, attract large numbers of nesting sea birds from all over the Red Sea (and possibly also from the Mediterranean and Gulf). Some 109 species have been recorded on the islands, including the Arabian bustard and osprey.

Eritrea also lies within a popular migratory fly way. Hundreds of species of wintering and migratory coastal and sea birds can be seen crossing between the continents of Africa and Arabia.

On the Bure peninsula, the ostrich and Arabian bustard are commonly seen. Sea birds include gulls, terns, boobies and, on the coastline and islands, many species of wader.

In the lush, evergreen, tropical forests in the Semenawi Bahri area north-east of Asmara, birdlife is particularly abundant. Species include the near-endemic white-cheeked turaco, and the Narina trogon.

Marine Life

Major marine ecosystems include the coral reefs, sea-grass beds and mangrove forests.

In the Red Sea, at least 129 species of coral are known to exist. Eritrea's coral is mainly found as 'patch reef' extending from the surface to around 15m to 18m; beyond this depth, coral development tends to be limited.

Lying on the northerly limits of the mangrove ranges, Eritrea is nevertheless home to at least three, possibly four, species (*Avicennia marina, Rhizophora mucronata, Ceriops tagal* and *Bruguiera gymnorrhiza*), which are found along the coast and on the Dahlak Islands.

Five species of marine turtle have been recorded. Most common are the green and

ERITREA

hawksbill turtles; the leatherback is occasionally seen, and the loggerhead and Ridley only rarely. The green turtle is quite often spotted around the Dahlak Islands.

Dolphins are also frequently seen around the Dahlak Islands. Four species occur: the common, humpback, bottlenose and spinner dolphins. Spinners are the very small type often seen in large groups. Shark species include the white and black-tipped reef, mako, nurse, whale, hammerhead and tiger sharks.

The dugong, or seacow (see the boxed text below), is now considered endangered. The Eritrean and Sudanese coastlines are thought to be home to at least half the 4000 to 5000 dugong estimated to inhabit the Red Sea. Sightings of the dugong in the sea are rare; most often they are caught in the nets of fishermen.

According to Article 12 of the Marine Reserves Act, spear guns are forbidden in the waters of the Dahlak Islands, as is the collection of coral, shells or any plant life from either the beaches or the waters. Leaving litter of any sort is also considered an offence, as is the disruption of the habitat of endangered species such as turtle.

For further information on marine life, see the special section 'Marine Life in the Red Sea'.

Endangered Species

Huge numbers of animals were killed during the war by hungry armies but the single greatest threat to wildlife today is the loss or degradation of habitat. Almost all of Eritrea's animals (with the exception of the baboon, ostrich and gazelle) are considered 'endangered' within the country's own national perimeters. Internationally, the Nubian Ibex (which has probably disappeared from Eritrea) is considered dangerously threatened. In recent years, concerns have been expressed for the elephant. A century ago, significant numbers inhabited Gash-Setit province. Today, it is thought that no more that 100 elephants exist, in a tiny pocket near Omhajer and Antore. The World Wide Fund for Nature (WWF) is expected to carry out a systematic survey of the area in the near future.

An even rarer animal, and one recently classed as 'critically endangered', is the African wild ass (Equus africanus; see the boxed text 'The Wild Ass' in the East of Addis Ababa section of the Ethiopia chapter).

The ass is found between Dankalia and the Bure peninsula, but numbers are extremely low (perhaps less than 100). It is not known for certain whether the population is truly wild ass, or – as is more common – a hybrid (donkey cross). Currently, research on wild asses is being carried out in the Bure peninsula.

Hunting and trapping are banned in Eritrea. However, turtles continue to be caught by the local people, who have long lived off them. At least 120 turtles a year, as well as turtle eggs, reach the fish market of Assab, and at least that number are caught for subsistence purposes.

Meaty Mermaids

The dugong (dugongo dugon), or seacow, has long intrigued humankind. Sailors of the ancient world took these marine mammals for mermaids: if honoured the 'mermaids' smiled upon you, but if dishonoured they lured your ship onto the rocks.

There is only one species of dugong, which is found throughout the Indian Ocean, in the Red Sea and the Gulf. The mammal is herbivorous, specialising in sea grasses found on sandy and muddy sea floors.

The dugong can measure up to 4m in length, and can weigh up to 1000kg. With a lifespan of over 70 years, the female does not bear a calf until she is between 10 and 25 years old, and then only every four to seven years. For this reason, a population is easily wiped out. Apart from the shark, humans are its only predator.

Until recently, the dugong made up an important part of the Eritrean coastal people's diet and way of life. All parts of the mammal were used: the fat, skin (which is very hard-wearing) and meat. The flesh in particular was highly prized for its rich, meaty taste and fine texture.

The only organised international trade in turtles or their products appears to exist on the island of Dohul in the Dahlak Islands. According to recent local reports, the islanders currently supply dried turtle penises to Saudi Arabia. One piece reportedly fetched a price of 100 Saudi riyals.

Endangered species of flora include the eucalypt *(Boswellia papyrifera)*, found in the provinces of Senhit, Gash-Setit and western Seraye; the baobab tree *(Adansonia digitata)*; and the tamarind tree *(Tamarindus indica)*.

National Parks

Although several wildlife reserves were established in colonial times, both land and wildlife were never properly protected.

Today, no national reserve or park exists formally, although their establishment is expected in the near future. Most likely sites are the province of Gash-Setit to the west, the Bure peninsula and the Semenawi Bahri ('Green belt', north-east of Asmara).

At present, there are no marine parks either, but several islands in the Dahlak group have been proposed, including Shumma, Black Assarca and Dissei.

Other government plans include the training of personnel in wildlife management, education of the local people, and their enlistment in both the creation and management of the new protected areas.

GOVERNMENT & POLITICS

The head of state, the president, holds wide powers and is elected for a five-year term, which is renewable once only.

The government is made of two branches: an executive branch composed of a 17-member cabinet; and a legislative branch, comprising the national assembly (parliament). Of the 150 seats in parliament, 75 belong to the central council of the ruling party, the PFDJ, and 75 nonparty members. Thirty percent of all seats are reserved for women.

The judiciary is composed of the head of the High Court and judges in the provincial and Sharia'a (Islamic law) courts. Currently, new criminal and civil codes are being drafted to replace the old Ethiopian ones.

Domestic politics are largely internal to the ruling PFDJ, who sees itself less as a party and more as a broad popular front, representing all spheres of the Eritrean population. In May 1997, a pluralist constitution was promulgated but opposition political parties remain illegal.

Ironically, the tragic and wasteful border conflict with Ethiopia that flared up in 1998 has sparked strong nationalist sentiment, which has not only ensured continuing support for the president and his government, but also internal stability.

ECONOMY

After independence, Eritrea began to enjoy strong economic growth and low inflation. However, the recent war with Ethiopia has put a swift stop to this, as the cost of the war has been high. In addition, the war has caused Eritrea to lose vital revenue from its port, Assab, where 90% of business was Ethiopian. Within a year of the conflict, GDP growth rate had halved to 4%, while inflation rose from 2% to 9%.

About 70% of the population are farmers, pastoralists or fishers. A major government priority – along with development of the infrastructure – has been to improve food security. Obstacles to the development of agriculture include serious soil erosion, outdated technology and lack of irrigation. Some horticultural projects are flourishing in the highlands, and may soon be developed in the western lowlands.

Other economic hopes include the huge resources of the Red Sea, especially high-value species such as lobster, fish and crab. Fishery cooperatives are currently being developed in Massawa and Assab.

Eritrea's main exports are salt, flowers, textiles, leather and livestock. Imports include fertilisers, machinery, spare parts and tools and construction materials.

Oil exploration has proved disappointing. However, there are hopes of developing exports of high-quality marble to the Middle East and Europe. Eritrea's traditional light industries continue to fill the shops of the capital with knitwear and sweaters, cotton, leather, glass, salt and processed food.

ERITREA

There are also moves to develop the private sector. Three government hotels have been sold recently, and the other eight are up for grabs. Takers are not forthcoming: the hotels are pretty shabby, and prices are high. A new five-star hotel has just opened in the capital, and joint US and Saudi plans for a casino and several hotels on the Dahlak Islands are finally under way.

POPULATION & PEOPLE

The population of Eritrea is estimated to be 3.5 million. There are nine ethnic groups: Tigrinya (the largest group), Afar, Bilen, Hedareb, Kunama, Nara, Rashaida, Saho and Tigré, each with their own language and customs (see the special section 'A Museum of Peoples'). The new banknotes illustrate some of these peoples. Some 1100 Italians are thought to live in Eritrea, 750 of whom live in Asmara.

Approximately 35% of the population are nomadic or semi-nomadic and around 80% live in the country. Just 3% of Eritreans have access to sanitation and waste disposal, and healthcare outside the capital is low.

UNAIDS estimates that at least 3.2% of the population are HIV+, though public awareness campaigns are limited by the deep conservatism of Eritrean society. You may notice a lack of young men around town; this is because they're almost all doing service at the front, although this may change if the dispute with Ethiopia is resolved.

Women enjoy far greater equality in Eritrea than in most other African countries (see the boxed text 'The New Woman' under Women Travellers in the Facts for the Visitor section later in this chapter). This liberal national attitude has been won by Eritrea's women themselves, contributing more than one-third of troops in both the recent wars against Ethiopia.

However, Eritrea remains a deeply conservative country and the 'double liberation' (for their country and for gender) expected after independence has not been as forthcoming as some had hoped. In rural areas, prejudices remain deeply rooted.

In the towns, several active and well-organised women's groups have sprung up in the last years (for more details, see Women Travellers in the Facts for the Visitor section in this chapter).

EDUCATION

Education is divided into three categories and is free to all: primary (for five years), middle (two years) and upper (four years). Some students then go on to university.

Improvements in education have been a high government priority. Despite the efforts, 80% of the population remain illiterate (though a greater percentage can read). The capital is well provided with primary and secondary schools, as well as a university with a capacity for 1300 students a year. Outside the capital, schools are few and far between, and enrolment anyway is low – from 50% in the primary schools, falling to just 10% in the upper schools.

Local languages are the medium for teaching at primary schools; English is used at secondary schools and above.

ARTS

Eritrean arts reflect the diversity of the country's many peoples. See also this heading in the Facts about Ethiopia section.

Dance

Dance plays a very important social role in Eritrea. Apart from marking the major events of life, such as birth and marriage, or celebrating special occasions and religious festivals, they traditionally also permitted the young girls and boys to meet, and the warriors to show off their prowess.

The dances of the Kunama and Hedareb are particularly exuberant. Well-known Eritrean dancers include Dahab Fatinga.

Music

Traditional musical instruments of Eritrea have their roots in Ethiopia (see Arts in the Facts about Ethiopia section). They include the *krar* and *wata*, both string instruments; the *shambko*, a type of flute; and the *embilta*, a wind instrument.

Though sharing some similarities, each of the nine ethnic groups has its own distinct melodies and beat.

Atewebrhan Segid is considered one of the leading traditional musicians and singers in Eritrea today. The famous Eritrean singer Yemane Gebremichael, known as the 'father of the poor', died in 1997.

Others singers, both traditional and modern, include Berekhet Mengisteab, Osman Abdel Rahim, Idriss Mohammed Ali, Teklé Kiflemariam, Tesfay Mehari and Samuel Berhane.

Literature

Eritrea's oral literature – in the form of folk tales, ballads, poetry, laudations etc – is rich and diverse (see the special section 'Oral Literature in the Horn').

Though inscriptions date from the 7th century, written works can be said to date from about the 15th century with the *Adkeme Melgaë* (a collection of rules and laws), as well as some Arabic writings.

The Italians imposed their own language and literature (and Latin alphabet) on the country, as did the British and later the Ethiopians. Woldeab Woldemariam is especially venerated for his part in fighting the suppression of the local languages and of encouraging their expression. His *Zanta Quedamot* was a collection of children's stories designed to make the Tigrinyan alphabet more easily understood by children. Other works of the 1950s and 1960s included *Embafrash*, *Awet dehri Sequay* and *Merab melash*.

During the Struggle for Independence from Ethiopia, writing in the vernacular was encouraged, expressed through such publications as the fighters' magazine *Mahta* (*Spark*) and *Fitewrari* (*Avant-garde*).

Today, increasing amounts of poetry, fiction and drama are being produced and published (mainly in Tigrinya and Arabic). Current novelists include Alemseged Tesfai, Solomon Drar and Bruk Habtemikael.

In recent times, the nine languages of the nine ethnic groups have adopted written scripts: six have adopted the Latin alphabet and one Arabic. The other two, Tigrinya and Tigré have always used the Ge'ez-derived script of ancient Aksum.

Architecture

Eritrean vernacular architecture depends on both its ethnic and geographical origin. In the cool highlands, the traditional house is the hidmo. Built on a rectangular plan, the house is constructed with dry-stone walls topped with a thick, earthen roof, supported both inside and out with strong wooden pillars (see the boxed text 'Heavy Hidmos' in Ecology & Environment earlier in this section).

In the lowlands, where warmth is less of a concern, people traditionally live in huts. Depending on the ethnic group, the hut walls are made of adobe (sun-dried brick), wood or stone, and have thatched roofs.

In Asmara and many of the larger towns such as Keren and Dekemhare the colonial heritage can be seen in the Italian-style buildings. Many, in Asmara and Massawa in particular, are remarkable historical and artistic pieces (see the special section 'Architecture in Asmara' in the Asmara section).

Painting

The country's ancient orthodox church has long provided an outlet for painting. Most church walls are painted with colourful and dramatic murals. Canvas and parchment manuscripts, some several hundred years old, are also illustrated with delightful and sometimes very beautiful biblical scenes.

Painters in various mediums today include Mikael Adonai, Tesfay Gebremikael, Ygzaw Mikael and Giorgis Abraham.

Pottery

Like most cultures, pottery is one of Eritrea's oldest arts. In rural areas, earthenware pots are still commonly used for cooking, food preparation and storage.

Even in the towns, earthenware pots are preferred over metal ones for the cooking of the traditional *zigni* (meat sauce).

Theatre

Theatre is an ancient art and, like painting, has its roots in Ethiopia. Traditionally, it was staged to celebrate religious festivals, and involved music, singing, dance and acting.

ERITREA

[Continued on page 334]

A MUSEUM OF PEOPLES

Since the beginning of time, Eritrea has attracted migrants, merchants and meddlesome foreign powers. Today, these influences are reflected in the country's diverse ethnic population. The Italian historian, Conti Rossini, described Abyssinia (an area comprising both Ethiopia and Eritrea) as 'un museo di populi' (a museum of peoples).

TIGRINYA

The Tigrinya make up 50% of the Eritrean population and inhabit the densely populated central highlands, extending over the provinces of Seraye, Hamasien and Akele Guzay. The people are sedentary farmers and are overwhelmingly Orthodox Christian, with just a small minority of Muslims, who are known as Jiberti. The very distinct plaited hairstyle of the women has been depicted for centuries in local art.

The people have always been fiercely attached to their land, which has been the cause of many a dispute. The Tigrinya community is traditionally tightly knit and deeply conservative. Tigrinya is one of the country's official languages.

TIGRÉ

The Tigré make up 31.4% of the population, and inhabit the northern lowlands, from the Sudanese frontier to the western limits of the Danakil.

A very heterogeneous people, the Tigré are divided into groups and clans. Most are Muslim, and they are both sedentary and nomadic. The sedentary farmers cultivate maize, *durra* (sorghum) and other cereals.

Tigrean society is traditionally hierarchical, with a small aristocracy known as *shemagille* ruling the masses. When the village leader dies, his power passes to his offspring.

Tigrean oral literature is rich and ranges from fables, riddles and poetry to funeral dirges, war cries and supernatural stories. The Tigré are also known for their love of singing and dancing, usually to the accompaniment of a drum and the *mesenko* (a type of guitar). Dances are celebrated on many occasions, such as when a new waterhole is found.

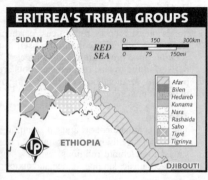

ERITREA'S TRIBAL GROUPS

SUDAN

RED SEA

0 — 150 — 300km
0 — 75 — 150mi

Afar
Bilen
Hedareb
Kunama
Nara
Rashaida
Saho
Tigré
Tigrinya

ETHIOPIA

DJIBOUTI

SAHO

The Saho make up 5% of the population; they inhabit the coast and the hinterland south of Asmara and Massawa. Towards the end of April, when the rains stop in the lowlands, many Saho leave the coastal area and trek with their livestock up to the highlands of Akele Guzay. When the rains stop in September, the people return for the wet season on the coastal lowlands.

The people are predominantly Muslim, but feelings of ethnic identity are less strong among them than other groups. Known as great pastoralists, the people fought for centuries with the highlanders over the pastures of the mountains. Today, the Saho often tend other people's cattle, including those of the Tigrinya, in exchange for grain. Many Saho children (up to the age of 16) wear little leather pouches around their neck, which are full of herbs and spices to ward off evil spirits.

Some Saho are sedentary farmers who have settled in the highlands of Akele Guzay. Honey is an important part of the Saho diet and the people are also known as good beekeepers. In the past, they were also reputed as warriors, and were often enlisted to escort trade caravans between central Ethiopia to the port of Massawa.

The Saho are organised in patrilineal descent groups. The leaders, elected by the male assembly, are known as *rezantos*, and were formerly the military chief in times of war.

AFAR

The Eritrean Afars, also known as the Danakils, make up 5% of the population and inhabit the long coastal strip stretching from the Gulf of Zula into Djibouti. Predominantly nomadic pastoralists, the people are Muslim, though elements of ancient ancestor-worship still persist.

Since early times, the Afar territory has been divided into kingdoms and ruled by individual sultans who have always remained fiercely independent of any foreign power.

The sole inhabitants of one of the most inhospitable regions on earth, during the last 100 years the Afars have acquired a fearsome reputation. In 1934, Nesbitt, an English engineer declared: 'the Danakil are ready to kill any stranger whom they come across'.

The men still carry the famous *jile* or curved knife, and some file their teeth to points. Afar oral literature reveals a high esteem for military prowess, with a whole repertoire of war chants. Today, their songs tend to extol the virtues of the camel.

HEDAREB

The Hedareb, along with their 'brother' tribes the Beni Amer and Beja, make up 2.5% of the population, and inhabit the north-western valleys of Eritrea, straddling the border with Sudan.

Most Hedarebs are nomadic and travel great distances in search of pasture. The people are Cushitic in origin (probably directly descended from the ancient Beja tribe) and speak mainly Tigré and an ancient Beja language.

The Beni Amer are a strongly patriarchal, socially stratified, almost feudal people. Their skills as camel drivers and in raising camels are legendary. Many of the men scarify their cheeks with three short, vertical strokes – the Italians called them the '111 tribe'.

BILEN

The Bilen inhabit the environs of Keren and make up 2.1% of the population. Cushitic in origin, the Bilen are either sedentary Christian farmers or Muslim cattle rearers.

Bilen traditional society is organised into kinship groups. The women are known for their brightly coloured clothes and their gold, silver or copper nose rings which indicate their means and social status. Like the Beja language, Bilen is slowly being replaced by Tigré, Tigrinya and Arabic, due to intermarriage, economic interactions and because Arabic is taught in local schools. Henna tattoos that mimic diamond necklaces or little freckles are fashionable among the women.

KUNAMA

The Kunama inhabit the Gash-Setit province in the south-western corner of Eritrea, close to the Ethiopian and Sudanese border, and make up 2% of the population. Barentu is their 'capital'. The Kunama people are Nilotic in origin, and very dark skinned. They are the original inhabitants of the region.

A few Kunama are Muslim, some Christian, but the great majority are animist. According to their beliefs, the higher divinity, Anna, created the sky and the earth but is largely indifferent to human fate. The spirits, by contrast, must be placated before every event, even the ploughing of a field.

Kunama society is patriarchal, but contains certain matriarchal elements, including inheritance through the female side. The society is strongly egalitarian, recognising only the authority of the elders and the village assemblies. The Kunama community is closely knit, and many educated Kunama abandon the city to return to the country.

KAHSSAI-TZEGUMENGHISTU

Land is often farmed co-operatively, and after the work is finished, the village unites to celebrate with feasting and dancing. The Kunama are known for their dances, and have developed more than 25 dance forms, often re-enacting great historical events or victories. This tradition was particularly well suited to the resistance movement against Ethiopia, when the dances were greatly popularised.

KAHSSAI-TZEGUMENGHISTU

NARA

The Nara, also known as the Baria, make up 1.5% of the population and inhabit the Barka Valley near the Sudanese border. Along with the Kunama, they are the only Nilotic (Negroid) Eritrean tribe, and are mainly Muslim.

The people are sedentary mixed farmers and share many customs with their neighbours the Kunama. Skirmishes and raids from other tribes have forced many of the people to flee, and the population is now thought to be endangered.

RASHAIDA

The Rashaida are the only true Eritrean nomads. Making up just 0.5% of the population, they roam the northern coasts of Eritrea and Sudan, as well as the southern reaches of the Nubian desert. Like their neighbours, the Beja (related to the Hedareb), they live by raising cattle and are Muslim.

The Rashaida were the last of the Semitic people to arrive in Eritrea in the middle of the 19th century. Their language is Arabic.

The magnificent Rashaida women are famous for their black-and-red geometrically patterned dresses, and their long, heavy veils, the *burga*, elaborately embroidered with silver thread, beads and sometimes seed pearls.

The Rashaida people are known for their great pride; marriage is only permitted within their own clan. The people are expert goat and cattle rearers, as well as merchants and traders along the Red Sea coasts.

[Continued from page 329]

During federation with Ethiopia, censorship was one of the principal constraints facing the development of local theatre. On the emergence of the EPLF in the 1980s, new works began to appear. One of them, *The Other War* by Alemseged Tesfay, has appeared in an English anthology of contemporary African plays.

SOCIETY & CONDUCT

Many traditional customs and ceremonies of Eritrea are identical to those in Ethiopia, and are covered fully under this heading in the Facts about Ethiopia section.

It is considered impolite to ask an Eritrean his ethnic origin, religion or whether or not he was a 'fighter' (in the Struggle for Independence). There is still a bit of a stigma attached to those who weren't – even if they made sacrifices in other ways.

RELIGION

The population is almost equally divided between Christians and Muslims. Christians are primarily Orthodox – the Eritrean Orthodox church has its roots in the Ethiopian one (see this heading in the Facts about Ethiopia section for more details). There are also small numbers of Roman Catholics and Protestants, as a result of missionary activity. The Muslims are primarily Sunnis, with a small Sufi minority (for general information

A Fighter's Salute

If you see two men banging their shoulders together, they're not having a wrestle. It is the 'shoulder greeting' popularised by the *tegadelti*, or freedom fighters. With right hands clasped, right shoulders are pressed together three times, the last a little more forcefully to push the two apart. It is a sign of great comradeship.

on Islam see this heading in the Facts about Djibouti section later in this book).

Roughly speaking, the agricultural Orthodox Christians inhabit the highland region, and the Muslims are concentrated in the lowlands, the coastal areas and towards the Sudanese border. Some animists inhabit the south-western lowlands.

There are at least 18 monasteries in Eritrea. Following the raids of the famous Muslim leader, Mohammed Gragn the Left-Handed, in the 16th century almost all of them were safely tucked away in very remote and inaccessible places. Three of the oldest and most important are Debre Bizen (near Nefasit), Hamm (near Senafe) and Debre Sina (near Keren).

LANGUAGE

In theory, Tigrinya, Arabic and English are all the official languages of Eritrea. In practice, Tigrinya is mainly confined to the highlands, Arabic to the coastal regions and along the Sudanese border and English to the educated urban populations (particularly in Asmara). Nevertheless a surprising number of Eritreans speak English.

Each of the nine ethnic groups speaks its own language: Afar, Arabic, Bilen, To Bedawi, Kunama, Nara, Saho, Tigre and Tigrinya. Amharic, a legacy of Ethiopian rule, is also still widely spoken.

Until independence, only Arabic, Tigre and Tigrinya had a written form. Nowadays, Eritrea is developing a Latin-based alphabet for the remaining six languages as a way of reinforcing regional culture and identity.

Wiles & Ways

For weddings, religious festivals and special occasions, Tigré and Tigrinya women love to get their hair done. The mass of tiny plaits go right up to the scalp, and can take a whole morning to prepare.

Married women can additionally have the palms of their hands and their feet tattooed with curvilinear patterns of henna. Fashionable teenagers prefer to have their gums tattooed. Pricked until they bleed, the gums are rubbed with charcoal. The resulting blue colour sets off a dazzling set of teeth, and is considered a mark of great beauty.

As English is the medium of instruction at secondary and tertiary level, travellers to Eritrea will find English surprisingly useful. This is also a legacy of the war, when most families had at least one member abroad; most returnees from Western Europe or North America speak it fluently. Also, some Italian words for greetings, food and beverage are spoken.

If you muster up a few words of Tigrinya, you'll amaze and delight the Eritreans and quickly win friends. See the Language chapter at the end of this book for useful words and phrases in Arabic and Tigrinya.

Facts for the Visitor

SUGGESTED ITINERARIES
Though Eritrea is a small country, bear in mind that travelling anywhere takes time. In Dankalia, the going can be as slow as 10km/h. From Asmara to Nakfa (around 200km to the north), count on a whole day's travel.

One Week
If you're really pushed for time, a week would give you just a glimpse of the country's main attractions. Asmara deserves at least half a day and serves as a base for excursions into the country.

The attractive town of Keren can be visited in a day from the capital; the tropical forest near Filfil (a must for bird-watchers and wildlife enthusiasts) is another good day trip. A hike to the monastery of Debre Bizen near Nefasit also makes a good excursion from Asmara.

Lying 115km to the east of Asmara is the old Turkish port of Massawa, which is worth a visit in itself, although it's better known as the starting point for visits to the Dahlak Islands. Spend a morning or afternoon snorkelling at the nearby reefs. South of Asmara lie the ancient ruins of Qohaito and Metara – allow at least three days there and back to visit both sites.

Two Weeks
With more days and money at your disposal, you could do everything suggested under

One Week, plus a diving or snorkelling trip off the Dahlak Islands. You'll need to book in advance either a cruise in one of the charter boats (minimum two days, but usually around six), or your own boat and equipment.

A trip to Nakfa in the far north, for years the centre of the Struggle, is another possibility, and would immerse you in the country's scenery and history.

Three Weeks & More
With around three weeks, the lowland savanna of the west and far north can be explored, giving a fascinating glimpse of some of Eritrea's most colourful inhabitants, though you'll need to hire a decent 4WD to get you there. In a tiny pocket of woodland between Antore and Awgaro, a small population of elephants still roams.

Penetration into the famously inhospitable Dankalia region to the south makes for an epic journey. It's possible by bus but could take between four days (in theory) and several weeks because of the conditions of the roads. In your own vehicle, it's expedition-style only.

For travellers with more time, there is good potential for hiking around Filfil, and in the mountains of the central highlands.

PLANNING
When to Go
Although Eritrea can be visited any time of year, the ideal time climate-wise is from September to October and from March to April (for more details, see Climate in the Facts about Eritrea section). If you can, avoid travelling during June to August, when it is the rainy season in the highlands and western lowlands, and the hot, torrid season in the eastern lowlands.

It's also worth trying to coincide with one or more of the country's colourful religious festivals. The most spectacular are Timkat (19 January) and Meskel (27 September) – for more details, see Public Holidays & Special Events later in this section. The other major religious event to look out for is the Muslim fasting month of Ramadan – see Planning in Facts for the Visitor in the Djibouti chapter for a discussion of the pros and cons of travelling at this time. For a table showing the dates of Ramadan, see Public Holidays & Special Events in the Djibouti chapter.

The effects of Ramadan are most felt in the Muslim-dominated areas along the coast and around the Sudanese border. It hardly features in the Christian-dominated areas such as the capital.

What Kind of Trip
Most places of interest in Eritrea can be reached by bus but travelling off the main routes is very slow and time-consuming. If you want to explore the real hinterland, you'll need to hire a 4WD (including driver) from the capital or take a tour. Both options are expensive.

Maps
A reasonable government-produced map of Eritrea (1995; 1:1,000,000) is sold in Asmara (Nfa85 to Nfa95), but it's sometimes hard to find. If you know you'll need a map, it's best to get one before leaving home.

The best map currently available – though far from perfect – is the one produced by the French Institut Géographique National or IGN (1997; 1:9,000,000). Most map suppliers should stock it, including Stanfords in London, UK (☎ 020-7836 1321, fax 7836 0189, ✉ sales@stanfords.co.uk, 12–14 Long Acre, London WC2E 9LP).

If you need navigational charts of the islands or ports, the ones produced by the British Admiralty are unsurpassed. Stanfords can order these for you, and delivery takes up to one week. The price per sheet is UK£15.30, and you'll need at least two – BA164 and BA171.

What to Bring
High-factor sunscreen, hat, mosquito net, and water bottle are probably the most important things for a trip to Eritrea. A torch is essential also; many towns have electricity until midnight only, and many villages have none at all. Reasonable snorkelling equipment can be bought or hired in Massawa. Personal items (such as contact lens fluid and tampons) are very difficult to find in Eritrea.

RESPONSIBLE TOURISM
The country receives relatively few tourists per year so impact on the environment is so far fairly minimal.

The beautiful coral reefs around the Dahlak Islands are perhaps most vulnerable to damage, and in addition receive more tourists (local and foreign) than many areas.

Eritrea is a party to the Convention on International Trade in Endangered Species (Cites), and it is therefore illegal to export any endangered species or their products, such as turtle or ivory. You may find turtle meat in restaurants, and turtle and elephant souvenirs in shops (particularly in Asmara); hawkers may offer you turtle eggs (particularly in Massawa). It's best to avoid these as all species of marine turtle are currently threatened. Coral and shell collection is now discouraged too.

Try to resist the temptation to buy any genuinely old artefacts, such as manuscripts, scrolls and bibles, found in some of the shops in the capital. Eritrea has already lost a huge amount of its heritage, particularly during the Italian era. Such exports will soon be illegal anyway.

Water is an extremely precious and scarce resource in Eritrea. Take care not to waste it.

TOURIST OFFICES
There is currently no national tourist office in the country, though one is planned in Post Office Square in Asmara. A Ministry of Tourism (☎ 12-00-73, ☎ 12-69-97) exists, but it's not really geared up to dealing with tourists. The best place to go for information is the Eritrean Tour Service or ETS (☎ 12-49-49, fax 12-76-95), PO Box 889, Asmara. For a long time it was the only travel agency, and for years it has acted as a kind of unofficial tourist office. Other, newer travel agencies will also help, but their interests obviously lie in selling you a tour.

Outside Eritrea, the Eritrean embassy or consulate in your home country (the few that exist) is your best bet, but tourist literature is generally very limited.

In the UK contact the British Eritrean Association (☎ 020-7736 3460), 6 Cortayne Rd, London SW6 3QA.

VISAS & DOCUMENTS

For general information on travel insurance, see the Facts for the Visitor in the Ethiopia chapter. You'll need an international driving permit if you are planning on driving in Eritrea.

Visas

All foreign nationals require visas for entry to Eritrea. Requirements tend to vary arbitrarily from one Eritrean embassy or consulate to another. Eritrea is also a very young country, and visa requirements are likely to change, so check with the embassy.

Visas should be obtained from the Eritrean embassy or consulate before you leave your home country. If there isn't any diplomatic representation in your home country, obtain a visa from the nearest one. If this is inconvenient, you can contact the consular section of the Ministry of Foreign Affairs in Asmara (☎ 12-71-08, fax 12-37-88, PO Box 190, Asmara). Normally, you'll be asked to fax your details to immigration in advance of your arrival. You'll then be issued with a visa at your port of entry. If you're planning to visit neighbouring countries, it might be easier to get a visa there, except in Ethiopia.

At the time of writing, an enterprising travel agent, Solomon Abraha of Travel House International (☎ 12-02-08, fax 12-00-64, @ soloabr@eol.com.er, PO Box 5579, Asmara), was offering a visa service for US$20. You'll need to fax him details of your passport pages and give him at least two weeks to organise the visa, which will then be faxed back to you.

For visa applications, you'll need your passport (valid for at least three months) and one passport photo. Some embassies also require some or all of the following: a valid return air ticket, travellers cheques worth US$40 per day for the duration of your visit, and an up-to-date yellow-fever vaccination certificate.

The visa application form may require an address in Eritrea and a 'reference'. If you don't have any, find a hotel and tour operator later in this book, and use these names. Applications can be made by post, and normally take 48 hours to process.

You usually have to travel within three months of the date of issue of the visa. If you're travelling to other countries for a period of three months or more before arrival in Eritrea, you should get a letter of recommendation from the Eritrean embassy before setting out – this will ease your arrival in Eritrea.

Visa Types Tourist visas are for single entry only, and are valid for 30 days from the date of arrival in Eritrea. They cost around US$30.

To get a business visa, you'll need a letter from your sponsoring company stating the purpose of the trip. Business visas cost US$60 (single entry, valid for one month) or US$75 (multiple entry, valid for three months).

Transit visas, which allow you to stay for seven days in Eritrea, can be issued provided you have an onward ticket and valid passport and visa for your country of destination. Transit visas (US$15) can be issued by Eritrean embassies abroad or at any official port of entry.

Visa Extensions The Department of Immigration (☎ 11-92-99, ☎ 11-40-11, fax 12-61-93) in Asmara will extend your visa up to two times for a further 30 days. This costs US$35 (except for US citizens, who pay US$20) and you will need one photo, photocopies of your passport details and visa page, and a 20-cent stamp. Payment must be made with cash, and with exact change. Applications must be made before the old visa expires. The office keeps normal business hours. The whole process takes about 1½ hours. The new visa is usually valid from the date of issue but if you need to, you can persuade the officials to post-date the start date to the expiry date of your present visa.

Travel Permits

Eritrea's 'national treasures' are protected by paperwork. To visit many places, you'll

ERITREA

need to get a special permit from the capital. Though this is a bit time-consuming and irksome, it means that the sites attract only those really interested in them – and those less likely to harm them.

To visit any of the archaeological sites of Eritrea, you will need to obtain a permission paper (good for all sites) from the National Museum office in Asmara (for contact details, see under National Museum in the Asmara section). If you're taking a tour, your agency should do this for you.

You need permission to visit the Dahlak Islands. This is obtainable from the Eritrean Shipping Lines office (☎ 55-26-29, fax 55-23-91) in Massawa. Note that you'll need US dollars cash to pay for the permit, so plan ahead – outside Asmara, no bank will be able to issue you with dollars.

You'll also need a permit to visit the monasteries, obtainable from the Orthodox Tewahedo Church Headquarters in Asmara. Ask for the 'monastery tour application'.

EMBASSIES & CONSULATES
Eritrean Embassies & Consulates
For the Eritrean embassies in Ethiopia and Djibouti, see under Embassies & Consulates in the other chapters. Eritrean embassies and consulates include the following:

Australia (☎ 6-282 3489, fax 282 5233) 26 Guilfoyle St, Yarralumla, ACT 2600
Canada (☎ 613-234 3989, fax 234 6213) Suite 610, 75 Albert St, Ottawa KIP 5E7
Egypt (☎ 303 0517, fax 303 0516) PO Box 2624, 87 Shahab St, Al Muhandesein, Cairo
France (☎ 01 43 06 15 56, fax 43 06 07 51) 1 Rue Miollin 75732, Paris CEDEX 15

Eritrean Embassies Closed

The Eritrean embassy in Addis Ababa, Ethiopia, was closed when this edition went to print. The embassy in Djibouti town was also closed. The embassy in Sudan is likewise vulnerable to volatile relations; at the time of writing it was closed but was rumoured to be about to reopen.

Germany (☎ 221-373 0168, fax 340 4128) Markt Str 8, 50968, Koln
Italy (☎ 6-4274 1305, 2474 1293) Via Boncompagni No 16 Int 6, 00187 Roma
Kenya (☎ 2-443 164, fax 443 165) PO Box 38651, New Woumin House, 4th floor, West Ianols, Nairobi
Saudi Arabia (☎ 672 7321, fax 676 2235) Ahmed Lary St, PO Box 770, Jeddah
South Africa (☎ 12-333 1302, fax 333 2330) PO Box 11371, 0121 Queenswood, Pretoria
Sudan (☎ 73165) PO Box 8129, Khartoum
UK (☎ 020-7713 0096, fax 7713 0161) 96 White Lion St, London N1 9PF
US (☎ 202-319 1991, fax 319 1304) 1708 New Hampshire Ave, NW Washington DC 20009
Yemen (☎ 1-209 422, fax 214 088) PO Box 11040, San'a

Embassies & Consulates in Eritrea
Ring your embassy for directions. All embassies and consulates are based in Asmara, and include the following:

Djibouti (☎ 18-10-10)
Egypt (☎ 12-49-35)
Ethiopia (☎ 12-07-36) Closed at the time of research
France (☎ 12-65-99)
Germany (☎ 18-29-01)
Italy (☎ 12-07-74)
Netherlands (☎ 18-59-06)
Norway (☎ 12-01-45)
Saudi Arabia (☎ 12-09-79)
Sudan (☎ 12-41-76)
Sweden (☎ 18-15-90)
Switzerland (☎ 18-17-01)
UK (☎ 12-01-45)
USA (☎ 12-00-04, fax 12-75-84) Franklin Roosevelt St, PO Box 211, Asmara
Yemen (☎ 11-44-34)

CUSTOMS
On arrival at the airport, any major electronic items (expensive cameras, laptops, video cameras etc) must be registered at customs. This is to deter black market business, and on departure the items will be signed off. If anything is stolen during your stay in Eritrea, make sure you obtain a police statement registering the loss immediately.

Duty-free allowances include 1L of alcohol, and 200 cigarettes. Rifles and shotguns for hunting require an import permit.

Declaration of foreign currency is not required. It is strictly forbidden in theory to export any nakfa from Eritrea. In practice, an allowance of up to Nfa50 is permitted to allow for any problems or needs. More than this, however, and there's a risk it will be confiscated.

MONEY
For general advice on safety issues, see Security in the Facts for the Visitor section in the Ethiopia chapter.

Currency
The nakfa (nfa) was introduced in November 1997 to replace the old Ethiopian birr. It is divided into 100 cents, in 5, 10, 25, 50 and 100 cent pieces, and in 1, 5, 10, 20, 50 and 100 nakfa notes.

Exchange Rates
Initially valued on a par with the Ethiopian birr, the nakfa was floated in mid-1998. Since then, military expenditure on the war has greatly weakened the economy, and the nakfa has suffered correspondingly (see the boxed text 'Fluctuating Currency Crisis' under Costs following). The official exchange rate was US$1 = Nfa10.50 at the time this book went to print, but the parallel rate had fallen to US$1 = Nfa15, and was falling fast.

Australia	A$1	=	Nfa6.29
Canada	C$1	=	Nfa7.13
Euro	€1	=	Nfa10.00
France	10FF	=	Nfa15.24
Germany	DM1	=	Nfa5.11
Japan	¥100	=	Nfa9.97
New Zealand	NZ$1	=	Nfa4.97
UK	UK£1	=	Nfa15.89
USA	US$1	=	Nfa10.50

Exchanging Money
US dollars (cash or travellers cheques) are the best currency to carry. Not only are US dollars easier to exchange outside the capital, but you have to pay for certain things in US dollars, including the government hotels, a permit to visit the Dahlak Islands, visa extensions, some air tickets and the departure tax. The rate of exchange for US dollars is also better than for other currencies.

Currently the only bank authorised to issue US dollars cash is the Commercial Bank in the capital, so be careful not to get stuck with cheques only.

There is one bank at Asmara airport and several in Asmara, as well as at least one exchange bureau. Some of the larger hotels in Asmara exchange money or travellers cheques, but you need to be a guest in the hotel.

Outside the capital, there are banking facilities in the main towns.

Banks Most banks open from 8 am to 11 am and from 2 to 4 pm Monday to Friday, and from 8 am to 12.30 pm on Saturday. Remember to take your passport; sometimes it's needed even for exchanging cash. Because of queues and bureaucracy, the process can be lengthy (particularly in the smaller rural branches, which have to telephone Asmara for the daily exchange rate).

All major currencies can be exchanged in the capital; in rural areas, sometimes only US dollars are exchanged. Banks charge a commission of around 1.3% for dollars and 1.5% for other currencies.

There are currently no ATMs in Eritrea.

Black Market You'll meet plenty of unofficial moneychangers around the main post office in Asmara, but exchanging money outside the banks is illegal. If you do indulge, you're taking a big risk for a small gain.

Travellers Cheques Most of the capital's major banks and hotels, some airline offices and some travel agencies accept travellers cheques. The Commercial Bank of Eritrea charges 0.5% commission, plus a postage charge of Nfa7.50 per three cheques cashed, and a revenue stamp of 40¢.

As with cash, travellers cheques are best carried in US dollars, although most major currencies can be exchanged in the banks in the capital and some banks outside.

Fluctuating Currency Crisis

Because of the serious economic problems currently afflicting the country (from the cost of the war with Ethiopia), the value of the national currency, the nakfa, has been depreciating every day. Prices quoted in this book are thus likely to have changed considerably.

Credit Cards The larger hotels in the capital, some airlines and, increasingly, some travel agents now accept credit cards. A commission of up to 5% is sometimes charged – check in advance. There are plans to introduce facilities for cash withdrawals with credit cards at the Commercial Bank of Eritrea – check on progress when you get there.

International Transfers In theory, a transfer by telex should take no more than 48 to 72 hours, though in practice it's often much longer, depending on the competence of both sender and receiver banks. The installation of computer link-ups should speed the process up in the future.

The Commercial Bank of Eritrea has accounts with the following banks: Midland Bank in the UK; Citibank in the USA; Credit Italiano, Citibank and Banca Nazionale del Lavora in Italy; Natexis in France; and the Commerce Bank in Germany.

Transfers can be made in all the major currencies but are expensive, and you'll be charged commission for conversion if you want the amount in local currency. In the future, the Commercial Bank plans to issues its own travellers cheques.

If you need a transfer urgently, the Western Union is the probably best bet, though it's not cheap. You will need someone at home to deposit the money; it will then be transferred immediately via a computer to the recipient bank. The whole process should take no more than a day (the transfer itself will take around 20 minutes). To send US$100 costs around US$20; to send US$500 costs around US$45. By credit card you'll be charged an additional 1.5% of the total amount sent.

Costs

In general, Eritrea is a very cheap country to visit. The only exceptions are car hire, some tours, and getting to and around the islands. Because of transportation costs, food and beer in the towns in the hinterland are a little more expensive than Asmara.

At the time of writing, some sample prices were Nfa2.06 for a litre of diesel fuel, 25¢ for a local phone call, Nfa15/30 for a meal in a town/country restaurant (without alcohol), and Nfa3 for a beer. Budget rooms without bathroom cost around Nfa40–50; mid-range rooms cost around Nfa 120–150.

Tipping & Bargaining

The practice of tipping has been introduced in Eritrea and is expected in the towns only. In the rural areas, you may even have your tip returned to you.

In the smaller restaurants in the towns, service is included, and Eritreans don't tip unless the service has been exceptional (in this case, Nfa2 to Nfa5 would be an appropriate amount to leave). In bars and cafes, loose coins are sometimes left. However, in the larger restaurants accustomed to tourists, at least 10% will be expected, and in the larger hotels, staff will expect a bare minimum of Nfa5 to Nfa10.

Unlike in other places in Africa, corruption is not the norm in Eritrea. Overcharging of tourists is very rare in the country, and prices are usually firmly fixed; haggling can offend Eritreans. However, all the usual discounts apply, and it's always worth asking for them – for long stays in hotels, extended car hire etc.

The one exception, where haggling is almost expected, is in the local shops and markets. In many of the shops, prices are rarely displayed. Haggling is meant to be an enjoyable experience, and if you're light-hearted and polite about it, you'll end up with a better price.

POST & COMMUNICATIONS
Post

The Eritrean postal service is considered quite reliable, albeit not the speediest, and it's rare for letters and parcels go astray.

Postage for the first 200g is Nfa3 worldwide, except for neighbouring countries, which are cheaper. Postcards cost Nfa2 worldwide.

If you want to send a parcel, take it already wrapped (but left open for customs inspection) to the parcel office at the back of the main post office, where it will be weighed. Postage costs from Nfa87 to Nfa128 per parcel, plus from Nfa9 to Nfa16 per kilogram, to Europe, the USA or Australia.

Express postal service (EPS) offers worldwide delivery of both letters and parcels, but it's relatively expensive. It costs Nfa116 to Nfa165 to send a 0.5kg parcel to Europe, the USA or Australia, and Nfa40 to Nfa45 for each additional 0.5kg. Courier services, such as DHL (☎ 12-02-10), are available in the capital, and cost between Nfa306 and Nfa366 per kilogram worldwide.

There is a free poste restante service in the capital; you'll need to show your passport to collect mail. Address mail to Poste Restante, Post Office, Asmara, Eritrea.

Telephone & Fax

When calling Eritrea from abroad, the country code is ☎ 291. The major towns (Asmara, Massawa, Dekemhare and Mendefera) must be prefixed by the number 1, followed by the six-figure number.

When calling abroad from Eritrea, call ☎ 00 followed by the country code. Direct dialling is only possible between main towns in Eritrea (Asmara, Dekemhare and Mendefera) and Europe and the USA. For all other countries, you'll need to go through the operator.

International calls are best made from the telecommunications office found in all the main towns. Outside the capital, international calls are made via Asmara. Faxes can be sent and received from some of the telecommunications offices. You can also send faxes from the post office in Asmara; rates are similar to the telecommunications office.

To make a call, you need to pay a deposit of Nfa200 then wait to be assigned a cabin. The cost is calculated by computer. Unfortunately, only one call at a time can be made, then you have to queue up again.

Early evening tends to be the busiest time, whereas early morning or late evening are the quietest. International rates are the same all day, and costs are calculated per minute: Nfa19.10 for the USA; Nfa25.15 for Europe and Canada; and Nfa27.90 for Australia and New Zealand.

National calls cost between Nfa1.50 and Nfa3, and you must leave a deposit of Nfa10. Telephone cards are available in denominations of Nfa25, Nfa50 and Nfa100.

It is possible to make calls and send or receive faxes from the larger hotels, but rates are expensive (up to 20% more than at the telecommunications offices).

For directory assistance call ☎ 97. For the international operator call ☎ 98.

For general information on Lonely Planet's eKno communication card, see Telephone & Fax in the Facts for the Visitor section in the Ethiopia chapter.

Email & Internet Access

Email is still in its infancy in Eritrea. Tfanus Enterprise (☎ 12-40-50, fax 12-64-57, ✆ tfanus@gemel.com.er) in Asmara offers access to the Internet, charging Nfa5 per incoming or outgoing message. For general information on accessing your email, see Email & Internet Access in the Facts for the Visitor section in the Ethiopia chapter.

INTERNET RESOURCES

There are a few Web sites with useful information on Eritrea, including the following:

Eritrea Network Information Centre (ENIC) is the best site on Eritrea, containing information on varied aspects of the country from quite detailed maps to economic information, book recommendations and practical information for organising your journey. It also has a currency converter.
http://eritrea.org/
Eritrea Online (Dehai) is another good site, with daily updated news on Eritrea gathered from various sources. This neatly organised site also has information on food, music and culture.
www.primenet.com/~ephrem/
NetAfrica is a governmental site with the usual information for tourists.
www.netafrica.org/eritrea/

ERITREA

BOOKS

Few books on Eritrea are available, at least in European languages. Italian is the one exception: colonial histories, travel accounts and novels of the late 19th and early 20th centuries abound. Some older books written about Abyssinia include the area covered by Eritrea (see Books in the Facts for the Visitor section in the Ethiopia chapter).

Guidebooks

Eritrea at a Glance, edited by Mary Houdek and Leonardo Oriolo, is an excellent, locally produced book. Despite its title, it's really a guide to Asmara rather than Eritrea, making it a good choice if you're going to be spending any length of time in the capital.

If you read Italian, *Eritrea* by Andrea Semplici is a very comprehensive, if rather idiosyncratic, guide to Eritrea. Though practical details and maps are a bit lacking, the depth of research and sheer enthusiasm for the country more than compensate. The best German guide is *Eritrea Ein Reiseführer*. In French, *Erythrée* by C Kutschera seems to be currently unavailable.

History & Politics

The Struggle has inspired a rash of gripping stories, many of them eyewitness accounts. Three of the best-known are *Against All Odds* by Dan Connell, *Even the Stones Are Burning* by Roy Pateman, and *Revolution at Dusk* by Robert Papstein. Sadly, no account in English by an Eritrean fighter or historian has so far emerged.

Women and the Eritrean Revolution by A Wilon recounts the important role of women throughout the Struggle. All four books can be found in Asmara.

NEWSPAPERS & MAGAZINES

The best-known of the local publications is the widely read *Haddas Eritrea* (*New Eritrea*), a newspaper published weekly in both Tigrinya and Arabic.

The *Eritrea Profile* is also published every week by the Ministry of Information. It's popular with the expat community in Asmara, and is available every Saturday from the tiny newsstand opposite the municipality (town hall), as well as from roaming street vendors. It's a good source of local information, including weather forecasts, pharmacies that do 'night duty' etc.

The *Eritrean Studies Review*, published by the Red Sea Press, is an excellent biannual book containing eclectic essays about the country. You can find it in bookshops in Asmara, but it's expensive (US$15 or the current nakfa equivalent).

RADIO & TV

Eritrean national radio, known as 'Voice of the Broad Masses', broadcasts three times a day in at least four of Eritrea's national languages. The BBC World Service can be picked up on short-wave radios (for frequencies, see Radio & TV in the Djibouti chapter).

Eritrean television broadcasts every evening except Sunday from around 7 pm. You can tune in to the hour-long BBC news bulletins at 9 pm. Various programs follow (sometimes in English), including sport, documentaries and feature films.

VIDEO & PHOTOGRAPHY

Eritrea, like Italy, uses the PAL system. It differs from France (which uses the SECAM system), and the USA, Canada and Japan (which use NTSC). The three systems are not compatible.

Decent print film is quite widely available in the capital and costs around Nfa27 for a 36-exposure Kodak film. Some slide film is also available, but only in the capital. Outside Asmara, it's difficult to find film except in the larger towns, and it may not always be within its use-by date.

Photographic equipment is very limited in Asmara, but photo development is of a good quality, fast (it can be done in around 20 minutes) and good value (Nfa8).

For technical tips on photographing in the Horn of Africa, see the boxed text 'Tips for Photographers in the Horn' in the Facts for the Visitor section in the Ethiopia chapter.

Restrictions

After 30 years of war, certain subjects in Eritrea are considered 'sensitive'. Avoid military and police installations and personnel, and even airports and bridges. Civil engineering and government buildings are off-limits too, as is the so-called tank graveyard in Asmara.

Outside the capital, it's fine to take pictures of war relics. You'll use up a whole film on your first burnt-out tank, but by the end of the journey, they won't even turn your head.

Photographing People

In some areas, people such as the colourful Rashaida and enigmatic Afars are more accustomed to photographers, and understandably want to benefit by it too. They may ask for money. The fee should always be agreed in advance. In some places, you may be charged a fee for video cameras, though this seems to be entirely randomly applied.

See also Photographing People in the Facts for the Visitor section in the Ethiopia chapter.

TIME

Eritrea is three hours ahead of GMT/UTC. When it's noon in Eritrea, it's 1 am in Los Angeles, 4 am in New York, 9 am in London, and 11 pm in Sydney. Eritrea uses the 24-hour clock.

ELECTRICITY

Confusingly, Eritrea uses both 110V and 220V at both 50Hz and 60Hz AC. If you're planning to take a laptop with you, make sure you have something to protect it against the variations in current, as power surges occur frequently. Alternatively, a UPS (Uninterrupted Power Supply) will protect it and can be bought locally.

A variety of electrical sockets are found around the country. Many are like the Italian type and take plugs with two round prongs rated at 600W. It's a good idea to bring an adapter; visitors from the US and Canada (with120V at 60Hz) should be careful to choose one appropriate for their equipment. Newer appliances in the US and Canada are made to run at both 50Hz and 60 Hz.

LAUNDRY

Laundries are found mainly in Asmara, and offer efficient and reasonably cheap ser-

vices (see under Information in the Asmara section).

Almost all hotels offer laundry services, for similar prices, and are probably more convenient. Prices in hotels tend to correspond to their room rates: budget hotels charge little, smart hotels a great deal.

TOILETS

Both the sit-down and squat types of toilet are found in Eritrea, reflecting Italian and Arab influences, respectively.

In the highlands, the sit-down type tends to prevail. In the Muslim lowlands such as in Massawa, the squat style is more commonly found (but only in the cheaper hotels). Toilet paper is very rare in either, so carry your own.

In the small villages of the torrid lowlands, you'll be lucky to find a bush. The inhabitants simply demarcate an area outside the village, point you in that direction, and off you trot.

If you're caught short in the towns, the hotels are the best places to head, and unlike in Europe, wouldn't dream of turning you away in your moment of need. Some of the Italian-designed cafes also have toilets.

HEALTH

Malaria is endemic on the coastal plain, in the western lowlands and around Keren (anywhere less than 2000m above sea level), particularly during the dry season. Get advice on malaria prevention before you go, but if you need to stock up on anti-malarials, the drugs are widely available in Asmara (with the exception of mefloquine or Lariam). Dengue fever is also prevalent, so wherever you go it's important to take steps to prevent mosquito bites. Other common conditions are travellers diarrhoea, giardia, dehydration and worm infestations. For more information on these and other health issues, see Health in the Facts for the Visitor section in the Ethiopia chapter.

Don't forget that the closer you get to the equator, the more vicious the sun becomes. If you're spending time outdoors, use a hat, sunglasses and high-protection sunscreen. The risk of skin infection is high in the heat,

ERITREA

Altitude in Asmara

If you arrive in Asmara directly from the lowlands, the sudden change to 2400m may induce a mild form of altitude sickness. Symptoms include headaches, light-headedness, insomnia and shortness of breath, but should soon wear off – take it easy, get plenty of rest and make sure you drink enough water to avoid dehydration. For more details, see Altitude Sickness under Health in the Ethiopia Facts for the Visitor section.

particularly in coastal areas such as Massawa, where humidity is also high.

If you're a diver or snorkeller, see Hazardous Marine Life in the special section 'Marine Life in the Red Sea'. Divers should note that there is currently no decompression chamber in Eritrea.

Asmara is reasonably well endowed with medical facilities, though it's always best to bring your own supplies of any prescription drugs you are on, as these may not be available locally. Blood, urine and stool tests are readily available.

The two best hospitals in the country are the large Mekane Hiwet Hospital (with a new intensive care unit), and the Italian hospital (Hospidem – Ospedale Italiano Ente Morale), both in Asmara. Outside the capital, a network of small village clinics can refer patients to the larger district hospital if necessary. Doctors often expect immediate cash payment for services.

WOMEN TRAVELLERS

With a very low national crime rate and an unusually liberal policy towards women, Eritrea must be one of the safest and least restrictive countries on the continent for women travellers.

Women NGO workers report few hassles in Eritrea, and in Asmara can be seen happily strolling the streets after dark. Use your common sense, though – all the usual precautions apply, such as safety in numbers.

Smoking or drinking and wearing lots of make-up are sometimes construed by the nation's less enlightened males as signs of

availability (as this is also the way the local prostitutes behave). As a result of Hollywood cinematic glamour, foreign women are sometimes considered easier 'prey' than local women. An invitation to the cinema, for example, isn't necessarily to watch a film.

There are a number of women's organisations in Eritrea. In Asmara, the National Union of Eritrean Women or NUEW (☎ 11-51-72, fax 12-06-28) welcomes visitors at its headquarters. It has a small library with a collection of books on women. Travellers can also call to arrange meetings with Eritrean women – ask for Ghenet.

GAY & LESBIAN TRAVELLERS

Homosexuality is severely condemned by both traditional and religious cultures, and remains a topic of absolute taboo. Eritrea's penal code concerning homosexuality is currently still based on Ethiopian law (see Gay & Lesbian Travellers in the Ethiopia chapter). Although gay locals obviously exist, they behave with extreme discretion and caution. Gay travellers are advised to do likewise.

SENIOR TRAVELLERS

Traditionally, older citizens are accorded great respect in Eritrea, and senior travellers will be made to be feel very welcome. Eritrea's capital is well equipped with top-

The New Woman

The new Eritrean woman is one of the most liberated in Africa. Not only has she won the right to vote, but women have a guarantee of 30% of seats in parliament. She enjoys her own national holiday, equal property rights, and the right to divorce and to the custody of her children in any settlement. She even has her own minister, ex-fighter Fawzia Hashim, Minister of Justice.

Eritrea's new woman has attitude. In Asmara, ex-fighters can be spotted sauntering down the street in old jeans and T-shirts, and in the little villages, women bark at men to form orderly lines outside their bakeries.

end hotels, restaurants and medical care, and should cater to most needs. Outside the capital, facilities are much more limited. Although most tourist sites can be visited in one- to three-day trips from the capital, roads are very rough in parts, and journeys are long, hot and hard, particularly on the back, even in the best 4WD.

DISABLED TRAVELLERS
Taxis are widely available in towns and are good for getting around, though none have wheelchair access. Car rental with a driver is easy to organise, if expensive. In Asmara, at least one hotel has facilities for travellers with wheelchairs. A few hotels have lifts.

Eritrea's Struggle for Independence left many of its inhabitants disabled. Land mines continue to maim the population. Disabled visitors can expect to find a sympathetic and accommodating attitude from Eritreans.

TRAVEL WITH CHILDREN
Eritreans are very welcoming and open towards children. However, many useful facilities for children – such as cots in hotels, safety seats in hired cars, and highchairs in restaurants – are almost totally lacking.

Items such as nappies, baby food and mineral water are available in the expat supermarkets of Asmara, but they are quite expensive. Should you need them, medical facilities in the capital are good. See also Travel with Children in the Facts for the Visitor section in the Ethiopia chapter.

DANGERS & ANNOYANCES
Crime
After independence, Eritrea's capital Asmara became known as the most peaceful capital on the continent. Muggings were unheard of, pickpocketings rare, and everyone let everyone else get on with their business.

Asmara is still an extremely peaceful place and the crime rate is incredibly low, but minor incidents of street crime are now occasionally reported. With the economy squeezed ever tighter by the ongoing war with Ethiopia, such incidents will inevitably increase. In early 2000, begging had certainly increased, particularly in Asmara.

Markets all over the world attract pickpockets, and no less so in Asmara, so it's sensible to take some basic precautions. Outside the capital, the crime rate is even lower.

In the far western and northern areas bordering Sudan, a few incidents of both bandit and terrorist attacks against Eritrean civilians were reported in the late 1990s. The Eritrean Islamic Jihad (EIJ) was blamed for some attacks. However, there is no evidence to suggest that foreign travellers are being targeted specifically. Foreign embassies are a good source of up-to-date information on security issues in the country.

Land Mines
After 30 years of war, the biggest threat outside the capital is the risk of land mines and unexploded munitions. Despite the government's best efforts, thousands still litter the countryside, and continue sporadically to kill and maim the population.

Most risks are confined to the sites of major battle fronts but there is obviously some element of risk anywhere fighting has occurred. Areas north and west of Keren and around Ghinda are thought to be heavily mined still.

Check with local government and local village officials before travelling in less-frequented areas. Never stray off the road. If you're walking, keep to well-trodden tracks and avoid hiking in river beds. Forget about 'war souvenirs' – you shouldn't touch anything. A useful phrase when out walking is *Fenjy allo?* (Are there mines here?).

LEGAL MATTERS
Foreign visitors are subject to the laws of the country in which they are travelling. Penalties for possession, use or trafficking of illegal drugs are strictly enforced in Eritrea. Convicted offenders can expect long jail sentences, fines and possible confiscation of personal property.

Note that consumption of the mildly intoxicating leaf *qat* is not permitted in Eritrea.

BUSINESS HOURS
In the 1997 constitution, in a bid to stoke up the recovery of the economy, the government decreed that working hours for the public sector should be 7 am to noon and 2 to 6 pm Monday to Friday.

Private businesses and shops keep various hours. In general, most open from 8 am to noon and 2 to 6 pm Monday to Friday, and on Saturday in the morning only. Many shops in the capital stay open until 7.30 pm.

For banking hours, see Exchanging Money earlier in this section.

In Massawa and Assab, government offices open from 6 am to 2.30 pm Monday to Friday during the hot season (June to September) and from 8 am to noon and 4 to 6.30 pm Monday to Friday the rest of the year. Private businesses open from 6 am to noon and 3 to 6 pm Monday to Friday the whole year.

In Muslim areas, business hours are shorter during Ramadan, and cafes and restaurants may be closed during the day.

Note that many restaurants close early (around 8 pm), particularly in rural areas, so don't leave dinner too late. In Asmara, most of the larger restaurants close around 10 pm.

PUBLIC HOLIDAYS & SPECIAL EVENTS
Eritrea's public holidays can be divided into three categories: national (secular) holidays, Christian Orthodox holidays and Islamic holidays.

The country follows the Gregorian (European) calendar, with 12 months to the year. However, the Eritrean Orthodox church, which is derived from the Ethiopian Orthodox church, follows the Julian calendar, which has 13 months (see Calendar in the Facts for the Visitor section in the Ethiopia chapter).

Some events therefore trail those of the Gregorian calendar by around one week. Muslim holidays are based on the Hejira calendar, which is 11 days shorter than the Gregorian calendar, so these holidays fall about 11 days earlier each year. The precise dates are determined by the sighting of the moon, so are known only a few days in advance.

National holidays include the following:

New Year's Day 1 January
International Women's Day 8 March
Workers' Day 1 May
Liberation Day 24 May
Martyrs' Day 20 June
Start of the Armed Struggle 1 September

The main Orthodox holidays are:

Leddet (Christmas) 7 January
Timkat (Epiphany) 19 January
Tensae (Easter) March/April (variable)
Kiddus Yohannes (Orthodox New Year) 11 September
Meskel (Finding of the True Cross) 27 September

Islamic holidays include Lailat al-Miraji, Eid al-Fitr, Eid al-Adha Arafa (the Muslim New Year), Al-Ashura, and Eid Mawlid al-Nabi (the Prophet's birthday). See Public Holidays & Special Events in the Djibouti chapter for a table of dates of Islamic holidays. For more information on the religious holidays listed in this section, see Public Holidays & Special Events in the Ethiopia chapter.

ACTIVITIES
Hiking & Camel Trekking
Eritrea has good potential for hiking in the various hills and mountain ranges in the east of the country. Another good place is the tropical forest around Filfil. However,

because of the recent war, travellers should check out carefully the safety of the areas they wish to visit with the local authorities first (for risk of land mines etc), and consider hiring a local guide.

A few travel agents in the capital now offer treks into the hinterland by camel (for details, see Organised Tours in the Getting Around section later in this chapter).

Water Activities

Eritrea's best-known and most developed tourism activity is diving in the Red Sea. The Dahlak Islands off the coast near Massawa and, to a very limited degree, Assab are currently the only places where organised diving and snorkelling takes place.

Diving is principally organised through various charter boats that tour the Dahlak Islands. Tours generally last a week, but occasionally two- or three-day trips are possible. If you're interested you should book well in advance through a travel agency in Asmara (see Organised Tours in the Getting Around section of this chapter for contact details). You can also organise your own day trips by motorboat. Diving equipment can be hired in Massawa.

Though the islands are opening up, access is still a little limited, monopolised by a few boat companies charging high prices. This may well serve to protect the reefs from too many tourists in the future. But at the moment, most destinations are out of the reach of budget travellers. However, if you can stretch to a trip – even just snorkelling – the opportunity is not to be missed. If you're prepared for the conditions and the demands, you're likely to be rewarded with some of the best diving of your life. Get there before the crowds do.

Water-skiing is possible in Massawa.

For more information on water activities, see the Dahlak Islands section, and also the special section 'Marine Life in the Red Sea'.

Fishing

Boats can be hired in Massawa for fishing trips in the Red Sea. Rods and gaffs can be borrowed free from the boat operators, but you'll need to bring your own hooks and lures. Metal spoons are good to lure king mackerel, tuna, kingfish, red snapper and barracuda. A trawling rod and weights (50g to 100g) are useful.

Fish are sometimes very large – some gropers can weigh 20kg or more, barracuda 30–35kg – so any equipment you bring should be durable. Strong hooks and trawling line are a must (at least 50lb). Steel line is essential for barracuda (which snap right through ordinary line).

The first three hours after sunset are particularly good for fishing (with a simple weighted line and hook) for large red snapper, groper and shark. These species tend to lurk on the sea bed; barracuda, jacks and kingfish are found at lesser depths. Trawl fishing is best from around 8 to 11 am and 4 to 6 pm.

ACCOMMODATION

Tourism is still in its infancy in Eritrea, and accommodation is limited. During the war, many of the old Italian hotels were destroyed. Those that remain are badly in need of decoration and, possibly, serious restoration.

The Eritreans are a very polite, soft-spoken people; what's missing in amenities is made up for in their hospitality and friendliness. Theft from hotels is very rare in Eritrea.

Asmara has hotels of all categories, though some of the popular medium-priced hotels are often booked up, and reservations are strongly advised. Currently, the government is trying to sell the dozen or so state-owned hotels in the capital.

Many of the country's cheaper hotels have cold water only (not a worry in the lowlands). Inevitably some double as brothels. Conversely, a few of the Muslim-run hotels allow only married or single-sex couples to share rooms. Though breakfast is provided by some hotels, you will usually be charged extra for it.

All the small towns have hotels, though they're often pretty basic affairs. Many rooms contain up to six beds (though you can pay for the whole room) and many lack running water (you get a bucket shower instead).

In the torrid lowlands, including Massawa, many people sleep on beds in the courtyards and on the verandas or rooftops. The cheap hotels, which don't have air-conditioning or ceiling fans, usually have similar arrangements.

In the rural areas, accommodation is sometimes little more than a bed in a hut, without running water, electricity or even washing facilities.

There are no official camping grounds. In theory, if you have your own tent, you are free to camp anywhere, apart from near the obvious off-limits sites, such as military installations. Be very careful to check that the area you are in is free of land mines (see Dangers & Annoyances earlier in this section). Take care not to start fires, and take all your litter away with you.

In Eritrea, a room with a double bed is usually called a 'single', and a room with twin beds a 'double'. However, in this book, the usual single/double definitions apply. Prices for one and two people are often the same.

FOOD

Eritrea is not exactly the gastronomic capital of Africa. The local food tends to provoke strong reactions – you either love it or loathe it. Or more commonly, you loathe it but grow to love it.

More important than the style or quality of the food is the ceremony. You won't forget your first meal, shared from a large plate with fellow diners. It's a great way of establishing and cementing local friendships. If you don't take to it, you could always try the ubiquitous, if rather bland and overcooked, pasta dishes.

Most types of food are very reasonably priced, the only exception being imported food in some of the capital's supermarkets. A dinner for two comes to around Nfa10. People eat early here (usually between 6.30 and 8 pm).

Italian

Along with their roads, towns and bridges, the Italians left another legacy: *macchiato* and spaghetti. Italian dishes are available in all restaurants throughout Eritrea. Outside the capital, these may be limited to just one dish, lasagne or spaghetti bolognese, which is based on a seemingly nationally agreed, fixed formula. However, it fills the gap.

In the capital, the choice is much better with both *primi piatti* (first courses), usually pasta, and *secondi piatti* (main dishes), usually fish or meat, on offer.

Traditional

Traditional Eritrean cuisine is the same as in Ethiopia – see Food in the Facts for the Visitor section of the Ethiopia chapter for a complete rundown of typical local dishes, ingredients and food etiquette, and for a glossary of food terms. Most of the terms used are the same as in Ethiopia, except for *wat*, the fiery and ubiquitous sauce, which is known as *tsebhi* in Tigrinya; *injera*, which is sometimes called *taitas* in Tigrinya; *tibs*, sometimes known as *tibsi*; and *kai wat*, known as *zigni* in Tigrinya.

If you like hot food, try the delicious *silsi*, a peppery fried tomato and onion sauce served for breakfast. Another very popular breakfast dish is *ful* (based on chickpea puree), with the ubiquitous *frittata*, omelette or scrambled egg pepped up with a bit of pepper.

Capretto often features on menus. It's roast goat, sometimes served like a rack of lamb.

Puddings aren't a traditional part of the diet and usually consist of fruit salad or synthetic creme caramel. Eritrean yoghurt (served in a glass) and the mild local cheeses are a much better bet. The latter are sometimes served with bread and exquisite local honey, which makes a terrific and easily prepared picnic.

In the western lowlands, look out for little boys selling *legamat*, a deep-fried dough sold hot in newspaper cones in the early morning; it's delicious for an early breakfast.

In the far west, the food is heavily influenced by the proximity of Sudan. One popular and very tasty dish is *sheia*, lamb drizzled with oil and herbs then barbecued on very hot stones until it sizzles. It's delicious. It's usually served with a lentil dish *ades*, and a stock-like soup known as *merek*.

In Massawa, the Arabic influence is evident. Kebabs and Yemeni-style charcoal-

A Fish for Life

'Eat fish and be happy' and 'A fish for life' are some of the slogans daubed about the coastal towns of Eritrea. Trying to improve the diet of its people, the government, pragmatic as ever, is also giving Eritrea's ancient but tiny fishing industry a much-needed boost.

Keeping the best – the shellfish, snapper and groper – for valuable exports, the people are informed of the delights of catfish, shark and barracuda.

Many Eritreans, unfamiliar with fish, view it with suspicion and disgust; others are afraid of choking to death on the bones.

Cookery lessons, recipes (including one for sweet, fishy biscuits for children) and, most popularly, cans of fish without bones, nasty fishy smells or complicated preparation have been distributed in the villages. But it's all still proving a bit too fishy for some.

baked fish are both widely available. A useful Tigrinya word that will please your host is *te-oom* (delicious).

Fast Food
In Asmara various fast-food restaurants have opened, serving quite decent fare, usually at a slightly higher price than local dishes.

The *latterias* (a kind of food shop) and cafes are great places for breakfast, serving egg dishes as you want them, or local breakfast dishes, good coffee and tea, and sometimes fruit juices and yoghurt.

Vegetarian
If you're after vegetarian food, ask for *nai tsom*, a selection of vegetable dishes traditionally served during times of fasting.

Self-Catering
The capital is well equipped with supermarkets, some stocked with a good selection of European imports. Outside the town, the local shops have a very limited selection of food products for sale, consisting of little more than dry biscuits from Yemen, milk powder and tins of tomato puree.

DRINKS
Nonalcoholic Drinks
In Asmara and, to a lesser degree, the larger towns, innumerable little cafes and bars dot the centre. In true Italian style, macchiato, espresso and cappuccino are all served, along with a selection of pastries and cakes.

The Eritreans seem to get a fix from large amounts of sugar, which is copiously applied to all hot drinks and even fresh fruit juices. If you don't want sugar, you'll have to make that clear when you order. Ask for *beze sukkar*.

Outside the capital and in the country, sweet black tea is the most common drink. Following Islamic traditions, it is often offered as a gesture of welcome to guests. In the lowlands, cloves are often added. In the west, near the Sudanese border, coffee is sometimes spiced with ginger. If you don't want it, ask for *beze gingebel*.

The water in Asmara is considered safe to drink but, as in many places, new arrivals may experience problems with it. Various makes of bottled water (known in Tigrinya as *mai gas*) can be bought in all the towns and some villages.

Local makes include Dongollo and Sabarguma (with a lighter fizz). Fresh fruit juices (most commonly mango, papaya, pineapple and banana) are sold in Asmara and some of the larger towns.

Various fizzy soft drinks are widely available, even in Dankalia, where without refrigeration they are served at room temperature, which in some places is as warm as tepid tea.

Glass bottles are recycled; save them and you can exchange them for full ones.

Alcoholic Drinks
In the capital and towns, all the usual favourites are available, including whisky, gin, vodka and beer. As many are imported, they tend to be expensive.

Local varieties include Asmara gin (also known as *ouzo*), which is a bit rough around the edges (especially the morning after drinking it), but it is soon knocked back. A shot of gin (Nfa1.50) is cheaper than either Coke or mineral water (Nfa2.50 to Nfa3).

ERITREA

ERITREA

The local beer, Melotti, is popular among both Eritreans and aid workers. It's manufactured in Asmara, and has a mild, quite smooth flavour and is very drinkable. It's also cheap at Nfa3. According to seasoned aid workers it can cause (in large quantities no doubt) a mild reaction among the uninitiated, known as 'Melotti botti'...

The red Asmara wine, though no huge cause for celebration, isn't at all bad, particularly with a good, hearty spaghetti bolognese. Local wines are very reasonably priced in restaurants, usually between Nfa6 and Nfa25 per bottle. Imported wine starts at about Nfa50.

If you're not catching an early bus out of town the next morning, try the local *araki*, a distilled aniseed drink, a little like the Greek ouzo. *Mies* is a delicious local wine made from honey, and comes in varying degrees of sweetness (the dryer it is, the more alcoholic). Don't miss it. If you're in Afar territory in Dankalia, try the delicious – but very powerful – doum palm wine.

ENTERTAINMENT

Most of the country's facilities for leisure and entertainment are in Asmara. Here, you'll find decent cinemas (showing films in English and sometimes Italian), nightclubs and bars. There's also a theatre (though plays are usually in Tigrinya).

Music in the bars is for the most part local (Tigrinya and Amharic pop), which, like the food, takes a bit of getting used to. But Western music and some reggae are also played. Most bars close around 10 or 11 pm during the week, but stay open until at least 2 am on Friday and Saturday.

Locals love to dance, and the traditional dancing is quite unique in style, with lots of variations on shaking body parts, but if you can give it a go, you'll win a lot of friends. Men should be aware that most of the women in the smaller bars and nightclubs are prostitutes.

A few of the larger hotels in the capital occasionally stage shows with local musicians and dancers.

Outside the capital, entertainment is limited to a few bars and cafes. Many of these have *biliardo* (Italian billiards) tables, which are rented by the half-hour or hour.

In many of the larger towns, bicycle races are organised. Streets are cordoned off, and everyone comes to watch.

SHOPPING

Though Eritrea's tourism industry is not yet greatly developed, there are a surprising number of shops catering to tourists in the capital. Most curios are imported from other countries (such as the wooden carvings and sculptures from Kenya).

Shops sell intricate silver and gold jewellery (priced by weight), fabrics, ceramics and basketware. Quality (and some might say taste) is very variable, so it's worth taking a good look around before you buy.

More unusual and interesting souvenirs include the little pewter crosses, which are often crudely fashioned. Although they are neither very old nor silver as some shopkeepers like to make out, they are attractive, and don't constitute a national treasure.

The local *gabi*, the white, light cotton togas worn by the local men, are also available, and make great, though bulky, travelling companions. They can be turned into blankets, pillows, mattresses, cushions (on long bus journeys) and wraps.

In some shops along Liberty Ave, ivory carvings and, less frequently, turtle shells are widely available. Apart from the environmental argument against buying these, it is also illegal to import them into most western countries.

Outside the capital, simple pottery, basketware and combs can be found in local markets.

Getting There & Away

Eritrea's ongoing conflict with Ethiopia has taken a heavy toll on its international land, sea and air links. Ethiopian Airlines used to provide a crucial link between Eritrea and the rest of the world. The ports have lost much traffic, and the roads connecting Eritrea and

Ethiopia are now closed. Until the conflict is resolved, the options for getting to and from Eritrea will remain somewhat limited.

For general information on travel and prices, and a glossary of travel terms, see Getting There & Away in the Ethiopia chapter.

AIR

Travel during the month of August, and over Easter, Christmas and New Year should be booked well in advance. Eritreans living abroad tend to visit their families during this time and some flights are more expensive.

Airports & Airlines

Eritrea's one international airport, 6km from the capital, was once reasonably well served by international carriers. However, the ongoing border conflict with Ethiopia has put an abrupt halt to that.

You should get to the airport well in advance of your departure (two hours is advised) to allow for security checks and other processing.

Departure Tax

International departure tax is US$15. All foreign nationals except those with residence permits are charged in US dollars. A 'security check tax' of Nfa3 is also levied.

The USA

So long as the conflict with Ethiopia continues, Ethiopian Airlines will not serve Asmara.

The alternatives are United Airlines or Lufthansa (via Frankfurt). Both fly three times a week from Washington to Asmara, and a return trip costs US$1600.

From the west coast, the same airlines fly from San Francisco three times a week for US$1700.

Europe

Ethiopian Airlines used to route some of its European flights to and from Addis Ababa via Asmara. Flights should resume again once the border issue is resolved. It connected Asmara directly with London, Rome and Frankfurt. Flights from other destinations came via Addis Ababa.

Other international airlines connecting Asmara to Europe include Lufthansa, which currently flies four times a week from Frankfurt for around US$1203. About the cheapest deal is offered by EgyptAir, which flies to London once a week via Cairo for around US$680.

The Middle East

Saudi Arabian Airlines has two flights a week between Asmara and Jeddah (US$210/420 one way/return) and two a week between Asmara and Riad (US$300/600). A special 'excursion' return fare valid for two months costs US$268/431 for Jeddah/Riad.

Red Sea Air (the Eritrean airline) also flies to Jeddah and occasionally to Dubai (through Daallo Airlines), though its prices and schedules are erratic.

Yemenia Yemen Airlines flies once a week between Asmara and San'a.

Africa

EgyptAir has two flights a week between Asmara and Cairo (via Addis Ababa) for US$418/548 one way/return.

Before the war, Ethiopian Airlines had daily flights from Addis Ababa to Asmara, and twice a week from Addis Ababa to Assab in southern Eritrea. These should resume eventually.

Flights to/from Djibouti have been suspended until relations between the two countries improve.

LAND
Border Crossings

Travellers should note that there is no formal border crossing established on the border between Eritrea and Djibouti in the south (see the Getting There & Away section of the Djibouti chapter).

Two posts on the border between Eritrea and Ethiopia serve as formal border crossings: Senafe and Adi Quala.

Djibouti

Despite many maps that cheerfully and misleadingly suggest otherwise, only tracks and dirt roads lead south of the town of Assab to Djibouti.

ERITREA

Almost no traffic runs south, apart from the occasional Afar and his camel. The civil unrest in the north of Djibouti has put an end to the old bus service that struggled the 1100km between Assab and Djibouti. (For possible alternatives, see Getting There & Away in the Assab section of this chapter.)

If you're thinking of taking your own vehicle south, see Eritrea in the Getting There & Away section of the Djibouti chapter.

Ethiopia

Since the outbreak of the conflict with Ethiopia, all roads connecting the two countries have been closed. The following information on routes and buses is included in case diplomatic relations are re-established and the roads are reopened in the near future.

Of the three tarmac roads connecting Eritrea to Ethiopia, the first goes from Asmara via Mendefera and Adi Quala to Aksum in Ethiopia – this is the choice if you want to travel Ethiopia's historical route (see the North of Addis Ababa section of the Ethiopia chapter).

The second route goes from Asmara via Dekemhare and Adi Keyh in Eritrea to Adigrat in Ethiopia, and though the journey is more comfortable, it is less interesting.

The third route, built originally by the Italians, connects Assab in the south with Addis Ababa in Ethiopia.

All border crossings closed on both sides at sunset (around 6.30 pm). On the Ethiopian side, you may be questioned about your itinerary and will have to fill in a currency declaration form.

Buses ran four times a week from Asmara to Addis Ababa (Nfa89, three days). For Aksum, you had to go to the nearby town of Shire first (also known as Inta Selassie) 60km from Aksum. Buses left every day at 5 am except Sunday (Nfa15, eight hours). Buses to Mekele from Asmara left four times a week (Nfa25, nine hours), stopping at Adwa (Nfa13, six hours) and Adigrat (Nfa15, seven hours).

Sudan

The current security situation in Sudan means the border is closed to foreigners.

However, at the time of research, relations between the two countries had improved and the border seemed likely to reopen. Check the current situation when you get there.

Formerly, it was possible to take a bus from Asmara to Kassala in Sudan (Nfa80, two or three weekly). The journey used to take three days, but with the extension of the sealed road from Asmara to Teseney on the Eritrean side of the border, the journey time should be reduced to two days.

SEA

Eritrea has two ports, Massawa and Assab. Although there are no scheduled passenger services, many cargo ships from other Red Sea countries use the ports, particularly the one at Massawa. It is often possible to hitch lifts.

Europe

In theory, it should be possible to hitch a lift on a vessel in Massawa or Assab, even as far as Marseilles. However, the practice is more difficult. Many commercial ships now seem to discourage passenger travel. The best thing is to ask around the port and town, particularly if a ship and its crew have just arrived in town.

The Middle East

The Saudi Baabour Line has a car and passenger service that sails once a week (usually Thursday) between Massawa and Jeddah, sometimes calling in at Suakin in Sudan. The journey takes 32 hours and tickets cost Nfa600 one way. Only third-class travel (on a bench), is possible so you're advised to bring a blanket. For information, reservations and tickets, you can call or visit the Eritrean Shipping & Transit Agency Service (☎ 12-30-90, fax 12-44-22) in Asmara. Saik Trading (☎/fax 11-91-68), above the Eritrean Tour Service in Asmara, also sells tickets and provides information; as does its office in Massawa (☎/fax 55-26-42).

Africa

To get to Suez (Egypt), you can take a passenger ferry first to Jeddah (see the Middle East section earlier) and change there.

Before you can be issued with tickets to Jeddah, you must have obtained a 72-hour transit visa for Jeddah, have bought an onward ticket to Suez, and have paid a deposit of US$150 towards 'living expenses' in Jeddah, in case you are required to stay there waiting for a connection. If the deposit is not used, it is reimbursed.

Travellers with vehicles (including motorcycles) must have paid the cost of freight for the vehicle, as well as a deposit for the onward journey.

Other options include the traditional dhows at both Massawa and Assab. They used to sail from Assab to Djibouti, but services rather depend on the recently rather volatile diplomatic relations between the two countries. You should check out the current situation, and if you do find a dhow willing to take you, be prepared to bargain hard.

Getting Around

As long as the conflict with Ethiopia continues, travel around the country may be slightly restricted, particularly at border towns. At the time of research, a permit was required for travel to Barentu in the west. However, check the situation when you get there.

The Italians were responsible for the construction of a small, but beautifully built, network of roads connecting Asmara to the north, east, south and west. During the war with Ethiopia, most of these roads were destroyed. After independence, the reconstruction of the network became one of the government's prime objectives. Much progress has been made, including the constructions of good roads connecting Asmara with Keren, Massawa and Ethiopia's Adigrat. Along many of the roads, you'll see platoons of young men in blue uniforms constructing roads as part of their military service.

Recent projects include the extension of the sealed road to Teseney, and the construction of sealed roads between Dekemhare and Barentu, and Keren and Barentu. It is hoped that, eventually, sealed roads will link Keren with Nakfa in the north, and Massawa with Assab in the south.

Some roads are in a very bad state of repair, or else little more than tracks, such as much of the way between Massawa and Assab. The road north of Keren to Nakfa and Sudan is also hard going.

Garis (horse-drawn carts) are used for short hops around the towns (see this section in the Ethiopia chapter).

AIR

Eritrean Airlines, based in the capital, flies to just one domestic destination: Assab. Flights leave from Asmara three times a week on Tuesday, Saturday and Sunday (Nfa274/548 one way/return).

There are plans to extend services from Asmara to Massawa, Teseney and eventually the Dahlak Archipelago. When relations with Ethiopia normalise, the twice-weekly flights from Assab to Addis Ababa should resume.

BUS

The bus service in Eritrea is reasonably efficient, comfortable and extensive. There are usually at least two buses a day between the larger towns (Asmara, Massawa and Keren), and at least one bus a day between the smaller ones. Fares are cheap, and services run between 6 am and 4.30 pm or 6 pm. For long-distance journeys (those taking three hours or longer), two buses often leave within an hour of each other, between 5.30 am and 6.30 am.

The major drawback of bus travel is that it's time-consuming. Progress on the road is often slow. Additionally, buses don't adhere to fixed timetables: they depart when they are full. For long-distance journeys, you need to be at the bus station by 6 am to buy a ticket and be guaranteed a seat. It's not usually possible to buy tickets in advance. From 6 am, you then wait any time up to 9 am for the bus to fill and depart.

TRAIN

The old Italian railway that stretched between Massawa, Asmara, Keren and Agordat was another casualty of war. Many of its tracks were pulled up to reinforce trenches.

However, a stretch of track inland from Massawa is being repaired. Over 60km has

The Old Railway

The old Italian railway, which climbed 2128m up the escarpment to Asmara, passing through three climate zones, 30 tunnels and 65 bridges, was a masterpiece of civil engineering.

At independence, Eritrea appealed for help to rehabilitate the old line. 'Impossible' said most, 'Too expensive' said some, and 'It depends' said others.

Undeterred, the Eritreans pulled the old railway workers, metal forgers and blacksmiths out of retirement, called for volunteers and set to work.

The first phase of the great line is soon to open. When the railway is eventually reconnected to Asmara, it will make for one of the most spectacular train journeys on the African continent.

so far been restored, as well as two old steam engines.

At the time of research, the track had been laid as far as Embatcalla, but locals were boarding the train at Ghinda to reach the Demas station on the outskirts of Massawa. Unfortunately, this is the least spectacular stretch of the journey, but if you're interested, ask at the station in Ghinda.

Before the current war you could walk down the railway line from Asmara to Nefasit, but as long as the conflict with Ethiopia continues, this walk looks likely to remain out of bounds for security reasons.

CAR & MOTORCYCLE

Over long distances, cars can be quicker than buses by half. If you're trying to calculate journey times by car, see the bus journey durations in each destination's Getting There & Away section, and cut the time given by about a third for short journeys or half for long journeys. For information on taxis see under Getting Around in the Asmara section.

Road Rules

Since Italian colonial days, driving has been on the right-hand side of the road.

The same road hazards that exist sometimes in Ethiopia also apply in Eritrea – precipitous roads, curfews, children playing, livestock wandering, land mines and roads impassable in the rainy season. (For detailed information, see Road Rules in the Getting Around section of the Ethiopia chapter.)

Fuel (both petrol and diesel) is quite widely available, apart from in the north after Keren, and south of Massawa into Dankalia. For travel in these places, it's essential to carry plenty of extra fuel. (See the boxed text 'Drive Safe' in the Getting Around section of the Ethiopia chapter.)

Rental

Vehicle rental is not cheap in Eritrea. The condition of many roads makes 4WD obligatory, though cars are adequate for Massawa and Keren.

Fortunately, the country is small, and with your own wheels, most of its attractions can be seen in quite a short period. If you're travelling solo, or as a couple, you can reduce the cost of vehicle rental by joining up with other travellers to hire a car plus a driver/guide. Most vehicles accommodate around five passengers, though some have extra benches in the back and can take about ten.

Cars can be rented from various agencies in Asmara (see Getting There & Away in the Asmara section; see also Organised Tours following in this section). To hire a car, you must have a valid international driving licence and be over 25 years old.

Prices vary and are usually open to a bit of negotiation, so it's worth shopping around. You should ask for a discount if you're hiring for more than a week. A deposit of around Nfa2000 is required to rent a 4WD; for a car it's around Nfa1000.

A driver usually comes automatically with a 4WD. Sometimes there's an additional charge if you want the driver to do more than eight hours in a day – check in advance.

Cars cost from Nfa200 to Nfa240 per day; a 4WD costs from Nfa600 to Nfa800 per day, including third-party insurance. The first 50 to 90km are free, and each additional kilometre costs between Nfa1.50 and Nfa3.

Purchase

If you're looking to buy a second-hand vehicle, expect to pay a minimum of Nfa105,000 (US$10,000) to Nfa157,500 (US$15,000).

If you're taking your own car or motorcycle into Eritrea, you should always carry with you and be ready to show your passport, a valid international driving licence, the vehicle ownership papers, and proof of insurance (third-party insurance is mandatory) covering all the countries you are visiting. Cars can be imported duty-free for a period of four months.

BICYCLE

Eritrea's climate, terrain and rough roads are not ideally suited to cycling. However, if you're totally self-sufficient with plenty of spare parts and tyres, as well as the capacity to carry plenty of water, there's nothing to stop you. One cyclist commented that the Eritreans' warm hospitality 'more than made up for the inhospitable terrain and climate'.

Bikes are hard to come by in Eritrea. The only place currently renting them is Explore Eritrea Travel Agency (see Organised Tours following), which requires you to rent for a minimum of two weeks; bikes need to be booked well in advance here. Eritrea has no bike repair shops, though the excellent local mechanics always do a great job by way of improvisation.

HITCHING

See Hitching in this section of the Ethiopia chapter for advice.

ORGANISED TOURS

In Asmara there are various reputable travel agencies that organise tours around the country. Tours can be tailored to your time, means and interests: from one-day bird-watching excursions from Asmara, or weekend trips to the beach in Massawa, to four-day safaris to look for elephants in Antore, or six-day expeditions through the Dankalia region to Assab. They also offer hotel and flight reservations and car hire.

The Eritrean Tour Service (☎ 12-49-49, fax 12-76-95), PO Box 889, Asmara, specialises in trips to Massawa, and has a de-

cent fleet of cars and 4WDs, usually with experienced drivers.

Explore Eritrea Travel Agency (☎ 12-12-42, fax 20-13-92), PO Box 2061, Asmara, is one of the newest on the scene, with enterprising and enthusiastic management and staff. Camping, diving and bicycling trips can be organised, as well as excursions by camel. Tailor-made trips using public as well as private transport can be arranged, which can cut costs a little.

The excellent agency Travel House International (☎ 12-02-08, fax 12-00-64, ✉ soloabr@eol.com.er), PO Box 5579, Asmara, is run by the efficient and very helpful Solomon Abraha, and offers similar services. Credit cards (Visa, Mastercard, AmEx, Eurocard and Diners among others) are accepted.

See Getting Around in the Asmara section for more information on car rental agencies.

Asmara

With a perfect climate, remarkable architecture and spotless, safe streets, Asmara ranks among the most pleasant capitals on the African continent. Perched on the eastern edge of the highland plateau, some 2356m above sea level, Asmara's climate is classed as 'tropical highland' – in other words, balmy and temperate, with cloudless blue skies for about eight months of the year.

With a population of 420,000 Asmara is easily the largest city in Eritrea, though by most African standards it's tiny. Following a government policy of 'positive discrimination'

Italian Apartheid

From 1922 to 1941, a system of discrimination existed in Eritrea and Ethiopia that was remarkably similar to the apartheid system of South Africa.

Local and Italian children were educated at different schools, with different textbooks, and to different levels. Non-Italian adults were prevented from learning basic skills or professions, or from opening shops, restaurants or businesses; they were expected to work as menials for the Italians.

On buses and in cinemas, Italian passengers sat in the front, whereas locals were obliged to sit at the back. Marriage between Italians and locals was forbidden by law, with a punishment of up to five years in prison for offenders. Following a decree in 1940, children of mixed Italian and local parentage were not considered Italian.

Thousands of locals were forcibly evicted from their houses and resettled in reservations far from where the Italians lived. The best agricultural land was seized, rent for town houses was not paid, and there were continual abuses of law in which locals were punished, fined and even killed without cause.

in favour of settlement of the countryside, Asmara has generally been spared the litter-strewn, sprawling ghettos of many developing-world cities and the bleak, Western-style high-rise office and apartment buildings of post-colonial Africa.

The town has long evoked cliched comparisons to 'southern Italian towns'. In some ways, Asmara is very Italian, not just in the tangible remnants of colonial days, such as the Centocinque taxis and Art Deco architecture, but also in the way of life – the morning cappuccino, the evening *passeggiata* (stroll) around town and the relaxed, unhurried pace of life.

However, that is just one facet of Asmara. It's also undeniably African and Arab. In the morning you'll hear the sound of the cathedral bells and the footsteps of the Orthodox monks on their way to Mass as well as the Muslim call to prayer.

These sounds are symbolic of the remarkable harmony that reigns in the city and throughout the country among the four different religions and nine ethnic groups. Apart from the Catholic cathedral, Asmara is home to 28 mosques and a thriving Muslim market, 12 Orthodox churches and a Jewish synagogue.

From October to March, Asmara is a riot of jacaranda, hibiscus and bougainvillea.

HISTORY

The town was first settled in the 12th century by shepherds from the Akele Guzay region. Encouraged by the plentiful supplies of water, they founded four villages on the hill that are now the site of the Orthodox church of Enda Mariam. The site became known as Arbate Asmere (Four Villages), from which the name Asmara is derived.

The little village then became a staging post for travellers making the long and arduous journey between the sea and the mountains. Soon it had developed into a small but bustling trading centre. In 1519, a visiting Ethiopian monk called it a 'great city'.

At the end of the 19th century, Ras Alula, the dashing Tigrinya *negus* (prince) had made it his capital and the centre of a flourishing caravan trade. By 1884, the town was home to some 2000 inhabitants and 300 houses, established on the hills where the city's water reservoirs now stand.

The town then caught the eye of the Italian general Baldissera and, in 1889, he took it over. A fort was built (some traces of which remain) and a square building (which later became the Governor's Palace) for the *Comando* (commander) Truppe. Italian architects and engineers got to work and had soon laid the foundations of the new town – Piccola Roma, as it was dubbed, was born.

In 1897, the first governor of Eritrea, Governor Martini, chose Asmara (in preference to Massawa) as the future capital of the Italian East African empire. During the Fascist years of Mussolini and amid dreams of great military conquests in Abyssinia, the town was greatly enlarged and a military base was installed.

ASMARA

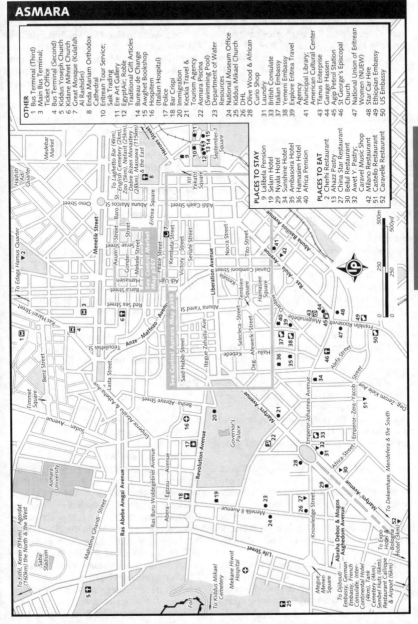

ERITREA

OTHER
1 Bus Terminal (Third)
3 Main Bus Terminal;
   Ticket Office
4 Bus Terminal (Second)
5 Kiddus Yoseph Church
6 Kidane Mihret Church
7 Great Mosque (Kulafah
   Al Rashidin)
8 Enda Mariam Orthodox
   Cathedral
10 Eritrean Tour Service;
   Saik Trading
11 Ere Art Gallery
12 EgyptAir, Roble
   Traditional Gift Articles
14 Bureau de Change
15 Awghet Bookshop
16 Hospitem (Italian Hospital)
17 Police
18 Bar Crispi
20 Immigration
21 Keckia Travel &
   Tourism Agency
22 Asmara Piscina
   (Swimming Pool)
23 Department of Water
   Resources
24 National Museum Office
25 Kiddus Mikael Church
26 DHL
28 Olive Wood & African
   Curio Shop
31 Laundry
33 British Consulate
37 Italian Embassy
38 Yemeni Embassy
39 Explore Eritrea Travel
   Agency
41 Municipal Library;
   American Cultural Center
43 Titanus Enterprise
44 Garage Hassen
45 Agip Petrol Station
46 St George's Episcopal
   Church
47 National Union of Eritrean
   Women (NUEW)
48 Star Car Hire
49 Ethiopian Embassy
50 US Embassy

PLACES TO STAY
9 Lalibela Pension
19 Selam Hotel
29 Nyala Hotel
34 Sunshine Hotel
35 Ambasoira Hotel
36 Hamasien Hotel
40 Africa Pension

PLACES TO EAT
2 Cherhi Restaurant
13 Ahaz Pastry
27 China Star Restaurant
30 Bellul Restaurant
32 Awet Y. Pastry
42 Caravel Music Shop
51 Milano Restaurant
52 Caravelle Restaurant
   Castello Restaurant

During the Struggle, Asmara was the last town held by the occupying Ethiopian army and, from 1990, it was besieged by the Eritrean People's Liberation Front (EPLF). By a fortuitous turn of events, the Ethiopian dictator Mengistu was overthrown in 1991, his troops fled from Eritrea and a final confrontation in the capital was avoided. Asmara was left intact. It was one of the very few Eritrean towns to survive the war undamaged.

ORIENTATION

Like most colonial towns, Asmara was built according to a strict urban plan, and divided into four main areas: the administrative centre, the colonial residential quarter, the 'native' quarter, and the outbuildings.

The administrative centre encompassed the area on and just north of Liberation Ave, marked by September 1 Square at the eastern end of Liberation Ave and the Governor's Palace in the west. Today, the municipality (town hall), Commercial Bank, many of the ministries, telecommunications and post office are still found in this area.

To the south of Liberation Ave lay the Italian residential quarter, at a safe distance from both the centre of town and the local quarter. Many of the Art Deco villas can be found in this area.

To the north-east, and well outside the confines of the town centre, lay the residential quarter of the local population. To this day, it is still the poorest area, made up of the Edaga Arbi, Hadish Adi and Abashawl quarters, and lies out of sight of most tourists.

The outbuildings – the larger garages, factories and assembly plants – were positioned outside the boundaries of the city, and grew to form a kind of industrial belt. Many of the old Italian factories can be found here, including the Melotti brewery, Tabacchi cement factory and Maderni match factory.

Street names have changed at least three or four times in the last 20 years, so are not really used for giving directions. Most people go by local landmarks such as government buildings, hotels or bars.

Maps

The Ministry of Tourism produces an adequate town map (Nfa15), which is available in some bookshops, souvenir shops and travel agencies in Asmara. The Eritrean Tour Service (ETS) just off September 1 Square usually stocks it. The central part of the map is a bit cramped, but it's good for general orientation as it shows the whole town. It also lists the main schools and institutions etc, which is useful if your desired destination draws a blank from the taxi drivers – do as the locals do, and describe where you want to go in relation to one of these landmarks.

INFORMATION
Tourist Offices

The best source of information in the capital is the Eritrean Tour Service (☎ 12-49-49, fax 12-76-95), which can be found through a passageway, off September 1 Square.

Money

There are various banks in Asmara, mostly on and around Liberation Ave; their exchange rates vary marginally. The Commercial Bank on Liberation Ave at the September 1 Square end offers reasonable rates and can change US dollars, pounds sterling, French francs and Deutschmarks.

Post

The main post office is on Tefebi Yazew St off the western end of Liberation Ave is open from 7 am to noon and 2 to 6 pm weekdays and from 8 am and 12.30 pm Saturday.

Telephone & Fax

The telecommunications building at the western end of Liberation Ave is open from 8 am to 10 pm weekdays, and to 9 pm on weekends and public holidays. You can make international calls in the special cabins or local calls. Phonecards (Nfa25, Nfa50 or Nfa100 denominations) are also available.

There's a fax office to the left of the entrance of the telecommunications building. Faxes cost between Nfa26 and Nfa34 for one minute's transmission, depending on the destination. The office is open 8 am to 9 pm Monday to Saturday and from 8 am to 1 pm and 3 to 7 pm on Sunday and public holidays. Faxes can also be sent from the post office.

If you want to receive faxes, the fax number is 12-29-04, and the fax should be clearly marked for your attention, c/o the Telecommunication Service of Eritrea, and marked 'For Collection'. The handling charge for incoming faxes is Nfa2 per page. If you leave a name and contact number, the office can let you know when a fax arrives for you.

Email & Internet Access

Tfanus Enterprise (☎/fax 12-40-50, ✉ maaza@gemel.com.er) on Maigenabebe Dantew St south of Liberation Ave offers Internet access. It is open from 8 am to noon and 2 to 6 pm weekdays and from 9 am to noon Saturday. It costs Nfa5 per email sent or received. Avoid Saturdays, as they're always busy.

Travel Agencies

The three main agencies are the Eritrean Tour Service (ETS ☎ 12-49-49, fax 12-76-95) off September 1 Square; Explore Eritrea Travel Agency (☎ 12-1242, fax 20-13-92), near the Yemeni embassy; and Travel House International (☎ 12-02-08, fax 12-00-64, ✉ soloabr@eol.com.er) near the Asmara Restaurant off the western end of Liberation Ave. For details of the sort of tours they offer, see the Getting Around section earlier in this chapter. Flights should be booked through the various airline offices in Asmara.

Bookshops & Newsagents

The Awghet Bookshop, on September 1 Square, has the widest selection of books on Eritrea, including history, politics and anthropology; prices range from about Nfa80 to Nfa100. It also stocks some novels by African writers, town maps and some rather uninspiring postcards.

UTTET, on Liberation Ave next door to the Luam Pension, is really a stationery shop, but it has a selection of books on Eritrea in English and Italian, and a decent selection of postcards.

For newspapers, head for Ghirmi newsagent near City Park, just south of Liberation

Ave, which sells *USA Today* and the *International Herald Tribune*, as well as magazines such as the *Economist*, *Time* and *Newsweek*. Occasionally, French, Italian and German newspapers and magazines are also sold.

Libraries & Cultural Centres

Alliance Français (☎ 12-65-99, fax 12-10-36) has a smaller library than the British Council. The library is separate from the main alliance building, behind the Ambassador Hotel off Liberation Ave. Occasionally, at the main building, exhibitions or concerts by local artists are put on and, twice a week, films in French are shown (free) at 7 pm. Before events, you can have a tasty *crêpe* (pancake) in the little garden.

American Cultural Center above the Municipal Library shows films every Friday at 6 pm, but you should get there early, as seating is limited.

British Council (☎ 12-34-12, fax 12-72-30) not far from the presidential office has a respectable library, as well as a reading room stocked with British newspapers and magazines. Temporary borrowing cards are available for up to two weeks (in exchange for some form of personal identification). It's open from 10 am to 12.30 pm and 2.30 to 5.30 pm Tuesday to Saturday (until 8 pm Thursday).

Municipal Library (☎ 12-70-44) on Ras Alula Ave near the Milano Restaurant has quite a good selection of books as well as American magazines and journals (provided by the United States Information Services). It's open to nonmembers, but only members can borrow books. It's open from 9.30 am to noon and 3 to 7 pm (until 6 pm on Saturday) Monday to Saturday.

Medical Services

If you are not feeling well, you could try talking to the sympathetic and knowledgeable pharmacist, Tesfay Menghes, at the Cathedral Pharmacy opposite the Catholic cathedral on Liberation Ave. He speaks English, Italian, a little French and Arabic.

If you need a doctor, you could try Dr Kibreab Fre (☎ 20-03-82) in the commercial centre off Liberation Ave, diagonally opposite the municipality. The doctor comes recommended by both the British consulate and the American embassy, and speaks excellent English. His surgery is open 8.30 am to noon and 3.30 to 8 pm weekdays.

[Continued on page 367]

ERITREA

ASMARA'S ARCHITECTURE

When Mussolini came to power in Italy in 1922, he nursed two ambitions relating to Italy's role in the Horn: to avenge Italy's defeat at Adwa (see the boxed text 'The Battle of Adwa' under Adwa in the North of Addis Ababa section); and to create a kind of new Roman Empire in Africa. To realise these dreams he needed a strong industrial base. Labour, resources and lire were thus poured into the new colony and, by the 1930s, it was booming. By 1940, Eritrea had become the second-most industrialised country in sub-Saharan Africa.

At the same time – and encouraged by Il Duce – a new and daring architectural movement called Rationalism was springing up in Italy. It was led by an alliance of young architects based in Milan known as the Gruppo 7.

Eritrea, in common with many colonies, became a kind of experimental architectural laboratory in which new and exciting ideas could be tested. Asmara, or Piccola Roma (Little Rome), soon came to epitomise the new philosophy: it was not just beautiful, but was well planned, well built and, above all, functional.

Isolated for nearly 30 years during its war with Ethiopia, Asmara escaped both the trend to build post-colonial piles and the push toward developing-world urbanisation. Today, it remains a model Art Deco town. The World Bank has just pledged funds for the preservation of Asmara's built heritage and the city is increasingly attracting interest from conservation groups in Italy, the US and UK.

As you walk around the town, you will see examples of the Art Deco, International, Cubist, Expressionist, Functionalist, Futurist, Rationalist and Neoclassical architectural styles.

Walking Tours

Asmara's greatest attraction is undoubtedly its fascinating collection of buildings. A tour by foot or by *gari* (horse-drawn cart) is a great way to spend a couple of hours.

For those lacking time, energy or inclination, a glimpse of Asmara's architecture can be had without even stepping outside Liberation Ave. For those with more time, a tour around the edge of the centre gives you a greater insight into the variety of buildings in Asmara, and is well worth the effort. However, some of the most interesting buildings lie further afield, and a gari provides the best way of exploring these. See Organised Tours later in this section.

If you want to step inside a church or mosque make sure that you are appropriately dressed. To visit any other interiors, you'll need to ask permission at the site.

ASMARA WALKING TOURS

1 Opera House	11 Bowling Alley	19 Piazza Mai Cew	28 Capitol Cinema
2 Ministry of Education	12 Zigzag Garage	20 Africa Pension	29 Selam Hotel
3 Catholic Cathedral	13 Old Bristol Hotel	21 Villa Roma	30 Asmara Piscina
4 Cinema Impero	14 Mai Khah Khah Fountain;	22 Hamasien Hotel	(Swimming Pool)
5 Synagogue	Gezzabanda	23 Odeon Cinema	31 Bar Zeili
6 Great Mosque	15 Villa Laila	24 Bristol Hotel	32 Irga Building
7 Red Sea Pension & Garage	16 Cohan's Villa	25 Greek Orthodox Church	33 Fiat Tagliero Building
8 Square & Market	17 Tobacco Factory	26 Enda Mariam Orthodox	34 Alpha Romeo Building
9 Wikianos Supermarket	18 Turreted Villa	Cathedral	35 Bar Aquila
10 Municipality	(Avram Villa)	27 Soap Factory	36 Alefa Street Piazza

TOUR 1 – Liberation Avenue

This short walk starts at the western end of Liberation Ave and ends at the Cinema Impero, about 500m further east.

At the western end of Liberation Ave is the old Governor's Palace. With its pediment supported by Corinthian columns and its spacious, elegant interior, it is thought to be one of the finest Neoclassical buildings in Africa. It is currently closed for restoration and its fate remains undecided; one possibility is that it may be converted into a guesthouse.

Heading east down Liberation Ave, you'll see the old Opera House on your right, near the telecommunications building. The Opera House is one of Asmara's most elegant early 20th century buildings. Designed by Cavagnari and completed around 1920, this eclectic building combines a Renaissance scallop-shell fountain, a Romanesque portico supported by Classical columns and inside, above multi-tiered balconies, a spectacular Art Nouveau ceiling painted by Saviero Fresa.

Next door is the Ministry of Education. Built during the 1930s as the Casa del Fascio (the Fascist Party headquarters), it mixes the Classical (the right-hand section) with the monumental and Fascist. Its massive stepped tower has strong vertical elements, including three gunslit windows. The steps, string courses (projecting bands of bricks) and mouldings give the building harmony.

Head eastwards along the avenue until you get to the Catholic cathedral. This building, consecrated in 1923, is thought to be one of the finest Lombard-Romanesque-style churches outside Italy. The altar is made of Carrara marble and the baptistry, confessionals and pulpit are carved from Italian walnut. The painting of Saint Mary by Carlo Maratta di Camerano (1625–1713) was presented by Vittorio Emmanuel III, king of Italy. According to a plaque inside the cathedral, Mussolini himself was a patron of its construction. Mass is celebrated every Sunday at 11 am in the cathedral.

The cathedral's narrow, Gothic bell tower makes a useful landmark and offers great views over the town. The tower is open every day from 8 am to 12.30 pm and 2 to 6 pm; entry is Nfa5. The new wooden staircase was a gift from two travelling German carpenters.

Continue heading east down Liberation Ave for another 100m or so and you will see the Cinema Impero and Bar Impero, part of a grand Rationalist terrace built in 1938. The imposing cinema is made up of three massive windows which combine strong vertical and horizontal elements with 45 porthole lamps. In the lobby, all the marble, chrome and glass features are original. The cavernous auditorium seats 1800 people and is decorated with motifs such as lions, nyalas and palm trees depicted in the Art Deco style. The Bar Impero, where cinemagoers traditionally enjoyed an aperitif before the film, is also original. Look out for the bevelled-glass cake cabinet, the porthole windows, the 'zinc' bar and the ancient gelato (ice cream) machine.

September I Square at the eastern end of Liberation Ave gets my 'hideous carbuncle' prize. It was built during the Ethiopian occupation as a parade ground and remains half-finished.

TOUR 2 – Around the Centre

If you want to see more, this walk covers the major architectural styles in Asmara and will take about 2½ hours to complete. It starts at the synagogue, just north of Liberation Ave near the Cinema Impero, and finishes at the Bristol Hotel, near the opera house at the western end of Liberation Ave.

Asmara's synagogue was built about 1905. Its pediment, Doric columns and pilasters make it very Neoclassical. As is usual in Asmara, the wrought-iron gates are handcrafted.

Turn right as you leave the synagogue, then right again at the first junction, then take a left turn at the next. This should bring you to the Great Mosque (Kulafah Al Rashidin). Completed in 1938 by Guido Ferrazza, this grand complex combines Rationalist, Classical and Islamic styles. The symmetry of the mosque is enhanced by the minaret, which rises at one side like a fluted Roman column above Islamic domes and arches. The mihrab (niche indicating the direction of Mecca) inside consists of mosaics and columns made from Carrara marble.

Ferrazza's style is also seen in the great square and market complex surrounding the mosque. The fountain is one of several still functioning in Asmara.

Head west from the mosque towards XII Yekatit Square. On the edge of the square, the Red Sea Pension & Garage with its sweeping facade is typical of the Moderne style.

Walk through the square, then head east, back towards the synagogue. Take the third turning to the left (Alema El Morgan St), and head south towards Liberation Ave. On the way look out for Wikianos Supermarket, formerly the Palazzo Mutton (residential palace), on Liberation Ave. This shop represents the curious 'corner solution' first used in Italy by Giuseppe Terragni, a founder of the Rationalist movement (Terragni is best known for his Novocomun flats and Casa del Fascio in Como, Italy). The cleverly curved corner entrance is studded with massive porthole windows.

Opposite Wikianos you'll see the Municipality building. Though built in the 1950s, the Municipality is firmly Rationalist. The two geometric wings are 'stripped Palladian' in style, and are dominated by a soaring central tower. The windows are beautifully detailed. Look out for the 'crazy majolica' facade in green and beige.

Head south from Liberation Ave down the street on the eastern side of the Municipality and turn left at Nocra St. The bowling alley is one of the few genuine 1950s alleys left in the world. This was probably built for US servicemen when they were manning military bases in the region. The reloading system is still manual; look out also for the bowling motifs on the balustrades and the carved wooden benches complete with Coke and popcorn holders. The colourful early 'pop art' window is spectacular at sunset.

Across the road from the bowling alley is a garage possibly built in the 1950s. Every part of the building features zigzags – there's probably no other building like it in the world.

Take a right turn down Abuna Basilios Ave. About 50m from the junction, on your right, you'll see the Old Bristol Hotel (now the Housing Commission). Built in the 1930s, this very unusual and innovative building was once a bordello. Its solid mass is still light and harmonious through the use of the 'rule of thirds': wing – loggia (porch) – wing. The windows and doors are in perfect proportion, too.

At the eastern end of Jubilee Ave is one of the most elegant pieces of architecture in Asmara – the Mai Khah Khah fountain. This cascades down the hillside in a series of rectangular steps. Above the fountain is the attractive suburb of Gezzabanda, which is full of impressive villas, and the Beverly Hills cafe with its 'jet engine' espresso machine.

From the fountain, head one block north onto Huru Selassie St. As you walk up this street, look out for the numerous villas standing in shady gardens. The Italian urban planners responsible for this area were honouring the age-old Classical tradition of rus in urbe (bringing a piece of the countryside into the town).

At the southern end of Ras Alula Ave is the Villa Laila, one of Asmara's finest Moderne villas.

Heading downhill on Ras Alula Ave past a row of old shops and 1950s Formica bars with fly-bead doors, you'll see at the next block an attractive villa, Cohan's Villa, with blue wraparound windows, a feature often used by architects in Miami, USA. At the rear is a Georgian-looking circular stairwell and, at the sides, nautically inspired balconies. The villa was built by one of the prominent Jewish trading families in the 1930s.

Still on Ras Alula Ave, a block downhill from Cohan's Villa is the tobacco factory, one of the most adventurous Art Deco buildings in Asmara. Look out for the very odd 'unfinished' pilasters, the tall slim windows and the massive cornice leading to the curved cantilever wings that give the building balance.

Heading west from the tobacco factory, you pass Ras Alula Hill, where the Tigrean negus (prince) once had a fort. The hill is now covered with lovely old villas including the Villa Grazia, a Cuban-style Moderne building.

The piazza nearby, which features a lone palm and tear-drop island, is beautifully designed. Heading east again along Zeude St, look out on the left for one of Asmara's grandest residences. Part Norman keep, part Riviera chateau, the three-storey Avram Villa (also known as the Turreted Villa) was built by the L'Atilla family in the 1930s. The roof terrace is topped by an unusual 'surfboard' loggia.

Head north towards Liberation Ave until you reach the Piazza Mai Cew, which was once the heart of the Greek community. On the corner on the east side is an old school that resembles a Greek temple, with a very Art Deco basketball stand in the grounds.

From the Piazza Mai Cew, head west through Tembien Square, and up the hill. Near the top of the hill, before you get to the Villa Roma, you reach the Africa Pension. This huge Cubist villa was built in the 1920s by a spaghetti millionaire. The villa is characterised by its elegant marble staircase and the ring of 40 marble urns. Today a solemn and slightly ludicrous bronze bust of Augustus Caesar stands guard in the once-formal garden. The villa is now a hotel (see Places to Stay – Budget later in this section).

At the top of the hill is the Villa Roma. This beautiful villa, built in 1919 by Gaetano L'Atilla, epitomises the Roman style. The marble staircases, louvred shutters, curving balustrades, shady portico, fountain and loggia with cascading purple bougainvillea are typical features of the ideal Roman villa. The interior is equally impressive and still contains some of its original Art Deco pieces. Today the Villa Roma is the residence of the Italian Ambassador.

Heading west from the Villa Roma brings you to the Hamasien Hotel, designed by the architect Reviglio around 1920. Most of the interior furnishings were lost during the Ethiopian occupation. The quirky chimney pots are designed to resemble miniature classical temples.

About 100m north, and just off Liberation Ave, is the Odeon Cinema with its authentic Art Deco interior. The box office, bar, bevelled mirrors, black terrazzo and Deco strip lights are a good introduction to the large auditorium.

Opposite the cinema is the Bristol Hotel. Built in 1941, the hotel, with its central stairwell tower surmounting geometric wings, is an example of classic Rationalist design. The strip-course separates the top-floor windows from the well-proportioned and well-made shutters, and the plain concrete balconies below.

TOUR 3 – Outside the Centre

Listed in this section are some buildings that are outside the centre. Although you could visit these on foot, a gari is probably the best way to see them. Garis can be found near the grain market on Eritrea Square at the city bus terminal. A morning or afternoon tour should cost around Nfa100. Some drivers don't speak English, so you may have to ask someone to explain to them which buildings you want to see.

The Enda Mariam Orthodox Cathedral, just north of XII Yekatit Square, was built in 1938 and is a curious blend of Italian and Eritrean architecture. Its central block is flanked by large square towers. Rather garish mosaics of stylised Christian figures are framed vertically above the entrance. Traditional elements of Aksumite architecture can be seen, such as the massive horizontal stone beams. The four objects that look like broken elephant tusks suspended in the middle of the compound are century-old 'bells'. These make a surprisingly musical sound when 'rung' (beaten with a stick).

On the western side of the market, the Greek Orthodox Church, with its frescoes, carved wood and candles, could almost be in Greece.

The old soap factory, on Ras Abebe Aregai Ave past the university, is typical of the International style, except that its dilapidated glass tower is nonfunctional. In Asmara, it was common for successful businesses to broadcast their wealth with such follies.

The Capitol Cinema, on Revolution Ave, north of the Governor's Palace, was built in 1937, and its massive horizontal elements and sweeping curves are typical of the Expressionist movement. Inside is Asmara's finest 'zinc' bar. The auditorium is pretty austere even by 1930s standards. One feature to note is the sliding roof that could be opened on warm summer nights.

Built in the 1930s, the Selam Hotel was one of a chain constructed by the Italian company Compagnia Immobiliare Alberghi Africa Orientale (CIAAO). Interesting interior details include the Arts and Crafts serving cabinets and the 'disc'-type lamps in the dining room, the old murals and the purple 'beehive' lamps in the rear courtyard. It's still run as a hotel (see Places to Stay – Top End).

The 1930s Asmara Piscina (swimming pool) is just south of the Governor's Palace. Take a peek inside – interior details include the 'Leonardo' sporting figures on the walls.

The facade of the extraordinary Bar Zeili, at the junction of Knowledge St and Martyrs' Ave, looks like a 1930s radio. The porthole windows and nautical balconies are separated into sections by mock-marble columns.

The beautiful Irga Building is both Neoclassical in its proportions and very modern.

Perhaps the best-known building in Asmara is the Fiat Tagliero building. This Futuristic l'aeroplano (aeroplane), on Emperor Teodros Square, in the south-west of town, was built in 1938 by the engineer Pettazzi. The central tower with its glass 'cockpit' is similar to many structures in Miami, USA.

The story goes that after the concrete had been poured, Pettazzi's workers refused to remove the shuttering supports of the cantilevered 'wings' for fear that the whole thing would collapse. Standing on one of the wings, with a revolver against his head, the engineer vowed he would shoot himself if his masterpiece did not hold together.

The dilapidated but majestic Alpha Romeo building on King Sahle Selassie St, with its Palladian proportions and striking bevelled arch and Futuristic antennas, is a strange mix of the old and the new.

The Bar Aquila, at the corner of Africa and Emperor Zera Yacob Sts, makes a good stop to have a rest and a drink. While there, admire the original Art Deco bar. Note the shelving, mirrors, chequered floor, rare antique billiard cue stand and scoring board.

If you head east from Bar Aquila, you'll get to the large piazza at the top of the hill from Alefa St. The piazza is surrounded by an incredible collection of Art Deco architecture, including two small Lubetkin-inspired villas, a crumbling 'Tuscan' tower and the Villa Venezia with its scored walls and Lion of Saint Mark in red and gold mosaics. Look out also for the vast and curious 'ocean liner' villa.

[Continued from page 359]

It's best to make an appointment; otherwise you can turn up and wait. Visits cost Nfa10; stool/blood tests cost Nfa5. Night calls to your hotel cost Nfa50 (call him on ☎ 18-41-93).

If you need a dentist, you can find Dr Surur Ali Abdu (☎ 12-05-62) at the Universal Dental Clinic just off the western end of Liberation Ave. A visit costs Nfa20, and a filling costs Nfa100. Phone in advance for an appointment, unless it's an emergency.

Other Services

There's a nameless laundry near the British Council and one close to the British Consulate that charges Nfa4/9 for T-shirts/trousers and Nfa2/3 for socks/underwear. Normal service takes 72 hours; express service takes 24 hours and costs double.

If your footwear has taken a battering and needs a bit of TLC, there's a cobbler next door to the Asmara Restaurant. The replacement of an entire leather sole costs Nfa55.

If your hair is in need of some TLC, try Abeba, which charges Nfa8/10 for men/women for a simple trim, including washing and drying.

For car care and repairs, head for Garage Hassen, near the Agip petrol station, on Ras Alula Ave.

Emergency

Emergency numbers (24 hour) include:

Ambulance (☎ 12-22-44)
Fire Brigade (☎ 11-77-77)
Police (☎ 11-55-55)

Dangers & Annoyances

It's safe to stroll around day or night in Asmara, barring some very atypical incidents recently. One area women travellers should be aware of is the red light district, known locally as Babylon, which has grown up in the vicinity of the Legese Hotel, just south of Liberation Ave. It's harmless enough but women walking home at night should be aware of it.

It used to be rare to see beggars in central Asmara, due to a government campaign to 'discourage' it. Recently, however, the numbers of beggars on the streets of Asmara appears to be increasing. The odd little street urchin creeps in – a favourite game is to try to extract money, usually successfully, from gullible tourists. Common appeals are for 'school books', 'footballs', 'English dictionaries' etc. If you oblige, you are sure to be shadowed for the rest of your trip. If you want to give alms, go to the Orthodox churches.

MARKET

The vibrant market is one of Asmara's major attractions. It takes place every morning except Sunday, but the best time to visit is early on Saturday (from 7 am), when people come in from all over the country. Highlights include the **spice market** (filled with colourful women from different ethnic groups), and the market area known as **Medebar**, which is like an open-air workshop where absolutely everything is recycled. The Medebar is a fascinating place. The air is filled with hammering, sawing and cutting; old tyres are made into sandals, corrugated iron is flattened and made into

ERITREA

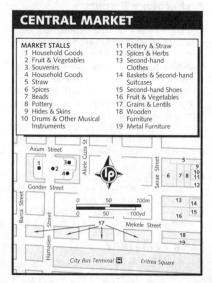

CENTRAL MARKET

MARKET STALLS	
1 Household Goods	11 Pottery & Straw
2 Fruit & Vegetables	12 Spices & Herbs
3 Souvenirs	13 Second-hand
4 Household Goods	Clothes
5 Straw	14 Baskets & Second-hand
6 Spices	Suitcases
7 Beads	15 Second-hand Shoes
8 Pottery	16 Fruit & Vegetables
9 Hides & Skins	17 Grains & Lentils
10 Drums & Other Musical	18 Wooden
Instruments	Furniture
	19 Metal Furniture

Axum Street

Akele Guza St

Gonder Street

Barca Street

Hamasien Street

Serae Street

0   50   100m
0   50   100yd

Mekele Street

City Bus Terminal 🚌   Eritrea Square

Eritrea Square

ERITREA

Passeggiata

Don't miss the evening passeggiata (between 5 and 6.30 pm), when the whole town takes a turn around the streets to see what's new, catch up with friends, hear the latest gossip, window shop, and generally take things easy. It's when Asmara most comes alive.

≪≪≪≪≪≪≪≪≪≪≪≪≪≪≪≪≪≪≪≪≪≪≪≪≪≪≪≪≪≪

metal buckets, and olive tins from Italy made into coffee pots and tiny scoopers. It's a salutary lesson in waste management.

The **souvenir market** is a great place to browse too, and is more interesting than the shops in the town. You can find, among other things, local basketwork, wooden masks, musical instruments, decorated gourds, warrior knives and skin paintings.

NATIONAL MUSEUM

The excellent National Museum is still closed, awaiting the completion of its new home. When it re-opens, it will include exhibits on the ethnic groups of Eritrea, the main archaeological sites of the country, and the Struggle for Independence. Don't miss it.

Archaeology Permits

To visit the archaeological sites of Eritrea, you'll need a permit. The National Museum office (☎ 11-99-02) PO Box 5284, Asmara, is in an old school building next door to the Comboni Sisters' convent school opposite the Department of Water Resources. It keeps normal business hours. You'll need your passport and Nfa30. The paper can be issued immediately; the staff are helpful and efficient. You can walk there in 15 minutes from Liberation Ave or take a taxi (Nfa10). Tell the driver it's next to the Barka school.

CITY PARK

This park is a pleasant place for a walk and an ice cream in the afternoon, or for a beer in the evening. It's open 6.30 am to 10.30 pm every day.

TANK CEMETERY

A few kilometres outside town, towards the airport, is the area known as Tsetserat and

the EPLF's Den Den military camp, home to the so-called Tank Cemetery, where hundreds of tanks, armoured cars and other detritus of war have been dumped. It's an impressive and rather chilling sight. But it may not be there forever; an enterprising local has decided to get into the scrap metal business fast. Photos aren't officially allowed.

ENGLISH CEMETERY

On the road to Massawa on the periphery of Asmara, 2km from the centre is the beautifully tended English Cemetery, dating from 1941. Interred here are 280 men killed during the African campaign. There is also a Hindu burial ground for the Indian soldiers fighting alongside the British.

ZOO

The zoo, 5km from town on the road to Massawa, is clean but small and cramped, and not worth an excursion.

ACTIVITIES

If you're grubby and tired after a long trip, you might fancy a **sauna** at the Expo Hotel (see Places to Stay – Top End, later in this section). It charges nonguests Nfa30 for two hours and provides towels. It's open 8.30 am to 2 pm Monday to Saturday for women and 2.30 to 10.30 pm daily for men.

The **Asmara Piscina** is a clean and well-kept swimming pool, open from 6 am to 9 pm every day. Entry is Nfa15.

There's a fun tenpin **bowling alley** opposite the Shell petrol station, not far from the Ghennet Hotel. It's open every day from 10 am to midnight, and costs Nfa4 per game, Nfa1 for shoe hire. Beer is available. **Billiardo** (billiards) is also possible here and costs Nfa5/10 for half/one hour. It's said that the president himself is not adverse to a game or two occasionally.

ORGANISED TOURS

The ETS does city tours – including the zoo, market, churches, mosques and panoramic views – for Nfa225 for one to three people (less if there's four or more of you). Explore Eritrea Travel Agency does a very basic architectural tour of the town for around Nfa150.

PLACES TO STAY – BUDGET

Many of the cheapest hotels, usually known as 'pensions', are dotted around the market place. Still cheap, but slightly better, are those just off Liberation Ave. Inevitably some double as brothels. All of the places listed in this section have communal showers (sometimes cold) and toilets. If you want to be in the thick of things, choose one on Liberation Ave, if you want some peace, opt for those south of Liberation Ave.

Rock-bottom but one of the best places in its class, is the *Melley Pension* (☎ 12-47-44), which has peeling but clean singles/doubles for Nfa22/33 and a hot communal shower. Similar but slightly better is the *Eritrea Pension* (☎ 12-45-93) with rooms for Nfa25/45. Both are a block or so north of Liberation Ave.

The *Green Island Pension* (☎ 12-17-02) just south of Liberation Ave, diagonally opposite the Catholic cathedral, has adequate rooms and a clean bathroom for Nfa35. Avoid the inappropriately named *Modern Hotel* nearby as it's falling apart.

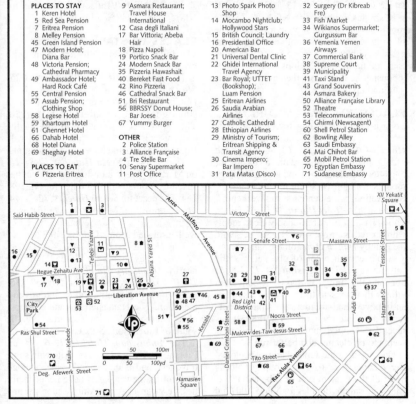

CENTRAL ASMARA

ERITREA

PLACES TO STAY
1 Keren Hotel
5 Red Sea Pension
7 Eritrea Pension
8 Melley Pension
45 Green Island Pension
47 Modern Hotel;
    Diana Bar
48 Victoria Pension;
    Cathedral Pharmacy
49 Ambassador Hotel;
    Hard Rock Café
55 Central Pension
57 Assab Pension;
    Clothing Shop
58 Legese Hotel
59 Khartoum Hotel
61 Ghennet Hotel
66 Dahab Hotel
68 Hotel Diana
69 Sheghay Hotel

PLACES TO EAT
6 Pizzeria Eritrea

9 Asmara Restaurant;
   Travel House
   International
12 Casa degli Italiani
17 Bar Vittoria; Abeba
   Hair
18 Pizza Napoli
19 Portico Snack Bar
24 Modern Snack Bar
35 Pizzeria Hawashait
40 Bereket Fast Food
42 Rino Pizzeria
46 Cathedral Snack Bar
51 Bri Restaurant
56 BBRSSY Donut House;
   Bar Joese
67 Yummy Burger

OTHER
2 Police Station
3 Alliance Française
4 Tre Stelle Bar
10 Senay Supermarket
11 Post Office

13 Photo Spark Photo
   Shop
14 Mocambo Nightclub;
   Hollywood Stars
15 British Council; Laundry
16 Presidential Office
20 American Bar
21 Universal Dental Clinic
22 Ghidei International
   Travel Agency
23 Bar Royal; UTTET
   (Bookshop);
   Luam Pension
25 Eritrean Airlines
26 Saudia Arabian
   Airlines
27 Catholic Cathedral
28 Ethiopian Airlines
29 Ministry of Tourism;
   Eritrean Shipping &
   Transit Agency
30 Cinema Impero;
   Bar Impero
31 Pata Matas (Disco)

32 Surgery (Dr Kibreab
   Fre)
33 Fish Market
34 Wikianos Supermarket;
   Gurgussum Bar
36 Yemenia Yemen
   Airways
37 Commercial Bank
38 Supreme Court
39 Municipality
41 Taxi Stand
43 Grand Souvenirs
44 Asmara Bakery
50 Alliance Française Library
52 Theatre
53 Telecommunications
54 Ghirmi (Newsagent)
60 Shell Petrol Station
62 Bowling Alley
63 Saudi Embassy
64 Mai Chihot Bar
65 Mobil Petrol Station
70 Egyptian Embassy
71 Sudanese Embassy

The **Victoria Pension** (☎ 12-16-48) opposite the Catholic cathedral is one of the better value central cheapies and has lots of character too. Clean doubles cost Nfa30–35 and twin-bed rooms cost Nfa50. Rooms 4 and 7 are among the best, and have views of the cathedral.

The **Red Sea Pension** (☎ 12-67-78) near XII Yekatit Square isn't bad, and has singles/doubles for Nfa35/45 arranged around a roof terrace. Despite the uninviting entrance, the **Lalibela Pension** (☎ 20-02-65) in front of the Shell petrol station on the opposite side of the square offers clean singles without shower for Nfa22, and doubles with bathroom for Nfa38 to Nfa50.

Another good choice, popular with the VSO aid workers, is the **Central Pension** (☎ 12-16-56), which has 13 simple but spotless singles/doubles for Nfa33/43. Some rooms have a basin (for an extra Nfa2). The place is Muslim-run so only married or single-sex couples can share a room. The hotel is a bit hard to find: look for the gates opposite the Bar Joese, then go through the yard and up the stairs.

PLACES TO STAY – MID-RANGE

Long a favourite among travellers and aid workers is the spotless and central **Legese Hotel** (☎ 12-50-54, fax 12-04-46), which offers singles/doubles with a basin for Nfa44/66. A safe deposit and luggage storage room is available (free) for the use of guests. Reservations are essential at the weekend.

The nearby **Hotel Diana** (☎ 12-15-29) on Tito St has just three reasonably clean rooms with shared bathroom for Nfa50/70. Avoid the grubby **Dahab Hotel** on the same street.

A place with a lot of character is the attractive **Africa Pension** (☎ 12-14-36) opposite the Italian embassy. A converted villa with a pleasant little garden, it's rather an impoverished aristocrat, but has 10 perfectly adequate rooms for Nfa50/80. It has recently changed management, and now seems to be cleaner and better run.

One step up is the atmospheric, old colonial **Keren Hotel** (☎ 12-07-40), a couple of blocks north of the western end of Liberation Ave, which has singles/doubles for Nfa75/100 (2nd

class) or Nfa85/114 (1st class). Prices don't include the 20% tax. The 2nd-class rooms have just a basin, the 1st-class rooms have shower, toilet and TV. In early 2000, the hotel was undergoing 'modernisation'.

The newly opened **Ghennet Hotel** (☎ 12-49-68), opposite the Ministry of Agriculture, about a 10-minute walk from the Catholic cathedral, is a modern and comfortable place with rooms without bathroom for Nfa81/126.

The clean and friendly **Sheghay Hotel** (☎ 12-65-62), a block south of the cathedral, has rooms with bathroom for Nfa88/110 and is clean and friendly. It's also got a roof terrace with great views over the town.

The **Khartoum Hotel** (☎ 20-13-94, fax 12-13-09) on Nocra St has rooms without shower for Nfa100/150 and with shower for Nfa150/200, including breakfast.

PLACES TO STAY – TOP END

The following hotels all offer rooms with private bathroom.

The **Bologna** (☎ 18-13-60, fax 18-26-86) and **Expo** (☎ 18-27-08, fax 18-42-42) Hotels both offer newish and comfortable singles/doubles for around Nfa165/220. The latter has a sauna. Both are in the Tiravolo district (a five-minute taxi ride from the centre) and have good restaurants.

The high-rise **Nyala Hotel** (☎ 12-31-11) on Martyrs' Ave is a bit lugubrious, but has spacious rooms with balconies for Nfa198/264. The peaceful **Selam Hotel** (☎ 12-72-44, fax 12-06-62) on Menelik II Ave just west of the Governor's Palace has comfortable, well-furnished rooms for Nfa240/320.

The **Hamasien Hotel** (☎ 12-34-11, fax 12-25-95) has rooms for Nfa252/336. The nearby **Ambasoira Hotel** (☎ 12-32-22, fax 12-25-95) offers rooms for Nfa252/336. Both hotels are colonial relics and government-run. The Hamasien has more atmosphere but the Ambasoira is smarter; both lie south of Liberation Ave so are peaceful.

The **Ambassador Hotel** (☎ 12-65-44) on Liberation Ave is an old favourite with some travellers, and is quite good value. Though some of the newer hotels have better facilities, few can beat the Ambassador's prime location at the heart of the town. Rooms are Nfa320/340, although they do offer some singles for Nfa212. Prices include a good buffet breakfast. However, it's in the process of being refurbished, so prices will probably go up. Credit cards are accepted.

The *Sunshine Hotel* (☎ 12-78-80, fax 12-78-66) is one of Asmara's newest hotels and offers comfortable albeit rather small rooms for Nfa328/456. Single/double suites cost Nfa517/960. All rooms have satellite TV and some have balconies. There is also a small garden.

Top of the pile, and the only five-star hotel in town, is the new *Hotel Inter-Continental Asmara* (☎ 15-04-00, fax 15-04-01, **@** inter con@eol.com.er), which opened in November 1999, apparently in response to Hillary Clinton's refusal to set foot in Eritrea because it lacked 'adequate facilities'! It lies 4km from the town centre on the airport road.

The hotel has 170 rooms with balconies, including six with facilities for the disabled. Other facilities include conference rooms, six restaurants, various cafes and bars, a fitness centre and swimming pool. Rooms cost from US$175/200 to US$1350 for the presidential suite. Prices don't include the 20% sales tax/service charge.

PLACES TO EAT

Apart from the smart places, most restaurants charge about the same for booze with your meal: Nfa6 to Nfa25 for local wine or Nfa50 for imported wine. Beer costs around Nfa 5/10 for local/imported varieties.

Restaurants

Local & Italian The market area is home to a rash of little restaurants. They're nothing fancy, but they offer the most authentic local fare in town.

The *Beilul Restaurant* near the Nyala Hotel is a good local joint, and offers cheap but decent mains for Nfa10 to Nfa12.

The *Asmara Restaurant* near the post office off the western end of Liberation Ave is a popular place with locals and is similarly priced. It's a simple place but the food is excellent.

There are two restaurants at the *Milano* on Ras Alula Ave: an inner restaurant offering good local food in a great, traditional setting; and an Italian restaurant out the front, which is also pretty good. At the inner restaurant, mains cost between Nfa15 and Nfa25. Try the house speciality, *tibs zil zil* (sizzling lamb).

The huge *Bologna Restaurant* (attached to the hotel) is another place offering both local and Italian food, at similar prices. Though less atmospheric than the Milano, the menu is more imaginative and the food more consistent in quality.

The *Nyala Hotel* (see Places to Stay – Top End) serves reasonable local food in little tents in its 7th floor restaurant for Nfa17 to Nfa23 (plus 15% tax). There's a good view of the city, too.

Italian The upmarket *Axum Restaurant* at the Legese Hotel (see Places to Stay – Mid-Range) is very popular locally for business and family lunches, with mains for around Nfa20. The Swiss-trained chef is known for his lasagne, meat balls and creme caramel.

The *Castello* just off Emperor Zera Yacob St is cheaper than the Axum but the food is not quite as good. Mains cost from Nfa12 to Nfa14 and its speciality is cannelloni. The outdoor seating area is very pleasant.

The *Caravelle* (☎ 12-38-30) just off the southern end of Martyrs' Ave was closed for restoration at the time of writing, but has a good reputation.

The *Restaurant Calliope* (☎ 18-17-70) near the Sembel Huts is a recently opened Italian restaurant, considered one of the best for Italian food in town. It has prices to match, with mains from Nfa 20–30, and you may need to book.

By far the best – and most authentic – pizzeria in town is *Pizza Napoli* on Itegue Zehaitu Ave at the western end of Liberation Ave. It has a selection of 22 pizzas ranging from Nfa9 to Nfa25, depending on the size. Try the *pizza della casa* which has 'a little of everything; for the very hungry'. There's also a great *pizza vegetariana* for Nfa10/13 for small/large size.

Despite its name, the *Pizzeria Hawashait*, just off the eastern end of Liberation Ave, is

ERITREA

a cheerful and popular little place. As well as pizzas, it does a good selection of cocktails (Nfa7 to Nfa12). The *Pizzeria Eritrea*, near the commercial centre opposite the municipality, does decent portions at good prices (Nfa10 to Nfa17). If you've rolled into town late, *Rino Pizzeria* near the taxi stand on Liberation Ave is open 24 hours.

Other Some of the smarter hotels, such as the Ambassador (see Places to Stay – Top End earlier in this section), have decent 'international' restaurants, though you're looking to pay around Nfa20 to Nfa30 plus tax. The Ambassador has a pasta and seafood night every Tuesday and Saturday. The Inter-Continental has six restaurants; mains go for Nfa35 to Nfa150.

The Chinese *Cherhi Bar & Restaurant* is set on a hill around 1½km from Liberation Ave north of the centre of town. The building looks more like an air-traffic control tower but it's got great panoramic views over Asmara. Mains cost from Nfa16 to Nfa28, and the food is authentic and good.

The new *Sembel Huts* complex on the airport road about 6km south-west of town has various restaurants offering different deals including a Sunday brunch for Nfa30 (10 am to 3 pm), and an international buffet on Wednesday and Friday, with traditional music. To get there at night, a taxi costs Nfa30 to Nfa40 one way.

In the centre of town, the Sudanese restaurant *Bri* just south of Liberation Ave provides some welcome variety. It's run by the larger-than-life patron, Arafat, who will suggest the day's dishes (there are no menus). Mains cost from Nfa10 to Nfa12. It's also a great place for vegetarians.

The *China Star* (☎ 12-58-53) restaurant on Knowledge St, near the Nyala Hotel, is a good place, much appreciated by the staff of the Chinese embassy. It has a wide-ranging menu, and does some fabulous soups.

Cafes & Pastry Shops

All of the places listed in this section serve pastries (usually made on the premises) and fruit juices, and are great for breakfast. Most are open by 7 am, some earlier.

The *Bar Royal* on Liberation Ave is considered one of the most chic places in town. It's cool, clean and quiet (if you don't mind the piped music and the 'Hello' badges on the waiters' uniforms). A coffee and freshly baked croissant costs Nfa3.50, and a freshly squeezed orange juice is Nfa5.

The *Bar Vittorio* is a simpler and cheaper place, with a good selection of cakes and great cappuccino (Nfa1.50). It's very popular with local students, who come to discuss girlfriend problems and the weather.

For quality and choice of cakes, probably the best place in town is the bright and spotless *Ahazz Pastry* on September 1 Square. Pastries include finger-licking chocolate eclairs, meringues and *millefeuilles* (puff pastry filled with pastry cream) and cost Nfa1. The smoky cappuccinos (Nfa2) make a great accompaniment.

The *Casa degli Italiani* at the western end of Liberation Ave, a block north of the avenue, was originally created for Italian expats but other visitors are welcome. It has a very pleasant, palm-shaded courtyard and is a great place to scribble a postcard or two over a coffee or a cocktail (Nfa12). Delicious sandwiches made with imported Italian cheese and salami are also available.

The *Cathedral Snack Bar* just opposite the Catholic cathedral is known for its fruit juices (Nfa2 to Nfa2.50). Try the 'mixture' – a terrific apricot colour as thick as soup. It's a good place for breakfast. The *Modern Snack Bar* also does great local breakfasts, and has the best yoghurt in town.

The *Bar Crispi* on Revolution Ave is newly opened and already very popular. It's an old Italian bar that's been very well restored by its current owner.

A coffee at the new *Inter-Continental Hotel* will set you back Nfa15; Nfa35 for an orange juice. The *Ambassador Hotel* is a great place for a buffet breakfast splurge (Nfa20 per person).

For a picnic, the *Awet Y. Pastry* near the British Consulate has a great selection of freshly baked pastries to take away. For early starters, the *Tre Stelle Bar* at the eastern end of Liberation Ave is open from 4.30 am and serves quite good coffee.

Fast Food

Yummy Burger on Nocra St, south of Liberation Ave, is a simple but clean place serving yummy burgers for Nfa4 to Nfa12 and fries for Nfa3. The best place in town for a fast feed is *Bereket Fast Food* next to the taxi stand on Liberation Ave. It's a clean, modern place, serving burgers (Nfa6) and fries (Nfa5). It also does good fruit juices for Nfa2.50 to Nfa4 and delicious fresh doughnuts. Breakfast fare includes omelettes and scrambled egg, served local style with pepper.

Portico Snack Bar at the western end of Liberation Ave is a very popular place with students and has burgers (Nfa5 to Nfa7) and sandwiches (from Nfa3). It's a great place for fruit juices (10 types including carrot and lemon) and milkshakes.

For *ice cream*, the cones and cups (Nfa1.50/3) served at City Park are considered among the best.

Self-Catering

Wikianos supermarket opposite the municipality has the best selection of products, and is a favourite with European expats. Most food is imported, so prices are much higher than in local supermarkets. If you're missing European beer, cigarettes or Heinz Baked Beans, it's the place to go. It also stocks imported baby food, mosquito nets, and useful travelling utensils (such as plastic plates, can openers etc). The cheese and meat counter provides good ammunition for a picnic.

Senay Supermarket near the Modern Snack Bar is a cheaper option, with a reasonable selection of groceries.

The *Asmara Bakery* on Liberation Ave across from the Ministry of Tourism sells freshly baked croissants and rolls each morning from 4.30 am. For fresh doughnuts, try the *BBRSSY Donut House* near the Central Pension.

ENTERTAINMENT
Pubs & Bars

Most bars stay open until 10 or 11 pm in the week, and until at least 2 am at the weekend.

The *Hard Rock Cafe* at the Ambassador Hotel (see Places to Stay – Top End) has become something of an institution with well-heeled locals, local returnees and expats from the embassies. The bar is open until midnight, and spirits cost from Nfa8.

The colonial-style dining room of the *Keren Hotel* (see Places to Stay – Mid-Range) is a good place for an early evening drink, just to see the fantastically rococo stuccowork ceiling.

The *American Bar* just off Liberation Ave at the western end is a popular place on Friday night with VSOs who catch up with friends who've come in from around the country. A beer/spirits costs Nfa3/7.

Gurgussum Bar (near Wikianos supermarket), the rough and ready *Hollywood Stars* (next door to Mocambo nightclub) and *Diana Bar* opposite the Catholic cathedral are considered among the best local bars for music, atmosphere and dancing. The Diana is a bit of a dive, but it is very popular with VSOs for its Western music and lively atmosphere.

More 'local' but just as lively is the *Mai Chihot Bar* on Ras Alula Ave. It's usually crammed with local bar girls, but it's fun and the music is diverse.

Discos & Nightclubs

Most clubs open only on Friday and Saturday (from around midnight to 5 am). Entrance is between Nfa30 and Nfa40, and local beer costs around Nfa5.

Pata Matas next to Cinema Impero on Liberation Ave is popular with adolescent Eritrean returnees.

Laghetto Bar on the road to Massawa is popular with a slightly less spotty crowd, but you'll need to organise a taxi there and back. The music is more varied and includes local hits.

The *Sembel Huts* complex out towards the airport has live music on Thursdays and Saturdays. Entrance is Nfa50, which includes a barbecue.

Mocambo, with its modern black and white decor, is regarded as one of the most hip nightclubs. During the week, it functions as a bar and entrance is free. It's a good place for live music, both traditional and Western.

Traditional Music

The larger hotels and restaurants sometimes put on reasonable performances by local musicians and dancers. The best time to see traditional performances is during the Orthodox religious festivals. Check out the listings in local papers such as the *Eritrea Profile*.

Cinemas & Theatres

One of the best places in town is the centrally located **Impero**. It charges Nfa3/5 for 1st/2nd-class seating (wooden flaps both categories), and shows action-packed American, Italian and Saudi films (in the original English, Italian or Arabic).

Generally, two films are shown twice a day at 2.30 and 4.30 pm, and at 7 and 9 pm Monday to Saturday (1.30, 3.15 and 5 pm on Sunday). Popcorn is available, if you can't see a film without it.

Currently, the few theatre productions staged are almost all in local languages. Local theatre tends to be quite spectacular and visual.

SHOPPING

For variety and colour, a trip to the market is a must – see Market earlier in this section.

Souvenirs & Handicrafts

Grand Souvenirs on Liberation Ave has the most interesting selection of souvenirs (and postcards) in town. It's run by an ex-fighter, Matusala, whose grandfather collected many of the items on sale. Items include traditional paintings, carved figures, jewellery, pottery and musical instuments.

There are goldsmiths and leather shops along Itegue Zehaitu Ave a block north of Liberation Ave. Gold goes for Nfa65 to Nfa100 per gram depending on the carat; silver is Nfa5 per gram (a simple pair of silver earrings costs around Nfa23).

The Olive Wood & African Curio Shop at the junction of Martyrs' Ave and Knowledge St has the best selection of musical instruments.

If you fancy some local art, check out the Ere Art Gallery just off September 1 Square, run by the ebullient Eritrean artist Kahssai. Canvas and skin paintings range from Nfa180 to Nfa300. Nearby, Roble Traditional Gift Articles (☎ 11-91-72) is run by Fattima Suleiman, a fighter for seven years during the Struggle. She makes most of the delightful traditional baskets herself. Other items include traditional clothing, horn mugs and musical instruments.

For traditional clothes, try the unmarked shop two doors down from the Assab Pension just south of the Catholic cathedral. Traditional cotton dresses range from Nfa350 to Nfa500 and *zurias* (shawls) from Nfa200 to Nfa500. Custom-made clothing can be made at no extra charge. Bring an Eritrean friend to interpret if your Tigrinya's not up to scratch.

Equipment

For film or batteries, head for Photo Spark, near the Casa degli Italia, which stocks both print and slide film at reasonable prices (Nfa 50-60). For cassettes of traditional as well as Western music, try Caravel Music Shop near Awet Y. Pastry on Martyrs' Ave. Snorkelling equipment can be bought at Travel House International near the Asmara Restaurant; a mask costs Nfa173 to Nfa257.

GETTING THERE & AWAY
Air

The airport is 6km south-west of Asmara. The Housing & Commerce Bank of Eritrea is near the exit of the airport. It changes cash only, and is open from 6.30 am to 2 am daily.

For details of international and national flights to/from Asmara airport, see the Getting There & Away and Getting Around sections earlier in this chapter. Note that as long as the dispute with Ethiopia lasts, there will be no services between the two countries.

Departure tax is Nfa15 for national flights and US$12 for international flights. The latter can only be paid in US dollars cash, so make sure you have some with you, as it's unobtainable at the airport bank.

Airlines with offices in Asmara include the following:

EgyptAir (☎ 12-70-34, fax 12-74-73) just off September 1 Square

Eritrean Airlines (☎ 12-55-00, fax 12-47-75) Liberation Ave, 50m west of the Catholic cathedral; also acts as agent for Lufthansa

Ethiopian Airlines (☎ 12-75-12, fax 12-68-27) Liberation Ave, opposite the Asmara Bakery; accepts credit cards

Saudi Arabian Airlines (☎ 12-01-66, fax 12-01-97) Liberation Ave, 50m west of the Catholic cathedral

Yemenia Yemen Airways (☎ 12-01-99, fax 12-01-07) Liberation Ave, near Wikianos supermarket

Bus

The city bus terminal lies next to the central market on Eritrea Square.

The long-distance bus station is about 10 minutes' walk due north of Liberation Ave, and is split into three different terminals. The ticket office at the main bus terminal is open from 5 am to 6 pm daily.

Buses east (to Massawa, Nefasit and Ghinda etc) leave from the main bus terminal; buses south (to Dekemhare, Segheneyti, Senafe, Adi Keyh etc) leave from the third bus terminal (also known as Edaga Hamus bus station); and buses west and north (to Keren, Nakfa, Agordat, Barentu and Teseney) leave from the second bus terminal (also known as Hamasien bus station).

For the east, buses leave hourly to Ghinda (Nfa4, two hours) via Nefasit (Nfa2, 30 to 45 mins), and to Massawa (Nfa9, 3½ to 4 hours). There are two buses a week to Assab (Nfa100, 3 to 5 days).

For the north, buses leave every half hour to Keren (Nfa8, 2½ hours). If you want to continue to Nakfa, you must change at Keren. One bus leaves daily to Agordat (Nfa13, six hours), Barentu (Nfa20, 6 to 7 hours) and Teseney (Nfa30, two days via Barentu).

For the south, buses leave every 15 minutes to Mendefera (Nfa5, 1½ hours), hourly to Adi Quala (Nfa7, 2½ hours), every 15 minutes to Dekemhare (Nfa3, 30 mins), every two hours to Segheneyti (Nfa5, 45 to 60 mins), every 1½ hours to Adi Keyh (Nfa9, 3 to 3½ hours) and hourly to Senafe (Nfa13, four hours).

GETTING AROUND

Central Asmara is so small that almost all places can be reached within 20 minutes on foot. Street names have changed at least three or four times in the last 20 years, so are not really used for giving directions. Most people go by local landmarks such as government buildings, hotels or bars.

To/From the Airport

A taxi from the town to the airport should cost around Nfa20–30 if you're alone, or Nfa10 each if there's a few of you, but you'll need to negotiate.

You can also take the city bus No 1, which passes in front of the cathedral on Liberation Ave. It costs 50¢; buses normally come every 20 to 25 minutes, but the service is erratic and you can wait up to 40 minutes.

From the airport, taxis may demand Nfa40 or more. Again, you'll need to negotiate. To catch the bus, bear left at the airport exit; the bus stop is a two-minute walk to the far end of the airport compound. The bus service runs from 6 am to 7.30 pm.

Bus

Red Mercedes buses serve all parts of the town. It costs 50¢ for journeys within town, and Nfa1 for journeys to the periphery and beyond. The No 1 bus, which runs along Liberation Ave and out to the airport, passing the Djibouti embassy and Sembel Huts complex, is probably the most useful for travellers.

Car & Motorcycle

With little traffic in town, parking is not a problem, and is allowed almost anywhere except on main thoroughfares such as Liberation Ave. If in doubt, ask a local. It's generally safe to leave your car parked.

Rental There are agencies that rent cars.

Ghidei International Travel Agency (☎ 12-38-38, fax 20-05-01) is one of the most competitive, with 4WDs for Nfa600 to Nfa700 per day (including driver)

Keckia Travel & Tourism Agency (☎ 12-04-83) also rents vehicles

Star Car Hire (☎ 12-68-49, fax 12-21-34) rents cars at good rates

ERITREA

Taxi

Taxis are used rather like buses. If you are on a main route, such as Liberation Ave, just flag one down. If there's space, it will stop, and you'll pay a shared price of Nfa1 per person.

If you hire the vehicle for yourself, or take it off the main routes, it costs Nfa10. There are no meters, so you should always agree the fare in advance. At night fares usually double. On Martyrs' Ave, taxis can be found 24 hours a day.

If you are planning on a few trips around town, or if you're out partying for the evening, you can hire a taxi for a few hours for a set rate of around Nfa50.

Garis are also plentiful, though few drivers speak much English; trips cost around Nfa50 depending on the length.

Around Asmara

FILFIL

The area around Filfil north of Asmara is home to Eritrea's last relic of tropical forest. It forms part of the Semenawi Bahri or 'Green Belt' area and, after the arid starkness of the surrounding landscape, rises up oasis-like before you: cool, lush and verdant. There are also plantations of coffee and fruit trees. The forest is evergreen, so it's good to visit any time of year, but it's particularly lush from October to February, after the heavy rains.

Filfil is one of the best places in Eritrea to see birds and mammals. Vervet monkeys and hamadryas baboons are easily seen, and gazelles, duikers, bushbucks, klipspringers and even leopards have been reported.

In December 1996, five tourists and their driver were killed by bandits on the Gahtielay to Filfil road. Though this incident was extremely atypical, you should check the current situation with your embassy before you set off.

Getting There & Away

Filfil lies 61km due north of Asmara, and the only way to reach it is along a rough dirt road. A 4WD (with driver to guide you ideally) is essential. The journey should take

around two hours (one way) from Asmara, and makes a great half-day trip. There are beautiful views along the way.

If you have more time, you could consider following the road south all the way down to the coastal plain, where it joins the road from Massawa to Asmara. The whole circuit takes around six hours (without a stop). The route is known as the Pendice Orientali, and takes you through some of the most dramatic and diverse landscape in Eritrea. It makes a great day excursion.

If your budget doesn't stretch to car hire, the only option is to take a bus to Keren – ask to be dropped off at the junction for Filfil, and try to hitch a lift with one of the trucks taking supplies to the village. There's very little traffic so it's a bit risky, but if you leave early enough you might be in luck.

DEBRE BIZEN MONASTERY

The monastery of Debre Bizen, near Nefasit, lies 2400m above sea level. It was founded in 1368 by Abuna Philippos. The library at the monastery contains over 1000 manuscripts as well as various church relics, including crowns, robes and incense burners. On a clear day, the view from the monastery is breathtaking – you can see the Dahlak Islands in the Red Sea. The birdlife is good in the woodlands around the monastery.

As with many Orthodox monasteries, Debre Bizen is not open to women (or any female creatures, including hens and she-donkeys!). However, even if you can't enter the monastery, the journey makes a great hike.

Men need to obtain a permit to visit the monastery (see Travel Permits in the Facts for the Visitor section) or they will be turned back. Bring lots of water (only rain-water is available). You will be welcomed with *sewa* (home-brewed beer) and bread when you arrive.

Men are welcome to stay at the simple monastery guesthouse (with just a bed or goatskin) for a couple of days. There's no charge but it's normal to make a contribution to the upkeep of the monastery. Simple gifts are a good idea too (sugar, coffee, candles etc).

Getting There & Away

To get to Debre Bizen, take the bus to Ghinda and get off at Nefasit (Nfa2, 30 to 45 mins). A taxi costs around Nfa175. From Nefasit, it's a 1½ to 2 hour steep walk. A local will show you the start of the path up to the monastery.

North of Asmara

With its combination of people, landscape and history, the north is one of the most rewarding – albeit demanding – travel destinations in Eritrea.

Easily accessible from Asmara is the attractive market town of Keren, long a crossroads for people of different religions, ethnic groups and languages.

Less accessible, in the remote and wild province of Sahel, is the remarkable town of Nakfa. The journey alone is a lesson in Eritrean history. During the Struggle for Independence, every inch of the road was fought over, and the carcasses of the tanks that line the road testify to the ferocity of the fighting. Few travellers ever get here, but Nakfa, like the site of a pilgrimage, is well worth the long, gruelling journey.

Though arid, eroded and bleak, the landscape of the north can be incredibly beautiful. Ancient baobab and acacia trees dot the plains, and at dusk, the Sahel mountains turn a kind of blue. Camels – making up sometimes-huge caravans – far outnumber vehicles. The patchwork tents of the Tigré nomads are everywhere visible, and around Keren, the beautiful Bilen women, adorned with large gold rings in their noses and henna tattoos on their necks and faces, can be seen squatting in the shade of acacia trees.

During the rains from July to September, the roads north can become impassable. Rivers rise quickly, leaving incredible debris on the roads. You should check road conditions before you set out.

KEREN

Set on a small plateau at 1220m above sea level, and surrounded by mountains, Keren is one of Eritrea's most attractive towns.

Trade thrived once Keren was connected to Asmara by the old Italian railway, and the little town grew. Today, it is the third-largest town in the country and is still an important centre of commerce.

Nevertheless Keren remains firmly small-town in flavour, and this is largely its attraction. Since Italian colonial days, the town has been a popular weekend retreat for the inhabitants of Asmara.

Controlling the northern gateway to Asmara, and the western route to Agordat, Keren's strategic position has always been very important. During World War II, it was the scene of bitter fighting between the Italians and the British. From the 1970s to the 1990s, it was fiercely contested during the Struggle for Independence.

On the roadside look out for the evergreen shrub known locally as *adaï* and used as a natural toothbrush (see the boxed text 'A Nomad's Toothbrush' in the Djibouti chapter).

Information

The centre of Keren is marked by the Giro Fiori (Circle of Flowers) roundabout.

A new tourist office (☎ 40-16-49) has opened not far from the Governor's Palace in the Ministry of Tourism building. It's open Monday to Friday from 7 am to noon and 2 to 6 pm. The staff can help you find guides to the town and suggest excursions out of town.

The Commercial Bank is open Monday to Friday from 8 to 11 am and from 2 to 5 pm, and on Saturday morning. Travellers cheques can be cashed here.

The post office is open Monday to Friday from 8 am to noon and from 2 to 6 pm, and on Saturday from 8 am to 12.30 pm.

The telecommunications office is open every day from 7 am to 1 pm and from 3 to 7 pm.

Things to See & Do

The scene of much fighting in the past, Keren is home to a number of graveyards. The **British War Cemetery** lies off the Agordat road north-west of town. In it, 440 Commonwealth troops lie buried, including the Hindu soldier Subadar Richpal Ram of the

Madonna of the Baobab

Close to Keren's market area there stands an ancient and gnarled baobab tree. Long venerated by the locals, it is believed to mark the spot from which fertility springs.

In the late nineteenth century, the Sisters of Charity built a small chapel in the tree, in the place where the city's orphans played, and it became known as St Maryam Dearit – the Madonna of the Baobab.

In 1941, some Italian soldiers took refuge in the tree from British planes. Though the tree was hit, it, the Italians and the shrine survived.

Today, according to local tradition, if a women desires a husband or a child, she must prepare coffee in the shade of the tree. If a traveller passes by and accepts a cup, her wish will be granted.

Sixth Rajputana Rifles, who was posthumously awarded the Victoria Cross, Britain's highest military decoration for bravery.

Just past the cemetery, a small **statue of the Madonna** watches over the road from Agordat in the west. The well-tended **Italian Cemetery** lies close by, and if you continue on foot a further 20 minutes, you come to the shrine of **St Maryam Dearit** (see the boxed text 'Madonna of the Baobab'), 2.3km out of town. On 29 May every year, there's a pilgrimage to the site, and hundreds of people congregate to dance and sing; if you're in the region at this time, don't miss it.

The old Italian **railway station** (now a bus station) and the old **residential area** testify to Keren's Italian heritage. As in Asmara, some of the architecture is exceptional for the period. Several Italian Roman Catholic churches dot the town, including **St Antonio** and **St Michael**.

Overlooking the town to the north-east is the **Tigu**, the Egyptian fort at 1460m, dating from the 19th century. At its foot lie the ruins of the old Imperial Palace, which were destroyed during the Struggle in 1977. There are good **views** from the top of the fort.

For information on Keren's markets, including the camel market, see Shopping later in this section.

Places to Stay

Bottom of the heap but not bad is the *Hotel Freselam*, which has basic rooms for Nfa10, and a proper if pongy communal shower and toilet.

The *Yohannes Hotel* has 22 clean and newish rooms for Nfa20/40/45 for singles/doubles/triples.

The best bet in town in the budget category is the old colonial *Albergo Sicilia* with a lovely, leafy courtyard. Clean singles with private bathroom cost Nfa50 (Nfa30 with shared bathroom). Doubles with sink cost Nfa36.

Just around the corner, the Muslim *Barka Hotel* is noisier, but has reasonable singles with shared bathroom for Nfa20 and doubles with private bathroom for Nfa40 (Nfa30 with shared bathroom). The veranda is a pleasant place for breakfast, and fruit juices are available.

One step up and with lots of character is the *Keren Hotel*, with fading but furnished singles/doubles with private bathroom for Nfa78/104 (Nfa60/80 with shared bathroom), plus tax. Some rooms are definitely better than others, so ask to see a few. It also has a great roof terrace with good views of the town, and an unusual 'observation tower'.

Places to Eat

The *Senhit Restaurant*, considered one of the best places in town, offers both Italian and local dishes. The *Eritrea Hotel* is popular among VSOs for its minestrone and macchiato.

The restaurant of the *Keren Hotel* is the smartest place to eat, and isn't bad if you can stomach the piped music. It does a good continental/English breakfast for Nfa9/12. On some Sundays, buffet lunches are laid on (Nfa26), and on Saturday nights, there's a lamb barbecue on the roof terrace (Nfa10).

The optimistically named *Peace & Love* restaurant is popular for its local fare; get there early (by 7.30 pm) or you may find most dishes have gone.

The *Latteria Semhar* near the Keren Hotel is good for a local breakfast, and has fruit juices. The *Addulis Pastry* is great for cakes, and also does mortadella sandwiches and yoghurt.

The **City Park**, with its flowers and garden, is a peaceful place for breakfast or a fruit juice. It's open from 7 am to 11 pm.

Entertainment

The verandas of the **Estifanos Bar** and the **Red Sea Hotel** are good places for a drink in the evening. Keren has its own cinema, the **Impero**, which shows films twice a day (at 5 and 7 pm) for Nfa1.50/2 depending on the seat.

Shopping

Keren's markets are some of the most interesting in the country, and are great for an afternoon's exploration. The covered area immediately behind the Keren Hotel sells fruit, vegetables, baskets and other household objects. Branching off the covered market are narrow alleyways, columns and low porticoes filled with the whirring machines of tailors and cloth merchants. Beyond, descending towards the Italian cemetery, lies the grain market.

In another quarter off the covered market, the workshops and boutiques of the silversmiths can be found. They're easy to track – follow the tapping and hammering ringing in the street. Keren is traditionally the place to buy silver. Although it's a little cheaper than in Asmara (Nfa3 to Nfa4 per gram), the choice may not be as good. The filigree jewellery is particularly recherche.

If you're in town on a Monday (between 9 am and 3 pm), don't miss the clamour of the camel market, 2km out of town on the road to Nakfa. It attracts people from all over the area. If you fancy buying a camel, they go for Nfa2500 to Nfa3000, but bargain hard.

Getting There & Away

Keren lies 91km north-west of Asmara on a good road.

For Nakfa, one bus leaves each morning at 5 am (Nfa17.75, eight to nine hours). To Asmara, nearly 50 buses depart daily (Nfa7.25, 2½ hours). For Massawa, change at Asmara. For Barentu, two buses leave

each morning (Nfa12.25, seven hours). For Teseney, two buses depart daily (Nfa22.75, 11 to 12 hours); for Agordat, three leave daily (Nfa6.50, 2½ hours).

Getting Around

If you're short of time, taxis are available. The main taxi stand is close to the Keren hotel. Most individual journeys cost between Nfa10 and Nfa20 (Nfa10 for the Italian cemetery; Nfa20 for Maryam Dearit), or you can hire a taxi for an hour (around Nfa50). For short hops within town, it's 50¢.

AROUND KEREN

There are a couple of monasteries around Keren, including the Debre Sina monastery, thought to date from the 6th century. The older, inner part of the church (which unlike many monasteries in Eritrea is open to both men and women) is hewn from the rock and, according to local tradition, is 2100 years old. The troglodyte dwellings of the 60 nuns and priests who live there can also be visited. The monastery lies around 35km east of Keren on the Gheleb road. You'll need a 4WD, then it's a 15-minute walk to the monastery. Without a vehicle, you could hitch to the approach, then walk from the main road.

AFABET

Afabet is best known for the battle which took place in and around the town, and which was the decisive confrontation of the entire thirty-year war (see the boxed text 'Victory at Afabet'). Around the town, you can still see the square-shaped trenches of the Ethiopian soldiers.

Although Afabet is the largest town north of Keren, it doesn't offer much to do, but if you're travelling north to Nakfa, you may get stuck here overnight. Afabet has a bank and a post office just off the main square.

Accommodation in Afabet is very basic – dirt floors, grill windows and no showers. The **Semhar Hotel** is the best of a sorry bunch. It has two twin-bedded rooms and two rooms with three and four beds, and costs Nfa6 per bed. The **Eritrea Hotel** has similar arrangements and prices. A new hotel will open soon on the outskirts of town.

Victory at Afabet

After over ten years of stalemate during the Eritrean Struggle for Independence, the morale of the conscripted Ethiopian troops was getting low. Realising this, the Eritrean People's Liberation Front (EPLF) took a gamble. On 17 March 1988 the guerrillas decided to abandon temporarily their effective hit-and-run tactics, and to hit the Ethiopian forces head-on at their strongest point – the strategic reserve at Afabet.

Within 48 hours, Afabet lay in ruins, three crack Ethiopian divisions had been wiped out, the largest ammunition depot in the whole country had been taken over, and 18,000 Ethiopian soldiers had been killed or captured.

At 1310 hours GMT on 21 March, British historian Basil Davidson described the battle on the BBC as 'one of the biggest (victories) ever scored by any liberation movement anywhere since Dien Bien Phu' (the famous battle that bought an end to the French colonial presence in Vietnam in 1954).

The **Selam Restaurant**, 200m from the mosque, is the favourite locally.

Buses going to Nakfa usually stop in Afabet; as do buses going south from Nakfa to Keren.

NAKFA

Lying some 221km from Asmara, at 1780m above sea level, Nakfa is little more than a tiny village perched high and remote in the mountains.

In 1978, after the famous 'Strategic Withdrawal', Nakfa became the EPLF's centre of resistance (see Eritrean Resistance in the Facts about Eritrea section). The town lies in a shallow dish at the edge of a mountain ridge that drops several thousand feet to the plain below. Facing south, the town guarded not only the headquarters of the EPLF, but also the essential trade and supply routes to Sudan. For this reason, Nakfa received some of the most intense and continuous assaults of the entire war.

At first sight, the corrugated-iron shacks of the village are hard to reconcile with the legendary Nakfa so venerated by Eritreans. However, Nakfa has become the symbol of the Eritrean resistance, and very recently even gave its name to the country's new currency.

With a little exploration, the town's extraordinary history soon shows itself. Nakfa is a fascinating place, even for those who are not normally military-minded. An incredible – and living – memorial to human endurance and courage, some of the sites may well make the hair on the back of your neck stand on end, or a lump form in your throat.

Few travellers get to Nakfa. Your interest in the town will really please the locals, who are among the friendliest and most hospitable people in the country.

Information

Presently, Nakfa resembles a large building site. New administrative buildings, a marketplace, housing, a hospital and a commercial area are all going up fast. Nakfa also has a fuel station.

Electricity shuts off in the whole town at 12.30 am; there are no telephones (radio contact only), and no running water except in the one big hotel. There is no public transport around Nakfa either. If you arrive by bus, you'll have to walk to those sites that can be reached on foot. It takes around two hours to get to the trenches on Mt Den Den.

Things to See

To get the most out of the place, you'll need at least half a day's touring with a good local guide. The local administration office can provide visitors with guides who are also ex-fighters. To tour a battlefield with one of the soldiers who fought on it is an extraordinary experience; but make sure the guide speaks adequate English – not all do.

Nakfa Mosque Flattened by the continual Ethiopian bombardments, the mosque was the only building left standing with more than two walls. The first sight of the building, standing tall and resolute amid the ruins, with a gaping hole blown in its cupola, is a memorable experience.

For many Eritreans, the mosque symbolised the unwavering faith of the fighters throughout the Struggle. The mosque is a beautiful sight at dawn or dusk; its maimed, very distinct profile has made it a favourite subject of Eritrean photographers and artists.

Den Den On the approach to Nakfa, look out for the distinct twin-peaked mountain known as Den Den. It was from here that the fighters broadcast news of the Struggle every day. The radio contact contributed – perhaps more than anything else – to maintaining the morale of the fighters, even when the odds against them looked hopeless.

You can climb up to the top of the mountain (around 1½ hours), from where the views are great. All around, the countryside is bare, denuded, not just by the continual aerial bombardments of the Ethiopians, but by demands for firewood and for the construction of the trenches. To the south-west, the plain is known as Furnello (furnace in Italian), because of the incessant bombing by Soviet-supplied MIGs.

Underground Towns Around the trenches, constructed underground, and carefully camouflaged from the Ethiopian planes, were a series of buildings: the famous underground towns. The functions of these buildings ranged from manufacturing weapons to printing literature (see the boxed text 'A Super Struggle' in the Facts about Eritrea section). At the time of research, many of these sites were closed because of lack of access. In future, the roads to them will be repaired and the sites will reopen.

The **Tsa'abraha Underground Hospital**, 12.5km from Nakfa on the road to Winna, can be visited. Between 1973 and 1991, at least 100 patients a day were treated in the hospital by five doctors working full time. The wounded were brought here by donkey, mule or camel, and important medical equipment was smuggled in from Sudan. The hospital was less sophisticated than the famous Orotta hospital, where even open-heart surgery was performed, but hundreds of lives were nevertheless saved here. Though little more than the dug-out foun-

> ## The Trenches
>
> The shoulder-deep trenches that run warren-like all over the southern ridges of the Den Den mountain give a vivid idea of the daily life of the fighters. Take a peek at the underground bunkers. In these tiny holes, measuring no more than 1m by 2m, five to six fighters ate, slept and carried on war for up to 18 months at a time without a break. The trenches are beautifully constructed, hewn into the stony ground and reinforced with neat, dry-stone walls. Stretching for over 25 miles, the trenches meander across the hillside in an apparently random manner. In fact, these irregular patterns made accurate targeting by Ethiopian long-range artillery almost impossible (see also the boxed text 'A Super Struggle' in the Facts about Eritrea section).
>
> Until quite recently, the trenches were littered with the bleached bones of soldiers from both sides. Most have now been buried. Shells of every type do still litter the landscape: rockets, mortar bombs, bullets, even napalm casings.
>
> To the north of the trenches, on a quiet and peaceful spot overlooking the hillside, lies Dig Dig, the fighters' cemetery. Graves are marked with simple painted metal plaques, with the fighter's name and date of death given in Tigrinya.

dations of two hospital buildings and a pharmacy remain, the site is still worth a visit. The 600m walk from the road to the hospital takes you through some beautiful woodland, teeming with birds.

Around 1.5km from the hospital lie the remains of some school buildings. The **Winna Technical College** was another installation dug into the mountainside. It will shortly be relocated to Nakfa. Today, students from all over the country compete for the 85 scholarship places available here.

Places to Stay & Eat

Barring one hotel, most accommodation in Nakfa is spartan – just dirt floors, corrugated-iron walls and no showers. It can get cold at night; if you haven't already got a *shamma* (a light cotton toga, worn by men) or a *gabi* (a slightly thicker version of the shamma), now might be the time to buy one.

The new **Nacfa Apollo Hotel** is the one exception, and offers 22 very comfortable rooms with double/twin beds with bathroom for Nfa77/110. With enough guests, an electrical generator is switched on and there's hot water between 7 and 11 pm. The rooms have balconies with beautiful views over the whole town.

The basic **Selam Hotel** on the street behind the mosque has four rooms containing three beds each at Nfa6 per bed. Though the accommodation is basic, the hospitality more than makes up for it.

Of the two restaurants currently operating, the **Den Den** is the best, offering basic but good local and Italian fare. If you want 'something exotic like chicken', it can be ordered in advance.

Getting There & Away

Though just 221km north of Asmara, the journey from the capital takes around 11½ hours. The road after Keren is very rough in parts and winds through the mountains. Add the heat to this equation and you'll be in for a long and tiring journey. One bus leaves each day for Keren at 6 am. You can change there for other destinations.

East of Asmara

The east of the country has two main attractions: the town of Massawa, Eritrea's largest port after Assab, and the nearby Dahlak Islands, which offer some of the best diving in the Red Sea.

Massawa is built on two coral islands rising from the Red Sea. It looks not west towards Asmara but east across the water towards Arabia. Massawa's ancient connections with the Arab world represent the other face of Eritrea's past. The town boasts some remarkable Islamic architecture but, like an old museum, the exhibits are spread out, covered in dust and gradually disintegrating. It is hoped that in the future funds will be found to restore these historical buildings.

The Dahlak Islands near Massawa give access to Eritrea's beautiful coral reefs. Though the dive-cruises around them are quite expensive, snorkelling is cheaper and easier to arrange, and is not to be missed. The islands are a very strange, unique environment, and a couple of days sailing around them or camping on their beaches makes for a memorable experience. Although it's hard to imagine a bleaker, more desolate landscape, they boast an enigmatic people and a surprising amount of life, including various wild animals and abundant birdlife. Some islands, such as Dahlak Kebir, also have an interesting and ancient history.

ASMARA TO MASSAWA

The journey from Asmara to Massawa is one of the most dramatic in Eritrea. In just 115km, the road descends nearly 2500m, plummeting through mountains often clad in mist, around hairpin bends and over old Italian bridges. Built by the Italians in 1935–36, the road was the most important in the country, linking the capital with the coast.

After leaving Asmara, the first village you come to is **Sheghrini**. Meaning roughly 'I've got a problem' in Tigrinya, these were supposedly the words uttered during the colonial era by an Italian whose car, like so many other vehicles, finally gave out at the top of the steep climb from Massawa.

Around 9km outside Asmara, the **Bar Durfo** and the **Seidici Restaurant** both make good places to stop, if you want to admire the views or take some photos.

Three kilometres further on from the Seidici is the little village of **Arborobu**. Its name means 'Wednesday-Friday' after its market days. The town is known for its *beles* (prickly pears) in season (mid-June to mid-September).

Around 25km east of Asmara lies the little town of **Nefasit**, the starting point for trips to the **Debre Bizen Monastery** (see Around Asmara earlier in this chapter). The monastery, perched high above the town, is just visible from the road.

From Nefasit, you can make a side trip to the **Maihabar Vocational Training Center &**

Center for the Disabled, which is 5km south of Nefasit on a good road. Founded in 1993 for victims of the war, it retrains ex-fighters in different vocations, including metalwork and woodwork, electronics and plumbing. This inspirational centre can be visited from 8 am to noon and 2 to 6 pm Monday to Friday. Sometimes the students' pottery is sold.

Back on the road to Massawa, **Ghinda** is 47km from Asmara and halfway to Massawa. It lies in a little valley that traps the warm, moist air from the coast. Rainfall is much higher than normal and its green, terraced hillsides supply the fruit and vegetable markets of Asmara and Massawa. The Jiberti, the Tigrinya Muslims, inhabit the area. Prohibited in the past from owning and cultivating land, they became instead great craftspeople, artists and scholars.

Dongollo and the springs of **Sabarguma**, 15km towards Massawa from Ghinda, are known as the sources of the Eritrean mineral water that bears their names.

Nearby, across the River Dongollo is the triple-arched **Italian bridge** with the inscription in Italian Piedmontese *Ca Custa Lon Ca Custa* (Whatever It Costs), said to be a reference to the Italian purchase of the Bay of Assab in the late 1860s.

MASSAWA

Though only about 100km to the west of Asmara, Massawa could not be more different from the capital. The history, climate, architecture and atmosphere of the town seem to come from another world. With its low, whitewashed buildings, porticoes and arcades, Massawa has a more Arab feel to it, reflecting its centuries-old connection with Arabia across the other side of the Red Sea.

Massawa's natural deep harbour and its position close to the mouth of the Red Sea and the Indian Ocean have long made it the target of foreign powers. It was occupied by the Portuguese, Arabs, Egyptians and Turks; finally, the British held it for a time before they all but handed it over to the Italians in 1885. Trade in Massawa flourished throughout these occupations – everything from slaves, pearls, giraffes and incense to ostriches and myrrh passed through the port.

Massawa's buildings reflect its history of occupation. The Ottoman Turks, who occupied the city for nearly 300 years, had the biggest influence on the architecture. Their

ERITREA

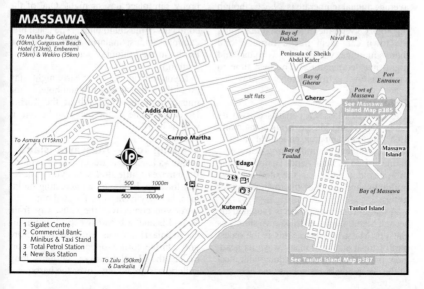

MASSAWA

To Malibu Pub Gelateria (10km), Gurgussum Beach Hotel (12km), Emberemi (15km) & Wekiro (35km)

To Asmara (115km)

Bay of Dakliat

Naval Base

Peninsula of Sheikh Abdel Kader

Bay of Gherar

salt flats

Gherar

Port Entrance

Port of Massawa

See Massawa Island Map p385

Addis Alem

Campo Martha

Edaga

Bay of Taulud

Massawa Island

Kutemia

Bay of Massawa

Taulud Island

0   500   1000m
0   500   1000yd

1 Sigalet Centre
2 Commercial Bank;
   Minibus & Taxi Stand
3 Total Petrol Station
4 New Bus Station

To Zulu (50km) & Dankalia

See Taulud Island Map p387

successors, the Egyptians, also left a legacy of buildings and public works, including the elevated causeways, an aqueduct and the governor's palace. In 1885 the Italians occupied Massawa, and the town became their capital until it was superseded by Asmara in 1897. During this time, many of the fabulous villas were built.

Once one of the most beautiful cities on the Red Sea, Massawa was all but flattened during the Struggle for Independence. Around 90% of the town was blitzed by Ethiopian blanket bombing, and great scars are still visible. Over the last decade, the town has been energetically reconstructed. Recently, a joint Unesco-Eritrean scheme has been drawn up to help preserve the town. In future, the height of buildings will be restricted to three storeys, further development will be controlled and the streets will be pedestrianised.

Although Massawa still far from merits its former accolade of 'Pearl of the Red Sea', it retains a very engaging, exotic character, which makes it an interesting place to explore. It's also hassle-free and pretty safe – no mean feat for a modern, international port. One major drawback is the heat. The average annual temperate is 29.5°C, though it often far exceeds that, sometimes reaching 46.5°C. With the high coastal humidity, the town can seem like a furnace, and there's marginal variation between day and night-time temperatures. The best time to visit Massawa is from October to May.

Orientation

The town of Massawa consists of two islands, Taulud and Massawa, and a mainland area. The mainland area, called Massawa, is largely residential, and a long causeway connects it to Taulud Island. Tualud is home to some old Italian villas, the administrative buildings, and a few of the town's smarter hotels.

A shorter causeway connects Taulud to the second island, Wushti Batsi, known simply as Batsi or Massawa Island. This is the oldest part of town and is in many ways its heart. Here the port can be found, along with most of the cheap hotels, restaurants and bars.

Information

Note that business hours in Massawa differ from those in the rest of the country. Government offices open from 6 am to 2.30 pm Monday to Friday from June to September and from 8 am to noon and 4 to 6.30 pm Monday to Friday from October to May. Private businesses open from 6 am to noon and 3 to 6 pm Monday to Friday the whole year.

The Commercial Bank on Massawa Island is open from 7 to 11.30 am and 4 to 5.30 pm Monday to Friday, 7 to 10.30 am on Saturday. It changes travellers cheques, as well as US dollars, British pounds and Deutschmarks (cash).

The post office on Massawa Island is open from 7 am to noon and 4 to 6 pm Monday to Friday, and Saturday morning. The telecommunications office is in the same building and is open from 6.30 am to 9.30 pm daily.

The Semhar Laundry on Massawa Island offers a six- to eight-hour service. It costs Nfa4/3/2 for trousers/T-shirts/socks. It's open 9 am to 1 pm and 4 to 10 pm Monday to Saturday.

Dangers & Annoyances Massawa is a pretty safe place day or night. One of the biggest problems is infected wounds (from coral cuts or mosquito bites). The usual precautions against malaria apply. (See also Health in the Ethiopia Facts for the Visitor section.)

If you're planning on an early night, stay away from the Massawa Island hotels – the music from the nightclub at the Torino Hotel and some of the bars can be felt as well as heard.

Walking Tour – Massawa Island

Massawa Island is a great place to explore. It's a maze of little streets, but you're never lost for long. It has some interesting buildings, but they have to be ferreted out.

As you come over the causeway from Taulud Island, a broad sweep of white, arcaded **palazzi** (palaces) stretches out before you. On the corner, opposite the transport office, the Hotel Savoiya, with its long gallery, has great views over the harbour.

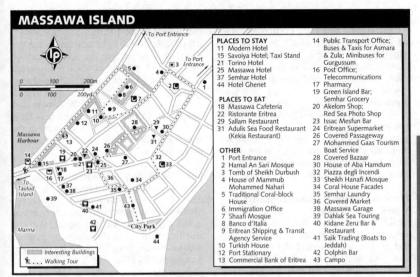

MASSAWA ISLAND

PLACES TO STAY
11 Modern Hotel
15 Savoiya Hotel; Taxi Stand
21 Torino Hotel
25 Massawa Hotel
37 Semhar Hotel
44 Hotel Ghenet

PLACES TO EAT
18 Massawa Cafeteria
22 Ristorante Eritrea
29 Sallam Restaurant
31 Adulis Sea Food Restaurant (Kekia Restaurant)

OTHER
1 Port Entrance
2 Hamal An Sari Mosque
3 Tomb of Sheikh Durbush
4 House of Mammub Mohammed Nahari
5 Traditional Coral-block House
6 Immigration Office
7 Shaafi Mosque
8 Banco d'Italia
9 Eritrean Shipping & Transit Agency Service
10 Turkish House
12 Port Stationary
13 Commercial Bank of Eritrea
14 Public Transport Office; Buses & Taxis for Asmara & Zula; Minibuses for Gurgussum
16 Post Office; Telecommunications
17 Pharmacy
19 Green Island Bar; Semhar Grocery
20 Akelom Shop; Red Sea Photo Shop
23 Issac Mesfun Bar
24 Eritrean Supermarket
26 Covered Passageway
27 Mohammed Gaas Tourism Boat Service
28 Covered Bazaar
30 House of Aba Hamdum
32 Piazza degli Incendi
33 Sheikh Hanafi Mosque
34 Coral House Facades
35 Semhar Laundry
36 Covered Market
38 Massawa Garage
39 Dahlak Sea Touring
40 Kidane Zeru Bar & Restaurant
41 Saik Trading (Boats to Jeddah)
42 Dolphin Bar
43 Campo

Interesting Buildings
.... Walking Tour

ERITREA

Keep left and head down the road along the harbour towards the port entrance. Near the port entrance is a good example of a traditional 17th-century **coral-block house**. For centuries, coral was the local building stone. Heading back towards the causeway, you'll pass the large **Banco d'Italia**, an exact copy of its 1920s original and a mishmash of architectural styles, including Gothic windows and towers. In a square beyond the Banco is a rare example of a **Turkish house** with a domed roof, now impressively restored. Turn back towards the port entrance, passing by the **Shaafi Mosque**. Founded in the 11th century but rebuilt several times since, it's worth a quick look.

If you keep heading towards the port, you'll come across the ancient house of **Mammub Mohammed Nahari** with soaring Ottoman-style windows on every side. Opposite the house is the 16th-century **tomb of Sheikh Durbush** enclosed in a small garden. Nothing is known about the sheikh. Around this area are some large and ornate 18th-century Armenian and Jewish **merchant houses**.

Turn right at the port entrance and head towards the southern tip of the island. On your right, about 150m from the port entrance, is the **house of Abu Hamdum**, with its magnificent *mashrabiyya* (trellised) balcony, which allowed cool breezes to enter and the air inside to circulate. It's a great example of Turkish Ottoman architecture, but awaits restoration. Continue on until you get to the Piazza degli Incendi (meaning 'Square of the Fire', after it was the scene of a great fire in 1885), in the centre of which is the **Sheikh Hanafi Mosque**. At over 500 years old, this mosque is one of the oldest surviving structures in the city. Sheikh Hanafi was a great teacher, who funded his students' studies in Egypt. The walls of the courtyard are decorated with stuccowork and inside hangs a remarkable chandelier from the glassworks of Murano near Venice in Italy.

Passing through the piazza, notice the small group of coral-block houses with finely detailed facades on your right. Then turn left into the remarkable **Campo**, a huge square lined on all sides by houses with trellised balconies and finely carved wooden doors and shutters of Turkish or Egyptian origin. Look out for the beautiful trilobate niches above the doors on the western side of the square.

To the north of the Campo is the **covered market**. Behind and to the north of the market lies the Massawa Hotel, bringing you into the main commercial artery of the town. Turn right towards the heart of the old town, which is reached though a covered passageway leading through unpaved streets lined with shops. Each of the shops is distinguished by individually carved mouldings and door hoods. At the end of the passageway lies the extraordinary old **covered bazaar**. Its ancient roof – in the Turkish style – is beamed like an upturned boat; it too awaits restoration.

Walking Tour – Taulud Island

A good way to start the walk is to have breakfast or lunch in the circular dining room of the **Dahlak Hotel** at the northern tip of the island, with its great views of the harbour. Just north of the gates of the Dahlak Hotel is the old **Imperial Palace** overlooking the harbour. The original palace was built by the Turkish Osdemir Pasha in the 16th century. The present building dates from 1872, when it was built for the Swiss adventurer Werner Munzinger. During the federation with Ethiopia, it was used as a winter palace by Emperor Haile Selassie, whose heraldic lions still decorate the gates. The palace also contained the first elevator in Eritrea. Look out for the beautifully carved wooden doors, said to come from India. The palace was badly damaged during the Struggle for Independence, and it may be converted into a regional museum. In its present state, it gives a very vivid idea of how all Massawa looked shortly after the war. It's usually possible to wander around the grounds.

Back on the causeway road, you'll see to your right the old Italian municipal buildings. Head south down the tree-lined road, past the Dahlak Hotel. Hotels and villas line the eastern shore. Some of the villas are exceptionally beautiful, combining elements of Art Deco style with traditional Moorish arcades and huge mashrabiyya balconies. After about 500m you'll find yourself at the Orthodox **St Mariam Cathedral**, which is at the end of the causeway from the mainland.

Opposite the cathedral is the massive **monument** to the Eritrean Struggle for Independence. Three huge tanks are preserved where they stopped in the final assault on the town in 1990, and now stand on a black marble base which is lovingly cleaned each morning.

South of the cathedral is the famous **Red Sea Hotel**, scene of many glamorous balls in the 1960s and 1970s. Devastated in the war, it has been rebuilt and is now the most luxurious hotel in Massawa.

At the southern tip of the island is the beautiful 1930s **Villa Melotti**, built by the owners of the Asmara brewery. There are plans to turn it into a state guesthouse. Much of its original furniture is preserved in the villa's huge vaulted rooms. With its stunning setting on the seafront, gardens and swimming pools, it has the decadent grandeur of a Fellini film set.

From the villa, take the road on the western side of Taulud and head north, passing by the causeway leading to the mainland. Look out for birds in the mud flats around the causeway. Pelicans are quite common visitors. Continuing north, you'll pass the original **railway station**, built during the fascist era, with its columns and elegant facade. It now functions as a medical clinic. There is access to the *sambuk* (dhow) **docks** just south of the train station, and it's worth taking a look at these beautiful traditional boats. There are always at least a couple around – the boats require a lot of maintenance (see the boxed text 'Indefatigable Dhows' later in this section).

Activities

Boat Trips Sometimes a private operator runs boat tours of the Bay of Massawa. Tours cost Nfa200 per hour per boat for one to four people – ask at the Dahlak Hotel.

Diving Massawa is the starting point for trips to the Dahlak Islands, Eritrea's main diving destination. Trips to the islands and equipment hire can be organised in Massawa. For full details on boat and equipment hire, see the Dahlak Islands section later in this chapter.

If you want to learn to dive, you can contact the Ministry of Marine Resources (☎ 55-20-10) on Taulud Island. Ask for the helpful English- and Spanish-speaking Dania Avallone, who can organise the usual PADI courses. Open-water courses (US$400) can usually be completed in three days. For those who just want a taste of Eritrea's underwater world, there's a 'Scuba Diving Introduction' for US$50 which runs over a half day.

Fishing If you want to go on a fishing trip, hire a boat and a captain and set off. A half-day's rental of a small boat in the Bay of Massawa costs Nfa500 for one to three people, including the boat captain.

Dahlak Sea Touring (☎/fax 55-24-89) on Massawa Island lends fishing rods free to clients who rent boats from them. You'll need your own hooks, but you can buy these in Massawa. The agency can also organise shark fishing.

For more information, see Fishing under Activities in the Facts for the Visitor section of this chapter.

Snorkelling Green Island (also known as Sheikh Saïd Island) is 10 to 20 minutes

from Massawa and is the most accessible place for decent snorkelling or good beaches (see Getting There & Away under Dahlak Islands later in this section). Equipment can be hired from Dahlak Sea Touring (see Fishing earlier in this section) on Massawa Island for Nfa50 per day (for mask, snorkel and fins). Eritrean Shipping Lines (☎ 55-26-29, fax 55-23-91) just beyond the Imperial Palace on Taulud Island rents masks and snorkels for Nfa28 per day, and fins for the same price.

Swimming In town, the beach off the Dahlak Hotel on Taulud Island is about the best bet. If you're not a guest, then it's polite at least to buy a drink or a snack on the premises.

On the mainland, the beach at the Gurgussum Beach Hotel is OK, though it suffers a bit from litter and algae due to tidal fluctuations. It can get crowded at weekends. The beach at the nearby Hamasien Hotel is a bit better.

Water-Skiing Water-skiing is possible through Dahlak Sea Touring (see Fishing earlier in this section) and costs Nfa400 per

ERITREA

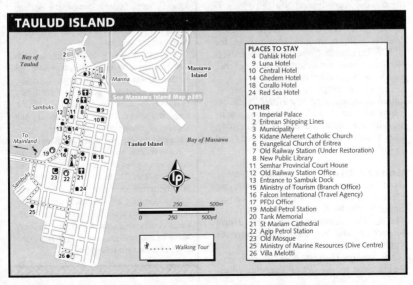

TAULUD ISLAND

Bay of Taulud

Massawa Island

Marina

See Massawa Island Map p385

Sambuks

To Mainland

Taulud Island

Bay of Massawa

Sambuks

0   250   500m
0   250   500yd

🚶 . . . . . . Walking Tour

PLACES TO STAY
4 Dahlak Hotel
9 Luna Hotel
10 Central Hotel
14 Ghedem Hotel
18 Corallo Hotel
24 Red Sea Hotel

OTHER
1 Imperial Palace
2 Eritrean Shipping Lines
3 Municipality
5 Kidane Meheret Catholic Church
6 Evangelical Church of Eritrea
7 Old Railway Station (Under Restoration)
8 New Public Library
11 Semhar Provincial Court House
12 Old Railway Station Office
13 Entrance to Sambuk Dock
15 Ministry of Tourism (Branch Office)
16 Falcon International (Travel Agency)
17 PFDJ Office
19 Mobil Petrol Station
20 Tank Memorial
21 St Mariam Cathedral
22 Agip Petrol Station
23 Old Mosque
25 Ministry of Marine Resources (Dive Centre)
26 Villa Melotti

hour, including all equipment and instruction for one to three people.

Places to Stay

Hotels on Massawa Island are cheap and in the thick of things, but noisy. Taulud is less central but much quieter. The mainland offers a couple of pricey hotels on the beach.

Taulud Island Bottom of the heap is the **Ghedem Hotel** (no telephone) with very basic but clean rooms (communal bathroom) for Nfa30.

The **Corallo Hotel** (☎ 55-24-06) is a very good place, with rooms to suit most budgets. Rooms without bathroom are Nfa44; with ceiling fan and bathroom Nfa66; and with air-conditioning Nfa132. It's a popular place with tour groups, and reservations are a good idea. The cheaper rooms are among the best value in town. Some rooms have balconies with sea views, and there's a good restaurant.

The **Luna Hotel** (☎ 55-22-72) is another good place. Rooms with bathroom are Nfa60 (Nfa130 with air-con).

The **Central Hotel** was closed at the time of writing for restoration, but should be good when it reopens. Rooms with bathroom and TV are around Nfa150.

The **Dahlak Hotel** (☎ 55-28-18, fax 55-27-82) has very comfortable singles/doubles with bathroom and air-con for US$26/35; payment is in US dollars only. It also has a good restaurant. At the weekend, reservations are essential.

Top of the range is the newly opened, Italian-designed, **Red Sea Hotel**. It has 50 rooms with satellite TV, and balcony. Facilities include disabled access, swimming pool, tennis court, private beach, jetty and motorboats.

Massawa Island The **Semhar Hotel** is about the cheapest option and is basic but adequate, with single/doubles with ceiling fan for Nfa20/40. A bed on the veranda costs Nfa10. The **Modern Hotel** and **Hotel Ghenet** are also not bad, with rooms for Nfa40.

The **Savoiya Hotel** (☎ 55-22-66) has simple but clean rooms around an untidy court-

Indefatigable Dhows

Since the 15th century, the ancient trading vessel, the dhow, has provided a link between Africa and Asia. Unmistakable on the sea for its single lateen (triangular) sail, the dhow is painted with multicoloured patterns, particularly around the castellated stern. Today, many dhows are also fitted with engines.

Three types of dhow are found in Eritrea and Djibouti – sizes range from the zaroug (the largest), to the zeima and the sambuk (the smallest). The boats are traditionally constucted without the aid of a plan, entirely from the expertise and memory of the master craftspeople who make them. Many Yemeni builders have inherited the art directly from the legendary builders of Mukallah. A sambuk costs from US$19,000 new, and takes around three months to build.

The vessel is lined with large planks of teak, impregnated with shark oil to prevent rot. A mixture of shark fat and lime is boiled together to make an extremely efficient, airtight filler, which still outperforms any modern equivalent. Weighing between 30 and 500 tonnes and measuring from 15m to 40m, the boats ply the waters between Eritrea, Djibouti, Sudan, Somalia, the Arabian Peninsula and the Gulf. The boats attain a maximum speed of only about 5 to 6 knots, even with a favourable wind.

The holds of the boats are crammed with every merchandise imaginable, from salt, cigarettes, animal hides and coffee, to dates, shark fins, electronic goods and dried fish. Even vehicles have been loaded – with the help of a lorry. Stories and rumours still abound of dhows filled with other cargo – smuggled goods, arms and even slaves.

Navigation is always without maps. Most sailors have plied the sea routes since their childhood days. The boat captains continue to fear the storms of the Red Sea – the dhows, though beautiful, are notoriously unstable. Pirates are said to scour the seas. During 1997, various boats were attacked off the coast near Assab by machine-gun-wielding pirates in the guise of fishermen selling fish.

yard for Nfa45 (Nfa60 with bathroom). A bed on its veranda costs Nfa15.

The *Massawa Hotel* is a good place despite the uninviting entrance. Rooms cost around Nfa50 for one or two people; beds on the veranda are Nfa15. The roof terrace has good views over the town.

The well-known *Torino Hotel* is very noisy. Rooms with shower cost Nfa150.

Mainland The *Gurgussum Beach Hotel* (☎ 55-29-11, fax 55-29-11) is 12km from Massawa on a moderate stretch of beach. Rooms for one or two people are Nfa240, suites are Nfa300 and pleasant 'family bungalows' (double bed, two twin beds, bathroom and living room) are Nfa420. Prices drop by Nfa60 in the low season (March to April and October to November). All rooms have air-con and satellite TV, and the suites and bungalows have fridges. Rooms are comfortable, if a little tired-looking.

The nearby *Hamasien Hotel* (☎ 55-27-25) has a better beach but rather run-down rooms with air-con for Nfa120 (Nfa144 with shower).

Places to Eat

Most restaurants, except the ones at the big hotels, are on Massawa Island.

Massawa Island One place not to be missed is the very simple but excellent *Sallam Restaurant*, owned by the genial Abubeker, who serves the Yemeni speciality of fresh fish sprinkled with hot pepper baked in a tandoori oven. The fish, served with a kind of *chapati* flat bread, is served in two sizes: medium (Nfa15) and big (Nfa20). Ask also for the *mokbusa*, the traditional accompaniment made with honey, butter and either dates or bananas (see the boxed text 'Poisson Yéménite' in the Djibouti town section of the Djibouti chapter). Beer (Nfa3) can be bought from the grocery opposite and drunk in the restaurant.

Ristorante Eritrea is considered to be the best place for Italian food in Massawa Island. It has a pleasant covered terrace, and offers a varied local and Italian menu,

including vegetarian dishes. The barbecued fish kebabs are delicious. Mains cost between Nfa15 and Nfa20.

For local food, the simple *Semhar Restaurant* at the Semhar Hotel is a favourite with Massawans, with mains around Nfa10. The menu is in Tigrinya, so you'll need to ask the waiter what's being served.

The *Adulis Sea Food Restaurant*, better known as 'Kekia Restaurant' after its owner, does great Yemeni and Middle-Eastern dishes, including the Yemeni baked fish dish and *bokhari* (meat and rice). Mains are around Nfa20. Despite the name, seafood needs to be ordered in advance. Alcohol is not served. It's open daily for lunch and dinner.

The *Massawa Cafeteria* opposite the post office has a great selection of fruit juices (Nfa2.50).

If you're preparing for a picnic, a camping trip to the islands or an expedition through Dankalia, the *Eritrean Supermarket* near the Massawa Hotel is the best stocked, and sells everything from dried noodles to chocolate and cereals. This is where most of the cruise captains come to stock up.

Taulud Island The big hotels have reasonable if somewhat bland food. The Dahlak Hotel has a good Saturday night buffet, and is a good place for breakfast – Corn Flakes/omelettes cost Nfa5/9. It's open from 7 am.

Mainland The *Gurgussum* has an imaginative menu, including curried dishes and unusual fish sauces. The *Malibu Pub Gelateria* near the Gurgussum is a great place to escape the heat. It's built like a traditional *tukul* (thatched roof hut) with an outdoor garden lit with lanterns. Mains cost around Nfa20–30; try the cool and delicious lemon sorbet or the vodka and orange. It's open from 10 am to 2 am.

Entertainment

There is a well-designed, open-air cinema at the *Sigalet Centre* (☎ 55-21-90) opposite the Total petrol station on the mainland, near the start of the causeway to Taulud Island. It shows slightly outdated Hollywood films in

ERITREA

English and sometimes Italian at 7 and 9 pm daily. The sound system is good, but the seats are a bit hard. Tickets cost between Nfa2 and Nfa7. Traditional or classical music concerts are sometimes staged. Check the notice board outside the Semhar grocery next door to the Green Island Bar in Batsi on Massawa Island for forthcoming programs.

There are plenty of lively but rather seedy little bars on Massawa Island, such as the *Green Island Bar* and the *Issac Mesfun Bar*; they close around 2.30 am. Single male travellers will soon find they have plenty of local female company.

A more peaceful place is the *Kidane Zeru* on Massawa Island. With its large terrace, it's great for an evening drink, and it also serves good food. The *Dolphin Bar* diagonally opposite is a lively outdoor venue, with a dance floor overlooking the harbour, and attracts a younger crowd.

On the mainland, the *Gurgussum Beach Hotel* has a nightclub. On Massawa island, the nightclub in the *Torino Hotel* (☎ 55-28-55) is a long-time favourite. It has a pleasant roof terrace as well as a dancing area inside with the obligatory sparkling silver ball, and it's fun and relaxed. It's open every day from 10 pm to 3am; entrance costs Nfa20 on the weekend, Nfa10 during the week.

Shopping
For diving and snorkelling equipment, the shop at the Gurgussum Beach Hotel on the mainland has the best selection, though it's not the cheapest. On Massawa Island, one of the best shops is Akelom near the Torino Hotel, which sells fishing gear (including spoons, hooks and weights), snorkelling gear (masks cost between Nfa45 and Nfa140), mosquito nets (by the metre), sun cream, and swimming and beach gear. It's open until 10 pm. The Red Sea Photo shop is the best place for film. There's not much in the way of souvenirs in Massawa, except for shells, which are best avoided.

Getting There & Away
Air A new international airport is currently being built and should open soon. If you need to reserve or reconfirm air tickets, go to Falcon International (☎/fax 55-21-08) on Taulud Island, opposite the Ministry of Tourism office.

Bus Buses leave for Asmara (Nfa9, 3½ to four hours) every hour from around 4 am to 3 pm. For Assab, you will have to go to Asmara and catch the bus there, as the buses pass through Massawa but don't stop. For Zula (to visit Adulis) in the south, two buses leave daily, at 6 am and 2 pm (Nfa6, 3½ to four hours). Buses leave from in front of the Public Transport Office on Massawa Island.

Car & Taxi The road to Massawa is sealed and in good condition. A normal car or taxi can make the journey in around three hours.

Taxis between Massawa and Asmara cost Nfa300. There's a taxi stand outside the Public Transport Office on Massawa Island.

Train The old Italian train linking Massawa to Asmara was being repaired at the time of writing; check with travel agencies in Asmara. (See also the boxed text 'The Old Railway' earlier in this section.)

Boat Cargo boats leave from Massawa to Assab every five to 14 days. The journey takes 18 to 48 hours depending on the boat. Passage is free, but you should bring food, water and a blanket for sleeping on the deck. Ask at the Eritrean Shipping & Transit Agency Services (Erstas) office near the port on Massawa Island.

Getting Around
Taxi Share-taxis for short hops around town cost Nfa1; if you take a taxi by yourself it costs Nfa10. You'll need to negotiate to get these fares. To the Gurgussum Beach Hotel it costs Nfa30. An unofficial taxi stand can be found outside the Savoiya Hotel on Massawa Island.

Bus The city buses cost 50¢, and bus stops are clearly marked around town. Buses only go to Gurgussum (Nfa1.50) on Sundays.

Minibus The town minibuses (with 'Taxi' written on the front) are plentiful, fast and efficient. They can be flagged down anywhere, and are great for hopping between the islands and to Gurgussum (Nfa5). Short journeys around town cost 60¢.

Bicycle The Dahlak Hotel has around 10 bikes for hire (Nfa10/30 for one hour/all day), though more often than not they're out of order.

AROUND MASSAWA

North of Massawa, stretching along the sandy coast into Sudan, lies the traditional territory of the enigmatic Rashaida people (for a description of the Rashaida, see the boxed text 'A Museum of People' in the Facts about Eritrea section). Around 4km out of Gurgussum, a track branches right off the Massawa road. A few Rashaida camps are visible between the villages of Emberemi and Wekiro.

You'll need a 4WD and, if you want to visit the Rashaida, a local guide who speaks Arabic. It's essential to show respect towards the people and not attempt to take any photos until you have clear permission. It's a good idea to bring some simple gifts, such as tea and sugar. You may well be expected to buy something, such as the traditional silver jewellery, and it's normal to haggle over the prices.

DAHLAK ISLANDS

Some 350 islands lie off the Eritrean coast, the majority – 209 – of which make up the Dahlak Archipelago. Largely arid, barren and flat, the islands have a maximum altitude of 15m. Fresh water is very scarce, and very few of the islands are inhabited (only three within the Dahlak Archipelago). At the time of writing, 21 islands could be visited, but more are opening all the time. The nine islands most popularly visited are Green Island (near Massawa), Dahlak Kebir (the largest island), Dissei, Madote, Seil, Dur Ghella, Dur Gaam, Dohul, Harat and Enteara. Note that these islands are not the tropical paradises you may be hoping for!

You need a permit to visit any of the Dahlak Islands, except Green Island. The permit costs US$30 for the first three days, then US$10 for each day on top of this. The

fee has to be paid in US dollars only (cash or travellers cheques). If you have to organise it yourself, go to the Eritrean Shipping Lines office (☎ 55-26-29, fax 55-23-91) just beyond the Imperial Palace on Massawa Island. It keeps normal government office hours, and is open until noon on Saturday. You need to fill out a form and pay the fee. The papers are then taken to the Ministry of Tourism on Taulud Island. The whole process takes between 30 and 60 minutes. If you're joining a tour or hiring a boat, the permit should be organised for you.

Dahlak Kebir

This is the largest island (over 650 sq km) in the archipelago, with nine villages and a population of 2300. The island has been inhabited for at least 2000 years and is known for its archaeological ruins. It may be declared a Unesco World Heritage Site in the future. The islanders speak their own dialect, guard their own customs and traditions, and seem to use the same centuries-old building techniques that their ancestors employed before them. Most islanders live from the sea, either fishing in village cooperatives or collecting sea cucumbers and shark fins for the Middle East, India, the Philippines and China.

The only hotel in the archipelago is on this island, and in early 2000, the controversial construction of a joint US-Saudi **casino** and huge tourist complex began. It will have facilities for diving, water sports and golf.

There's a post office on the island not far from Luul Hotel, and a wonderful old wind-up Italian telephone, which even does for international calls (via Asmara).

On the southern coast of the island, 300m south-east of the village of Dahlak Kebir, lie some of Eritrea's most ancient relics, including 360 or so **underground cisterns**, cut from the madreporic (coral) limestone. According to local tradition, there was a different well for every day of the year. The cisterns catch rainwater and are the main source of water for the islanders, though the water from some is not drinkable now. Water was the reason for the island's importance in the past: for centuries, with fresh water limited in Massawa, passing ships were obliged to call on the island.

Around 50m south-west of the cisterns lies a huge and ancient necropolis, with literally thousands of **tombs** marked by small, upright basalt stones, beautifully inscribed with Kufic (ancient Arabic) script. The tombs are thought to date from at least AD 912 to the 15th century. James Bruce, an 18th-century Scottish traveller and explorer, described the site as 'one of the wonders of the ancient world'. Look out for the incredible fossils scattered everywhere. Needless to say, nothing should be removed from the site.

Adel is a fascinating and totally unexcavated site near the village of Selawit, around 30km north of Dahlak Kebir village, on the journey back to the Luul Hotel. Even less is known about the mysterious ruined buildings, but the site may be even older than Dahlak Kebir, possibly dating from pre-Islamic times. There is also a necropolis with uninscribed tombstones. The buildings are beautifully constructed, with very straight, thick walls, arches and some columns.

Currently the only way of getting to the sites is by hiring a car from the only hotel on the island, the Luul Hotel. From the hotel, it's a 44km journey (around 1½ to two hours) to the village of Dahlak Kebir, along a bumpy road. Keep an eye out for gazelles on the way (several hundred are said to inhabit the island); it's also a good place to see raptors (birds of prey). It's polite to stop at the village (before or after a visit to the ruins), where you'll be offered tea and biscuits. You should leave a tip. Though not expected, any income is much appreciated – life is tough here for the islanders.

If you want to go on a fishing trip on a traditional sambuk, this can usually be arranged through the Luul Hotel. Ask for the charming and helpful manager, Tselalu Azzene.

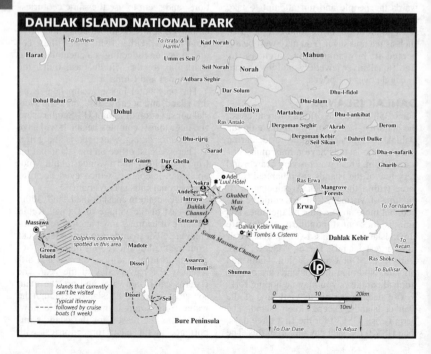

DAHLAK ISLAND NATIONAL PARK

Nokra

The island of Nokra was the site of a once notoriously harsh Italian penitentiary, as well as a large Russian military base. The island is currently off-limits, but may well open in the future. It's an interesting site; if you're particularly keen to visit it, ask at the Eritrean Shipping Lines office in Massawa.

Diving

One of the very few positive effects of the Struggle for Independence is that Eritrea's reefs have been allowed to flourish. During the war, the fishing industry ground almost to a halt. The reefs were also spared pollution from industry and marine traffic, and the invasions of tour boats and divers. As a result, the fish population has grown to an incredibly dense level, and the reefs may well become home to one of the last pristine subaquatic coral environments in the Red Sea. The variety of wreck diving around the Dahlak Islands is also good, ranging from well-preserved Ethiopian cargo boats and WWII Italian warships to rusting Russian tanks. At least 67 wrecks are known to lie off the islands, and the true figure is probably three times this. Currently, only a few are 'open' to divers; more will become accessible in the future.

To really appreciate the reefs, you need to bear a few things in mind. Lying on a shallow continental shelf, there are no vertical drop-offs or 'deep blues' around the Dahlak Islands and the coral growth is not as profuse here as in the northern Red Sea. During the summer, the water temperatures on the plateau rise to the upper limit of coral tolerance. Dense algae, plankton spore and sediment are also thought to inhibit growth. Most coral is found as fringing 'patch' reefs, ranging from the surface to around 15 to 18m. At greater depths, coral colonies tend to drop off. Although the abundant plankton does attract pelagic species such as manta ray and whale shark, these species, along with other 'crowd-pullers' such as dugongs, tiger sharks and hammerhead sharks, are only very occasionally seen.

The biggest cause of disappointment – particularly for underwater photographers – is visibility, which is notoriously erratic. The clarity of the water depends on the influx of cooler waters and plankton and nutrients from the Indian Ocean. Visibility frequently drops to 10m to 13m, or even less. The best time for water visibility seems to be during the summer months (end of June to end of August), when temperatures outside touch 45°C. At this time, the sea can seem like a bath – surface temperatures of up to 36°C have been reported. Many cruise boats are not, or not adequately, air-conditioned, and sleeping on deck is the only option.

All divers must be certified (you will be asked for evidence), and each dive must be accompanied by a local divemaster.

See also the special section 'Marine Life in the Red Sea'.

Equipment Hire You can hire diving equipment from several places in Massawa. Dahlak Sea Touring rents equipment to its clients for Nfa200 per day. Eritrean Shipping Lines charges Nfa216 for equipment per dive per person (for air cylinder, weight belt and divemaster). A BCD and regulator cost an additional Nfa83 each per day; mask and snorkel cost Nfa28. Extra air cylinders cost Nfa110. Rental is also possible by the week.

The Dive Centre at the Ministry of Marine Resources rents out equipment for Nfa60 for a BCD and regulator, Nfa75 for each air cylinder and Nfa30 for mask and snorkel.

Organised Tours

Cruises around the islands, usually lasting a week, can be organised through Travel House International in Asmara (see Travel Agencies in the Asmara section for contact details). Boats range from beautiful, but correspondingly pricey, twin-masted, 30m-long Turkish caiques with private cabins and

Decompression Facilities

Note that there is no decompression chamber in Eritrea, though it's hoped that one will be installed at the Massawa hospital soon.

Major Dive Sites of the Dahlak Islands

	Characteristics	Highlights
Dur Gaam	Small island populated with some acacias and conifers; ruined Italian gun installations; camping possible	Good coral and fish species, very occasionally manta rays; blue-spotted rays quite common; crown-of-thorns starfish
Madote	Not officially part of Dahlak Archipelago; good beaches and birdlife; one of best islands for camping	Good coral and fish species including angelfish, parrotfish, surgeons and cardinals
Dahlak Kebir	Largest island, known for its archaeological ruins	Hammerhead sharks; wrecks in bay including Ethiopian cargo ship and three Russian tanks; British and Italian warships should 'open' soon; large batfish
Dahlak Channel	Channel is fault crack 50–150m deep	No coral, just fish species; also manta ray and pelagic species including various types of shark
Dissei	Not officially part of Dahlak Archipelago; most attractive of the islands, with vegetation, hills and good beaches; one of best islands for camping (fresh water available)	Good variety of hard and soft corals; profuse fish life; schools of jack and rays occasionally seen
Dohul	Two villages on island; ruins of seven Italian gun placements; seagrasses found	Dugongs seen very occasionally; good coral in southern area
Harat	Several islets off northern tip; ruined village; mangroves and doum palms found; fresh water available	Quite good hard coral species including Favites, Goniopora and Porites
Enteara	Near Dahlak Kebir; island is completely devoid of vegetation; unsuitable for camping	Many lined and spotted snapper
Green Island	Lies just off Taulud island, 10 minutes by boat; consists of beach and mangrove swamp	Quite good coral and fish species including wrasse, butterfly and parrotfish; blue- spotted ray
Dur Ghella	Close to Dur Gaam; shallow reef ranging from around 1m to 10m	Abundant and diverse fish species; many large bumphead parrotfish; spotted sweetlips, Arabian angelfish

Comments

Currents around western side attract some sharks; shallow reef; good for snorkelling and diving

Good snorkelling and diving to east and west of island

Look out for the giant groper inhabiting the Ras Degan wreck

Excellent drift diving; August is best month for mantas

Better for diving than snorkelling; reef is slightly deeper than other areas (20m); particularly good diving off northern tip; visibility can be very poor

Dugong sightings increasingly rare, but still the best place to see them

Good for snorkelling

Shallow diving (around 10m); good for snorkelling

The most accessible island, the cheapest to get to and good for snorkelling

Soft corals are generally found in north, hard corals in south (to 10m); good for snorkelling and diving; waves and wind can limit access

bathrooms to converted sambuks. Chefs, divemasters and crew are provided, as well as air cylinders (boats have their own compressors). Some also have diving and fishing equipment for rental.

Six-day cruises (minimum of six people) cost from US$190/280 for a single/double cabin with bathroom. Weekend cruises (1½ days) cost US$260/400 for single/double cabins. Day trips cost US$60 per person (minimum 12 people) including lunch on board. Prices include full board but not drinks or equipment hire.

Places to Stay

It's possible to *camp* on some of the islands, including Dissei, Madote, Dur Gaam and Dahlak Kebir. Some boat operators rent full camping equipment; fresh water for showering is included in the price. Dissei (the east or north of the island) and Madote are probably the best for camping.

The Eritrean Shipping Lines owns the only hotel on the islands, the *Luul Hotel* (no telephone) on Dahlak Kebir. It costs Nfa165/297/347 for one/two/three people in a small, pleasant bungalow and Nfa297/495/594 for a suite. Breakfast costs Nfa24, lunch or dinner (two courses) Nfa55. You can also use the kitchen for a small fee (all provisions must be brought from the mainland). Camping in the hotel grounds costs Nfa66/88 per day for one/two people. Prices include all tax, but must be paid in cash in US dollars.

Snorkelling gear can be hired (Nfa28 for mask and snorkel) from Luul Hotel. Prices go up by a few nakfa during the high season (June to September).

Getting There & Away

Unless you've got your own boat, you'll need to hire one. The journey from Massawa to most of the islands takes between 1½ and two hours by motorboat.

Boats can be hired for picnic excursions, fishing, snorkelling or diving trips to the islands. It's worth shopping around, as prices vary from company to company and also depend on the season (low season is from October to February). If you come in low

ERITREA

season, you should be able to get a good discount. Boat operators advise reservations one week to 10 days in advance. However, if you just turn up, something can almost always be organised within 24 hours. If a boat is available, it takes about an hour to get it ready. The services of a boat captain are always included in the price. You may be offered cheaper deals for sambuks; check they look reasonably seaworthy (some are very rickety) and are carrying sufficient life jackets and supplies of water. Most are infested with mice and cockroaches.

No boats are currently fitted with compressors. A maximum of 10 air cylinders can be carried at one time.

Eritrean Shipping Lines (☎ 55-26-29, fax 55-23-91) on Taulud Island in Massawa can organise transport to the Luul Hotel on Dahlak Kebir. A round trip costs Nfa1980 (Nfa1500 in the low season, from October to May). It also has three motorboats for hire, and can supply tour guides and divemasters. Excursions to Green Island cost Nfa180 per person for up to four people. If there are more than four people, it's Nfa45 per person. For trips to the other islands, it costs between Nfa1452 and Nfa2244 for one to five people, depending on the distance. In the low season, prices are about 10% cheaper. Mattresses, gas stove and cooking equipment are included with the price of the boats.

Dahlak Sea Touring (☎/fax 55-24-89) on Massawa Island, run by the efficient Buzuamlak Gebre Selassie who is better known as 'Maik', also has various boats to hire. A trip to Green Island costs Nfa200 for one to three people. Boats for one to five people to all the other islands cost Nfa1700, except to Dohul and Harat (Nfa2000) and Dahlak Kebir (Nfa2500). Bigger boats (for up to 10 people) can also be organised. Maik also has tents, mattresses, ice boxes, gas stoves, cutlery and dishes for hire. The office is open from 7 am to 6 pm every day.

Mohammed Gaas Tourism Boat Service (☎ 55-26-67) on Massawa Island can supply bigger boats (traditional sambuks) for up to 20 people for Nfa2000 per day, including a cook, but facilities are basic: just

mattresses to sleep on below deck and a toilet and stove.

A new boat owner on the scene is Robel Asfaha (☎ 18-19-07, fax 18-20-33).

Various travel agencies, including the Eritrean Tour Service (see Travel Agencies in the Asmara section), offer weekend (two-day) tours to the islands which cost US$170, including all transport, one night's accommodation on Dahlak Kebir and food.

Getting Around

Boats can be hired from the Luul Hotel for trips to the surrounding islands and cost between Nfa528 and Nfa2244 (depending on the distance) for round trips with up to two hours spent on the island. Additional hours are charged at Nfa100 per hour.

A couple of village cars can usually be hired on Dahlak Kebir Island for Nfa400 to Nfa600 per day, including driver, petrol and mileage. The villagers have a monopoly so they can ask what they like but you can try bargaining. You'll need to give two to three days' notice to organise a car.

West of Asmara

Must-see tourist attractions are few and far between in the west. It's hot, dusty and hard-going on the roads, and facilities for travellers are basic.

However, the fact that the region sees so few travellers is a major part of its attraction. Some of the ethnic groups inhabiting the west – such as the Kunama – are among the more enigmatic and 'untouched' in Eritrea (see the special section 'A Museum of Peoples' in the Facts about Eritrea section).

The towns of the west are all easily accessible by bus. Many have an interesting character, and some seem to have more in common with Muslim Sudan than the neighbouring highlands of Eritrea. In climate, geography, religion, industry, people and way of life, the Muslim lowlands could not be more different from the Christian highlands.

Undisturbed by people or traffic, wildlife is abundant, and includes several Eritrean-Ethiopian endemics. Gash-Setit province boasts more wildlife than any other province in Eritrea. Near the town of Antore roam Eritrea's last remaining elephants.

With your own 4WD, the west is a great place to explore. However, the roads are very rough in places, and during the rainy season, can become impassable. Fuel is easily obtained in the big towns, but extra jerry cans of fuel are useful for exploring remoter areas.

During the Struggle, many towns in the west witnessed some bloody fighting. The relics of war are everywhere visible: tank carcasses, blown-up bridges, rubble and bullet holes. Along these roads too, thousands of Ethiopian soldiers tragically perished, fleeing in panic to Sudan at the end of the war. Most just collapsed on the roadside from thirst, hunger or exhaustion.

Like all Muslim peoples, western Eritreans honour the Islamic tradition of hospitality: they are friendly, and genuinely pleased to see the few visitors who come their way.

AGORDAT

Lying 160km west of Asmara, Agordat is the capital of Barka province, with a population of 14,000.

The Commercial Bank is open from 8 am to noon and 4 to 5.30 pm Monday to Friday, and 8 to 11.30 am on Saturday. Travellers cheques can be cashed.

The post office is near the old Italian railway station. It's open from 8 am to 2 pm Monday to Saturday. The telecom building, near the police station, is open from 7 am to 6 pm every day.

Like most towns in the west, Agordat has an overwhelmingly Arab feel to it – even the colonial governor's **palace** is Moorish-inspired. Other major Muslim landmarks include the **mosque** – the second-largest in Eritrea – and the bustling **marketplace**, one of the most important in the lowlands.

Places to Stay

Rock-bottom is the **Lem Lem**, which has beds in male and female dorms for Nfa5. The **Agordat Hotel** has clean rooms with ceiling fan for between Nfa18 and 25; a bed outside costs Nfa6.

Travelling on a Budget

Around the towns of Agordat, Teseney and Barentu, a new ethnic group has made its home. The people known as the *Tacaruri* (Black Ones) are believed to originate from Nigeria.

According to local tradition a group of tacaruri set off from Kano in Nigeria 100 years ago on a long and difficult pilgrimage to Mecca. But on their return journey, funds ran short, and they were obliged to finish their journey where they stood: in the Eritrean lowlands.

To this day, the tacaruri speak their own Nigerian dialect and earn their livlihood by fishing in the rivers and catching and skinning crocodiles.

The **BG Sellassie Pension**, better known as 'Belamberas', is quite a pleasant, clean place situated near the Commercial Bank. It has triple rooms for Nfa60, a proper shower and an attractive garden patio. Almas, the owner, is friendly and speaks good English.

A step up is the upmarket **Alwaha**, which has clean, more modern twin-bedded rooms for Nfa40, Nfa50 (upstairs and quieter) and Nfa80 (with private shower and toilet).

Places to Eat

Very popular locally is the **M'sika Restaurant**, close to the Photo Barka, run by the indefatigable G'dai, whose *zigni* (peppery stew with beef or lamb) is well known. Get there early, as there's always a rush and the food goes quickly. It's open all day and both beer and fruit juices are available.

The **Ambaswera Restaurant** is popular for *sheia* (lamb drizzled with oil and flavoured with herbs, then barbecued).

The large, colonial **Barka Hotel & Restaurant** is noisy to sleep in, but it's a good place for a drink, with views over the town. It serves beer and spirits, as well as a good selection of fruit juices. There's also a billiards table. If you're very lucky, you might be in town for the big fortnightly disco (Nfa10).

Getting There & Away

Buses leave from the main square, close to the ticket office. Two buses depart early each morning for Asmara (Nfa13.75, four to five hours); six to eight buses travel daily to Keren between 6 am to 4 pm (Nfa6.50, nearly two hours); one bus leaves daily for Ghirmayka on the Sudanese border (Nfa17, five hours); one bus goes to Barentu (Nfa5.75, three hours). For Teseney, you should go to Barentu and change.

If you have your own vehicle, you must be off the roads outside the town by 6 pm.

BARENTU

Lying 65km south-west of Agordat, Barentu has a population of around 8000. It is the heartland of the Kunama people, one of the most fascinating of Eritrea's ethnic groups (see the boxed text 'Museum of People' in the Facts about Eritrea section).

Barentu serves three main purposes: it is a small market town for the local Kunama, it is the site of a military camp (at the top of the hill it sits on), and it provides a stopover for buses on their way to and from the west; many local travellers stay overnight here. Though it offers little to do, Barentu is a very peaceful, laid-back sort of place.

The Commercial Bank is open from 7 to 11.30 am and 4 to 5.30 pm Monday to Friday, and from 7 to 10.30 am Saturday. It doesn't accept travellers cheques but it does accept cash in the major currencies.

The post office is open from 7 am to 2.30 pm Monday to Saturday, and 7 am to 2 pm Saturday. The telecom office, found in the same building, is open from 8 am to 6 pm daily. Electricity runs from 8 am to noon and 4 pm to midnight. Thursday is the main market day in Barentu, but Saturday is also good; both days are busiest around lunchtime.

Places to Stay & Eat

A good, cheap bet is the *Selam Hotel*, which is peaceful and clean; a double costs Nfa20, a bed in the courtyard costs Nfa6.

A little noisier but long considered one of the best hotels is the *Asmara Hotel* with six clean double rooms for Nfa28. It has a bucket shower. A bed on the veranda with a mosquito net costs Nfa6. The hotel has a pleasant terrace overlooking the town, and is a popular place among aid workers.

Lacking the location, but quieter, is the excellent *Hotel Lalmba* with seven spotless double rooms (Nfa20) set around a pleasant leafy courtyard. It's one of the few hotels with a proper shower. The restaurant is good.

The *Sahel Latteria*, not far from the Selam Hotel on the main road, has a pleasant terrace and serves good Eritrean fare. The *Matlel Latteria* is good for breakfast and fruit juices.

The *Diana Restaurant* offers decent local and Italian dishes and is popular with NGOs, though one traveller claimed to have suffered ill effects after eating there. At the *Adal Hotel*, you should ask for the Sudanese dish *sheia*.

Getting There & Away

The bus station is in the main square. For Mendefera (Nfa16), there's just one bus a week direct. If you miss it you can hop between towns: first go to Shambiko (Nfa8, 3½ hours, two daily) and then take a minibus to Molki (Nfa8, 3½ hours) and another from Molki to Mendefera (Nfa8, four hours).

For Asmara, two buses leave daily between 6 and 8.30 am (Nfa19.50, eight to nine hours). Two buses go daily to Keren (Nfa12.25, six hours). To Teseney, five or six buses leave daily (Nfa10.50, five to six hours). For Agordat (Nfa5.75, three hours), take the bus to Keren or Asmara. To get to Sittona, south of Barentu, you must go first go to Tokombiya (Nfa6.50, three hours).

If you have your own vehicle, the night curfew comes into effect here too: be off the road by 6 pm.

TESENEY

Situated 119km west of Barentu, and just 45km from the Sudanese border, Teseney is a large frontier town with a population of some 30,000 people.

At first sight the town seems like a large, sprawling, rubble-strewn conglomeration devoid of trees, beautiful architecture or anything of interest. But Teseney has an intriguing character and is unlike any other town in Eritrea.

A crossroads between two countries, the town has long been a meeting place, trading station and smuggling post for various ethnic groups – Sudanese as well as Eritrean.

During the war, the town was hotly contested – lost and won again and again by the Eritrean fighters. It was liberated finally in 1988, but not before it had suffered serious damage. Gradually the town is rebuilding itself, and new hotels and restaurants are springing up to cater to the large numbers of itinerant merchants and travellers.

Information
The Commercial Bank is open Monday to Saturday from 7 to 11.30 am and 4 to 5.30 pm (Saturday to 10.30 am only). Travellers cheques can be changed, as can cash.

The post office, near the Nacfa Hotel, is open Monday to Friday from 7.30 am to noon and from 1 to 4 pm. On Saturday it opens from 8 am to 3 pm. Diagonally opposite is the telecom building, open daily from 7 am to noon and 2 to 5 pm.

Dangers & Annoyances With the continuing instability in Sudan, the border remains closed – at least to foreigners. If you're thinking of crossing, you should first check out the situation while you're in Asmara.

Land mines were laid in the hills and plains all around the town during the war, so hiking in these areas is not advised. In the late 1990s, there was a bit of terrorist activity in the area (see Dangers & Annoyances in the Facts for the Visitor section). The situation seems to have stabilised now; if you're concerned, check with your embassy in the capital.

Malaria is rife; take precautions.

Places to Stay & Eat
The *Shafaray Hotel* is one of the best and newest places in town. It's quiet, has a pleasant little garden, and there's a proper shower. Four-bed rooms cost Nfa40, or you can sleep outside (Nfa7).

The *Harena* is also adequate though a bit noisy, with rooms for Nfa20 and a bucket shower. One of the better places is the *Luna Hotel* with doubles for Nfa30. It's well maintained and very clean.

The *City Park* is a good, shady place for breakfast and has fruit juices. The *Beilul*

Bar & Restaurant not far from the Nakfa Hotel is also good. The *Diana Restaurant* is considered the best eatery in town.

The *souq* area, known locally as 'Shuk al Shab' (Market of the Masses in Arabic) is straight out of Sudan. It's home to a huge open-air restaurant; you just join the rabble (most of them truck drivers from Sudan) at the long wooden tables and wait to be served. It's lively and fun and the evening air fills with the smoking and sizzling of the sheia. Beer is not available.

The Gelhanti Hotel is a good place for a drink. From June to August, watermelons are sold on the roads around the town.

Getting There & Away
Teseney's bus station lies 1.4km from the town centre. Five buses run daily to Barentu (Nfa10.50, five hours); three go every morning to Omhajer (Nfa9.50, five hours); one goes to Agordat (Nfa16.25, eight hours); and two buses every morning go to Asmara (Nfa30), overnighting at either Agordat or Keren. To Keren two buses depart daily (Nfa22.75, 10 hours).

With your own vehicle, you could consider looping back to Agordat via Sebderat, north of Teseney. There's a hard (bumpy) road as far as Sebderat, then it's a dirt track. It will take you through hot, open plains, then, just outside Agordat, acres of banana plantations, irrigated by the Barka River. As around Barentu and Agordat, you must be safely off the roads by 6 pm.

South of Asmara

Southern Eritrea is like a vast, open-air archaeological site.

Many of the country's 8000 or so sites are located here, just a fraction of which have been excavated. Though less spectacular than the more famous ruins found to the south in Ethiopia, some ruins are no less important. It is hoped that Qohaito and Metera will eventually be declared Unesco World Heritage Sites.

Even the local settlements – the farmsteads, wells and terraces – are just a continuation of those settled millennia earlier. In the same way, many of the Tigré and Saho peoples' traditions and customs remain completely unchanged. The yoke and plough used to break up the dry, stony, unyielding soil hasn't changed since its development centuries ago. The autumn winnowing – when the chaff is thrown high in the air and trampled by a wheeling team of oxen – is a beautiful, almost biblical, sight.

This interweaving of past and present, along with the new discoveries made almost every day and the mystery that still surrounds Eritrea's ancient past, makes the south a fascinating place to explore. Unfortunately, at the time of writing there was no information available on the sites themselves, and there were no official guides.

The south is the most densely populated area of Eritrea as well as one of the most cultivated. Euphorbia, eucalyptus and the prickly pear cactus are the most common natural vegetation; the Orthodox churches perched on the hilltops are among the most common built features.

There are two roads leading south to the Ethiopian frontier. One goes to Dekemhare, Segheneyti, Adi Keyh and finally to Senafe; the other goes south via Mendefera and Adi Quala. The roads are generally good, apart from the odd pothole.

Women & The Struggle

By 1990, women made up 30% of the Eritrean People's Liberation Front (EPLF), and 13% of frontline combatants. All the women fighters – like the men – were involved in often very risky guerrilla activity: some women learnt to drive tanks, others even commanded battalions.

Behind the lines, women benefited from EPLF training programs that discriminated in their favour. Women became doctors, dentists, mechanics, administrators and teachers. When the Struggle was over, it was inevitable that traditional perceptions of women's roles and capabilities would change – just as they did in Europe after the two world wars.

If the border crossing with Ethiopia reopened, a good excursion would be around the historical Aksumite sites of the area: the trip from Asmara to Aksum, Adigrat, Senafe and back to Asmara amounts to just 514km, and could be done in three days.

DEKEMHARE

The Italians had planned to make Dekemhare the industrial capital of Eritrea. Bypassing Asmara, a road ran directly from the port of Massawa to the uplands, and Dekemhare became an important industrial centre where offices, warehouses and factories were concentrated. During the war of independence, however, the town suffered much damage, and today just two of the old factories still operate: a pasta factory and the biscuit factory Red Sea Geneva Mills. Other remains of colonial days include the old market with its iron roof to protect the fruit, vegetables and grain.

Dekemhare was also famous for its wine industry, and grapes feature in the decorations adorning many balconies.

Information

The Commercial Bank is open Monday to Friday from 8 to 11.30 am and 2 to 5 pm, and on Saturday morning from 8 to 11.30 am. Travellers cheques cannot be changed.

The post office is open Monday to Friday from 8 am to noon and 2 to 5.30 pm, and on Saturday morning; the telecom office is open daily from 7 am to 8.30 pm.

Places to Stay & Eat

One of the best cheapies is the *Oasis Hotel*, with doubles/twins without private shower for Nfa15/20. The *Sellas Hotel* is also good with singles/doubles for Nfa20/30. The newly refurbished *Paradise Hotel* (☎ 64-13-16) is the smartest place in town, with rooms with private bathroom for between Nfa50 and Nfa100. It has a good restaurant.

Getting There & Away

For Asmara there are 30 buses a day (Nfa3.25, one hour); Adi Keyh has ten buses daily (Nfa5.50, two hours); for Massawa there is just one bus that goes direct at 6 am (Nfa10.75, around three hours); for Senafe, you'll need to change at Adi Keyh.

There's a rough road that winds from Dekemhare to just north of Mendefera. Three buses travel to Mendefera daily (Nfa3.75, around two hours).

AROUND DEKEMHARE

At the exit from a gorge, at the approach to some experimental agricultural nurseries, is the village of **Segheneyti**, 57km from Asmara. It is dominated by the huge Catholic Church of Saint Michael and two forts from which there are good views.

The *Va Bene Bahta Hotel* has a reasonable restaurant, and simple but clean rooms for Nfa15/20 for one/two people.

In season (mid-June to mid-September), Segheneyti and the surrounding area are known for the delicious and surprisingly thirst-quenching *beles* (prickly pear fruit). Little boys sell them for just Nfa0.10 each. Watch out for the skins – they're notorious for their almost invisible thorns.

Continuing south of Segheneyti, the road traverses the plain of Deghera, known popularly as the **Valley of the Sycamores** for the magnificent sycamore figs which march across the plain (see the boxed text 'Stately Sycamores'). At dusk, the trees make one of the most beautiful natural sights in all of Eritrea. Many are at least 300 years old and there are hopes to declare the whole valley a protected site in the future.

ADI KEYH

Adi Keyh, 104km from Asmara, boasts one green mosque and a chaotic afternoon market. Otherwise it's little more than a staging post for visiting the archaeological ruins of Qohaito.

The Commercial Bank is open Monday to Friday from 8 to 11 am and 2 to 4 pm, and on Saturday morning.

The post office is open Monday to Saturday from 7 am to noon and 2 pm to 5.30 pm, plus Saturday morning. The telecom office is open daily from 7 am to 10 pm.

The town's electricity is switched off at midnight.

Stately Sycamores

The sycamore fig *(Ficus sycomoros)* is one of the most common but also most beautiful figs in the Horn. Growing at an altitude of between 500m and 2400m high, it is found along rivers and lake margins, in woodlands, evergreen bushlands, forest edges and forest clearings.

Many people in the Horn consider the tree sacred. The Oromo people in Ethiopia have blazoned the tree on their ethnic flag.

The sycamore is used by the local people in many ways: the wood is used for carvings, the fruit is eaten during times of hardship, and the bark is used as traditional medicine.

The tree also serves a very important social purpose: under its branches in many regions of the Horn, village assemblies take place, as well as popular tribunals, community debates and disputes and advisory sessions from the elders.

The tree is also greatly appreciated for its beauty, for its generous shade, and as a fruitful home for beehives.

Places to Stay & Eat

The *Keste Demena Hotel* has adequate double rooms for Nfa10. One of the best places is the *Quahayto Hotel*, which has simple but clean and quiet rooms (without shower) for Nfa18 for up to three people. The *Bana Hotel* has well-kept doubles or twins for Nfa20. The *Adi Kaih* (☎ 41) is considered the best in Adi Keyh, but is usually booked out if there are archaeologists in town. Its nine double and twin rooms cost Nfa30; the doubles have private toilet. The restaurant here is reasonable.

The *Piazza Latteria* is a good place for a local breakfast. The *Agersh Hotel* has a reasonable restaurant. For fast food, you can try the new self-styled *Macdonald's Restaurant* on the main road near St Mary's church. Its burgers aren't a bad imitation.

Getting There & Away

Around 20 buses leave daily for Senafe (Nfa2, 45 mins); five go to Dekemhare (Nfa6, three hours); four go to Asmara (Nfa9, four hours); and four to Zala Ambassa on the Ethiopian border (Nfa4, 1½ hours).

QOHAITO

In the 2nd century AD, the famous Egyptian geographer Claudius Ptolemy (who wrote in Greek) made reference to an important ancient town named Koloe. This town flourished at the time of the great Aksumite kingdom (see Aksumite Civilisation in the Facts about Eritrea section) and provided a staging post between the ancient port of Adulis in the north and the capital of the kingdom, Aksum, in the south. It has long been thought that Qohaito was that town.

But even if it is not (some modern scholars favour nearby Metera), Qohaito's importance in the ancient world during this time is obvious.

Very little is known about the exact history of the settlement. A few ancient chronicles record that Qohaito was still flourishing in the 6th century AD. However, like Adulis and Metera, it then vanished very suddenly in the next one or two hundred years.

At an altitude of 2700m, Qohaito lies high above the port of Adulis and the baking lowlands, and may also once have served as a kind of summer retreat for the Aksumite merchants. The traces of cultivated areas found between the buildings have led to the belief that Qohaito was once a garden city.

Orientation & Information

Lying some 121km south of Asmara, Qohaito's impressive ruins are spread over a large area measuring 2.5km wide by 15km long. You'll need a good half day to see all the sites. As much as 80 to 90% of the ruins remain unexcavated, and information – even the age of the sites – remains obscure. In 1996 and 1997, a German expedition surveyed both Qohaito and Metera: new hypotheses were ballooning and bursting in a single day.

A short walk from Qohaito takes you to the edge of a vast canyon that drops away dramatically. The views of the surrounding mountains, including Mt Ambasoira (3013m) to the south (the highest peak in Eritrea), are stunning. Far below, you can make out the terraced fields and tiny *tukuls* (thatched conical huts) of a seemingly totally inaccessible Saho settlement. Get there

early in the morning, as it tends to cloud over later.

If you want to visit the rock art sites (described later in this section) or the viewpoint, you should ask at the village of Qohaito for a guide. One who speaks English is Ibrahim. The older but charming Suliman Ali speaks Tigrinya and Arabic, not English, but he knows the rock art sites like the back of his hand.

Temple of Mariam Wakiro

Among Qohaito's most important ruins is the so-called Temple of Mariam Wakiro, where four columns rise out of a mass of stones and fallen pillars. One of the columns is topped by an unusual four-sided capital. The temple was built on a rectangular plan on a solid platform, and may have been the site of a very early Christian church or even a pre-Christian temple. Nearby, other pilasters and platforms attest to the existence of at least half a dozen other temples. In the local language this site has long been referred to as 'abode of the prestigious ones'.

Egyptian Tomb

To the north, a little less than a kilometre from the ruins of Mariam Wakiro, lies an ancient underground tomb dug out of sandstone. Discovered in 1894, the tomb was nicknamed 'Meqabir Ghibtsi' or the Egyptian Tomb because of its impressive size. The tomb faces east, overlooking the Hedamo River. Rectangular in shape and built with large blocks of stones, its most distinctive features are the two quatrefoil (flowershaped) crosses carved on the inside walls.

Saphira Dam

This remarkable structure, lying just beyond the new village mosque, is Qohaito's greatest claim to fame. Measuring 67m long and 16m deep, the dam is constructed of large rectangular blocks of stone that measure close to 1m by 0.5m. The masonry is quite beautifully dressed – one of the reasons perhaps for the dam's incredible longevity. For around 1000 years, it has served the local Saho people as the main source of water.

Following recent investigations carried out by the German team, it has been suggested – amid hot controversy – that the structure may actually be a water cistern dating to the Aksumite period, and not a dam dating to the pre-Aksumite period as had previously been thought. However, until the site is properly excavated and investigated, most theories concerning Qohaito are likely to remain highly hypothetical, even wildly speculative.

On one of the walls inside the dam are some inscriptions in ancient Ge'ez, the religious language of ancient Aksum. The inscription, made up of 79 words, is the longest yet found in Ge'ez.

Rock Art Sites

At Iyago, near Qohaito, south-east of Mt Faquiti, an open shelter around 9m long is covered in rock paintings dating from approximately 4000–5000BC. Nearly 100 figures painted in ochre, black and reddish-brown adorn the rock face, depicting cattle, antelopes and perhaps lions. To get there, it's an easy 15-minute walk from Qohaito.

Another site that's easily accessible is the cave of Adi Alauti. Getting there involves a beautiful 30-minute walk along a mule path down the edge of a gorge. A large number of animals, including camels and gazelles, are depicted in ochre and white.

Other rock shelters in the area include Ba'atti Abager, Zebanona Libanos and Mai Ayni, where figures include warriors with long spears and oval-shaped shields, and Ona Addi Qantsa, where masked dancers wearing animal skins seem to be indulging in a ritual dance.

Getting There & Away

From Adi Keyh, it's an 11km drive south until you reach the left-hand turn-off from the main road, marked by a signpost; then it's a further 10km along a dirt road to the village of Qohaito.

If you don't have your own vehicle, you can take a bus from Adi Keyh to Senafe (Nfa1), and ask to be dropped at Egila, at the junction for Qohaito. From there, you'll have to walk the remaining 11km (about

three hours). Make sure you take lots of water and a hat. When you return, you can flag down any bus or minibus travelling on the main road in the direction of Adi Keyh.

You can also try getting a lift with other travellers. Ask around at the hotels.

AROUND QOHAITO
Toconda

The Aksumite ruins of Toconda lie 4km south of Adi Keyh in a wide valley. The ground is littered with potsherds, broken pillars and chiselled stones. Close to the dirt road there are two pillars: one standing, another with a curious rounded head. On a hill west of the site, there is an early inscription curved on a large basalt rock. Toconda is unexcavated and very little is known about it.

Keskese

Keskese lies in a small valley about 400m from the main road, 128km south of Asmara. This huge, unexcavated site is considered exceptional for its pre-Christian and pre-Islamic remains, which include the ancient tomb of a local prince or lord.

Lying among the barley fields like elongated, upturned boats are various huge monoliths, including one measuring a giant 14m long. Some stelae bear ancient inscriptions in Ge'ez; from their style, it is believed that they are at least 2500 years old. Elephants are offered as the most likely explanation for the way the immense stones were transported, though this, like everything else here, is shrouded in mystery.

SENAFE

Lying 139km from Asmara, Senafe is the last Eritrean town of any size before the Ethiopian border and is famous as the site of the ancient city of Metera. The latter lies clearly visible on a large plain to the east of the road, 2km south of Senafe.

The town has no bank. The post office is open Monday to Friday from 8 am to noon and 2 to 6 pm. The telecom office is open from 8 am to 8 pm every day. Senafe suffers from serious water shortages; most hotels have just bucket showers. Electricity shuts down at 11 pm each evening.

ERITREA

Things to See & Do

Apart from the site of Metera, Senafe is known for the huge rocky outcrops that dominate the plain. You can hike to the top of Amba Metera, one of the outcrops, in about an hour, though there are various routes with varying degrees of difficulty. Local boys soon appear and will guide you for a small tip. The most popular route takes 45 to 60 minutes and is in parts a scramble over boulders; in one place, a fixed rope helps you up a short section in which grooves are chiselled into the rock. Heavy or bulky camera equipment should be left behind. From the top there is a great panoramic view that recalls Senafe's name, which is supposedly derived from the Arabic: 'Can you see Sana'a?'.

Recently the local village priest has started to charge travellers Nfa50 to climb Amba Metera. Make sure you go early in the morning, as it gets very hazy later on. If you want to walk further in the area, you can find guides easily around the bus station.

The Senafe market, located just over a kilometre outside town, is worth a peek, particularly on Saturday, the major market day.

Places to Stay & Eat

Avoid the grubby *Bissrat Hotel* on the edge of town. The *Embasoira Hotel* with clean doubles/twins for Nfa10/12 is very adequate. The spotlessly clean and peaceful *Pension Fiori* is probably the best bet, with single/double rooms for Nfa10/15, and two-bed rooms for Nfa25.

A step up, and the only hotel in its class, is the *Hotel Mamona (☎ 12)* which has 15 rooms: four with private bathroom for Nfa40 for one or two people, and 11 without for Nfa20 to Nfa30. Reservations at the weekend are recommended, or arrive early.

The *Mama Roma* restaurant in the Sahel Hotel is run by an Eritrean woman married to an Italian, and is considered the best in town. Italian dishes need to be ordered in advance.

Getting There & Away

Buses from Senafe go to Adi Keyh at least every hour (Nfa2, 45 mins). To Asmara, five or six buses run every day (Nfa11, four hours); to Dekemhare, four or five buses leave daily (Nfa7.50, 3½ hours).

When the border with Ethiopia was open, there were buses to Zala Ambessa every hour from 6 am to 5.30 pm (Nfa2, one hour).

AROUND SENAFE
Enda-Tsadqan

The rock-hewn church of Enda-Tsadqan near the village of Bareknaha, 17km due south of Metera, makes an interesting half-day excursion. You'll need a guide from Senafe to show you the rough track to the village (ask at one of the hotels or the bus station). The church recalls the ancient architectural tradition of Lalibela in Ethiopia (see the North of Addis Ababa section in the Ethiopia chapter). According to tradition it dates from AD 486, when it was built by Gebre Meskel, the son of King Kaleb.

Monastery of Debre Libanos

An excursion to the monastery of Debre Libanos (also known as Debre Hawariyat) is strongly recommended. Debre Libanos is the oldest church in Eritrea, and is accessible from the very remote village of Hamm, perched dramatically on a high plateau, with sweeping views all around.

The monastery is thought to date from the 6th century; the library is open only to men but other parts on the other side of the valley can be visited by women, including a collection of 60 mummified bodies (supposed to date from the 4th century).

The walk alone is worthwhile for its scenery of dramatic peaks and valleys and views south into Ethiopia. There is a guesthouse where you can stay free (on a goat skin on a floor). Remember to leave a contribution for the monastery. You'll be offered bread and *sewa* (home-brewed beer).

Hamm can be reached in about two hours by foot from Senafe. From Hamm, a steep but not difficult descent takes you down to the monastery (around 45 minutes down, and around 1¼ hours back up).

A fun alternative is to approach Debre Libanos from Tsorena to the north-west. Some of the travel agencies in Asmara, such as Explore Eritrea (see Organised Tours in the Getting Around section earlier in this chapter), can organise two- to three-day camel safaris there. Or you can go independently. But you'll need to register at the administration office in Tsorena first, and find camels to hire for the following morning. In theory, it should take around four hours to reach Hamm from Tsorena. However, it took the author 25½ hours when her guide got lost! Bring water.

METERA

Situated 20km south of Qohaito, near the little village of Metera, are some of Eritrea's most important historical sites. Like Qohaito, Metera flourished around the time of the ancient civilisation of Aksum. (For more information on the Aksumite civilisation, see History in the Facts about Eritrea section.) The scattered ruins testify to the existence of a once large and prosperous town.

Metera is important for three main reasons: for its age – some of it, from about the 5th century BC, actually pre-dates Aksum; for its huge size – it spreads over at least 20 hectares, so it is much the largest Aksumite site after Aksum itself and Aksum's port, Adulis; and for its unusual character – it is the only place in the Aksumite civilisation where a large bourgeois community is known to have thrived.

If you've visited Aksum in Ethiopia (see the North of Addis Ababa section in the Ethiopia chapter), you'll soon recognise the typical Aksumite architectural features present at Metera, such as construction in tiers. But there are also big differences from Aksum, such as the plan and layout of the buildings. Nevertheless, it is clear that there were very strong cultural ties between Aksum, Adulis and Metera, not just during the Aksumite period, but earlier too.

The Stele

One of Metera's most important objects is its enigmatic stele. Unique in Eritrea, the stele is known for its pagan, pre-Christian symbol of the sun over the crescent moon, engraved on the top of the eastern face. Like the famous Aksum stelae, it faces eastward.

Standing 2.5m tall, the stele has an inscription near the middle in Ge'ez. An unknown king dedicates the stele to his ancestors who had subjugated the 'mighty people of Awanjalon, Tsebelan'.

Inexplicably, the stele was uprooted from its original position on the hill, and was at one time broken into two pieces. Today it sits in its new location at the foot of the hill Amba Saim, in front of the open plain.

Excavations

Metera's 'discovery' came in 1868, when Frenchman Denis de Rivoire reported its existence. In 1903, an Italian officer made a few amateur excavations in two places. The first scientific survey was carried out by the German Aksum Expedition in 1906. In 1959, the Ethiopian Institute of Archaeology began major excavation under the French archaeologist Francis Anfray.

From 1959 to 1965, various sites were excavated. A large mound located 100m northwest of the stele revealed a big, central building – perhaps a **royal palace** or a villa – attached to an annexe of living quarters. A huge wall surrounds the whole complex. Several burial chambers were found in the larger building; in one of them, the skeleton of a chained prisoner was discovered.

Between 1961 and 1962, two additional mounds were investigated. A large, square, multiroomed complex was found, built on a sturdy podium. A **tomb chamber** was also unearthed – but curiously it was empty. During the 1964 excavations the focus was on a cluster of rock-cut tombs on the Amba Saim hill south of the site.

Anfray's excavations also uncovered four large villas, some smaller houses, three Christian churches and a residential quarter – perhaps for the common people.

In the middle of the ruins, one of the building structures, made from finely chiselled, large blocks of limestone, contains a stairway that descends into a corridor. Though collapsed, the remains of what seems to be an **underground tunnel** are visible. According to local legend, this tunnel dates from the time of King Kaleb, and leads all the way to Aksum, hundreds of kilometres to the south.

ERITREA

Curiously, a similar entrance is said to exist in Aksum, but blocked by a large boulder. A more modern hypothesis – and almost as exciting – is that the 'tunnel' is a deep burial chamber containing great sarcophagi.

Objects unearthed at Metera in the last 50 years include some beautiful and amazingly well-preserved **gold objects** – two crosses, two chains, a brooch, necklaces and 14 Roman coins dating from between the 2nd and 3rd centuries AD – found in a bronze vase. **Bronze coins** minted by the great Aksumite kings have also been found, as have many 'household' items including bronze lamps, needles and daggers, Mediterranean amphorae, and the remains of large marble plates.

Only a tiny part of Metera has been excavated. Big mounds lie tantalisingly untouched all around. The ancient people's tombs – hidden somewhere among the rocks – still await exploration, and may yield remarkable finds.

Getting There & Around
Metera lies just 2km from Senafe, so is easily reached on foot. Currently, a sole caretaker looks after the site and will record your visit in a book. In the future, guides will work here. Admission is free.

MENDEFERA
Mendefera, the capital of Seraye province, is a bustling market town. Reflecting the old rivalry, the town is dominated by two churches: the Orthodox San Giorgio and the Catholic church school, situated on hills opposite from one another.

Mendefera's name derives from the high hill around which the town grew up. Meaning 'No One Dared' it is a reference to the fierce resistence put up by the local people against Italian colonialism. The hill was never taken. Today, there's little of interest to the traveller, but the town makes a convenient stop-off point on your way to or from the south.

Information
The Commercial Bank is open Monday to Friday from 8 to 11 am and 2 to 5.30 pm,

and Saturday morning. Travellers cheques can be changed.

The post office, near the Nacfa Hotel, is open Monday to Friday from 8 am to noon and 2 to 6 pm, and on Saturday until noon. The telecom office is open daily from 8 am to 9 pm.

At around 11 pm, the town's electricity shuts down.

Places to Stay & Eat
The *Awet Hotel* is a good, very clean place with singles or doubles with common shower for Nfa20.

The Semhar Hotel, popular with VSOs, has adequate single or doubles with common shower for Nfa25. It also has a good restaurant.

The *Embasa Hotel* is about to reopen with new rooms with private bathroom for between Nfa30 and Nfa50. Rooms without bathroom will cost Nfa20–25.

A favourite restaurant among aid workers is the bright *Restaurant N*. It serves local and Italian dishes and a few snacks such as hamburgers (Nfa5). The *Galaxy Pastry* is popular for its cakes. It also does fruit juices.

Getting There & Away
Mendefera's bus station lies around 20 minutes' walk from the town centre. If your bus is continuing south, ask to be dropped off at one of the hotels on the main street.

To Adi Quala, 20 buses leave daily (Nfa2.50, 45 mins); for Barentu there's just one direct bus weekly (Nfa16). It's best to hop between towns: first to Molki (Nfa8, four hours), then by minibus to Shambiko, and bus to Barentu. To Dekemhare, two buses go daily (Nfa4, two hours); to Asmara, at least 50 buses depart daily (Nfa5, 1½ hours).

The road west to Barentu is just a gravel track, and there's just one fuel station, at Shambiko, so if you're driving, make sure you fill up before setting off.

AROUND MENDEFERA
At Tera-Emni, 32km north of Mendefera, is the new *Green Island Hotel* (☎ 61-15-76). Rooms with private bathroom cost Nfa60

for one or two people. The hotel has an outdoor swimming pool, a garden, and horses for hire (Nfa50 per hour). There's good potential for hiking in the area too.

To get there from Asmara, take a bus heading for Mendefera, and ask to be dropped off at the hotel in Tera-Emni.

ADI QUALA

Adi Quala functions as a frontier town (it's the last town of any size before the Eritrean border). At the time of writing there was no bank in Adi Quala. The post office is open Monday to Friday from 8 am to noon and 2 to 6 pm, and Saturday until noon. The telecom office is open daily from 8 am to 9 pm.

Things to See

Adi Quala is home to two rather different institutions: a high-security prison and an attractive tukul church. The church has some interesting **frescoes**, including a depiction of the battle of Adwa painted on the eastern face of the its *maqdas* (inner sanctuary). Look out for General Baratieri (see the boxed text 'The Battle of Adwa' in the North of Addis Ababa section in the Ethiopia chapter) with moustache and striped jodhpurs. It's a good place to see traditional Eritrean religious painting if you haven't already; if you want a guided tour of the frescoes, ask for the resident priest Gebremichael. He'll expect a small tip.

A few kilometres west of town lies the Italian monument in honour of those who fell at Adwa. There are good **views** from the top.

Places to Stay & Eat

The *Mareb Hotel* is one of the best cheapies with 11 clean and peaceful rooms for Nfa10 for one or two people. The *Tourist Hotel* has good rooms with private shower for Nfa20 (Nfa10 without private shower). It also has a good restaurant. The *Bahari Eritrea Hotel* is another good place to eat.

Getting There & Away

To Mendefera, 23 buses leave daily (Nfa2.50, 45 mins); to Asmara, at least 10 buses run daily (Nfa7, 2½ hours). If you're trying to get to Ethiopia (when the border is

open), four buses run daily to Adwa (Nfa7, three hours).

Dankalia

For my part, I travel not to go anywhere, but to go. I travel for travel's sake.
Robert Louis Stevenson, *The Quotable Traveler*, **Running Press, London, 1994**

If there's one place in Eritrea where travel is for travel's sake, it's Dankalia. The region is known as one of the hottest and most inhospitable on earth: there's little to see, nothing to do, and no great destination awaiting you at the other end. The journey is hot, tiring and demanding; very few travellers come here. But the sense of exploration is real, even on the rickety old bus. If you drive, the journey is likely to be one of the most memorable and challenging of your life.

Dankalia is the name given to the volcanic desert that stretches from the Red Sea south of Massawa into northern Ethiopia and north-western Djibouti. It is also the territory of the legendary Afar people, described as one of the fiercest tribes on earth (see the boxed text 'A Museum of Peoples' under Population and People in the Facts about Eritrea section). A journey into Dankalia gives a fascinating glimpse into their lives.

The best time to go is from November to December or from March to April. At the height of summer, the heat is unbearable; in winter, the sparse rain can quickly turn the tracks and wadis into a mire.

If your time and budget are limited, an excursion as far as Thio will give you a good idea of the region, and the Buri Peninsula will give you a good idea of the wildlife. A trip taking in Adulis and going as far as Irafayle (87km from Massawa) at the start of the Buri Peninsula is just possible in a day.

ADULIS

Lying 59km to the south of Massawa, near the village of Foro, are the ancient Aksumite ruins of Adulis. Once numbering among the greatest ports of the ancient world, Adulis was the site of large and elegant

A Case of Mistaken Identity

In some of the remote villages, where Western visitors are rare, little children may approach you calling 'Tilian, Tilian', a corruption of the word 'Italian' that is used to address all white people.

'Teacher, Teacher', or 'Doctor, Doctor' are other titles accorded you. Many of the children will assume you're one of the white breed of aid workers visiting their villages.

Sometimes you'll get a 'Helen, Helen' or 'John, John', depending on your sex, and according to the name of the last – probably the only – white person they have met.

buildings and a bustling international port. Inhabited since at least the 6th century BC, the site is the oldest in Eritrea.

Adulis' present condition belies its former grandeur, and many travellers are disappointed. It remains around 98% unexcavated; almost everything remains underground. Nevertheless, Adulis is impressive for its sheer size, and if you're with your own vehicle, and have a bit of imagination, the ruins are definitely worth a stop.

Like modern-day Massawa, Adulis' importance lay in its port, and by the 3rd century AD the port had grown to become one of the most important on the Red Sea. Trade at this time flourished from the Mediterranean all the way to India.

Adulis' fortunes waxed and waned with the ancient kingdom of Aksum (see Aksumite Civilisation in the Facts about Eritrea section). Like Aksum, its heyday came during the 3rd and 4th centuries AD, then it went into decline, before a brief revival in the 7th century. The town supplied all the major Aksumite towns of the interior: Aksum, Qohaito, Metera and Keskese (see the South of Asmara section).

Orientation & Information

To visit Adulis, it's best to pick up a guide at Foro. Try asking for Salhé, who has long accompanied the archaeologists working on the site. He speaks quite good Italian and Arabic, but no English; ask for him at one of the cafes or bars. From Foro it's around 8km to Adulis, in the direction of Zula.

Don't forget that you need a permit from the National Museum Office in Asmara to visit the site (see National Museum in the Asmara section of this chapter). It is hoped that Adulis will eventually be declared a Unesco World Heritage Site.

If you have to overnight in Zula, there's at least one no-name place where a bed can be had (Nfa5). Ask any of the locals to show you the way.

Getting There & Away

The road from Massawa as far as Zula and Adulis is quite good. If you're driving, you can usually find a guide at Foro.

From Massawa, two buses leave daily for Zula at 6 am and 2 pm (Nfa6, four hours). You'll need a guide to take you to the ruins, which lie a few kilometres north-east of Zula. To return to Massawa, there's a bus from Zula at 6 am. Sometimes bush taxis also make the journey. Ask around at Zula.

ADULIS TO ASSAB

After Zula, the road begins to deteriorate. So do most of the maps. Due to the war, land mining, weather conditions etc, the roads have invariably shifted course. The locals are the best source of information, either as guides or to give you directions. A compass comes in handy too.

Most villages on the Danakil coast survive from a mixed economy of fishing, salt mining and animal husbandry. The millennia-old trading contact with the Arabian peninsula still thrives; in some places smuggling with Yemeni merchants has proved a more lucrative means of income.

The little fishing village of **Irafayle** (meaning 'Place of Elephants' – slim chance now) lies 87km from Massawa and marks the boundary between the provinces of Akele Guzay and Dankalia. Here Afar territory and its desolate landscape begins. The village offers simple refreshments and accommodation.

The bay around the **Gulf of Zula** is the site of Napier's landing in 1868, during the expedition to rescue the hostages held by the

Emperor Tewodros (see History in the Facts about Ethiopia section earlier in this book). It has good sandy beaches and snorkelling, and birdlife is plentiful along the shore.

The **Bure Peninsula** is probably one of the best places in Eritrea for wildlife. Ostriches, hamadryas baboons, and gazelles (Soemmering's and Dorca) are all quite frequently seen. The wild ass is also reported, though it's now very rare (see Endangered Species in the Facts about Eritrea section). Mangroves, good beaches and huge salt flats also characterise the area. If you have the time, a detour into the peninsula is worthwhile.

Marsa Fatma (188km from Massawa) is the starting point for a visit to the crater lake known as **Lake Badda**, around two hours (43km) west of the village of **Adaito**. Lying below sea level, seasonal water from the Tigré Mountains collects here, feeding the agricultural plantations. Unless you have lots of time, it's probably not worth a special excursion. Unfortunately, the administration at Badda (very atypical for Eritrea) seems more interested in extracting guide fees from tourists than offering any help or advice.

South of Marsa Fatma, the fishing village of **Thio** (305km from Massawa) offers food and accommodation and has a couple of excellent workshops which are good for repairs and sell new tyre inner tubes. They're run by ex-fighters. The village, with its brightly painted wooden huts, is worth a stroll.

Afambo (485km from Massawa), lying in some rocky hills and the site of a ruined Italian fort, also offers food and accommodation.

South of **Beylul** (621km from Massawa) around the headland known as Ras Termine are some mangroves, good beaches and islands which attract nesting seabirds. Sometimes the beaches are littered with shark carcasses; the local fisherman sell the fins to the Middle East and Far East.

ASSAB

Assab, Eritrea's largest port, is hot, windy and industrial, and has none of the charm of small-town Massawa. At the southern extremity of the desolate and inaccessible Dankalia region, Assab has always been a bit of an outpost. Tourism facilities are almost totally lacking.

Assab was Italy's first foothold in Eritrea, bought by the Rubattino Shipping Company in 1882, and taken over soon afterwards by the Italian government. For centuries and right up until recently, it was Ethiopia's principal port of access to the Red Sea. However, the dispute with Eritrea in 1998 put an end to all that. The deviation of all Ethiopian commerce via Djibouti has made Assab even more of a backwater.

Lying less than 100km from Ethiopia, Assab has an Ethiopian feel about it. Ethiopians (24,000) outnumber Eritreans by at least two to one. Assab's average annual temperature is 29.5°C, though it can reach 46.5°C. Annual rainfall is just 58mm. The coolest time is between November and February.

Orientation & Information

The town can be divided into three parts. To the north-east lies Assab Seghir (little Assab), home to the large Yemeni community with their many restaurants, fruit shops and small shops. In the centre lies Assab Kebhir (big Assab), which makes up the administrative centre and includes the port.

ERITREA

Popular Palms

Situated on a large plain dotted with *amba* (flat-topped mountains), the village of Wade, around 70km south-east of Afambo, is the site of an oasis of doum palms. The whole area from Wade to Beylul is known for its production of the very alcoholic doum palm 'wine'. You'll see old lemonade bottles in the villages frothing over with a milky liquid.

Don't miss the chance to try some; you may be invited into one of the local 'pubs', discreet enclosures made from the wood and palms of the doum trees. A litre bottle costs between Nfa1.5 and Nfa7, depending on the quality.

In Wade, the drink has become almost a village addiction, and the authorities have tried to ban consumption; fines of up to Nfa100 have been introduced, though they don't seem to be levied.

Most of the hotels can be found here. To the west, lies Campo Sudan, the residential quarter for many of the town's Ethiopians and the main area for 'nightlife'.

There is no tourist office in Assab. See Business Hours in the Facts for the Visitor section.

The Commercial Bank is open Monday to Friday from 7 am to noon and 4 to 6.30 pm, and Saturday from 7 to 11.30 am. Travellers cheques are accepted.

The post office is open normal business hours and Saturday morning, but closes early on Friday morning (11.30 am).

The telecom office is open daily from 7 am to 8 pm; the fax office keeps normal business hours.

The *Eritrean Profile* can be bought in front of the Kebal International Hotel.

Dangers & Annoyances There are significant red-light districts, requiring vigilance, around both Campo Sudan and the port. Heat rash is a common problem and is best relieved by cold showers. Sometimes there are electrical power cuts.

Things to See & Do

To **swim** in town, head for the Ras Gembo Hotel; nonguests pay Nfa3, but can use the hotel's shower. Alternatively, the pleasant and sandy **Bayeta beach** lies 4km to 5km from town on the airport road. A contract taxi costs around Nfa20. Minibuses also run there.

The only boat visiting the **islands** off Assab is that belonging to the Ras Gembo Hotel. In theory, a boat leaves every Sunday (from March to the end of September) at 7.30 am for Ras Fatuma Island, returning at 4 pm. (US$20 per person, 1 to 1½ hours.) However, a minimum of 10 people are normally required; for fewer, you may have to pay more per head. The only other way of getting there is with the local fisherman. You can also try the Ministry of Marine Resources (Asmara ☎ 66-07-54), which rents out its boats if they're not being used.

Apart from Fatuma Island and Sennabar (the nearest island with a beach on the western side), a permit is required to visit the other 28 islands in the Bay of Assab. This can be obtained from the Ministry of Tourism in Asmara (see Tourist Offices in the Eritrea Facts for the Visitor section). The best place for **snorkelling** is Fatuma Island.

Places to Stay

In most of the hotels in Assab, the showers are cold.

In Assab Kebir, one of the best cheapies in town is the *Asmara Hotel* north-west from the Kabal International Hotel on the edge of Campo Sudan. It's simple but spotless, friendly and secure. It has 10 double rooms with shared bathroom for Nfa15.

The old colonial *Assab Hotel*, near the Kebal International, has adequate double rooms with shared bathroom and ceiling fan for Nfa20 to Nfa25; or with private bathroom and ceiling fan for Nfa35; or with private bathroom and air-con for Nfa90.

The *Zeray Deres Hotel*, at the far end of the port is a bit lugubrious (perhaps not for those on Lariam), but has good-value rooms with fan and shower for Nfa48; or with air-con, telephone, toilet and shower for Nfa72; or with bath for Nfa84.

The *Kebal International Hotel* (☎ 66-17-08) is often still known by its old name, the Nino. It has peeling double/twin-bed rooms with shower for Nfa25/30 (those at the Assab are better). The newly renovated rooms at Nfa120, with air-con, shower and toilet (and some with fridge) are very comfortable, as are those that also include TV, fridge and telephone, for Nfa150.

Top of the range is the *Ras Gembo Hotel* (☎ 66-05-21), the old Port Club, which lies near St Michael's Church outside the main port area. It has comfortable but overpriced rooms with air-con from Nfa195 to Nfa325. Its greatest advantage is its beach.

Places to Eat

For self-catering, *Dankalia Provision Supplies* not far from the Zeray Deres Hotel is one of the best-stocked places.

The *Portico Snack Bar* in a small, cool park in Assab Kebir is a good place for a beer or coffee. Decent food is also available. The *Sunshine Snack* near the Aurora restaurant is popular locally.

As Assab Seghir is Muslim, no alcohol is served at restaurants.

In Assab Kebir, the *Aurora Restaurant*, not far from the Zeray Deres Hotel, is considered the best place for Italian dishes (Nfa8 to Nfa10). It's run by Signora Giuseppina Fracasso, whose Italian father built the telephone line in Assab.

The large, open restaurant of the *Kebal International Hotel* has good local food (Nfa8 to Nfa10). Seafood can be ordered in advance at the *Port Club Hotel*, but it's expensive: lobster costs around Nfa110.

The restaurant of the *Ras Gembo Hotel* serves good grilled fish and, unlike most restaurants in Assab, is open all day to 10 pm. A bit cheaper and good for local food is the popular but simple *Stella Restaurant* near the municipality.

Assab Seghir has some cheap but excellent Yemeni restaurants serving fresh fish baked in a tandoori oven. The *Moosa Restaurant* is a good choice, though check the price of the fish as it's brought out to you. It's traditionally served with a doughy mixture: *fatta assal* (with honey), *fatta tamor* (with dates) and *fatta moz* (banana). Try the *fasoliya* (white beans) too.

The *Sahel Cafeteria* on the seafront serves some great barbecued fish and meat.

Entertainment

Assab Cinema Hall shows action-packed Hollywood films in English every night at 7 pm for Nfa2.

The *Ras Gembo* and *Kebal International Hotels* are popular places for an evening drink. Sometimes the latter puts on a nightclub (usually during holidays).

Campo Sudan is a great place at night, though you'll need to take care: bring with you the minimum amount of money, and women should be accompanied.

Bars and outdoor 'beer gardens' (usually a gravel or cement courtyard plus a single tree decorated with Christmas lights) can be found everywhere and open from around 6 pm to midnight. Ethiopian *azmaris* (minstrels) often do the rounds singing and playing with traditional instruments.

Getting There & Away

Air The airport is little more than a shack with a few wooden tables set up inside.

Eritrean Airlines (☎ 66-00-28) is open every day. There are three flights a week to Asmara (Nfa274 one way), usually on Tuesday, Saturday and Sunday.

Ethiopian Airlines (☎ 66-01-85) used to sell tickets to Addis Ababa for US$102 one way (US dollars only). These flights should resume when Eritrea's relations with Ethiopia normalise.

Bus & Truck Incredibly – almost miraculously – a bus service (of sorts) connects Assab to Massawa. The service is erratic, unreliable and very uncomfortable. After any rain when the track becomes muddy services are often cancelled. If you do want to give it a go, allow plenty of time. The journey can take days and days, and much of the journey can be spent outside the bus pushing it! Bring all the food and water you can carry. Two buses a week (usually Saturday and Tuesday) depart for Asmara (Nfa100); the journey take three to five days depending on the going.

Don't forget that hitching always carries a risk (see Hitching in the Getting Around section in the Ethiopia chapter).

Ethiopia When the border with Ethiopia was open, two buses a week (usually Sunday and Thursday) ran to Addis Ababa (Nfa60, two days) via Awash and Nazret, departing at 4 am.

Before the dispute, many trucks ran from Assab port to Addis Ababa (1½ days). Lifts (for one to three people) were easy to organise and were faster, more comfortable and cheaper (Nfa50 per person) than the buses. Adi Nefas, 2km from central Assab on the Assab–Addis Ababa road, is the best place to find a truck. Buses leave every hour to Adi Nefas, or you can take a share-taxi.

Djibouti There are no buses between Assab and Djibouti. The best option for Djibouti is to go to Adi Nefas then hitch a lift with a truck towards Addis Ababa and get off at the junction to Galafi on the border between

ERITREA

Ethiopia and Djibouti; from there, it's an easy hitch to Djibouti town.

The alternative route via Rahaita (around 112km from Assab) in the south is difficult to organise, as there's almost no traffic between the two towns. The author got there (just) in a hired minibus (Nfa250), but a 4WD is really required. From Rahaita, you have to hire another taxi (only one is available) to the border (23km) and then you have to try and hitch (there's even less traffic) to Djibouti town.

For more information, see the main Getting There & Away in the Djibouti chapter.

Boat A cargo boat usually sails to Djibouti every five days, and it's normally possible to hitch a lift; the trip takes seven to 10 hours.

Cargo boats also go to Massawa every week or fortnight; two accept passengers (Nfa75 one way). You can book a place at the Eritrean Shipping Lines office

(☎ 66-04-77) next door to the Ministry of Finance in Assab Kebir. You should bring food, water and a blanket for sleeping on the deck. In the future, there will be a passenger ship connecting the two ports.

Currently it's not possible to hitch a ride on boats to Yemen (special permission is needed).

Getting Around

To/From the Airport Ignore the taxis jostling for custom at the exit; you can take a minibus, which costs Nfa10 into town.

Minibus The yellow minibuses serve as taxis about town. Journeys cost between 50¢ and 75¢ depending on the distance. You can also hire the whole bus (Nfa10). Buses to Assab Seghir can be taken from near the Zeray Deres Hotel. One of these travels via Port Sudan.

FRANCES LINZEE GORDON

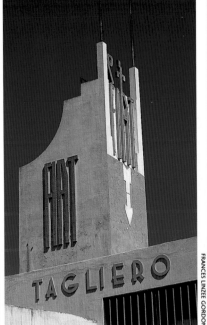

FRANCES LINZEE GORDON

FRANCES LINZEE GORDON

In the 1920s and 1930s, Asmara was a showcase for contemporary international architectural design. Today, it features a delightful and eclectic mix of buildings.

Taking in a spectacular view

An international archaeological team inspects the ruins of an AD 3rd-century city near Adi Keyh

The winding road to Senafe, near the Eritrea-Ethiopia border

Rock paintings and engravings from the southern region of Eritrea date from 2000 BC.

Priestly regalia at the festival of Timkat

Finger lickin' good!

Eritrean baskets show a fine attention to detail.

The waters off the largest island in the Dahlak Archipelago are home sweet home to this dolphin.

Hawksbill turtles are happy to snooze in the sea.

Jackfish find safety in numbers.

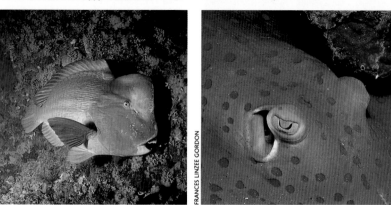

Napolean wrasses add colour to the reef.

Don't mess with the blue-spotted eel!

FRANCES LINZEE GORDON

MARINE LIFE IN THE RED SEA

The Red Sea possesses physical characteristics found nowhere else in the world. Geologically, it is classed as a basin, ie, a partially enclosed area of water. The Gulf of Suez in Egypt and the Gulf of Aqaba in Jordan mark the northern limits, and the Straits of Bab al Mandab in Djibouti the southern limits, 2350km away. This isolation for the past 2.5 million years in a semi-enclosed environment has given rise to an incredibly rich marine life, as well as a high proportion of endemism – nearly 20% of the fish in the Red Sea are found nowhere else. Up to 50% of some species, such as the butterfly fish, are endemic. The variety of coral is also enormous, with over 400 species recorded. See also Diving & Snorkelling in the Facts for the Visitor section in the Djibouti chapter, and Water Activities in the Facts for the Visitor section in the Eritrea chapter.

Inhabitants of the Reef

The reef is home to more major animal groups than any other ecosystem in the world. At first glance, the reef appears to be bedlam. It teems with creatures of all shapes and colours, mingling with one another in what appears to be a completely chaotic and random manner. Beneath this apparent confusion there is a complex pattern of behaviour and specialisation that allows the vast numbers of the reef's inhabitants to coexist.

Fish

The Red Sea is home to several thousand species of fish, ranging from the tiny **blennies**, **anthias** and **basslets** to large **barracuda** and **shark**.

The **cardinal fish**, **angelfish**, and **triggerfish** are among those found feeding off or near the coral; **gropers** and **rock cod** lurk in crevices and caves; schooling fish, such as **snappers**, **unicornfish** and **surgeonfish**, patrol the reef; pelagic (open-sea) species such as the **hawksbill turtle** and **white-tipped shark** just visit it.

Some particularly exotic Red Sea inhabitants to look out for include the **frogfish**, the **crocodilefish** and the **trumpetfish**.

Echinoderms

The name, meaning 'spiny-skinned', denotes a large group of animals including **sea urchins**, **starfish**, **brittle stars**, **feather stars** and **sea cucumbers**. The **crown-of-thorns starfish** is found in the Red Sea, but in moderate numbers.

In general, these animals live either on the surface of the reef or on the sandy sea bed, so are easily seen. Sea urchins prey on coral and in moderate numbers play an important role in creating reef sediment and stemming the growth of the reef out to sea.

Crustaceans

Protected by a hard external skeleton like a jointed suit of armour, crustaceans, such as **shrimps**, **crabs** and **prawns**, are abundant on the reef, and can usually be found hidden in crevices. Some, like the **lobster**, feed at night. Very little is known about crustaceans and the often complex relationships they have with other animals on the reef.

Molluscs

These animals make up a huge family and are more numerous on the reef than fish. Molluscs are classed as invertebrates, and have soft, unsegmented bodies. They include gastropods (with a shell) such as **snails**, bivalves (with two hinged valves) such as **oysters**, **clams** and **scallops**, and cephalopods (with a head and tentacles) such as **octopus** and **squid**.

Molluscs are a vital link in the food chain, providing up to 20% of the diet of many species of fish.

Sponges

These multicelled creatures are among the most primitive on the reef, and are little more than living pumps. Many sponges are poisonous, though some are preyed upon by certain species of molluscs, fish and especially turtles. Some also provide a home for certain animals that live in the sponge, without apparently contributing any benefit to them in return. Among these 'squatters' are small **crabs**, **worms**, **shrimps** and sometimes **brittle stars**.

Mammals

Mammals are strictly speaking reef visitors rather than reef inhabitants. Many, such as **dolphins**, visit the reef to feed, or can be seen playing around boats heading to or from the reef. The **dugong** (see the boxed text 'Meaty Mermaids' under Fauna in the Facts about Eritrea section) is seen only very occasionally on the reef. It prefers the protection offered by the murky sea-grass beds, which are also its main food source. The dugong has suffered a sharp decline in recent years and is now considered endangered. It has long been hunted for its meat which is highly prized among some fishing communities of the Red Sea (including Eritrea and Djibouti), and is further threatened by loss of habitat and human activities such as power-boating.

Reptiles

Turtles are frequently spotted hanging around the reefs. The **hawksbill turtle** feeds on invertebrates and sponges, and can sometimes be seen snoozing or resting on a comfortable plateau of the reef. The **green turtle** is also seen, though it prefers habitats where its diet of seaweed and seagrass is more abundant.

Turtles have long been hunted by humankind for their eggs, shell, meat and skin. Now all species of marine turtle are threatened, and according to the Convention on International Trade in Endangered Species, they number among the most endangered species in the world.

Other Marine Life

Many other lesser known or less conspicuous animals inhabit the reef. The **marine worm** is one of the most common, and comes in a multitude of colours and varieties. Some of the most attractive are the **fan worms** and the **Christmas tree worms**, both of which use their brightly coloured crowns of tentacles to filter food.

Other colourful animals to look out for include the **anemone**, found on the rocky surfaces of reef drop-offs, and the **jellyfish** which belongs to the same family as the anemone and coral.

Hazardous Marine Life

Though most marine creatures have some form of self-defence or means of showing displeasure, some marine life in the Red Sea should be given a wide berth.

Many poisonous sea creatures lurk on the reef bottom, hidden or camouflaged in the sand or coral. The **stonefish**, **lionfish**, **turkeyfish** and **rabbitfish** all have venomous spines or fins; the stonefish is the most dangerous of these and has a potent venom. **Sea urchins** are another hazard of the reef floor, and their spines are occasionally poisonous. Even if they are not, the spines can break off under the skin and become troublesome. **Stingrays** administer stings through one or more barbs on the top of the tail. Stingrays are sea-bed dwellers and usually only sting when trodden on or trapped. If you are stung by a venomous fish or stingray or step on a sea urchin, carefully remove any remaining spines, wash off any remaining venom with water then bathe the wound in hot water (this helps relieve the pain) and apply a clean dressing. Get medical help for severe stings.

Some species of **cone shells** are highly dangerous. If you are stung by a cone shell, wash the wound then apply a pressure bandage over it and get medical help quickly.

Most **jellyfish** sting, but few in the Red Sea are dangerous. Other stingers include **stinging plankton**, which are often difficult to see and which stick to skin. If you get stung by a jellyfish, pour vinegar on the affected area and get medical advice if the sting is severe.

Barracuda can give a painful bite, though it's unusual for them to attack. In fact, divers are much more likely to be bitten by another sharp-toothed, albeit more diminutive, aggressor, the **triggerfish**, which sometimes protects its nest very fiercely. Its bite can draw blood even through a wetsuit. The **moray eel** is probably responsible for more bites to divers than any other creature, albeit unwittingly. The eel is actually quite a passive creature, and will not bite unless provoked or threatened. Divers collecting shells, reaching for lobsters in holes, or removing anchors are the most common victims of bites. The eel has fearsome teeth, but is more notorious for its vice-like hold: once it has bitten, the moray will often not let go. If you are bitten by any of these fish, clean the wound carefully and cover it with sterile dressing – get medical help if the wound is large.

Staying Safe on the Reef

Don't forget to look after cuts which, if neglected or ignored, can be more troublesome than stings or bites. Scratches and scrapes are commonly caused by coral, barnacles or sharp metal from wrecks. Unless cuts are properly cleaned and disinfected after each dive, they are likely to become infected. For larger wounds, you may have to stay out of the sea for a few days to allow them to heal.

A few basic precautions, as follows, will ensure that neither party is harmed or threatened.

The best advice of all if you're swimming, snorkelling or diving on the reef is not to touch anything. Some dive centres may even ask you to remove your gloves to oblige you to respect this rule. Always wear shoes when swimming and if you have to walk any distance along the sea bottom, try to do so in a shuffling movement. In this way, you have a chance of edging venomous creatures out of your path. Don't assume that shoes or fins will protect you; many poisonous spines are sharp enough even to penetrate rubber.

Fish should never be fed. Apart from potentially harming them and upsetting their ecosystem, many, even the innocuous-looking species, have nasty bites if your fingers should get in the way.

Remove all jewellery. Some species such as barracuda are known to go for flashing objects, mistaking them, perhaps, for prey such as sardines.

Diving in Eritrea & Djibouti

The southern waters of the Red Sea around Eritrea and Djibouti are known principally for four things: the huge shoals of fish, the large size of individual specimens of fish, their apparent lack of fear of humans and the significant number of unusual species, even by Red Sea standards.

Snappers, jackfish, sweetlips, unicornfish and fusiliers all form enormous schools, frequently numbering in the hundreds. The larger species of reef fish, such as groper, parrotfish and wrasse, reach the extreme upper limit of their growth range. Giant specimens of groper are quite frequently seen, and large Napoleons, bumphead parrotfish and lyretail cod are common sightings.

The southern Red Sea was once famous for its shark populations but shark life is not as abundant as it once was. In both Eritrea and Djibouti, commercial shark fishing, mostly by Yemeni fisherman, has had a significant impact on the shark population. Though their trade is an ancient one, the demand for shark fins for the Asian markets has made the profession a much more lucrative one.

However, reef sharks (particularly the white-tipped),grey, hammerhead, nurse, tiger and mako sharks, turtles, stingrays and dolphins are also common. Manta rays and dugongs are occasionally seen.

Water temperatures range from 27° to 29°C (though 36°C has been reported in the summer), so a swimskin or 3mm tropical wetsuit offers more than adequate protection.

Further Reading

Coral Reef Fishes published by Collins is a handy illustrated pocket guide. Although it covers the Indo-Pacific and Caribbean too, it includes many of the more common fish species of the Red Sea.

Diving & Snorkeling Guide to the Red Sea published by Lonely Planet is brimming with colour and good advice.

Red Sea Fishes by Dr John E Randall is a good book on the area.

Red Sea Fishwatcher's Field Guide published by Seahawk Press, Florida, is a laminated waterproof card that is useful for quick identification of around 60 species.

Djibouti

Calcareous 'chimneys' make for almost apocalyptic landscapes

Tadjoura's Islamic architecture

Rest huts on Goda Mountain

Salt crystallizes on Lac Assal

The lush lowlands of the Goda Mountains

Dive tours off Les Sept Frères Islands

Djibouti

Before crossing this country, even the jackal makes his will.

Djiboutian Somali proverb

Measuring just one sixth the size of England, and roughly equal in size to diminutive El Salvador, Djibouti is one of Africa's tiniest countries. Dwarfed by giants – Ethiopia to the south and west and Somalia to the south-east – the country is little more than a port. But its position at the southern entrance to the Red Sea gives the country an importance wholly disproportionate to its size.

Situated at the crossroads of Europe, Africa and Asia, Djibouti has long drawn the covetous eye of great powers and empires. Mythicised by the ancient Egyptians, highly prized by the Greeks and Romans, the area was claimed finally by French colonisers trying to thwart British ambitions across the waters in Yemen.

The country's history as a tourist destination is less dazzling. Many early visitors came to Djibouti with gritted teeth. The majority took up second-rate colonial posts, or lingered as little as possible, waiting for transport to other destinations. Most early travellers were unimpressed by the stark landscape and the torrid, tropical climate that greeted them. Reports and letters home described an 'apocalyptic wasteland', and 'the devil's cauldron'. Rimbaud, the famous French poet, described Djibouti as 'this awful colony' and 'filthy country'; the British explorer Wilfred Thesiger called it 'a godforsaken spot'.

The dwindling French presence in the country still brings travellers – some just as reluctantly – to visit relatives posted in the port. Others go on using Djibouti as a transit point, hurrying in and hurrying out as fast as modern transport allows them.

Travellers still vie with one another for pejoratives to describe the little country. The greatest cause for grumbling among visitors today is the high cost of living. Although disproportionately expensive compared to

DJIBOUTI AT A GLANCE

Capital City: Djibouti town
Population: 750,000 (including refugees)
Time: 3 hours ahead of GMT
Land Area: 21,000 sq km
International Telephone Code: ☎ 253
GDP/Capita: US$1200
Currency: Djibouti franc (Dfr170 = US$1)
Languages: Arabic, French
Greeting: *Salam 'alekum*

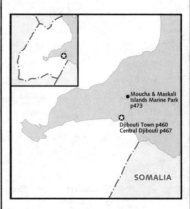

- Moucha & Maskali Islands Marine Park p473
- Djibouti Town p460 Central Djibouti p467

SOMALIA

Highlights

- Visit the weird, lunar landscape of Lac Abbé at dawn
- Dive or snorkel off the stunning coral reefs of Djibouti's Red Sea
- Explore the great salt lake and black volcanic landscape of Lac Assal
- Spot birds and animals in the lush and verdant Fôret du Day National Park
- Trek behind the Afar nomads and their caravans along the ancient salt route
- Chew *qat* (mildly intoxicating leaves) with the locals
- Scoff a poisson *yéménite* (fish supper) with the locals
- Gorge on the sumptious local seafood

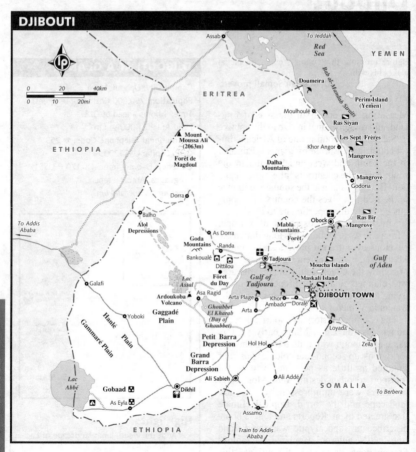

DJIBOUTI

other African countries, costs in Djibouti are far from extortionate. A slight scratch below the surface reveals alternatives even for the budget traveller.

For the visitor who hangs around for more than a day or two, for those with less restrictive schedules, outlooks and preconceptions, the country may well hold a surprise or two. With the current trend in tourism towards 'natural attractions', Djibouti turns out to be a destination richer and better endowed than anyone might have imagined.

The landscape, though bleak in parts, can be strikingly beautiful. Some places, such

as the vast salt lake of Lac Assal and the bizarre lunar landscape of Lac Abbé, are unique and strangely unforgettable. The beautiful coral reefs off the coast undoubtedly rank among the best-kept secrets of the Red Sea.

For lovers of nature, Djibouti boasts a geological landscape matched by few other countries in the world. The country's range of birds is surprisingly diverse, and includes Djibouti's very own indigenous species. For those interested in people and culture, a trip around the country can provide a fascinating glimpse into the life of two remarkable and enigmatic nomadic tribes: the legendary Afars and Somalis.

Catering for years to the demands of a French administration and military presence, the capital is quite well geared up for the visitor. With hotels and restaurants to satisfy the most demanding or diffident of travellers, there's plenty also for those in search of the exotic.

Djibouti's blend of African, Arab, Indian and European influences presents an interesting and unusual cultural experience: from chewing qat and tasting milk fresh from a nomad's camel, to gorging on exquisite seafood from the Red Sea, there's plenty to keep the visitor entertained.

Finally – the result perhaps of an incredibly inhospitable climate – the people are incredibly hospitable. For those who make the effort, the Djiboutians prove to be a generous, eloquent and quite charming people, whose welcome to their much-maligned and little-visited country is genuine, heartfelt and never forgotten. A visit to Djibouti should prove to be worth every begrudged penny ... but don't go in the hot season!

Facts about Djibouti

HISTORY
Prehistory
With the discovery in recent years of spectacular fossil finds in the Rift Valley of East Africa, the region has been dubbed the 'Cradle of Humanity'; it is believed that humankind may have its origins here. Such discoveries shed a little more light on our still very obscure evolution. Fossils offering the first undisputed evidence for human evolution date from about five million years ago and belong to the group known as *Australopithecus*. East Africa has proved to be particularly rich in fossils dating from this period. 'Lucy', the most famous, was unearthed in 1974 in Ethiopia (see the boxed text 'Lucy in the Sky' under History in the Facts about Ethiopia section earlier in this book) in an area known as the Afar Triangle

Land of Many Names

The area now called East Africa has long been known to the outside world. The Red Sea linked Egypt and the Mediterranean with India and the East, providing antiquity with a crucial and much coveted commercial route. It also gave access to the rich African continent itself, which yielded highly prized valuables such as gold, ivory, incense, myrrh and slaves.

The Egyptian Pharaohs called this part of the world the 'Land of Punt' and frequently travelled here for commercial purposes (see also the boxed text 'Land of Punt' under History in the Facts about Eritrea section earlier in this book). Although it's still hotly disputed by historians, this quasi-legendary land most probably comprised present-day Eritrea, Djibouti and parts of Ethiopia.

The Greeks were also familiar with the area. The *Periplus of the Erythraean Sea*, an anonymous trade manual written in the 1st century AD, refers to various commercial ports such as Zeïla in modern-day Somalia.

To the Romans, the area was known as the Land of Spices, alluding to the seemingly limitless supplies of incense and myrrh that issued from the region.

– a geographical area overlapping Djibouti (see Geography later in this section).

Many believe that similar finds are waiting to be discovered in Djibouti itself. Recent discoveries include evidence of *Homo erectus* and *Homo sapiens*, dating from around 1½ million years ago. The most important of these finds was a jawbone discovered at Hara Idé in 1984.

Although little is known about subsequent periods in Djibouti, there is evidence of very early agriculture in the region. Research carried out in the late 1980s by a French team of palaeontologists revealed evidence of prehistoric, specialist societies that had apparently exploited their environment. Located near Lac Abbé, one site revealed large basalt millstones that were 4000 years old. These tools suggest the presence of agriculture, though no evidence of grains has yet been discovered. Mammal

DJIBOUTI

and numerous fish bones have also been uncovered in the same location, along with pottery, tools made from obsidian and evidence of stoves. The discovery of burial places, including the remarkable tomb of a young girl dating from 2000 BC, has further increased interest in the site.

Paleoanthropology is still in its infancy in Djibouti, but the richness of recent finds suggests that a great deal awaits discovery. A key question facing researchers is whether prehistoric populations did indeed practise farming, or were sedentary, or still belonged to the larger group of hunter-gatherers that inhabited the rest of Africa at this time.

The Kingdom of Aksum

Around the 1st century AD, Djibouti made up part of the powerful Ethiopian kingdom of Aksum, which included modern-day Eritrea and even stretched across the Red Sea to parts of southern Arabia. It was during the Aksumite era, in the 4th century AD, that Christianity first appeared in the region. However, as the empire of Aksum gradually fell into decline, a new influence arose that would supersede forever the Christian religion in Djibouti.

The Arrival of Islam

Islam was brought to Djibouti not by the sword, but by the sea. From around the 9th century AD, Muslim merchants crossed the Red Sea from southern Arabia and settled some of Djibouti's trading ports, such as Tadjoura. As the influence of Islam expanded, consolidated by the rise of local Muslim potentates, a clash with the Ethiopian Aksumite Christians became inevitable.

In 1542, at the head of a large army, the famous Muslim *imam* (religious leader) and warlord Mohammed Gragn the Left-Handed invaded Ethiopia from his sultanate in the East. Although the Muslim leader was defeated in battle, his religion was not, and Islam continues its hold over Djibouti to the present day (see Religion later in this section).

The Ottoman Empire & Egypt

After the fall of Constantinople in 1453, Ottoman influence gradually began to expand.

By the 16th century, the empire controlled most of south-eastern Europe, the Middle East, North Africa, and later the whole of the eastern coast of the Red Sea, including the area now known as Djibouti. Following the decline of the Ottomans, the Egyptians briefly held sway in the region.

After the 16th century, Ottoman power gradually went into decline, and by the middle of the 19th century, new powers had entered the scene. The Egyptians took over the region, subduing even the rich commercial town of Harar, far into Ethiopia.

European Colonialism

The opening of the Suez Canal in 1869 let loose a stampede of Europeans into East Africa (see the boxed text 'The Scramble for Africa' under History in the Facts about Eritrea section earlier in this book). Keen to grab those territories that had eluded them, Great Britain, Italy and France all arrived in the region. The area now known as Djibouti attracted particular interest for its strategic location on the Red Sea.

The British took over Aden in Yemen, and replaced the Egyptians along much of the Somali coast, with the exception of a tiny area in the far north. This enclave was occupied by France, which hoped to counter British trading influence in the area, and came to be known as French Somaliland. It was then that the current boundaries of present-day Djibouti were drawn.

The French initially chose to settle in Obock, north of Djibouti town, in 1862. However, keen to establish a harbour with better access to the Red Sea, they later opted for a site further south, on the southern shore of the Gulf of Tadjoura, which was to become known as Djibouti town.

The Rise & Fall of Djibouti Town

Djibouti town grew rapidly, helped in particular by the construction of a great railway, which connected the new town of Addis Ababa in Ethiopia to the Red Sea. As trade flourished around the port, Djibouti town grew still more. Djibouti's good fortunes were briefly interrupted by WWII. At this time, Britain imposed a blockade on the port in opposition to the Vichy regime of occupied France.

However, by the 1950s, the port's prosperity was soon revived as Djibouti became a kind of service station for traffic in and out of the Red Sea. By the 1960s, the French territory of Afars and Issas, as Djibouti was then known, ranked among France's biggest ports, surpassed only by Marseilles and Le Havre. However, the closure of the Suez Canal in 1967 dealt a serious blow to the port, from which it has still not perhaps fully recovered.

Independence

On 27 June 1977, the colony finally won its sovereignty from France. The last French colony on the African mainland to gain its independence, the country became the new Republic of Djibouti. Just one month later, however, the Ogaden War broke out. Ethiopia and Somalia, which had long had designs on the territory of Djibouti as well, began to wage a long and bloody war, in which Djibouti became unwittingly involved. The effect on Djibouti's economy was catastrophic: the railway to Addis Ababa in Ethiopia was closed, and traffic in and out of the port was reduced to practically nothing. Djibouti was as good as bankrupt.

Post-Independence

From the 1970s ethnic tensions within the country grew as rival groups jostled for power. These came to a head in late 1990, with the outbreak of the civil war. In December 1994, a peace accord was signed between the government and rebel forces, and the country has remained relatively stable ever since (see also Government & Politics later in this section).

When the Gulf War broke out in 1990, Djibouti's strategic position was recognised again. During the conflict, the country's president, Hassan Gouled Aptidon, played a shrewd double game, posing as all things to all people. While appearing to oppose the military build-up in the Gulf, he simultaneously allowed France to increase its military personnel in the country, as well as giving the Americans and Italians access to the naval port. Throughout the conflict, Saudi Arabia and Kuwait continued to lend support for the modernisation of Djibouti's port. Djibouti is a member of the Arab League.

War in the Horn

Since independence, Djibouti has tried to present – at least nominally – a neutral political face in the Horn of Africa. Since 1986, it has styled itself as a regional conciliator, attempting to promote the resolution of conflict and economic integration within the region through the East African organisation of IGAD (Inter-Governmental Authority on Development), the brainchild of ex-president Hassan Gouled Aptidon.

In 1998 the border dispute between Ethiopia and Eritrea broke out. IGAD proved ineffective in its role as conciliator, but the conflict presented an unexpected windfall for Djibouti. With Ethiopia's access to the Red Sea blocked at Eritrean ports, Ethiopian foreign trade was diverted through the port of Djibouti. Relations with Eritrea inevitably turned sour, and in November 1998 were formally broken off.

There can be little doubt that Djibouti at least has emerged smirking from this tragic and wasteful war. Initial figures suggest a five-fold increase in cargo transiting to and from Ethiopia, growing by 300% in 1998 alone. Other economic benefits to the country include greater income, employment and business opportunities in the port, as well as an increase in commerce along the roads connecting the country to Ethiopia.

Future Outlook

Since its birth as a nation, Djibouti has always been poised rather uneasily between its larger and more powerful neighbours. The geographical position of the country, sandwiched between three stronger nations, and its strategic value as a port, as well as its limited natural resources, have made the maintenance of good international relations absolutely vital.

Relations with Ethiopia have improved greatly in the last couple of years; Somalia

DJIBOUTI

– with clan rivalries similar to those that dog Djibouti – is still a potential source of destabilisation. Many Djiboutians admit in private to a lack of confidence in the country's survival as an independent nation-state.

In 2000, Djibouti was coming under increasing pressure from external economic aid agencies to raise revenue by increasing tariffs at its port. Ethiopia is resisting increases, and relations between the two countries will require careful handling. In the meantime, Djibouti continues to support Ethiopia against Eritrea and in Somalia and in its relations with the Arab states through the Arab League.

Another source of political and economic anxiety is the flood of refugees that has been arriving in the country since the early 1980s. As a result of conflicts in Ethiopia, Eritrea and Somalia, nearly 200,000 refugees are estimated to have arrived. Quite apart from the huge economic burden this places on the country, it also threatens to upset the ethnic balance of its people.

Relations with France continue to be ambivalent. A large French naval base is still maintained in Djibouti, providing France with a staging post between it and its outposts in the Indian Ocean, and Djibouti with much-needed revenue. In the past, the French presence had additionally guaranteed Djibouti's existence against potential threats from Somalia and Ethiopia both before and after independence. However, many Djiboutians are keen to at last shake off what they consider the final shackles of French influence and interference, in both the economic and political spheres.

In July 1997, in line with a general policy of reducing France's military presence in Africa, it was announced that the garrison in Djibouti would be scaled down from 3800 people to 2600 over the next five years. However, France remains Djibouti's largest bilateral aid donor.

GEOGRAPHY

Djibouti covers an area of 21,000 sq km, in which at least three different geographical zones can be identified. To the east lie the coastal plains, fringed with white, sandy

Monfreid's Hell

It is truly a valley of hell here, hemmed in by stark mountains, and where everything seems tormented by an endless and hopeless struggle. Everywhere there are thorns: on the ground, on the bushes, on the trees; everything seems to want to scratch, to tear, to harm; soils in glassy hues of metallic oxide, rocks jutting out like monsters from the Apocalypse, trees with tortured boughs, it is all the stuff of nightmares and, in the distance, the howling of hyaenas seems to personify the dismal voice of this harrowing nature.

From *Le roi des abeilles* by Henri de Monfreid, Gallimard, France, 1937 (translated by Frances Linzee Gordon)

beaches and coral reefs, which make up much of the 350km coastline.

To the north lie the mountain ranges, where the altitude reaches more than 2063m above sea level, and pockets of forest and dense vegetation are found.

By far the largest zone, however, and the one most characteristic of Djibouti is the volcanic desert: an arid, rock-strewn, desolate wasteland spreading out from the centre.

The country forms part of the Afar Triangle: a triangular depression that makes up part of the East African Rift Valley. This landscape is characterised by a series of volcanic plateaus, sunken plains and salt lakes. Djibouti's landscape is little cultivated and sparsely populated.

GEOLOGY

Millions of years ago, the area now known as Djibouti was under water. Volcanic activity under the sea pushed up the rock and lava that forms the land mass of today. Much of the country still lies below sea level, and most its lakes are saline.

Salt is abundant in the country, and has been mined for centuries by the Afar people, who once used it like currency to trade for goods (see the boxed text 'Salt for Gold' under Danakil Desert in the North of Addis Ababa section of the Ethiopia chapter).

CLIMATE

Djibouti's climate is classed as 'semi-arid tropical' – in other words torrid – and temperatures can get very high. The year can be divided into two seasons: hot and dry, and cool and (relatively) wet.

The hottest period is between June and August, when the temperature can reach 45°C in the shade. The Danakil Depression in Dankalia is one of the hottest areas on Earth. Additionally, two hot, dusty winds, the Khamsin (from the north-west) and the Sabo (from the south-west), blow from the desert during this period. Like the North African Sirocco, they can make conditions seem even more uncomfortable. On the coast, humidity can be very high too during this period.

The coolest time is from mid-October to mid-April, when temperatures average 25°C, and the wind from the east brings some rain. The annual rainfall is very low, averaging less than 125mm.

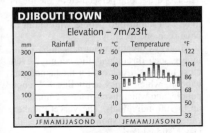

DJIBOUTI TOWN
Elevation – 7m/23ft
Rainfall / Temperature

ECOLOGY & ENVIRONMENT

Djibouti's arid land is among the least productive in Africa. Agricultural production is very limited, and even where irrigation is possible, it is thought that no more than 6000 hectares can be cultivated in total. Livestock rearing is the most important type of agriculture, and it is estimated that nearly 1½ million cattle, sheep, goats and camels roam the country.

As demand for grazing land mounts, Djibouti's richest habitats, the forests of the north, are coming under threat. The greatest offenders of overgrazing are the sheep and the goat. Other threats to the forest include the local people's demand for firewood, for-

Oh What a Beautiful Day!

Djibouti is not known for its seasons; rainfall is incredibly low, and the number of hours of sunlight are incredibly high. When the sun's burning and relentless presence is obscured by clouds on the occasional grey day, Djiboutians cannot conceal their delight: 'Comme il fait beau!', they exclaim, raising their hands to heaven – 'Oh, what a beautiful day!'.

est clearance, and even army manoeuvres and exercises in the fragile Fôret du Day National Park, the country's only national park. In 1973 measures were taken to protect an endemic tree species, the Mont Goda palm, which was threatened with extinction.

Hunting was banned in 1971 in Djibouti, and this has helped the more vulnerable species such as the gazelle and certain types of birds. Nevertheless, the frequent periods of drought and the destruction of the forests through overgrazing are threatening the existence of much wildlife, especially animals that have adapted over the years to the very particular foods and conditions.

A Ministry of Environment was established in 1998.

FLORA

Despite the dry conditions of most of the environment, Djibouti's flora is surprisingly rich, with 650 species of plants registered in the country. The most interesting are the indigenous palms of Bankoualé, the ancient junipers found in the Fôret du Day National Park, the doum palms and the dragon trees.

Corresponding to its geography, Djibouti's flora can be found inhabiting three different zones: coastal plains, mountain ranges and volcanic desert.

Along the coastal plain, particularly along the northern coast, and on the islands of Moucha and Maskali, mangrove forests can be found.

In the mountains, where the massif of the Mabla and Goda Mountains shelters the only forests in the country, the juniper is the most successfully established tree, thriving on the upper slopes between 900 and 1600m above

DJIBOUTI

Dragon Tree

Dotted about the country, the dragon tree (*Dracaena ombet*) is Djibouti's most striking tree. The Greek name, meaning 'female dragon', is derived from the tree's spiky appearance and its strange red sap – used in antiquity and by Djiboutian nomads today as a dye and medicine. More remarkable is the tree's longevity: on the Spanish island of Tenerife, one famous specimen is believed to date from the time of the Egyptians – over 5000 years ago.

sea level. It is found particularly in the magnificent Fôret du Day National Park and around the massif of the Goda Mountains north-west of the Gulf of Tadjoura, where it can reach heights of 20m or more. Numerous other species of trees, shrubs and herbaceous plants also grow in these woods, including the box, the wild olive, the false camphor and various species of fig and mimosa.

On the lower hills below 350m and on the plains, vegetation is scarce, and only the acacia flourishes. Keep an eye out for areas where water is sometimes found, or along the *oueds* (riverbeds), where acacias and tamarisk can be found carpeting the banks.

Some areas are too arid even for the acacias: these include the area around Lac Assal and the Bay of Ghoubbet, where the soil is very saline; the plain of the Grand Barra, which is very rich in clay; and the many plateaus around the country that are too rocky.

Other plants found include wallow, restharrow, saltwort, bellflowers, rock or sun roses, and just one species of orchid (*Holothrix arachnoidea*).

FAUNA

Djibouti's mammals have had to adapt to the harsh environment in which they live. Many of them share common evolutionary characteristics, such as consuming and urinating small amounts of water, leading seminocturnal lives, seeking out shade, and resting during much of the day.

Herbivores inhabiting the country include a good variety of gazelles (Speke's,

Pelzeln's, Waller's and Soemmering's), and various species of antelope including the little klipspringer and the diminutive dik-dik.

Until just a few years ago, the larger antelope, the beisa oryx, could be seen around the Gobaad area. Sadly, it seems to have left the territory because of the lack of food. Smaller herbivores commonly seen include the Abyssinian hare, the porcupine and sometimes the warthog, which frequents more humid areas.

Reptiles include vipers, cobras, mambas, pythons and various tortoises. There are large numbers of butterflies and other insects, many of which remain unclassified.

Carnivores in Djibouti are much feared and hated by the local herdsmen, who protect their animals at night by penning them into enclosures, which are made from drystone walls or thorny acacia branches. The common jackal, the spotted hyaena and less often the wild cat are quite commonly seen. The leopard – long persecuted by the locals – has become rare if not extinct, though you may well bump into people who claim to have seen one recently.

Monkeys are the mammals most commonly seen throughout the country, even close to towns. Look out for the hamadryas baboon, which looks a bit like a French poodle, and which lives in large colonies of up to 100 individuals. The vervet monkey can sometimes be spotted in the Fôret du Day National Park.

Birds

Birdlife in Djibouti is surprisingly rich, with 342 species reported (compared to 250 in Britain, which is six times the size of Djibouti). Of the ten families endemic to the African mainland, three are found in Djibouti: the ostrich, mousebird and barbet. One bird, the Djibouti francolin, is endemic to the country (it's also threatened – just 1500 are thought to remain). The Somali starling is near-endemic.

Considered the highlights for those keen on birds are a sighting of the francolin, the autumn passage of migrants over the Bab el Mandeb Straits, and the selection of northeast African specialities – such as the Arabian

Fussy Females

One bird even the determined nonbirder can't fail to spot is a delightful little yellow bird, hard at work constructing pendulous nests from acacia branches. It is the weaver bird, which is found throughout the Horn. Curiously, it's the male who builds the nest, and the female who inspects it. If it's not up to scratch, it – and presumably he – gets the boot.

golden sparrow, Rueppell's weaver and the shining sunbird.

The Fôret du Day National Park is home to the francolin, as well as an excellent selection of other birds. Obock, at the north-east corner of the Gulf of Tadjoura, is good for seabirds such as the white-eyed and sooty gulls.

The Bab el Mandeb Straits are known as a spectacular crossing point for migrants, particularly raptors moving between Africa and the Middle East in autumn (September to November). Nearly 250,000 birds have been counted crossing during this period. Doumeïra and Ras Siyan in the far north-east of Djibouti are considered the two best spots to witness this spectacle. These sites offer exceptional views of the birds, which pass through a narrow coastal strip at very low altitudes.

Other places to look out for birds include in and around the capital itself, the village of Arta and its surrounding scrubland, the Dorra Desert near Dorra, and the saline wetlands of Lac Abbé.

See also the boxed tips in the special section 'Birds in Ethiopia'.

Marine Life

Situated at the southernmost point of the Red Sea, and at the junction of the Gulf of Aden and the Indian Ocean, Djibouti's position is unique. The combination of the Red Sea's endemic species and the Indian Ocean's variety and number of species makes the country's marine life exceptionally rich. Additionally, the relative isolation of the Gulf of Tadjoura has given rise to a still unknown number of species endemic to Djibouti.

The confluence of these seas in the Bab el Mandeb Straits causes considerable currents, which in turn attract large pelagic species such as sharks and manta rays. The reefs around the group of islands known as Les Sept Frères are particularly known for these; sharks such as the grey, whale, hammerhead, tiger and whitetip reef are all seen here.

Djibouti's waters are also known for the sheer numbers of fish they support (over 250 species) as well as for the size of individual specimens. Colourful reef fish include at least 20 speciesm of angel and butterfly fish and various species of parrot and clown fish. Enormous Napoleon wrasse and giant groper are quite commonly seen, as well as huge schools of snapper, surgeon and blue triggerfish. Schooling barracuda, tuna, king fish, lionfish and scorpionfish are common sightings, as are large moray eels (including the giant and honeycomb). Puffer, box and frog fish and the spotted eagle ray also occur frequently, as do various species of dolphins and the leatherback and hawksbill turtles.

The dugong or sea cow is sadly on the verge of global extinction and sightings have become increasingly rare in this region. These mammals, which can weigh between 200 and 300kg and grow several metres long, used to flourish in the Indian Ocean and the Red Sea.

Djibouti's reefs are also brimming with coral growth, with a density and pristine quality rarely seen further north. Over 140 types of reef coral have been recorded including soft corals and sea fans.

Measures to protect the marine environment have been introduced. An area to the east of the islands of Moucha has been declared an underwater marine park, in which all fishing and hunting is banned. Turtle hunting and the collection of turtle eggs is also forbidden, as is hunting with scuba diving equipment or using gas-charged spearguns.

For more information, see the special section 'Marine Life in the Red Sea' in this chapter.

GOVERNMENT & POLITICS

The Republic of Djibouti's constitution is largely modelled on the French system. The

DJIBOUTI

president, who holds enormous power, is elected by universal suffrage, for a six-year period. The country's parliament, the Assemblée Nationale, is made up of 65 members who are elected every five years (also by universal suffrage). The legal system owes much to the French Code Napoléon, but also incorporates Islamic law.

Djibouti is made up of two main ethnic groups, the Afars and Somalis. The tension and conflict between these rival groups has long made up the whole basis of the country's politics. As early as 1947, anticolonial demonstrations were staged by the Somalis. The Afars, on the other hand, supported French rule, and in 1958 the French placed Ali Alef and his fellow Afars in control of local government.

Independence From France

Protests against French rule continued, but in the 1967 referendum, the country appeared to opt for a continued association with France. However, serious allegations of foul play by the French and vote rigging in favour of the Afars provoked demonstrations and led to pressure on France, both inside and outside the country, to reconsider its position.

In 1976, Ali Alef was forced to resign following huge demonstrations in support of the opposition party, the Rassemblement populaire le progrès. The RPP was a moderate interethnic party led by Hassan Gouled Aptidon, an Issa Somali, and Ahmed Dini, an Afar. Aptidon became president, Dini became prime minister, and in 1977, France reluctantly granted the country its independence.

Ethnic Rivalries

Afar-Somali rivalries continued to simmer, and in December 1977, a near crisis point was reached when five Afars including the prime minister, Ahmed Dini, resigned from the cabinet. Nevertheless, throughout most of the 1980s, President Aptidon adeptly managed to suppress outright conflict between the two main tribal groups.

In 1981, the RPP was declared the only legal party. However, through Aptidon's complex but crafty system of personal and clan patronage within the party, a degree of political stability was maintained. The RPP won the elections of 1982 and 1987.

Afar Rebellion

Tensions rose to the surface again in 1990. Amid calls both inside and outside Djibouti for political pluralism (a multiparty system), the government suddenly cracked down on Afar unrest in the capital. An armed Afar insurgency was launched, led by Ahmed Dini and the Front pour la restauration de l'unité et de la démocratie (FRUD).

In the north, the Afars' traditional territory, the rebellion spread fast. After four months of bloodshed, several hundred casualties, and under pressure from France, a new constitution was at last approved in the 1992 referendum, and a multiparty system introduced. However, only four parties were legally recognised, and almost all power still resided in the presidential office.

By the middle of 1993, the government had regained control of the north, and the Afar movement was left not only defeated but also divided. Towards the end of 1994, the government signed a peace accord with a minority faction of FRUD, and two of its leaders joined the cabinet.

Ismaël Omar Guelleh

The policy of a kind of 'divide and rule' of the opposition seemed to pay off, and the strategy has been continued by the new president, Ismaël Omar Guelleh. Aptidon's cabinet director for over two decades, Guelleh has long been considered the prince regent to the septuagenarian and apparently failing president.

Since 1993, Guelleh has consolidated his power behind the scenes, skilfully and ruthlessly using his control of the security services not only to purge the government of the military threat posed by the Afar rebels in the north, but also to weed out political rivals within his own party. In April 1999, Guelleh won a convincing victory over the rival Issa Somali RPP candidate, Moussa Ahmed Idriss.

The new cabinet has been extensively reshuffled and some new and younger blood introduced. However, in a continuation of

Aptidon's tradition, real power looks likely to remain firmly in the hands of the president and his immediate political cronies. At the end of May 1999, President Guelleh made a state visit to France, where he seemed at pains to promote good relations between the two countries, particularly in the economic field.

Although portraying himself and his policies as liberal and reformist, Guelleh's opponents predict little break with the past, and are critical of both the president's authoritarian style, and the country's human rights record. Some political prisoners have been held without charge for nearly two years, and in May 1999, the European Parliament demanded the release of all political prisoners in Djibouti.

The Opposition

Political parties in opposition to the government – such as the Parti pour le renouveau démocratique (PRD) and the Parti national démocratique (PND) – remain small, internally divided and virtually powerless. In the presidential elections of April 1999, an attempt was made to unite opposition parties and a total of one quarter of the vote was gained. However, the RPP-FRUD alliance continues to hold all seats in parliament.

Ahmed Dini, the leader of the illegal faction of FRUD, remains in exile in Paris. During the 1990s, however, some attempts were made to unite the different factions of FRUD both inside and outside Djibouti. In the meantime, Dini's illegal faction continues to wage a kind of guerilla warfare on army units in the mountains to the north of Djibouti. This does not seem to pose a serious threat to the country's security as a whole.

The next legislative elections are scheduled for 2003; presidential elections are scheduled for April 2005.

ECONOMY

Djibouti's economy is small and struggling. Natural resources are practically nonexistent, manufacturing is basic, and agriculture is severely limited by shortages of both land and water. Djibouti's hopes lie in its port; its future economic outlook depends on its success in improving the port's facilities and increasing trade, particularly with Ethiopia. France's plans to scale down its military presence in Djibouti over the next five years make new enterprise particularly important.

Most of the country's economic assets – along with most of the population – are concentrated in the capital. Service industries, which made up nearly 70% of GDP in 1999, form the basis of the economy, and revolve around the port, civil service, railway and French military garrison.

The 1991–94 civil war did not help the economy: foreign aid dwindled, expenditure escalated and debt increased. Since 1991, Djibouti has tackled major problems with quick-fix, short-term economic solutions. Under increasing pressure from international donors, particularly France, the government attempted to introduce cuts into the proposed budget of 1996. Unrest and a general strike followed, and the government was forced to reverse its policy.

Economic Reforms

Later in 1996, with the help of the IMF, the World Bank and France, another reform program was drawn up. Credit from the IMF and some limited French budgetary assistance was gained, and in May 1997, a program sponsored by the United Nations Development Programme (UNDP) promised limited funds for continued reforms. In October 1999, the IMF approved further loans to Djibouti. Though the figures are modest (no more than US$25 million), it is hoped that the sums will consolidate the country's moves toward economic reform, and will lead to loans from other donors.

Past economic programs have included plans to improve agriculture and livestock breeding, decentralising the economy and developing a free-trade zone. However, a lack of external funding, as well as large internal deficits, has meant that most plans have had to be shelved. The state's Boûl'aos electricity generator, in desperate need of new investment, seems to epitomise the country's ailing economy, and power cuts frequently cripple the capital.

A long-proposed privatisation plan is expected to be implemented by the government in 2000. All the main public utilities are expected to be sold off, including electricity, the railway and the port. There are also hopes to attract private investment in future projects to create free-trade zones. Other hopes for the future include the development of the port and the airport to boost the fishing and tourism industries. In 1997, a US mining company even acquired the rights to search for gold.

Future Outlook

Although Djibouti's economy is fragile, and is almost entirely port-dependent, the ever-increasing commerce through the port (as a result of the Ethiopia-Eritrea war), and the promise of economic reform in exchange for international aid, make Djibouti's economic prospects look rosier than they have for decades. However, progress will depend on the implementation of reforms; in particular restraining state salaries and reforming the civil service and labour market.

It will be a little time before Djibouti's ordinary inhabitants feel the benefits of the changes. In the meantime, many Djiboutians choose to escape temporarily the realities of their daily struggle through the mass consumption of *qat*, an intoxicating leaf. This national pastime, which verges on addiction, is in itself thought to impede the development of the economy. (For more information on qat, see the boxed texts 'Qat & Mouse' under Dangers & Annoyances in the Facts for the Visitor section of this chapter, and 'Chat Among the Pigeons' in the East of Addis Ababa section of the Ethiopia chapter.)

POPULATION & PEOPLE

The population is currently estimated at 750,000, of which up to 200,000 may be refugees fleeing recent conflicts in Ethiopia and Somalia (though figures are difficult to calculate). Roughly half the people are Afars, ethnically linked to Eritrea and Ethiopia, and the other half are Somalis, ethnically connected to Somalia. The Somalis are further divided into clans, of which the Issa is the largest (and whose name is often

Murder Most Foul

Since time immemorial, two famous nomadic peoples have inhabited the territory of Djibouti: the Afars (also known as the Danakils) and the Somalis. Both groups are descended from the same ethnic group (oriental Hamitic), speak related languages (Cushitic), share the same religion (Islam), and belong to tightly knit clan systems that are both patriarchal and hierarchical.

Despite their similarities, the two groups have never seen eye to eye – even up to the present day. In the not-so-distant past, the murder of a member of an opposing tribe brought great glory and prestige to its perpetrator. Warfare and feuds were common, and as recently as 1935, 300 people died in a single clash.

Since the middle of the 19th century, travellers have brought back sensational tales of the bellicose tribes, culminating in Wilfred Thesiger's account of his epic journey through Afar territory in the 1930s (see the boxed text 'The Dreaded Danakils' in the East of Addis Ababa section of the Ethiopia chapter). Many travellers are still shocked and scandalised by what they consider the crude and barbaric customs of these peoples – such as those today surrounding the rites of male and female circumcision (see the boxed text 'A Scream So Strong, It Would Shake the Earth' in the West of Addis Ababa section of the Ethiopia chapter).

However, the very harsh environment and difficult conditions in which the nomads live – in which survivors must compete fiercely for very limited resources – have given rise to a culture in which physical courage and individual initiative are exalted, pain is despised, suffering ignored, and death accepted with serenity.

Both Afar and Somali nomadic cultures are ancient, complex and fascinating, but like so many African tribes are little understood and too quickly condemned or dismissed by western cultures.

For more information on the Afars, see the boxed text 'A Museum of Peoples' under Population & People in the Facts about Eritrea section earlier in this book.

FOUAD DAOUD YOUSSOUF

Street vendor in Djibouti town

used erroneously to denote all Djiboutian Somalis), followed by the Gadabursis and Issaqs. At least 40 different Afar tribes inhabit Djibouti.

The geographical distribution of these groups also reflects their ethnic origin: the Afars inhabit the northern regions of the country; the Somalis the southern.

There is also a minority of Arabs – mainly from Yemen – who number about 14,000; many work as traders and merchants. Around 8000 Europeans live in Djibouti, many of them French, including the 3000 or so troops stationed there. Other nationalities include Greeks, Armenians, Italians, Hindus, Pakistanis, Chinese and Vietnamese.

A huge proportion of Djibouti's population (nearly 80%) lives in urban areas, at least half of them in the capital itself, and the rest lead largely nomadic lives in the country. The population is growing at a rate of 4.4% a year.

EDUCATION

Like the country's political system, the educational one is largely French-inspired. Primary schools accept children from the age of six. From the age of 11 pupils join a *lycée* (secondary school), where at the age of 15 they choose in theory between a vocational education and an academic one (considered more prestigious).

A few students in the latter category can sit for the university entrance exam called the *baccalauréat* (often shortened to *le bac*). Djibouti has no university, so students must apply for places abroad, most often in France. Technical training is also basic, leaving the workforce with a serious shortage of skills.

Education is free in Djibouti, but is not compulsory. The small percentage of children going to school (just 39% attend primary school, and 14% attend secondary school) live in the towns. In the country, children continue to tend the herds of their nomadic families. Djibouti's statistics for education are far below the African average.

According to a recent government survey, 66% of the working population can read, but a tiny 4.5% can read and write. Again, Djibouti is placed well below the average for Africa.

ARTS
Music & Dance

Djibouti's music is diverse, and like the rest of its culture, reflects African, Arab and European influences. Singers range in style from the more traditional, such as Somali singer Amina Farah and Afar singer Abaïzid, to Neïma Moussa, who combines a kind of soul-jazz mix with traditional Somali rhythms. Aïdarous, with his solo guitar, is considered the leader of modern Djiboutian music.

Other particular styles to look out for include the Somali *Guux*, 'the expression of frustrated desire', whose protagonists include Abdi Bobow, Aden Farah and Mohammed Quarchileh. Leading Guux musician Taha Nahari has toured Europe with his band La Troupe du 4 Mars.

Djibouti boasts a rich tradition of dance, both Afar and Somali. The best time to see traditional dancing is on 27 June, Djibouti's Independence Day, which is celebrated in villages and towns across the country. The show staged in the capital is the largest, albeit the most artificial.

DJIBOUTI

Dancing in Djibouti

Dance has always played an important social role in the lives of Djibouti's nomads. Accompaniments are simple: just a drum, a chorus and the rhythmical clapping of hands. Sometimes the words are fixed, sometimes improvised.

Some dances celebrate major events in life, such as birth or circumcision. The *Barimo* is performed at wedding ceremonies, and is a dance of seduction in which two protagonists, a young man and a young woman, dance together.

The *Hirwo* is a dance in praise of nature, which takes place once the rains have come; the *Bismillah* is a dance of love, allowing young lovers to make known long-suppressed feelings towards one another.

The *Laale* dance allows the young men to show off their agility and athleticism. The *Barri Horra* and the *Wiwileh* are war dances, which are designed to stoke up the warriors before they depart for battle; they are characterised by high-pitched cries and impressive manoeuvres with spears. The *Dinkara* dance celebrates the coronation of the new Afar sultan (see also the boxed text 'Drumming the Dinkara' in the Tadjoura section later in this chapter).

Literature & Poetry

By culture and temperament, Djiboutians are a very verbal people. A long tradition of oral literature exists, passed down from generation to generation, and includes beautiful poetry, traditional tales and proverbs, nomadic songs, and local history. (See the special section 'Oral Literature in the Horn' for more information on this tradition.) It was not until 1972 that a written form of Somali was established.

Today, literature continues to flourish, but is increasingly committed to paper – not, unfortunately, in the native Somali and Afar languages (which seem to be considered unsuitable for the written word), but in French. One benefit of Djibouti's alliance with France is the encouragement given by French publishing houses to local writers. Many works are available in bookshops both in Paris and

in Djibouti (see Books in the Facts for the Visitor section).

Perhaps the most famous Djiboutian poet is William JF Syad (1930–93), best known for his lyrical, sometimes semi-erotic collections of poems, such as *Khamsine* and *Cantiques et Harmoniques*.

Other Arts

Though the tradition of theatre is less strong, modern playwrights of note include Aïcha Mohammed Robleh *(La Toubib* and *La Devoilée)*, whose plays explore the typical conflicts of a traditional society meeting a modern world.

Visual artists include Djama Elmi God (1948–96), who for ten years designed the stamps of the republic. Many of his sketches of nomads can be seen reproduced about the capital. Others of note include Nawal Awad, Mouhoumed Mohammed Houssein and Fouad Daoud Youssouf, whose pastels give a Toulouse Lautrec-like glimpse into the seedier side of Djibouti town – from prostitutes in bars to qat chewers in the *mabraz* (qat dens).

See also Shopping in the Facts for the Visitor section.

SOCIETY & CONDUCT
Traditional Culture

The culture of Djibouti's two main ethnic groups, the Afars and Somalis, is traditionally nomadic (see the boxed text 'A Nomad's Life' following in this section). Since colonisation there has been an increasing tendency towards a more sedentary lifestyle, with a steady drift towards the towns. Difficult climatic conditions such as drought, as well as the war in the north, has aggravated the trend. Less than a quarter of the population are now thought to lead nomadic lives.

Nevertheless, town dwellers still retain strong links with their nomadic past. Ties to the family and clan, and all the laws and traditions governing these institutions, remain extremely important. The strong nomadic tradition of hospitality has also retained its importance.

The country's beautiful beaches, clean water and stunning diving are lost on most

Djiboutians. Like their nomadic parents, they prefer to keep their feet firmly on the land; most cannot swim, and keep the Red Sea seafood firmly away from their tables. Look out for local nomads marching past the fish market with fingers firmly pegged to their nose.

If you see a man with ferocious-looking pointed teeth, he is likely to be Afar; many Afar nomads still file their front teeth in this way. The men walking about town in *foutahs* (sarongs) held up with wide coloured belts are probably Afar or Somali nomads on day trips to town. By law, they must leave their *jile* (curved knives), which are normally hung from these belts, behind.

Modern Living

Most Djiboutians live with their family until they marry (women most often in their late teens, and men in their early twenties). Although arranged marriages are becoming less common in the towns, the rules of dowry still apply. The video recorder now forms an important part of the furnishings offered to newlyweds. The car is a very significant status symbol – the newer the better. This might explain the plethora of brand-new 4WDs, despite the *crise* (economic crisis).

Many professional Djiboutians are educated in Europe (mainly France) and return to employment in the civil service.

The life of most Djiboutian males revolves entirely around the consumption of qat, the mildly stimulating leaf. At least five hours per day, several days a week, are spent in conversation in the mabraz (see the boxed texts 'Qat & Mouse' under Dangers & Annoyances in the Facts for the Visitor section of this chapter).

Status of Women

Women do not consume qat in public, and as in many Islamic countries, they keep a lower profile than men. Although significantly fewer girls than boys still go to school, women are entering the workforce.

One of the most contentious issues facing women in Djibouti today is female circumcision (see the boxed text 'A Scream

A Penchant For Poetry

If people can boast national attributes, then Djiboutians can claim perhaps two above all: an unusual power of memory and a remarkable eloquence.

Without a hint of a written record, hotel receptionists effortlessly recall complicated telephone messages, and operators recall long international numbers. Waiters and taxi drivers wax lyrical at the slightest provocation, and any inhabitant can, on demand, recite the entire family tree, and in conversation retell hundreds if not thousands of proverbs and traditional tales.

Such gifts are considered the product of a nomadic culture, in which the spoken word has always been more important than the written one. Individuals carry in their heads their nation's culture and their ancestors' artistry; great memories are developed and a remarkable diction learnt. For the visitor willing to learn, Djiboutians can bring a new meaning to the 'art of conversation'.

So Strong, It Would Shake the Earth' in the West of Addis Ababa section of the Ethiopia chapter). All women in Djibouti are circumcised in one way or another from the age of eight. The average woman bears 6.6 children.

See the boxed text 'A Nomad's Life' later in this section for more on nomadic women.

Where there is a woman, a fire blazes.
Djibouti proverb

Dos & Don'ts

Djiboutians are a friendly, open people who love to chat. However, a few subjects are best treated as taboo, or at least accorded more sensitivity than others. Never ask an inhabitant about their ethnic origin, whether they are Afar or Somali, or, if Somali, to which clan they belong. Religion and politics are also probably best left alone; many Djiboutians feel strongly about the former, and fearfully about the latter. It is also said

A Nomad's Life

Nomads' lives are spent entirely following their animals: seeking out the country's limited grazing and scant sources of water. The herds, which constitute their sole wealth, are made of camels, fat-tailed sheep and above all – due to ever harsher conditions – goats.

Camels are used as sources of milk as well as beasts of burden, but are never ridden in Djibouti (except for transporting the sick and the elderly). They are loaded instead with the household possessions: mats and camel skins for bedding, some simple wooden utensils for cooking, goatskins for carrying water, and some traditional arms: a knife, an axe, and sometimes a spear and shield.

A nomad's shelter consists of long, thin, wooden poles bent into arcs, and covered with matting woven from vegetable fibres or leaves from the doum palm. The Afar huts are usually spherical, the Somali huts more quadrangular in design.

The materials are light, easily transportable, and can be dismantled very quickly, an important attribute in areas where relations between clans and tribes are less than amicable. Raids on rival herds or property still occur, and many nomads now carry Kalashnikovs, in addition to their traditional arms.

It is the women's job to set up the huts, cook, fetch water and weave the mats for the huts, while the men and children tend to the animals and travel to market to barter goods. Usually just one meal is taken a day: a kind of porridge made from sorghum, butter and milk.

Although game abounds in some regions, nomads do not hunt. Traditionally, harmless creatures are respected. Supper is only eaten once all the animals have been safely penned for the night. Hyaenas pose the biggest threat to the herds, and are hated and feared by the herdsmen.

Major events in life, such as circumcision, marriage, widowhood, adultery and death, are all marked by ancient, strictly applied rules. The Afar nomads celebrate the *Rabéna* or Festival of the Dead, which is thought to date from times when ancestor worship was still practised. *L'apsouma*, another old Afar tradition, dictates that a girl cannot marry without her uncle's permission, and she is sometimes 'promised' in matrimony to her first cousin.

that some taxi drivers, hotel staff and waiters act as government informers.

As Muslims, some Djiboutians feel ashamed to admit outright to consuming qat, drinking or smoking. If you want to invite someone to do any of these things, or get invited, you should try and go about it with subtlety. Don't expect the French expats to line up as qat-chewing partners; French law classifies it as a drug and forbids consumption on the territory (see the boxed text 'Qat & Mouse' under Dangers & Annoyances in the Facts for the Visitor section).

If you make a rendezvous with someone, make sure you determine if it's on *temps djiboutien* (Djiboutian time) or *temps européen* (European time). The latter means keeping the appointment punctually; the former means rolling up anytime during the rest of the day. However, western visitors are expected to arrive punctually, and not doing so is considered rude.

RELIGION

The great majority of the country's inhabitants (96%) are Sunni Muslim, albeit not strictly orthodox. The nomads in particular adhere only loosely to the five Islamic 'pillars' (see Islamic Practices following). Some rituals still practised by the nomads are thought to date back to the days of ancestor worship.

Fundamentalism is uncommon in Djibouti, and it is rare to see women wearing the *hijab* (veil), though the majority wear either headscarves or *shalmas*, a gauze-thin length of fabric draped around the head, shoulders and torso. Female visitors are not expected to do so (see Women Travellers in the Facts for the Visitor section , and the boxed text 'Islamic Form' following).

Islam & Other Faiths

Allahu akbar, Allahu akbar ... Ashhadu an la Ilah ila Allah ... Ashhadu an Mohammedan rasul Allah ... Haya ala as-sala ... Haya ala as-sala ...

Of all the sounds that assault the ears of the first-time visitor to a Muslim country, it is possibly the call to prayer that leaves the most indelible impression. The midday prayers on Friday are considered the most important; on this day, the sheikh of the mosque delivers the *khutba*, or weekly sermon.

Contrary to popular belief, Islam shares similarities and origins with the other great monotheistic faiths: Judaism and Christianity. Islam is quite a bit younger than the other two, but like them, springs from the harsh lands of the Middle East.

Again contrary to what is generally believed, Muslims traditionally attribute a place of great respect to Christians and Jews, referring to them as *ahl al-kitab*, the People of the Book. Muslims recognise, respect and even embrace some of the other faiths' teachings. The pages of the Quran (Islam's holy book) carry many references to the earlier prophets of both older religions: Adam, Abraham (Ibrahim), Noah, Moses and others all feature.

Jesus, however, is seen merely as another prophet; one in a long line that ends definitively with Mohammed. The Quran also differs from either the Torah of the Jews or the Christian Gospels in that it is said to contain the word of God, directly communicated through the Prophet Mohammed in a series of revelations.

For Muslims, therefore, Islam represents the apogee of the monotheistic faiths from which it derives. Christianity is seen in effect as a kind of 'new and improved' version of the teachings of the Torah, and Islam as a kind of improved version of Christianity. And so Islam is seen to represent the 'definitive' religion.

The History of Islam

In AD 570, Mohammed was born into a trading family inhabiting the Arabian city of Mecca (in present-day Saudi Arabia). From AD 610, the Prophet began to receive his revelations, and after a time started to impart the content of Allah's message to the Meccans. In essence, his teachings were a call to submit to God's will – the word 'Islam' means submission. However, not all Meccans were initially impressed by these revolutionary ideas.

In AD 622, Mohammed was forced to flee Mecca for Medina – also in Saudi Arabia and today Islam's second most holy city. Mohammed's flight from Mecca or *hijra* (migration) marks the beginning of the Muslim calendar.

In Medina, Mohammed continued to preach the new religion and gradually his power began to increase. Soon he and his supporters began to clash with the Meccans, led by powerful elements of the Quraysh tribe, possibly exacerbated by disputes over trade routes.

By AD 632 and with growing support, Mohammed was able to return to Mecca. Many of the tribes in the surrounding area then swore allegiance to him and his new faith. From then on, the city became the symbolic centre of the religion, and contained, most significantly, the Ka'aba, which housed the black stone said to have been given to Abraham by the archangel Gabriel. Muslims thereafter were instructed to turn towards the direction of Mecca when praying outside the city.

On Mohammed's death in AD 632, the four *caliphs* (successors or companions of Mohammed) became determined to continue spreading the word. Soon all of modern Syria was conquered followed by Iraq, Lebanon, Israel and Palestine. The caliphs were succeeded by the Umayyad dynasty (AD 661–750) in Damascus, and then the Abbassid line (AD 749–1258) in the newly built city of Baghdad.

Islam then spread west, first taking in Egypt and then fanning out across North Africa. By the end of the 7th century AD, the Muslims had reached the Atlantic - by this stage they saw themselves as being sufficiently in control of the Gezirat al-Maghreb (the 'Island of the West' or North Africa beyond Egypt) to consider marching on Spain in AD 710.

One hundred years later, Islam started to touch the coast of modern-day Djibouti, brought not by the sword, but by ship. From around the 9th century AD, Muslim merchants crossed the Red Sea from southern Arabia and settled some of Djibouti's trading ports, such as Tadjoura.

DJIBOUTI

Islamic Form

More than any other religion, Islam governs not only religious life, but also daily and civil activity. Five times a day, Muslims are called to prayer; if they are unable actually to enter a mosque to pray, then they must take the time to do so where they are – whether at home, in the office or elsewhere.

Two phrases above all else strike the listener when in conversation with a Muslim: the phrase 'insh'allah', meaning 'if God wills', and placed obligatorily at the end of any reference to the future; and 'el hamd'llalah', or 'thanks be to God', to express gratitude, such as after an inquiry about someone's health.

Dress and behaviour are also governed by rules – for men as well as women. Travellers in Muslim countries should try and respect these rules. Muslims consider excessive display of flesh offensive; women should try and keep their shoulders and upper arms covered and opt for long trousers or skirts. Low-cut, revealing and very tight clothes are frowned upon!

Men are best advised to opt for trousers (or the local *foûtah* or sarong, which is great for air circulation) rather than skimpy shorts, and should never walk around without a shirt. Nudism on the beaches is forbidden.

Public displays of affection are common among friends of the same sex, but are not normally seen between local couples (even married ones).

Although the consumption of alcohol is prohibited by Islam, discreet consumption is tolerated in many Islamic countries including Djibouti. However, drunken behaviour of any kind is considered a serious offence. Muslims are also prohibited from eating pork (which is considered unclean) and are expected to refrain from gambling, fraud, usury and slander. As in all religions, practitioners follow the teachings with varying degrees of zeal. Many Muslims smoke and drink, though usually discreetly, among good friends, or in the confines of their own homes.

Any effort made to respect this code is greatly appreciated by the locals, and travellers will be accorded greater respect in return.

Sunnis & Shiites

Following Mohammed's death, a power struggle developed between Ali, Mohammed's son-in-law (and the last of the four caliphs), and the emerging Umayyad dynasty in Damascus. A great schism developed at the heart of the new religion.

Those who favoured the Umayyad caliph became known as the Sunnis. Making up the majority of Muslims, Sunnis are considered the orthodox mainstream of Islam.

The Shiites, on the other hand, recognise only the successors of Ali. Most of the Shiites are known as 'Twelvers', because they believe in 12 *imams* (religious leaders), the last of who has been lost from sight, but who will appear some day to create an empire of the true faith. The rest of the Shiites are called the 'Seveners' because they believe that seven imams will succeed Ali.

Islamic Practices

In order to lead a good life, the devout Muslim is expected to adhere to the Five Pillars of Islam.

Shahada This is the profession of faith, the basic tenet of the Muslim faith. 'There is no god but Allah, and Mohammed is His Prophet', is a phrase commonly heard as part of the call to prayer and at many other important events throughout life, such as births, marriages and deaths. The first half of the sentence has become virtually an exclamation, good for any time of life or situation. Muslims can often be heard muttering it to themselves, as if seeking a little strength or consolation in order to get through the trials of the day. Most famously, it was the phrase uttered again and again by the co-pilot in the EgyptAir crash in 1999.

Sala Sometimes written 'salat', it is the obligation to pray, ideally five times a day, when *muezzins* (mosque officials) call the faithful to pray. Although Muslims can unroll their prayer mats anywhere (thought to have evolved with the nomadic lifestyles of the Arabs), it is considered more laudable to worship together in a *masjid* or *jami'* (mosque). The important midday prayers on Friday (roughly the equivalent of Sunday Mass for Christians) are held in a *jami'*, a special kind of mosque that serves as the main district mosque.

Zakat Alms-giving to the poor was, from the start, an essential part of the social teaching of

Islam. In some parts of the Muslim world, zakat later developed into a kind of tax, which was redistributed as funds to the needy. Muslims' moral obligation towards their poorer neighbours continues to be emphasised at a personal level, and exhortations to give are often posted up outside the mosques.

Sawm Ramadan, the 9th month of the Muslim calendar, commemorates the revelation of the Quran to the Prophet. Muslims are expected to participate in a demonstration of a renewal of faith. From dawn to dusk every day of the month, the faithful must abstain from letting anything – even water – pass their lips. Restraint from physical 'indulgences' such as smoking, drinking (when Muslims do), sex and even 'unclean thought' is also expected (see the boxed text 'Ramadan' under Planning in the Facts for the Visitor section).

Hajj The pinnacle of a devout Muslim's life is the pilgrimage to the holy sites in Mecca. Ideally this should be undertaken in the last month of the year, Zuul-Hijja, when Muslims from all over the world join together in the pilgrimage and the subsequent feast. A pilgrim who has accomplished this journey can expect to be addressed as *Hajj*, a title that still elicits considerable respect.

Islamic Customs

When a baby is born, the first words uttered to it are the call to prayer. A week later, a ceremony follows, in which the baby's head is shaved and an animal is sacrificed.

The major event of a boy's childhood is circumcision, which normally takes place between the ages of seven and 12.

Marriage ceremonies are colourful and noisy affairs that usually take place in summer. The ceremony usually takes place in either the mosque or the home of the bride or groom. After that, the partying goes on until the early hours of the morning.

The death ceremony is simple: a burial service is held at a mosque and the body is then buried with the feet facing Mecca.

Before praying, certain rituals must be observed. First, hands, arms, feet, head and neck must be washed in running water; all mosques have an area set aside specifically for this purpose. If no water is available, clean sand suffices, and where there is no sand, just the motions of washing are gone through.

Worshipers then turn to face Mecca – all mosques are oriented so that the *mihrab* (prayer niche) marks the correct direction. A set pattern of gestures and genuflections are then performed. In Djibouti, Muslims can often be seen praying by the side of the road or in the street as well as in mosques.

LANGUAGE

Somali and Afar are the local languages; French and Arabic are the official languages. Most street and shop signs are in French (as are menus), and most educated Djiboutians speak French beautifully. If you can get by in French, you're in for a treat: the Djiboutians are a gregarious, eloquent and hospitable people. Lonely Planet's *French phrasebook* will ease your travels among the people of Djibouti.

Outside the larger towns few people speak French; outside Djibouti town very few people speak English. Even in the capital English is not widely spoken. If you can't muster French, head for the larger hotels. Many have English-speaking staff who are happy to act as interpreters or to accompany you on errands.

See the main language section at the back of this book for more information.

Facts for the Visitor

SUGGESTED ITINERARIES

Although Djibouti is a tiny country, roads are poor and getting anywhere takes time. The country's major attractions can be seen comfortably in ten days, adequately in a week, and at a push in four days.

If you're keen on diving or snorkelling, another couple of days should be budgeted in. Given the distance to the well-known diving destination of Les Sept Frères Islands (around 96km from Djibouti town), a trip there plus a few dives will take the barest minimum of 48 hours.

Arta, the Bay of Ghoubbet, Lac Assal, Tadjoura and the Fôret du Day National Park can all be seen on one trip of three days or more. Venturing into the south and west to Lac Abbé via Dikhil and Ali Sabieh should be a separate excursion and is best seen over 1½ to two days. Of all the highlights, perhaps Lac Abbé in the extreme south-west is the one that shouldn't be missed.

PLANNING
When to Go
The best time to visit Djibouti is during the cooler months from mid-October to mid-April. Visiting in the months from June to August, when Djibouti can seem like a furnace, should be avoided at all costs (see Climate in the Facts about Djibouti section earlier in this chapter). Air travel can be hard to arrange during the school holidays.

Travel during Ramadan (the traditional month of fasting, which takes place during the 9th month of the Islamic calendar) can have its drawbacks. During this period, many cafes and restaurants close throughout the day, business hours are reduced, and the working day goes into a kind of slow motion, when little is accomplished. Additionally, many guides, drivers and those with physically demanding jobs are reluctant to work at this time.

On the other hand, traditional Islamic hospitality comes into its own during this period, and travellers can get an unrivalled opportunity to meet the local people (see

Ramadan

Ramadan – particularly when it falls during the hottest months – can be a demanding time in Djibouti. Productivity goes down, road accidents go up, and everywhere tempers boil over. Even visitors can feel a bit uncomfortable while eating and drinking when those around them go without.

Each day ends with an almost audible sigh of relief with the *fitr*, the breaking of the fast. Visitors may well be invited to join families to celebrate this meal.

On the final day of Ramadan is the *Eid al-Fitr*, an even bigger feast, which is like a kind of Christmas and bonfire night combined, but lasting four or five days. During this time, almost everything comes to a halt; visitors should not miss the chance to join in the celebrations.

Public Holidays & Special Events later in this section).

What Kind of Trip
Djibouti is not yet properly geared up for tourism, at least not the independent sort. The only way of getting to some of the country's principal attractions is by hiring a 4WD with driver-come-guide, or by taking a tour (see the Getting Around section).

Although tours are well organised and allow you do a lot in a short time, they are expensive. Some tour companies offer more unusual trips, such as sorties into the bush to visit the nomadic peoples. These can offer fascinating, unique and rewarding experiences, and if you've got the time and the means, should not be missed.

Many facilities outside the capital are geared towards groups rather than independent travellers. Rolling up to these places is impossible – you'll need to book in advance. Travelling alone presents no problems (for men or women) but if you want to cut costs by sharing an organised tour or vehicle hire, it pays to be part of a group (don't expect tour agencies to bring a group to you as this is against their interests). Try scouting the more popular hotels and cafes of the capital for like-minded fellow travellers. You could also try contacting the agencies in advance from your home country to find out if there are any scheduled group tours that you can join.

If you're contemplating diving off the famous Les Sept Frères group of islands from one of the live-aboards, you will need to book well in advance of your trip (preferably several months), through the local tour agencies in Djibouti town (see Travel Agencies in the Djibouti Town section).

Maps
Decent maps of Djibouti are practically nonexistent in the country itself, so obtain one before leaving home, especially if you need any degree of detail and accuracy. A basic map of the country (and town) is available from the tourist office in Djibouti town.

A much better option – and practically the only one available – is the 1:200,000 physical map, published in 1992 by the well-respected French Institut Géographique National (IGN). Most map suppliers should stock it, including Stanfords in London (☎ 020-7836 1321, fax 7836 0189, ✉ sales@stanfords.co.uk), at 12–14 Long Acre, London WC2E 9LP, UK. The retail price is UK£8.95.

If you need navigational charts, those of the British Admiralty are unsurpassed. Stanfords can order them (they take up to one week to arrive). The price is £15.30 per sheet; you'll need at least one (No: BA253).

RESPONSIBLE TOURISM

The country receives relatively few tourists per year so the impact on the environment is so far fairly minimal. The beautiful coral reefs off Djibouti's coasts are perhaps most vulnerable to damage since they have become a favourite playground of expats. Travellers planning to do a bit of diving or snorkelling should see the considerations for responsible diving under The Threat to the Reef in the special section 'Marine Life in the Red Sea'.

In particular, try and steer away from turtle soup or meat, or from buying turtle products such as shells in the markets. Unfortunately, these items are commonly encountered in Djibouti. All species of marine turtle are threatened, and according to the Convention on International Trade & Endangered Species (CITES), they number among the most endangered animals in the world.

For more information on etiquette, see Dos & Don'ts and the boxed text 'Islamic Form' in the Facts about Djibouti section earlier in this chapter. For advice on being a responsible photographer, see under Photography & Video later in this section, as well as in the Facts for the Visitor section of the Ethiopia chapter. For travel agencies that offer ecofriendly tours and put money back into the local economy, see Travel Agencies in the Djibouti Town section .

See also Responsible Tourism in the Facts for the Visitor section of the Ethiopian chapter.

TOURIST OFFICES

Tourism in Djibouti is still in its infancy. The only tourist office in the country is that found on the main square, Place Ménélik, in the capital (see the Djibouti Town section).

Information for tourists is hard to come by outside the country. In Europe, the Djiboutian embassy in Paris does its best to provide friendly suggestions and some rather weary-looking brochures.

A much better option is the excellent and enthusiastic Association Djibouti Espace Nomade or ADEN (☎/fax 1-43-98-96-02, ✉ aden@club-internet.fr) at 25 Avenue du Château, 94300 Vincennes, France. The organisation was set up by Dominique Lommatzsch, a French national, following a visit to the country. She liked it so much, that she became a kind of self-appointed ambassador, and her organisation functions as a kind of tourist office abroad.

Outside Europe, travellers can try either the Djiboutian embassy in their home country, or the French embassy, which acts *en lieu*.

VISAS & DOCUMENTS

All travellers to Djibouti need visas; the one exception is French nationals, who can visit for up to three months without a visa.

Visas can be obtained from Djiboutian or French embassies. They cost around US$20 and are valid for ten days to one month depending on the embassy. Entry visas can also be obtained at the airport upon arrival; a ten-day visa costs Dfr3000 and a one-month visa costs Dfr5000.

Travellers thinking of visiting neighbouring countries such as Ethiopia, Eritrea, Kenya or Yemen, but returning to Djibouti at the end of their trip (for flights home etc), should consider getting a multiple-entry visa (also around US$20). Note that overland travel between Eritrea and Djibouti may have implications for your ability to leave or to organise visas and extensions in either country (see Border Crossings in the Getting There & Away section).

Travellers also require evidence of a recent yellow fever vaccination, which should be stapled into your passport.

Visa Types

Transit visas cost around US$10, are valid for 72 hours, and can be obtained at the airport for nationals of Belgium, Denmark, Finland, Germany, Italy, Japan, Luxembourg, Netherlands, Norway, Sweden, the UK and the USA. However, you must have an onward ticket before a transit visa is issued; if you do not, you will be expected to buy a ticket.

Visa Extensions

Up to three visa extensions are permitted in theory, and each extension is for up to three months – make sure you extend your visa *before* your current visa expires. Extensions are issued by the Service d'Immigration or immigration office (☎ 35-00-23) at the Police Nationale building in the capital for between 24 hours and ten days (Dfr3000); or between ten days and three months (Dfr5000). Prices are the same for all nationalities, and for both tourists and business travellers. You'll need your passport, one photo (in black and white *not* colour), the immigration form (available from the immigration office and some hotels), and usually also a *garant* (stamp) on the form showing that you are resident at a hotel (ask your hotel).

The office is open from 6.20 am to 1 pm every day except Friday.

EMBASSIES & CONSULATES
Djiboutian Embassies & Consulates

Djiboutian diplomatic representation abroad is scarce. For the Djiboutian embassies in Ethiopia and Eritrea, see Embassies & Consulates in the other chapters. In countries without diplomatic representation, travellers should head for the French embassy, which acts *en lieu* for the issuing of visas.

Egypt (☎ 336 6435) 15 Dr Muhammed Abdel Said St, Dokki, Cairo
France (☎ 01 47 27 49 22, fax 45 53 50 53) 26 Rue Emile Menier 75016, Paris
Japan (☎ 4815 252, fax 4810 476) 2 2 17 201 Shoto, Shibuya-ku, Tokyo 150
Saudi Arabia (☎ 454 3182) BP 94340 Riyadh 11693
US
  Washington: (☎ 202-331 0270, fax 331 0302) Suite 515, 1156 15th St NW, Washington DC, 20005

  New York: (☎ 212-753 3163) 866 United Nations Plaza, Suite 4011, New York, 10017
Yemen (☎ 415 985, fax 412 186) 84 Amman St, 06 As-Safiya al-Gharbiya

Embassies & Consulates in Djibouti

If you're planning to spend a long time in a remote or unstable area (such as parts of the north), it's a good idea to register with your embassy or consulate. See also Embassies & Consulates in the Facts for the Visitor section of the Ethiopia chapter for general information on your own embassy.

All embassies and consulates (many of them honorary) are based in the capital, often around the area known as the Plateau du Serpent, and include:

Belgium (☎ 35-09-60)
Denmark (☎ 35-10-65)
Egypt (☎ 35-12-31)
Eritrea (☎ 35-03-81) closed at the time of research
Ethiopia (☎ 35-10-27)
France
  Embassy: (☎ 35-09-63)
  Consulate: (☎ 35-25-03)
Germany (☎ 35-21-51)
Italy (☎ 35-00-11)
Netherlands (☎ 35-20-22)
Norway (☎ 35-10-65)
Spain (☎ 35-63-53)
Sweden (☎ 35-10-65)
Switzerland (☎ 35-62-74)
Somalia (☎ 35-35-21)
Sudan (☎ 35-14-83)
UK (☎ 35-38-44)
USA (☎ 35-39-95, fax 35-39-40, emergency ☎ 35-13-43)
Yemen (☎ 35-29-75)

MONEY
Currency

The unit of currency is the Djibouti franc, which like the French franc is divided into 100 centimes. Coins are in denominations of Dfr1, 2, 4, 5, 10, 20, 50, 100 and 500. Notes are available in Dfr1000, 2000, 5000 and 10,000.

Unlimited amounts of local or foreign currency can be taken into or out of the country.

Exchange Rates

Since 1973, the Djibouti franc has been pegged to the US dollar, and each day follows the US dollar's variations.

country	unit		franc
Australia	A$1	=	Dfr102
Canada	C$1	=	Dfr116
euro	€1	=	Dfr163
France	10FF	=	Dfr250
Germany	DM1	=	Dfr82
Japan	¥100	=	Dfr160
New Zealand	NZ$1	=	Dfr80
UK	UK£1	=	Dfr257
USA	US$1	=	Dfr170

Exchanging Money

Currency exchange is not possible at the airport, but there are plenty of banks in the capital. As Djibouti is little more than a one-city state, there are few banking facilities outside the capital (in Tadjoura and Ali Sabieh only), and travellers are best advised to rely on cash.

Bank opening hours are Sunday to Thursday from 7.30 to 11.30 am. Remember to have your passport with you for all exchanges of money, even cash. The process is generally quite quick and efficient, and long queues are rare as Djiboutian banks are generally well-run and efficient. There is no commission or service charge for cash exchanges. The authorised bureaus de change are open from 8 am to noon and 4 to 7.45 pm every day except Friday, and are fast and convenient and offer quite good rates.

Travellers Cheques The major banks and hotels, the bureaus de change, some airline offices, and car hire companies accept travellers cheques (in US dollars and French francs only). A commission of between 1.5 and 4% is normally charged.

Proof of purchase of the cheques (the slip issued with them by your bank) is sometimes required when trying to cash travellers cheques – banks usually insist, bureaus de change usually do not.

ATMs There are currently no ATMs (cash withdrawal machines) in Djibouti, though

there are plans to introduce at least one in the near future. Check with the Banque Indosuez Mer Rouge.

Credit Cards All the capital's larger hotels, restaurants and shops (and increasingly the smaller ones) accept major credit cards. Most airline offices and car hire agencies also take them. A commission of up to 5% is usually charged but you should check in advance.

The standard commission on cash exchanges at bureaus de change(for all currencies) with credit cards is US$12 per US$100 (US$6 commission, plus US$6 for telephone verification).

At some banks, such as the Banque Indosuez Mer Rouge and BCIMR, major French credit cards can be used to obtain cash.

International Transfers Transfers are possible in US dollars only. In theory, by telex they should take no more than 48 hours, though in practice it's often much longer, depending on the competence of both banks.

There is no limit to the amount of the transfer but be aware that a flat fee of US$70 is charged by the bank for this service! You'll also be charged a further commission for conversion into the local currency.

A few banks have special agreements with banks in France. The Banque Indosuez Mer Rouge is a correspondent with the following French banks: Crédit Agricole, Crédit Lyonnais, Societé Générale, Banque Populaire, CIC, CCF and the Banque Transatlantique.

Black Market There is a flourishing and currently well-tolerated black market in the capital. However, don't forget that it is officially illegal, and by indulging you're taking a big risk for a small gain. Though the transactions don't present a danger in themselves, the area around Les Caisses market is renowned for pickpockets and sometimes muggings, particularly at night.

The only reason to use the black market is if you're caught out over the Muslim weekend (the banks are closed Friday and Saturday), or you're desperate to get rid of leftover 'nonexchangable' currencies such as the Ethiopian birr.

DJIBOUTI

Tips for Tight Travelling

Despite popular travellers' lore, it is possible to visit Djibouti on a budget. The following are a few pointers to assist:

- In the capital, avoid the European Quarter and particularly Place Ménélik, where even a cup of coffee can be three times the local price.
- Stick to local hotels, restaurants, bars and markets.
- A water bottle saves spending too much on soft drinks in the heat.
- If you want to taste the seafood but can't afford the restaurants, buy it direct from the fishermen.
- If you want to snorkel but can't afford a boat trip to the islands, catch the ferry to Tadjoura and snorkel from the beach – it's just as good.
- If you want to swim but can't afford the boat to Moucha Island, head for the beaches in town, or for Doralé, where there are cheap cabins if you want to stay overnight.
- Use the local minibuses for travel in the capital. For the country, use the buses.
- If you want to learn about Djibouti's culture, try the tourist office and IRIS (see under Information in the Djibouti Town section).

You'll need to ask a local for help in finding a moneyexchanger; many are women and are well camouflaged as street vendors who keep their wads of cash hidden up their skirts!

Most major currencies can be exchanged, including the nonexchangables such as the Ethiopian birr, Eritrean nakfa and Yemeni rial, but not in very large amounts.

Security

Because of the paucity of banking facilities outside Djibouti, you'll have to carry fair amounts of cash with you. Fortunately, the risk of theft and pickpocketing diminishes considerably outside the capital, though you'll still need to be vigilant – never ever leave money or documents on beaches!

Pickpockets are adroit in Djibouti, so a moneybelt – ideally concealed under clothing – is still the best way of carrying around cash and documents. Most travellers experience no problems in Djibouti. See also the Dangers & Annoyances section later in this section and in the Djibouti Town section. For general information on security, see Security in the Facts for the Visitor section of the Ethiopia chapter.

Costs

Djibouti is not cheap compared to other African countries, but neither is it extortionate, as the majority of travellers and guidebooks love to make out. If your budget is limited, you can get by adequately on Dfr5000–6000 (US$28–33) a day (including food and accommodation). A rock-bottom room costs around Dfr1500 and a budget meal around Dfr500. A can of soft drink costs Dfr50; a soft drink or coffee in an average cafe costs between Dfr100 and Dfr200.

If you're after a few more creature comforts, such as a wider choice of food, you should budget for around Dfr12,000 (US$68) per day. For the run of the city's best hotels and restaurants, be prepared to spend Dfr30,000 (US$170) and upwards per day.

Transportation and customs duties make many French imports very expensive. Products in the French supermarkets, bookshops, newsagents etc retail for between two and three times their original retail value in France.

Tipping & Bargaining

Service charges are generally included in the bill and tipping is not normally expected. However, in the restaurants, bars and hotels frequented by Europeans (particularly on and around Place Ménélik), the locals have come to expect a tip of around 10% of the bill.

Bargaining is normal in all the markets, particularly in the capital, where the Arab influence from across the Red Sea is most felt. You should also haggle with the taxi drivers in the capital whose rates seem to fluctuate according to your nationality, naivity and negotiation skills (see Local Transport in the Getting Around section).

POST & COMMUNICATIONS

The main post office in Djibouti town has poste restante services (see Information in the Djibouti Town section). The postal system works with French efficiency and organisation, but remember to put *par avion* (airmail) on letters and postcards destined for abroad; delays have been reported without.

A stamp for a postcard costs Dfr50 for France, and Dfr100 everywhere else. A letter weighing up to 10g costs Dfr120 for France, Dfr125 for Europe, and Drf135 for the USA, Canada or Australia.

Parcels weighing up to 2kg can be sent from the main post office. The price per kilo is Dfr1410 to France, Dfr1740 to Europe, and Dfr1840 to the USA, Canada or Australia.

Parcels weighing between 2kg and 20kg, should be taken to the large parcel office near the main post office. Parcels need to be prepared in advance. A 5kg parcel costs Dfr8700 to Europe, Dfr12,890 to the USA or Canada, and Dfr18,105 to Australia.

Telephone & Fax

When calling from abroad, the country code for Djibouti is 253; there are no other town or area codes. When calling abroad from Djibouti, wait for the first tone, dial 00, wait for the second tone, then dial the country code followed by the rest of the number. For directory assistance in Djibouti call ☎ 12.

The cheapest place to make an international call is the main post office in the capital. You will be asked to pay a deposit, then allocated a cabin. You can make as many calls as you like, and pay afterwards. However, calls are expensive: a one-minute call costs Dfr500 to France, Dfr700 to most European countries, and Dfr1050 to the USA, Canada or Australia. Rates remain the same all day.

If you just want to send a short 'I'm still alive' message, you could consider a telegram. It costs Dfr56 per word to France, and Dfr105 to Europe or Australia, and Dfr105–121 per word to the USA or Canada. Telegrams can be sent from the main post office in the capital.

Outside business hours and sometimes until quite late in the evening, calls can be made (and faxes sent and received) from private phone centres or shops in the capital; look out for the 'Fax' or 'Téléphone' signs. Many of the larger hotels also send and receive faxes, though rates are pricey.

There are a number of phone boxes around town, that take both cash and *telecartes* (phonecards). Phonecards are available in fifty-unit increments from 50 to 300, and cost from Dfr2500 to 12,000. The main post office and small local shops on Place Ménélik sell them. For general information on Lonely Planet's eKno communications card, see Telephone & Fax in the Facts for the Visitor section of the Ethiopia chapter.

Email & Internet Access

Email services are still nascent in Djibouti, with just one service provider, Societé des Telecommunications Internationales de Djibouti (STID), for residents only. The Chambre Internationale de Commerce de Djibouti in the capital, among others, hopes to introduce facilities soon (see Post & Communications in the Djibouti Town section). Ask the tourism office for an update on progress.

INTERNET RESOURCES

There are a few Web sites on Djibouti.

Africa News Online News about Djibouti as reported by its neighbours.
www.africanews.com

CIA The World Factbook Lots of facts about Djibouti to complement this chapter. Follow the links to the World Factbook.
www.odci.gov

Deja News Follow the Travel/Africa links for a bulletin board forum on Djibouti similar to Lonely Planet's Thorn Tree.
www.deja.com

Djiboutian Sightings A beautiful site illustrating Djibouti's past.
www.multimania.com/soulard

Gateway Sites Busting with links useful for travellers to Djibouti.
www.woyaa.com
www.travel-finder.com

Middle East Internet Directory Search for Djibouti in this comprehensive database.
www.arab.net

US State Department Bureau of Consular Affairs This site is informative in the usual very alarmist sort of way.
www.travel.state.gov

DJIBOUTI

BOOKS

Books on the country are a bit limited (though there are more options if you read French). Many titles are available in Djibouti town.

Travel

For travellers tales, you can't beat Wilfred Thesiger's *The Danakil Diary*, which records the explorer's epic journey in the 1930s across uncharted Afar territory (in Ethiopia and Djibouti), in search of the source of the Awash River. His account of the Afars and their way of life is largely responsible – albeit unwittingly – for their somewhat sensational status as 'one of Africa's fiercest tribes'.

In French, one of the best books currently available is *Djibouti l'Ignoré* by Marie-Christine Aubry. It's really a collection of travellers tales, but offers interesting, amusing and sometimes penetrating insights into the country – from travellers and traders, to disgruntled administrators and adventurers.

Other travellers accounts in French include the swashbuckling adventures of Henri de Monfreid, of which *Les Secrets de la Mer Rouge* is perhaps his best. Keep an eye out also for Joseph Kessel's *Fortune Carrée*, possibly the most lyrical book to have come out of the country – at least from an outsider.

History & Politics

The very few books in English include *Djibouti: Pawn of the Horn of Africa* by Robert Saint-Veran, which looks at the politics of the country, during and since colonial days, and *Naval Strategy East of Suez: The Role of Djibouti* by Charles Koburger, which is more interesting than it sounds, and gives some insights into the country.

General

For those interested in the remarkable geology of the country, the French-language *Djibouti Itinéraires Géologiques* by Pierre Vellutini is an excellent and well-illustrated publication. Attractive coffee-table publications include *Djibouti: Terre des Extrèmes* by Jean Claude Nourault & Giles Nourault, and *Djibouti* by Eric Weiss, though both seem to be currently out of print.

NEWSPAPERS

Various local newspapers are available, all published weekly in French. *La Nation* is probably the most professionally produced, but is strongly pro-government. The others are also party-produced, among them *Le Populaire* (for the opposition parties), *Le Renouveau* (PRD), *République* (PND) and *Liberté* (FRUD). Although ostensibly demonstrating the freedom of press, they tend to lose credibility with rabid rants against opposing parties.

A good range of international newspapers and magazines can be found in the newsagents and bookshops off Place Ménélik.

RADIO & TV

Broadcasting is controlled by the government. Television broadcasts start at 6 pm and last for between four and six hours. Programs are in Somali, Afar, Arab and French. Some of the big hotels have satellite TV.

Radio Djibouti can be found at 92.25 MHZ FM 24 hours per day. The BBC World Service can be received in Djibouti on shortwave radio, but frequencies vary according to the time of day (try 9630, 11940 and 17640).

PHOTOGRAPHY & VIDEO

A good range of print and slide film is available in Djibouti (including both Kodak and Fuji products). Processing is of a high standard, but is expensive at Dfr2400 for 24 exposures and Dfr4000 for 36. For film, head for the One Hour Photo Services on Rue Clochette in Djibouti town, which has an excellent though pricey range of print and slide film. Film processing is also good quality.

Djibouti, like France, uses the SECAM video system. This differs from the rest of Western Europe and Australia (which use PAL), and the USA, Canada and Japan (which use NTSC). The three systems are not compatible.

For more information, see Photography & Video in the Ethiopia chapter.

Dos & Don'ts

With the recent civil war and unrest, Djibouti's security services are active, sensitive and unsympathetic. You should avoid photographing all military- or police-related subjects, even airports and bridges. The presidential palace in the capital is also off-limits. Attempts to photograph socially sensitive subjects such as protest marches or demonstrations are quickly noticed too, and may well end up in film confiscation.

Always smile at your subject and ask permission first – even with basic sign language. Best of all, use a local as a kind of interpreter or go-between. If you show a little respect, patience and sympathy for the people, the rewards will be great: the Djiboutians are a proud, colourful and very photogenic people. Evelyn Waugh, a British writer travelling in Djibouti in the 1930s, described the people as a 'race of exceptional beauty'.

TIME
Djibouti is three hours ahead of GMT/UTC. When it's noon in Djibouti, it's 1 am (earlier) in Los Angeles, 4 am in New York, 9 am in London, and 11 pm in Sydney.

Like France, Djibouti uses the 24-hour clock. Often an 'h' is used between hours and minutes; thus 00h30 is 12.30 am.

ELECTRICITY
Djibouti runs on 220V at 50Hz AC. Sockets are like the old French type that take plugs with two round prongs rated at 600 watts. Most travel adapters accommodate this, though travellers from the US and Canada (with120V at 60Hz) should be careful to choose one appropriate for their equipment. Newer appliances are made to run at both 50 and 60Hz.

See Dangers & Annoyances later in this section for information on Djibouti's electricity supply problems.

LAUNDRY
There are no laundries in Djibouti, just *pressings* (dry cleaners). The best place to get clothes washed is in your hotel, where prices tend to correspond to the room rate: budget hotels will charge little, smart hotels a great deal.

For those on business, dry cleaning costs a little less than in Europe: Dfr2300 for a dress, Dfr1500 for a skirt, Dfr1000 for a pair of trousers and Dfr700 for a shirt.

TOILETS
Both the sit-down and squat types of toilet are found in Djibouti, reflecting French and Arab influences respectively. The smarter hotels and restaurants go *á l'Européen*, but the budget establishments (particularly in the smaller towns) favour the Arab way. In the small villages and country areas, you'll be lucky to find a bush.

HEALTH
For general information on health, see the Facts for the Visitor section of the Ethiopia chapter.

One of the biggest hazards in Djibouti, and the one taken least seriously by travellers, is the sun. A writer early in the 20th century called it *le soleil qui tue*, 'the sun that kills'. Never embark on a journey outside town without a good supply of water.

Malaria and dengue fever pose problems outside the town, especially in the cool

---

Toilet Troubles

Many travellers to Djibouti are shocked to see the country's males responding to calls of nature in public. Inhabitants display an enviable ease and self-assurance while urinating in the streets of their capital. A particular partiality for the central road reservations – all green and grassy one assumes – can cause consternation for unsuspecting motorists pulling up at red lights.

Djiboutian society is traditionally nomadic and it is thought that old habits die hard. Additionally, there are very few public toilets in Djibouti, and those there are, are certainly not green and grassy. Nomads express disgust at the 'revolting custom' of visiting these places.

Travellers caught out in the capital are lucky enough to have a better option: head for the smart hotels and restaurants. Unlike in Europe, staff wouldn't dream of turning you away in your moment of need. Outside the capital? Head for the green and grassy bits.

season, and particularly in the region of Ali Sabieh, in the south-east near the Ethiopian border. Antimalaria prophylactics should be taken; these can easily be bought in Djibouti.

Divers should be aware that there is currently no permanent decompression chamber in Djibouti – if you get decompression sickness, it could be fatal.

Djibouti is very well endowed with excellent French-supplied pharmacies, laboratories, medical practices and hospitals. Blood, urine and stool tests are readily available.

Sexually Transmitted Infections (STIs)

STIs are rampant, particularly gonorrhoea, syphilis and increasingly HIV/AIDS. Abstinence is the best protection; condoms are another alternative in practising safer sex. Good-quality and reliable condoms are widely available from pharmacies, kiosks and supermarkets.

WOMEN TRAVELLERS
Attitudes Towards Women

With the large French presence, Djiboutians are well used to having European women wander their capital and countryside. However, as in all Muslim countries, it's greatly appreciated if women dress conservatively (see the boxed text 'Islamic Form' under Society & Conduct in the Facts about Djibouti section earlier in this chapter).

Swimming and sunbathing on the beaches is no problem (but not topless or nude), and you may well find some of Djibouti's younger female population already in the water.

Djiboutians are taught to be well-mannered, courteous and respectful towards women. Almost the only attention you're likely to receive are the little poetic complements sung out in the street from women and children as well as from men, and to which it's impossible to take offence. Most often you'll hear a *Soyez bienvenue* (Welcome). Whistling or cat calls are considered very rude, so don't worry about the builders!

Djibouti is practically hassle-free, and compared to many other countries – including European ones – is an absolute treat for a woman traveller, either alone or as part of a group. If you show the Djiboutians a little respect, an openness of mind, and an interest in their culture, you'll find them a charming, respectful and extremely hospitable people.

The organisation IRIS (see Cultural Centres under Information in the Djibouti Town section) promotes 'cultural exchanges', and always welcomes foreign travellers. It can also put you in touch with local women's clubs in Djibouti.

HIV/AIDS in Djibouti

AIDS is thought to pose a particularly serious threat to Djibouti. As a port, it harbours a high population of prostitutes; as a country in an unsettled region, it is home to thousands of refugees; as an ex-colony of France, it is the military base for a large number of French soldiers (more than any other country in Africa).

Other particular problems include the influence (albeit disputed) of qat, said to promote promiscuity; social difficulties such as the lack of education; economic problems, which mean that men are marrying later; the cultural obstacles that make any mention of sex taboo; and the religious doctrines that state that the use of condoms is against the teachings of Islam.

A local doctor estimates that at least 15% of Djibouti's population is HIV+. Unless serious measures are taken soon, Djibouti's population has a very bleak future.

The Djibouti Droops

New arrivals to Djibouti often complain of fatigue, insomnia, cramps in the legs, lack of appetite and sometimes diarrhoea. These symptoms are thought to relate to the sudden exposure to heat, and usually disappear rapidly. Prickly heat is another very common complaint, and can become severe. Air-conditioned rooms and frequent cold showers usually bring relief.

Safety Precautions

Local women generally hurry home before dark. If you want to go out in the evening and explore the local areas, try and find a companion (ideally male). Never wander the streets after nightfall alone (mugging is the greatest risk). If you're trying to get back to your hotel after visiting a restaurant etc, ask the manager or a waiter to find a taxi for you.

Only prostitutes are seen chewing qat, drinking or smoking in public, and although allowances are made for foreign women, a few local men may construe these habits as signs of 'availability'.

If you want to try qat, it's harder to find women's *partis* or circles than it is to find men's. It's fine to partake with men if you're invited, but make sure it's with a group you know or are comfortable with – never accept the invitation of a sole man. It

might be a good idea to tell your hotel where you are going, and dress extremely conservatively – in very long, baggy clothes that cover even your ankles.

See also the boxed texts 'Qat & Mouse' later in this section and 'Qat Among the Pigeons' in the East of Addis Ababa section of the Ethiopia chapter.

GAY & LESBIAN TRAVELLERS

Recent legislation has declared that homosexuality is illegal in Djibouti. It is also severely condemned by both traditional and religious cultures, and remains a topic of absolute taboo. Although reports of male prostitution in the capital have emerged recently, the French military has been blamed for creating the market. Although gay locals obviously exist, they behave with extreme discretion and caution. Gay travellers are advised to do likewise. The best source of information is the International Lesbian and Gay Association Web site at www.ilga.org.

DISABLED TRAVELLERS

For wheelchair-using travellers, taxis are widely available in the capital and are good for getting around the town, though none have wheelchair access. Car rental with a driver is easy to organise, if expensive (see the Getting Around section). See also Disabled Travellers in the Facts for the Visitor section of the Ethiopia chapter.

SENIOR TRAVELLERS

Traditionally, older citizens are accorded great respect in Djibouti, and you will be made to feel very welcome. Djibouti's capital is well equipped with first-class hotels, restaurants and medical care, which should cater to most needs. Outside the town, though, many facilities are lacking.

Although most tourist sites can be visited in a one- to two-day trip from the capital, roads are very rough in parts, and journeys are long, hot and hard (particularly on the back) even in the best 4WD.

TRAVEL WITH CHILDREN

The Djiboutians are very welcoming and open towards children and there are no

---

Prostitution in Djibouti

After nightfall, almost all 'decent women' are safely tucked away at home. So male travellers should be aware that almost 100% of the 'local' women (many in fact Ethiopian) encountered in the bars, cafes and nightclubs of Djibouti town are prostitutes.

Many are young, attractive and often soberly dressed; some travellers mistake them for ordinary local girls, and are flattered by their attention. However, responding to their attentions will raise expectations, and cost you at least a round or two of high-priced drinks (many girls have agreements with the establishment where they work).

Also, be careful not to tread on the toes of the local *legionaires* (Foreign Legionaries). Some have 'favourite friends', and don't appreciate strangers muscling in, particularly after a drink or two.

Should you be tempted by the invitations of the girls, remember that HIV/AIDS is said to be rampant in Djibouti town. One local French doctor described an unprotected encounter of this kind as 'paramount to suicide'. Infection in this group has been estimated at between 68 and 80%.

particular reasons for not taking them with you. However, many important facilities for children, such as cots in hotels, safety seats in hired cars, and highchairs in restaurants, are almost totally lacking.

Items such as nappies, baby food and mineral water are easily available in the well-stocked French supermarkets (but are between two and three times their normal price). Medical facilities are also good.

DANGERS & ANNOYANCES
Crime
Djibouti is a relatively safe country, and serious crime or hostility aimed specifically at travellers is very rare. However, the recent influx of thousands of refugees into Djibouti has significantly pushed up the crime rate in the capital, particularly at night (see also Dangers & Annoyances in the Djibouti Town section).

Popular tourist spots the world over attract thieves; beaches such as those at Doralé, Ambado and Khor Ambado are particularly infamous for thefts. Use the bungalows, and don't leave more than a towel or old clothes on the beach, particularly if you're swimming. You can't rely on friendly neighbours as thefts happen in the blink of an eye. Never leave valuable possessions in a car, not even in the boot.

Land Mines
Some areas of Djibouti (the Djibouti-Eritrea border and parts of Obock and Tadjoura) were heavily mined during the civil war. Never stray off the beaten track when driving or walking in these areas. If you're planning on trekking, check the security situation with authorities such as the local police. In 1999, more than 50 people were killed or wounded by land mines in Djibouti.

Electricity Supply
For the inhabitants of Djibouti town, the greatest annoyance is the frequent power failures. Cuts take place when demand is greatest – in the morning as people get up, between 6 and 7 am, and at lunchtime between noon and 1 pm. Blackouts can last several hours or sometimes all day.

If you rely on electricity at this time to power laptops, shavers, recharging video camera batteries etc, work around these periods. If you really need a constant supply of electricity, or if air-con or even a basic fan to cool your room is important to you, make sure you inquire if your hotel has a *groupe* (generator). If you're planning to take a laptop with you, make sure you have something to protect it against the variations in current and the frequent power cuts in the capital.

Dealing with Police
With the rebel insurgency in the north, Djibouti's security services are sensitive and active. There is no reason why travellers should attract the attention of the police, but if it happens, it's usually pretty harmless information-gathering.

You'll be taken to the station, interviewed, asked to sign a statement, then released. It's important to remain polite and calm. Even the police in Djibouti are friendly and courteous, and they'll probably give you a lift back to your hotel.

BUSINESS HOURS
Business hours vary widely with the season, the sector (private or public) and the occasion (such as Ramadan). Note that Friday is the day of rest. Just like on Sunday in the west most shops close on Friday, but many restaurants (particularly in the capital) and places of entertainment remain open. The 'weekend' in Djibouti refers to Friday only; Saturday and Sunday are normal working days.

Most government offices and institutions are open from Sunday to Thursday from 7.30 am to 1.30 pm. Note that banks close earlier at 11.30 am (but bureaus de change are open later). Shops and private enterprises are generally open from around 7 am to 12.30 pm, and then from 4 to 6.30 pm. Some of the Yemeni-owned shops stay open until late (up to 11 pm).

Most restaurants open around 7 pm and close around 11 pm, though outside the capital they close earlier; you shouldn't leave dinner for much later than 8.30 pm.

During Ramadan, most shops close during the day and open in the evening

Qat & Mouse

Visitors to Djibouti may be surprised by the sudden commotion that bursts each day upon the otherwise torrid and torpid streets of the capital. At 1.20 pm on the dot, a cacophony of car horns and shouting breaks out heralding some marvellous news: qat, the mildly intoxicating leaf, and the nation's daily addiction, has arrived.

Two hours later, the capital is a ghost town again, abandoned to the cats, the Foreign Legionaries and the occasional tourist. Locals are firmly ensconced behind closed doors in the sacred confines of the *mabraz* (qat den).

Every day, or at least several times a week, qat consumers meet their circle of friends or peers in the mabraz, to *mâcher la salade* (munch up the salad). There, a minimum of five hours is spent reclining on cushions, smoking cigarettes and sipping tea; all *en brutant* – while 'grazing' on the leaves.

Gathered members gossip, joke and exchange local and international news. Later, lively debates and heated discussions break out, and the mabraz becomes perhaps Djibouti's real parliament. Chewers, with inhibitions and a natural diffidence suppressed by the leaf, find themselves elbow to elbow with an eminent politician or affluent businessman. With wild gestures and wide, shining eyes, opinions are voiced, explanations demanded, and remedies promised.

Eight tonnes of qat are flown in daily to Djibouti from Ethiopia. Easily the most significant commodity consumed in the country, qat is estimated to account for a staggering 40% of household expenditure. While the health effects of the drug are debatable (see the boxed text 'Chat among the Pigeons' in the East of Addis Ababa section of the Ethiopia chapter), its economic impact in Djibouti is clearer and more disturbing. Expenditure is grossly distorted, and huge amounts of working time and efficiency are lost. It is estimated that two months and 16 days are lost per worker per year in the consumption of qat in Djibouti.

Social repercussions are alarming too. Long known to cause discord in the home (as husbands spend all their time and money on qat), divorce is ever on the increase, and now affects nearly 50% of the population. As a result, children are underperforming at school, and many wives themselves are increasingly seeking comfort in – of all things – qat. Over 10% of women in Djibouti are thought to consume the plant regularly.

The government has long wrung its hands over the problem – or ruminated over a leaf or two. In 1977, President Hassan Gouled Aptidon tried to ban outright the importation and consumption of qat in the country. Unprecedented protest broke out from all levels of the population, the black market boomed, and qat consumption thrived. The government was forced to back down.

Although the social role of the mabraz is recognised, it is also seen as possibly ghetto-ising Djibouti. The mabraz functions as a kind of club affiliating members of the same ethnic, cultural or social background. Integration and exchange of the different groups is therefore retarded, exacerbating existing ethnic and political tensions already threatening the precarious unity of the country.

Qat has also been called the opium of the people. On election day, the daily supplies from Ethiopia suddenly arrive miraculously early. And the day passes smoothly and without so much as a voice, let alone a vote, raised in protest. The solution to weaning the nation from its addiction is complex and difficult. The nation's dependency is in part explained by a struggling economy. With unemployment chronic (at least 40%) and living conditions very poor, qat provides a daily refuge from reality.

Many measures have been proposed to tackle the problem in Djibouti, including education programs, controlled sales of qat on certain days of the week, the development of leisure facilities and activities, and the reintroduction of the old working day (to 5.30 pm). But nothing has yet been implemented. In the meantime, the game of qat and mouse continues.

If you fancy a chew of qat, head for the markets in the African Quarter. Qat costs from Dfr300 for a small bundle of inferior-quality leaves, to Dfr5000 for 1kg of top-quality stuff (up to Dfr10,000 when in demand).

Islamic Holidays

Hejira Year	New Year	Prophet's Birthday	Ramadan Begins	Eid al-Fitr	Eid al-Adha
1421	06.04.00	14.06.00	27.11.00	27.12.00	06.03.01
1422	26.03.01	03.06.01	16.11.01	16.12.01	23.02.02
1423	15.03.02	23.05.02	05.11.02	05.12.02	12.02.03
1424	04.03.03	12.05.03	25.10.03	24.11.03	01.02.04

from 7 to 11 pm (see also the boxed text 'Ramadan' under Planning earlier in this section).

PUBLIC HOLIDAYS & SPECIAL EVENTS
National Holidays
New Year's Day 1 January
Labour Day 1 May
Independence Day 27 June
Christmas Day 25 December

Islamic Holidays
Islamic holidays include Lailat al-Miraji, Eid al-Fitr, Eid al-Adha, Arafa the Muslim New Year, Al-Ashura, and Eid Mawlid al-Nabi (the Prophet's birthday). The exact dates all vary from year to year, as they depend on the lunar calendar.

For more information on the festival of Ramadan see the boxed text 'Ramadan' under Planning earlier in the section.

ACTIVITIES
Djibouti's tourism potential is still relatively unexploited; there are few organised leisure activities for the traveller besides those that revolve around the sun and the sea.

Occasionally an enterprising expat installs other activities, but these usually last the length of the expat's sojourn in Djibouti. At the time of writing, there was a centre for windsurfing on wheels set up on the desert sands of the Grand Barra. See also the activities listed separately in the Djibouti Town section later in this chapter.

Diving & Snorkelling
The one outstanding activity that makes up for the dearth of others is diving. Even if you're a nondiver, you shouldn't miss the chance to snorkel off Djibouti's beautiful coral reefs. All diving gear can be hired in Djibouti, though it's expensive.

Bring a mask and snorkel if you plan to explore the reefs. If you're planning to dive, don't forget your diving proficiency card and logbook, and check that your insurance policy covers this activity. If you're heading for Les Sept Frères Islands, bring a night-diving torch and a diver's float or surface marker. Some dive operators don't bother with buoyancy control devices (BCDs); if you're concerned about this, you should take your own.

Most snorkelling and diving takes place off the islands of Maskali and Moucha in the Gulf of Tadjoura. The islands can be quite easily visited through organised boat trips from the capital, particularly at the weekend (Friday), when the French expat population like to go there. Budget travellers who can't afford a boat trip should hop on the ferry to Tadjoura. From the beaches there, you can snorkel at leisure off the reefs.

Other interesting diving destinations include the Bay of Ghoubbet and Les Sept Frères Islands. For both, you will have to organise a custom-made tour; trips to Les Sept Frères Islands are very expensive because of the distance. Chartered, week-long live-aboard tours also go there. If you're lucky you may be able to get a space on one of these, but in general, all tours need to be organised well in advance. In theory, boats can be rented to almost any destination, but unless there are several of you to share the cost, they are very expensive.

All the major schools including the American PADI and NAUI, British BSAC, and the French FFESSM are recognised in Djibouti.

DJIBOUTI

Camel's milk is a welcome drink for this nomad.

Somali refugees near Hol Hol

Fishing in the 'Gulf of the Demons'

Fishermen trying their luck in the Red Sea

Nomadic Afars gathering salt, Lac Assal

Form follows function

Henna hand tattoos are often worn by married women.

Traditional Afar and Somali tribal knives, which are worn from the belt, are banned in the towns.

Afar nomad women weave these (very portable) *fiddima* mats from the leaves of the doum palm.

Note that there is still no permanent decompression chamber in Djibouti. Sometimes the French military ship the *Jules Vernes* docks for a few months in Djibouti; it has its own chamber but it is unwise to rely on this. Some diving operators and divers try to limit their dives to 30 or 40m as a precaution.

For more information, see Snorkelling & Diving in the Djibouti Town section. For information on local marine life, see Fauna in the Facts about Djibouti section earlier in this chapter, and the special section 'Marine Life in the Red Sea'.

ACCOMMODATION

Djibouti's accommodation is limited: there are no formal camping grounds, hostels or university campuses, and self-catering facilities are mainly geared towards the expat population. The Résidence de l'Europe in the capital has some suites with kitchen facilities, but these are expensive.

Most hotels are in the capital, with very few options outside. Some privately owned *tukuls* (traditional huts) are beginning to mushroom up around the major tourist attractions in the hinterland, such as at Lac Abbé and the Fôret du Day National Park. Though quaint and comfortable, facilities are fairly basic with shared showers and toilets.

Hotel categories are also limited in range; most of them fit into the upper echelon, and are expensive. At the lower end, the few budget hotels that exist tend to be pretty seedy. There's a limited choice in between.

Because of the *crise* (economic crisis), it is possible to negotiate quite big discounts with the mid-range and top-end hotels, particularly if you're staying for more than a week. Also check in advance if an accommodation tax is levied.

In the cheaper hotels, travellers should make sure the hotel has a *groupe* (generator) that kicks in when Djibouti's erratic electricity supply kicks out. Without one, you may end up paying for an air-conditioned room without actually getting one.

If you have your own tent you can camp anywhere except on private property (not recommended in the hot season).

FOOD

Djibouti's cuisine reflects the diverse influences on its culture. For sheer choice and quality of food, Djibouti has to be one of the best places in East Africa. If it weren't for the high prices, it might be one of the best places on the continent.

Imported originally from India, rice and tea have been incorporated into the national diet, as well as coffee from Ethiopia, pasta from Italy (via Somalia and Eritrea), and baked dishes and kebabs from the Middle East. The local preference is for meat – often served without a sniff of a vegetable or other accompaniment.

One quirk of Djibouti's restaurants is the pen and paper sometimes left on the table along with the menu. When you are ready, you write down your order on the pad and wait for it to be collected. Also note that in the majority of the cheaper and Muslim-run restaurants, alcohol is not served.

Local Meat Dishes

Though Djibouti has no national cuisine per se, a few local dishes have established themselves. Specialities worth tasting are either the *cabri farci* (stuffed kid) or the *méchoui* (lamb), both of which are traditionally roasted whole on a spit. Djiboutian families serve these dishes on special occasions such as weddings or public holidays. In the restaurants, they must be ordered in advance. The meat can be tender, moist and full of rich, herby flavours, or equally it can be tough as a boot, dry and insipid.

The local Somali-influenced breakfast, *foie* (liver), is also worth tasting, and can be delicious. Chopped liver (sheep, goat or even camel) is fried with onions, and served with bread. It's also very reasonably priced (from Dfr200).

Local Seafood

The local seafood is certainly Djibouti's *pièce de la résistance*. Along with the sun and the sea, the seafood probably comprises the country's greatest resource. The locals don't care for it one bit, and what little is caught is flogged to the expat population.

Major Dive Sites of Djibouti

	Getting There	Species & Highlights
Arta Plage	Pebbly beach around 50km west of Djibouti town, north of Arta. Also known as Ras Eïro. Accessible by boat or 4WD (last stretch of road requires 4WD).	White-tipped reef sharks, grey sharks, occasionally whale and hammerhead sharks. Plenty of barracuda and turtles, large gropers, rays and sometimes manta rays.
Les Sept Frères Islands	Arid archipelago made up of seven volcanic islands. Situated in the Straits of Bab el Mandeb, south of the the Yemeni island of Périm in the far north of Djibouti. Boats leave from Djibouti town. Minimum visit is 48 hours (given the distance); between three and seven hours by boat, depending on the size and speed of the vessel.	Most famous and spectacular dive site of Djibouti. Known for sheer size of shoals as well as large dimensions of individual species: huge Napoleon fish, groper and barracuda are common. Sharks include white-tipped reef, grey, nurse, whale and very occasionally tiger. Dolphins are frequently seen as are turtles and sometimes manta rays. Abundant and diverse corals and sponges. Various species of moray eels. Stunning.
Bay of Ghoubbet	Large bay about 100km from Djibouti town. Connected to the Gulf of Tadjoura by a narrow gully. Accessible by boat, bus or car from Djibouti town.	Known as one of best places to spot whale sharks and manta rays. Less coral, and not as rich in fish as other areas, but interesting, sometimes large, and possibly indigenous species inhabit enclosed water (see the boxed text 'Gulf of the Demons' under Bay of Ghoubbet later in this chapter).
Moucha & Maskali Islands	Archipelago in the Gulf of Tadjoura, north of Djibouti town. Most accessible diving destination. Around 20 minutes by boat from Djibouti town.	Barracuda, various species of moray eels, Napoleon fish, jacks, rays, starfish, turtles, box fish, puffer fish. Good variety of fish, and soft and hard corals.
Tadjoura	Various beaches and coral reefs around Tadjoura, north-west of Djibouti town. Lies 173km by road from Djibouti town. Best reached by boat or ferry.	Diverse reef fish including box fish, parrot fish and butterfly fish. Also turtles and moray eels.
Obock	Coral reefs lying off the coast near the town of Obock, north-east of Tadjoura (235km by road from Djibouti town). Road from Tadjoura is rough; best reached by boat or ferry from Djibouti town.	Large variety of hard and soft corals, great numbers and varieties of moray eels. Turtles and dolphins are commonly seen.

DJIBOUTI

Information

Site known locally as Plateau des Tortues is good for abundant turtles. Ras Eïro site good for large numbers of white-tipped reef sharks. No facilities on beach; bring your own food and water. Should register with Foreign Legionaries at base on beach. Good for snorkelling and diving.

Sometimes strong currents underwater, and strong winds above. In theory, divers should be Advanced (PADI) or Niveau 2 (FFESSM) or have logged at least 30 dives. Dives are to an average of 25m, though some sites up to 40m. Night and drift dives are both good. Sea is calmest between September and November. Some live-aboards run during certain months of the cool season only (September to May). Main sites include le Grand Ile (and Jardin Japonais), l'Ile de l'Est, le Boeing, la Grotte (for bat fish) and Tolkalle du Sud.

Basically an underwater fault, interesting for its geological aspect as much as for marine life. Depth unlimited (bay is 200m deep). Gully can be dangerous outside tidal slack, because of strong currents. More easily approached by land than sea.

Reefs on the eastern side of Moucha Island have been declared a marine park. Sites include Epave de Moucha (a sunken cargo boat at 20m), known for large groupers and Napoleon fish; Ilot de Moucha, known for coral species; and Tombant de Moucha for moray eels.

Beaches (with facilities) that give access to coral reefs include Plage des Sables Blancs (east of Tadjoura) and Ambabo (west of Tadjoura). Good for snorkelling and diving; snorkelling equipment for hire.

Sites include Banc de Surcouf (boat only). Various beaches give access to coral reefs. Good for snorkelling and diving.

Some of the top-end restaurants serve seafood including prawns, lobster and crab, but it is inevitably rather pricey. Additionally, and contrary to claims, much of it has been frozen. If you want to be sure of fresh seafood, see the manager of the restaurant and order exactly what you want in advance.

International Cuisine

There is an excellent range of international cuisine available in Djibouti, ranging from top-notch French haute cuisine to good Chinese and Vietnamese fare, along with interesting Ethiopian and Somali dishes, Italian pizzas and, at the bottom of the price range, the dirt-cheap but delicious *poisson yéménite* (Yemeni fish suppers), which are served on a newspaper, *á la yéménite*. Don't miss these! (see the boxed text 'Poisson Yéménite' under Places to Eat in the Djibouti Town section).

Self-Catering

Djibouti boasts a good selection of local and French supermarkets. The latter stock a mouth-watering range of all those things you're probably dreaming about – and will perhaps continue to dream about as the price of these imports is two to three times higher than their equivalent in France.

One very affordable treat is the delicious sticks of freshly baked French bread, which are available from a number of *boulangeries* (bakeries) about town from the early morning. A bit more indulgent, but in the same line, are the delicious croissants and the *pâtisseries* (pastries).

The food markets in the capital are stocked throughout the year with a good range and quality of fruit and vegetables. Those from Ethiopia and Kenya are quite cheap; those from France are predictably expensive – up to five times the cost of local products.

DRINKS
Nonalcoholic Drinks

You shouldn't really drink the tap water, though it's fine for rinsing fruit or brushing your teeth. Bottled water is widely available in shops, restaurants and hotels. The local bottled water (ONED) is fizzy, and has a slightly salty, mineral taste, but it's refreshing

DJIBOUTI

served cold. The only alternative is expensive French mineral water (fizzy or still), which can be bought from French supermarkets.

International soft drinks are widely available; both coffee and tea are quite widely available and are well prepared. Both are served without milk (tea sometimes with lemon) unless you instruct otherwise.

Alcoholic Drinks

Although alcohol is frowned upon by Islam, alcohol consumption is freely tolerated in Djibouti. Beer is widely available, as are wines, spirits and liqueurs (many of them French imports). All alcohol is relatively expensive; the cheapest place to buy it is in the local supermarkets. The cheapest place to drink it is in the local unlicensed bars (see the boxed text 'Banning the Bars' under Entertainment following).

ENTERTAINMENT

Djibouti's diversions are mainly geared towards the entertainment of the several thousand French soldiers stationed in the capital. Outside the town, there are few leisure and entertainment facilities. For details of theatres, concerts, exhibitions and cinemas, see the Djibouti town section .

European Bars & Clubs

Like the city's hotels and restaurants, most establishments in Djibouti town can be divided into the local joints and those purportedly 'European' in style. European bars tend to be considerably more expensive, but offer a greater variety of western drink, food and music. The cafes, pubs and bars around Place Ménélik are European in style, as are some of the nightclubs just off the square.

The nightclubs don't get going until at least 10 or 11 pm at the weekend (Thursday night). Entrance fees are charged and drinks are quite pricey. Some places have reasonable sound systems. Foreign Legionaries in and out of uniform, and local working girls form the majority of the clientele.

Local Bars & Clubs

Local joints take the form of small, rather lugubrious bars and clubs, which are dotted all about town, except in the Europeanised centre. Trickier to locate, they have adopted a kind of camouflage as the best way around the government restrictions on licences.

In the bars, decor is very simple: just wooden tables and chairs, and a simple bar attended by a madame and her retinue pouring out measures of alcohol. There is no entrance charge, alcohol is much cheaper, and the music and clientele more local.

Along with drinking and smoking, frequenting such locales is frowned upon by Islam. The prohibition explains the rather dismal, diffident and contrite but nevertheless fascinating atmosphere of these places. Ordinarily the haunt of men, women travellers should understand that their presence may seem a bit intrusive (though Djiboutians are too polite to show it). Women who want to visit these places should do so with male companions and act discreetly.

The local clubs seem to suffer from a serious lack of punters, particularly on weekdays, but are brimming over with prostitutes (who in boredom dance depressingly

Banning the Bars

In 1995, in a bid to crack down on vice in the city, the government issued a decree that restricted the sale of alcohol to nightclubs, restaurants and hotels.

Undeterred, Djibouti's rash of tiny bars simply switched the 'Bar' signs above their doorways to 'Restaurant'. Many places – as unsuspecting travellers soon found out – served not so much as a crust of bread, and 'restaurant' owners seemed as surprised by the demand for food as the hungry traveller was by the reply that there was none.

Late in 1999, the police retaliated with another crackdown and closed around 40 of the 'restaurants', as well as targeting some nightclubs and discos.

However, with the 3200 French army personnel providing a good and reliable demand, it seems likely that these bars – or restaurants – will metamorphose miraculously into some other unlikely form.

to mirrors or with one another). A mixture of Ethiopian and western music is played. There is usually a small entrance fee, and drinks are less expensive than in their European counterparts, but that doesn't compensate for their rather depressing atmosphere.

SHOPPING

Many of the goods and souvenirs found in the shops and markets of the capital are not really Djiboutian at all, but are imported (sometimes smuggled) from neighbouring countries. Les Caisses market has the best selection of goods (see Shopping in the Djibouti Town section).

Popular items include hookah pipes, jewellery made of amber, malachite and silver (usually imported from Yemen), traditional clothing, pots and animal-skin paintings (from Ethiopia), and various sculptures made of wood, alabaster and soapstone (from Kenya). Look out for leather goods too, which are usually made from the large local herds of animals; sheep, cow, goat and camel skins can all be found. Simple but attractive leather belts, bags and shoes (including traditional nomad sandals, which cost between Dfr1300 and Dfr2000) are sometimes available.

One indigenous souvenir, and a favourite with tourists, is the traditional Afar and Somali *poignard* or knife, which is still carried by nomads in the hinterland. They cost between Dfr1500 and Dfr5000, depending on the quality – which varies widely, so take your time choosing one. The blades of the Afar knives are slightly broader than those of the Somali ones.

Ivory carvings are widely available. Apart from the environmental argument against buying these, it is illegal to import them into most western countries.

Outside the capital, particularly in the northern villages around Randa (such as Ardo), look out for the very attractive and geometrically designed Afar *nattes* or woven straw mats (known in Afar as *fiddima*), which are light and easily rolled up for transportation home. Tadjoura is considered the capital of production. The fiddima takes at least one month to weave, and in-

corporates a complex and symbolic series of patterns (see the boxed text 'The Fabulous Fiddima' under Ardo in the Around the Gulf of Tadjoura section later in this chapter), so it is relatively expensive at Dfr8000–10,000 (US$45–56). Other items such as baskets cost between Dfr800 and Dfr3000.

Getting There & Away

For general information on travel to/from the region, and a glossary of travel terms, see Getting There & Away in the Ethiopia chapter.

AIR

Djibouti's one international airport, in the capital, is reasonably well served by international carriers including Air France, Air Djibouti, Ethiopian Airlines, United Airlines and Yemenia. (For information on airline offices, see Getting There & Away in the Djibouti Town section .)

Travel during the month of August, and over Easter, Christmas and New Year, should be booked well in advance. Djiboutians living abroad tend to take advantage of the school holidays to visit their families during these times. Flights can also be more expensive.

Departure Tax

Departure tax is Dfr3000 for flights to neighbouring countries (including Yemen), and Dfr5000 for elsewhere. It is usually included in the price of the ticket.

The USA

Ethiopian Airlines has four flights a week from Djibouti town (via Addis Ababa) to Washington and New York. The cheapest flight is the Saturday flight (back on a Friday) from Newark, New York (US$1200 return).

From San Francisco, Ethiopian Airlines and United Airlines both offer Saturday flights (back on Friday) for US$1600 return.

DJIBOUTI

Europe

Flights from Europe are best served by Air France, which has three flights a week between Paris and Djibouti (via Jeddah in Saudi Arabia) for around Dfr170,000 (US$988). Minimum stay is seven days; maximum stay is two months.

Air Djibouti also flies to Paris twice a week.

For those on a budget, probably the cheapest way of getting to Djibouti is to fly to Addis Ababa and take the train or bus overland from there.

The Middle East

For flights across the Red Sea to Yemen, Yemenia has two flights a week to San'a, and one per week to Aden (Dfr23,814) and Ta'izz (Dfr24,881).

Air Djibouti flies once a week to Ta'izz (Dfr20,000/Dfr30,000 single/return) and Dubai, UAE (Dfr50,000/65,000), and twice a week to Jeddah, Saudi Arabia (Dfr50,000/65,000).

Africa

For Ethiopia, Ethiopian Airlines has direct daily flights between Djibouti and Addis Ababa (Dfr52,800 return). Air Djibouti also

FOUAD DAOUD YOUSSOUF

Baskets are made in many parts of the country.

> ### Humour Heals
>
> 'A man with a sense of humour is never at a loss', goes a Somali-Djiboutian proverb. When asked for the four secrets of life, a nomad once replied: 'courage, alertness, religious faith, and a sense of humour'.
>
> Humour in a nomadic society is thought to teach tolerance towards others, and humility for oneself. It protects against the fear of failure, and consoles in the event of death. In the harsh and sometimes brutal environment in which a nomad lives, a sense of humour is seen as prerequisite for survival. Survivors of the Holocaust have attested to the same theory.

flies daily to Addis Ababa (Dfr34,700/52,800 single/return), and four times a week to Dire Dawa (Dfr16,500/ Dfr26,500).

Flights to Asmara in Eritrea by both Ethiopian Airlines (formerly Dfr67,800) and Air Djibouti have been suspended since 1998, because of the border conflict between the two countries. Formerly, it was possible to charter (at a reasonable cost) a five- to 48-seater plane from Djibouti to Asmara or Assab. Services should resume eventually.

For Kenya, Ethiopian Airlines flies to Nairobi (Dfr146,1000) via Djibouti.

For Somalia, Air Djibouti flies three times a week to Hargeisa (Dfr13,000/18,000 single/return), and twice a week to Mogadishu (Dfr39,200/71,000).

LAND

The development of a national network of roads linking Djibouti with Eritrea, Somalia and particularly Ethiopia is high on the government's 'to do' list. At the moment, road links to Eritrea and Somalia are very limited.

If you're planning to take your car to neighbouring countries, you'll need all the car documents, proof of insurance (third-party is mandatory) covering all the countries you're visiting, driving licence, a list of all passengers with their passport numbers, a *laissez passer* (pass) from the Ministry of the Interior, and a certificate releasing your car from the Republic of Djibouti from the police nationale.

Border Crossings

Travellers should note that there is no formal border post at the Eritrea border in the north. Also note that at the time of research Somalia was not considered safe for travellers.

Eritrea

Beyond the town of Tadjoura, only tracks and dirt roads lead further north to Eritrea.

Afar guerrilla activities still smoulder in a pocket to the north-west of Djibouti, so any forays here are viewed by the authorities with nervousness and suspicion (as the author can testify as she was flatteringly mistaken for a spy). After all, there's little here in the way of traditional tourist attractions: just kilometre after kilometre of parched desert scrubland.

Little traffic runs north apart from the occasional Afar camel or government military truck on manoeuvre. The civil unrest has also put an end to the old bus service that struggled the 1100km between Djibouti and Assab in Eritrea.

Taking a vehicle there yourself, apart from the problems outlined already, is a tricky proposition. You'll have to travel in convoy and be properly equipped for a full expedition; it's easy to get stuck in the sand, and mechanical problems such as overheating radiators are common. If you do have problems, you're unlikely to meet another living soul for days, if not weeks or even months. Leftover landmines from the civil war are also a hazard off the main tracks.

The other problem that can cause real agro is the absence of formal border posts between the two countries. Without an entry stamp in your passport, you may well have problems leaving Eritrea, or if you're coming from Eritrea, problems leaving Djibouti. Obtaining visas or visa extensions will be difficult too. If you still insist on coming this way, make sure you visit the Djiboutian or Eritrean diplomatic representative in the country you are coming from, and get a letter explaining your route and purpose.

See Getting There & Away under Assab in the Dankalia section of the Eritrea chapter for more information on this difficult crossing.

Ethiopia

Road The quickest route to Ethiopia is via Dikhil, Yoboki and Galafi in the west. See Djibouti under Land in the Getting There & Away section of the Ethiopia chapter for more details.

Train The old Djibouti-Ethiopia train link – though rather dilapidated and slow – probably still presents the best means of travelling between the two countries (at least until Dire Dawa in Ethiopia then continuing by bus to Addis Ababa). See Getting There & Away in the Djibouti Town section for prices and schedules, and see also under Land in the Getting There & Away section in the Ethiopia chapter for general information on the service.

Somalia

In the past, there were quite good road links with Somalia; cars, trucks and buses all made regular journeys to Berbera and Hargeisa. In late 1999 the breakaway self-styled Somaliland Republic closed its land borders with Djibouti.

SEA

Europe

Djibouti's port is its *raison d'être*. Thousands of boats and ships each year use its facilities. In theory, it should be possible to hitch a lift on one of these vessels, even as far as Marseilles in France. However, in practice it's more difficult, particularly as access to Djibouti's port is restricted. Additionally, many commercial ships seem to have a policy of discouraging passenger travel. The best thing to do is to ask around Djibouti town, particularly if a ship and its crew have just arrived.

The Middle East

Travel on the traditional dhows that cross the Red Sea should be easier to arrange, though you'll need a flexible schedule and good bargaining skills. Dhows ply the waters between Djibouti and Aden and Al-Makha in Yemen.

Examples of fares include Dfr5000 one way to Aden in Yemen although you'll have to bargain hard for this – you'll be quoted around Dfr10,000 at first. The journey to Aden (Yemen) takes between 14 and 20 hours depending on the load in the boat; food is provided by the crew. All dhows leave from Quai 5 in the port. You'll need to explain your purpose at the *gendarmerie* (police) checkpoint at the entrance to the port.

Africa

Formerly, both cargo boats and dhows sailed to Berbera (Somalia), Assab (Eritrea) and Sudan, but as with land travel, travellers to these countries should check the political situation before heading out. Ask around at the port.

ORGANISED TOURS

Very few travel agents abroad run tours to Djibouti. One that does and which can be recommended is Club Aventure Signature (☎ 01 44 32 09 30, fax 44 32 09 59) at 18, rue Séguier, 75006, Paris, France. A varied nine-day itinerary is offered, including contact with the local nomads and hiking. The price per person (sharing a double in hotels) is FF12,000 all inclusive.

Getting Around

It's possible to travel almost anywhere in the country. The only places that present a problem due to rebel Afar insurgency are a pocket in the north-west, and the road north of Tadjoura to Obock and on to Eritrea. For trips off the beaten track, check first with the tourist office or your embassy in the capital.

Of the four district capitals, Ali Sabieh and Dikhil can be reached by bus, while Obock and Tadjoura are best reached by ferry from Djibouti town. For many other destinations, you'll need to hire a 4WD and driver or join an organised tour.

AIR

The country has just one national airline: Air Djibouti. Its service is safe and reliable, albeit a bit limited. The only domestic flights run daily between Djibouti town and Obock and Tadjoura. Air Djibouti flies each

day to Tadjoura and Obock for Dfr3000/6000 single/return.

Private planes can also be chartered from the Aéro-Club (☎ 34-08-24) next door to the airport in the capital. If you fancy a 'flight below sea level' at Lac Assal, or over the chimneys of Lac Abbé, you can organise it through the club, though advance notice (around 48 hours) is required. Prices (for up to three passengers) and journey times are:

Lac Abbé and Lac Assal (Dfr57,200) 1½ hours
Lac Assal (Dfr30,500) 1¼ hours
Moucha and Maskali Islands (Dfr13,500) 20 minutes
Obock (Dfr25,000) one hour
Tadjoura (Dfr21,000) 50 minutes

BUS

Public transport is limited in Djibouti; most buses just connect the main towns to the capital. Buses are simple affairs with few comforts and travelling on them can be hard work: journeys are hot, dusty and bumpy.

For most buses, you pay once you're on the bus. Baggage is usually strapped on the roof and there's usually a supplement to pay of between Dfr200 and Dfr500 per item, depending on the size.

Buses only leave when they are full, so there are often long waits before departure. One-way fares between the capital and all other towns in the country range between Dfr300 and Dfr500.

For minibus information, see Getting Around in the Djibouti Town section .

TRAIN

The train linking Djibouti town to Addis Ababa in Ethiopia (see the Getting There & Away section earlier in this chapter) makes several stops en route. Services from Djibouti town to Hol Hol (Dfr900, 3rd class only) and Ali Sabieh (Dfr1200, 1st class only) are of most interest to travellers. The journey is grindingly slow and the jointly owned railway is badly in need of an overhaul. If you're short on time, you may prefer to fly.

CAR & MOTORCYCLE

Only 10% of the country's 2800km of road is tarred. To get to most places in Djibouti, you'll need a 4WD vehicle. Apart from Lac Assal, most of Djibouti's principal attractions, including Lac Abbé and the Fôret du Day National Park, are only accessible in this way. Fortunately, the country is small, and with your own wheels, most of its attractions can be seen in quite a short period. If you're travelling solo, or as a couple, you can reduce the cost of a vehicle by joining up with other travellers, and either hiring a car plus driver-guide (for many places such as Lac Abbé, you'll need a good guide) or taking an all-inclusive tour. Most vehicles accommodate around five passengers, though some have extra benches in the back and can take about ten.

Road Rules

If you're travelling with your own vehicle, or you hire one without a driver, some local road etiquette might be useful.

In theory, Djibouti subscribes to the same highway code as France. In practice, it is little respected. For those unfamiliar with the French system, driving is on the right, and the most important thing to bear in mind is the notorious *priorité á droite* (give way to your right) traffic law – the rule that confuses and terrorise travellers unused to the system.

In a nutshell, any car entering an intersection (including a T-junction) from a road on your right has right of way (unless specifically indicated), no matter how small the road it's coming from. To put it a different way: if you're turning right from a side road onto a main road, you have priority over vehicles coming from your left. If you're turning left, though, you must wait for cars coming from your right!

In Djibouti, speed is limited to 30km/h in the centre of town, 50km/h in the suburbs, and 80km/h anywhere else. The last is a fairly optimistic figure; the state of the roads often demands a much lower speed.

Rental & Purchase

Like many things in Djibouti, rental vehicles don't come cheap, as cars, spare parts and

Priscilla Queen of the Desert?

Peculiarities of modern-day Djiboutian culture include the sumptuous decoration of vehicles, particularly the public buses. Feathers, frills, flags, stickers, streamers and painted pictures adorn vehicles; some are even 'christened' with names – usually after a rock star or other cultural icon – from Colonel Gadaffi and Charlie Chaplin to Princess Diana.

fuel are all imported. A basic 4WD will set you back around Dfr25,000–30,000 (US$145–175) per day, plus third-party insurance for about Dfr5000. To hire a car, you need to be at least 21 years old, have had a licence for at least a year, and be able to leave a deposit of Dfr350,000 (US$2030); only major credit cards and cash are accepted.

If you're looking to buy a second-hand vehicle, expect to pay a minimum of US$10,000–15,000 (see Getting There & Away in the Djibouti Town section).

Road Hazards

The streets of the capital are potholed and, at night, dimly lit. Look out for people, particularly children playing on the road.

Outside the capital, livestock is the main hazard; camels wandering onto the road can cause major accidents.

In the north, land mines still pose a threat; drivers should stay on paved roads or existing dirt tracks, particularly on the approach to villages, towns, airstrips and bridges and other places of strategic importance.

If you're heading north, take lots of extra fuel, as north of Tadjoura, petrol stations are few and far between.

When driving in the south-east of the country, watch for railway crossings as these are often unmarked.

For general safety tips, see the boxed text 'Drive Safe' in the Getting Around section of the Ethiopia chapter.

BICYCLE

Djibouti's climate, terrain and rough roads are not ideally suited to cycling. However,

DJIBOUTI

if you're totally self-sufficient with plenty of spare parts and tyres, as well as a capacity to carry large amounts of water, there's nothing to stop you. There are no bicycles for hire in Djibouti, nor any repair shops, though the garages will do their best to help.

HITCHING

For general information (and a warning) on hitching, see Hitching in the Getting Around section of the Ethiopia chapter. With trucks and private 4WD vehicles providing the only transport along many roads in Djibouti, hitching is a tempting option for travellers on a restricted budget. Dozens of trucks make the long, hot journey from Djibouti to Addis Ababa in Ethiopia each day. In the future, trucks will run again to Eritrea in the north and Somalia in the south (both currently off-limits).

If you're determined to hitch, you could try hanging around outside Djibouti's port in the early morning (access to the port itself is restricted), or at one of the main petrol stations in or just out of town.

Getting a lift may prove pretty difficult, but if you succeed, make sure you agree from the outset how much you are expected to contribute to the journey (for fuel etc). Remember that hitching is always a risky option.

SEA

There are various boat services connecting the capital with different destinations on the coast. All of them leave from l'Escale marina in the capital.

Ferry

The ferry (known as *le bac*) crosses regularly between Djibouti town and Tadjoura and Obock, north of the Gulf of Tadjoura (see Getting There & Away under Tadjoura later in this chapter for prices and schedules).

Motorboat

Private *vedettes* (motorboats) can be hired (with captain) for one day to a week and will take you almost anywhere you wish, but they are expensive, particularly if you go through a travel agent. If you get a big enough group together, you could approach the boat owners

directly at l'Escale marina in the morning between 8 and 9 am. If you bargain hard you can get quite reasonable prices: a boat for the whole day for Dfr20,000 (maximum 15 people) instead of the official price of Dfr35,000.

A good day's excursion is to Moucha or Maskali Islands. If you can't get a large group together, there are smaller boats available for up to four people. The official price is Dfr20,000 (US$112), but you should be able to reduce this.

Dhow

Less comfortable and slower, but more picturesque, are the traditional *boutres* (dhows) that carry cargo between Obock, Tadjoura and Djibouti. If there's space, they accept passengers for a nominal charge (check that the boat carries life jackets).

Dhows can also be hired for the day, but you'll need a good-sized group to share the cost. Dhows carry between 10 and 50 people and cost Dfr35,000–85,000 (US$200–500) to hire.

See also the boxed text 'Indefatigable Dhows' in the East of Asmara section of the Eritrea chapter.

LOCAL TRANSPORT
Taxi

Djibouti town boasts one of the most rickety and ramshackle fleet of taxis you are ever likely to see. Expenditure on much-needed maintenance and repair work is diverted to the national addiction instead: qat. Still, drivers show admirable ingenuity in coaching their bangers into motion with wire, string, stockings, sticky tape – anything goes.

Taxis are not cheap, and visitors are almost always expected to fork out more for them than the locals. Meters (if they work) are not used, so you should *always* negotiate the price of your fare first. Few drivers speak any European languages other than French. It's a good idea to swat up on a few numerals (such as 500 or 1000!) if your command of this language is shaky.

If you think you will need a taxi for more than a few journeys, a good system is to befriend one driver. In exchange for promising him your business, you can ask him for a decent rate per journey, or negotiate a fee for the whole day or even for your whole stay.

Taxis and taxi stands are numerous in the capital. The only time when taxis seem a bit scarce is at dusk, when Djibouti's women rush home Cinderella-like, before the first hour of night strikes.

Bush Taxi
Outside of the capital, there is a limited network of *taxis-brousses* (bush taxis); these are usually Toyota pick-ups that connect major villages. Most leave in the morning from a designated place when they are full, and cost a flat rate of Dfr500 per person to any destination. The best thing is to ask the locals for the day's schedule.

ORGANISED TOURS
There are just a handful of agencies providing tours within the country. All are based in the capital, and offer excellent, albeit rather pricey, excursions to all the major sites of the country for between one day and a week or more. The hiking or trekking excursions, or those offering contact with the nomads, are probably the most worthwhile, since they are difficult to organise independently without the knowledge and experience of local guides.

Djibouti Town

For many travellers, Djibouti town is little more than an overpopulated, ramshackle and filthy little village that seems to be on the verge of collapse. However, with a little exploration, the town reveals an interesting character with many vestiges of its unusual past. Djibouti continues to act as a crossroads where African, Arab, Indian and European influences all converge.

From its beginning, Djibouti town was an artificial creation. In many ways it still is. The town is the sedentary capital of a nomadic people, an African city designed like a European town, a seedy port in an Islamic country, and a kind of French Hong Kong in the Red Sea. With the dawning of the 21st century, the country is struggling to find a

new identity; whatever happens it will be based, as always, around the port.

HISTORY
At the end of the 19th century, the French, keen to establish a refuelling station for their ships between Suez and Saigon, planned the building of a great port. After an initial attempt at Obock failed, a deserted, desolate spot further south was chosen. In 1889, the building of the new capital began.

By 1900, the town had sprouted mushroom-like from the surrounding desert. Djibouti town owed its rapid growth to its superb strategic position. Its large, natural harbour at the entrance to the Red Sea provided protection from the ferocious winds of the Straits of Bab el Mandeb, and the town represented the natural terminus of the shortest and simplest route from Ethiopia.

With the harbour, the road and later the railway to Ethiopia, trade flourished and the town boomed. Travellers at the turn of the 19th and 20th centuries described Djibouti town as a colourful, cosmopolitan town bustling with merchants from all parts of the Indian Ocean, as well as intrepid adventurers, smugglers, gunrunners, secret agents and slave-traders.

Today, the port, railway and French military garrison still form the mainstay of the economy, contributing nearly three-quarters of the country's GDP. Over half of the population lives in the capital. In recent years, the town has been inundated by refugees from Somalia and Ethiopia. Inevitably, strains have been placed on the city's resources.

ORIENTATION
Djibouti town's centre can be divided into two quarters: the *quartier Européen* (European Quarter), laid out on a grid system to the north, and the *quartier Africain* (African Quarter), which spills out to the south.

The Place du 27 juin 1977, still better known by its former title, Place Ménélik, marks the heart of the European Quarter, and is lined with French cafes, bars, restaurants and shops.

South of Place Ménélik lies Place Mahmoud-Harbi, also better known by its former

DJIBOUTI TOWN

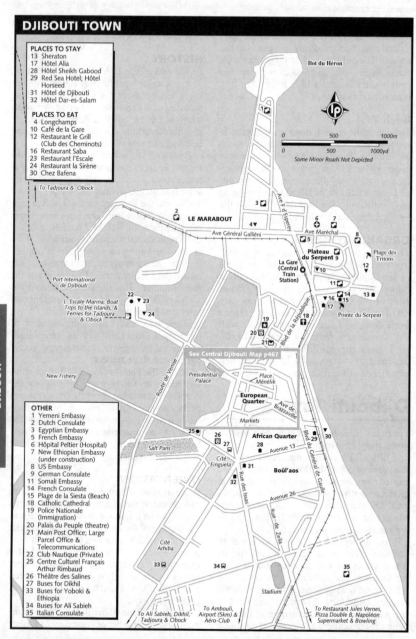

PLACES TO STAY
- 13 Sheraton
- 17 Hôtel Alia
- 28 Hôtel Sheikh Gabood
- 29 Red Sea Hotel; Hôtel Horseed
- 31 Hôtel de Djibouti
- 32 Hôtel Dar-es-Salam

PLACES TO EAT
- 4 Longchamps
- 10 Café de la Gare
- 12 Restaurant le Grill (Club des Cheminots)
- 16 Restaurant Saba
- 23 Restaurant l'Escale
- 24 Restaurant la Sirène
- 30 Chez Bafena

OTHER
- 1 Yemeni Embassy
- 2 Dutch Consulate
- 3 Egyptian Embassy
- 5 French Embassy
- 6 Hôpital Peltier (Hospital)
- 7 New Ethiopian Embassy (under construction)
- 8 US Embassy
- 9 German Consulate
- 11 Somali Embassy
- 14 French Consulate
- 15 Plage de la Siesta (Beach)
- 18 Catholic Cathedral
- 19 Police Nationale (Immigration)
- 20 Palais du Peuple (theatre)
- 21 Main Post Office; Large Parcel Office & Telecommunications
- 22 Club Nautique (Private)
- 25 Centre Culturel Français Arthur Rimbaud
- 26 Théâtre des Salines
- 27 Buses for Dikhil
- 33 Buses for Yoboki & Ethiopia
- 34 Buses for Ali Sabieh
- 35 Italian Consulate

Îlot du Héron

0   500   1000m
0   500   1000yd
Some Minor Roads Not Depicted

To Tadjoura & Obock

LE MARABOUT

Ave Général Galliéni

Ave F d'Esperey

Ave Maréchal

Plateau du Serpent

Plage des Tritons

Port International de Djibouti

La Gare (Central Train Station)

L'Escale Marina; Boat Trips to the Islands, & Ferries for Tadjoura & Obock

Pointe du Serpent

Blvd de la République

New Fishery

See Central Djibouti Map p467

Presidential Palace

Place Ménélik

European Quarter

Ave de Brazzaville

Route de Venise

Markets

Salt Pans

African Quarter

Avenue 13

Cité Einguela

Boûl'aos

Avenue 26

Blvd du Général de Caulle

Rue des Issas

Rue de Zeila

Cité Arhiba

Stadium

To Ali Sabieh, Dikhil, Tadjoura & Obock

To Ambouli, Airport (5km) & Aéro-Club

To Restaurant Jules Vernes, Pizza Double B, Napoléon Supermarket & Bowling

DJIBOUTI

name, Place Rimbaud. Here the European Quarter ends (marked symbolically by the sealed road coming to an abrupt halt) and the African Quarter begins. Many Djiboutians consider Place Rimbaud the real soul of the city. On and around the square some of the local markets are found. Further south are the local residential quarters known as Boûl'aos.

North-west of town, a causeway known as l'Escale leads past the presidential palace to a small marina, which is the point of departure for trips to the islands and to Tadjoura and Obock. Further north, running almost parallel to l'Escale, is the town's port proper, access to which is restricted.

North-east of town is the Plateau du Serpent, where many of the foreign embassies and residences can be found, and the so-called 'European beaches'. The Plateau is attached artery-like to the centre of town by the Boulevard de la République, along which many of the principal administrative buildings can be found.

In the far north is the Ilot du Héron, where the country's rich, the fat and the famous keep their lavish villas.

Djibouti town is small enough to explore on foot. However, walking at night, during the heat of the day, or – in some areas –unguided, is not really recommended (see Dangers & Annoyances later in this section).

INFORMATION
Tourist Offices
The Office National du Tourisme et de l'Artisanat (☎ 35-28-00, fax 35-63-22), BP 1938, Djibouti town, is open from 7.30 am to 12.30 pm and 4.30 to 6.30 pm every day except Friday. Though it lacks many resources and almost any useful written information, the staff do their best to help. If you have any particular needs, ask for the enterprising and very helpful Mohammed Abdillahi, the director.

Reasonable but rather outdated *plans de ville* (town maps) are sold here for Dfr300. Free exhibitions on Djibouti's culture and wildlife are often staged here.

Money
Most banks, such as the Banque Indosuez Mer Rouge (☎ 35-30-16, fax 35-16-38), can

Beautiful Henna

Djibouti's older generation of males seems to have a penchant for henna; perhaps in an attempt to disguise unwelcome signs of greying. The results can seem a bit incongruous: pink, orange or scarlet beards and hair. Women also use henna, but after the Yemeni way – to decorate their palms and feet with beautiful curvilinear patterns and designs. This is particularly *recherché* (in demand) for big occasions such as weddings, and is traditionally the mark of married women.

be found around the Place Lagarde north of Place Ménélik. The Bureaus de Change are on the south-eastern side of Place Ménélik. The black market operates among the stalls of the market known as Les Caisses, east of Place Rimbaud.

See Money in the Facts for the Visitor section of this chapter for more information.

Post & Communications
The main post office is on Blvd de la République; it's open from 6.20 am to 1 pm every day including holidays. From 1 to 8 pm, only the telephone facilities remain open. The large *messagerie postale* (parcel office) is one block down from the main post office, and is open from 7 am to 1 pm every day. For information on postal prices, see Post & Communications in the Facts for the Visitor section of this chapter.

Email and Internet access is still in its infancy in Djibouti. The Chambre Internationale de Commerce (☎ 35-10-70, fax 35-00-96) on Place Lagarde is hoping to install a cybercafe on its ground floor in the near future. It will cost around Dfr500/200 to send/receive email. The chambre is open from 7 am to 1 pm and 4 to 6 pm every day except Friday. For inquiries, travellers should ask for Nimaan.

Travel Agencies
The Caravane du Sel travel agency (☎/fax 35-66-18) off Place Ménélik is run by the accommodating and knowledgeable Baragoïta Saïd. A proponent of ecotourism

Walking Tours

Djibouti town is well worth a wander. Beneath the dusty, noisy and shambolic facade, there's plenty of life and lots of interest.

European & African Quarters

A convenient spot to start a walking tour is **Place Ménélik**. With its whitewashed houses and Moorish arcades sheltering Parisian-style cafes and elegant shops, it's a strange mix of the Arab and the European.

The **crisscrossing alleyways** to the south of the square are a strange mix of the past and present. Selling lengths of muslin, silk and linen, as well as perfumes, fragrances, incense and myrrh, merchants also stock Taiwanese televisions, and gimmicky gadgets from Hong Kong.

Two hundred metres to the south lies **Place Rimbaud**, named after the French poet and adventurer Arthur Rimbaud. During his days as gunrunner to the Ethiopian emperor Menelik, Rimbaud is said to have stored provisions here (see the boxed text 'Arthur Rimbaud – The Revolting Genius' in the East of Addis Ababa section of the Ethiopia chapter). Dominated by the minaret of the great **Hamoudi mosque**, this vast, chaotic square teems with life: market-goers with their donkeys and carts, nomads exchanging news, pickpockets and street urchins, and herds of sheep and goats trotting to and from the auction yards.

The **marché central** (central market) extends west from Place Rimbaud and east along Blvd de Bender. To the west, fruit and vegetables are sold. Eastward, women hawkers sell cooking spices, clothes dyes and every type of medicinal herb. The qat sellers, behind their rickety stalls, keep the precious leafy sprigs fresh and free from dust with damp towels and sacking.

Spreading along Blvd de Bender are the stalls of **Les Caisses market**. Crammed with every type of souvenir from stuffed cobras, frogs and bats to moth-eaten leopard skins, it's a colourful place for shopping.

Marina

In the early evening, the walk along l'**Escale causeway** makes a very pleasant stroll. The Moorish-inspired presidential palace (not open to the public) marks one end, the harbour of l'Escale, the other.

The little marina is home to a variety of boats, from the traditional and very picturesque Arab dhows, to the simple local fishing skiffs and sleek international yachts. A drink at the Restaurant l'Escale overlooking the gulf at sunset is a great way to end the day.

---

and the sponsoring of local communities, his *randonnées en brousse* (walks in the bush), and caravane du sel route (in which tourists follow the Afar nomads along the ancient salt route) have become something of a speciality. Most tours cost from Dfr13,000 per person per day all-inclusive.

Also recommended is le Goubet (☎ 35-45-20, fax 35-11-03), which issues air tickets as well as running tours inside and outside the country including to neighbouring Ethiopia and Yemen. Excellent geological day tours (in French) are also on offer; these cost Dfr44,000 for up to four people including vehicle hire. An overnight trip to the Fôret du Day National Park costs Dfr8000 per person plus vehicle hire for up to eight people (Dfr50,000). This is also the agency to contact if you're interested in visiting Les Sept Frères Islands on a live-aboard diving boat. Ask for Valérie, who is efficient and helpful.

ATTA (☎/fax 35-48-88), near Place Lagarde, organises excursions, as well as car hire (Dfr40,000/30,000 with/without driver).

Bookshops

Djibouti town's bookshops are quite well stocked, but books are expensive and almost exclusively in French. The excellent Librairie Omar Khayyâm on Place Ménélik boasts a small but comprehensive collection of books on Djibouti, including some coffee-table publications and travellers accounts, such as those by Henri de Monfreid (see the boxed text 'Monfreid's Hell' under History in the Facts about Djibouti section). It also sells a selection of decent postcards (Dfr100–150).

The Librairie Couleur Locale, nearby, is good for local literature. English-French-Afar dictionaries and French-Somali phrase-books are available for sale, plus a few useful guides, such as to the reef fish of the Red Sea. Both bookshops stay open until 7.30 pm.

For international newspapers and maga-zines the Maison de la Presse, also nearby, has a good collection.

Cultural Centres

The excellent, nonprofit organisation IRIS (☎ 35-43-77), off Place Lagarde, is run by an enthusiastic team of volunteers trying 'to promote culture (in the Horn)'. Folk music, dance, slide shows, exhibitions, lectures and debates are organised, and some cultural publications are available. The staff can also organise classes in Afar, Arabic and Somali. It's open from 5 to 8 pm every day except Friday.

Close to the site of the old Prisunic su-permarket, just south-west of the centre, is the Centre Culturel Français Arthur Rim-baud (☎ 35-24-00, fax 35-10-38, ❷ ccfar@intnet.dj). The centre hosts various French and African cultural events, including films in French twice a week (Dfr1000), two dance, theatre or musical evenings per month (Dfr3500), and an art exhibition once every two months (free). The library contains a collection of books on Djibouti, and is open to all (but you can't borrow books). There's also a *salle de presse* (news room) if you're keen to catch up on the news. It's open from 9.30 am to noon and 4 to 7 pm every day except Friday and Saturday.

Hairdressers & Barbers

If you're desperate for a haircut, head for Coiffure Vijay just north of Place Ménélik. A dry cut for men/women costs from Dfr500/1500, and a shave from Dfr500. It stays open until 9 pm.

Medical Services

Two European doctors, Patrick Guillard and Bruno dell'Aquila, keep a surgery (☎ 35-27-24) in the building opposite Maison de la Presse, off Place Ménélik, and between them speak French, English, German and Italian. Surgery times are from 8 am to noon and 4 to 7 pm, every day except Friday; ap-pointments are not necessary. A consulta-tion costs Dfr6000; an on-the-spot malaria test costs Dfr5000. In an emergency, you can call the doctors at home (☎ 35-50-70, ☎ 35-41-57).

In the same building as the surgery, on the first floor, Dr Djaoui (☎ 35-52-78, home ☎ 35-57-40) has a well-respected dental practice, which is open from 8 am to noon and 4 to 8 pm every day except Fri-day. He speaks French, Italian and some English. Appointments are preferred. Visits cost Dfr5000 for a check-up, and between Dfr7000 and Dfr11,000 for dental work.

The well-equipped Hôpital Peltier (☎ 35-27-14) is on the Plateau du Serpent.

The Pharmacie de l'Indépendence near the centre is very well stocked, with helpful, knowledgeable staff and an international drugs directory if you need one. It also stocks contact lens solution.

Emergency

For the police call ☎ 17; for fire and ambu-lance services call ☎ 18.

Dangers & Annoyances

Though Djibouti is in general pretty safe, the recent influx of thousands of refugees has significantly pushed up the crime rate of the capital, particularly at night.

The area immediately on and off Place Ménélik is pretty safe at all times of the day, but travellers should never stray fur-ther afield after dark. If in doubt, take a taxi.

Pickpocketing is the biggest problem and is rife in and around the market. Keep an eye particularly on the tiny, angelic-looking boys, who usually work in pairs: one will bump into you or distract you while the other frisks your pockets.

Outside the immediate centre of town, snatch-thieving is increasingly common, even through open car windows, or while walking in or out of restaurants. Money belts offer the best protection. Muggings with knives (particularly at night) have also been reported.

Most thieves (largely desperate refugees) are after cash, or items that can be easily exchanged for cash: jewellery, watches and clothes. In 90% of cases, stolen passports, credit cards and travellers cheques are later found abandoned. If you have something stolen, keep checking with the police – it may be handed in. Cameras are not usually targeted either, but are best left at your hotel when not in use. (The author retrieved important documents by letting it be known that there was a large reward of qat for their recovery!)

ORGANISED TOURS

The organisation IRIS (see Cultural Centres under Information earlier in this section) offers excellent half-day guided tours of the centre of town, including an introductory slide show and a traditional lunch at a local's home. Tours cost Dfr5000, and depart at 8.30 am and 12.30 pm, but should be booked at least a day in advance. Tours are in French, but English-language tours can be organised with enough notice.

If you're short of time, or it's just too hot, you could consider a flash around the town in a taxi. It should cost no more than Dfr2000 (for up to four people).

SWIMMING

If you're looking for a beach, those on the islands of Moucha are the best; the sand is fine and the water incredibly clear. In town, you can try the Plage des Tritons and Plage de la Siesta on the Plateau du Serpent, though they're not as clean as they might be. An alternative is to head for Doralé west of Djibouti town.

The only pool in town is at the Sheraton at Pointe du Serpent, where a day's dip will set you back Dfr2500 (US$14)!

Djibouti's Architecture

Like many colonial towns, Djibouti town was laid out in a series of zones. Place Ménélik and its environs comprised the administrative quarter. The Plateau du Serpent, placed at a safe distance from the town, served for the colonial, residential quarter. Place Rimbaud, well outside the European Quarter, was the site of the 'native quarter'. Lastly, at some distance south of town, was Ambouli, the quarter for outbuildings, where the abattoirs, camel stables, quarries, lime ovens and military arsenals could be found.

Cut blocks of coral along with lime cement (made from baked coral) were used to construct Djibouti. Stylistically, many of the older buildings are Arab – rather than French – inspired. Many buildings are square and two-storeyed with arcades and terraces. The walls are whitewashed, very thick, and sometimes perforated with *mashrabiyya* (Moorish screen) designs to keep the building cool and allow the air to circulate.

Other features include *azulejos* (the Moorish coloured tiles), horseshoe arches, and small stained-glass windows, which allow a gentle and calm light to penetrate the interior. Some buildings look more oriental in design – particularly the Indian merchant houses – with door and window frames ornately decorated, sometimes with lavish wooden canopies or balconies.

SNORKELLING & DIVING

Currently just two dive operators exist in the whole of Djibouti. Both are properly certified, have good safety records, and can provide boats, full diving equipment (except wetsuits which aren't necessary), and proper supervision.

The Palandris (☎ 35-18-56 at home) are an Italian father-and-son team who, between them, speak Italian, French and English. Mr Palandri senior makes an entertaining underwater guide, if you can persuade him to take you. Deep-sea fishing can also be organised for Dfr10,000 per hour.

The other operation, the Centre de Plongée des Iles des Sept Frères (☎ 34-17-29 at home), is run by a local diving instructor, Mr Assowe Rirache, who speaks French and a little English, and also makes an excellent guide. If you want to join a tour to Moucha or Maskali Islands, just sign up on the list posted in the reception of the Sheraton.

For the islands of Moucha or Maskali, Assowe charges Dfr4000 per person for day trips, including boat, equipment and one dive. For an extra Dfr1000, you can have lunch and a leisurely afternoon on either island. Palandri charges Dfr4500 for the dive plus Dfr3000 for lunch. Reservations with either should be made at least 24 hours in advance.

For Les Sept Frères Islands, Palandri offers a 48-hour tour (the barest minimum, given the distance), which includes four dives (two each day), and one night's camping on the islands. A minimum of five people are required. The boat rental costs Dfr150,000 including all diving equipment, and meals are an extra Dfr1000 per person (or you can bring your own). For extra days, the boat costs Dfr20,000 per day, plus Dfr10,000 for meals for five people. Reservations should be made a week in advance.

Other destinations include the Bay of Ghoubbet (Dfr120,000 per boat for a two-day excursion, plus bottles of air at Dfr3000 each).

Finally, if you've never dived before, but always rather fancied a go, here's your chance: Assowe offers a *baptême de plongée*, a 'dive christening' for a reasonable Dfr5000 per person, including all equipment, training and supervision. The depth is limited to just 10m. If you can afford it, the chance to glimpse Djibouti's reefs is not to be missed.

Live-Aboard Diving Tours

If you're interested in a live-aboard tour (outside the hot season – from around September to May only), there's a choice of at least three large motorised sailing boats offering different facilities and prices. However, not all are in service all the time, and it's best to check with le Goubet travel agency in the capital first (see Travel Agencies earlier in this section). Reservations should be made several

months in advance, particularly for tours during holiday periods. Occasionally it's possible to fill spaces on a tour at short notice.

All boats have onboard air compressors, but supply weight belts and air cylinders only, so you'll need your own kit (though this can be rented in Djibouti town). Prices include three meals (but not alcohol) and two dives per day.

La Flibuste is a very comfortable 36m-long boat that accommodates between six and 14 people in two-person, air-con cabins with private bathroom. Tours to Les Sept Frères Islands cost Dfr20,000–23,000 per person per day and usually last a minimum of six days (though occasionally three-day tours are possible).

The *Breiz-Izel* is a 20m-long converted tuna trawler from Brittany, France. It has three double cabins, one single, and one cabin containing four bunk beds. Cabins have air-con but the bathroom and toilets are communal. Examples of tours for a group of between six and 15 people include: one day at Plage des Sables Blancs near Tadjoura (Dfr12,900 per person); a weekend (Thursday to Friday) at the Bay of Ghoubbet (Dfr20,000); a week at Les Sept Frères Islands (Dfr23,000 per day per person). A half-day tour at Moucha or Maskali Islands costs Dfr5400 per person for a group of between 10 and 15 people.

WINDSURFING

If you fancy windsurfing – on wheels – an enterprising ex-legionary has set up a centre on the desert sands of the Grand Barra (see Grand Barra & Petit Barra later in this chapter).

PARACHUTING

Parachuting is possible through the Paraclub, though proof of proficiency and insurance are essential. It costs Dfr5000 per jump. Book through Marill travel agency and car hire (☎ 35-11-50).

HIKING

Many tour operators in the capital offer hikes and walks around the country. A cheaper option is to take public transport to

Bankoualé or Dittilou and explore the mountains yourself (see these headings in the Around the Gulf of Tadjoura section later in this chapter).

PLACES TO STAY – BUDGET

The hotels in the African Quarter are the cheapest but also the roughest option; some double as brothels.

The *Hôtel Sheikh Gabood* (☎ 35-10-67) on Avenue 13 is one of the cheapest places in town, with 16 air-con rooms with one/two beds for Dfr1500/3000 (air-con at night only). Bathrooms are shared. Rooms are clean, but small and gloomy.

The *Red Sea Hotel* (☎ 35-23-09) nearby has nine basic air-con rooms, three of which have private shower and toilet. All rooms cost Dfr2000/4000 for one/two people. A better bet is the peaceful, clean and well-run *Hôtel Horseed* (☎ 35-23-16) nearby, which has 12 simple doubles with air-con for Dfr5000 (one or two people). Bathrooms are communal.

The noisy and rather seedy *Bienvenue Hotel* (☎ 35-46-22) on Blvd de Bender is really only for the desperate. Air-con rooms with communal bathroom cost Dfr3000/5000/7000 for one/two/three people.

The *Hôtel Dar-es-Salam* (☎ 35-33-34, fax 35-12-22), south-west of the centre opposite the Cité Einguela on the Ali Sabieh road, has 17 clean air-con rooms. Those with communal bathroom cost Dfr2500 per bed; those with bathroom and TV cost Dfr5000/6000 for twin/double beds.

By far the best budget option is the friendly, family-run *Hôtel de Djibouti* (☎ 35-64-15, fax 35-46-70) on Avenue 13. It has 32 air-con rooms with telephone (and some with TV). Singles/doubles on the second floor with communal bathroom cost Dfr2500/3000. Rooms on the first floor with private bathroom cost Dfr5000/7000/10,500 for singles/doubles/triples.

PLACES TO STAY – MID-RANGE

The following are only marginally more expensive than the budget places, but all are in the European Quarter.

The cavernous *Djibouti Palace Hotel* (☎ 35-09-82, fax 35-37-82), east of the cen-

tre, has air-con rooms with private bathroom, telephone and TV for one/two/three people for Dfr4500/6000/9000 (plus tax of Dfr200 per person per day).

The central *Hôtel des Alpes* (☎ 35-58-68) offers quite good value with 11 clean and well-decorated rooms with air-con for Dfr6000 for one or two people. The bar next door can be noisy. *Hôtel Ali Sabieh* (☎ 35-32-64, fax 35-50-84) across the road has 27 air-con rooms with private bathroom for Dfr7500/9000 for one/two people. Rooms are comfortable, with fridge and telephone, but some are a bit on the small side. There's an Italian restaurant below serving good mains and pizzas for around Dfr1500.

PLACES TO STAY – TOP END

All of the following hotels accept credit cards (but not always AmEx), and charge a tax of Dfr300 per person per day.

The *Ménélik Hôtel* (☎ 35-11-77, fax 35-46-82) on Place Ménélik offers good, well-decorated singles/doubles with telephone and fridge for Dfr10,000/14,500.

Also three-star, but not such good value, is the '70s creation *Hôtel Plein Ciel* (☎ 35-38-41, fax 35-68-57), west of Place Ménélik, with rather brown, weary and overpriced rooms for Dfr14000/16000/18000 for one/two/three people.

The *Hôtel Bellevue* (☎ 35-80-88, fax 35-24-84) is a new, well-furnished hotel north of the centre. It has 30 rooms with bathroom, TV, telephone, and kitchenette for Dfr10,000/14,000 and suites for Dfr16,000. The *Hôtel Alia* is another new place, on Pointe du Serpent, due to open at the time of writing with rooms expected to go for Dfr15,000.

A step up, the *Résidence de l'Europe* (☎ 35-50-60, fax 35-61-08) on Place Ménélik offers modern, spacious and well-furnished suites (with kitchenette) for Dfr17,500/20,500 for singles/doubles. Mobility-impaired travellers should note that there is no lift in the hotel.

At the very top of the range is the recently renovated *Sheraton* (☎ 35-04-05, fax 35-58-92) on the Plateau du Serpent. It has 200 sin-

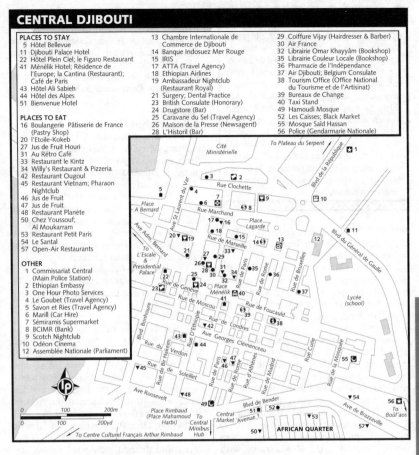

CENTRAL DJIBOUTI

PLACES TO STAY
5 Hôtel Bellevue
11 Djibouti Palace Hotel
22 Hôtel Plein Ciel; le Figaro Restaurant
41 Ménélik Hotel; Résidence de l'Europe; la Cantina (Restaurant); Café de Paris
43 Hôtel Ali Sabieh
44 Hôtel des Alpes
51 Bienvenue Hotel

PLACES TO EAT
16 Boulangerie Pâtisserie de France (Pastry Shop)
20 l'Etoile-Kokeb
27 Jus de Fruit Houri
31 Au Rétro Café
33 Restaurant le Kintz
34 Willy's Restaurant & Pizzeria
42 Restaurant Ougoul
45 Restaurant Vietnam; Pharaon Nightclub
46 Jus de Fruit
47 Jus de Fruit
48 Restaurant Planète
50 Chez Youssouf; Al Moukarram
53 Restaurant Petit Paris
54 Le Santal
57 Open-Air Restaurants

OTHER
1 Commissariat Central (Main Police Station)
2 Ethiopian Embassy
3 One Hour Photo Services
4 Le Goubet (Travel Agency)
5 Savon et Ries (Travel Agency)
6 Marill (Car Hire)
7 Sémiramis Supermarket
8 BCIMR (Bank)
9 Scotch Nightclub
10 Odéon Cinema
12 Assemblée Nationale (Parliament)

13 Chambre Internationale de Commerce de Djibouti
14 Banque Indosuez Mer Rouge
15 IRIS
17 ATTA (Travel Agency)
18 Ethiopian Airlines
19 Ambassadeur Nightclub (Restaurant Royal)
21 Surgery; Dental Practice
23 British Consulate (Honorary)
24 Drugstore (Bar)
25 Caravane du Sel (Travel Agency)
26 Maison de la Presse (Newsagent)
28 L'Historil (Bar)

29 Coiffure Vijay (Hairdresser & Barber)
30 Air France
32 Librairie Omar Khayyâm (Bookshop)
35 Librairie Couleur Locale (Bookshop)
36 Pharmacie de l'Indépendance
37 Air Djibouti; Belgium Consulate
38 Tourism Office (Office National du Tourisme et de l'Artisinat)
39 Bureaux de Change
40 Taxi Stand
49 Hamoudi Mosque
52 Les Caisses; Black Market
55 Mosque Saïd Hassan
56 Police (Gendarmarie Nationale)

gles/doubles/suites starting from Dfr20,300/ 24,300/60,000 including breakfast. Prices depend on room views and the length of your stay (discounts are offered for stays of eight days or more). The rooms on the 5th and 6th floors have just been redecorated and so, unsurprisingly, are a bit more expensive (Dfr30,300/ 35,300 for singles/ doubles). The hotel's facilities include two restaurants, a pool, cocktail bar and casino.

PLACES TO EAT
During Ramadan, most restaurants close during the day (until sunset). If you're

after a spot of lunch head, for the larger hotels.

Cheap Eats
Bottom of the rung are the little *food stalls* along the Route de Venise. They are open every evening until 1 am, and sell delicious and filling sandwiches and brochettes for around Dfr300.

The cheaper hotels, such as *Hôtel Horseed* and *Hôtel de Djibouti*, and the *restaurant* next to the Hôtel Dar-es-Salam, also do reasonable but hearty fare; pasta costs from Dfr200, and fish or steak and chips costs

Djibouti by Night

By night, Djibouti town takes on an altogether different character. The open-air restaurants along Avenue 13 and south of Blvd de Bender are filled with diners, and the streets with colourful characters. Itinerant peddlers hawk their wares, bootleggers sell alcohol from the safety of deep shadows, and middle-aged women sustain a flourishing black market of currencies from under the folds of their skirts.

Merchants, sailors and awestruck nomads wander the town; prostitutes try to detain them, calling softly from balconies, or by advertising discreetly, by draping bras over balconies and balustrades.

Dfr500–800. They're also good places for a cheap breakfast: a continental/Djiboutian breakfast costs from Dfr250/300.

Other places for a cheap meal include the row of local open-air restaurants along Avenue 13 and Ave de Brazzaville. They're basic, but clean and serve more or less the same fare: brochettes, pasta, chicken etc, all for Dfr200–500.

South of Les Caisses market stalls and Blvd de Bender are a number of other small cheap restaurants where mains with chips or rice cost no more than Dfr700. One of the best is **Restaurant Petit Paris** on Avenue 1, where pasta/chicken costs from Dfr150/700. Try the excellent shish kebabs (Dfr300). It's open every night from 6 pm to around 3 am. Other even cheaper places nearby include **Al Moukarram** with pasta/chicken and chips for Dfr100/500. Look out for the lethal local *pastis blanc* or *doma*, a kind of liqueur made with the doum palm.

Yemeni
The **Restaurant la Sirène** at l'Escale is a basic but excellent place, cooled by sea breezes. It's also one of the best and cheapest places in town to try the famous *poisson yéménite* (fish supper), which costs Dfr1500 for two people. Fresh, grilled fish alone costs Dfr300–500, depending on size. Other good-value fare includes spaghetti (Dfr200),

chicken and chips (Dfr700), and steak (Dfr800). The restaurant is open every day.

Other popular Yemeni restaurants include **Chez Youssouf** near the central market, which charges Dfr1500–2000 for the poisson yéménite for two, and, on the Pointe du Serpent, the **Restaurant Saba**.

Seafood
Perhaps the best place in town for seafood is the **Restaurant Ougoul** (☎ 35-36-52) south of Place Ménélik. Mains start at Dfr1000; for a splurge, try one of the excellent set menus at Dfr3500/4000/5000, which generally include an aperitif, seafood, dessert and wine. Lobster costs from Dfr2600. If you want to guarantee that the seafood is fresh, order it in advance from the obliging Ahmed, whose family has owned the restaurant since 1959. It's open for lunch and dinner every day (until midnight).

The **Sheraton Beach Club** hosts a BBQ every Friday on Moucha Island (see Moucha & Maskali Islands later in this chapter).

French
The most famous cafe in Djibouti town, the **Café de Paris** (☎ 35-50-60), sits on the southern side of Place Ménélik (next door to Ménélik Hôtel). With powerful air-con, waiters in black ties, and good French cuisine served both in the brasserie and the more upmarket restaurant on the first floor, it's also the most upmarket. A coffee costs from Dfr350, a beer/aperitif Dfr650/700, and a simple sandwich Dfr800. If you can afford the odd indulgence or two, try the ice cream or sorbet (Dfr 800–1000); the *coupe colonel* (lemon sorbet and vodka) is heavenly. The cafe is open every day (including Ramadan) from 6 am to 11 pm.

The famous **Longchamps** (☎ 35-37-01) is still considered one of the best restaurants in town (and one of the most expensive). Mains go for around Dfr4000; two set menus offer better value at Dfr4500/8000. Wine costs from Dfr2900 for a half bottle. Cooking is classic French haute cuisine. It's open evenings only (closed Friday), from 6.30 pm, and reservations are advised, particularly on Thursday.

Poisson Yéménite

Though actually Yemeni in origin, and not relished at all by the carnivorous Djiboutians, the *poisson yéménite* has become something of an institution in the capital. Large groups of well-heeled tourists can sometimes be seen cramming rather uncomfortably into the simple surrounds of the Yemeni restaurants. And though simple, and prepared in a flash, it's a meal not to be missed.

Take one fish fresh from the sea, clean it with a quick flick of the knife, sprinkle it inside with a little hot pepper, and slap it onto the side of a large tandoori oven.

After a couple of minutes, fetch it from the coals with a long, pointed stick and turn it onto a newspaper. Serve it accompanied by a chapati-like bread and honey, along with some *mokbusa* made with butter, honey and either dates or bananas. A feast fit for a king – but not for a nomad!

The *Restaurant Le Kintz* (☎ 35-27-91) north of Place Ménélik, and *Le Figaro* (☎ 35-38-41) in the Hôtel Plein Ciel, are also upmarket French restaurants with good reputations. The atmosphere in Le Figaro is more intimate; it's decorated like an English dining room. Mains in both places cost Dfr2500–4500; wine costs from Dfr2200 a bottle.

Other International

There are a number of restaurants on or just off Place Ménélik, but almost all are 'European' in style and price.

The *Pizzeria Carlo & Elena* (☎ 35-30-30) has pizzas for Dfr1400–2400. A little more expensive, but popular with Foreign Legionaries, is *Willy's Restaurant/Pizzeria* (☎ 35-65-22). Designed like a French bistro, it offers a wide menu including salad/meat/pizza dishes from Dfr800/1600/1800. It also does great fondues (Dfr2200–2800). A lively bar gets swinging from 5 pm to midnight.

For cheap pizza, you could try the simple *Pizza Double B* (☎ 35-80-33) opposite the Shell station 3.3km from town on the road to the airport. Over 20 different pizzas

(Dfr1500–2200) are served. Cheaper options include sandwiches, hamburgers, omelettes and crepes (all from Drf600). If you're feeling jetlagged, under the weather or just plain lazy, the restaurant will deliver to your hotel.

An excellent modern Italian restaurant is the relatively new *Café de la Gare* (☎ 35-75-51) near La Gare central train station. Mains start at Dfr1500, wine from Dfr1800 a bottle.

For Tex-Mex, head for the new restaurant *La Cantina* in the basement of the Résidence de l'Europe on Place Ménélik. Mains go for around Dfr1500, though you may have to wait a while for them. It's open every day from 6 pm to 2 am.

The *Restaurant Vietnam* (☎ 35-17-08) near Place Rimbaud, with a Chinese owner and chefs, prepares excellent Chinese and Vietnamese food, and is open every evening except Tuesday from 6.30 to 10.30 pm. Another oriental (and very elegant) place is *Le Santal* (☎ 35-37-91) east of the centre on Ave de Brazzaville; it's open every day except Saturday. Both places have mains from around Dfr1500.

Ethiopian

For something more exotic, you could try the Ethiopian restaurant *Chez Bafena* (☎ 35-32-38) south-east of the centre. The *assortiments* (assortments) for Dfr3000 per person give you a taste of six different dishes, plus salad; other mains cost around Dfr1500. Vegetarians can order special dishes in advance. From September to April, you can eat on the pleasant roof terrace, and there's live traditional, Ethiopian music and dance every night from 7.30 pm to closing. The restaurant is open even on Friday and holidays. Another good Ethiopian restaurant is *l'Etoile-Kokeb* (☎ 35-04-10) on Rue de Marseille.

The *Restaurant l'Escale* (☎ 35-22-12), on a terrace overlooking the marina at l'Escale, has to be one of the coolest and most pleasant places in town. European and Ethiopian dishes are available for around Dfr1500, and it's open on Friday but closed Saturday. Friday's all-you-can-eat buffet costs Dr2000 per person. Don't confuse this restaurant with

Fresh is Best

If you're desperate to try the seafood, but can't afford restaurant prices, there is an alternative. Fresh, reasonably priced seafood can be bought (or ordered) directly from the local fisherman who gather each morning outside the Sémiramis supermarket, north of Place Ménélik. Crab goes for around Dfr1500 per kilogram and lobster goes for Dfr2500 per kilogram, though prices depend on both the seasons and your ability to barter. If you don't speak French, ask an English-speaking local to help you.

If you ask very politely, you can normally persuade the small local restaurants to prepare and cook it for you (with a decent tip and consumption of the restaurant's own food or drink) – although you may have to direct operations yourself! Or if your hotel has a kitchen, you can ask there.

This could be too much hassle for some, but it's one way of ensuring that the seafood is fresh, while also directly supporting the local fishing industry.

the adjacent *Club Nautique*, which is open only to travellers with their own boat.

French Djiboutian

The *Restaurant Jules Vernes* (☎ 35-14-09), 5km south of town, is a great family-run affair with a pleasant garden and diverse menu. Main courses cost from Dfr1500. If you want to try a *cabri farci* (stuffed kid), Abdi, the owner, prepares the dish every Thursday evening; it costs Dfr2000 per person. The restaurant is open on Friday.

Perhaps the best place in town for its combination of excellent, reasonably priced food and pleasant, tranquil location on the Plateau du Serpent is the *Restaurant le Grill* (☎ 35-72-93) at the Club des Cheminots (the old rail-workers club). Tables are placed outside in the garden, where the cool sea breeze and shade from the old acacia trees create a very welcome respite from the heat and dust of the town. Try the delicious fish or beef *brochettes* (kebabs) for Dfr1000. Ismaël, the charming owner, keeps standards high. It's open every day for lunch and din-

ner. Minibuses from Place Rimbaud can drop you near the club's gates.

Fruit-Juice Bars & Pâtisseries

The *Restaurant Planète* (☎ 35-17-12), located above a gym on Rue d'Ethiopie, is more like an upbeat cafe, and serves a good range of fresh fruit juices, fruit cocktails and milkshakes (all from Dfr200–700). Salads, sandwiches and hot dishes are also available (Dfr400–1000). The big attraction, though, are the views over the market and mosque in Place Rimbaud – bring your camera.

One of the best and cheapest places for a fresh fruit juice is the *Jus de Fruits Houri*, just off Place Ménélik. It has a good selection of juices (from Dfr100), as well as tea and coffee (Dfr50–150), and some good snacks (such as samosas – known as *sambousas* – for Dfr30) made by the Indian owner. It's open from 7 am to 1 pm and 4.30 to 8 pm every day except Friday.

The *Au Rétro cafe* on Place Ménélik is a popular place with Djibouti's young 'intelligentsia' who meet for an early morning cup of coffee. It's quite a good place for breakfast with croissants for Dfr150, omelettes for Dfr250, and the delicious Djiboutian breakfast of *foie* (liver) for Dfr350.

The *Boulangerie Pâtisserie de France* is one of the best pâtisseries in town with a good selection of bread/cakes/pastries from Dfr30/100/130. A baguette costs Dfr120. It's open every day from 6.20 am to 12.30 pm and 5.30 to 7.30 pm.

Self-Catering

The *Sémiramis* supermarket is the best-known French supermarket, and is crammed with all kinds of goodies from paté de foie gras to Belgian chocolates, but as products are imported, prices are high. (It also stocks sunscreen, nappies and tampons.) A packet of Corn Flakes cost Dfr595; bottles of milk/beer/wine cost from Dfr210/265/450.

Cheaper than Sémiramis and open 24 hours is the *Napoléon* supermarket around 2km south of the centre, which is also reasonably well-stocked and functions as a supermarket, stationer and chemist all in one.

ENTERTAINMENT

Events are advertised in *La Nation* weekly newspaper, or you can check with the tourist office for details. See also Arts in the Facts about Djibouti section and Entertainment in the Facts for the Visitor section of this chapter.

Bars & Clubs

All the following are European in style, and attract mainly legionaries. They stay open until around 11 pm to midnight.

There are three OK clubs on Place Ménélik. For a pleasant outdoor terrace, with western music and satellite TV, check out *l'Historil*. Beer costs from Dr700. The *Drugstore* is a modern-looking cafe-come-restaurant and bar, which plays music videos. A coffee/soft drink/beer costs Dfr400/500/800. Hamburgers cost Dfr800. The *Café de Paris* (see French under Places to Eat in the previous section) is popular with well-heeled Djiboutians, who come here for an aperitif.

The *Ambassadeur Nightclub* (disguised as the *Restaurant Royal*), next door to the l'Etoile-Kokeb restaurant on Rue de Marseille, is considered the best 'European' nightclub in town. Other good places include the ever-popular *Scotch* north of the centre on Rue Clochette, and the *Pharaon* nightclub below the Restaurant Vietnam near Place Rimbaud.

If you're into karaoke, you could head for the *Sheraton* between 8 pm and midnight. Nonguests pay only during the month of May.

There are a few rather dismal Ethiopian nightclubs to the south of Place Ménélik. The Djiboutian bars are even harder to locate, and tend to come and go very quickly (see the boxed text 'Banning the Bars' under Entertainment in the Facts for the Visitor section of this chapter). The best thing to do is to ask the locals for the latest lowdown.

Cinemas

The only cinema in town is the *Odéon* on the Blvd du Générale De Gaulle. There are generally two programs every night (starting at 6.30 and 9.30 pm), usually featuring action-packed if somewhat *dépassé* (old-fashioned) Hollywood movies, which are dubbed into French. Entrance costs Dfr500. Films in French are also shown at the Centre Culturel Français Arthur Rimbaud (see Cultural Centres under Information earlier in this section).

Films in English are shown usually every Thursday at Association House in the US embassy on Plateau du Serpent (Dfr400); book in advance with the security officer (☎ 35-39-95).

Theatre & Concerts

The *Palais du Peuple (☎ 35-42-00)*, north of the centre, and the *Théâtre des Saline* (closed at the time of writing but due to re-open), both host a variety of spectacles, including plays and concerts. Musical performances range from traditional and classical to modern. Events normally take place two to four times a month.

Bowling

Bowling (☎ 35-41-07) is possible at the alley that lies 2.1km south of the centre on the Boûal'os road, opposite the abattoir. It's open from 6 to 8 pm every day except Friday and costs Dfr1200 per person (Dfr700 for students).

SHOPPING

If you're in search of souvenirs, head for Les Caisses, east of Place Rimbaud on the edge of the African Quarter, named after the ramshackle and numerous crates that make up the market. Many stalls sell almost identical products, but prices and quality vary greatly, so take your time choosing. Bargaining is very much the order of the day. The market is open from 8 am to noon and 4 to 8 pm every day except Friday.

See also Shopping in the Facts for the Visitor section earlier in this chapter.

GETTING THERE & AWAY
Air

All airlines have offices in the centre of town (on or around Rue de Marseille) with the exception of Yemenia and Air Tanzania,

DJIBOUTI

who are represented by Savon et Ries travel agency. All accept credit cards, with the exception of Air Djibouti. Airlines serving Djibouti are:

Air Djibouti (☎ 35-10-06, fax 35-24-29)
Air France (☎ 35-20-10, fax 35-06-05)
Air Tanzania (☎ 35-23-51)
Ethiopian Airlines (☎ 35-10-07)
Yemenia (☎ 35-23-51)

The Air France office is closed Thursday afternoon as well as Friday. The airport (☎ 35-16-41) has neither banking nor left-luggage facilities.

Bus

Buses leave from various departure points south of town (see the Djibouti town map). Buses leave hourly for Ali Sabieh (Dfr500, 1½–2 hours), three buses leave daily for Arta (Dfr400), four buses leave daily for Dikhil (Dfr500), there is a daily bus to Hol Hol (Dfr400, two hours), and two buses depart daily for Randa (Dfr500, 3½ hours).

One or two buses leave daily for Tadjoura (Dfr500, 2½–3 hours) at 1pm. There are no buses to Bankouale, Dittilou, Foret du Day or Obock; take a taxi-brousse to these places from Tadjoura.

Train

The Djibouti-Ethiopia train departs three times a week on Wednesday, Friday and Sunday at 5.45 am, arriving in Dire Dawa, Ethiopia, at 6 pm. To continue west to Addis Ababa, you can either catch the train for the second leg or catch the (more rapid) bus.

Tickets (one-way) cost Dfr3900/2500 in 1st/2nd class; on Wednesday, 3rd-class tickets (Dfr1200) are also available. Tickets can be bought 24 hours in advance (but not further ahead) at the train station (☎ 35-80-70), which is open every day from 7.30 am to 2 pm.

Car & Motorcycle

Marill (☎ 35-11-50, fax 35-23-56) sells new and second-hand cars and rents out vehicles. It's got a good reputation, but is not the cheapest place; a 4WD costs from Dfr30,000/186,000 (US$166/1046) per day/week including tax. There is a 20% discount for vehicles rented for more than a week. It's also got a good garage, if you need repairs for your vehicle. It's open from 9 am to 5 pm weekdays and 9 am to 6 pm Saturday.

Boat

Le bac (ferries) to Tadjoura and Obock depart from l'Escale. For information on fares and schedules call ☎ 35-23-51; see also Getting There & Away in the Tadjoura section later in this chapter.

Boats and captains can be hired from the dive operators (see Snorkelling & Diving earlier in this chapter). You can also try asking around at l'Escale and talk to boat owners directly.

If your boat is in urgent need of some TLC contact Franc Huibaut (☎ 35-40-41 or ☎ 35-02-74) at Club Nautique.

GETTING AROUND
To/From the Airport

There is no bus service between the town and the airport, 5km south of town. A taxi ride should cost no more than Dfr1000 (sometimes Dfr100 is charged per item of luggage).

Minibus

The central hub for city minibuses is on Place Rimbaud. The majority operate from 5.30 am to 11 pm every day.

Minibuses belt around almost the whole of the city. For hops within the centre, it costs Dfr30 (Dfr50 after 10 pm) and Dfr100 for longer journeys. You just ask the driver to stop when you want to get off.

Basically, there are two minibus routes of interest to travellers: the first is the 'Ligne Daktar' or 'Hôpital Peltier' (named after the terminus). Destinations are not marked on the minibuses but are shouted out. Minibuses leave at least every five minutes and pass the Odéon cinema, Police Nationale, the train station, Club de Cheminots, the Sheraton, Plateau du Serpent and the beaches. The second route, 'l'Escale', leaves less regularly (you may have to wait 10 to 20 minutes) for l'Escale via various routes.

Taxi

Taxi stands can be found in various parts of town including Place Ménélik, outside the Sémiramis supermarket, and various large banks and hotels (including the Sheraton on Plateau du Serpent, and Hôtel de Djibouti in the African Quarter).

Short journeys during the day around the centre of town, to the Sheraton, l'Escale, Plateau du Serpent and the port should cost no more than Dfr500. At night, and for longer journeys, you will be expected to pay twice as much – around Dfr1000. For general information on taxis in Djibouti town, see the main Getting Around section earlier in this chapter.

Around Djibouti Town

There are several places around Djibouti town that make good one-day snorkelling or diving excursions, including the islands of Moucha and Maskali, off the coast northeast of Djibouti town. (See also Snorkelling & Diving earlier in this chapter.)

If you're just after relief from the heat, there are a few beaches that make reasonable half- or full-day excursions from Djibouti town. Unfortunately, none of these beaches are served by bus. Taxi, hitching a lift (which is difficult) or walking for around two hours are the only options. There are few facilities at these beaches (no showers). If you're desperate for a shower,

you can normally get a bucket of water from one of the restaurants.

MOUCHA & MASKALI ISLANDS

The beaches on the islands of Moucha (mou-sha) are among the best in the country. Snorkelling is excellent too, since much of the area is a designated marine park. Mangrove forests border some of the islands; they're worth exploring if you're keen on birds.

The islands are most accessible on Friday (the Muslim weekend). Between 8 and 8.30 am, dhows and motorboats assemble at l'Escale; if you're not in a group big enough to hire your own boat, you can almost always find a place on another (during the week it can be more difficult). A return trip to the islands costs Dfr3000 per person (returning to Djibouti town around 4.30 pm). For other transport options, see Motorboat in the main Getting Around section earlier in this chapter.

Camping is permitted on the islands, though you'll have to be totally self-sufficient with your own food, water and sleeping facilities, and either hire your own boat, or organise for one to pick you up.

If you fancy a deluxe picnic on an island, you can join the so-called *Sheraton Beach Club* (a bungalow) on Moucha Island. At noon on Friday, the Sheraton puts on an excellent though rather pricey buffet with barbecued fish on the beach for Dfr3500. Reservations are essential, and you'll have to organise your own transport (possible by boat charter, plane or on an organised tour).

DJIBOUTI

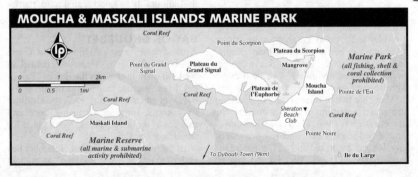

MOUCHA & MASKALI ISLANDS MARINE PARK

Coral Reef

Point du Scorpion

Plateau du Scorpion

Marine Park
(all fishing, shell &
coral collection
prohibited)

Point du Grand Signal

Plateau du Grand Signal

Mangrove

0   1   2km
0   0.5   1mi

Coral Reef

Plateau de l'Euphorbe

Coral Reef

Moucha Island

Pointe de l'Est

Sheraton ▼ Beach Club

Coral Reef

Maskali Island

Coral Reef

Pointe Noire

Marine Reserve
(all marine & submarine
activity prohibited)

To Djibouti Town (9km)

Ile du Large

DORALÉ

Situated 8km west of Djibouti town, Doralé is a simple but reasonably clean beach with few facilities and no shade. It can seem a bit dismal, but if it's peace you're after, this is a better choice than Khor Ambado. Sometimes a bit of litter strews the beach, but the water is clean.

Three restaurants face the seafront. The **Trou Normand**, the first one you come to, is probably the best bet with a pleasant veranda and parasols. It's open every day until midnight or later. Mains cost from Dfr1100, beer costs Dfr800.

Personal belongings should be left at the restaurant or locked up in your car or taxi, as things can disappear in a flash. The thieves of Doralé are considered among the most adroit of any in Djibouti!

Four simple but reasonably pleasant cabins (one with its own shower) are available for Dfr3000. There is no air-con, just a ceiling fan. If you want to reserve a cabin (advisable on Thursday nights), call ☎ 35-73-26. It's also possible to camp on the beach (again leave everything you don't want to lose at the restaurant).

A taxi from Djibouti town to Doralé and back should cost no more than Dfr4000 (they come back later to pick you up). Coming from Djibouti town, look out on the right for the remains of the old lime factory, which once coughed out 8 to 10 tons of lime every day, used for the construction of the capital. A little railway connected the factory to a jetty, from where barges transported it to the capital.

KHOR AMBADO

Khor Ambado, 7km west of Doralé (15km from Djibouti town), is larger, more attractive and has better facilities than Doralé. It's also more lively, and on Fridays can get pretty crowded and noisy with both expat families and adolescent locals.

There are two or three restaurants serving the usual selection of snacks/mains for around Dfr500/1500. The **Traité Ambado** is probably the best bet, and is open every day. It's run by an old and well-known Djiboutian poet and actor, Aden Farah Samatar.

If there are a few of you (ideally around five), you could ask Aden to prepare a cabri farci (Dfr12,000). It makes a terrific feast in the evening after a swim.

Once people head home, the beach takes on a completely different character. Cool, close to the sea, in the light of the moon and under an old acacia tree, this might provide the perfect location for an outdoor *parti* of qat, if you fancy it! – though you'll need to bring supplies with you from Djibouti town. It's also possible to camp here.

The road to Khor Ambado is bumpy, and you may have trouble persuading a taxi to take you there. Like Doralé, it should cost no more than Dfr4000 to go and come back.

Around the Gulf of Tadjoura

The north of the country contains many of the country's highlights. The Bay of Ghoubbet and Lac Assal can be visited easily on a day trip from the capital. Tadjoura, which is best reached by boat, also makes a good day trip from Djibouti town. The beautiful Fôret du Day National Park will require at least two days there and back.

Known as Route de l'Unité, the road leading around the gulf and to the north is aptly named: built after the civil war in the early 1990s, the road links the capital and the Somali south with the Afar north, as far as Tadjoura. It's a good sealed road, particularly as far as Lac Assal.

BAY OF GHOUBBET

Around 90km west of Djibouti town, and barely connected by a narrow channel to the Gulf of Tadjoura, lies the Bay of Ghoubbet. In the narrow gully at the mouth of the bay, violent currents can reach speeds of up to 9 knots, forming a rushing bore and troughs of up to 4m across. Not a place for small boats or little boys!

In the middle of the Bay of Ghoubbet lies Guinni Koma or 'Devil's Island', an ancient

Gulf of the Demons

Known to the local Afar people as Ghoubbet al Kharab (Gulf of the Demons), the vast Bay of Ghoubbet is surrounded by myth. Like Loch Ness in Scotland, the strange, still waters have an enigmatic quality – sometimes appearing almost black.

According to the legend, there was once a mountain on this spot, which was crowned by fire. One day, it was engulfed by a terrible deluge, and since that time, the gulf has been inhabited by demons who drag to the bottom all those who venture onto the waters. Many locals boys are said to have lost their lives in the waters, and few fisherman venture there even today.

Cousteau himself, the famous scuba-diving pioneer, is said to have encountered strange creatures while diving here. Surrounded by steep cliff faces, the bay is thought to be around 200m deep, and is almost cut off from the Gulf of Tadjoura by a narrow gully, just 750m long. Curiously – and like at Loch Ness – researchers now believe that large specimens of underwater fauna may lurk in these deep, dark, isolated waters.

underwater crater, at the top of which fossilised oysters have been found.

If you have your own vehicle, there's a very good view of the bay from a bend in the road, just after it turns north as you approach the bay. The bus journey between Djibouti town and Tadjoura or Randa gives you a very good view of the bay.

AROUND THE BAY OF GHOUBBET

The area between Lac Assal and the Bay of Ghoubbet is considered one of the most remarkable – geologically speaking – in the world. It marks the point of convergence between three continental plates, in which the Arabian and African plates are gradually drifting apart (see the special section 'Geology in Djibouti').

Because of this constant plate movement, the area is very active volcanically. In early

November 1978, the volcano now known as Ardoukoba erupted. Active for no more than a week, the little volcano nevertheless was cited as tangible proof of the geologists' theory that in a few million years a new ocean will have formed here; one that will one day measure as large as the Atlantic.

In the meantime, the Assal rift between Lac Assal and the Bay of Ghoubbet gets ever wider. Already measuring over 12km long, the rift attracts geological tours. Visitors can literally walk along an embryonic ocean bed. For information on geological tours, see Travel Agencies under Information in the Djibouti Town section earlier.

LAC ASSAL

At 153m below sea level, Lac Assal is the lowest point on the African continent, and the third-lowest in the world (after Israel's Dead Sea at 400m, and the Sea of Galilee at 208m). Entrepreneurs used to fly private planes here in order to issue tourists with certificates of their flight '150m below sea level'.

Some geologists believe that the lake was once linked to the nearby Bay of Ghoubbet and the Gulf of Tadjoura. Although a volcanic zone still separates them, it is thought that the lake may be fed sea water through underground fracture lines. This would compensate for the very high rate of evaporation that occurs in the lake; the water is totally saturated with salt (330g per litre), so there's not much chance of a swim.

Encircled by dark, dormant volcanoes, the vast depression is an impressive sight. The banks of salt and gypsum surround the lake for more than 10km, and the blinding white contrasts starkly with the black lava fields around it. At dusk, the colours of Lac Assal change and can look almost fluorescent.

As you approach the lake, there are several bubbling hot springs (where guides like to boil eggs). Towards the northern end, look out for the smooth, spherical formations of the halite (rock salt), which fill the shallow water like large, white mints. Boys sometimes sell these, and grim animal skulls caked in salt crystals.

DJIBOUTI

[Continued on page 480]

GEOLOGY IN DJIBOUTI

In a few million years, Djibouti as we know it will not exist: it will have been superseded by a new continent floating in a new ocean. At this very minute that new ocean is being born.

'Open textbook of geology' and 'natural laboratory' are both phrases coined recently to describe this country. Over the past twenty years, Djibouti has drawn geologists, volcanologists and geophysicists from all over the world; more recently, geological tours have been on the agenda.

A little knowledge of the geological landscape of the country – its volcanoes, basins, fumaroles, sunken plains, salt lakes and rifts – enhances a traveller's understanding and discovery of Djibouti. The discovery is worth making: few countries in the world, with the possible exception of Iceland, offer such geological interest, or the chance to witness first-hand the evolution of the world. This section is designed for the unescorted traveller who has little or no knowledge of geology.

For Djibouti's geological hotspot see Bay of Ghoubbet in the Around the Gulf of Tadjoura section later in this section.

Djibouti Itinéraires Géologiques by Pierre Vellutini is an excellent and well-illustrated publication, albeit rather expensive. It's available in Djibouti town for Dfr4500.

The Theory of Tectonics

The following is the theory of plate tectonics in a nutshell. The outermost part of the Earth, the lithosphere (which includes the crust), is thin and brittle. It has broken up into a number of giant, rocky fragments called plates. These plates 'float' like giant icebergs on top of the asthenosphere (the softer, warmer layer below the lithosphere). Thermal convection currents circulating deep within the mantle (the hot, middle layer between the Earth's core and crust) drive the plates about. The movement of these plates generates a great deal of geological activity, particularly when they come into contact with one another along their edges or plate margins. Earthquakes and volcanoes are the most obvious signs of this movement.

Top: Perfectly rounded spheres of halite crystal, formed from evaporating salt water at Lac Assal.

Bottom: Gypsum crystals, which carpet the banks and bottom of Lac Assal.

In short, tectonic plate activity has influenced the composition of the Earth, the formation of the atmosphere, the development of climatic zones and the evolution of life itself. The theory has become a kind of master key in geology; we now understand a great deal better the structure, history and dynamics of the Earth's crust.

Tectonics in Djibouti

Six large tectonic plates and a number of smaller ones make up the Earth's surface. Djibouti is situated at the meeting point of three major tectonic axes: those of the African, Somali and Arabian plates, which are at 120° angles to one another.

The other two axes, marked by the mid-ocean rifts of the Red Sea and the Gulf of Aden, are opening at a speed of 2cm per year; in other words, five times faster than the African rift. The Arabian plate, which is shifting in a north–north-east direction, is responsible for this rapid widening, and it is now almost completely free of the African plate. Just one 'bridge' ties it still to Africa: the Afar Depression, which comprises the territory of Djibouti.

According to current findings by geologists, the continental crust under the Afar Depression has already been stretched by plate movement to a thickness of just 2km or 3km (as opposed to several dozen kilometres under normal circumstances). More thinning of the crust will have to take place before the two plates are completely separated. Further tectonic activity – such as earthquakes, volcanoes and open fractures – will help bring this about, but the whole process will take several million years.

The Clash of the Titans

There is nowhere in the world with so many extinct volcanoes, so much lava spread on the ground. If the ancients had known of this land, it would never have been in Sicily that they placed the clash of the Titans against the gods, nor the fiery furnaces of the Cyclopes.

Rochet d'Héricourt, *Second voyage sur les deux rives de la mer Rouge*, A Bertrand, France 1846 (translated by the author)

Top: View from the top of La Grande Cheminée (the big chimney), Lac Abbé.

Nonetheless, some signs of these dramatic future developments are already emerging in Djibouti: sea water from the Bay of Ghoubbet and the Gulf of Tadjoura has begun to enter the Assal axis, and the 'bridge of lava' that separates Assal from the Bay of Ghoubbet has already started to collapse. The future ocean, which will comprise the Gulf of Aden and the Red Sea, will start to expand, and eventually a free passageway to the Mediterranean will open. Geologists believe that in some 200 million years the new sea, dubbed the 'Eritrean Ocean', will be as large as its big brother, the Atlantic, is today. In our lifetime, separation of continental plates has occurred only under water – with the exception of the movement in Djibouti. So Djibouti is currently the only place in the world where it is possible to witness first-hand the birth of an ocean. A new passageway, a new sea and a new East African continent are being born!

Volcanism in Djibouti

Located at the convergence of three plates, the territory of Djibouti is quite active volcanically. Slight tremors are frequent, but only two volcanic eruptions are known to have occurred in the country within living memory: Kammourta in the north-west of the country in 1928, and Ardoukoba near Lac Assal in 1978.

Smaller volcanoes are found all over the country, such as in the area between Ghoubbet and Lac Assal. The large amounts of igneous rock that litter the landscape, giving it the 'apocalyptic' appearance so fondly described by travellers, testify to significant volcanic activity in the past.

Basalt is Djibouti's most common igneous rock, and many large lava flows of basalt can be seen in the north of the country. Rhyosite is also found, along with pumice and obsidian. The region around Ali Sabieh, in particular, is rich in basalt and rhyolite that dates from 19 to 27 million years ago.

Top: Geologists examining halite crystals at the edge of Lac Assal.

Bottom: Boiling hot spring, Lac Abbé.

Lac Assal and **Lac Abbé**, due east of the capital, are both bodies of water that are in the process of drying up. Because of the gradual evaporation, the salinity of the water is very high, and some interesting mineral formations can be found around the edges of Lac Assal, including large crystals made of gypsum and halite (see Lac Assal in the Around the Gulf of Tadjoura section).

Lac Abbé is famous for its extraordinary 'lunar' landscape which is populated by large, spike-like deposits of travertine. Hot springs dot the landscape, and fumaroles can also be found. To the south-east of the capital, the **Grand** and **Petit Barra** are examples of vast plains that have collapsed, and they are surrounded by basalt plateaus or mountains (see the South-West to Lac Abbé section later in this chapter for all of these).

Geothermal Energy in Djibouti

Groundwater is heated when it comes into contact with hot rock. This hot water can be harnessed to produce energy. Geothermal energy has been used for over 50 years in areas of the world that have witnessed recent volcanic activity: New Zealand, Iceland, the USA and Italy are all examples.

Geothermal energy is not only cheaper than other types of energy – a fraction of the cost of fuel oil or electrical heating – it is also much cleaner. As the world's oil reserves decline, geothermal energy is becoming an attractive alternative fuel. Djibouti is keen to exploit its natural resource in order to reduce a little its dependence on imported forms of energy such as oil and gas. Plans have been drawn up to this end, and the first steps, in the form of research, have been taken recently in the area around Lac Assal. Unfortunately, the equipment required for the harnessing of geothermal energy is specialised and expensive. Considerable capital investment will have to made if the search for a new type of energy is to get beyond the drawing board in Djibouti.

Top: Geologists examining a fumarole, near the Ardoukoba volcano.

All photos in this section are by Frances Linzee Gordon.

[Continued from page 475]

Getting There & Away

Lying 107km west of the capital and connected by a decent sealed road, Lac Assal is within easy reach of Djibouti town. Most visitors to Lac Assal come with tours or hire their own vehicles from the capital. Though the car hire agencies don't like it, it is perfectly possible to take a normal car there (not just a 4WD).

If you can't stretch to car hire, the only option is to take a bus as far as the junction to Tadjoura, and hike the 17km or so to Lac Assal. You may be able to hitch a lift on the return journey, particularly on the salt miners' trucks when they return to Djibouti town.

Hitching or driving, it's worth making an early start; temperatures can soar in the depression of Lac Assal, and the light reflected off the salt can seem blinding. There are no facilities at all at Lac Assal, so bring lots of water. If you're hiking, you should bring several litres per person, as well as a hat and plenty of sunscreen. If you have water left over, and don't need it for the return journey, give it to the salt workers, who always appreciate it. Working conditions are tough here.

AROUND LAC ASSAL
Ardoukoba Volcano to Randa

Around half an hour's drive from the road near Lac Assal, there's a good walk to the Ardoukoba volcano. The landscape is an extraordinary geological showcase of faults, folds and recent and ancient lava; the most recent lava (that of Ardoukoba) is the blackest. There's a good view of Lac Assal and the Bay of Ghoubbet from the crater. The walk takes around two hours there and back; bring lots of water with you.

If you have your own vehicle, you can continue around 80km on the rough track north of Lac Assal, to the little village of Balho, situated close to the Ethiopian border. It is the site of some beautiful rock carvings that were discovered quite recently.

From Balho, there's a lovely drive to Randa (via the village of Dorra) which

Keen on Carvings

Finely chiselled rock carvings, thought to date from between the 2nd and 4th centuries BC, are found throughout Djibouti, etched on slabs of basalt and on cliff faces. Engravings often feature large savage mammals, as well as antelopes, giraffes or ostriches, and provide the palaeontologist with an invaluable glimpse into the economic, artistic and social life of the ancient Djiboutian.

Particularly remarkable in Djibouti are the very beautiful depictions of cows with long, exaggerated, lyre-like horns, which are thought to date from the 2nd or 3rd century BC. More recent drawings show warriors mounted on camels and armed with spears and shields.

The tradition of rock carving continues among the local inhabitants to this day. Travellers should look out for the numerous abstract signs etched on rocks by nomads along the caravan routes, or to mark out the grazing ground of their herds. The different signs represent the country's different (and sometimes still antagonistic) nomadic tribes.

takes you close to the foot of the highest peak in Djibouti, Mt Moussa Ali (2063m).

RANDA

Situated 35km west of Tadjoura is the little town of Randa. At 700m above sea level, Randa benefits from a cooler climate than much of the rest of the country, and was originally built by the French as an administrative post and summer retreat. Today, it mainly serves as the starting point for hikes and expeditions by 4WD to the Fôret du Day National Park and its environs.

A higher rainfall (falling on the nearby massif of Mt Day) has traditionally allowed the little town to cultivate gardens and orchards. Randa is a pleasant place to stroll around, but there's not much else to see or do in the town.

The *Centre Touristique de Randa* (☎ 42-40-31) is currently the only hotel in town and has nine rooms for Dfr2000 per person. Meals can also be arranged (Dfr1000 for breakfast and Dfr2000 for lunch or dinner).

Reservations for rooms and meals need to be made in advance, as tour groups often fill the place.

Getting There & Away
Off the main Djibouti town–Tadjoura road lies Randa. The road from the junction (10km south-west of Tadjoura) is one of the few in the country that is sealed.

Buses connect Randa with Djibouti town. From Tadjoura, you can take a *taxi-brousse* ('bush taxi' or Toyota pick-up) for Dfr500, which takes about one hour. Go to the Shell station in Tadjoura between 3 and 4 pm each afternoon, and look out for the Toyota pick-ups. Check with the locals for information on taxis that day.

BANKOUALÉ
Not far from Randa is the green and fertile oasis of Bankoualé, known for its year-round waterfalls and small, terraced gardens. Though not as spectacular as nearby Dittilou, it is a pleasant place to spend a day and a night, particularly if you're keen on hiking.

A variety of walks take you up to the waterfalls, streams, fruit trees and little gardens around Bankoualé. Don't get too excited about *la Grande Cascade* (the Great Waterfall). The volume of water varies with the season – sometimes dwindling to the kind of trickle you'd expect from the shower of your budget bunkhouse in Djibouti town.

Recommended walks include Randa (three hours return), the Fôret du Day National Park or Dittilou (three hours one way), and the Plateau de Bassale to the north (five hours return).

Bankoualé is rich in flora. Look out for the indigenous palm of Bankoualé *(Livistonia carinensis)*, rising around 20m high, with a thick crown of fanlike leaves. Fruit trees include banana, mango, orange, lemon and pomegranate.

Places to Stay & Eat
The *Campement de Bankoualé (☎ 35-66-18)* has several *daboyta* (traditional Afar huts) equipped with simple but comfortable beds and mattresses. Showers and toilets are communal. Huts and meals in the camp both cost Dfr2000 per person.

The enterprising Mohammed Chehem Mohammed *(☎ 35-27-12)* owns *tukuls* (traditional cone-shaped huts), which cost Dfr2500 per person including breakfast. Other meals cost Dfr2000, though you can take your own food. Guided walks cost Dfr500 per person; 10% of all takings go back to the community. Reservations for both camps are essential.

Getting There & Away
To reach Bankoualé from Tadjoura, take a taxi-brousse (Dfr500) and get off at Amisso. From Amisso to Bankoualé, it's a 7km walk. Sometimes a taxi-brousse goes on to Ardo, 2km from Bankoualé.

From Randa, you can walk to Bankoualé (about one hour), but you'll need a guide. Ask at the Centre Touristique de Randa (see the preceding Randa section). Guides cost Dfr1000–2000, depending on the size of your group and your ability to bargain.

ARDO
On the way to or from Bankoualé – just 2km down the road – you'll pass the little village of Ardo. The Afar villagers will rush out to display along the side of the road their bright, geometrically designed straw baskets and mats.

If you're interested, ask to be taken to the 'exhibition' in the village, where you'll have a better choice. It's a great opportunity to see the well-known and highly accomplished Afar basketware. Because of tourist traffic to Bankoualé, prices are a bit on the high side, so it's worth trying to bargain – but prices, choice and quality are still much better than those found in Djibouti town. Additionally, any purchase you make will directly benefit the community. *Fiddimas* (mats) cost Dfr8000–10,000; baskets cost Dfr800–3000.

FORET DU DAY NATIONAL PARK
Rising above the Gulf of Tadjoura, the massif of Mt Goda (1750m) shelters one of the rare speckles of green on Djibouti's topographical map: the famous Fôret du Day National Park.

Measuring just 3.2 sq km, this tiny pocket of vegetation has been declared the country's only national park. Despite its size, plant life is incredibly diverse (including several endemic and very rare species), and wildlife abundant. The forest is home to the country's only endemic bird species, the Djibouti francolin. Trees species include ancient juniper (some thought to date back some 1500 years), box wood, wild olive and various types of fig.

Situated at 1500m above sea level, the forest benefits from its proximity to Mt Goda. As rain clouds and mist from the mountain drift into the forest, considerable condensation forms. The soil, as wet as after a storm, releases humidity, which allows the plants and trees to flourish despite the infrequent rains. In winter (from December to March), the temperature at night can drop sometimes to just above freezing.

The Fôret du Day National Park is an exceptional ecosystem, the last remains of a primeval forest that once must have stretched over a far greater area. The forest also gives ecologists a picture of how the mountains of Arabia and the Sahara would have once looked before the profound climatic changes on the continent, and later the systematic destruction of the forests by mankind.

Unfortunately, the destruction continues (see Ecology & Environment in the Facts about Djibouti section).

Getting There & Away

The Fôret du Day National Park is a protected park. Access to it is from the various camps situated on its periphery. These tend to come and go with the fluctuating fortunes of the local entrepreneurs who run them. If you're planning a visit to the forest, check out the current situation with the tourist office in the capital.

DITTILOU

A visit to Dittilou, at the edge of vegetation around the Fôret du Day National Park, should not be missed. This explosion of green amid a desert land is extraordinary by any standards, not just Djiboutian ones. With the rain pattering on your hut in the early morning and mist swirling outside, you could be

---

The Fabulous Fiddima

Ornaments are possessions that few nomads, limited by the constraints of travel and transportation, can afford. But the Afars in Djibouti have developed one art form which allows them artistic expression, serves an intensely practical purpose, and plays a very important social role too.

Designed by Afar women as mattresses for newlyweds, prayer mats for the faithful, and even mortuary cloths for the deceased, the *fiddima* or Afar mat serves a multitude of functions. Finely woven from the leaves of the doum palm, and designed in just three colours – natural straw, black and red – each mat incorporates complex, stylised symbols and patterns suitable for every occasion.

Some mat designs such as *suquudita* (good luck) follow set formulae, adhered to for generations; others are based on new inspirations and ideas. Some incorporate propitious, figurative designs, such as the *urri-ibbate* (the little children's feet); while others record their geographical origin: the fluid motifs of the *terdo* mat recall the mists that swirl around the mountain.

Great social prestige surrounds the craft of the fiddima, as do rivalry and local competition. Sometimes as many as fifty are demanded in the dowry of a bride.

---

forgiven for thinking you're back in your native Scotland, New Zealand or Canada – well, anywhere except dry old Djibouti. Visitors find it impossible to believe that Dittilou belongs to the same country as the one they left on the burning plain just one hour before.

Wildlife Walks

Set 700m above sea level on the flank of Mt Goda, Dittilou shares the Fôret du Day National Park's luscious vegetation and rich wildlife. The walks around Dittilou take you through an almost enchanted landscape of dense, dripping forest, tiny abandoned villages, and viewpoints swirling with mist. Sometimes the woods – with their twisted boughs and festoons of old man's beard – seem reminiscent of a Grimm's fairy tale.

If you want to see animals and birds, hire a guide (in a group no bigger than four), and move about the undergrowth stealthily and quietly. The forest is one of the few places where leopards are still seen. Common sightings include various species of monkey and deer, and several birds of prey, including Bonelli's eagle.

Guides can be hired from the camps, and can take you on beautiful walks in the surrounding forests and mountains, including to the summit of Mt Goda (1750m), from where there's a view of the Gulf of Tadjoura.

Other hikes take you to the waterfall of Toha (three to four hours return), to the plateaus of Mandah and Dawdayya (four to five hours return), and the Fôret du Day National Park (seven hours return).

Places to Stay & Eat

Various entrepreneurs have set up accommodation in daboytas at Dittilou. Baragoïta, of the Caravane du Sel travel agency in Djibouti town (see Travel Agencies in that section), was one of the first, and has established a well-designed, 'ecofriendly' camp with around 20 traditional huts, with communal showers and toilets. Produce from his own orchards and vegetable gardens furnishes the tables of the restaurant. Accommodation costs Dfr2000 per person, lunch and dinner cost Dfr2000, and breakfast and guided walks cost Dfr1000.

Getting There & Away

The road to Dittilou is little more than a very bumpy track – there are no buses or taxi-brousses to Dittilou from either Djibouti town or Tadjoura. Apart from taking a tour from Djibouti town or hiring a 4WD from Tadjoura (expensive at Dfr10,000 one way), the only option is to walk. Take a taxi-brousse (Dfr300) from Tadjoura bound for Randa or Bankoualé as far as the *carrefour* (crossroads), where the track to Dittilou begins (around 11 km from Tadjoura), then walk the remaining 13km (around three hours) to Dittilou.

On Thursdays, a vehicle takes supplies up to the camp. You may be able to hitch a lift

(ask around at the ferry terminal in Tadjoura or call the Caravane du Sel travel agency in the capital). It takes around one hour to drive the 24km from Tadjoura to Dittilou.

TADJOURA

Set against the Goda Mountains and lying at the at the edge of the Gulf of Tadjoura, the whitewashed town of Tadjoura is a picturesque little place. One of the oldest towns on the East African coast, its long commercial history is attested to by several 12th-century Arab texts. For centuries, the town has served as the capital of the sultans of Tadjoura. During its heyday, it was the departure point for countless caravans making the very arduous and dangerous journey to the empire of Abyssinia (modern-day Ethiopia). The French poet Rimbaud was forced to spend a year here in 1886, while waiting to begin his gunrunning exploits to the Ethiopian emperor Menelik.

Today, the town's main assets are its good beaches of white sand. It's also home to the famous curved *poignard*, or knife of Tadjoura, carried by all the Afar nomads of the region.

The town itself, with its palm trees, whitewashed houses and seven mosques, has rather an Arab feel to it. There's little to do here besides swim and stroll around, but it's a pleasant place to spend a morning or afternoon. Facilities in the town include a BCIMR bank, post office and telecommunications building.

On the beaches, look out for the camels waiting patiently to be loaded with foodstuffs brought by the dhows; later they'll return with the nomads to the arid interior of the country. In the town itself, the houses are built close together to keep out the sun, with narrow alleyways creating shade. Afar women sit here weaving the famous fiddima, considered the finest in the country.

If you're keen on birds, the silty beach to the west of the port is a good place for sea birds.

Places to Stay & Eat

The *Hôtel Restaurant le Golfe* (☎/fax 42-40-91), around 2km west of Tadjoura, is a

DJIBOUTI

sizeable complex with its own restaurant, pebbly beach, coral reefs, terrace, table tennis and pool table. A tennis court and swimming pool are planned. It has 14 pleasant, air-con bungalows with double bed and private bathroom for Dfr8000; supplementary beds cost Dfr1500. Reservations should be made well in advance, as the hotel is popular with weekenders from the capital. The Italian owner, Mr Mondino, can collect you from Tadjoura. The restaurant is also open to nonguests; mains cost around Dfr1500, soft drinks cost Dfr400, wine from Dfr2000 a bottle.

The *Restaurant á la Brise de la Mer* (☎ 42-40-31), just a stone's throw from the jetty, offers four basic (but due for renovation) rooms for Dfr2000 per person with communal shower, or Dfr7000 for a room with three meals included. This place is better known for its restaurant (with mains around Dfr1000). If you want anything special or vegetarian dishes, it's a good idea to order in advance. The restaurant is open from 7 am to 10 pm.

A cheaper option is the row of little eating places along the seafront, though these tend to close early in the evening. The *Restaurant le Marso* charges just Dfr100 for spaghetti, Dfr150 for fish and Dfr60/50 for a fruit juice/soft drink.

About 1km from the jetty, on the main road to Dittilou, there's a bakery, and opposite, a supermarket advertised with just a Coke sign.

Getting There & Away

Road The bus is a good idea for the return journey to Djibouti town as it takes you through some interesting landscape, including the volcanic neck that separates the Bay of Ghoubbet from Lac Assal. From Tadjoura, buses depart each day between 7 and 9 am from near the jetty. There are 4WD taxi-brousses also going to Djibouti town (Dfr1000), departing at around 6 am (2½ hours).

Buses leave every day from Cité Arhiba in Djibouti town at 1 pm (Dfr500, 2½ to three hours).

Sea Although there's a reasonable 173km-long sealed road connecting Djibouti town

Drumming the Dinkara

For the Afar sultan of Tadjoura, the *dinkara* is his sceptre, the emblem of royal power. Made up of two copper drums covered in cow's hide, the dinkara is hidden in a secret place in the sultan's house, only brought out for special celebrations, when just the village virtuoso is allowed to beat a rhythm.

On the sultan's death, the skin on the drums is ruptured with a single stroke of the knife. Buried in the deceased sultan's house for a period of twelve months, it is not retrieved until the period of mourning is over. Then a new skin is stretched across the drums, and the new sultan is crowned.

with Tadjoura, travel by boat provides the simplest, most comfortable and picturesque way of reaching the little town (as you leave the port of Djibouti, look out for dolphins).

The ferry departs from l'Escale on Thursday at 1 pm (departing Tadjoura between 3 and 4 pm) and Saturday at 9 am (departing Tadjoura at noon), and takes 2¼ hours. It costs Dfr600 (one way) per person, Dfr4500 for a car.

One or two *vedettes* (motorboats) also depart Djibouti town each day (Dfr1000, 45–60 mins), but at no fixed hour and with only 30 places; ask at l'Escale for the day's schedule.

Dhows usually leave Djibouti between 1 and 2 pm each day, but their schedules are irregular, and passenger places depend on the volume of cargo they are carrying. Ask around just behind the Restaurant La Sirène at l'Escale. Trips cost Dfr400–500 (one way) and take 2½ to three hours.

AROUND TADJOURA
Plage des Sables Blancs

A good excursion (particularly if you snorkel) is to the Plage des Sables Blancs, around 7km east of Tadjoura. Beaches are white, clean and sandy, and there are good coral reefs.

The *Centre Touristique des Sables Blancs* is a new development with traditional huts on the beach and two communal showers and toilets. Huts (with simple beds and mats) sleep up to three people and cost Dfr2000 per person. Lunch or dinner costs Dfr3000 but reservations for food are essential (call le Goubet or Caravane du Sel travel agencies in the capital; see Travel Agencies in the Djibouti Town section earlier in this chapter), otherwise you'll have to come entirely self-sufficient (including water). Bring mosquito repellent too!

In the future, masks and snorkels (Dfr300 per day) and windsurfers (Dfr2000 per hour) should be available to hire. Diving, fishing, volleyball and water-skiing activities are also planned.

To get there, you can take a *petite vedette* (small motorboat), which costs Dfr3000/4000 for one/two or more people, from the jetty in Tadjoura. The other option is to walk (one to 1½ hours), but you'll need to take a guide from the village.

Ambabo

Lying 9km west of Tadjoura, another camp, Ambabo, has been set up offering accommodation on the beach, fishing, access to coral reefs, and walks in the area. It costs Dfr9500 per person for accommodation and all meals, and transport there can be organised if you're in a group. For (essential) reservations contact ☎ 35-76-75, ⊜ mibrathu@softhome.net.

OBOCK

Obock, lying 62km north-east of Tadjoura, is where French colonialism all began. In 1862, the Afar sultans of Obock sold their land for 10,000 thalers to the French, and construction of the town began. By 1888, its population had grown to 2000.

But Obock's future was doomed. Isolated from the hinterland by high mountains, without sufficient sources of potable water, and above all lacking a harbour suitable for the future development of the colony, Obock was soon eclipsed by Djibouti town.

Since then, the little town has remained something of a backwater, and survives primarily from its small fishing industry. For the visitor, Obock's greatest attraction is the beaches and coral reefs, which are among the best in the country.

The town itself is a pleasant enough place, though it's not as picturesque as Tadjoura. The civil war in the 1990s destroyed much of the town, and the old factories and shops visibly crumble all around – some still strewn with bullet holes. Beware of leftover land mines!

All that remains of its past glory as the capital is the governor's house (the first official building erected on the site), and a French Legionary graveyard with the graves of French soldiers who died from fever on their way to Indochina between 1885 and 1889. There's also a house – yet another – credited with the dubious distinction of housing the famous poet and adventurer Arthur Rimbaud. The early morning fish market is also worth a peek.

It's possible to buy the Afar fiddimas here, as well as the poignard knives. Prices are cheaper than in Djibouti town and the quality is better. A local artist, Omar Mohammed Aman, makes little wooden models of dhows (Dfr3000–5000). The locals will help you find them if you're interested.

Facilities in Obock include a small telecommunications building and post office.

Places to Stay & Eat

Accommodation in Obock is hard to come by, but a new 'tourist village' is planned in the future. The only hotel in town, and one of the few restaurants, is the **Restaurant Machallah** (☎ 42-80-11), with a pleasant terrace. Follow the road that bears left from the jetty for around 400m. It boasts just two doubles for Dfr10,000 (with air-con and TV) and Dfr7000 (with fan); the bathroom is shared. The restaurant offers fish/meat dishes for Dfr500/800, and continental breakfasts for Dfr300. It closes at 10 pm.

The **Restaurant le Ras Bir** (☎ 42-80-22) is pleasantly situated on the seafront to the west of the jetty. It usually caters to tourist groups, and if there's a group in town or you order in advance, you can eat there. If you're desperate for accommodation, ask the owner, Assia Souleiki, for a bed on the veranda.

For cheaper fare, try the row of eateries (little more than shacks advertised with soft-drink bottles) that line the seafront. On the main street, there is a grocery and some fruit-juice bars where you can get cheap snacks.

Getting There & Away

Air If you get stuck in Obock and can't wait for the next boat, you can usually hitch a lift with the private plane that flies no fewer than 45 sacks of qat from Djibouti town every day. It normally leaves Obock between 1 and 3 pm, costs Dfr5000 (one way) and takes 25 minutes. For inquiries, call Djibouti airport (☎ 34-01-01).

Road At the time of writing, there was no petrol station in Obock, though there are plans to install one soon. Travellers with their own vehicles should bring lots of spare fuel from Djibouti town, particularly if continuing north.

To head north from Obock, there are a few taxis-brousses to Khor Angor (Dfr2000 per person), Moulhoulé (Dfr2000), and even Assab in Eritrea. If you want to go to Ras Siyan for its coral reefs or bird-watching, you'll probably need to charter a taxi-brousse (Dfr30,000 for up to ten people).

There's only a rough road between Obock and Tadjoura; no buses connect the towns.

See also Land Mines under Dangers & Annoyances in the Facts for the Visitor section of this chapter.

Sea From Djibouti town, the ferry is the best option. It leaves l'Escale at 9 am on Monday, it costs Dfr600/4500 (one way) for a passenger/car and takes between three and 3½ hours. From Obock to Djibouti town, the boat simply turns around, leaving between 12 and 1 pm the same day.

Commercial dhows go to Obock from l'Escale up to five times a week (departing between 8 and 9 am) when there's enough business and there's space for passengers. The trip costs Dfr500–600 (one way) and takes around 4½ hours. From Obock, dhows usually leave for Djibouti town on Friday and Monday.

The other option is to ask a fisherman to take you, but make sure that the boat is equipped with two motors and is in decent condition.

AROUND OBOCK
Mt Mabla

Due west of Obock is the massif of Mt Mabla (1250m). Site of the second green pimple on the map of Djibouti, it boasts the only other significant forest besides the Fôret du Day National Park. The road there is just a narrow, snaking track and you'll need a 4WD, guide, camping gear and all provisions; but for hikers, climbers and lovers of wildlife, the possibilities are good.

To the North & Les Sept Frères Islands

The landscape north of Obock is little more that a vast, semidesert plain. There's little reason to come here unless you're on your way to Eritrea. The road is little more than a dusty track.

Visible for the entire journey off the coast are the Straits of Bab el Mandeb (Gate of Lamentations), which mark the crossroads between the Red Sea and the Indian Ocean. The coast is fringed with white, sandy beaches and good coral reefs.

Rising out of the sea, you can also make out the sandy-coloured islands known as Les Sept Frères. Legendary in local folklore, they have also been mythicised by the diving community for the stunning coral reefs surrounding them.

Despite the bleak conditions, there is a surprising amount of wildlife – from various gazelles and antelopes to coveys of sandgrouse. The journey to Moulhoulé, the

---

Bandit Brothers

Legend has it that seven wicked brothers once pillaged the coast of Yemen, and committed terrible crimes and untold flagrances. One night at sea, just beyond Périm Island, the lawless bandits were surprised by a violent storm. Transformed into seven rocks, they were condemned to be whipped forever by the ocean waves. The islands known as Les Sept Frères, or The Seven Brothers, can be seen to this day, subjected to the harsh winds and angry seas of the Straits of Bab el Mandeb.

last Djiboutian outpost before the Eritrean border, will take around 4½ hours by car.

South-West to Lac Abbé

Benefiting from the road links to Ethiopia, most places south-west of Djibouti town are accessible by public transport. The major exception, unfortunately, as it's the major highlight of the south-west, is Lac Abbé. The only means of visiting this remarkable site is by taking a tour or hiring a 4WD with driver-guide from the capital.

ARTA
Arta, lying 41km outside Djibouti town, was built as a little summer retreat. Perched 800m above sea level in the mountains, here temperatures are up to 10°C cooler than in the capital. It's a popular place with expats and well-healed Djiboutians, who like to keep weekend houses here.

Although there's not much to do in the town, there are great panoramic views across the Gulf of Tadjoura, which are worth a stop if you're driving by. On the way to Arta, look out for nomads selling smoky-tasting camel's and goat's milk on the side of the road. It's fine to just have a taste if you fancy it, though it's good to leave a tip for this. A litre costs Dfr400, but you'll need your own receptacle.

Places to Stay & Eat
The **Centre d'Estivage Arta** (☎ 35-13-51) officially caters to the French army stationed in Djibouti. However, if there's space, travellers are sometimes allowed to use the centre – call in advance to check. Rooms for up to three people, with bathroom, cost Dfr1700 (Dfr5000 Thursday night). Bungalows (for up to four people) with shower cost Dfr2000 (Dfr6000 Thursday night), and studios (for up to six people) with bathroom cost Dfr2500 (Dfr6000 Thursday night). Facilities include tennis, volleyball, football, billiards and minigolf; the pool is open from March

Local Landmarks

If you're wondering about the little piles of stones littering the landscape, here's a quick key. The piles of black stones resembling upright cylinders are ancient burial mounds, thought to belong to the Galla period, and still shrouded in mystery. The piles of pebbles marked by little red flags are Muslim marabouts, denoting the graves of holy men.

The short, dry-stone walls mark the temporary shelter of nomads, protecting them against the wind and the sand, and their animals against the hyaenas and jackals.

The mounds of stones in the form of pyramids, in the Afar region, mark the graves of nomads who have met an unnatural death – whether by accident, violence or misfortune.

to October. The restaurant does decent fixed menus for Dfr1800 (Dfr3000 Thursday evening).

The **Ecole Hôtelerie d'Arta** (☎ 42-20-52) was set up for the training of future chefs and hotel staff. It used to be possible to eat there and stay in one of the four rooms. These were being renovated at the time of writing, but should reopen in the future; you can try calling, or check with the tourist office in Djibouti town for details.

Currently the only place to eat in town is the simple **Restaurant Darar**, which is open only in the evenings (until midnight), and serves mains for around Dfr200.

Getting There & Away
There are between two and four buses a day to and from Djibouti town (Dr400), leaving between 8 and 9 am and around noon. There are no buses from Arta to Ali Sabieh. A taxi to/from Djibouti town costs Dfr4000 (Dfr6000 return).

GRAND BARRA & PETIT BARRA
Situated around 70km south-west of Djibouti town, the two great sunken desert plains of the Petit and Grand Barras are the remnants of an ancient lake. The Grand Barra measures 25km by 10km, and is basically a plain of white clay, which has dried

DJIBOUTI

and cracked in the desert sun. The trucks bound for Ethiopia can't resist letting rip here (it's almost the only place on the entire journey where they can), and the trail of white dust blazing behind them can be seen for miles as you pass through the area.

Look out for mirages, which are often seen here, and the wildlife, which despite the very bleak conditions is abundant: gazelle, dik-dik, antelope, hyaena, jackal and fennec (African fox).

On the Grand Barra, you can go wind-surfing on wheels. A centre has been set up just past the Djibouti town–Ali Sabieh–Dikhil crossroads. It's open from September to May, though by prior booking only. Ali Liaquat, an ex-legionary, can be contacted on ☎/fax 35-46-95. Windsurfing costs Dfr4000 per person per hour, or Dfr26,600 for three people with transport from Djibouti town included. It makes a half- or full-day excursion – it can get pretty windy out there! You can also book a barbecued meal here (Dfr4000), and refreshments are available (Dfr300/500 for soft drinks/beer).

Getting There & Away

Buses going to Ali Sabieh, Dikhil, Yoboki and on to Ethiopia can all drop you on the edge of the Grand Barra (Dfr500). From the road, you will have to walk the last couple of kilometres to the windsurfing centre.

DIKHIL

Dikhil lies 118km south-west of Djibouti town and is the second district capital of the south. In 1928 the French decided to set up an administrative post here; the village has grown from a few huts into the town of today with a population of some 35,000 in-habitants.

Dikhil has always been a meeting place for nomads, providing a kind of crossroads from the surrounding plains of Hanlé, Gob-aad and the Petit and Grand Barra. Today it prospers further from its position on the main Djibouti-Ethiopia road. Dikhil is also where traditional Somali *bilaawe* nomad knives are made.

As with many places in Djibouti, the plea-sure lies more in the trip than the destination.

Tourist groups usually use the little town as a base for trips to Lac Abbé. However, with new accommodation, albeit simple, at Lac Abbé, it's probably now better to stay there.

Perched on a small rocky promontory, the town is reasonably attractive. The most interesting thing is the ancient *palmeraie* (palm grove), which makes a good stop after a long, hot journey. Cool and shady paths wind past limpid pools nourishing the abundant palm and fruit trees (including lemon, mango, banana and pomegranate). Look out also for Fatima, the semi-tame fe-male ostrich that inhabits the place.

Facilities in Dikhil include a grocery, petrol station, and post and telecommunica-tions building, but no bank.

Place to Stay & Eat

The only hotel in town is the *Hôtel la Palmeraie* (☎ 42-01-64), just beyond the Mobil petrol station. It's similar in style to its sister hotel in Ali Sabieh, and has ten (rather peeling) twin-bedded rooms for Dfr2500 (Dfr5000 with air-con).

There are a number of cheap food joints around the bus station. The *Al Baraka* is probably the best bet and does good meat and rice dishes for around Dfr200.

The restaurant *Lac Abbé* near the mar-ketplace is also recommended. Very popu-lar with the locals is the *Okar* restaurant, which does mains such as beef and beans for Dfr150. The supermarket next door is a good place for stocking up on provisions if you're planning a sortie to Lac Abbé.

Getting There & Away

Three or four buses leave Dikhil every day for Djibouti town (Dfr500), the first around 7 am, the last around 4 pm. Buses leave twice a day for Ali Sabieh (Dfr400), at 7.30 am and 2 pm. A taxi-brousse leaves every day for Yoboki (Dfr400), on the road to Ethiopia, around noon.

There are no buses to Lac Abbé. How-ever, with three days' notice, the Hôtel la Palmeraie can organise day trips with a ve-hicle and guide for Dfr15000, everything included (maximum ten people), or for a day and a night for Dfr9000 per person.

LAC ABBÉ

Spreading over 350 sq km, Lac Abbé is a vast lake; at least 6000 years old, it's also a very ancient one. Many fossils have been found in the vicinity, including elephant, antelope and hippo remains, and shells and fish. These, along with other finds such as grinding stones, suggest that the area was once marshy and fertile.

Not so today. The landscape of Lac Abbé is thought to rate among the most desolate on Earth. The hundreds of calcareous chimneys that march across the plain, and stand up to 50m high, have made the lake famous. And the sulphurous gas emitted from the chimneys has given the lake its name: Abbé means 'rotten' in the local Afar dialect.

Described as 'a slice of moon on the crust of the Earth', the lake is an extraordinary place and should not be missed. The film *Planet of the Apes* was filmed here; no need for props and backdrops – the landscape is truly 'lunar', 'apocalyptic' or 'otherworldly', as travellers for generations have loved to describe it.

Until recently, the lake was fed by the Awash River from Ethiopia – the source also of the desiccated fish on the shores of the lake. Because water from this source seems to be dwindling, it is thought that the vast lake of Lac Abbé may be in the process of dying.

Guided Tours

A guide to Lac Abbé is essential. Not just to get there, but also to steer you clear of the quicksand and pits said to riddle certain areas of the banks. Local people and animals still lose their lives here. At the time of writing, a local Afar girl, tending goats, fell into a pit and drowned. Guides can also give you a proper tour of the site, which should include the chimneys, the boiling, sulphurous-smelling springs (which nourish the meagre pastures on which the nomads' herds exist) and the flamingos. Pelicans and ibis can sometimes be seen mingling in the crowd too. For a decent snap of them, you'll need a lens of at least 300mm. A walk to the edge of the lake to see the birds takes between 1½ and two hours there and back. Don't forget sun-

Lac Abbé Revealed

Thousands of years ago, Lac Abbé lay 400m below its current level. From deep in the Earth's mantle, hot ground water started to gush up in the form of hot spring water, full of dissolved minerals. When it mixed with the cold water at the bottom of the lake, these minerals solidified into deposits, forming little by little concretions in the water. When the level of the lake eventually subsided, these formations were left freestanding – the 'chimneys' you see at Lac Abbé today.

screen and lots of water. In the afternoon, a hat is essential!

The banks immediately surrounding the lake are covered in strange geometrical patterns created by the drying mud. Look out for the paw prints of jackals and hyaenas. The animals themselves are often seen – and heard – in the very early morning, if you keep a sharp eye or ear out.

Some of the chimneys can be climbed, if you fancy it. There's a great view of the lake and surrounding plain from *la Grande Cheminée* (the Big Chimney), but you should take care, as the shifting shale can make it a bit treacherous underfoot. A guide can point out the best routes, though most prefer their party to keep two feet firmly on the ground.

When to Go

The best time to visit the lake is in the early morning, when the chimneys appear to belch smoke in the cool morning air. It's also the time to see the thousands of flamingos, which feed on the lake until around 9 am.

An even better plan is to arrive in the late afternoon, stay the night, and leave after sunrise the following morning. In the evening, when the sun sets behind the chimneys and the animals are driven home across the plain, the landscape can look almost magical.

Places to Stay

At the time of writing, there was only one camp at Lac Abbé. Set up late in 1998, the *Gîte d'Etape* sits on a small plateau overlooking the lake. Known as Asboley

(Where There's Salt) in Afar, the camp comprises traditional nomad shelters (with camp beds and mattresses), and a communal shower and toilet. Reservations are essential; call Mr Ougouré at the Hôtel Calypso in Djibouti town (☎ 35-11-99, fax 35-81-98).

A minimum of five people are required for an excursion from Djibouti town to the site. Tours leave Djibouti town at 1 pm and arrive in time for sunset. The following morning, there's a guided tour of the site, returning to Djibouti town by 5 pm. The trip costs Dfr11,500 per person, including meals and accommodation. Transport to and from the camp costs an additional Dfr7000 per person (minimum six people).

If you have your own vehicle, and want to stay at the camp, it costs Dfr3000 per person for a bed in a hut. Reservations are still required.

If you have a tent, you can camp anywhere, but keep away from the quicksand around the lake!

Getting There & Away
Buses and taxis-brousses run nowhere near Lac Abbé. The only way of getting there is by hiring a car and driver-guide either from the capital or from Dikhil, or by taking a tour.

From Djibouti town, it's a long, hot and dusty journey to Lac Abbé (around four hours nonstop), so bring lots to drink. Look out for the ostriches halfway between Dikhil and As Eyla (around 200km out of Dikhil).

Don't bother stopping in the village of As Eyla; it's the one place in Djibouti where you're likely to be mobbed by villagers demanding money and offering their services as guides. There is no longer accommodation in town, and there are few places for refreshments.

South to Ali Sabieh

The south of the country is well served by the Ethiopia-Djibouti railway. And that's the most likely reason for coming here – on your way to or from Ethiopia. There are few breath-stopping attractions here, and

the old maxim 'it's better to travel than to arrive' is rather appropriate in this region.

If you have your own vehicle (4WD only), a possibility is to loop back from Dikhil or Lac Abbé to Djibouti town via Ali Sabieh (rather than the normal route via Arta). You'll need lots of time and a guide or good driver; the road is in parts little more than a track, and the direction isn't always clear so bring a compass.

HOL HOL
The little village of Hol Hol is a pretty dusty, ramshackle little place, with no hotels and few other facilities. Its *raison d'être* was – and apparently still is – the viaduct carrying the Ethiopia-Djibouti train across a narrow valley.

In 1900, the viaduct represented the greatest engineering feat of the entire railway, measuring 136m long and 29m high. In 2000, it's hard to get too excited about it, though. Unless you're on your way somewhere else, it's very difficult to justify a special expedition.

If you do stop and are feeling thirsty, the *Restaurant Miriam* is about the best bet.

Buses leave every day to and from Djibouti town (Dfr400, two hours). The train to and from Ethiopia also stops here (Dfr400).

ALI SABIEH
Lying 95km south-west of Djibouti town, Ali Sabieh is the last stop in Djibouti on the train journey to Ethiopia. The town's trade thrives from the connection with the railway, and local markets are lively and colourful.

Set amid red sandstone rock at an altitude of 750m, Ali Sabieh serves as the administrative capital of the southern region. Though quite attractive, with houses washed in different pastel shades, the town is not terribly exciting.

There are a few vestiges of French colonial rule, such as a hospital and a little church, but the most interesting thing about the town are the markets. There's usually at least one every morning from around 6 am until noon.

Ali Sabieh also boasts two petrol stations, a post office, a BCIMR bank, and a small telecommunications building.

Places to Stay & Eat

Currently the only hotel in town is the *Hotel Palmeraie d'Ali Sabieh* (☎ 42-61-98), 2km from the centre of town. If you come by bus, ask to be dropped here; if you come by train, it's about a 15-minute walk. Six simple twin-bedded rooms with private bathroom cost Dfr3500 (Dfr5000 with air-con). A cheaper option are the traditional huts that sleep up to four and cost Dfr1000 per person (even if you're alone). Reservations are advised. The restaurant is open to nonguests and is a good place for lunch. Sandwiches, salads and hamburgers (Dfr450–500), chicken and chips (Dfr750) and steak (Dfr1300) are on the menu.

The large restaurant *Etoile du Mont Arrey* (☎ 42-61-91), just off the main square, is considered the best restaurant in the centre of town and does mains such as chicken or steak for Dfr700. Make sure you check your order and bill, as there have been reports of overcharging. In the future, the restaurant is hoping to rent out around ten air-con rooms with private bathroom for Dfr3500/5000 for one/two people.

The cheapest places for a bite to eat can be found around the bus station. The restaurant *Dur Dur* is a small place covered in bright murals, and is a favourite with the locals.

Getting There & Away

Ali Sabieh can be reached by bus or train from the capital.

Buses to/from Djibouti town (Dfr500, 1½ to two hours) leave almost every hour until an hour before sunset. There are three

A Nomad's Toothbrush

If there is one thing in Djibouti that has defied the industrial revolution, it's the toothbrush. Disdaining the modern variety, Djiboutians in both town and country have stuck with their traditional version, the adaï. Cut from the evergreen shrub *Salvadora persica*, which grows in low bushes throughout the country, the little wooden sticks are collected in neat little piles and sold at the side of the road.

Scientific analysis has shown that the Djiboutians' preference for home products may be a wise one. With a bit of chewing, the very fibrous and spongy wood forms into long, strong 'bristles'. And contained in the wood are, among other things, chloride, various antibacterial agents and vitamin C. In other words, the adaï is a kind of toothbrush-toothpaste neatly packaged as one.

Recently, a certain brand of popular toothpaste, 'Sarakan', manufactured in the Middle East, turned out to be manufactured from a local shrub. No prizes for guessing which one.

buses a day to/from Dikhil (Dfr400, 45 mins), two buses to Ali Addé (Dfr400, 45 mins), and two buses to Hol Hol (Dfr400, 1½ hours).

Trains to Djibouti town leave on Tuesday, Thursday and Saturday (Dfr1200/800/600 for 1st/2nd/3rd class, 2½ hours).

Trains to Dire Dawa in Ethiopia leave on Wednesday, Friday and Sunday (Dfr2700/2000/1700 for 1st/2nd/3rd class, six to seven hours).

DJIBOUTI

Language

ARABIC

Arabic is one of Eritrea's three national languages (the other two being English and Tigrinya), and one of Djibouti's two national languages (the other being French). In Eritrea it's spoken mainly in coastal regions and along the Sudanese border. In Djibouti you can try your hand at Arabic if you find that French doesn't work for you.

Arabic is subject to much dialectal variation. While the following guide is based on the variety spoken in Egypt, it should be fine for basic communication in both Eritrea and Djibouti.

Pronunciation
Vowels

a	as in 'had' (sometimes very short)
e	as in 'bet' (sometimes very short)
i	as in 'hit'
o	as in 'hot'
u	as in 'book'
aw	as the 'ow' in 'how'
ay	as the 'y' in 'by'
ei	as in 'vein'

Long vowels are indicated by a macron (stroke above the letter).

ā	as the 'a' in 'father'
ē	as the 'e' in 'ten', but lengthened
ī	as the 'e' in 'ear', only softer
ō	as the 'o' in 'for'
ū	as the 'u' in 'nude'

Consonants

Most consonants in Arabic are pronounced as they would be in English. Here are some that may cause confusion:

th	as in 'thin', not as in 'this'
g	as in 'go' or as in 'rage'
H	strongly whispered 'h', almost like a sigh of relief
kh	as the 'ch' in Scottish *loch*
dh	as the 'th' in 'this'
r	a rolled 'r', as in Spanish *caro*
s	as in 'so', never as in 'wisdom'

sh	as in 'ship'
'	a glottal stop – pronounced like the closing of the throat when saying 'Oh oh!'
gh	a guttural sound like Parisian 'r'
q	a strongly guttural 'k' sound; sometimes pronounced as a glottal stop
h	as in 'ham'
w	as in 'wet'
y	as in 'yes'

Note that when double consonants occur in transliterations, both are pronounced. For example, *el-hammām* (toilet), is pronounced 'el-ham-mam'.

Greetings & Civilities

Arabic greetings vary according to whether you're addressing a male, a female or a group of people.

Hello.	*salām 'alēkum*
(response)	*wa 'alēkum es salām*
Hello/Welcome.	*ahlan wa sahlan*
(response)	*ahlan bīk* (to m)
	ahlan bīkī (to f)
	ahlan bīkum (to group)
Pleased to meet you.	*tasharrafna* (polite)
	fursa sa'īda (informal)
Goodbye.	*ma'as salāma*
Please.	*min fadlak* (to m)
	min fadlik (to f)
	min fadlukum (to group)
Excuse me.	*'an iznak, esmaHlī* (to m)
	'an iznik, esmaHīlī (to f)
	'an iznukum, es maHūlī (to group)
Thank you (very much).	*shukran gazīlan*
You're welcome.	*'afwan, al-'affu*
No thank you.	*la' shukran*
Yes.	*aywa*
No.	*la'*
Sorry.	*'assif*

What's your name?	*ismak ēh?* (to m)
	ismīk ēh? (to f)
My name is ...	*ismī ...*

Language Difficulties

I understand.	*ana fāhem*
I don't understand.	*ana mish fāhem*
Do you speak English?	*enta bititkallim inglīzī?* (to m)
	entī bititkallimī inglīzī? (to f)

Getting Around

How far is ...?	*kam kilo li ...?*
I want to go to ...	*ana 'ayiz arūH ...*
Does this bus go to ...?	*al-otobīs da yerūH ...?*
Which bus goes to...?	*otobīs nimra kam yerūH ...?*
What is the fare to ...?	*bikam at-tazkara li ...?*
Stop here, please.	*wa'if/hassib hena, min fadlak*

When does the ... leave/arrive?	*emta qiyam/wusuul ...?*
boat	*al-markib*
ferry	*ma'atiya*
bus	*al-otobīs*
train	*al-'atr*

Where is the ...?	*fein ...?*
airport	*matār*
bus station	*maHattat al-otobīs*
bus stop	*maw'if al-otobīs*
station	*al-maHatta*

Where can I rent a ...?	*fein e'aggar ...?*
bicycle	*'agala*
boat	*markib*
car	*sayyāra/'arabiyya*

Directions

Where is the hotel ...?	*fein al-funduq ...?*
Can you show me the way to the hotel ...?	*mumkin tewarrīnī at-tarīqlil-funduq ...?*
Where?	*fein?*
here	*hena*
there	*henek*

this address	*al-'anwān da*
north	*shimāl*
south	*ganūb*
east	*shark*
west	*gharb*

Accommodation

I'd like to see the rooms.	*awiz ashūf al-owad*
May I see other rooms?	*mumkin ashūf owad tānī?*
How much is the room per night?	*kam ugrat al-odda bil-laila?*
Do you have any cheaper rooms?	*fī owad arkhas?*
It's too expensive.	*da ghālī 'awī*
This is fine.	*da kwayyis*
air-conditioning	*takyīf hawa*

Around Town

Where is the ...?	*fein ...?*
bank	*al-bank*
embassy	*as-sifāra*
female toilet	*twalēt al-Harīmī*
male toilet	*twalēt ar-ragel*
market	*as-sūq*
police station	*al-bolīs*
post office	*al-bōsta/ maktab al-barīd*
restaurant	*al-mat'am*

I want to change ...	*ana 'ayiz usarraf ...*
money	*fulūs*
travellers cheques	*shīkāt siyaHiyya*

Where can I buy ...?	*fein mumkin ashtirī ...?*
How much is this/that ...?	*bikam da ...?*
It costs too much.	*da ghālī 'awī*
Do you have ...?	*fī 'andak ...?*

Time & Numbers

What time is it?	*sā'ah kam?*
When?	*emta?*
today	*el nharda*
tomorrow	*bokra*
yesterday	*mberrah*
early	*badrī*
late	*mut'akhar*
daily	*kull yōm*

Sunday	(yōm) al-aHadd
Monday	(yōm) al-itnīn
Tuesday	(yōm) at-talāt
Wednesday	(yōm) al-arba'a
Thursday	(yōm) al-khamīs
Friday	(yōm) al-gum'a
Saturday	(yōm) as-sabt

1	١	wāHid
2	٢	itnein
3	٣	talāta
4	٤	arba'a
5	٥	khamsa
6	٦	sitta
7	٧	sab'a
8	٨	tamanya
9	٩	tis'a
10	١٠	'ashara
11	١١	Hidāshar
100	١٠٠	miyya
1000	١٠٠٠	'alf

Health

I need a doctor.	'awiz doktōr
Where is the hospital?	fein el mustashfa?
I feel dizzy.	ana dayikh

I'm allergic to ...	'andī Hasasiyya dodd ...
antibiotics	el entībiyotik
penicillin	el binisilīn

I'm ...	'andī ...
asthmatic	hasāsiyya fi sadri
diabetic	marad es sukkar
epileptic	marad es sar'

accident	Hadsa
antiseptic	mutahhir
aspirin	asbirin
condoms	kabābīt
diarrhoea	is-hāl
fever	sukhūna
headache	sudā'
hospital	mustashfa
pharmacy	agzakhana
pregnant	Hāmel
sanitary napkins	kotex
stomachache	waga' fil batn
tampons	hifāz al-'āda al-shahriyya

ETHIOPIAN AMHARIC

Amharic is the national language of Ethiopia. It belongs to the Afro-Asiatic language family, in the Semitic language sub-group that includes Arabic, Hebrew and Assyrian.

While regional languages such as Oromo, Somali and Tigrinya are also important, Amharic is the most widely used and understood language throughout the country. It is the mother tongue of the 12 million or so Amhara people in the central and north-west regions of the country, and a second language for about one third of the total population.

Amharic word-endings vary according to the gender and number of people you're speaking to, indicated in this guide by the abbreviations 'm' (to a male), 'f' (to a female) and 'pl' (to more than one person). There are also general modes of address that can be either informal or polite; these are indicated by the abbreviations 'inf' and 'pol' respectively.

For a more comprehensive guide to the language, get a copy of Lonely Planet's *Ethiopian Amharic phrasebook*. It has useful introductory sections on pronunciation and grammar, and includes Amharic script throughout.

Pronunciation

While many of the sounds of Amharic will be familiar to you, there are some sounds for which there are no English equivalents. Keep your ears tuned to the way Ethiopians pronounce their language – this will be a good start in mastering pronunciation.

In general, stress falls equally on each syllable. Like English, a raised tone at the end of a sentence signifies a question.

Vowels

a	as in 'mamma'
e	as in 'her', without the 'r' sound
ë	as the 'a' in 'ago'; shorter and flatter than e above
ea	as in 'head'
i	as in 'bit'
o	as in 'hot'
u	as in 'flute' but shorter

ai	as in 'bait'
ie	as in 'pie'
ō	a cross between the 'oa' in 'coat' and the 'au' in 'haul'; similar to French *au*

Consonants

ch	as in 'church'
g	as in 'get', not as in 'rage'
gw	as in 'gwen'
h	as in 'him'; at the end of a sentence it's like a short puff of breath
k	as in 'kick'
kw	as the 'q' in 'queen'
j	as in 'jump'
p	as in 'pop'
s	as in 'plus' (never a 'z' sound)
sh	as in 'shirt'
t	as in 'time'
z	as in 'zoo'
ny	as the 'ni' in 'onion'
r	a rolled 'r'

You should also be aware of the Amharic consonant sounds that have no English equivalents – 'glottalic' or 'explosive' consonants, made by tightening and releasing the vocal chords. Explaining these sounds in any depth would take more space than we have here so they haven't been included in this guide. Instead, their nearest English equivalents have been used.

Greetings & Civilities

Hello/Greetings/ Goodbye.	*teanastëllën* (lit: 'may you be given health')
Hello.	*tadiyass* (inf)
Hello.	*selam* (lit: 'peace be with you')
How are you?	*dehna neh?* (m)
	dehna nesh? (f)
	dehna not? (pol)
	dehna nachu? (pl)
I'm fine.	*dehna*
Good night.	*dehna der* (m)
	dehna deri (f)
	dehna yideru (pol)
	dehna deru (pl)
Goodbye.	*dehna senbët* (m)
	dehna senbëch (f)
	dehna yisenbëtu (pol)
	dehna senbëtu (pl)

The Ethiopic Syllabary

The unique Ethiopic script is the basis for the alphabets of Amharic, Tigrinya and Tigre. The basic Ethiopic syllabary has 26 characters; Amharic includes another seven, and Tigrinya another five characters to cover sounds specific to those languages.

The alphabet is made up of root characters representing consonants. By adding lines or circles (representing the vowel sounds) to these characters, seven different syllables can be generated for each consonant (eg, *he, hu, hi, ha, hë, ho*). As with Roman script, the characters are written from left to right on a page.

Goodbye/See you.	*chow*, as in Italian *ciao* (inf)
Have a nice trip.	*melkam guzo*
Yes.	*awo*
OK.	*ëshi*
No. (not the case/ not true)	*ie*
No. (not there/ not available)	*yellem*
Maybe.	*mënalbut*
Please.	*ëbakëh* (m)
	ëbakësh (f)
	ëbakon (pol)
	ëbakachu (pl)
Thank you.	*amesegënallō*
Thank you very much.	*betam amesegënallō*
You're welcome.	*ënkwan dehna metah* (m)
	ënkwan dehna metash (f)
	ënkwan dehna metu (pol)
Excuse me.	*yikërta*
Sorry.	*aznallō*

Small Talk

What's your name?	*sëmëh man nō?* (m)
	sëmësh man nō? (f)
	sëmëwot man nō? (pol)
My name is ...	*sëmea ... nō*
What country are you from?	*ke yeat ager neh?* (m)
	ke yeat ager nesh? (f)
	ke yeat ager not? (pol)

I'm from ...	ke ...
Africa	afrika
America/USA	amearika
Australia	awstraliya
Canada	kanada
Djibouti	jëbuti
Egypt	gëbs
Eritrea	earëtra
Ethiopia	itëyopiya
Europe	irop
South Africa	debub afrika

Are you married?	agebtëhal? (m)
	agebtëshal? (f)
I'm married.	agëbëchallō
I'm not married.	alagebahum
May I take your	(anten/anchën/ërswōn)
photograph?	foto mansat
	yichalal? (m/f/pol)

Language difficulties

Do you speak ...?	... tëchëlalleh? (m)
	... tëchëyallesh? (f)
	... yichëlallu? (pol)
English	ënglizënya
Amharic	amarënya

Yes, I speak	aow, (ënglizënya)
(English).	ëchëlallō
I don't speak	(amarënya) alchëllëm
(Amharic).	
Do you understand?	gebbah? (m)
	gebbash? (f)
	gebbawot? (pol)
I don't understand.	algebanyëm
I understand.	gebëtonyal
Do you have/Is	astergwami alle?
there a translator?	
Does anyone here	ënglizënya yemichël
speak English?	alle?
Please speak	ëbakëh kess bëleh
slowly.	tenager (m)
	ëbakësh kess bëlesh
	tenageri (f)
	ëbakon kess bëlō
	yinageru (pol)
Please write it in	ëbakon be ënglizënya
Roman script.	alfabeat yisafuliny
	(pol)

Getting Around

Where is the ...?	yeat ... nō?
airport	awroplan marefiyaw
bus station	awtobës tabiyaw
bus stop	awtobës makomiyaw
city centre	mehal ketemaw
taxi stand	taksi makomiyaw
ticket office	tikeat biro/
	tikeaṭ meshchaw
train station	babur tabiyaw

Which bus goes	yeatënyaw awtobës
to ...?	wede ... yiheadal?
Does it go to ...?	wede ... yiheadal?
Please tell me	ëbakon ... sënëderss
when we get	yinëgeruny? (pol)
to ...?	
I want to get off	ëzzih mōred ëfellëgallō
here.	

What time does	... mechea
the ... arrive/leave?	yidersal/yinesal?
boat	jelba
bus	awtobës
car	mekina
minibus	wëyëyët
plane	awroplan
train	babur
truck	ye chënet mekina

next	yemiketëllō
How much is it	wede ... sënt(ë) nō?
to ...?	
I'd like to reserve	wede ... tikeat bekëd
a ticket to ...	miya megzat ëfellë
	gallō
I'd like a one way	wede ... meheaja tikeat
ticket to ...	ëfellëgallō
I'd like a return	wede ... derso mels
ticket to ...	tikeat ëfellëgallō

I want to rent a ...	... mekerayet ëfellëgallō
bicycle	bëskleat
car	mekina

Directions

I want to go to ...	wede ... mehead ëfellë
	gallō
How do I get	wede ... ëndeat
to ...?	ëheadallō?

Is it near/far?	*kërb/ruk nō?*
Can I walk there?	*begër yaskeadal?*
Can you show me on the map?	*kartaw lie yasayunyal?* (pol)
Where?	*yeat?*
Turn ...	*be ... bekul tatef* (m)/ *tatefi* (f)
Go straight ahead.	*beketëta hid* (m)/*hij* (f)
on the (left/right)	*be (gra/keny) bekul*
at the next corner	*yemiketëllō metatefiya*
to the north	*wede semean*
to the south	*wede debub*
to the east	*wede mësrak*
to the west	*wede më'ërab*
in front of/behind	*fit le fit/beholla*
highway	*awra godana*
main road	*wanna menged*
street	*menged*
village	*meneder*

Around town

Where is a/the ...?	*... yeat nō?*
bank	*bank*
church	*beate kërëstëyan*
city centre	*mehal ketema*
... embassy	*ye ... eambassi*
hotel	*hoteal*
market	*gebeya*
mosque	*mesgid*
pharmacy	*farmasi/ medhanit beat*
police station	*polis tabiya*
post office	*posta beat*
public toilet	*ye hëzb mesedaja beat*
restaurant	*mëgëb beat*
tourist office	*ye turist biro*
university	*yuniversiti*

What time does it open/close?
sënt se'at yikefetal/yizzegal?
I want to change money/travellers cheques.
genzeb/travlers cheaks mekeyer ëfellë gallō
I want to make a (local/international) call.
(ager wëst/wëch ager) sëlk medewel ëfellëgallō

Open	ክፍት ነው
Closed	ተዘግቷል
Entrance	መግቢያ
Exit	መውጫ
Information	ማስታወቂያ
Danger	አደጋና
No Smoking	ማጨስ ክልክል ነው
Toilets	መፀዳጃ ቤት/ ሽንት ቤት
Men	የወንዶች
Women	የሴቶች

Accommodation

Where is a ...?	*... yeat nō?*
hotel	*hoteal*
good hotel	*tëru hoteal*
cheap hotel	*rëkash hoteal*
bed	*alga*
room	*këfël*
Do you have/ Is there ...?	*... alle?*
a room/bed	*alga*
a single room	*and alga*
a room with two beds	*bale hulett alga*
a quiet room	*set yale këfël*
showers	*shawer*
water for bathing	*metatebiya wuha*
hot water	*muk wuha*
How much is the room/bed for ...?	*alga le ... sëntë nō?*
one night	*and mata*
one week	*and samënt*

Does it include breakfast?
kursënëm yichemëral?
I'd like to see the room.
këflun mayeat ëfellë gallō
Can I see a different room?
leala këfël mayeat ëchëlallō?
I leave tomorrow.
nege ëheadallō

Food

breakfast	*kurs*
lunch	*mësa*
dinner	*ërat*

| Is there a cheap (restaurant) near here? | *ëzzih akababi, rëkash (mëgëb beat) alle?* |

I want to eat ... food.	*ye ... mëgëb ëfellëfallō*
Ethiopian	*itëyopiya*
Arab	*arab*
Italian	*talyan*
Western	*faranji*

| I'm vegetarian/ I don't eat meat. | *sëga albellam* |
| Can I have it mild? | *alëcha yimëtallëny?* |

bread/bread rolls	*dabbo*
round bread	*ambasha*
chips	*ye dënëch tëbs*
salad	*selata*
sandwich	*sandwich* (usually spicy meat between plain bread)
soup	*merek* (usually a spicy lamb or beef broth)
yoghurt	*ërgo*

water	*wuha*
water (boiled)	*ye fela wuha*
water (sterilised)	*ye tetara wuha*
mineral water	*'ambo wuha'*
soda/soft drink	*leslassa*
juice	*chëmaki*
milk	*wetet*
tea	*shai*
coffee	*buna*
strong/weak	*wefram/kechën*
with/without	*be/yale*
honey	*mar*
sugar	*sëkwar*
beer	*bira*

Shopping

Where is a/an ...?	*... yeat nō?*
bakery	*dabbo beat*
bookshop	*mesëhaf beat*
clothes shop	*ye lëbs suk*
general store	*sheketa sheket medebër*
market	*gebeya*

Emergencies

Help!	*ërdata!*
It's an emergency!	*aschëkwie nō!*
There's been an accident!	*adega nebber!*

Call ...!	*... tëra/tëri! (m/f)*
the police	*polis*
an ambulance	*ambulans*

Danger!	*adegenya!*
Fire!	*ësat!*
Thief!	*leaba!*
Go away!/ Leave me alone!	*temelless!*
I'm lost.	*menged teftobënyal*
Where is the toilet?	*mesedaja beatu yeat nō?*

| stationers | *steashenari* |
| shop | *suk* |

Where can I buy ...?	*... yeat yigenyal?*
I'm just looking.	*ëyayo nō*
I want a (larger/ smaller) ...	*(tëllëk yale/annes yale) ... ëfellëgallō*
How much is it?	*sëntë nō?*
That's (very) expensive.	*(betam) wëdd nō*
Do you have anything cheaper?	*rëkash alle?*

Health

I'm sick.	*amonyal*
I need a doctor (immediately).	*hakim (baschëkwie) ëfellëgallō*
doctor	*hakim*
hospital	*hospital*
medical centre	*ye hëkëmëna tabiya*

I'm allergic to ...	*... ies-mamanyëm*
antibiotics	*antibiotiks*
penicillin	*penisillin*

I have ...	*... allebëny*
diabetes	*sëkwar beshëta*
epilepsy	*yemitël beshëta*
nausea/vomiting	*yasmelësenyal*
stomach ache	*hodean yamenyal*

Time & Dates

When?	mechea?
What time is it?	sënt se'at nō?
It's (one) o'clock.	(and) se'at nō
It's a quarter past (one).	(and) se'at kerub nō
It's half past (one).	(and) se'at tekul nō
the morning	tëwatu
the evening	mëshëtu
the night	lealitu

now	ahun
today	zarea
tonight	zarea mata
tomorrow	nege
day after tomorrow	ke nege wediya
yesterday	tënantëna

Monday	senyo
Tuesday	maksenyo
Wednesday	rob
Thursday	hamus
Friday	arb
Saturday	këdamea
Sunday	ëhud

Numbers

Although there are Amharic script numerals, Arabic numerals are now commonly used throughout Ethiopia. Amharic is used to refer to numbers in speech.

½	gëmash
1	and
2	hulett
3	sost
4	arat
5	amëst
6	sëdëst
7	sebat
8	sëmënt
9	zeteny
10	assër
11	assra and
12	assra hulett
13	assra sost
14	assra arat
15	assra amëst
16	assra sëdëst
17	assra sebat
18	assra sëmënt
19	assra zeteny
20	haya
21	haya and
30	selassa
31	selassa and
40	arba
50	hamsa
60	sëlsa
70	seba
80	semanya
90	zetena
100	meto
101	meto and
200	hulett meto
1000	and shi
2000	hulett shi
100,000	meto shi

one million	and milliyon

FRENCH

French and Arabic are the official languages in Djibouti. French is spoken by almost all educated people in the country – a few words and phrases will win you many friends.

Basics

Hello.	Bonjour.
Goodbye.	Au revoir.
Yes.	Oui.
No.	Non.
Please.	S'il vous plaît.
Thank you.	Merci.
You're welcome.	Je vous en prie.
Excuse me.	Excusez-moi.
Sorry. (forgive me)	Pardon.
Do you speak English?	Parlez-vous anglais?
How much is it?	C'est combien?

Getting Around

When does the next ... leave/arrive?	À quelle heure part/ arrive le prochain ...?
boat	bateau
bus	bus
train	train

1st class	première classe
2nd class	deuxième classe
left luggage (office)	consigne

timetable	*horaire*
bus stop	*arrêt d'autobus*
train station	*gare*
ferry terminal	*gare maritime*

I'd like a ... ticket.	*Je voudrais un billet ...*
one-way	*aller simple*
return	*aller retour*

I'd like to hire a car/bicycle.	*Je voudrais louer une voiture/un vélo.*
Where is ...?	*Où est ...?*
Go straight ahead.	*Continuez tout droit.*
Turn left.	*Tournez à gauche.*
Turn right.	*Tournez à droite.*
far/near	*loin/proche*

Around Town

a bank	*une banque*
the ... embassy	*l'ambassade de ...*
post office	*le bureau de poste*
market	*le marché*
chemist/pharmacy	*la pharmacie*
newsagency	*l'agence de presse*
a public telephone	*une cabine téléphonique*
the tourist office	*l'office de tourisme/ le syndicat d'initiative*

What time does it open/close?	*Quelle est l'heure de ouverture/ fermeture?*

Accommodation

the hotel	*l'hôtel*
the youth hostel	*l'auberge de jeunesse*

Do you have any rooms available?	*Est-ce que vous avez des chambres libres?*
for one person	*pour une personne*
for two people	*deux personnes*

How much is it ...?	*Quel est le prix ...?*
per night	*par nuit*
per person	*par personne*

Time, Days & Numbers

What time is it?	*Quelle heure est-il?*
today	*aujourd'hui*

Emergencies

Help!	*Au secours!*
Call a doctor!	*Appelez un médecin!*
Call the police!	*Appelez la police!*
Leave me alone!	*Fichez-moi la paix!*
I'm lost.	*Je me suis égaré/ée.*

tomorrow	*demain*
yesterday	*hier*
morning/afternoon	*matin/après-midi*

Monday	*lundi*
Tuesday	*mardi*
Wednesday	*mercredi*
Thursday	*jeudi*
Friday	*vendredi*
Saturday	*samedi*
Sunday	*dimanche*

1	*un*
2	*deux*
3	*trois*
4	*quatre*
5	*cinq*
6	*six*
7	*sept*
8	*huit*
9	*neuf*
10	*dix*
100	*cent*
1000	*mille*

one million	*un million*

TIGRINYA

Tigrinya is the predominant language of Eritrea and is also widely spoken in Tigray province in Ethiopia. It belongs to the Ethiopic branch of the Semitic language family. Like Amharic, it uses the syllabic alphabet of classical Ethiopic or *Ge'ez* (see the boxed text 'The Ethiopic Syllabary' earlier in this chapter).

Tigrinya words vary their endings according to the gender of the person you are speaking to; this is indicated in this guide where relevant by the abbreviations 'm' (to a male) and 'f' (to a female).

Pronunciation
Vowels

a	as in 'mamma'
e	as in 'men'
ee	as in 'heed'
i	as in 'bit'
o	as in 'or', with no 'r' sound
oo	as in 'cool'
u	as in 'put'
ai	as in 'bait'
ie	as in 'pie'
ō	a cross between the 'oa' in 'coat' and the 'au' in 'haul'; similar to French *au*

Consonants

Most consonants are pronounced as per their English counterparts but, like Amharic, there are some consonant sounds not found in English. The transliterations in this guide are designed for ease of use and are not meant as a detailed phonetic representation of all the consonant sounds in Tigrinya. By pronouncing the words and phrases clearly you should be able to make yourself understood. Listening to the everyday speech of the people is the best way to master some of the more complex sounds of the language.

ch	as in 'church'
g	as in 'get', not as in 'gel'
h	as in 'him'
j	as in 'jump'
k	as in 'kick'
ny	as the 'ni' in 'onion'
p	as in 'pop'
q	like a 'k' from far back in the throat
r	as in 'run'
s	as in 'plus' (never a 'z' sound)
sh	as in 'shirt'
t	as in 'time'
ts	as the 'ts' in 'its'
z	as in 'zoo'

Greetings & Civilities

Hello.	*selam*
Welcome.	*merhaba*
Good morning.	*dehaando hadirka* (m)
	dehaando hadirkee (f)
Good afternoon.	*dehaando weelka* (m)
	dehaando weelkee (f)
Good evening.	*dehaando amsika* (m)
	dehaando amsikee (f)

Good night.	*dehaan hideru*
Goodbye.	*dehaan kun* (also Italian *ciao*)
Yes.	*u-we*
No.	*aykonen*
Please.	*bejaka* (m)
	bejakee (f)
Thank you.	*yekanyeley/yemesgin*
That's fine, you're welcome.	*genzebka* (m)
	genzebkee (f)
Excuse me.	*yikrie-ta*
I'm sorry.	*aytehazeley*
How are you?	*kemay aleka?* (m)
	kemay alekee? (f)
I'm fine, thanks.	*tsebuk, yekeniyeley*
Pleased to meet you.	*tsebuk afleto/ leila yigberelna*
What's your name?	*men semka?* (m)
	men semkee? (f)
My name is ...	*shemey ... iyu*
Where are you from?	*kabey metsika?* (m)
	kabey metsikee? (f)
I'm from ...	*a-nne kab ... iye*
Are you married?	*temereka dikha?* (m)
	temerekee dikhee? (f)
How many children do you have?	*kenday kolu-oot (deki) alowuka?* (m)
	kenday kolu-oot (deki) alowukee? (f)
I don't have any children.	*deki yebeleyn.*
I have a son.	*wedi aloni*
I have a daughter.	*gual alatni*
May I take your photograph?	*kese-alekado?*

Language difficulties

Do you speak (English)?	*(engiliznya) tezarebdo/ tezarebido?* (m/f)
I don't speak Tigrinya.	*a-nne tigrinya ayzareben*
I understand.	*yirede-anee iyu/ teredioonee*
I don't understand.	*ayeterede-anen*

Getting Around

Where is the ...?	*abey alo ...?*
airport	*aryaporto/maerefi nefarit*
bus station	*maerefi autobus*
bus stop	*autobus tetew tiblelu*

What time does the next ... leave/arrive?
tikitsil ... saat kenday tinekel/te-atu?

boat	*jelba*
bus (city)	*autobus (ketema)*
car	*mekina*
plane	*auroplan/nefarit*
taxi	*taksi*
train	*babur*

I want to go to ...	*nab ... kikeid delye*
Where is ...?	*abey alo ...?*
How do I get to ...?	*kemey geire naboo ... yikeid?*
Is it far/near?	*rehooq/kereba diyu?*
Can I walk there?	*baegrey kikedo yikealdo?*
Can you show me the direction?	*ket-hebreni tikealdo?*
Go straight ahead.	*ket elka kid*
Turn left/right.	*netsegam/neyeman tetewe*

Around Town

I'm looking for ...	*ne ... yenadi alekoo*
a bank	*bank*
the embassy	*embasi*
the hospital	*hospital/ beit hikmena*
my hotel	*natey hotel*
the market	*idaga/shooq*
a pharmacy	*farmacha/ beit medhanit*
a post office	*beit busta*
a public telephone	*nay hizbi telefon*
the tourist office	*nay turist haberieta beit tsihfet*

What time does it open?	*saat kenday yikifet?*
What time does it close?	*saat kenday yi-etso?*
Do you have ...?	*... alekado?*
How many/ How much?	*kenday?*
this	*eizee*
that	*etee*

Accommodation

| Where is ...? | *abey alo ...?* |
| hotel | *hotel* |

guesthouse	*maeref agaish/ albeirgo*
youth hostel	*nay mena-esey hostel*
camping ground	*metkel dinquan/ teinda bota*

Do you have any rooms available?	*medekesi kiflee alekado?*
How much is it per night/person?	*neha-de leiti/seb kenday yikifel?*
Is breakfast included?	*kursi mesoo hisub d'yu?*
single bed	*kelete arat*
double bed	*hadde arat*
for one/two people	*neha-de/kelete seb*
for one/two nights	*neha-de/kelete leiti*

Food

breakfast	*kursi*
lunch	*mesah*
dinner	*dirar*
restaurant	*beit megbi/restront*

water	*mai*
beer	*beera*
mineral water	*mai gas/aqua minerale*
coffee	*boon* (Italian words such as *capuccino* and *macchiato* also)
tea	*shahee*
with	*mis*
without	*bizey*
milk	*tsaba*
sugar	*shukar*
bread	*banee*
eggs	*enkakuho*
potato	*dineesh*
rice	*ruz*

Shopping

How much is it?	*kenday iyu waga-oo?*
I'm just looking.	*nikeree tirah iye*
That's too expensive.	*aziyu kebiruni*
bookshop	*mesheta metsahifti*
clothes shop	*mesheta kidawenti*
market	*idaga/shouq*
local products	*nay kebabi etot/firyat*

Health

| I need a doctor. | *a-nne hakim/doctor yedliyeni a-lo* |

Where is the hospital?	*hospital/beit hikimina abey alo?*
I have a stomachache.	*a-nne kirtset aloni*
I'm diabetic.	*a-nne shikor/shikoria himam aloni*
I'm epileptic.	*a-nne minfirfar himam aloni*
I'm allergic to penicillin.	*a-nne nay pencillin kute-at aloni*
diarrhoea	*witse-at*
medicine	*medhanit/fewsi*
nausea	*egirgir/segedged*

Time, Days & Numbers

What time is it?	*saat kenday koynoo?*
today	*lomee/lomee me-altee*
tomorrow	*tsebah*
yesterday	*timalee*
morning	*niguho*
afternoon	*dehri ketri*
night	*leytee*
Monday	*senui*
Tuesday	*selus*
Wednesday	*reboo*
Thursday	*hamus*
Friday	*arbi*
Saturday	*kedam*
Sunday	*senbet*

Emergencies

Help!	*hagez/redi-at!*
Leave me alone/ Go away!	*hidegeni/kid bejakha!*
I'm lost.	*a-nne tefi-a aloku*
Call ...!	*... tsewe-a!*
a doctor	*hakim/doctor*
the police	*police*

1	*hadde*
2	*kelete*
3	*seleste*
4	*arba-ate*
5	*hamushte*
6	*shedushte*
7	*shewate*
8	*shemonte*
9	*tesh-ate*
10	*aserte*
20	*isra*
30	*selasa*
40	*arba-a*
50	*hamsa*
60	*susa*
70	*sebe-a*
80	*semanya*
90	*tese-a*
100	*mi-eetee*
1000	*sheh*

one million	*hadde million*

Glossary

This glossary covers some of the local words the traveller is likely to encounter. For information on culinary terms, see Food in the Facts for the Visitor sections; for general information on the languages of the Horn, see the Language chapter.

abba – a prefix used by a priest before his name; means 'father' (Ethiopia, Eritrea)

abuna – archbishop of the Ethiopian and Eritrean Orthodox church, from the Ge'ez meaning 'our father'

adaï – evergreen shrub used as toothbrush (Ethiopia, Eritrea, Djibouti)

agelgil – round, leather-bound 'lunch boxes' carried by country travellers (Ethiopia, Eritrea)

amba (also *emba*) – flat-topped mountain (Ethiopia, Eritrea)

araki – grain spirit (Ethiopia, Eritrea)

ato – literally 'sir'; equivalent of 'Mr' (Ethiopia, Eritrea)

azmari – itinerant minstrel (Ethiopia)

bac – ferry (French – Djibouti)

beat – Amharic word meaning 'place', which is attached to the end of other words, eg, *buna beat, shint beat* (Ethiopia)

boulangerie – bakery (French – Djibouti)

boutre – see *dhow*

brousse – French colonial term for the hinterland outside towns, like the English 'bush' (Djibouti)

buluko – heaviest type of *shamma*, used in cold areas such as the Bale Mountains (Ethiopia)

buna beat – literally 'coffee house' but more often than not a bar! (Ethiopia)

campement touristique – tourist camp (French – Djibouti)

caravane de sel – ancient salt caravan (French – Djibouti)

chat – see *qat*

contract taxi – private taxi, ie, nonshared taxi

daboyta – traditional Afar hut (Djibouti)

Derg – Socialist military junta that governed

Ethiopia from 1974 to 1991 under Lt Colonel Mengistu Haile Mariam; derived from the Ge'ez meaning 'committee'

dhow – traditional Arab vessel rigged with a lateen (triangular) sail, plying the Indian Ocean and the Red Sea; known in Djibouti by its French name, *boutre*, and in Eritrea as *sambuk*

dula – wooden staff carried by many Ethiopian men when travelling

emba – see *amba*

enset – false-banana tree found in much of southern Ethiopia, used to produce a bread-like staple

épicerie – grocery store (French – Djibouti)

EPLF – Eritrean People's Liberation Front; victorious guerrilla army in the 'Struggle for Independence'

Falasha – Ethiopian Jew

faranji – foreigner, especially a western foreigner (Ethiopia)

fiddima – straw mat woven by the Afar people (Djibouti)

foutah – sarong-like wrap worn by men in Djibouti and in lowland parts of eastern Ethiopia and Eritrea; known in Ethiopia as *shirit*

gabeta – ancient board game (Ethiopia, Eritrea)

gabi – slightly thicker version of the *shamma*, worn by men (Ethiopia, Eritrea)

gada – age system of male hierarchy among the Oromo people of eastern Ethiopia

gari – horse-drawn cart used for transporting passengers and goods in the towns (Ethiopia, Eritrea)

Ge'ez – ancient language, like a kind of Latin, still used by priests today (Ethiopia, Eritrea)

gommista – tyre repair shop (Italian – Ethiopia, Eritrea)

gotera – granary with a little thatched roof (Ethiopia)

grocery/grocerie – more often than not a liquor shop! (Ethiopia)

hookah – in Ethiopia, water pipe used to smoke marijuana or tobacco; known in Djibouti as *nargile*

hotel – often a restaurant! (Ethiopia, Eritrea)

jellabia – hooded cloak with wide sleeves (Eritrea)

jile – the curved knife carried by Afar nomads in Ethiopia; see also *poignard*

jus beat – juice bar offering fresh fruit juices (Ethiopia)

keak beat – cake shop (Ethiopia)

Kebra Negast – 14th-century collection of legends that describe the origins of the Solomonic dynasty (Ethiopia)

kemis – white cotton dress worn by Ethiopian highland women

Kiddus – Saint, eg, Kiddus Mikael translates to St Michael (Ethiopia, Eritrea)

mabraz – *qat* den; designated room where qat chewers customarily meet (Djibouti)

maqdas – inner sanctuary of a church (Ethiopia, Eritrea)

masjid – mosque (Djibouti)

mesob – hourglass-shaped woven table from which traditional food is served (Ethiopia)

messagerie – parcel office (French – Djibouti)

mies – see *tej*

muezzin – mosque official who calls the faithful to prayer (Djibouti)

nargile – see *hookah*

natala – women's equivalent of a *shamma*, but with a decorated border or *tibeb*

negus – king (Ethiopia)

negus negast – king of kings; the traditional and official title of Ethiopian emperors

oued – a river that is dry except in the rainy season (French – Djibouti)

palmeraie – palm grove (Djibouti)

poignard – French term used in Djibouti to describe the knife carried by both Afar and Somali nomad men; see also *jile*

poisson yéménite – Yemeni fish supper (French – Djibouti)

qat – mildly intoxicating leaf that is widely consumed in Djibouti and eastern Ethiopia; known in Djibouti as *qat* and in Ethiopia as *chat* (it is illegal in Eritrea)

Ramadan – ninth month of the Muslim calendar, 30 days long, during which strict fasting is observed from sunrise to sunset (Ethiopia, Eritrea, Djibouti)

ras – title of nobility equivalent to duke or prince (Ethiopia, Eritrea)

sambuk – see *dhow*

sewa – see *tella*

shamma – white, light cotton toga worn in Ethiopia and Eritrea; see also *gabi*, *natala* and *buluko*

shifta – traditionally a rebel or outlaw; today a bandit or roadside robber (Ethiopia, Eritrea)

shint beat – toilet (Ethiopia)

shirit – see *foutah*

tabot – replica of the Ark of the Covenant, kept in the inner sanctuary of every Orthodox church (Ethiopia, Eritrea)

tankwa – traditional papyrus boat used on Lake Tana (Ethiopia)

taxi-brousse – bush taxi (French – Djibouti)

tef – an indigenous grass cultivated as a cereal grain; the key ingredient in injera, a bread-like staple (Ethiopia, Eritrea)

tej – wine made from honey, popular in Ethiopia; known in Eritrea as *mies*

tella – home-brewed beer made from finger millet, maize or barley, popular in Ethiopia; known in Eritrea as *sewa*

tibeb – the decorative border of a woman's shawl (Ethiopia)

tukul – traditional cone-shaped hut with thatched roof; like South Africa's rondavel (Ethiopia, Eritrea, Djibouti)

vedette – small motorboat (French – Djibouti)

VSO – Volunteer Service Overseas worker; an aid worker sent by the charity of the same name

weizero – literally 'lady', now equivalent of 'Mrs' (Ethiopia)

Lonely Planet Guides by Region

Lonely Planet is known worldwide for publishing practical, reliable and no-nonsense travel information in our guides and on our Web site. The Lonely Planet list covers just about every accessible part of the world. Currently there are 16 series: Travel guides, Shoestring guides, Condensed guides, Phrasebooks, Read This First, Healthy Travel, Walking guides, Cycling guides, Watching Wildlife guides, Pisces Diving & Snorkeling guides, City Maps, Road Atlases, Out to Eat, World Food, Journeys travel literature and Pictorials.

AFRICA Africa on a shoestring • Botswana • Cairo • Cairo City Map • Cape Town • Cape Town City Map • East Africa • Egypt • Egyptian Arabic phrasebook • Ethiopia, Eritrea & Djibouti • Ethiopian Amharic phrasebook • The Gambia & Senegal • Healthy Travel Africa • Kenya • Malawi • Morocco • Moroccan Arabic phrasebook • Mozambique • Namibia • Read This First: Africa • South Africa, Lesotho & Swaziland • Southern Africa • Southern Africa Road Atlas • Swahili phrasebook • Tanzania, Zanzibar & Pemba • Trekking in East Africa • Tunisia • Watching Wildlife East Africa • Watching Wildlife Southern Africa • West Africa • World Food Morocco • Zambia • Zimbabwe, Botswana & Namibia
Travel Literature: Mali Blues: Traveling to an African Beat • The Rainbird: A Central African Journey • Songs to an African Sunset: A Zimbabwean Story

AUSTRALIA & THE PACIFIC Aboriginal Australia & the Torres Strait Islands •Auckland • Australia • Australian phrasebook • Australia Road Atlas • Cycling Australia • Cycling New Zealand • Fiji • Fijian phrasebook • Healthy Travel Australia, NZ & the Pacific • Islands of Australia's Great Barrier Reef • Melbourne • Melbourne City Map • Micronesia • New Caledonia • New South Wales • New Zealand • Northern Territory • Outback Australia • Out to Eat – Melbourne • Out to Eat – Sydney • Papua New Guinea • Pidgin phrasebook • Queensland • Rarotonga & the Cook Islands • Samoa • Solomon Islands • South Australia • South Pacific • South Pacific phrasebook • Sydney • Sydney City Map • Sydney Condensed • Tahiti & French Polynesia • Tasmania • Tonga • Tramping in New Zealand • Vanuatu • Victoria • Walking in Australia • Watching Wildlife Australia • Western Australia
Travel Literature: Islands in the Clouds: Travels in the Highlands of New Guinea • Kiwi Tracks: A New Zealand Journey • Sean & David's Long Drive

CENTRAL AMERICA & THE CARIBBEAN Bahamas, Turks & Caicos • Baja California • Belize, Guatemala & Yucatán • Bermuda • Central America on a shoestring • Costa Rica • Costa Rica Spanish phrasebook • Cuba • Cycling Cuba • Dominican Republic & Haiti • Eastern Caribbean • Guatemala • Havana • Healthy Travel Central & South America • Jamaica • Mexico • Mexico City • Panama • Puerto Rico • Read This First: Central & South America • Virgin Islands • World Food Caribbean • World Food Mexico • Yucatán
Travel Literature: Green Dreams: Travels in Central America

EUROPE Amsterdam • Amsterdam City Map • Amsterdam Condensed • Andalucía • Athens • Austria • Baltic States phrasebook • Barcelona • Barcelona City Map • Belgium & Luxembourg • Berlin • Berlin City Map • Britain • British phrasebook • Brussels, Bruges & Antwerp • Brussels City Map • Budapest • Budapest City Map • Canary Islands • Catalunya & the Costa Brava • Central Europe • Central Europe phrasebook • Copenhagen • Corfu & the Ionians • Corsica • Crete • Crete Condensed • Croatia • Cycling Britain • Cycling France • Cyprus • Czech & Slovak Republics • Czech phrasebook • Denmark • Dublin • Dublin City Map • Dublin Condensed • Eastern Europe • Eastern Europe phrasebook • Edinburgh • Edinburgh City Map • England • Estonia, Latvia & Lithuania • Europe on a shoestring • Europe phrasebook • Finland • Florence • Florence City Map • France • Frankfurt City Map • Frankfurt Condensed • French phrasebook • Georgia, Armenia & Azerbaijan • Germany • German phrasebook • Greece • Greek Islands • Greek phrasebook • Hungary • Iceland, Greenland & the Faroe Islands • Ireland • Italian phrasebook • Italy • Kraków • Lisbon • The Loire • London • London City Map • London Condensed • Madrid • Madrid City Map • Malta • Mediterranean Europe • Milan, Turin & Genoa • Moscow • Munich • Netherlands • Normandy • Norway • Out to Eat – London • Out to Eat – Paris • Paris • Paris City Map • Paris Condensed • Poland • Polish phrasebook • Portugal • Portuguese phrasebook • Prague • Prague City Map • Provence & the Côte d'Azur • Read This First: Europe • Rhodes & the Dodecanese • Romania & Moldova • Rome • Rome City Map • Rome Condensed • Russia, Ukraine & Belarus • Russian phrasebook • Scandinavian & Baltic Europe • Scandinavian phrasebook • Scotland • Sicily • Slovenia • South-West France • Spain • Spanish phrasebook • Stockholm • St Petersburg • St Petersburg City Map • Sweden • Switzerland • Tuscany • Ukrainian phrasebook • Venice • Vienna • Wales • Walking in Britain • Walking in France • Walking in Ireland • Walking in Italy • Walking in Scotland • Walking in Spain • Walking in Switzerland • Western Europe • World Food France • World Food Greece • World Food Ireland • World Food Italy • World Food Spain **Travel Literature:** After Yugoslavia • Love and War in the Apennines • The Olive Grove: Travels in Greece • On the Shores of the Mediterranean • Round Ireland in Low Gear • A Small Place in Italy

Lonely Planet Mail Order

Lonely Planet products are distributed worldwide. They are also available by mail order from Lonely Planet, so if you have difficulty finding a title please write to us. North and South American residents should write to 150 Linden St, Oakland, CA 94607, USA; European and African residents should write to 10a Spring Place, London NW5 3BH, UK; and residents of other countries to Locked Bag 1, Footscray, Victoria 3011, Australia.

INDIAN SUBCONTINENT & THE INDIAN OCEAN Bangladesh • Bengali phrasebook • Bhutan • Delhi • Goa • Healthy Travel Asia & India • Hindi & Urdu phrasebook • India • India & Bangladesh City Map • Indian Himalaya • Karakoram Highway • Kathmandu City Map • Kerala • Madagascar • Maldives • Mauritius, Réunion & Seychelles • Mumbai (Bombay) • Nepal • Nepali phrasebook • North India • Pakistan • Rajasthan • Read This First: Asia & India • South India • Sri Lanka • Sri Lanka phrasebook • Tibet • Tibetan phrasebook • Trekking in the Indian Himalaya • Trekking in the Karakoram & Hindukush • Trekking in the Nepal Himalaya • World Food India **Travel Literature:** The Age of Kali: Indian Travels and Encounters • Hello Goodnight: A Life of Goa • In Rajasthan • Maverick in Madagascar • A Season in Heaven: True Tales from the Road to Kathmandu • Shopping for Buddhas • A Short Walk in the Hindu Kush • Slowly Down the Ganges

MIDDLE EAST & CENTRAL ASIA Bahrain, Kuwait & Qatar • Central Asia • Central Asia phrasebook • Dubai • Farsi (Persian) phrasebook • Hebrew phrasebook • Iran • Israel & the Palestinian Territories • Istanbul • Istanbul City Map • Istanbul to Cairo • Istanbul to Kathmandu • Jerusalem • Jerusalem City Map • Jordan • Lebanon • Middle East • Oman & the United Arab Emirates • Syria • Turkey • Turkish phrasebook • World Food Turkey • Yemen **Travel Literature:** Black on Black: Iran Revisited • Breaking Ranks: Turbulent Travels in the Promised Land • The Gates of Damascus • Kingdom of the Film Stars: Journey into Jordan

NORTH AMERICA Alaska • Boston • Boston City Map • Boston Condensed • British Columbia • California & Nevada • California Condensed • Canada • Chicago • Chicago City Map • Chicago Condensed • Florida • Georgia & the Carolinas • Great Lakes • Hawaii • Hiking in Alaska • Hiking in the USA • Honolulu & Oahu City Map • Las Vegas • Los Angeles • Los Angeles City Map • Louisiana & the Deep South • Miami • Miami City Map • Montreal • New England • New Orleans • New Orleans City Map • New York City • New York City City Map • New York City Condensed • New York, New Jersey & Pennsylvania • Oahu • Out to Eat – San Francisco • Pacific Northwest • Rocky Mountains • San Diego & Tijuana • San Francisco • San Francisco City Map • Seattle • Seattle City Map • Southwest • Texas • Toronto • USA • USA phrasebook • Vancouver • Vancouver City Map • Virginia & the Capital Region • Washington, DC • Washington, DC City Map • World Food New Orleans **Travel Literature:** Caught Inside: A Surfer's Year on the California Coast • Drive Thru America

NORTH-EAST ASIA Beijing • Beijing City Map • Cantonese phrasebook • China • Hiking in Japan • Hong Kong & Macau • Hong Kong City Map • Hong Kong Condensed • Japan • Japanese phrasebook • Korea • Korean phrasebook • Kyoto • Mandarin phrasebook • Mongolia • Mongolian phrasebook • Seoul • Shanghai • South-West China • Taiwan • Tokyo • Tokyo Condensed • World Food Hong Kong • World Food Japan **Travel Literature:** In Xanadu: A Quest • Lost Japan

SOUTH AMERICA Argentina, Uruguay & Paraguay • Bolivia • Brazil • Brazilian phrasebook • Buenos Aires • Buenos Aires City Map • Chile & Easter Island • Colombia • Ecuador & the Galapagos Islands • Healthy Travel Central & South America • Latin American Spanish phrasebook • Peru • Quechua phrasebook • Read This First: Central & South America • Rio de Janeiro • Rio de Janeiro City Map • Santiago de Chile • South America on a shoestring • Trekking in the Patagonian Andes • Venezuela **Travel Literature:** Full Circle: A South American Journey

SOUTH-EAST ASIA Bali & Lombok • Bangkok • Bangkok City Map • Burmese phrasebook • Cambodia • Cycling Vietnam, Laos & Cambodia • East Timor phrasebook • Hanoi • Healthy Travel Asia & India • Hill Tribes phrasebook • Ho Chi Minh City (Saigon) • Indonesia • Indonesian phrasebook • Indonesia's Eastern Islands • Java • Lao phrasebook • Laos • Malay phrasebook • Malaysia, Singapore & Brunei • Myanmar (Burma) • Philippines • Pilipino (Tagalog) phrasebook • Read This First: Asia & India • Singapore • Singapore City Map • South-East Asia on a shoestring • South-East Asia phrasebook • Thailand • Thailand's Islands & Beaches • Thailand, Vietnam, Laos & Cambodia Road Atlas • Thai phrasebook • Vietnam • Vietnamese phrasebook • World Food Indonesia • World Food Thailand • World Food Vietnam

ALSO AVAILABLE: Antarctica • The Arctic • The Blue Man: Tales of Travel, Love and Coffee • Brief Encounters: Stories of Love, Sex & Travel • Buddhist Stupas in Asia: The Shape of Perfection • Chasing Rickshaws • The Last Grain Race • Lonely Planet … On the Edge: Adventurous Escapades from Around the World • Lonely Planet Unpacked • Lonely Planet Unpacked Again • Not the Only Planet: Science Fiction Travel Stories • Ports of Call: A Journey by Sea • Sacred India • Travel Photography: A Guide to Taking Better Pictures • Travel with Children • Tuvalu: Portrait of an Island Nation

LONELY PLANET

You already know that Lonely Planet produces more than this one guidebook, but you might not be aware of the other products we have on this region. Here is a selection of titles which you may want to check out as well:

Read this first: Africa
ISBN 1 86450 066 2
US$14.95 • UK£8.99

Healthy Travel Africa
ISBN 1 86450 050 6
US$5.95 • UK£3.99

Trekking in East Africa
ISBN 0 86442 541 4
US$17.95 • UK£11.99

East Africa
ISBN 0 86442 676 3
US$24.99 • UK£14.99

Africa on a shoestring
ISBN 0 86442 663 1
US$29.99 • UK£17.99

Kenya
ISBN 0 86442 695 X
US$19.95 • UK£12.99

Tanzania, Zanzibar & Pemba
ISBN 0 86442 726 3
US$17.95 • UK£11.99

Egyptian Arabic phrasebook
ISBN 1 86450 183 9
US$7.99 • UK£4.50

Ethiopian Amharic phrasebook
ISBN 0 86442 338 1
US$5.95 • UK£3.50

French phrasebook
ISBN 0 86442 450 7
US$5.95 • UK£3.99

Available wherever books are sold.

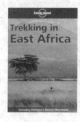

Index

Abbreviations

Djib – Djibouti   Eri – Eritrea   Eth – Ethiopia

Text

Bold indicates maps.

509

Bold indicates maps.

Boxed Text

MAP LEGEND

CITY ROUTES

Freeway .... Freeway	─ ─ ─ ─ .... Unsealed Road
Highway .... Primary Road	──────── .... One Way Street
Road .... Secondary Road	════════ .... Pedestrian Street
Street .... Street	▥▥▥▥▥ .... Stepped Street
Lane .... Lane	════════ .... Footbridge

REGIONAL ROUTES

═══════ ....Tollway, Freeway
═══════ .... Primary Road
═══════ .... Secondary Road
─────── .... Minor Road

BOUNDARIES

━ ▪ ━ ▪▪ ▪ .... International
━ ▪ ━ ▪▪▪ .... State
─ ─ ─ ─ .... Disputed
─────── .... City Wall

HYDROGRAPHY

~~ .... River, Creek	◯◯ ◯◯ .... Dry Lake; Salt Lake
─▪─▪─▪─ .... Canal	◉ ↘ .... Spring; Rapids
◯◯◯ .... Lake	◐ ╢ ◁ .... Waterfalls

TRANSPORT ROUTES & STATIONS

─┼─◯─┼─ ....Train	─────── .... Walking Trail
+ + + + ... Underground Train	• • • • • • • .... Walking Tour
▬▬▬▬ ....Tramway	~~~~~~ .... Path
─────🚏 ....Ferry	─────── .... Pier or Jetty

AREA FEATURES

▭ .... Building	▭ .... Market	🌴 .... Beach	▭ .... Campus
❀ .... Park, Gardens	◯ .... Sports Ground	+ + + ... Cemetery	▭ .... Plaza

POPULATION SYMBOLS

✪ **CAPITAL** .... National Capital	● **CITY** .... City	● Village .... Village
◉ **CAPITAL** .... State Capital	● **Town** .... Town	▭ .... Urban Area

MAP SYMBOLS

● .... Place to Stay	▼ .... Place to Eat	● .... Point of Interest

✉ .... Airport	⊞ .... Cinema	▥ .... Museum	⊠ ..... Shopping Centre
⚓ ◥ ... Anchorage; Dive Site	▣ ..... Embassy/Consulate	▦ .... National Park	▥ .... Stately Home
⊞ ... Animal Viewing/Hide	⊕ .... Hospital	▣ .... Parking	⊠ .... Synagogue
⊖ .... Bank	⊡ .... Internet Cafe	◉ .... Petrol Station	⊠ .... Telephone
▣ ▣ ... Bus Terminal; Taxi	▲ .... Islamic Shrine	◼ .... Police Station	▲ .... Temple
▲ .... Camping Ground	※ .... Lookout	▭ .... Post Office	▣ ... Tomb/Mausoleum
⌂ ▲ .... Cave; Volcano	▲ .... Monument	▣ .... Pub or Bar	❶ ... Tourist Information
▬ ▣ .. Church/Monastery	⦿ .... Mosque	▣ ⊠ ......Ruins; Battlefield	▭ ... Zoo/Wildlife Sanctuary

Note: not all symbols displayed above appear in this book

LONELY PLANET OFFICES

Australia
Locked Bag 1, Footscray, Victoria 3011
☎ 03 9689 4666 fax 03 9689 6833
email: talk2us@lonelyplanet.com.au

USA
150 Linden St, Oakland, CA 94607
☎ 510 893 8555 TOLL FREE: 800 275 8555
fax 510 893 8572
email: info@lonelyplanet.com

UK
10a Spring Place, London NW5 3BH
☎ 020 7428 4800 fax 020 7428 4828
email: go@lonelyplanet.co.uk

France
1 rue du Dahomey, 75011 Paris
☎ 01 55 25 33 00 fax 01 55 25 33 01
email: bip@lonelyplanet.fr
www.lonelyplanet.fr

World Wide Web: www.lonelyplanet.com *or* AOL keyword: lp
Lonely Planet Images: lpi@lonelyplanet.com.au